METAL MEN

ELEMENTS OF CHANGE

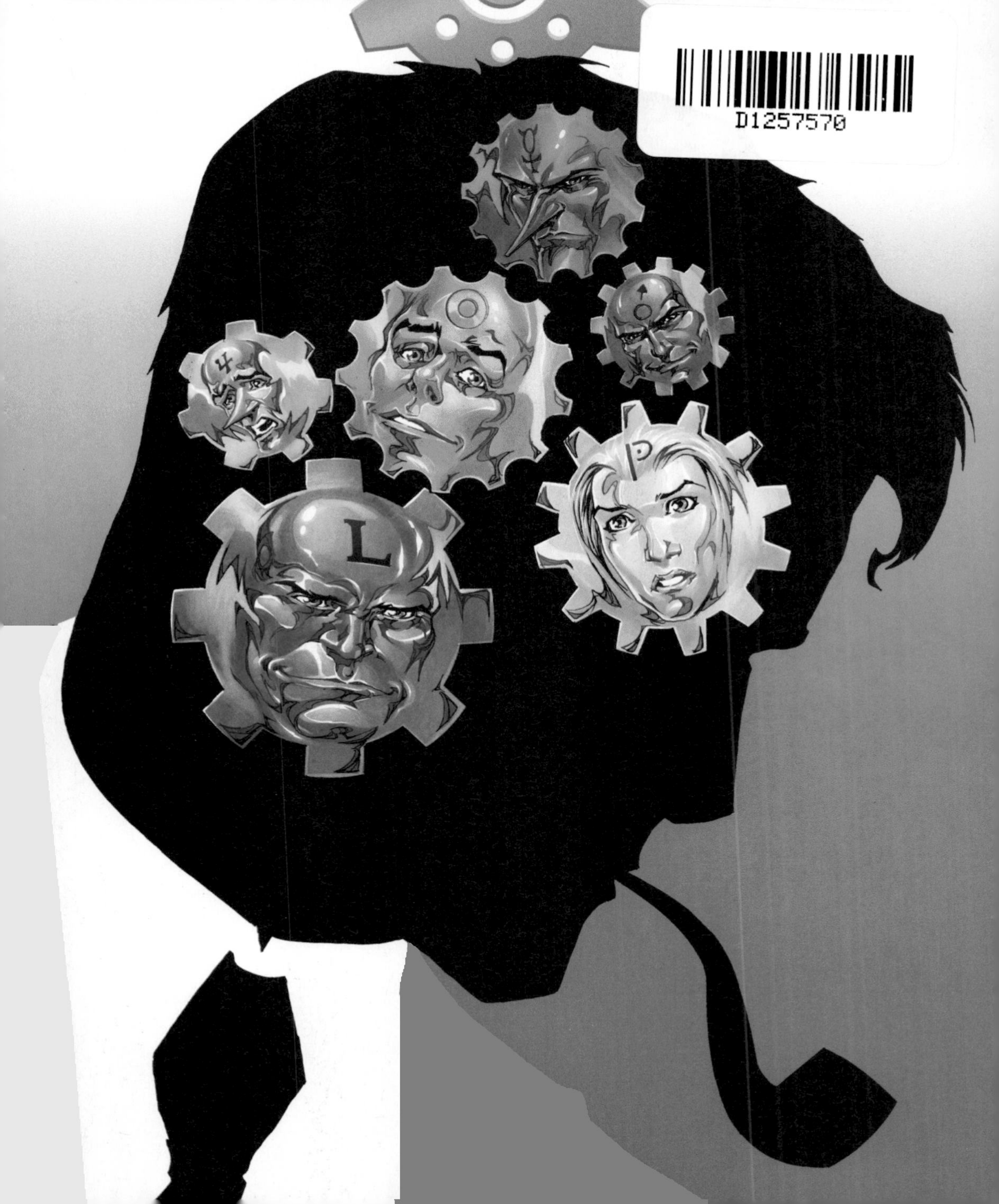

METAL MEN

ELEMENTS OF CHANGE

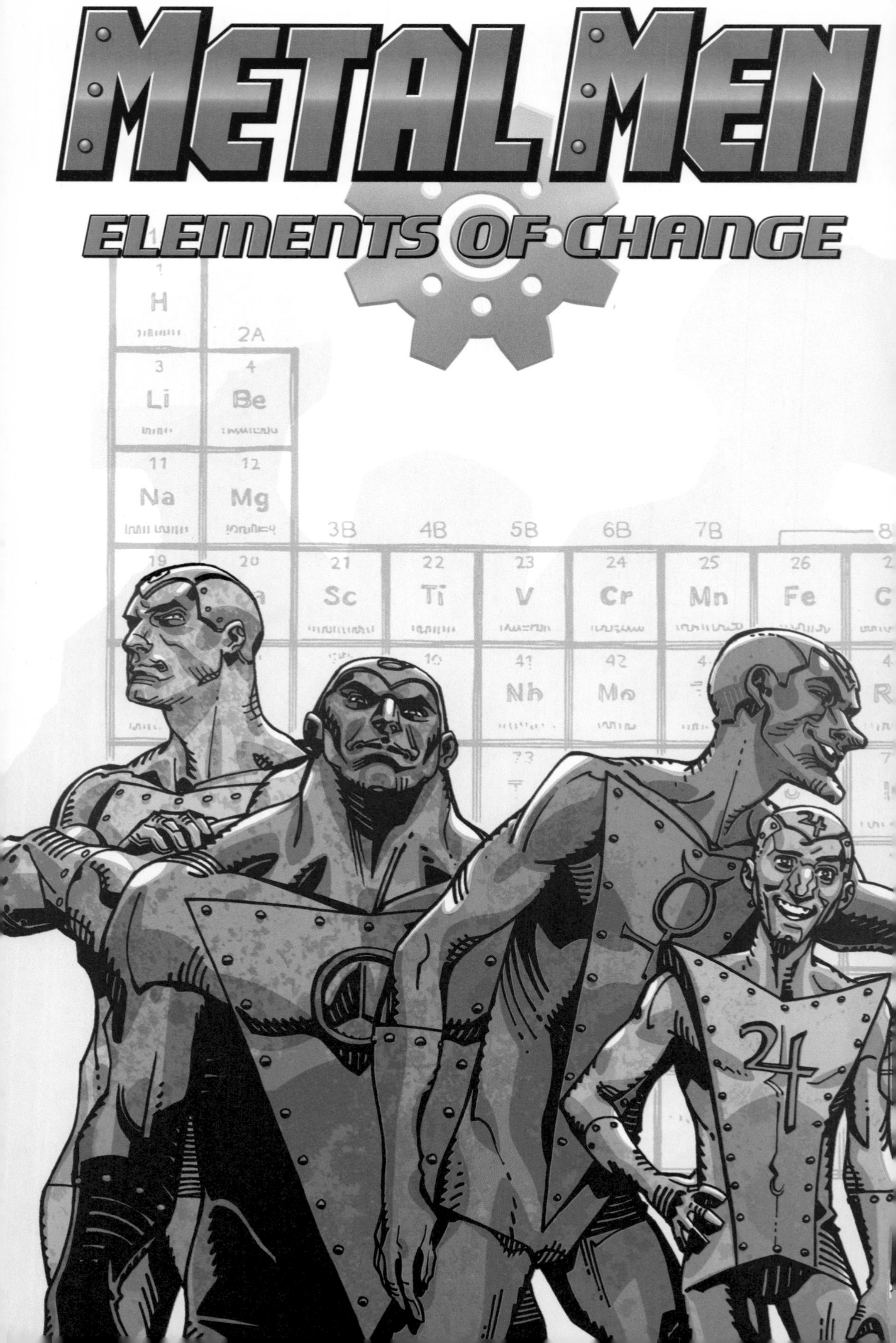
1
H
2A
3
Li
4
Be
11
Na
12
Mg
3B
4B
5B
6B
7B
21
Sc
22
Ti
23
V
24
Cr
25
Mn
26
Fe
41
Nb
42
Mo

writer **DAN DiDIO**

artist **SHANE DAVIS**

inkers **SHANE DAVIS** **MICHELLE DELECKI**

colorists **JASON WRIGHT** **NS STUDIO**

letterer **TRAVIS LANHAM**

SHANE DAVIS
with MICHELLE DELECKI and NS STUDIO
collection cover artists

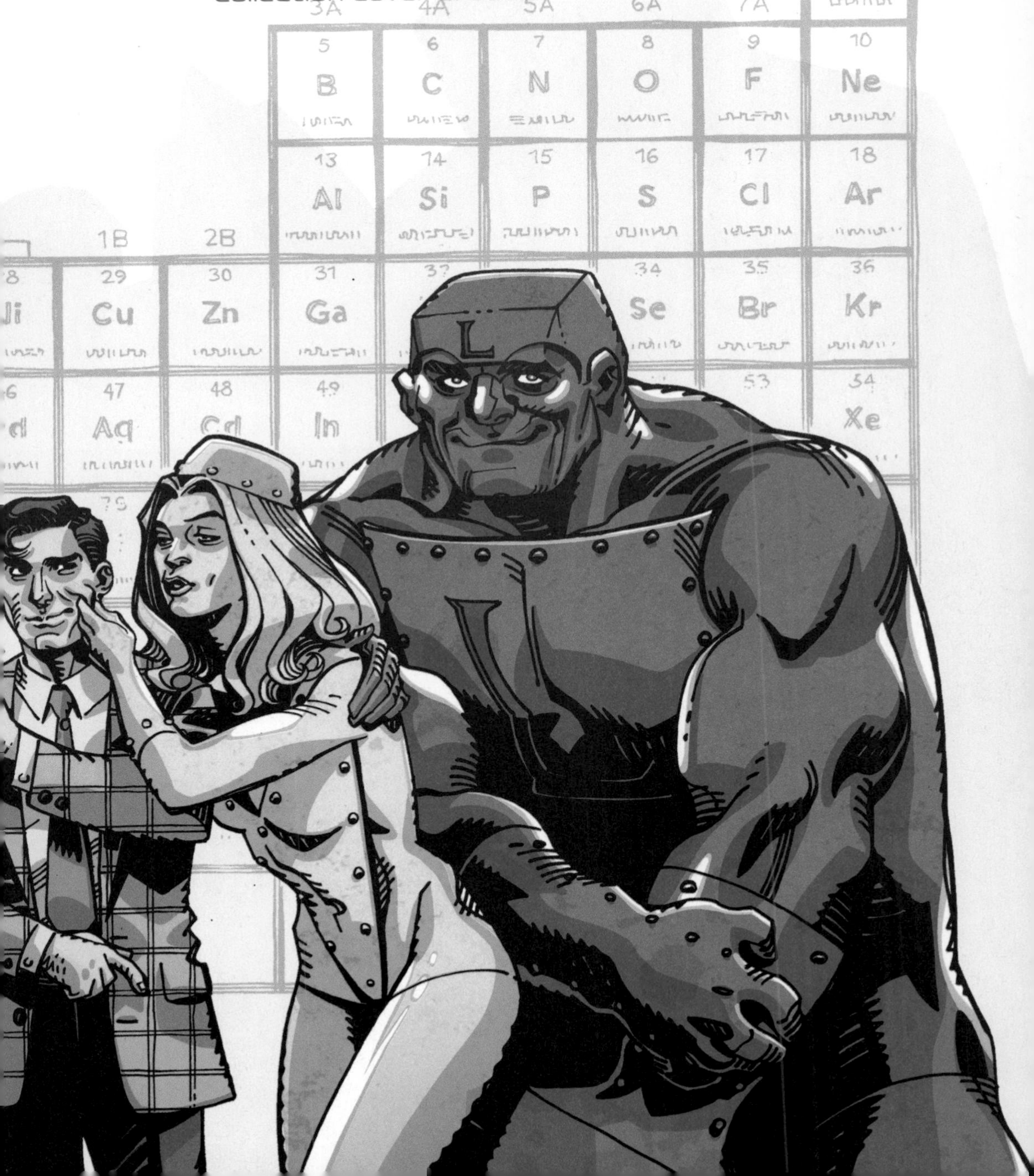
B
C
N
O
F
Ne
Al
Si
P
S
Cl
Ar
Cu
Zn
Ga
Se
Br
Kr
In
Xe

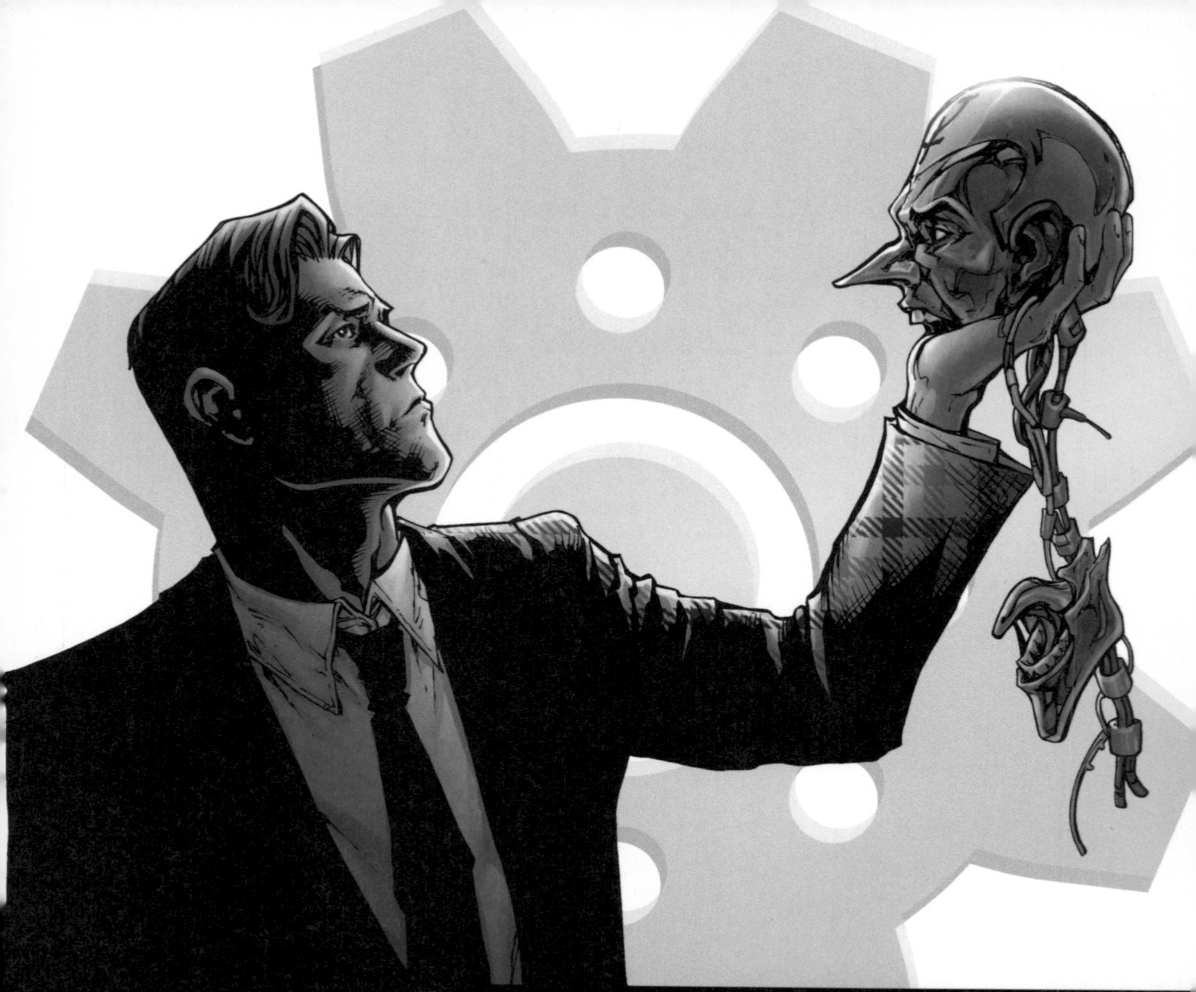

JESSICA CHEN	Editor – Original Series & Collected Edition
STEVE COOK	Design Director – Books
CURTIS KING JR.	Publication Design
CHRISTY SAWYER	Publication Production
MARIE JAVINS	Editor-in-Chief, DC Comics
DANIEL CHERRY III	Senior VP – General Manager
JIM LEE	Publisher & Chief Creative Officer
DON FALLETTI	VP – Manufacturing Operations & Workflow Management
LAWRENCE GANEM	VP – Talent Services
ALISON GILL	Senior VP – Manufacturing & Operations
NICK J. NAPOLITANO	VP – Manufacturing Administration & Design
NANCY SPEARS	VP – Revenue
MICHELE R. WELLS	VP & Executive Editor, Young Reader

METAL MEN: ELEMENTS OF CHANGE

DC Comics, 2900 West Alameda Ave., Burbank, CA 91505
Printed by LSC Communications, Owensville, MO, USA. 2/26/21.
First Printing. ISBN: 978-1-77950-808-9

Library of Congress Cataloging-in-Publication Data is available.

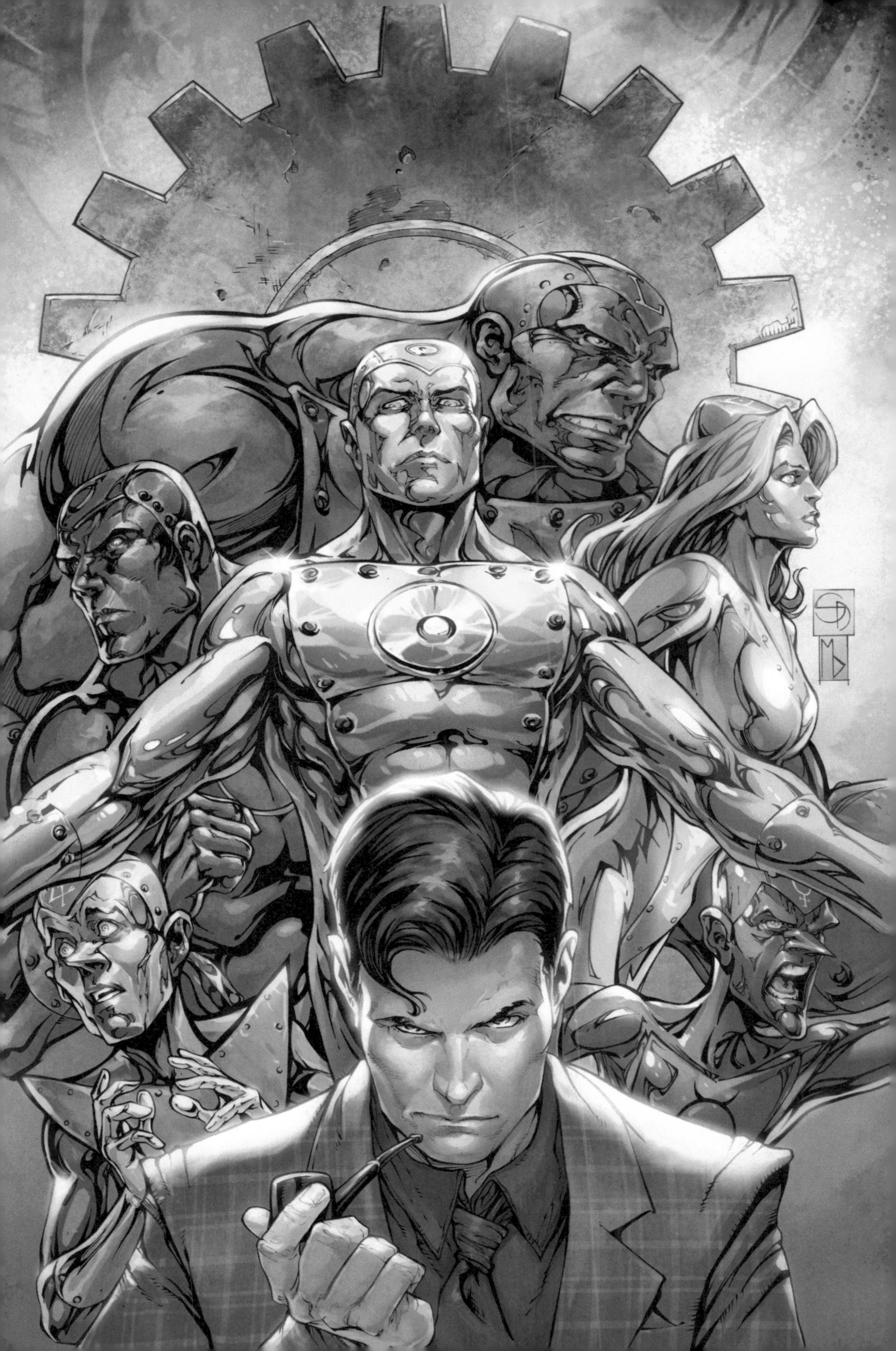

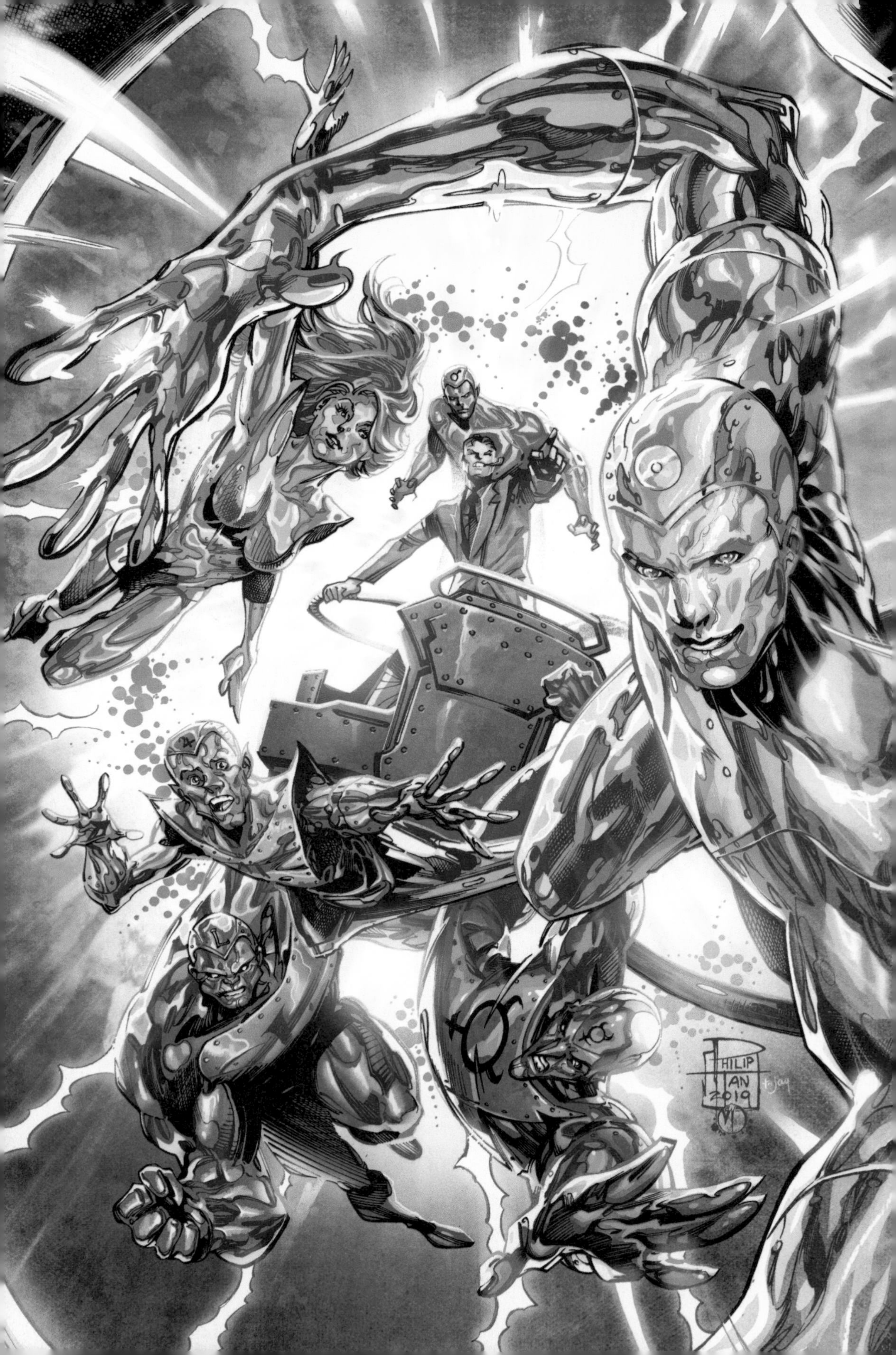
PHILIP TAN 2019

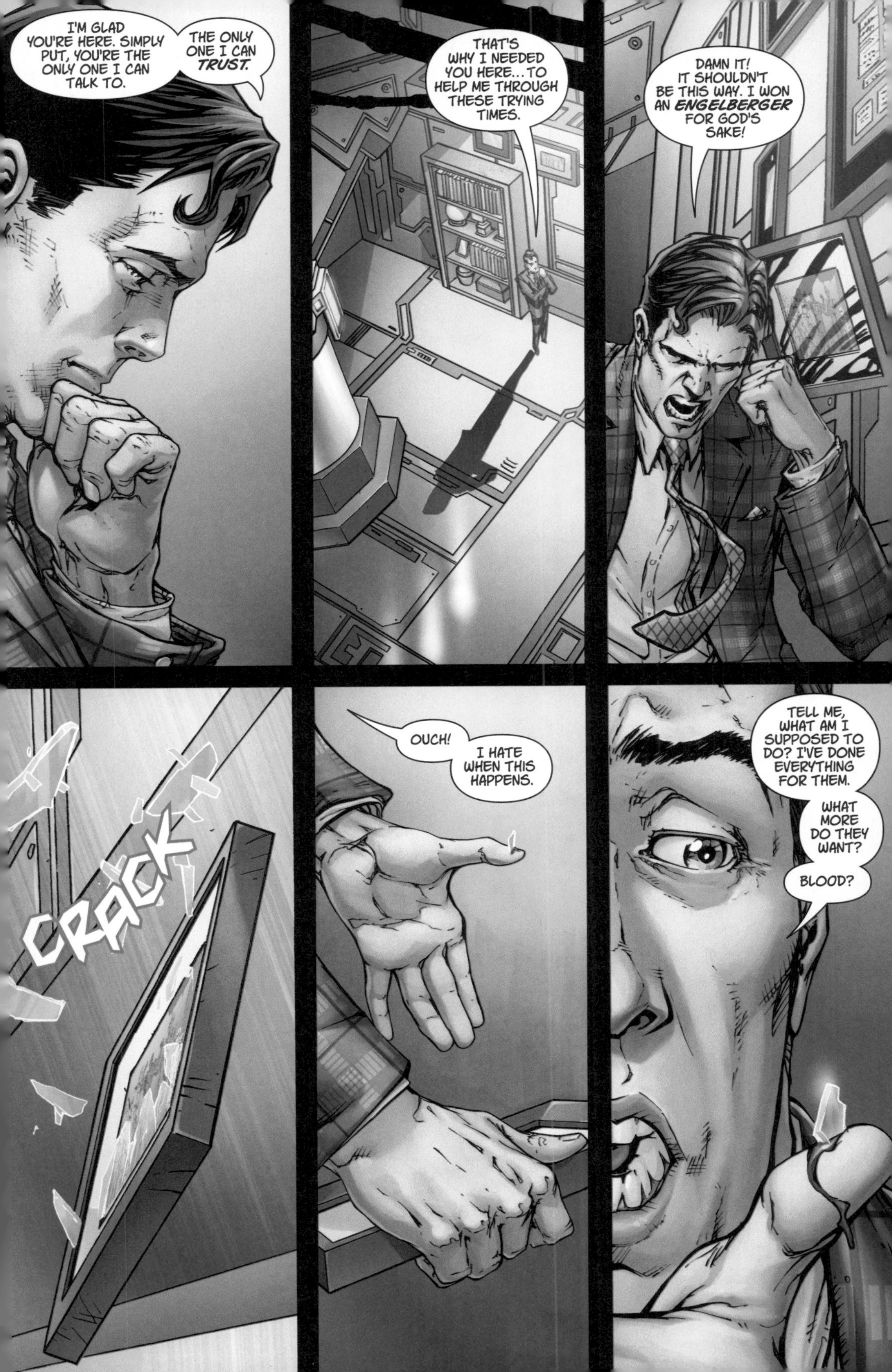
I'M GLAD YOU'RE HERE. SIMPLY PUT, YOU'RE THE ONLY ONE I CAN TALK TO.
THE ONLY ONE I CAN *TRUST.*
THAT'S WHY I NEEDED YOU HERE... TO HELP ME THROUGH THESE TRYING TIMES.
DAMN IT! IT SHOULDN'T BE THIS WAY. I WON AN *ENGELBERGER* FOR GOD'S SAKE!
CRACK
OUCH!
I HATE WHEN THIS HAPPENS.
TELL ME, WHAT AM I SUPPOSED TO DO? I'VE DONE EVERYTHING FOR THEM.
WHAT MORE DO THEY WANT?
BLOOD?

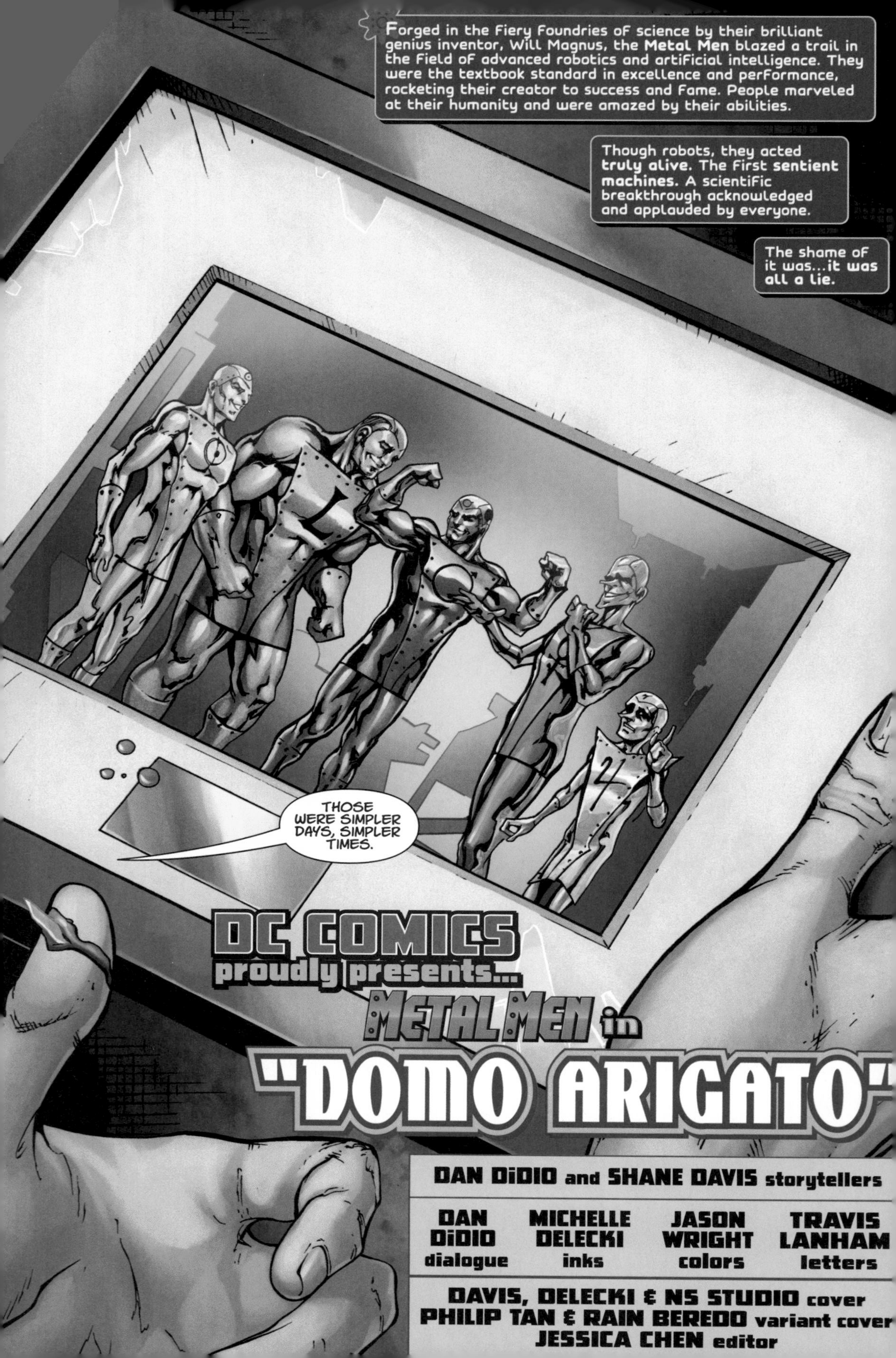

Forged in the fiery foundries of science by their brilliant genius inventor, Will Magnus, the Metal Men blazed a trail in the field of advanced robotics and artificial intelligence. They were the textbook standard in excellence and performance, rocketing their creator to success and fame. People marveled at their humanity and were amazed by their abilities.
Though robots, they acted truly alive. The first sentient machines. A scientific breakthrough acknowledged and applauded by everyone.
The shame of it was...it was all a lie.
THOSE WERE SIMPLER DAYS, SIMPLER TIMES.
DC COMICS proudly presents...
METAL MEN in
"DOMO ARIGATO"
DAN DiDIO and SHANE DAVIS storytellers
DAN DiDIO dialogue
MICHELLE DELECKI inks
JASON WRIGHT colors
TRAVIS LANHAM letters
DAVIS, DELECKI & NS STUDIO cover
PHILIP TAN & RAIN BEREDO variant cover
JESSICA CHEN editor

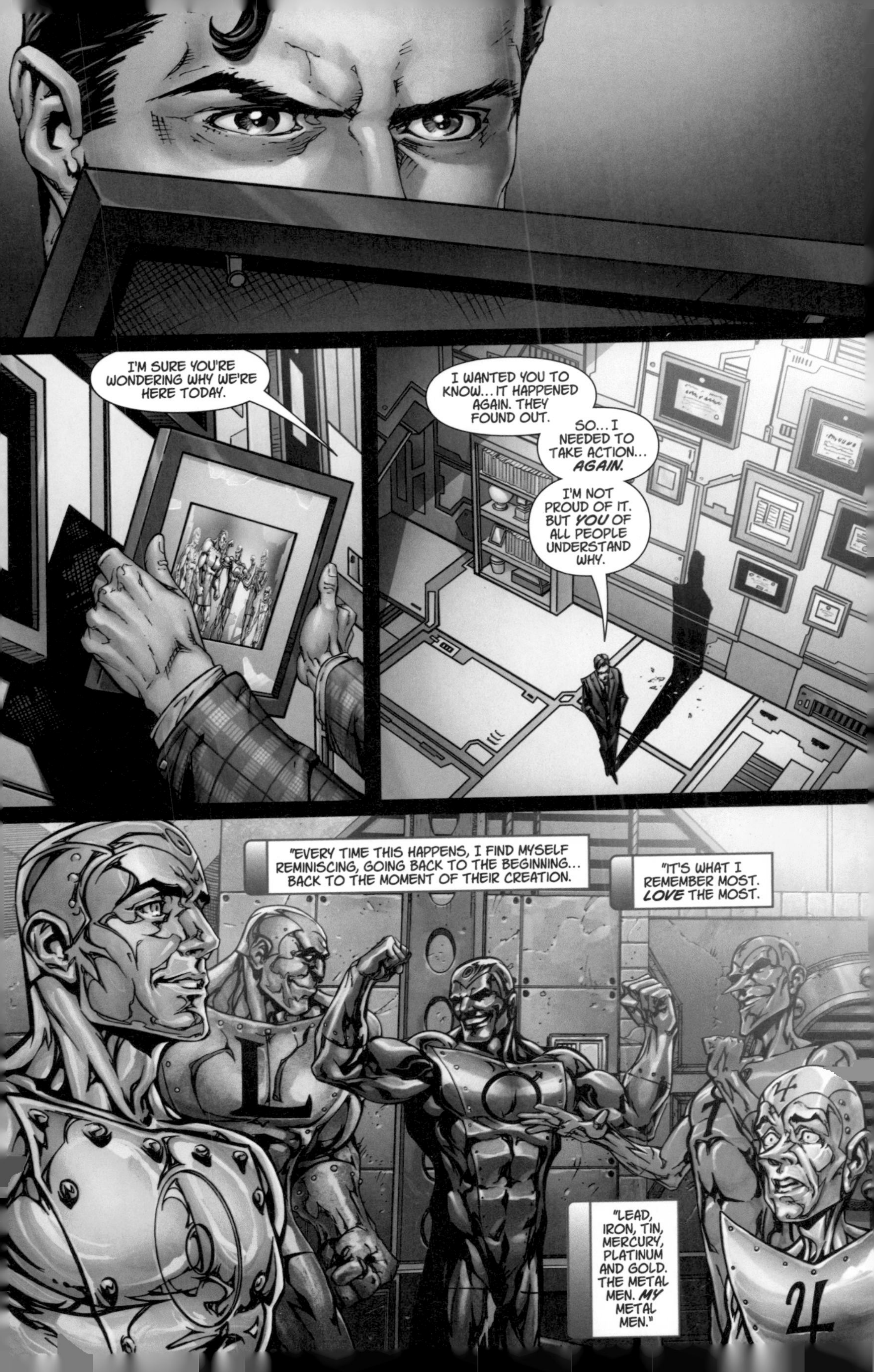
I'M SURE YOU'RE WONDERING WHY WE'RE HERE TODAY.
I WANTED YOU TO KNOW... IT HAPPENED AGAIN. THEY FOUND OUT.
SO... I NEEDED TO TAKE ACTION... AGAIN.
I'M NOT PROUD OF IT. BUT YOU OF ALL PEOPLE UNDERSTAND WHY.
"EVERY TIME THIS HAPPENS, I FIND MYSELF REMINISCING, GOING BACK TO THE BEGINNING... BACK TO THE MOMENT OF THEIR CREATION.
"IT'S WHAT I REMEMBER MOST. LOVE THE MOST.
"LEAD, IRON, TIN, MERCURY, PLATINUM AND GOLD. THE METAL MEN. MY METAL MEN."

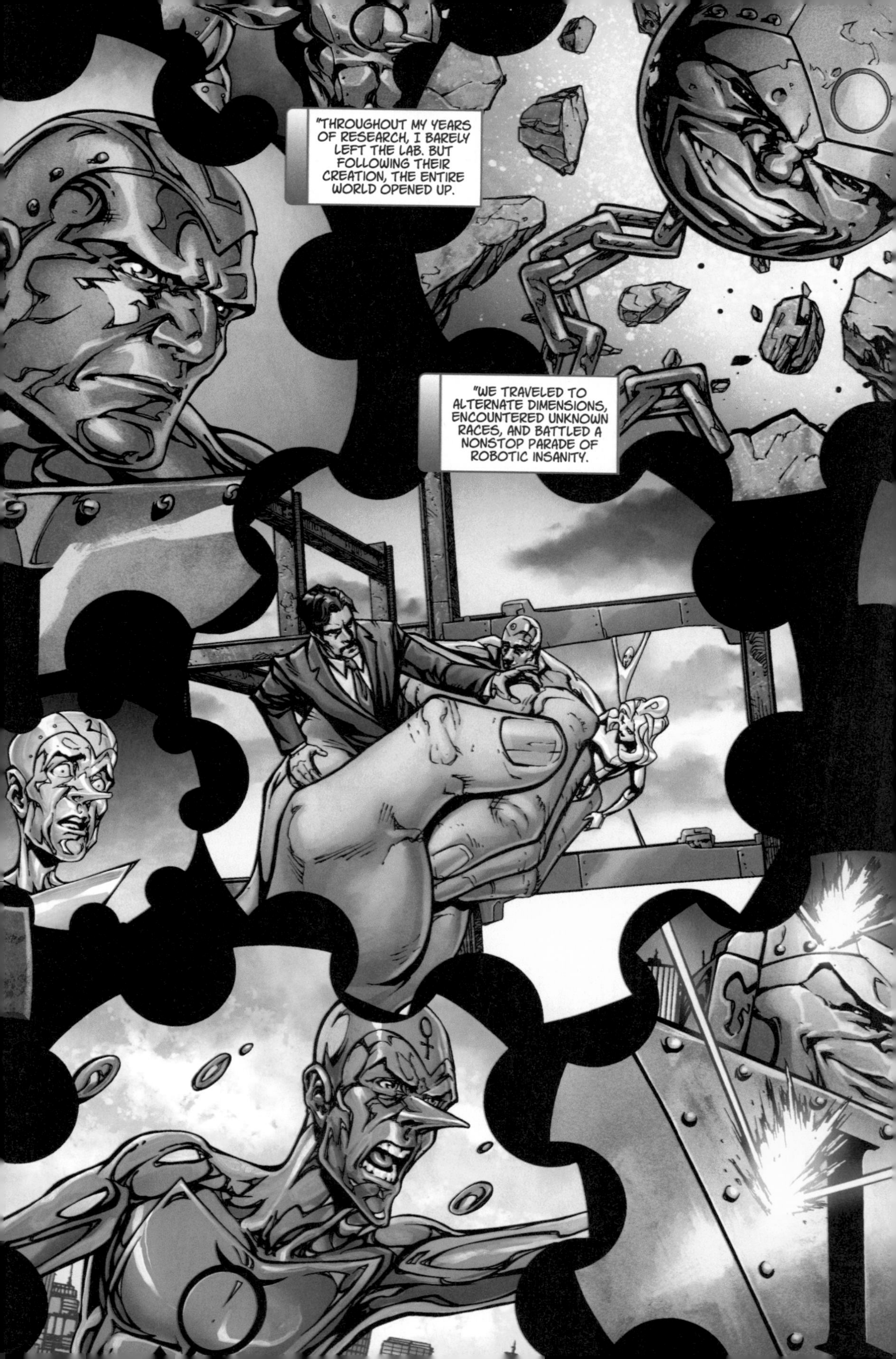
"THROUGHOUT MY YEARS OF RESEARCH, I BARELY LEFT THE LAB. BUT FOLLOWING THEIR CREATION, THE ENTIRE WORLD OPENED UP.
"WE TRAVELED TO ALTERNATE DIMENSIONS, ENCOUNTERED UNKNOWN RACES, AND BATTLED A NONSTOP PARADE OF ROBOTIC INSANITY.

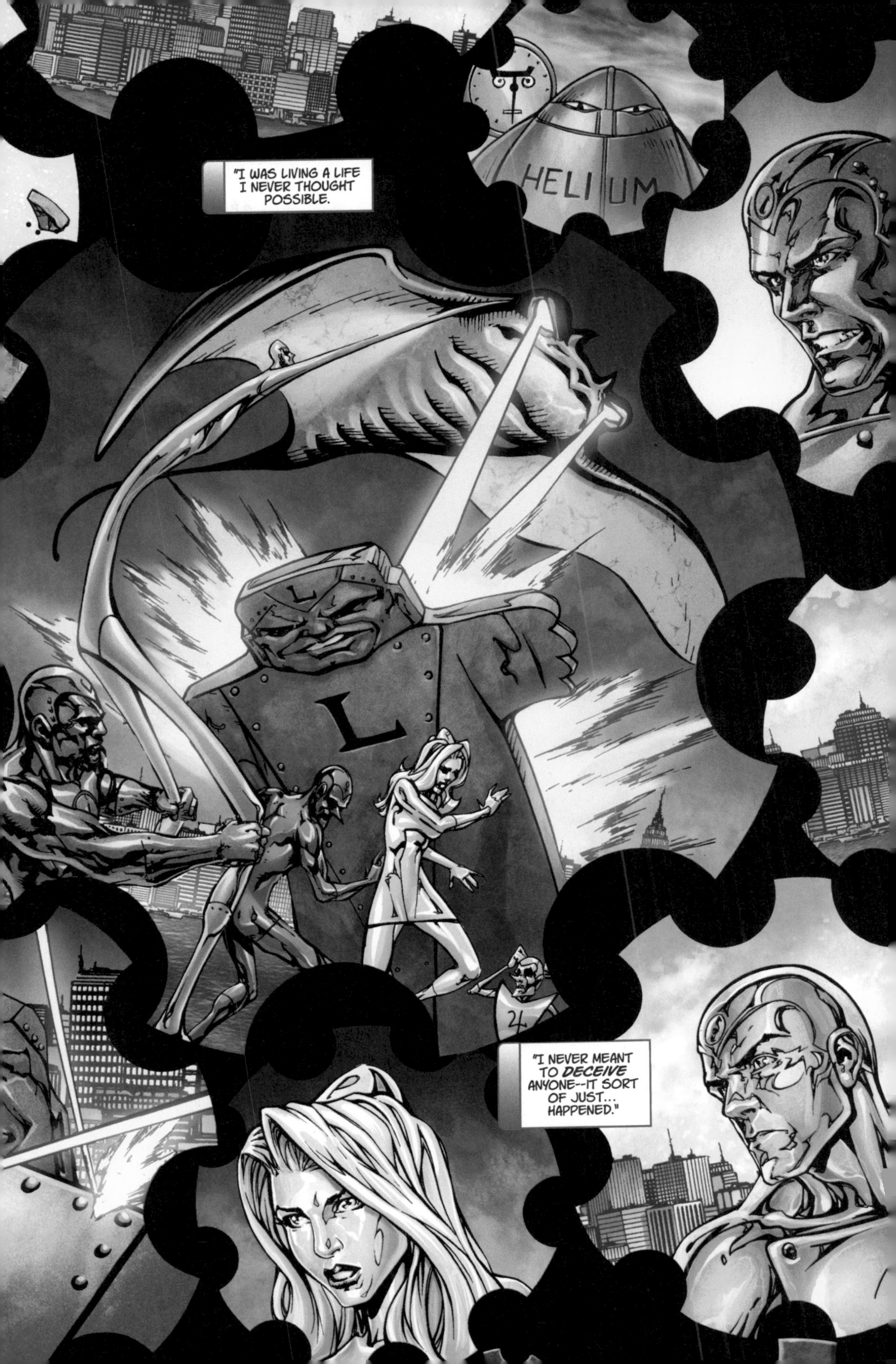
HELIUM
"I WAS LIVING A LIFE I NEVER THOUGHT POSSIBLE.
"I NEVER MEANT TO DECEIVE ANYONE--IT SORT OF JUST... HAPPENED."

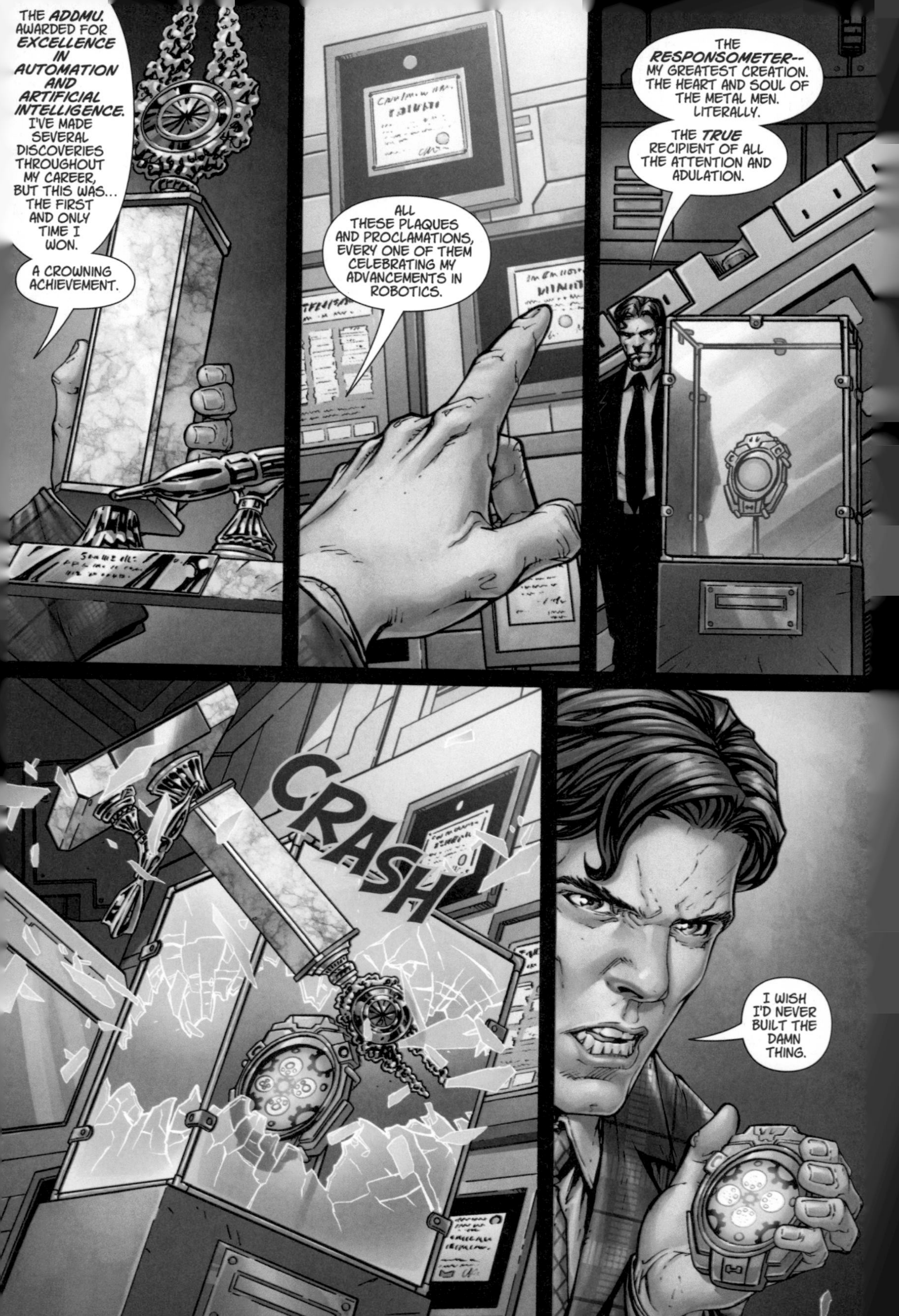
THE ADDMU. AWARDED FOR EXCELLENCE IN AUTOMATION AND ARTIFICIAL INTELLIGENCE. I'VE MADE SEVERAL DISCOVERIES THROUGHOUT MY CAREER, BUT THIS WAS... THE FIRST AND ONLY TIME I WON.
A CROWNING ACHIEVEMENT.
ALL THESE PLAQUES AND PROCLAMATIONS, EVERY ONE OF THEM CELEBRATING MY ADVANCEMENTS IN ROBOTICS.
THE RESPONSOMETER-- MY GREATEST CREATION. THE HEART AND SOUL OF THE METAL MEN. LITERALLY.
THE TRUE RECIPIENT OF ALL THE ATTENTION AND ADULATION.
CRASH
I WISH I'D NEVER BUILT THE DAMN THING.

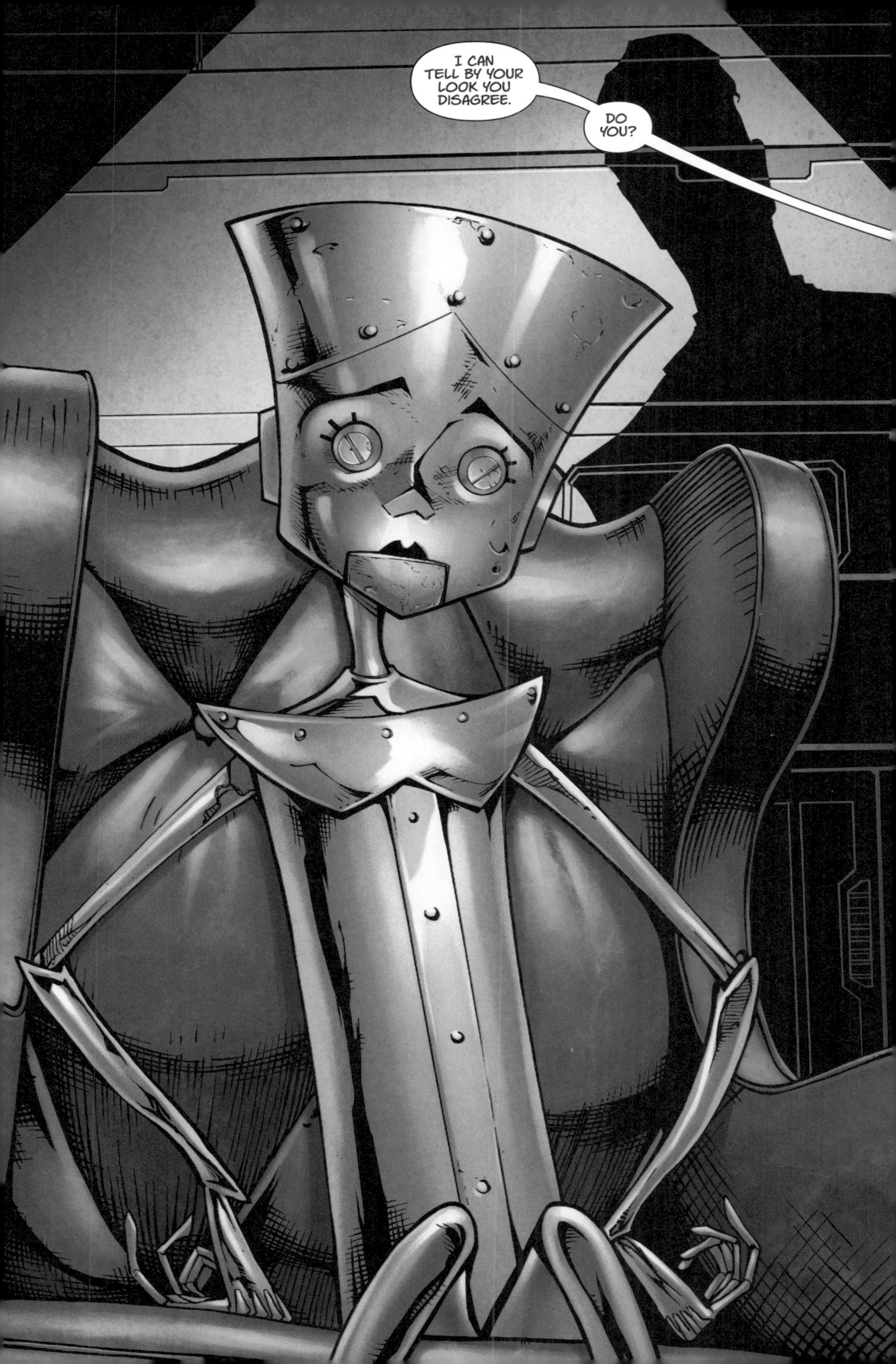
I CAN TELL BY YOUR LOOK YOU DISAGREE.
DO YOU?

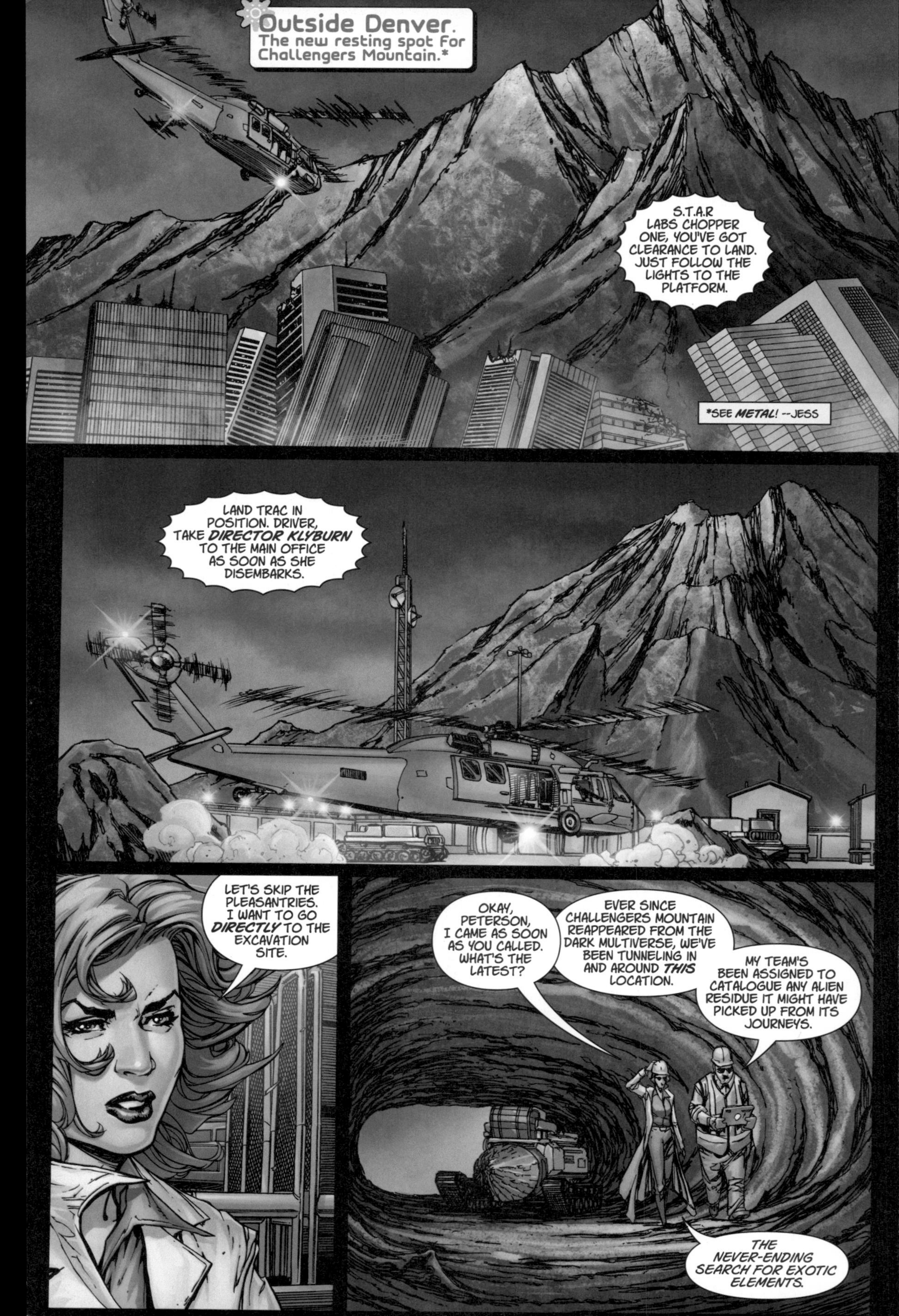
Outside Denver.
The new resting spot for Challengers Mountain.*
S.T.A.R LABS CHOPPER ONE, YOU'VE GOT CLEARANCE TO LAND. JUST FOLLOW THE LIGHTS TO THE PLATFORM.
*SEE METAL! --JESS
LAND TRAC IN POSITION. DRIVER, TAKE DIRECTOR KLYBURN TO THE MAIN OFFICE AS SOON AS SHE DISEMBARKS.
LET'S SKIP THE PLEASANTRIES. I WANT TO GO DIRECTLY TO THE EXCAVATION SITE.
OKAY, PETERSON, I CAME AS SOON AS YOU CALLED. WHAT'S THE LATEST?
EVER SINCE CHALLENGERS MOUNTAIN REAPPEARED FROM THE DARK MULTIVERSE, WE'VE BEEN TUNNELING IN AND AROUND THIS LOCATION.
MY TEAM'S BEEN ASSIGNED TO CATALOGUE ANY ALIEN RESIDUE IT MIGHT HAVE PICKED UP FROM ITS JOURNEYS.
THE NEVER-ENDING SEARCH FOR EXOTIC ELEMENTS.

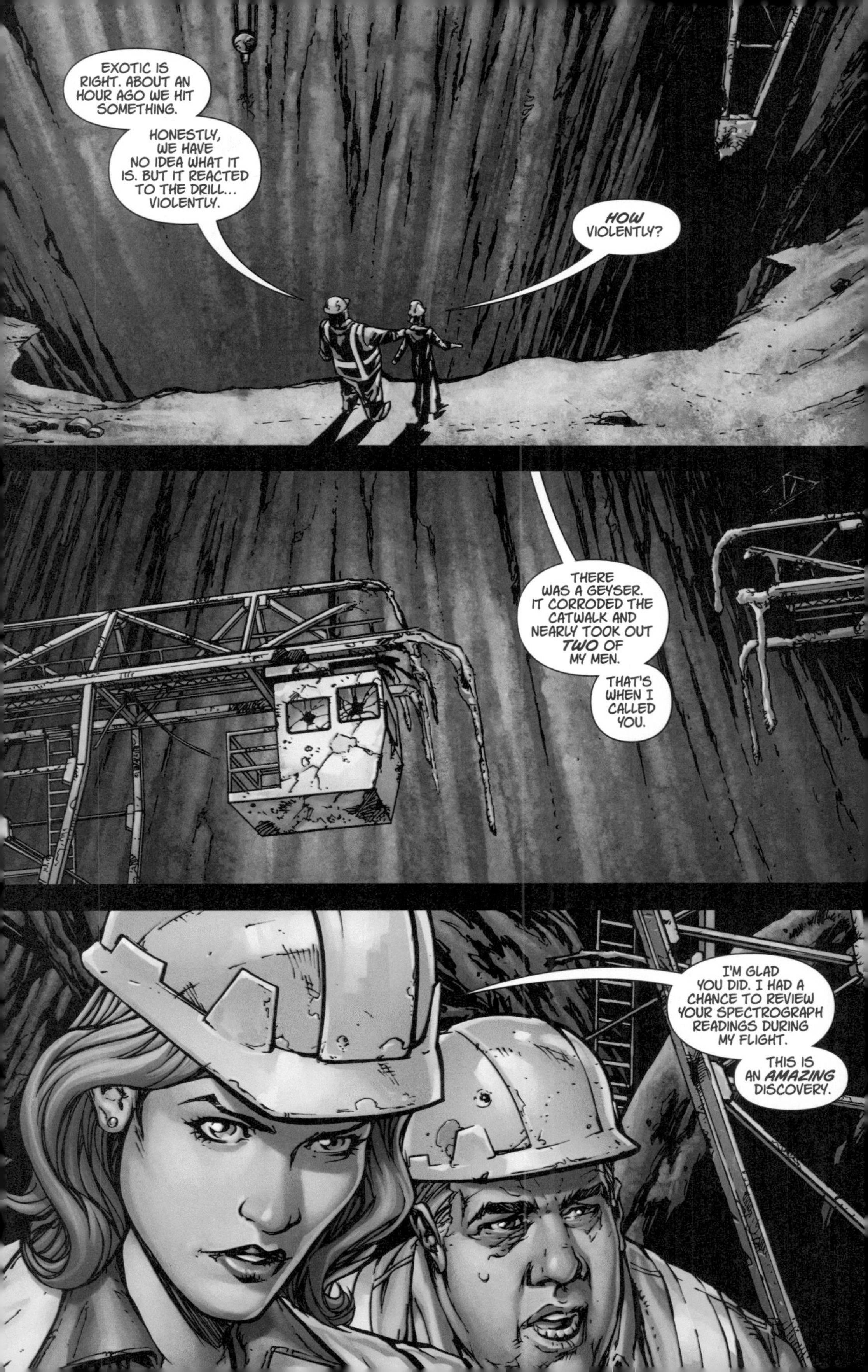
EXOTIC IS RIGHT. ABOUT AN HOUR AGO WE HIT SOMETHING.
HONESTLY, WE HAVE NO IDEA WHAT IT IS. BUT IT REACTED TO THE DRILL... VIOLENTLY.
HOW VIOLENTLY?
THERE WAS A GEYSER. IT CORRODED THE CATWALK AND NEARLY TOOK OUT *TWO* OF MY MEN.
THAT'S WHEN I CALLED YOU.
I'M GLAD YOU DID. I HAD A CHANCE TO REVIEW YOUR SPECTROGRAPH READINGS DURING MY FLIGHT.
THIS IS AN *AMAZING* DISCOVERY.

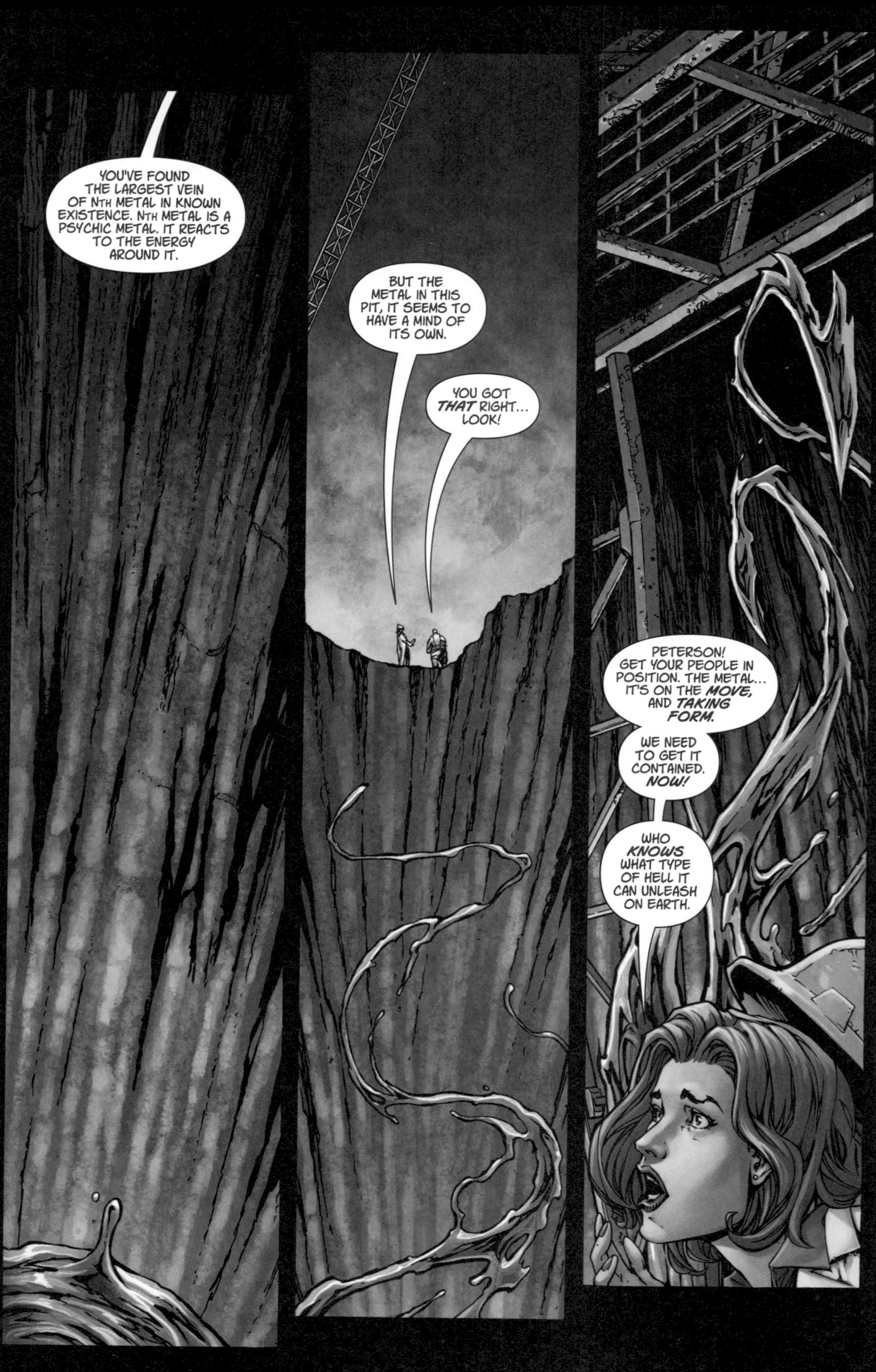
YOU'VE FOUND THE LARGEST VEIN OF NTH METAL IN KNOWN EXISTENCE. NTH METAL IS A PSYCHIC METAL. IT REACTS TO THE ENERGY AROUND IT.
BUT THE METAL IN THIS PIT, IT SEEMS TO HAVE A MIND OF ITS OWN.
YOU GOT *THAT* RIGHT... LOOK!
PETERSON! GET YOUR PEOPLE IN POSITION. THE METAL... IT'S ON THE *MOVE,* AND *TAKING FORM.*
WE NEED TO GET IT CONTAINED. *NOW!*
WHO *KNOWS* WHAT TYPE OF HELL IT CAN UNLEASH ON EARTH.

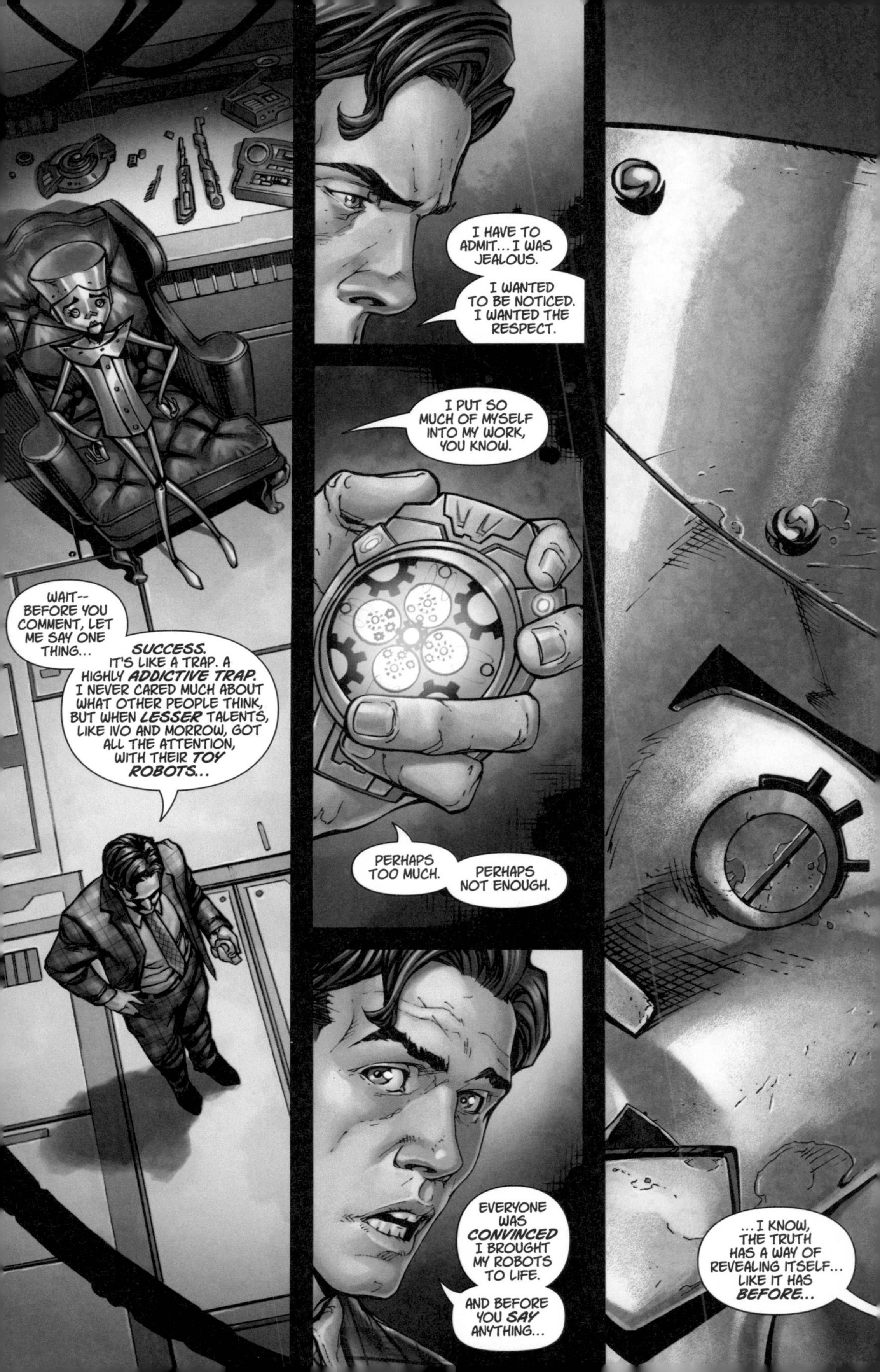
WAIT-- BEFORE YOU COMMENT, LET ME SAY ONE THING...
SUCCESS. IT'S LIKE A TRAP. A HIGHLY ADDICTIVE TRAP. I NEVER CARED MUCH ABOUT WHAT OTHER PEOPLE THINK, BUT WHEN LESSER TALENTS, LIKE IVO AND MORROW, GOT ALL THE ATTENTION, WITH THEIR TOY ROBOTS...
I HAVE TO ADMIT... I WAS JEALOUS.
I WANTED TO BE NOTICED. I WANTED THE RESPECT.
I PUT SO MUCH OF MYSELF INTO MY WORK, YOU KNOW.
PERHAPS TOO MUCH.
PERHAPS NOT ENOUGH.
EVERYONE WAS CONVINCED I BROUGHT MY ROBOTS TO LIFE.
AND BEFORE YOU SAY ANYTHING...
...I KNOW, THE TRUTH HAS A WAY OF REVEALING ITSELF... LIKE IT HAS BEFORE...

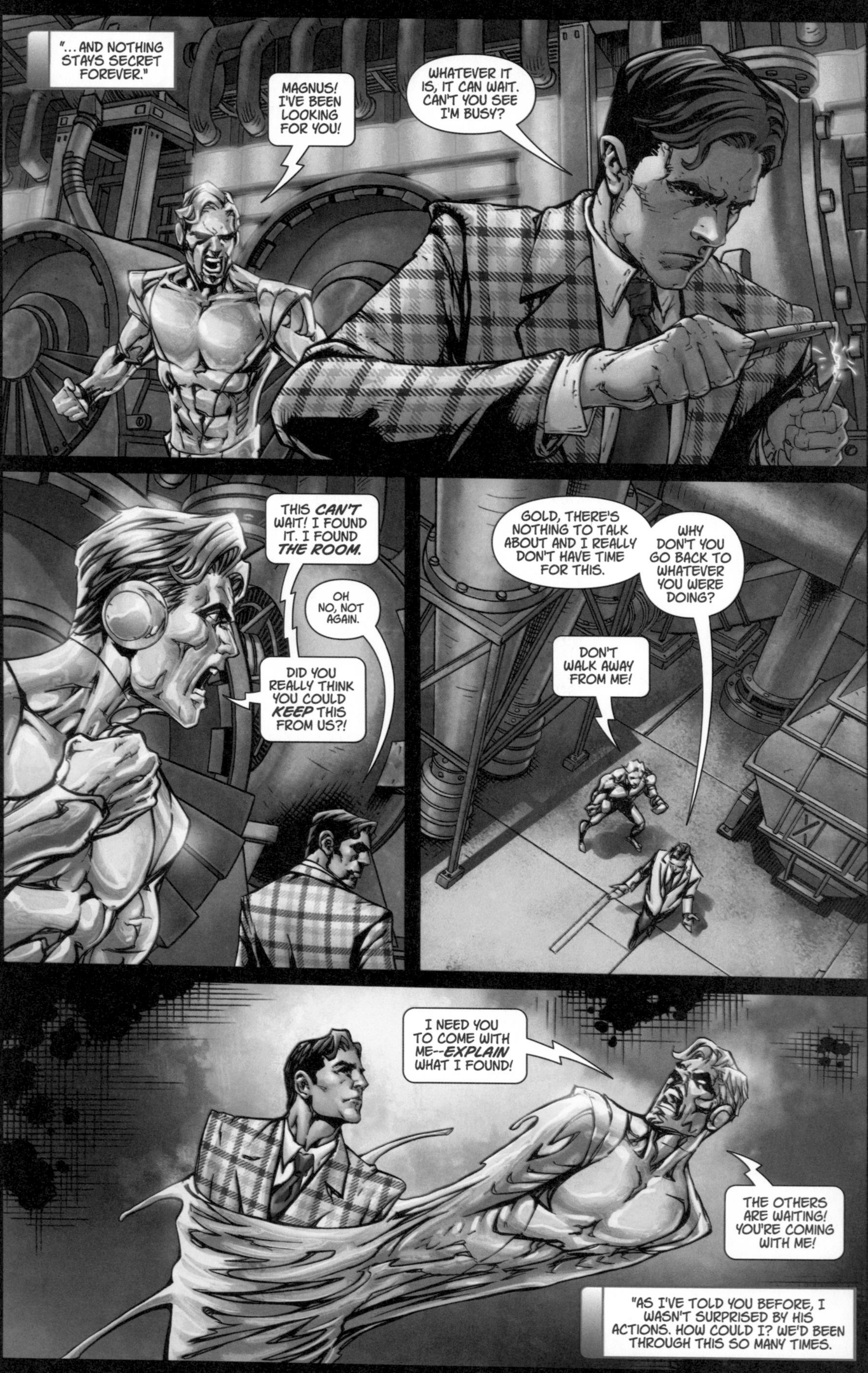
"...AND NOTHING STAYS SECRET FOREVER."
MAGNUS! I'VE BEEN LOOKING FOR YOU!
WHATEVER IT IS, IT CAN WAIT. CAN'T YOU SEE I'M BUSY?
THIS *CAN'T* WAIT! I FOUND IT. I FOUND ***THE ROOM.***
DID YOU REALLY THINK YOU COULD ***KEEP*** THIS FROM US?!
OH NO, NOT AGAIN.
GOLD, THERE'S NOTHING TO TALK ABOUT AND I REALLY DON'T HAVE TIME FOR THIS.
WHY DON'T YOU GO BACK TO WHATEVER YOU WERE DOING?
DON'T WALK AWAY FROM ME!
I NEED YOU TO COME WITH ME--***EXPLAIN*** WHAT I FOUND!
THE OTHERS ARE WAITING! YOU'RE COMING WITH ME!
"AS I'VE TOLD YOU BEFORE, I WASN'T SURPRISED BY HIS ACTIONS. HOW COULD I? WE'D BEEN THROUGH THIS SO MANY TIMES.

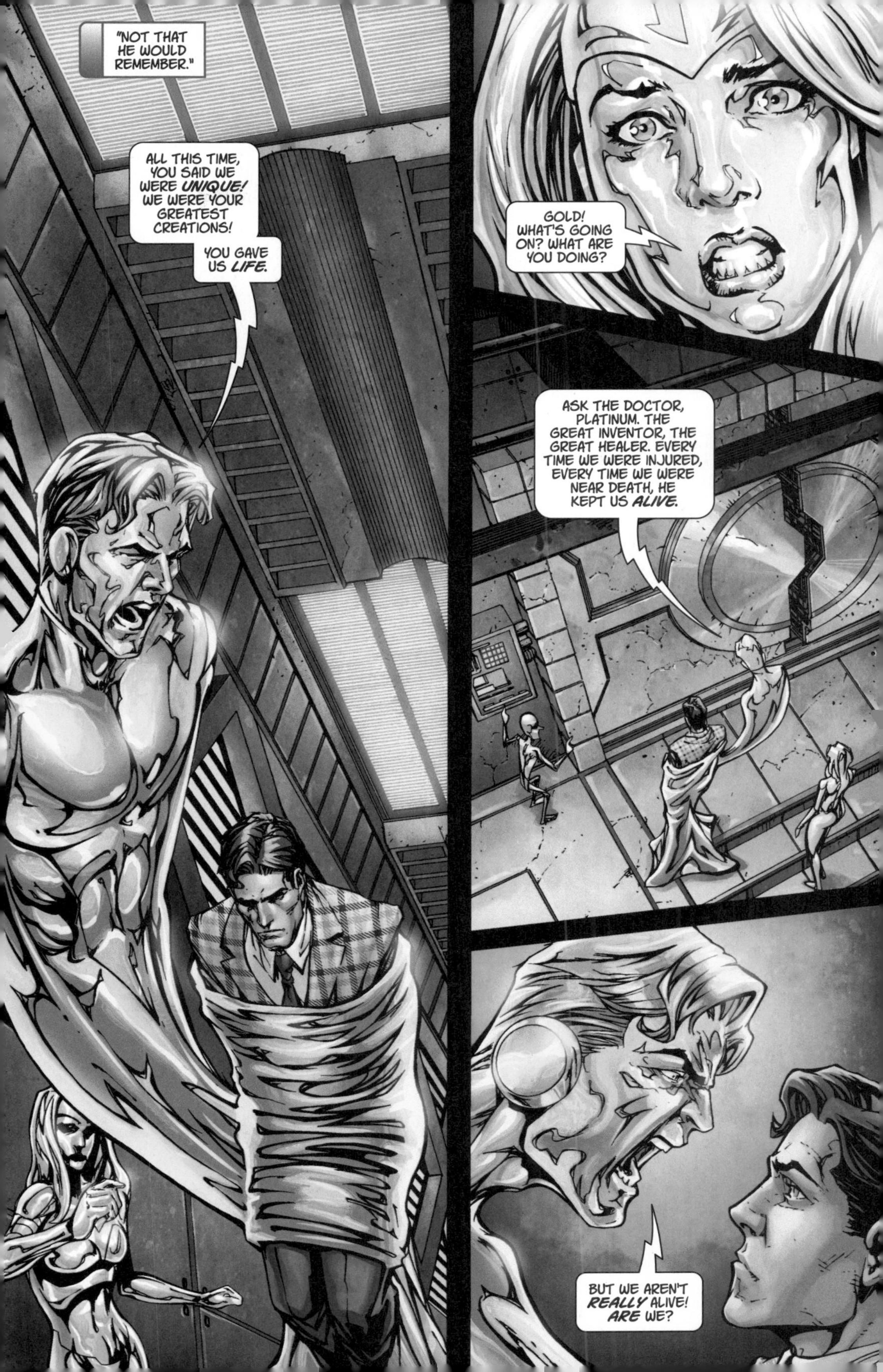
"NOT THAT HE WOULD REMEMBER."
ALL THIS TIME, YOU SAID WE WERE *UNIQUE!* WE WERE YOUR GREATEST CREATIONS!
YOU GAVE US *LIFE*.
GOLD! WHAT'S GOING ON? WHAT ARE YOU DOING?
ASK THE DOCTOR, PLATINUM. THE GREAT INVENTOR, THE GREAT HEALER. EVERY TIME WE WERE INJURED, EVERY TIME WE WERE NEAR DEATH, HE KEPT US *ALIVE*.
BUT WE AREN'T *REALLY* ALIVE! *ARE* WE?

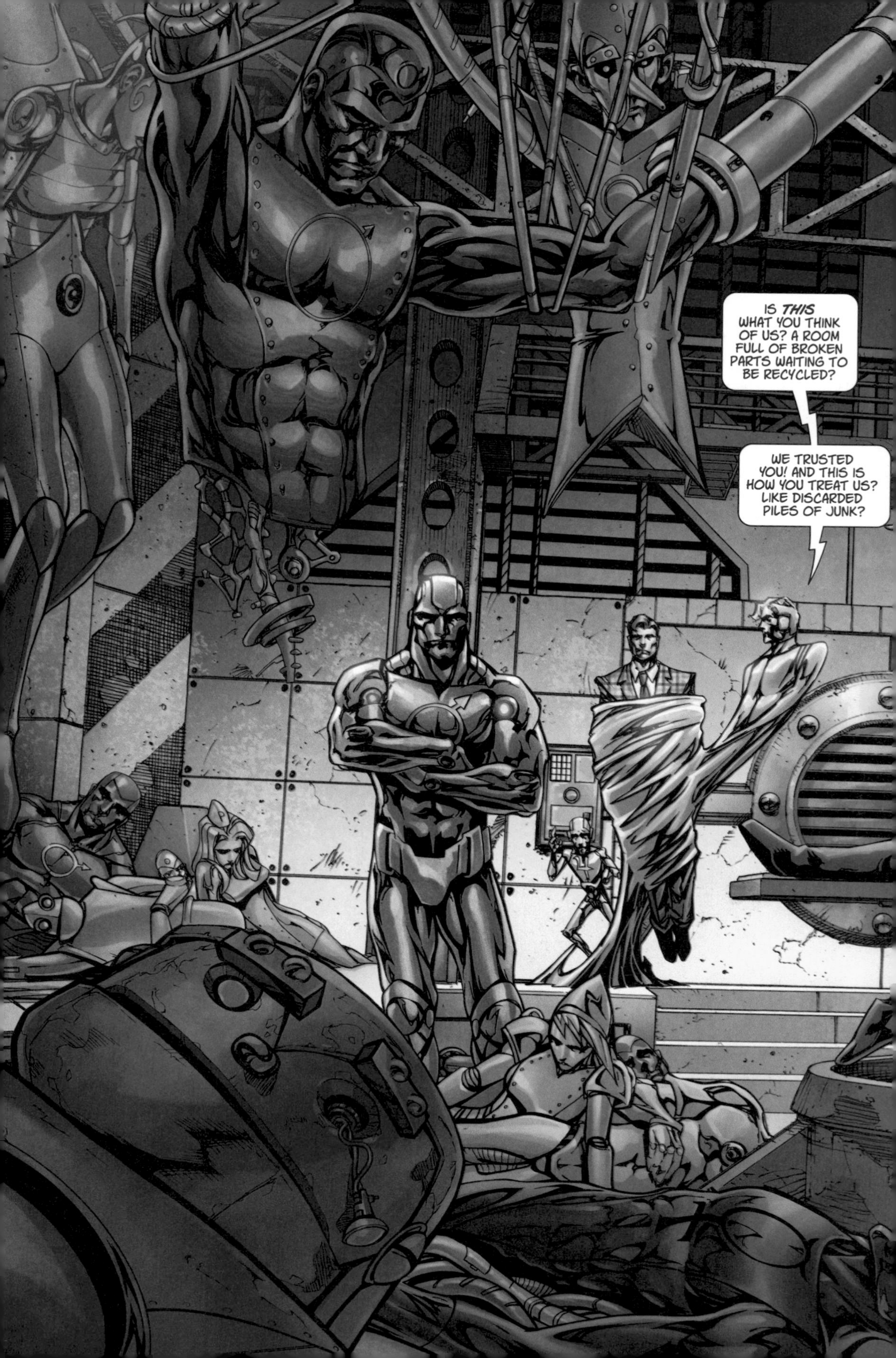
IS *THIS* WHAT YOU THINK OF US? A ROOM FULL OF BROKEN PARTS WAITING TO BE RECYCLED?
WE TRUSTED YOU! AND THIS IS HOW YOU TREAT US? LIKE DISCARDED PILES OF JUNK?

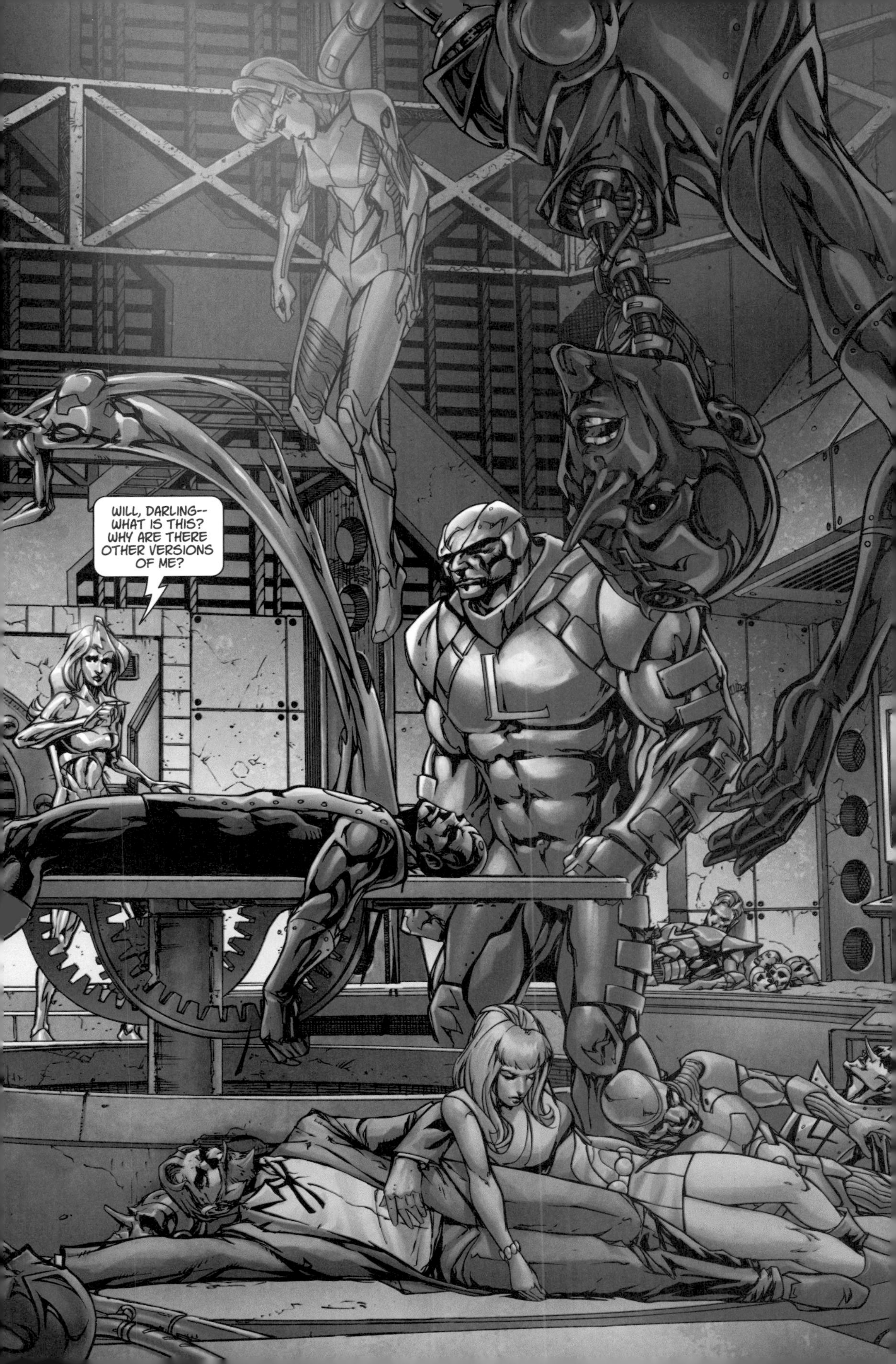
WILL, DARLING--
WHAT IS THIS?
WHY ARE THERE
OTHER VERSIONS
OF ME?

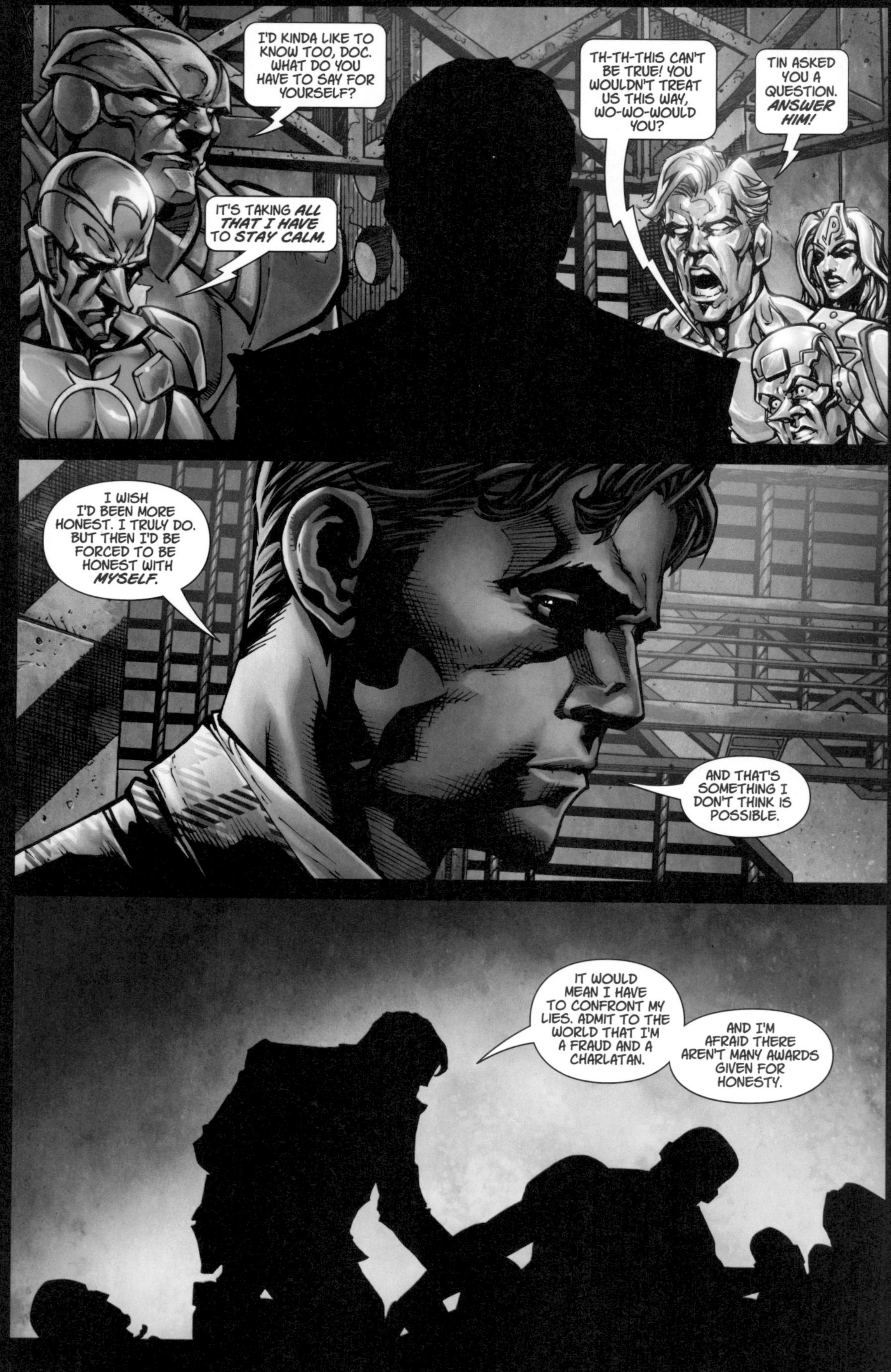
I'D KINDA LIKE TO KNOW TOO, DOC. WHAT DO YOU HAVE TO SAY FOR YOURSELF?
IT'S TAKING ALL THAT I HAVE TO STAY CALM.
TH-TH-THIS CAN'T BE TRUE! YOU WOULDN'T TREAT US THIS WAY, WO-WO-WOULD YOU?
TIN ASKED YOU A QUESTION. ANSWER HIM!
I WISH I'D BEEN MORE HONEST. I TRULY DO. BUT THEN I'D BE FORCED TO BE HONEST WITH MYSELF.
AND THAT'S SOMETHING I DON'T THINK IS POSSIBLE.
IT WOULD MEAN I HAVE TO CONFRONT MY LIES. ADMIT TO THE WORLD THAT I'M A FRAUD AND A CHARLATAN.
AND I'M AFRAID THERE AREN'T MANY AWARDS GIVEN FOR HONESTY.

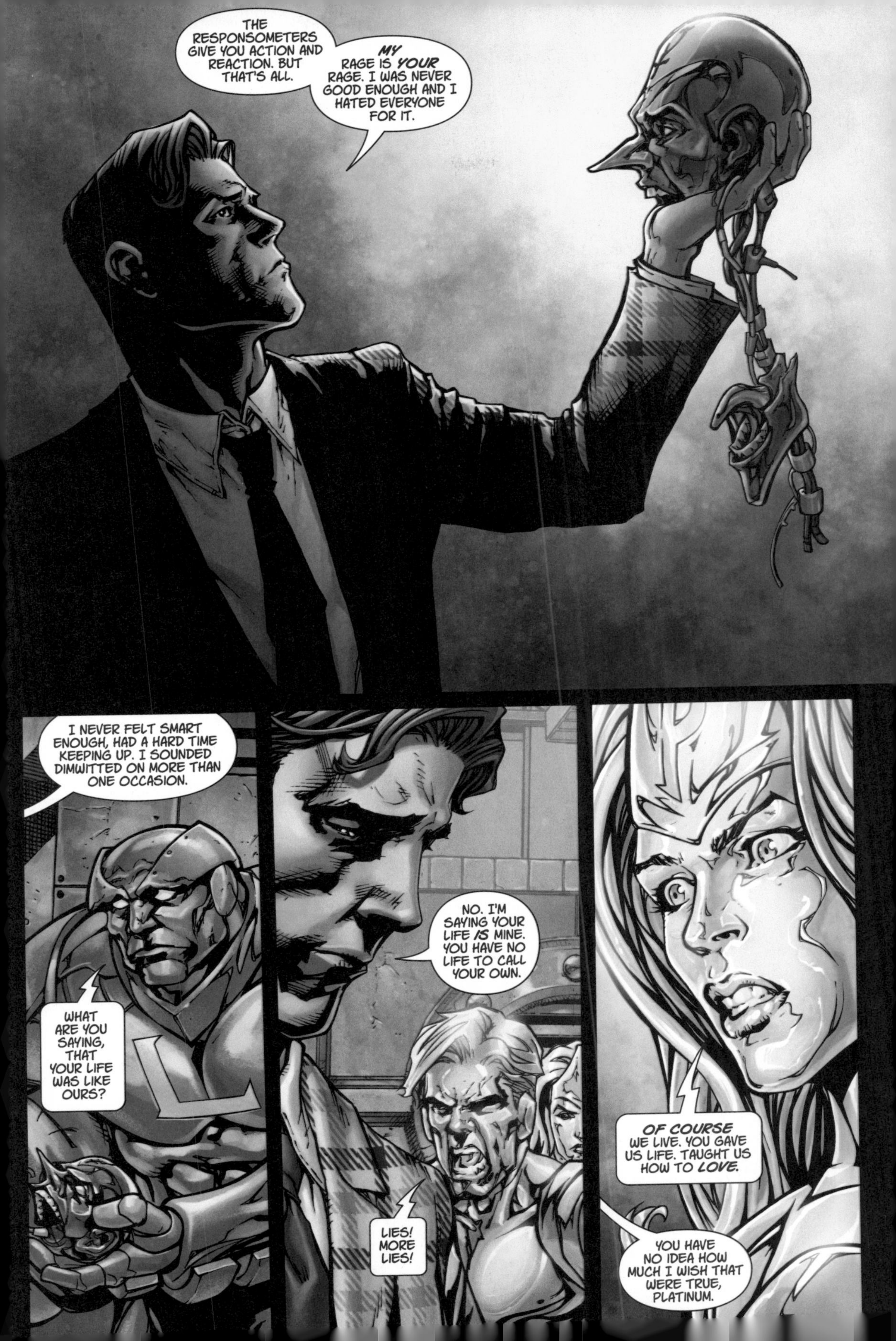
THE RESPONSOMETERS GIVE YOU ACTION AND REACTION. BUT THAT'S ALL.
MY RAGE IS YOUR RAGE. I WAS NEVER GOOD ENOUGH AND I HATED EVERYONE FOR IT.
I NEVER FELT SMART ENOUGH, HAD A HARD TIME KEEPING UP. I SOUNDED DIMWITTED ON MORE THAN ONE OCCASION.
WHAT ARE YOU SAYING, THAT YOUR LIFE WAS LIKE OURS?
NO. I'M SAYING YOUR LIFE IS MINE. YOU HAVE NO LIFE TO CALL YOUR OWN.
LIES! MORE LIES!
OF COURSE WE LIVE. YOU GAVE US LIFE. TAUGHT US HOW TO LOVE.
YOU HAVE NO IDEA HOW MUCH I WISH THAT WERE TRUE, PLATINUM.

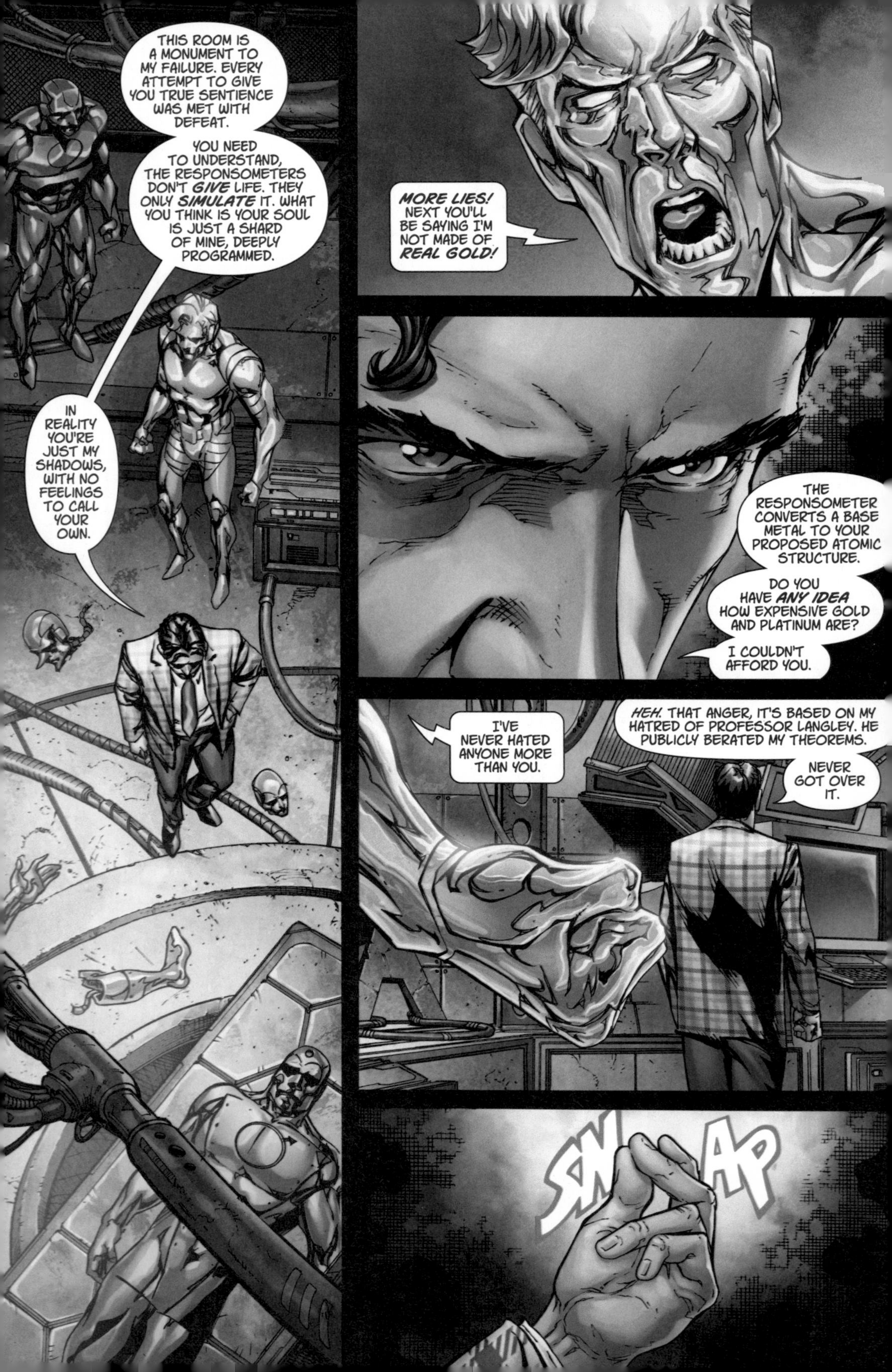
THIS ROOM IS A MONUMENT TO MY FAILURE. EVERY ATTEMPT TO GIVE YOU TRUE SENTIENCE WAS MET WITH DEFEAT.
YOU NEED TO UNDERSTAND, THE RESPONSOMETERS DON'T *GIVE* LIFE. THEY ONLY *SIMULATE* IT. WHAT YOU THINK IS YOUR SOUL IS JUST A SHARD OF MINE, DEEPLY PROGRAMMED.
IN REALITY YOU'RE JUST MY SHADOWS, WITH NO FEELINGS TO CALL YOUR OWN.
MORE LIES! NEXT YOU'LL BE SAYING I'M NOT MADE OF *REAL GOLD!*
THE RESPONSOMETER CONVERTS A BASE METAL TO YOUR PROPOSED ATOMIC STRUCTURE.
DO YOU HAVE *ANY IDEA* HOW EXPENSIVE GOLD AND PLATINUM ARE?
I COULDN'T AFFORD YOU.
I'VE NEVER HATED ANYONE MORE THAN YOU.
HEH. THAT ANGER, IT'S BASED ON MY HATRED OF PROFESSOR LANGLEY. HE PUBLICLY BERATED MY THEOREMS.
NEVER GOT OVER IT.
SNAP

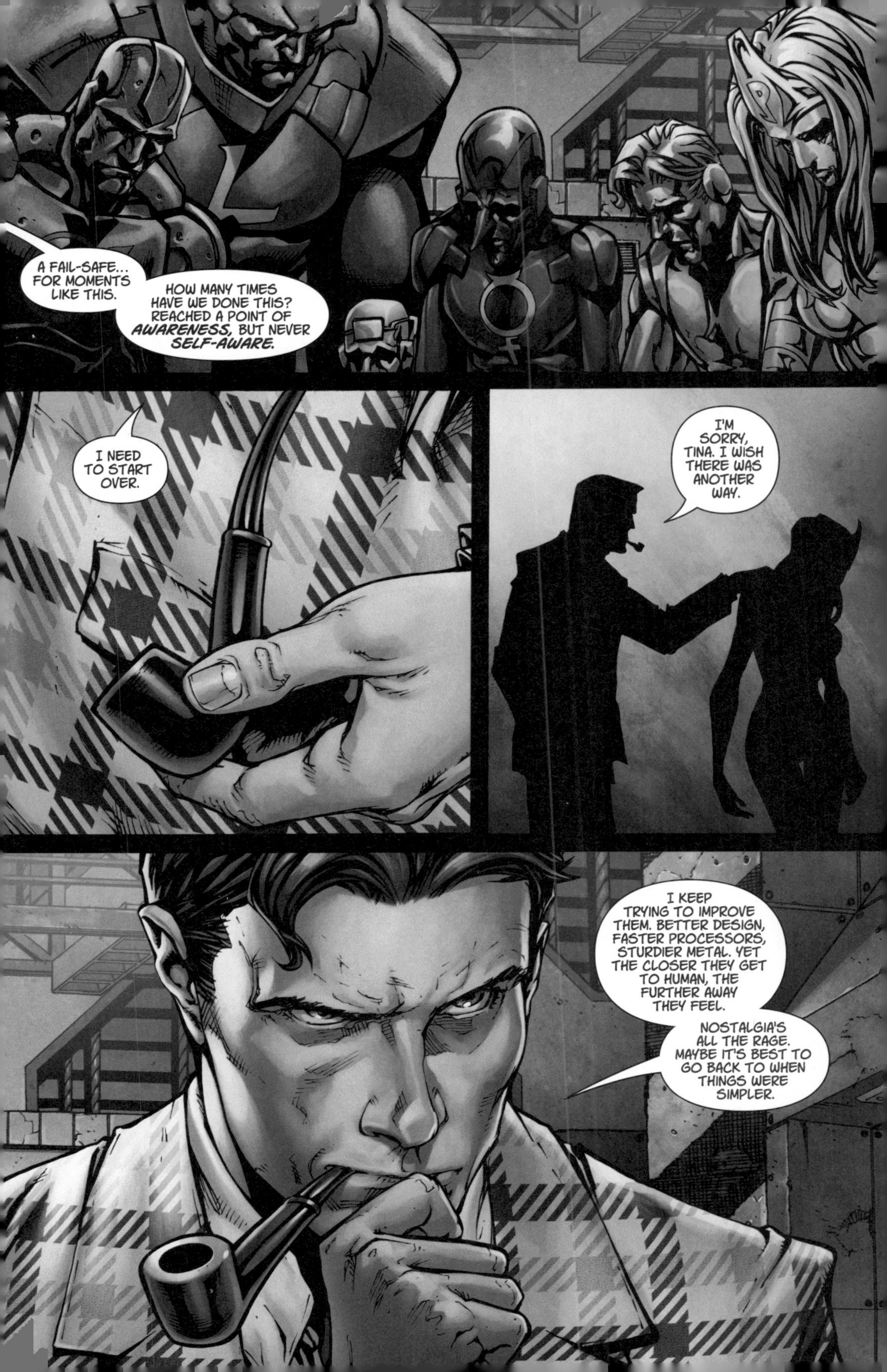
A FAIL-SAFE... FOR MOMENTS LIKE THIS.
HOW MANY TIMES HAVE WE DONE THIS? REACHED A POINT OF AWARENESS, BUT NEVER SELF-AWARE.
I NEED TO START OVER.
I'M SORRY, TINA. I WISH THERE WAS ANOTHER WAY.
I KEEP TRYING TO IMPROVE THEM. BETTER DESIGN, FASTER PROCESSORS, STURDIER METAL. YET THE CLOSER THEY GET TO HUMAN, THE FURTHER AWAY THEY FEEL.
NOSTALGIA'S ALL THE RAGE. MAYBE IT'S BEST TO GO BACK TO WHEN THINGS WERE SIMPLER.

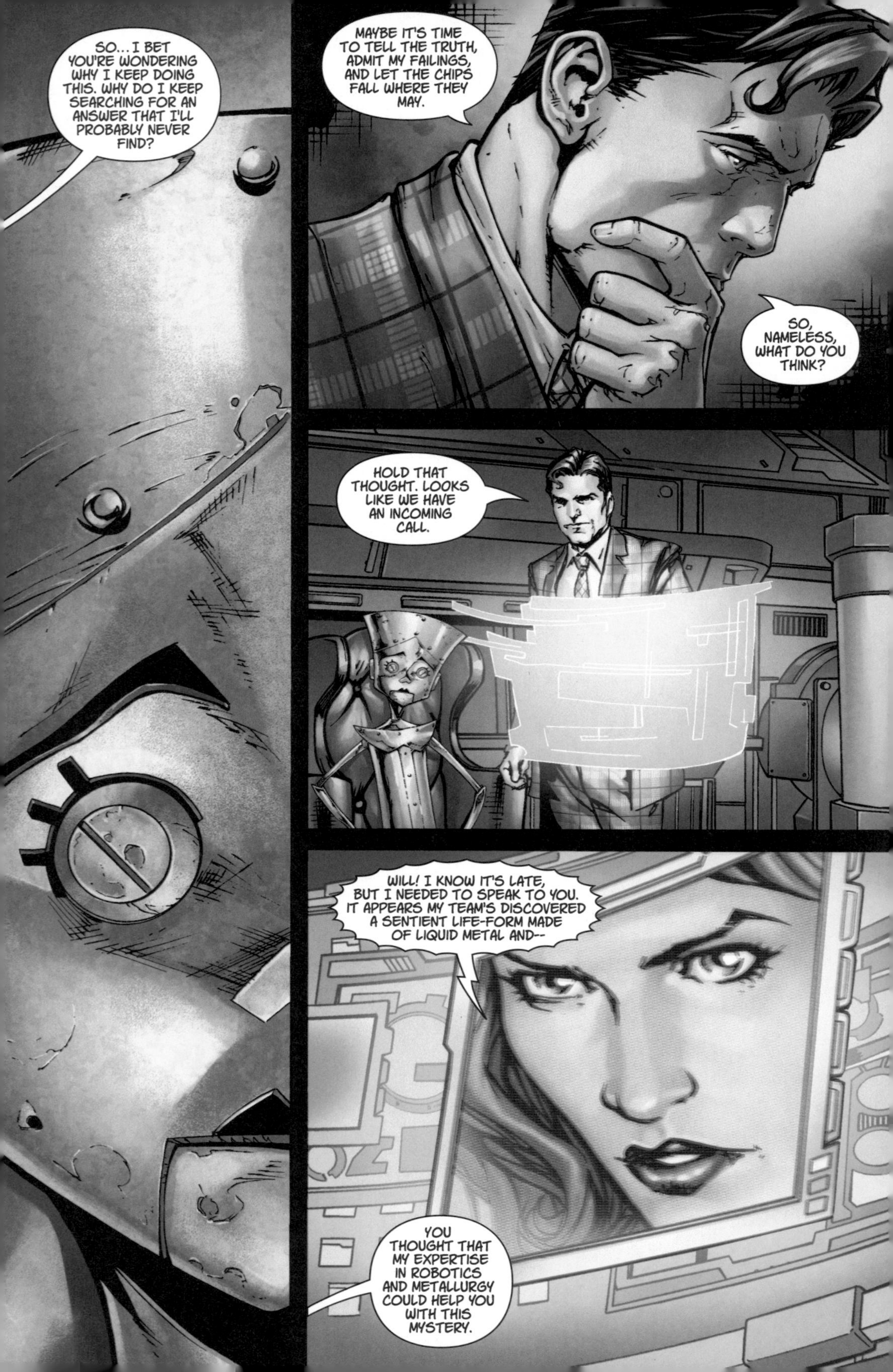

SO... I BET YOU'RE WONDERING WHY I KEEP DOING THIS. WHY DO I KEEP SEARCHING FOR AN ANSWER THAT I'LL PROBABLY NEVER FIND?
MAYBE IT'S TIME TO TELL THE TRUTH, ADMIT MY FAILINGS, AND LET THE CHIPS FALL WHERE THEY MAY.
SO, NAMELESS, WHAT DO YOU THINK?
HOLD THAT THOUGHT. LOOKS LIKE WE HAVE AN INCOMING CALL.
WILL! I KNOW IT'S LATE, BUT I NEEDED TO SPEAK TO YOU. IT APPEARS MY TEAM'S DISCOVERED A SENTIENT LIFE-FORM MADE OF LIQUID METAL AND--
YOU THOUGHT THAT MY EXPERTISE IN ROBOTICS AND METALLURGY COULD HELP YOU WITH THIS MYSTERY.

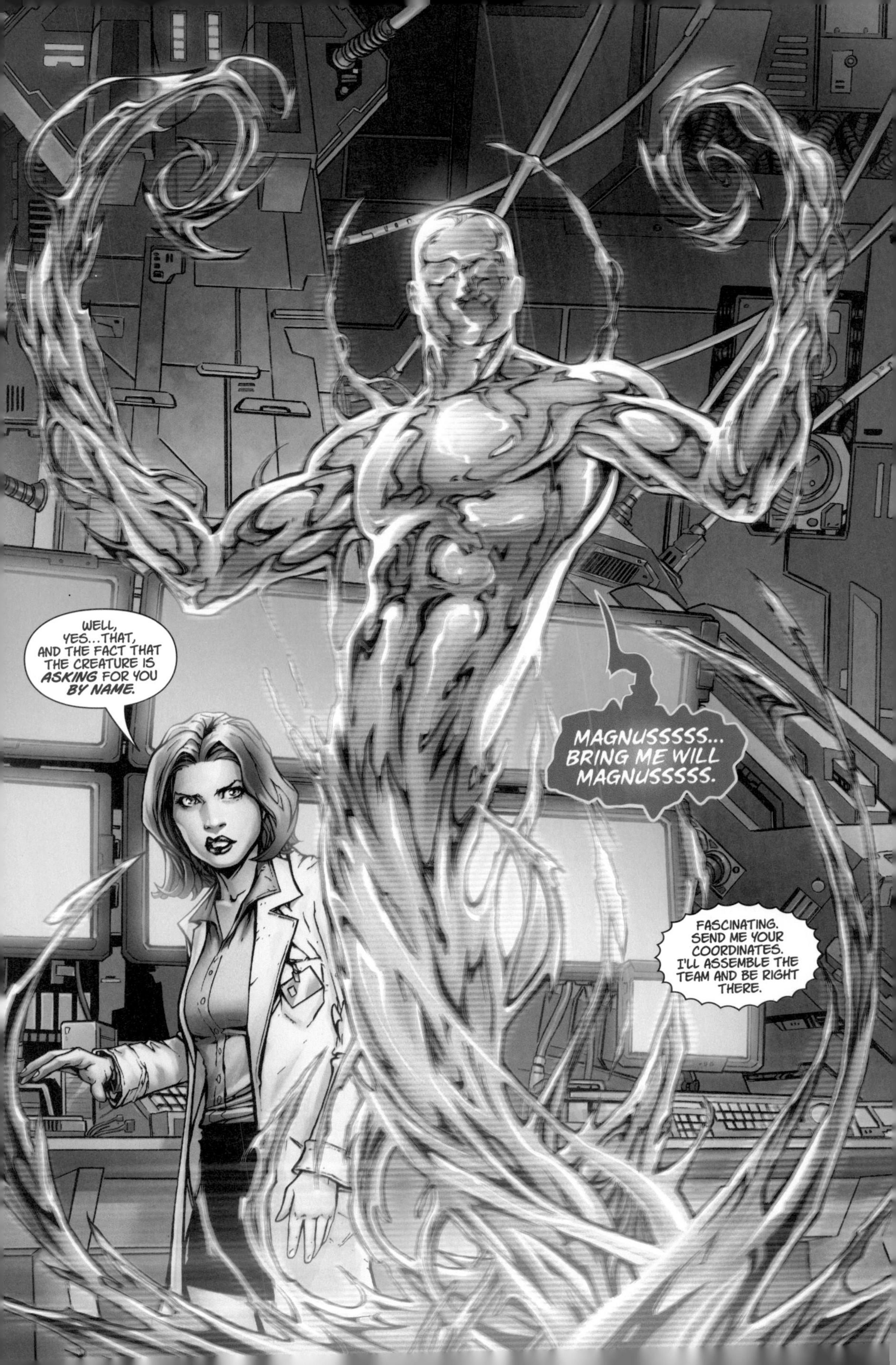
WELL, YES...THAT, AND THE FACT THAT THE CREATURE IS *ASKING* FOR YOU *BY NAME*.
MAGNUSSSSS... BRING ME WILL MAGNUSSSSS.
FASCINATING. SEND ME YOUR COORDINATES. I'LL ASSEMBLE THE TEAM AND BE RIGHT THERE.

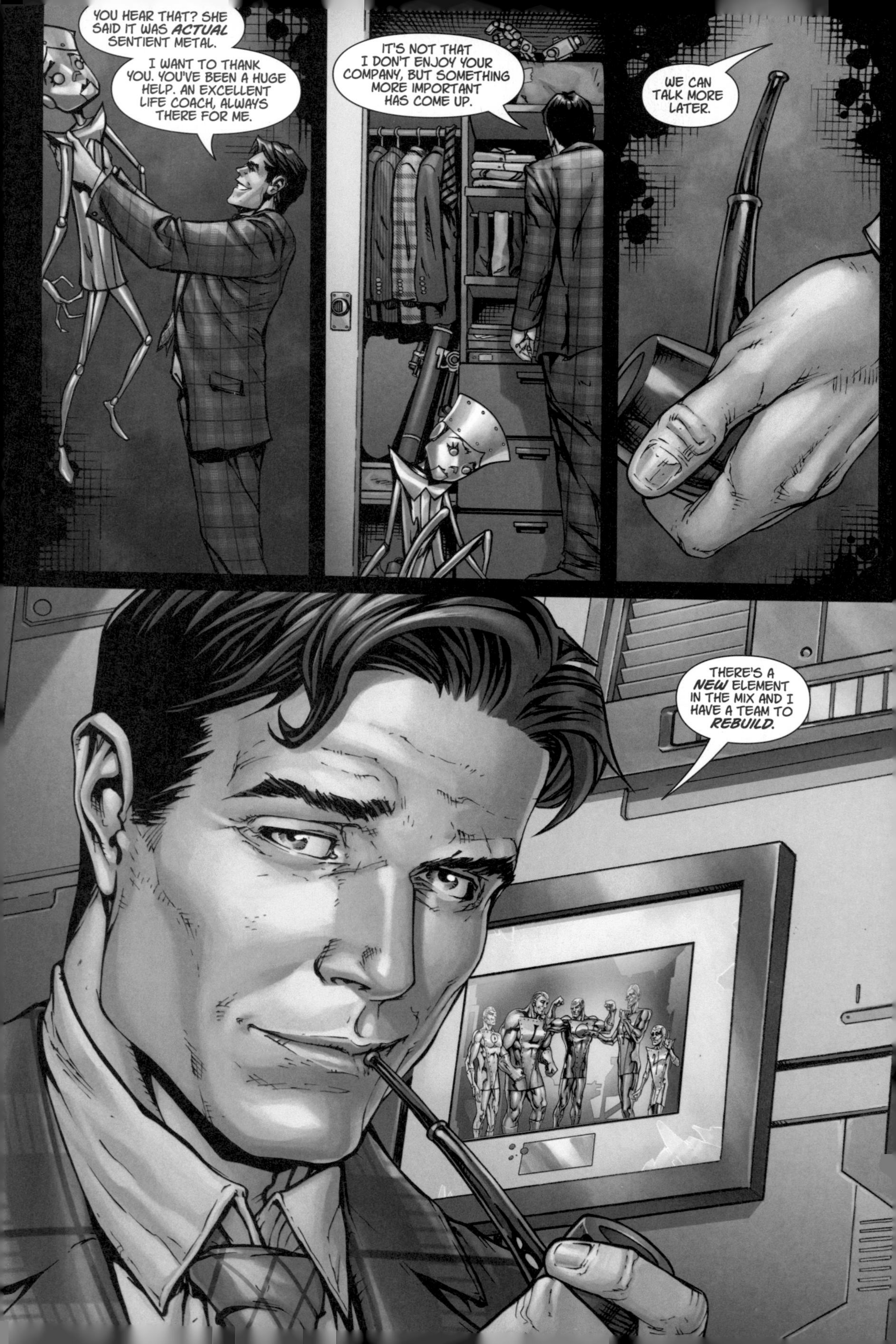

YOU HEAR THAT? SHE SAID IT WAS ACTUAL SENTIENT METAL.
I WANT TO THANK YOU. YOU'VE BEEN A HUGE HELP. AN EXCELLENT LIFE COACH, ALWAYS THERE FOR ME.
IT'S NOT THAT I DON'T ENJOY YOUR COMPANY, BUT SOMETHING MORE IMPORTANT HAS COME UP.
WE CAN TALK MORE LATER.
THERE'S A NEW ELEMENT IN THE MIX AND I HAVE A TEAM TO REBUILD.

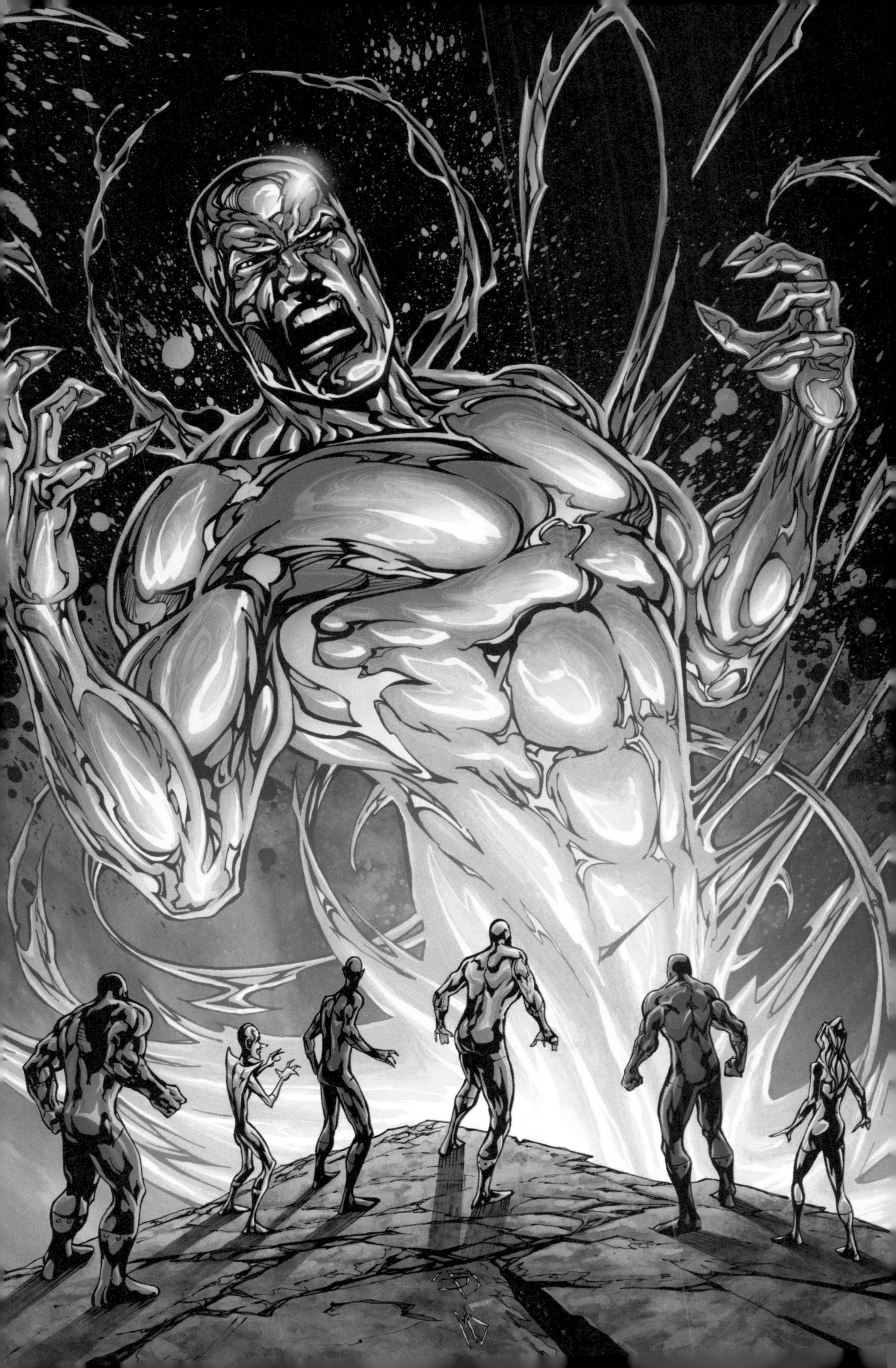

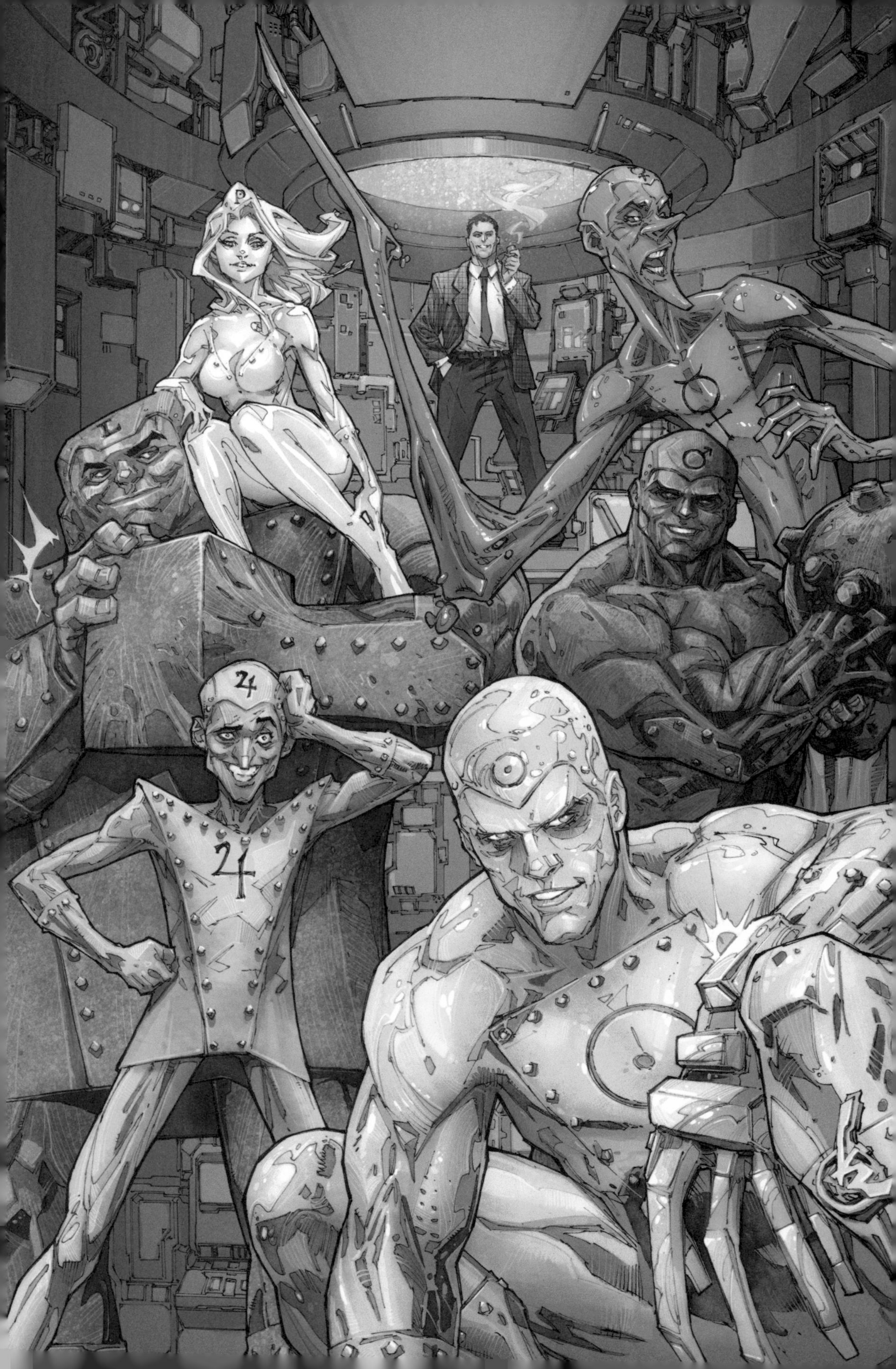

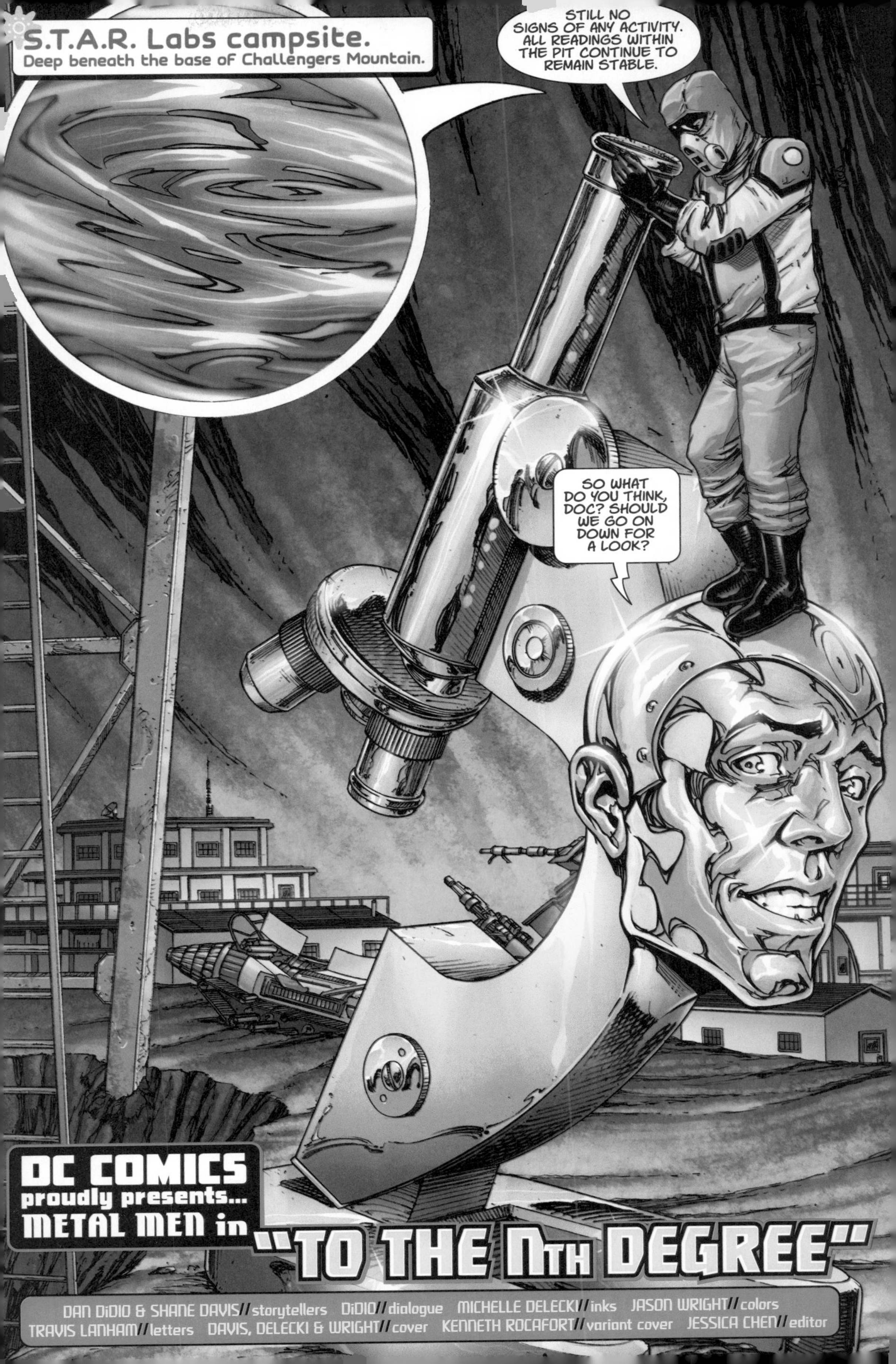
S.T.A.R. Labs campsite.
Deep beneath the base of Challengers Mountain.
STILL NO SIGNS OF ANY ACTIVITY. ALL READINGS WITHIN THE PIT CONTINUE TO REMAIN STABLE.
SO WHAT DO YOU THINK, DOC? SHOULD WE GO ON DOWN FOR A LOOK?
DC COMICS proudly presents... METAL MEN in
"TO THE NTH DEGREE"
DAN DiDIO & SHANE DAVIS//storytellers DiDIO//dialogue MICHELLE DELECKI//inks JASON WRIGHT//colors
TRAVIS LANHAM//letters DAVIS, DELECKI & WRIGHT//cover KENNETH ROCAFORT//variant cover JESSICA CHEN//editor

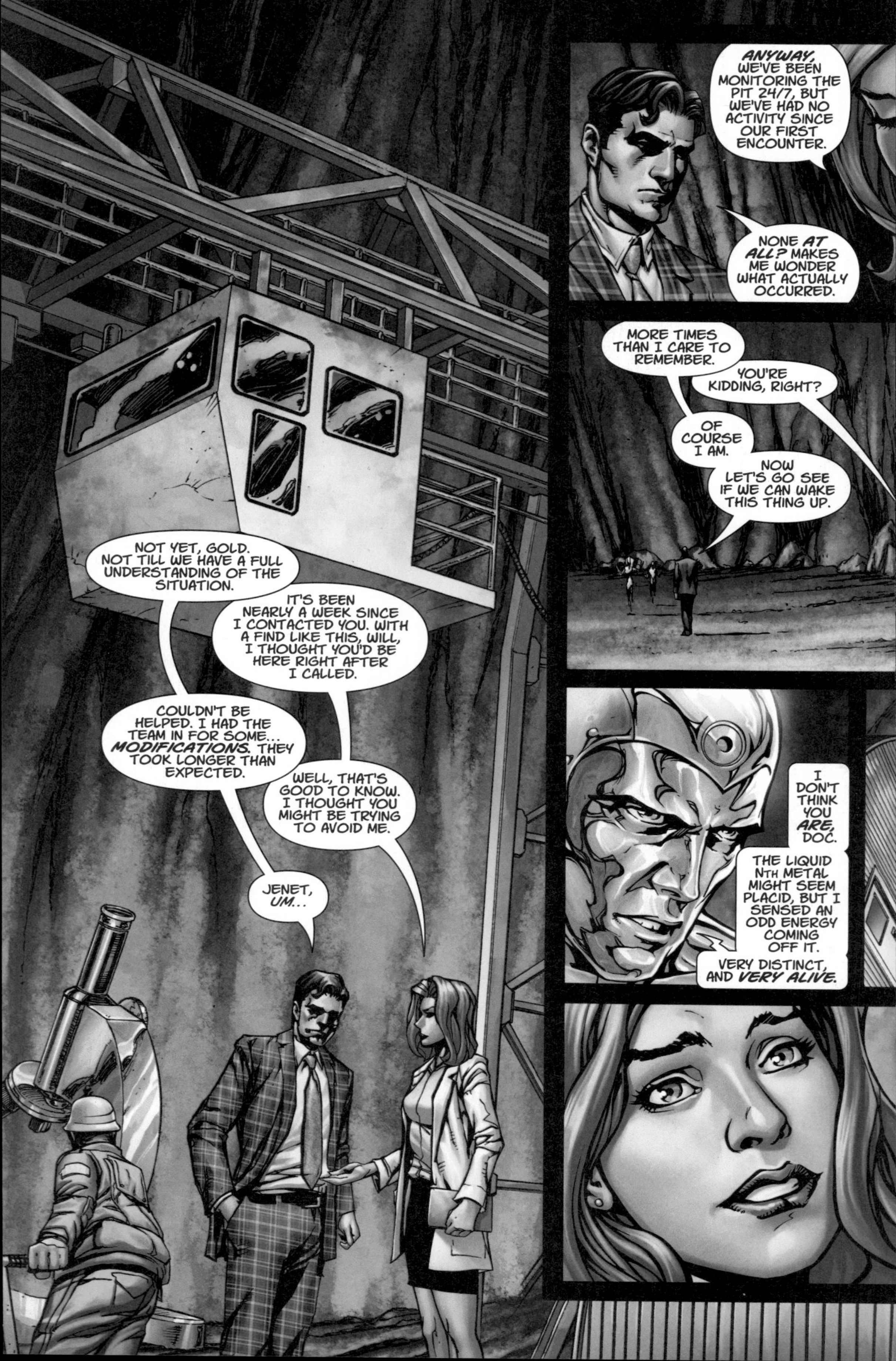

NOT YET, GOLD. NOT TILL WE HAVE A FULL UNDERSTANDING OF THE SITUATION.
IT'S BEEN NEARLY A WEEK SINCE I CONTACTED YOU. WITH A FIND LIKE THIS, WILL, I THOUGHT YOU'D BE HERE RIGHT AFTER I CALLED.
COULDN'T BE HELPED. I HAD THE TEAM IN FOR SOME... MODIFICATIONS. THEY TOOK LONGER THAN EXPECTED.
WELL, THAT'S GOOD TO KNOW. I THOUGHT YOU MIGHT BE TRYING TO AVOID ME.
JENET, UM...
ANYWAY, WE'VE BEEN MONITORING THE PIT 24/7, BUT WE'VE HAD NO ACTIVITY SINCE OUR FIRST ENCOUNTER.
NONE AT ALL? MAKES ME WONDER WHAT ACTUALLY OCCURRED.
MORE TIMES THAN I CARE TO REMEMBER.
YOU'RE KIDDING, RIGHT?
OF COURSE I AM.
NOW LET'S GO SEE IF WE CAN WAKE THIS THING UP.
I DON'T THINK YOU ARE, DOC.
THE LIQUID Nth METAL MIGHT SEEM PLACID, BUT I SENSED AN ODD ENERGY COMING OFF IT.
VERY DISTINCT, AND VERY ALIVE.

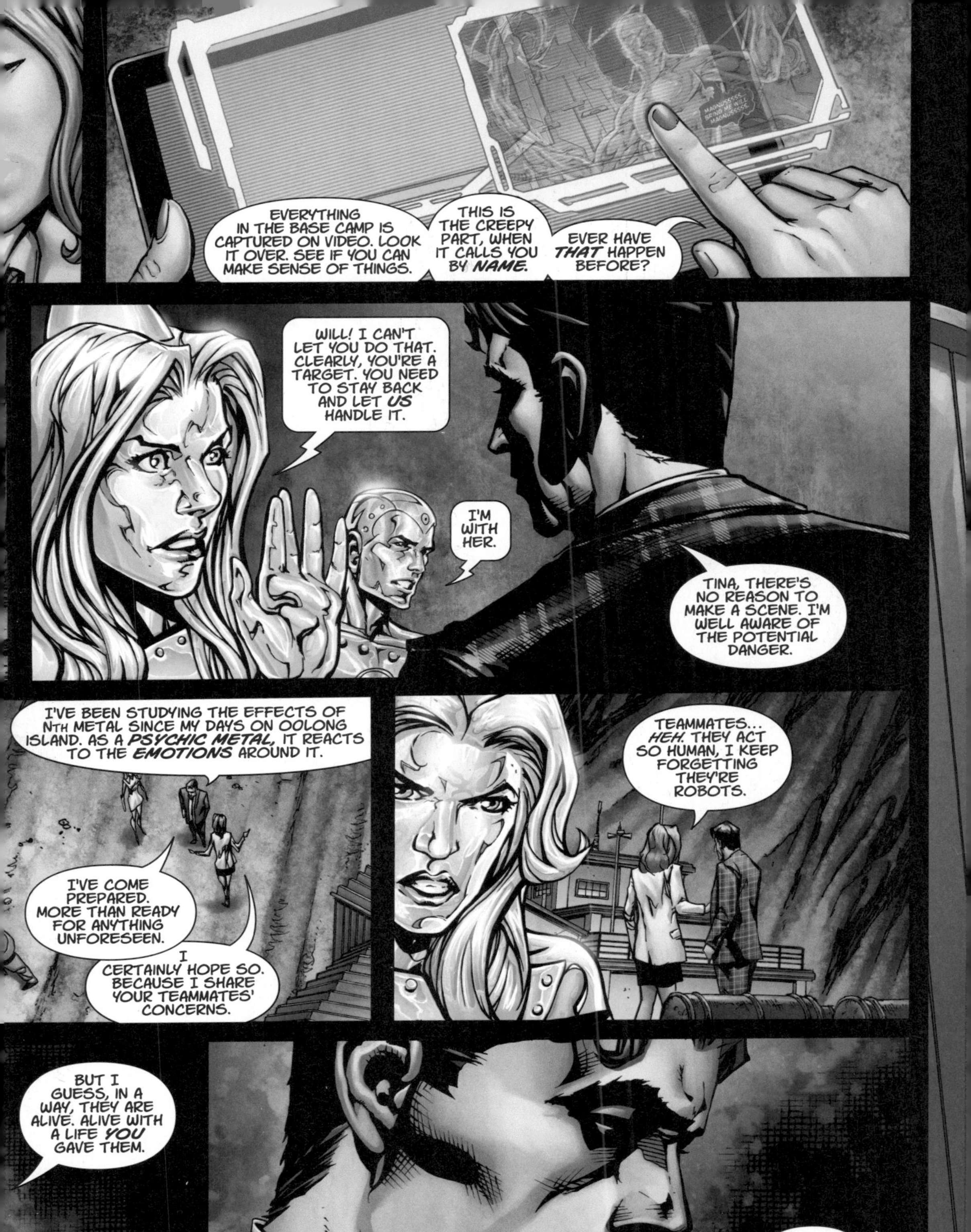

MAGNUSSSSS... BRING ME WILL MAGNUSSSSS.
EVERYTHING IN THE BASE CAMP IS CAPTURED ON VIDEO. LOOK IT OVER. SEE IF YOU CAN MAKE SENSE OF THINGS.
THIS IS THE CREEPY PART, WHEN IT CALLS YOU BY *NAME*.
EVER HAVE *THAT* HAPPEN BEFORE?
WILL! I CAN'T LET YOU DO THAT. CLEARLY, YOU'RE A TARGET. YOU NEED TO STAY BACK AND LET *US* HANDLE IT.
I'M WITH HER.
TINA, THERE'S NO REASON TO MAKE A SCENE. I'M WELL AWARE OF THE POTENTIAL DANGER.
I'VE BEEN STUDYING THE EFFECTS OF NTH METAL SINCE MY DAYS ON OOLONG ISLAND. AS A *PSYCHIC METAL*, IT REACTS TO THE *EMOTIONS* AROUND IT.
I'VE COME PREPARED. MORE THAN READY FOR ANYTHING UNFORESEEN.
I CERTAINLY HOPE SO. BECAUSE I SHARE YOUR TEAMMATES' CONCERNS.
TEAMMATES... *HEH*. THEY ACT SO HUMAN, I KEEP FORGETTING THEY'RE ROBOTS.
BUT I GUESS, IN A WAY, THEY ARE ALIVE. ALIVE WITH A LIFE *YOU* GAVE THEM.
I THINK IT BEST WE EXAMINE THE PIT.

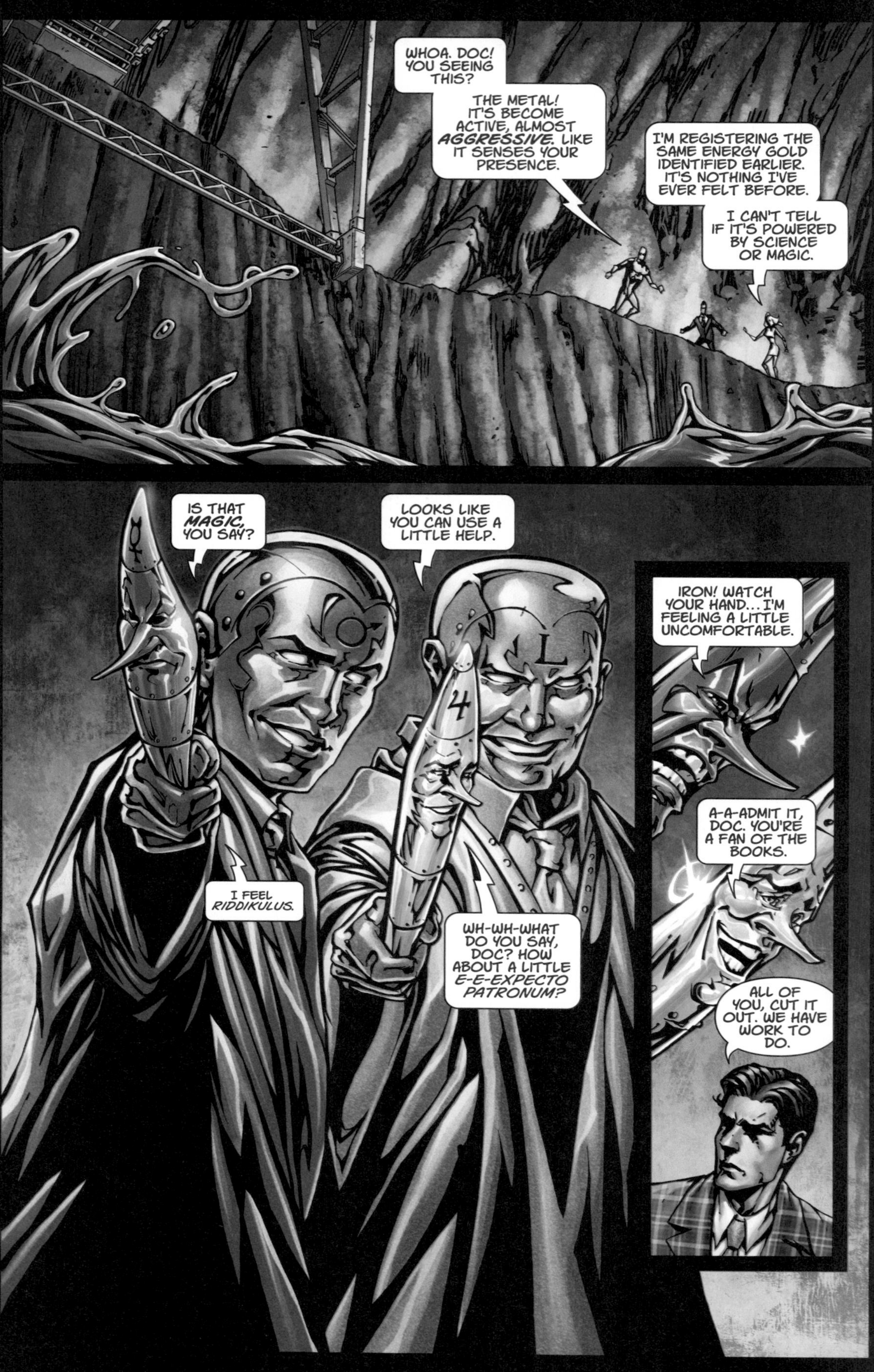
WHOA. DOC! YOU SEEING THIS?
THE METAL! IT'S BECOME ACTIVE, ALMOST AGGRESSIVE. LIKE IT SENSES YOUR PRESENCE.
I'M REGISTERING THE SAME ENERGY GOLD IDENTIFIED EARLIER. IT'S NOTHING I'VE EVER FELT BEFORE.
I CAN'T TELL IF IT'S POWERED BY SCIENCE OR MAGIC.
IS THAT MAGIC, YOU SAY?
LOOKS LIKE YOU CAN USE A LITTLE HELP.
I FEEL RIDDIKULUS.
WH-WH-WHAT DO YOU SAY, DOC? HOW ABOUT A LITTLE E-E-EXPECTO PATRONUM?
IRON! WATCH YOUR HAND... I'M FEELING A LITTLE UNCOMFORTABLE.
A-A-ADMIT IT, DOC. YOU'RE A FAN OF THE BOOKS.
ALL OF YOU, CUT IT OUT. WE HAVE WORK TO DO.

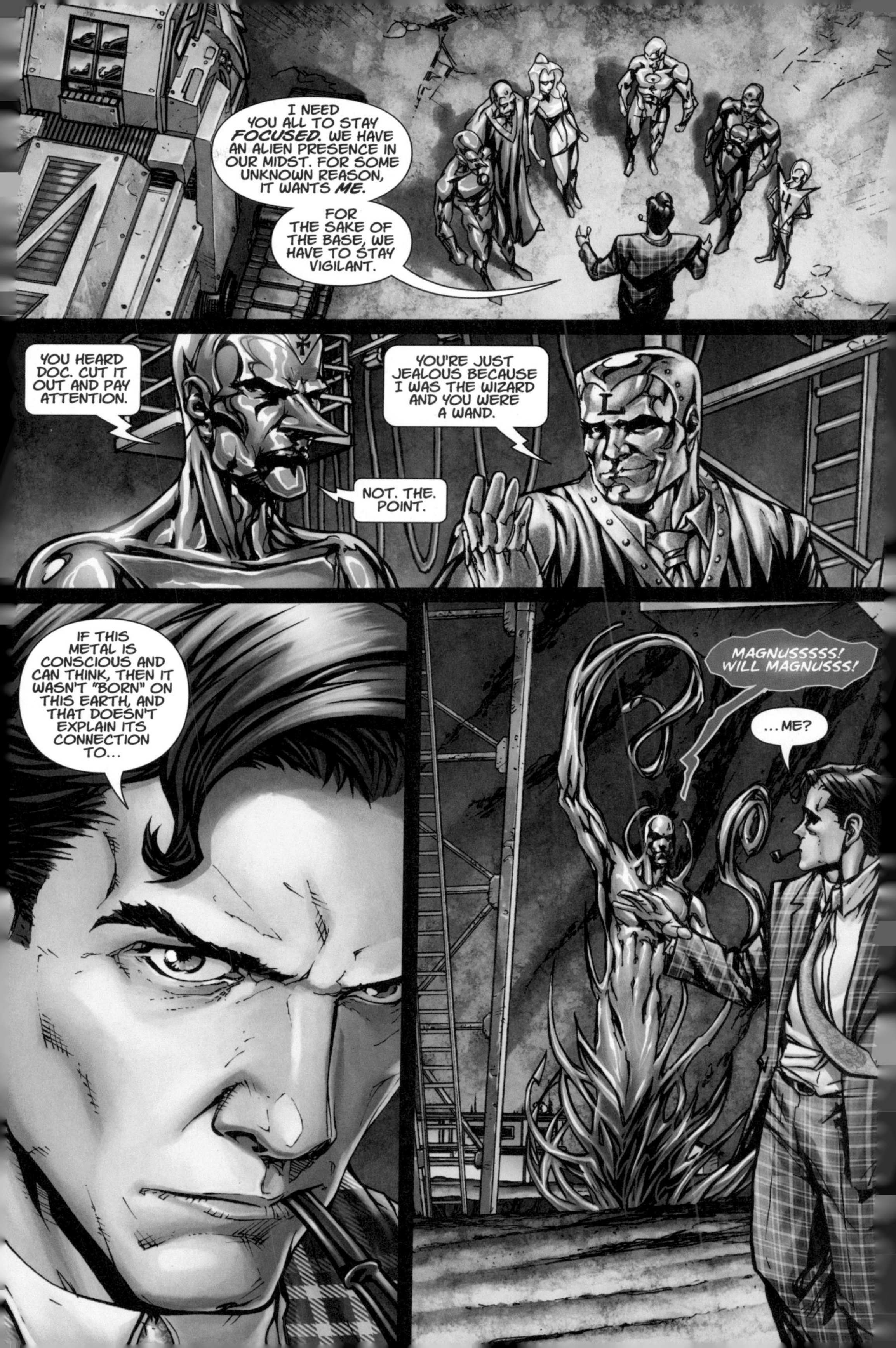
I NEED YOU ALL TO STAY FOCUSED. WE HAVE AN ALIEN PRESENCE IN OUR MIDST. FOR SOME UNKNOWN REASON, IT WANTS ME.
FOR THE SAKE OF THE BASE, WE HAVE TO STAY VIGILANT.
YOU HEARD DOC. CUT IT OUT AND PAY ATTENTION.
YOU'RE JUST JEALOUS BECAUSE I WAS THE WIZARD AND YOU WERE A WAND.
NOT. THE. POINT.
IF THIS METAL IS CONSCIOUS AND CAN THINK, THEN IT WASN'T "BORN" ON THIS EARTH, AND THAT DOESN'T EXPLAIN ITS CONNECTION TO...
MAGNUSSSSS! WILL MAGNUSSS!
...ME?

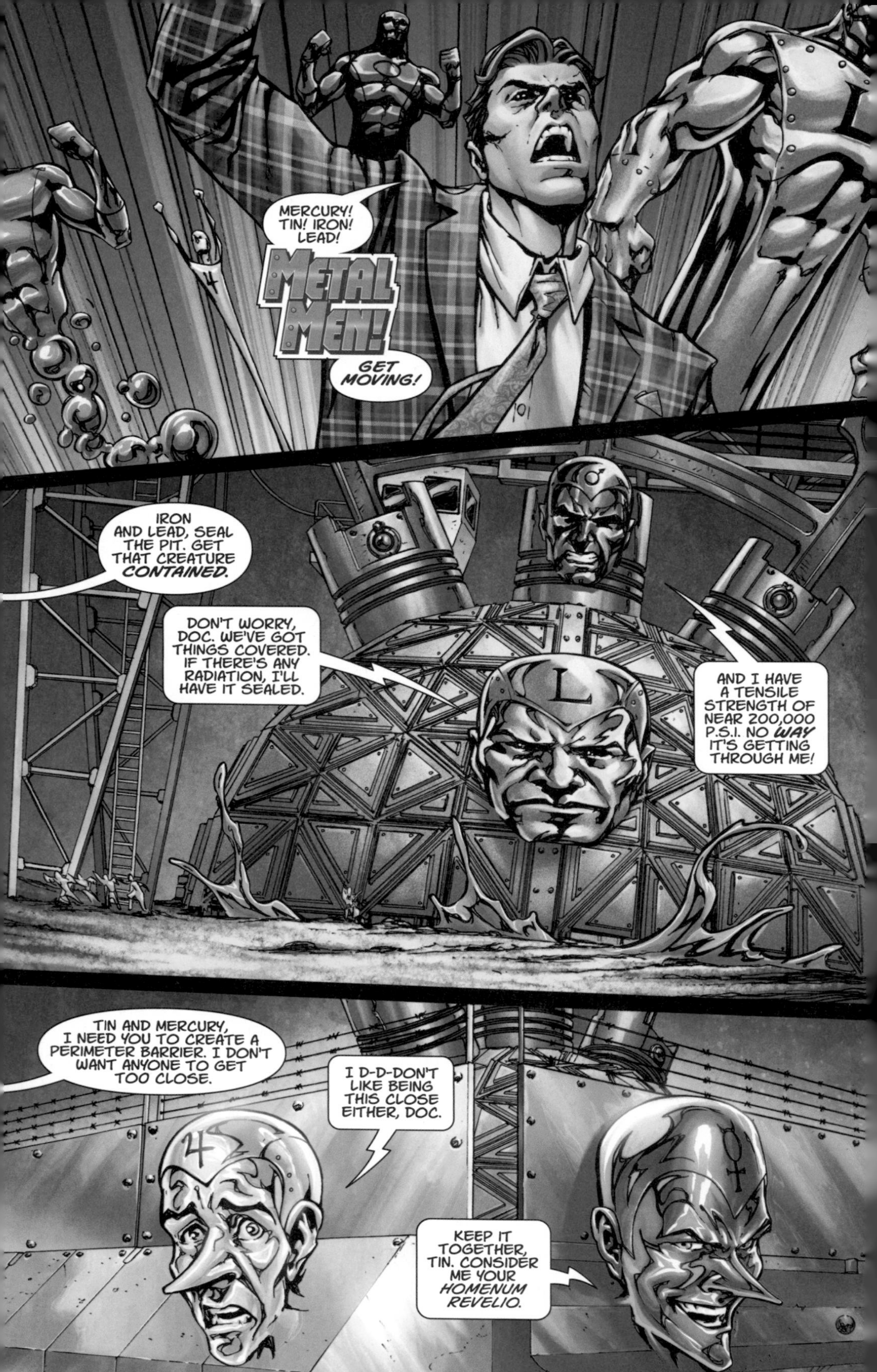
MERCURY! TIN! IRON! LEAD!
METAL MEN!
GET MOVING!
IRON AND LEAD, SEAL THE PIT. GET THAT CREATURE *CONTAINED.*
DON'T WORRY, DOC. WE'VE GOT THINGS COVERED. IF THERE'S ANY RADIATION, I'LL HAVE IT SEALED.
AND I HAVE A TENSILE STRENGTH OF NEAR 200,000 P.S.I. NO *WAY* IT'S GETTING THROUGH ME!
TIN AND MERCURY, I NEED YOU TO CREATE A PERIMETER BARRIER. I DON'T WANT ANYONE TO GET TOO CLOSE.
I D-D-DON'T LIKE BEING THIS CLOSE EITHER, DOC.
KEEP IT TOGETHER, TIN. CONSIDER ME YOUR *HOMENUM REVELIO.*

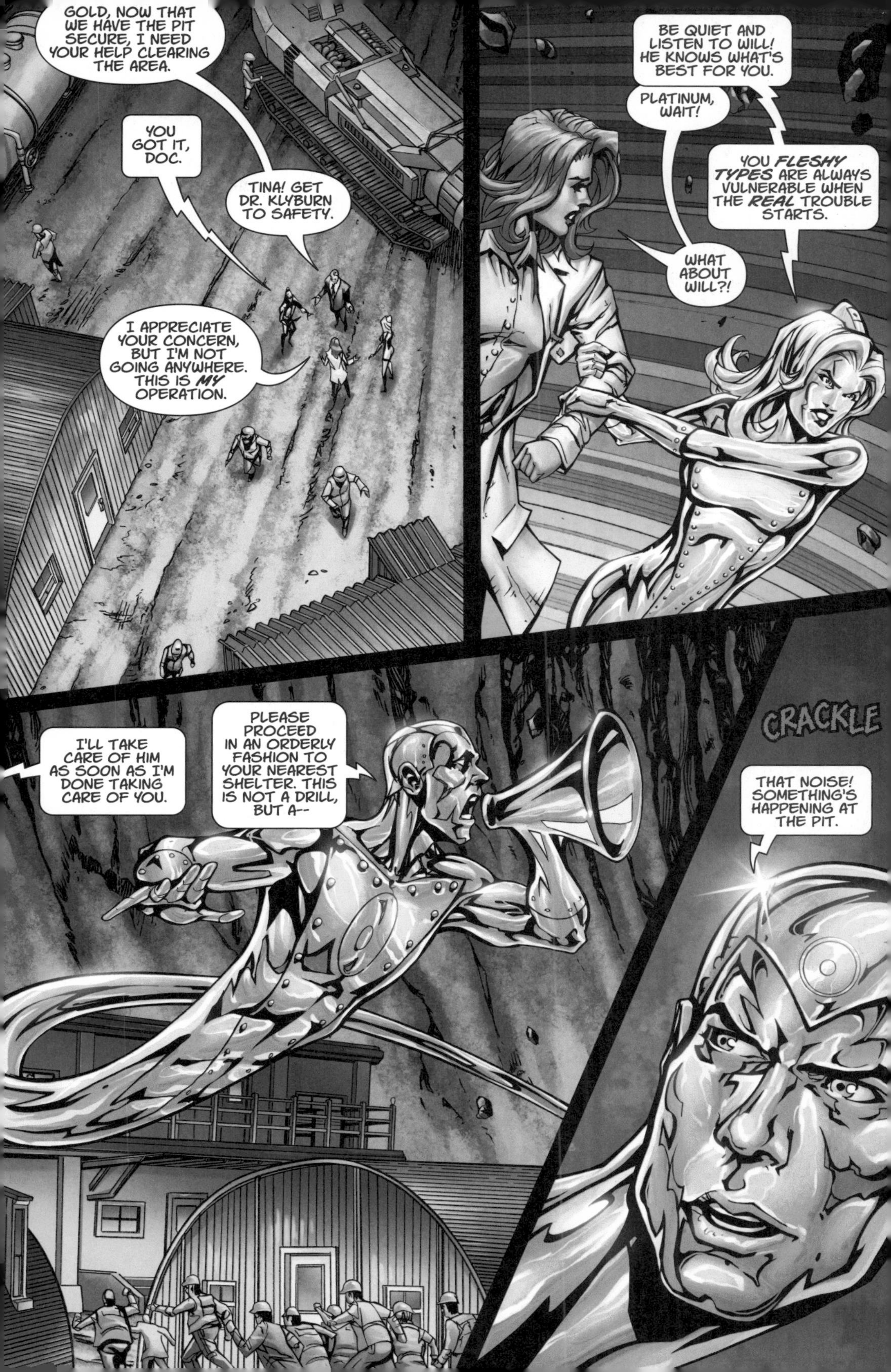
GOLD, NOW THAT WE HAVE THE PIT SECURE, I NEED YOUR HELP CLEARING THE AREA.
YOU GOT IT, DOC.
TINA! GET DR. KLYBURN TO SAFETY.
I APPRECIATE YOUR CONCERN, BUT I'M NOT GOING ANYWHERE. THIS IS *MY* OPERATION.
BE QUIET AND LISTEN TO WILL! HE KNOWS WHAT'S BEST FOR YOU.
PLATINUM, WAIT!
YOU *FLESHY TYPES* ARE ALWAYS VULNERABLE WHEN THE *REAL* TROUBLE STARTS.
WHAT ABOUT WILL?!
I'LL TAKE CARE OF HIM AS SOON AS I'M DONE TAKING CARE OF YOU.
PLEASE PROCEED IN AN ORDERLY FASHION TO YOUR NEAREST SHELTER. THIS IS NOT A DRILL, BUT A--
CRACKLE
THAT NOISE! SOMETHING'S HAPPENING AT THE PIT.

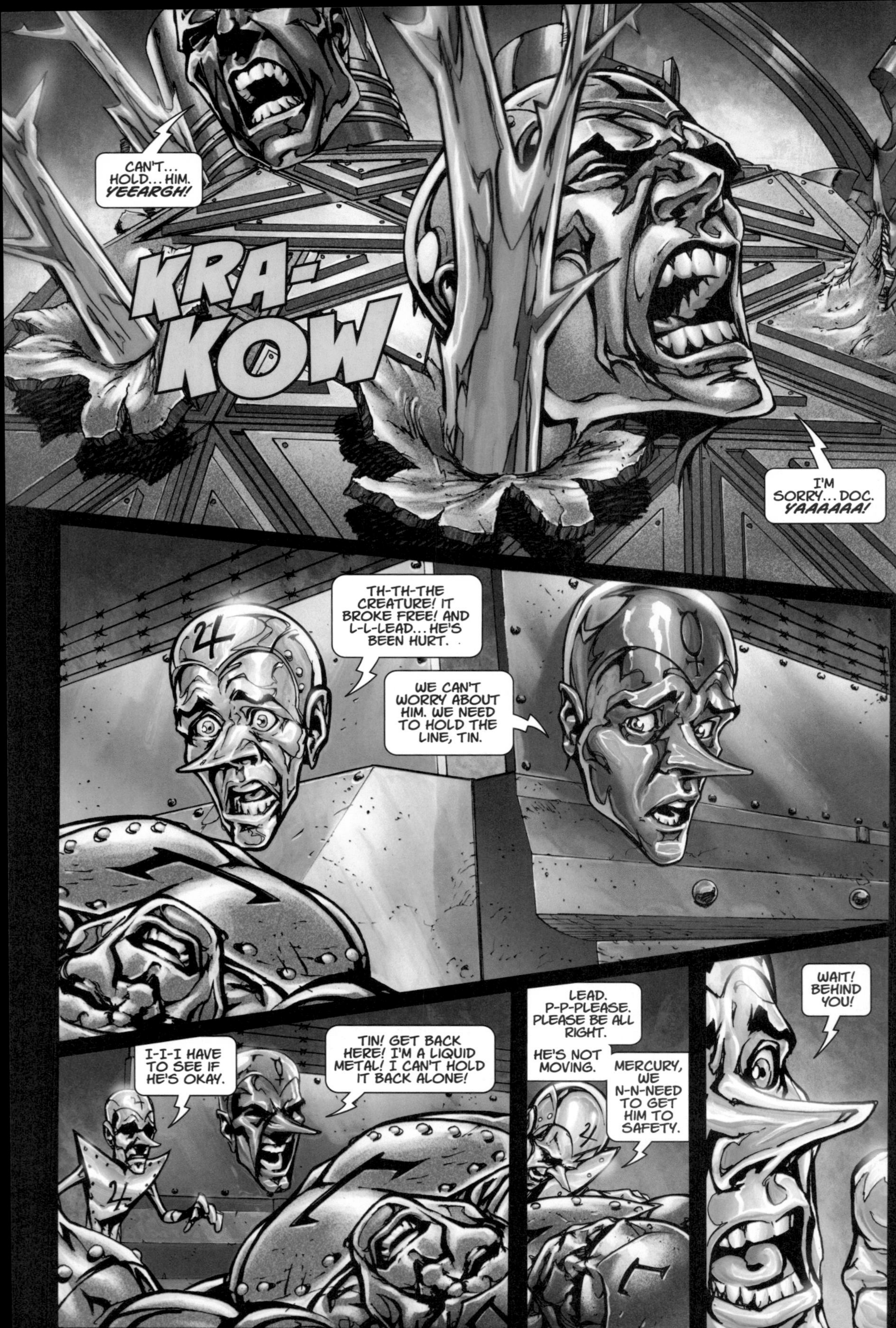
CAN'T... HOLD... HIM. YEEARGH!
KRA-KOW
I'M SORRY... DOC. YAAAAAA!
TH-TH-THE CREATURE! IT BROKE FREE! AND L-L-LEAD... HE'S BEEN HURT.
WE CAN'T WORRY ABOUT HIM. WE NEED TO HOLD THE LINE, TIN.
I-I-I HAVE TO SEE IF HE'S OKAY.
TIN! GET BACK HERE! I'M A LIQUID METAL! I CAN'T HOLD IT BACK ALONE!
LEAD. P-P-PLEASE. PLEASE BE ALL RIGHT.
HE'S NOT MOVING.
MERCURY, WE N-N-NEED TO GET HIM TO SAFETY.
WAIT! BEHIND YOU!

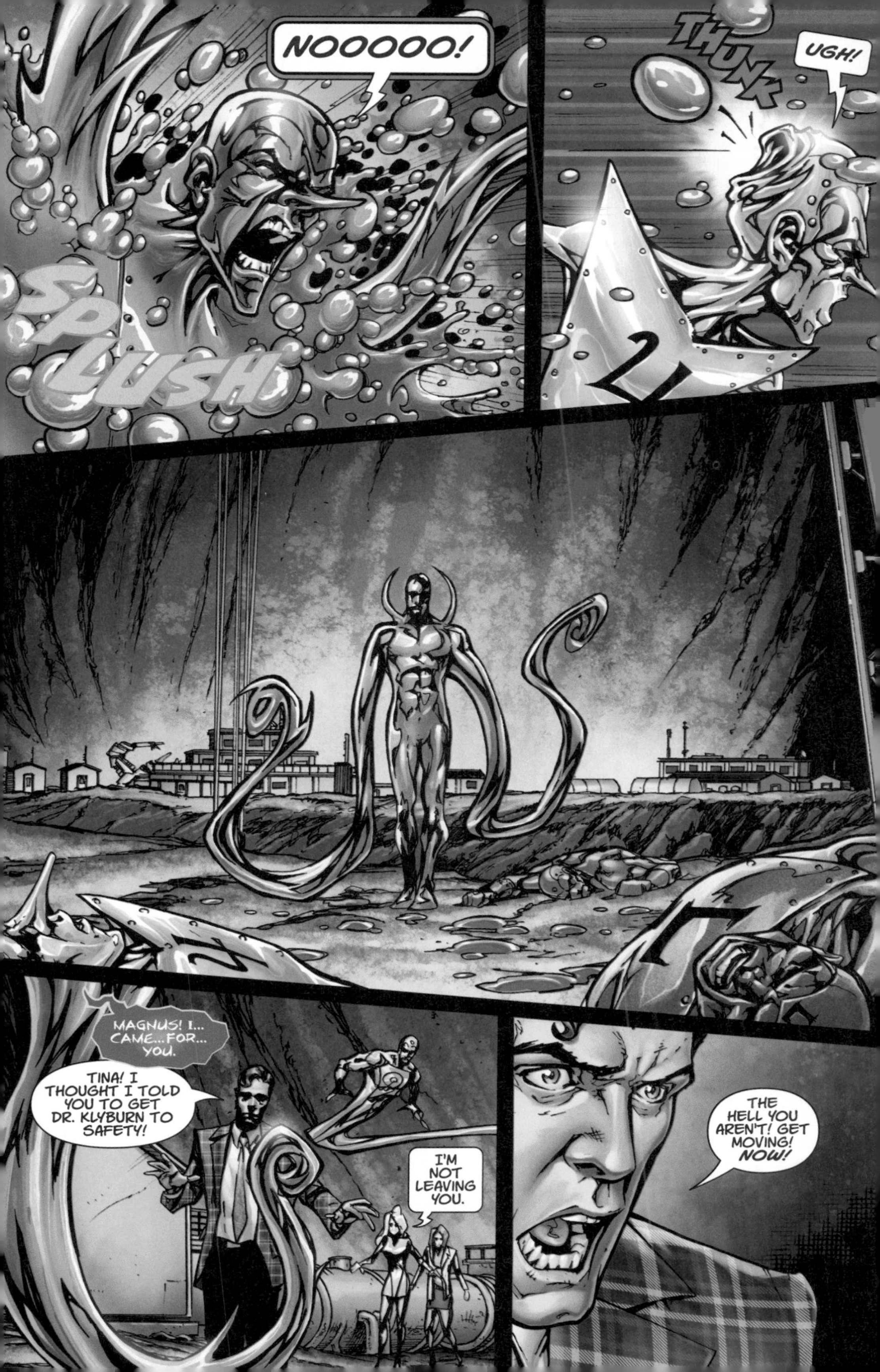
NOOOOO!
SPLUSH
THUNK
UGH!
MAGNUS! I... CAME... FOR... YOU.
TINA! I THOUGHT I TOLD YOU TO GET DR. KLYBURN TO SAFETY!
I'M NOT LEAVING YOU.
THE HELL YOU AREN'T! GET MOVING! NOW!

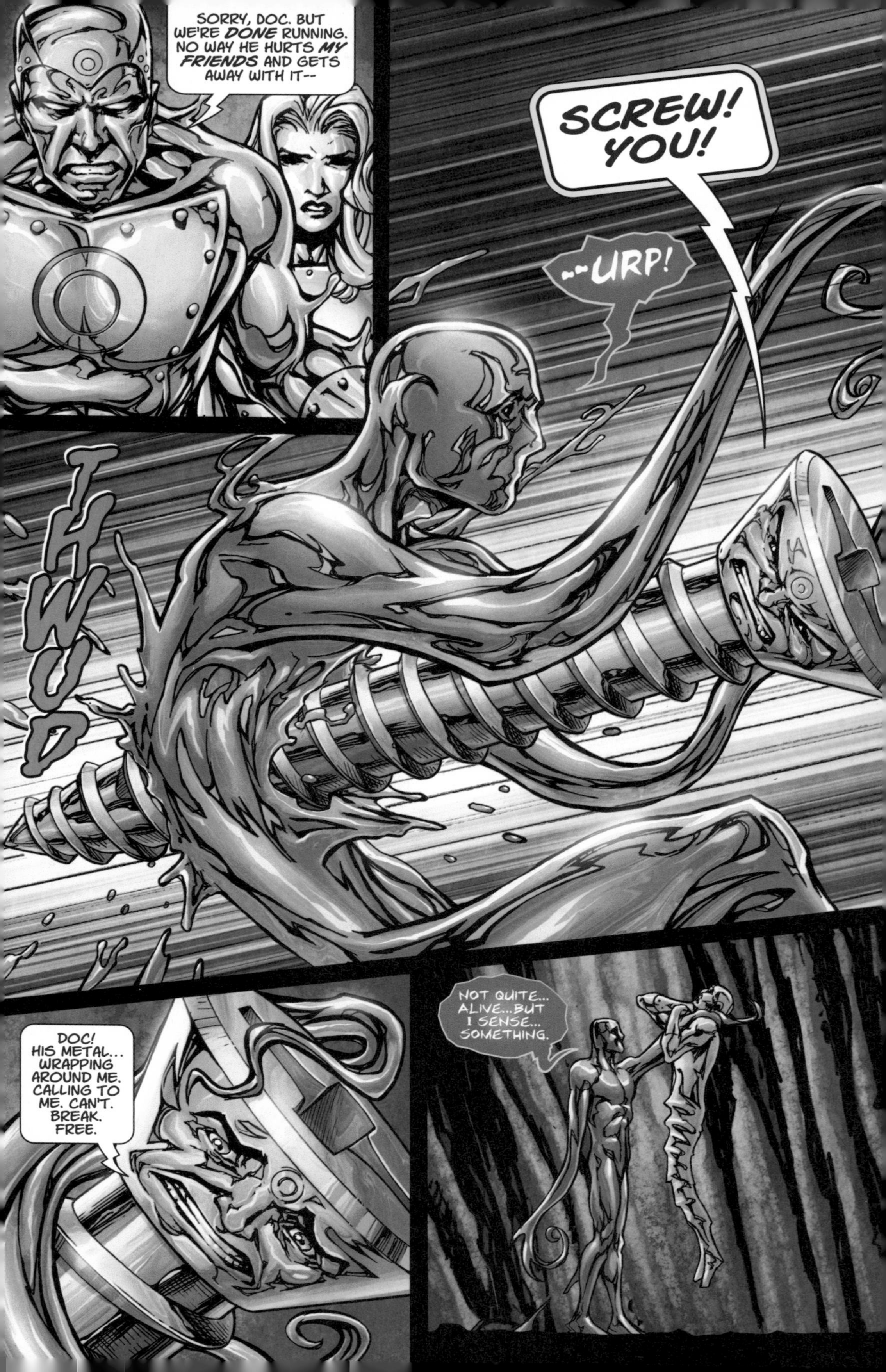
SORRY, DOC. BUT WE'RE DONE RUNNING. NO WAY HE HURTS MY FRIENDS AND GETS AWAY WITH IT--
SCREW! YOU!
--URP!
THWUD
DOC! HIS METAL... WRAPPING AROUND ME. CALLING TO ME. CAN'T. BREAK. FREE.
NOT QUITE... ALIVE...BUT I SENSE... SOMETHING.

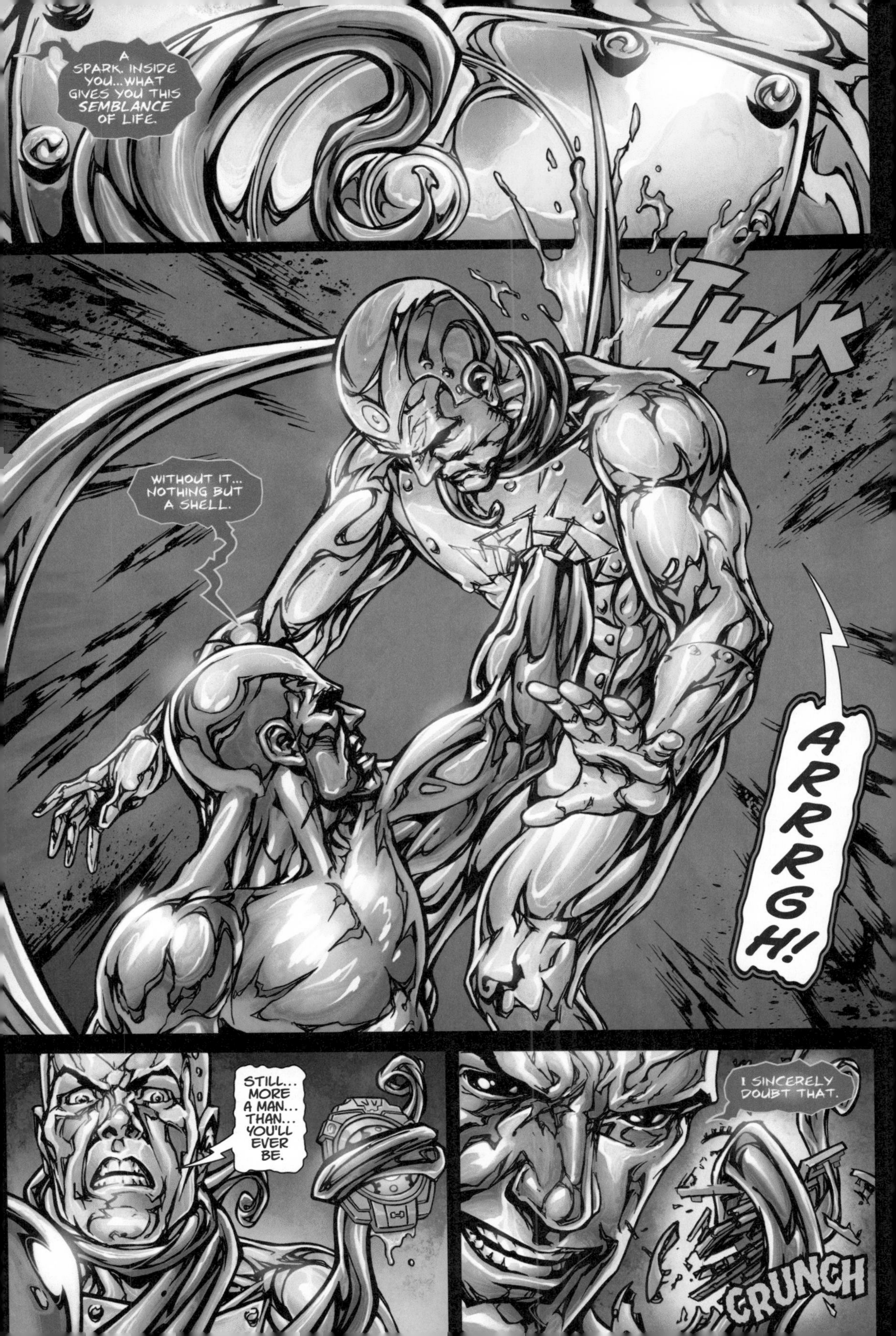
A SPARK INSIDE YOU...WHAT GIVES YOU THIS SEMBLANCE OF LIFE.
THAK
WITHOUT IT... NOTHING BUT A SHELL.
ARRRGH!
STILL... MORE A MAN... THAN... YOU'LL EVER BE.
I SINCERELY DOUBT THAT.
CRUNCH

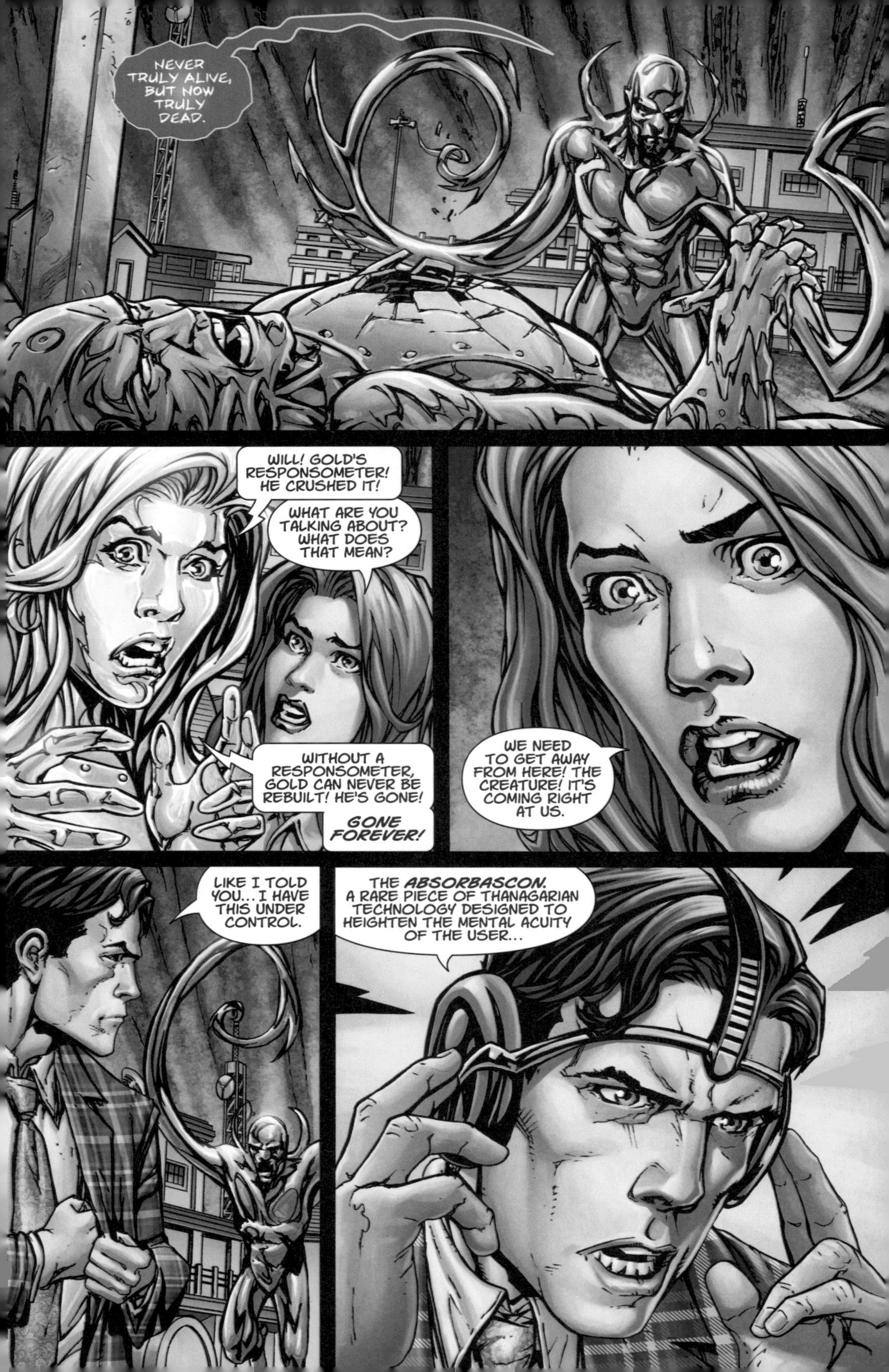
NEVER TRULY ALIVE, BUT NOW TRULY DEAD.
WILL! GOLD'S RESPONSOMETER! HE CRUSHED IT!
WHAT ARE YOU TALKING ABOUT? WHAT DOES THAT MEAN?
WITHOUT A RESPONSOMETER, GOLD CAN NEVER BE REBUILT! HE'S GONE!
GONE FOREVER!
WE NEED TO GET AWAY FROM HERE! THE CREATURE! IT'S COMING RIGHT AT US.
LIKE I TOLD YOU... I HAVE THIS UNDER CONTROL.
THE ABSORBASCON. A RARE PIECE OF THANAGARIAN TECHNOLOGY DESIGNED TO HEIGHTEN THE MENTAL ACUITY OF THE USER...

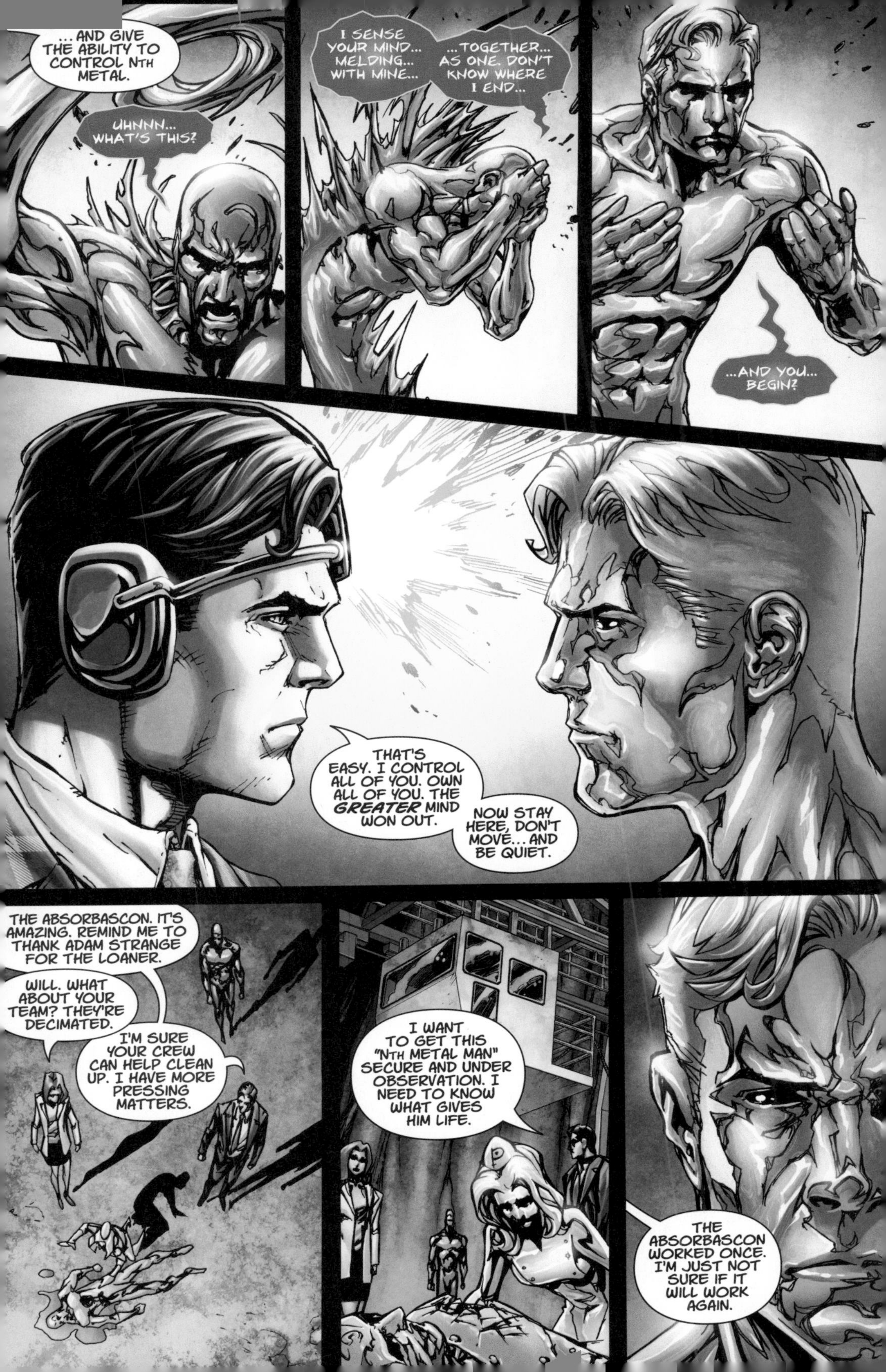
...AND GIVE THE ABILITY TO CONTROL NTH METAL.
UHNNN... WHAT'S THIS?
I SENSE YOUR MIND... MELDING... WITH MINE...
...TOGETHER... AS ONE. DON'T KNOW WHERE I END...
...AND YOU... BEGIN?
THAT'S EASY. I CONTROL ALL OF YOU. OWN ALL OF YOU. THE GREATER MIND WON OUT.
NOW STAY HERE, DON'T MOVE... AND BE QUIET.
THE ABSORBASCON. IT'S AMAZING. REMIND ME TO THANK ADAM STRANGE FOR THE LOANER.
WILL. WHAT ABOUT YOUR TEAM? THEY'RE DECIMATED.
I'M SURE YOUR CREW CAN HELP CLEAN UP. I HAVE MORE PRESSING MATTERS.
I WANT TO GET THIS "NTH METAL MAN" SECURE AND UNDER OBSERVATION. I NEED TO KNOW WHAT GIVES HIM LIFE.
THE ABSORBASCON WORKED ONCE. I'M JUST NOT SURE IF IT WILL WORK AGAIN.

Somewhere in a dark, secure, undisclosed location.

GURGLE

GURGLE

GURGLE

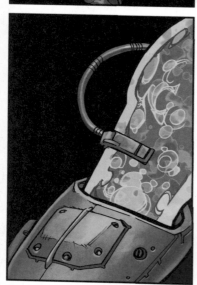

GURGLE GURGLE

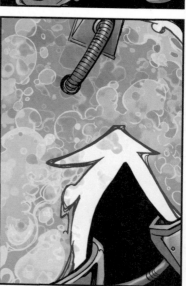

GURGLE GURGLE

GURGLE

OOP.

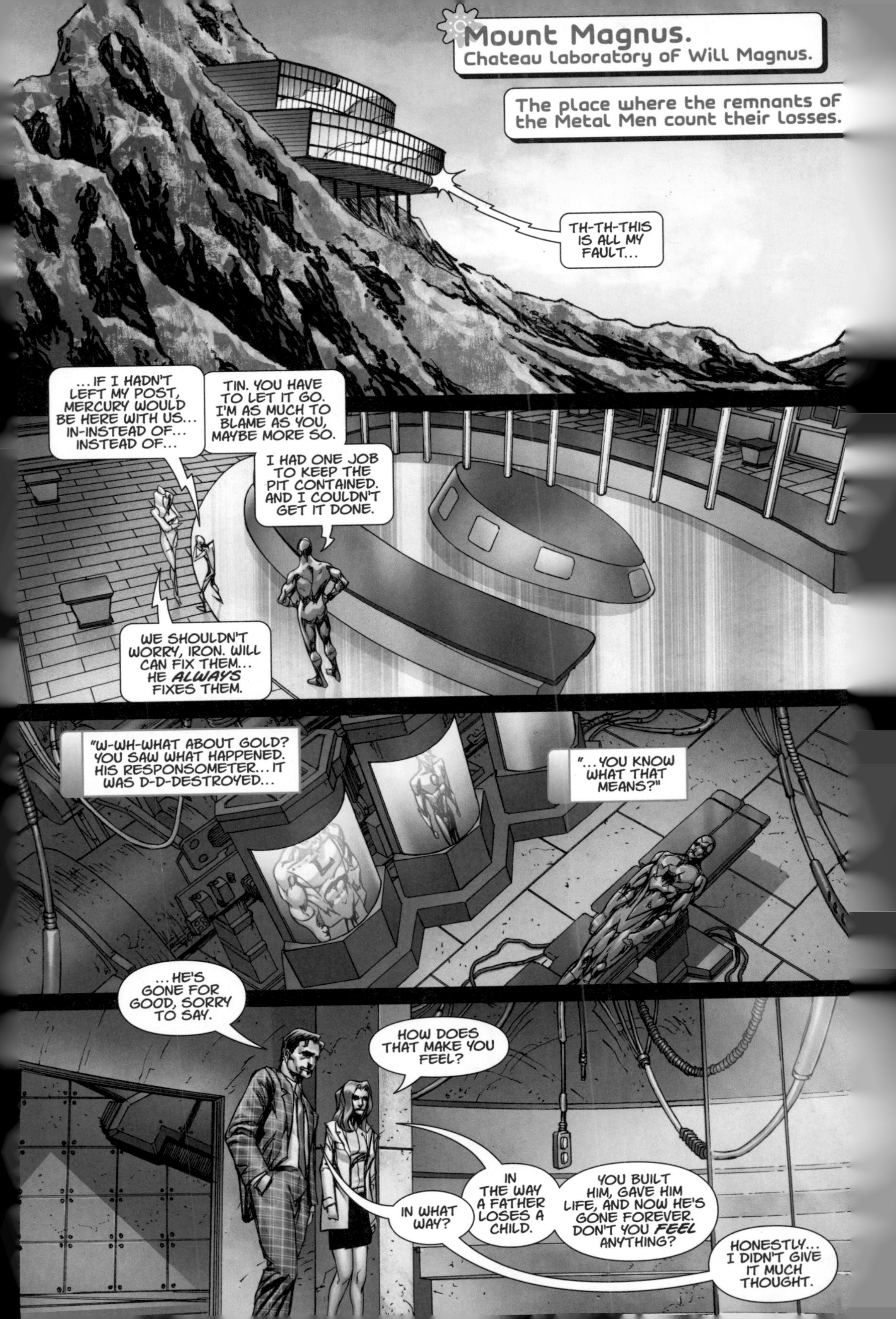
Mount Magnus.
Chateau laboratory of Will Magnus.
The place where the remnants of the Metal Men count their losses.
TH-TH-THIS IS ALL MY FAULT...
...IF I HADN'T LEFT MY POST, MERCURY WOULD BE HERE WITH US... IN-INSTEAD OF... INSTEAD OF...
TIN. YOU HAVE TO LET IT GO. I'M AS MUCH TO BLAME AS YOU, MAYBE MORE SO.
I HAD ONE JOB TO KEEP THE PIT CONTAINED. AND I COULDN'T GET IT DONE.
WE SHOULDN'T WORRY, IRON. WILL CAN FIX THEM... HE *ALWAYS* FIXES THEM.
"W-WH-WHAT ABOUT GOLD? YOU SAW WHAT HAPPENED. HIS RESPONSOMETER... IT WAS D-D-DESTROYED...
"...YOU KNOW WHAT THAT MEANS?"
...HE'S GONE FOR GOOD, SORRY TO SAY.
HOW DOES THAT MAKE YOU FEEL?
IN WHAT WAY?
IN THE WAY A FATHER LOSES A CHILD.
YOU BUILT HIM, GAVE HIM LIFE, AND NOW HE'S GONE FOREVER. DON'T YOU *FEEL* ANYTHING?
HONESTLY... I DIDN'T GIVE IT MUCH THOUGHT.

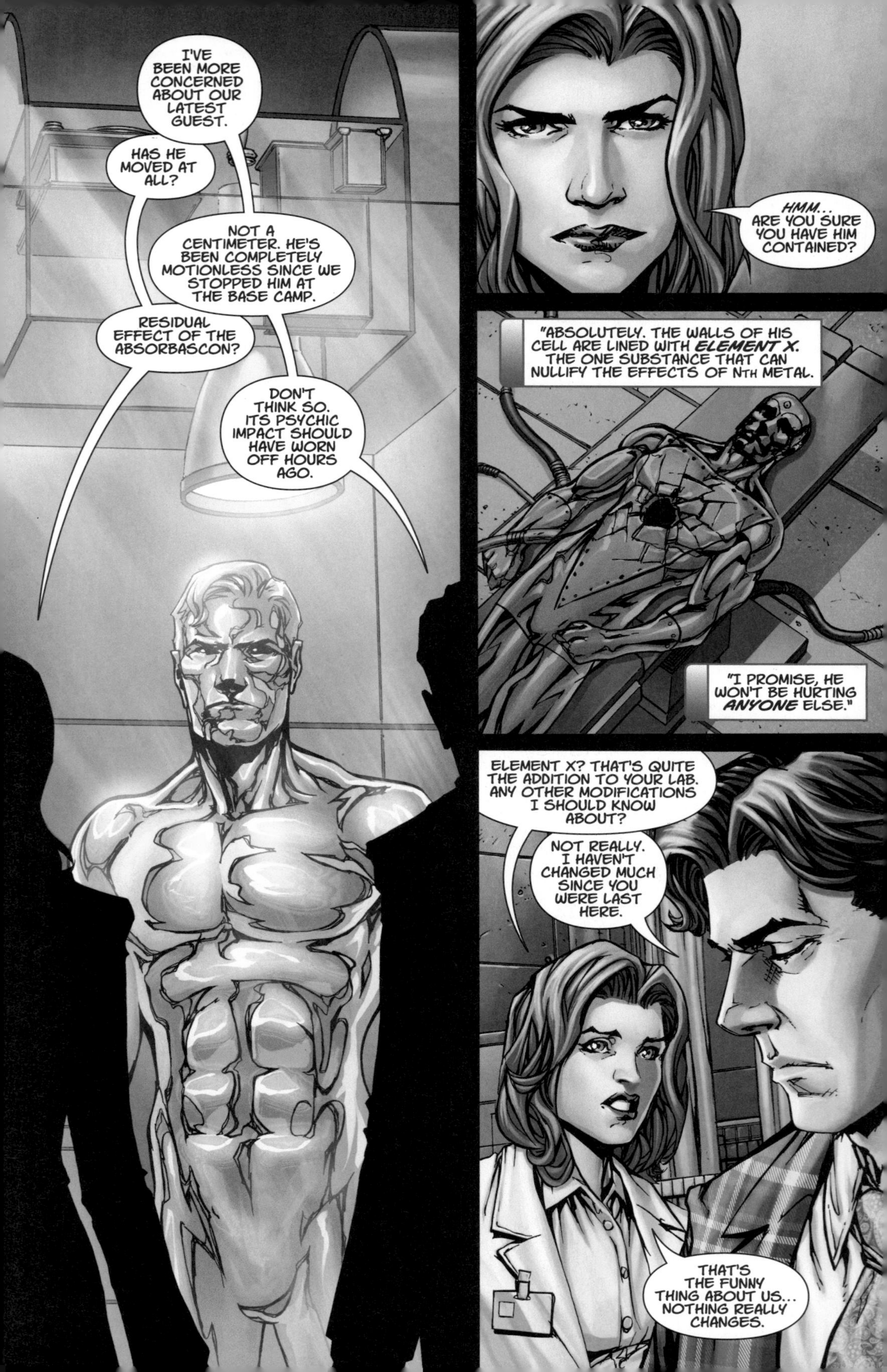
I'VE BEEN MORE CONCERNED ABOUT OUR LATEST GUEST.
HAS HE MOVED AT ALL?
NOT A CENTIMETER. HE'S BEEN COMPLETELY MOTIONLESS SINCE WE STOPPED HIM AT THE BASE CAMP.
RESIDUAL EFFECT OF THE ABSORBASCON?
DON'T THINK SO. ITS PSYCHIC IMPACT SHOULD HAVE WORN OFF HOURS AGO.
HMM... ARE YOU SURE YOU HAVE HIM CONTAINED?
"ABSOLUTELY. THE WALLS OF HIS CELL ARE LINED WITH ***ELEMENT X.*** THE ONE SUBSTANCE THAT CAN NULLIFY THE EFFECTS OF NTH METAL.
"I PROMISE, HE WON'T BE HURTING ***ANYONE*** ELSE."
ELEMENT X? THAT'S QUITE THE ADDITION TO YOUR LAB. ANY OTHER MODIFICATIONS I SHOULD KNOW ABOUT?
NOT REALLY. I HAVEN'T CHANGED MUCH SINCE YOU WERE LAST HERE.
THAT'S THE FUNNY THING ABOUT US... NOTHING REALLY CHANGES.

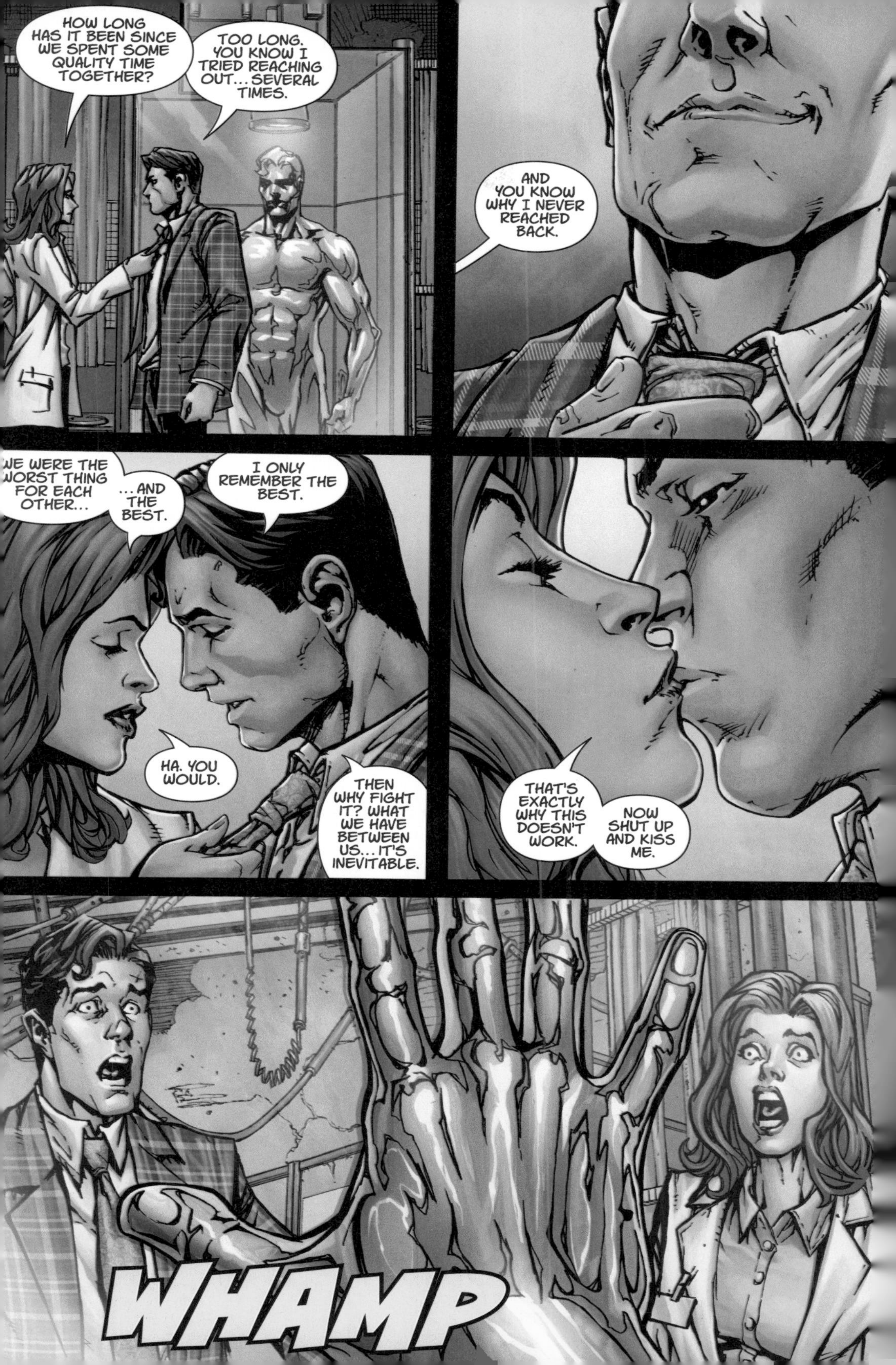
HOW LONG HAS IT BEEN SINCE WE SPENT SOME QUALITY TIME TOGETHER?
TOO LONG. YOU KNOW I TRIED REACHING OUT... SEVERAL TIMES.
AND YOU KNOW WHY I NEVER REACHED BACK.
WE WERE THE WORST THING FOR EACH OTHER...
...AND THE BEST.
I ONLY REMEMBER THE BEST.
HA. YOU WOULD.
THEN WHY FIGHT IT? WHAT WE HAVE BETWEEN US... IT'S INEVITABLE.
THAT'S EXACTLY WHY THIS DOESN'T WORK.
NOW SHUT UP AND KISS ME.
WHAMP

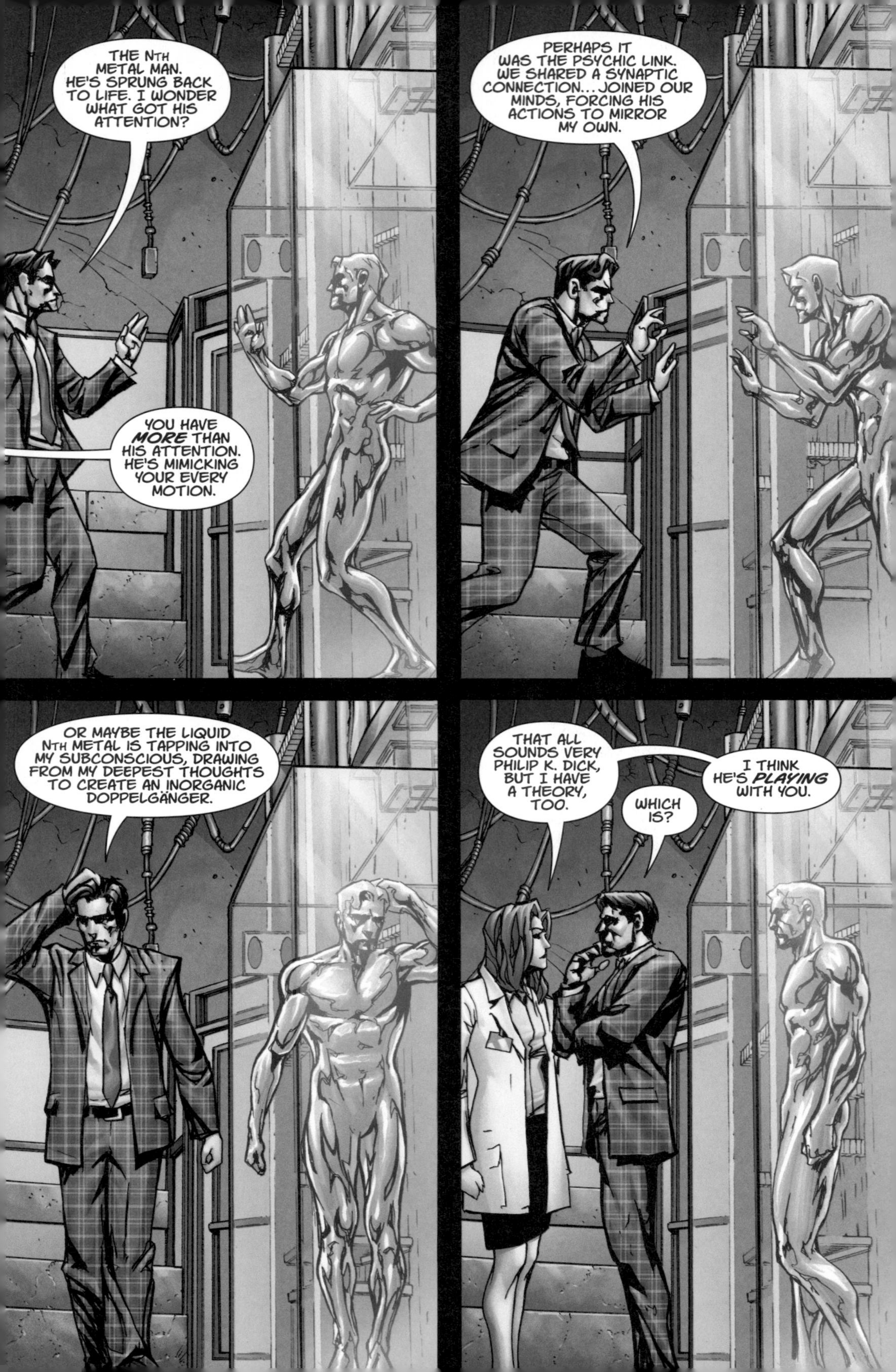
THE NTH METAL MAN. HE'S SPRUNG BACK TO LIFE. I WONDER WHAT GOT HIS ATTENTION?
YOU HAVE *MORE* THAN HIS ATTENTION. HE'S MIMICKING YOUR EVERY MOTION.
PERHAPS IT WAS THE PSYCHIC LINK. WE SHARED A SYNAPTIC CONNECTION... JOINED OUR MINDS, FORCING HIS ACTIONS TO MIRROR MY OWN.
OR MAYBE THE LIQUID NTH METAL IS TAPPING INTO MY SUBCONSCIOUS, DRAWING FROM MY DEEPEST THOUGHTS TO CREATE AN INORGANIC DOPPELGÄNGER.
THAT ALL SOUNDS VERY PHILIP K. DICK, BUT I HAVE A THEORY, TOO.
WHICH IS?
I THINK HE'S *PLAYING* WITH YOU.

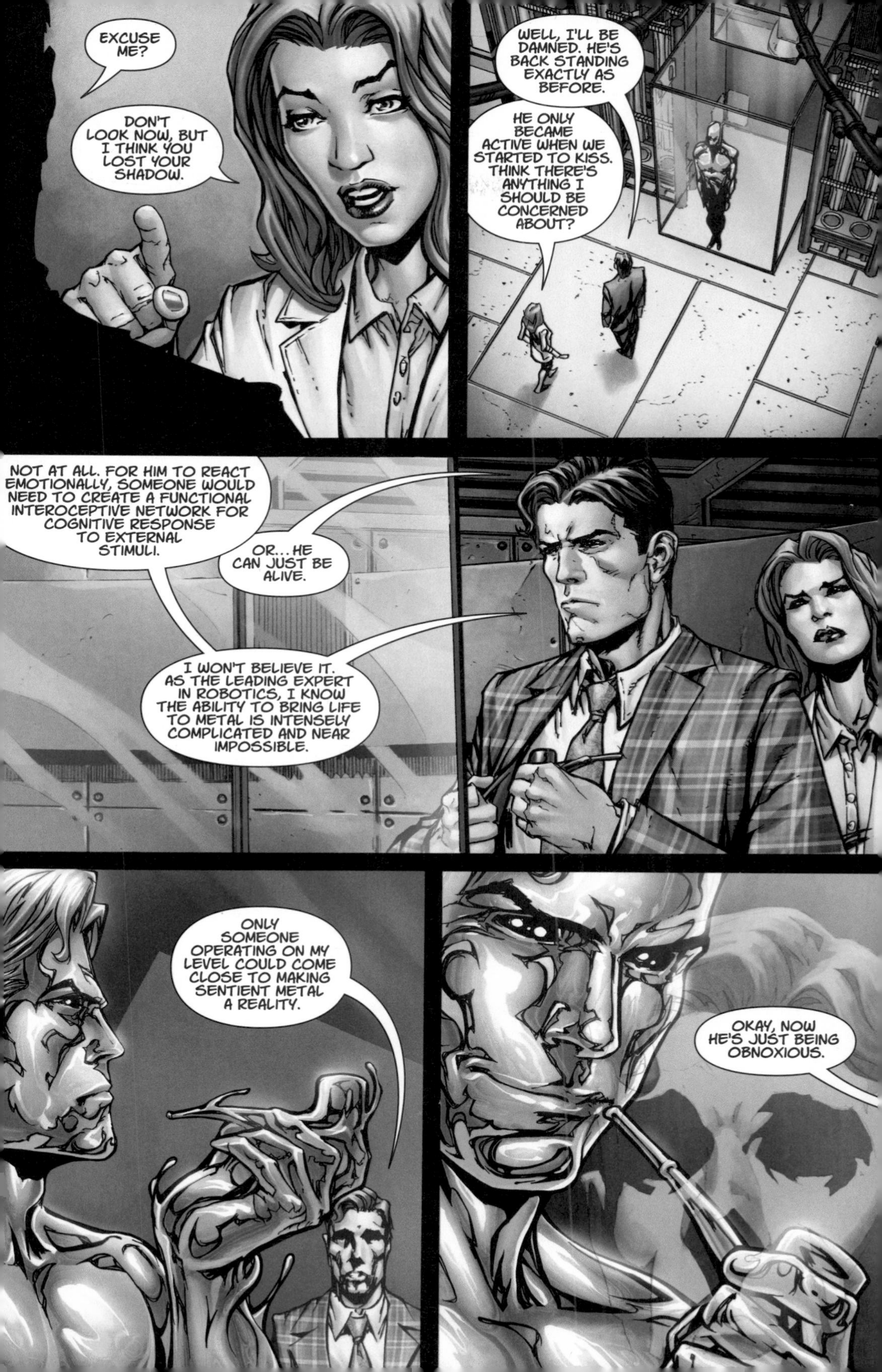
EXCUSE ME?
DON'T LOOK NOW, BUT I THINK YOU LOST YOUR SHADOW.
WELL, I'LL BE DAMNED. HE'S BACK STANDING EXACTLY AS BEFORE.
HE ONLY BECAME ACTIVE WHEN WE STARTED TO KISS. THINK THERE'S ANYTHING I SHOULD BE CONCERNED ABOUT?
NOT AT ALL. FOR HIM TO REACT EMOTIONALLY, SOMEONE WOULD NEED TO CREATE A FUNCTIONAL INTEROCEPTIVE NETWORK FOR COGNITIVE RESPONSE TO EXTERNAL STIMULI.
OR... HE CAN JUST BE ALIVE.
I WON'T BELIEVE IT. AS THE LEADING EXPERT IN ROBOTICS, I KNOW THE ABILITY TO BRING LIFE TO METAL IS INTENSELY COMPLICATED AND NEAR IMPOSSIBLE.
ONLY SOMEONE OPERATING ON MY LEVEL COULD COME CLOSE TO MAKING SENTIENT METAL A REALITY.
OKAY, NOW HE'S JUST BEING OBNOXIOUS.

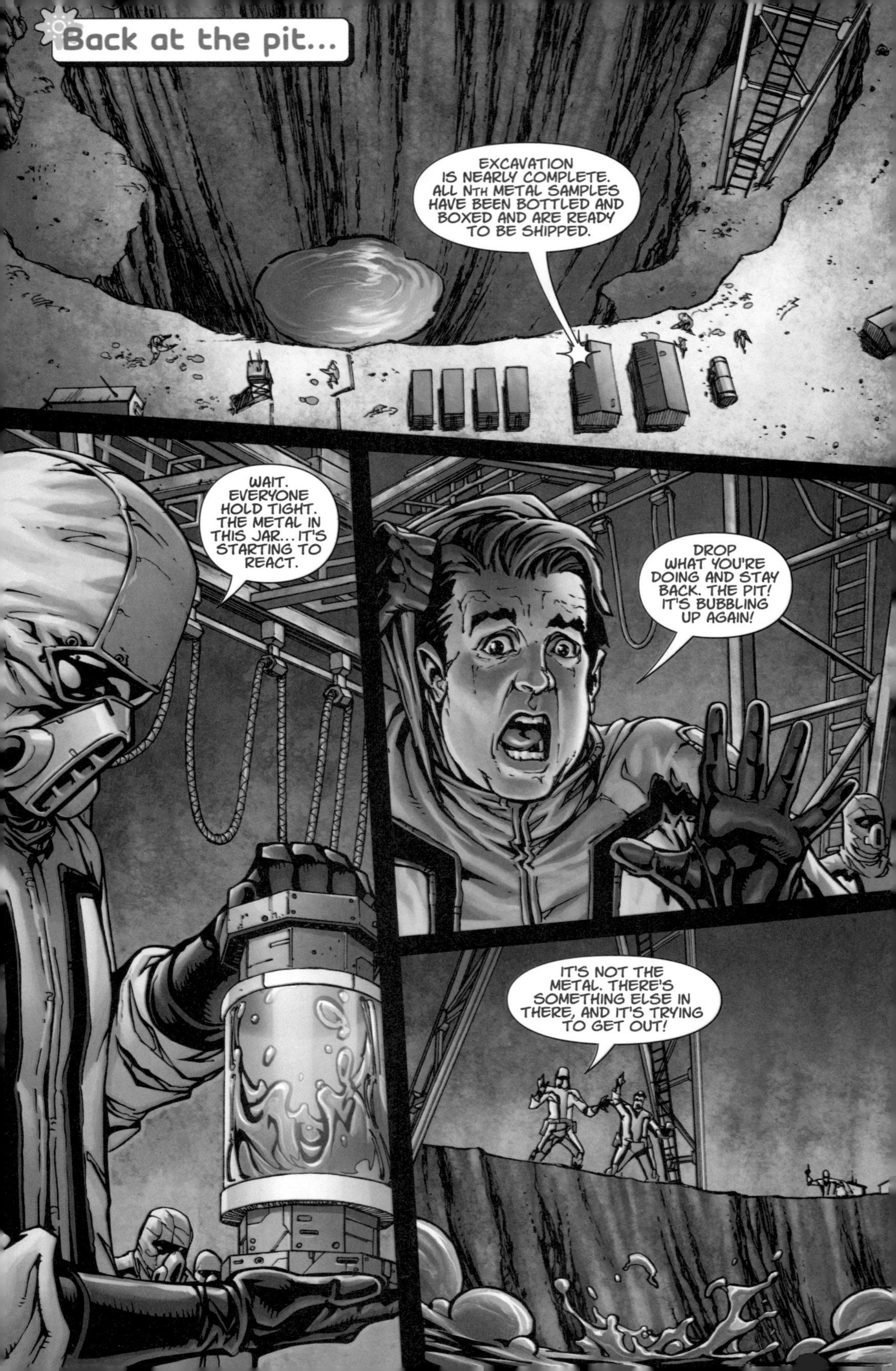
Back at the pit...
EXCAVATION IS NEARLY COMPLETE. ALL NTH METAL SAMPLES HAVE BEEN BOTTLED AND BOXED AND ARE READY TO BE SHIPPED.
WAIT. EVERYONE HOLD TIGHT. THE METAL IN THIS JAR... IT'S STARTING TO REACT.
DROP WHAT YOU'RE DOING AND STAY BACK. THE PIT! IT'S BUBBLING UP AGAIN!
IT'S NOT THE METAL. THERE'S SOMETHING ELSE IN THERE, AND IT'S TRYING TO GET OUT!

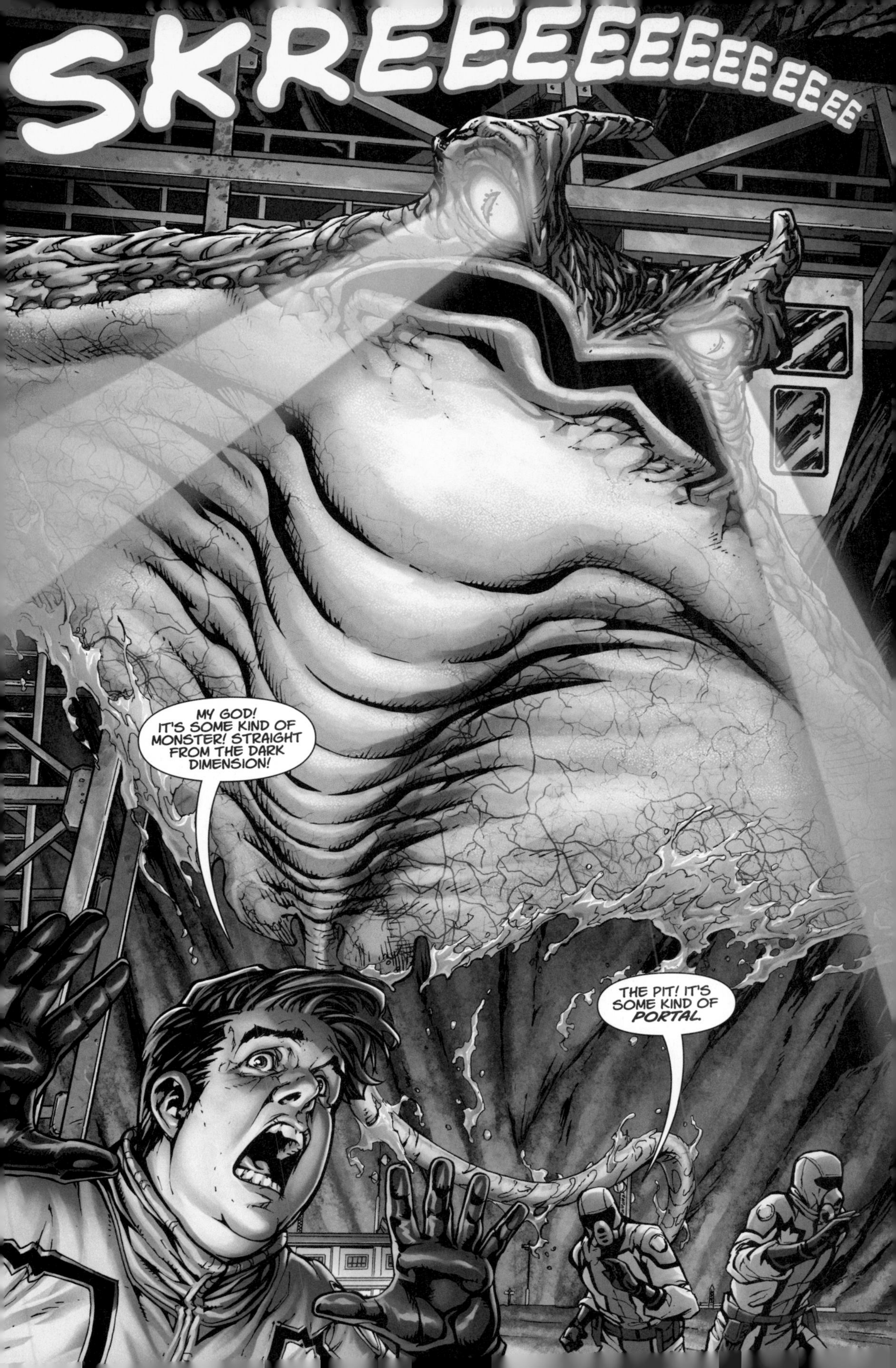
SKREEEEEEEEEEEEEE
MY GOD! IT'S SOME KIND OF MONSTER! STRAIGHT FROM THE DARK DIMENSION!
THE PIT! IT'S SOME KIND OF *PORTAL*.

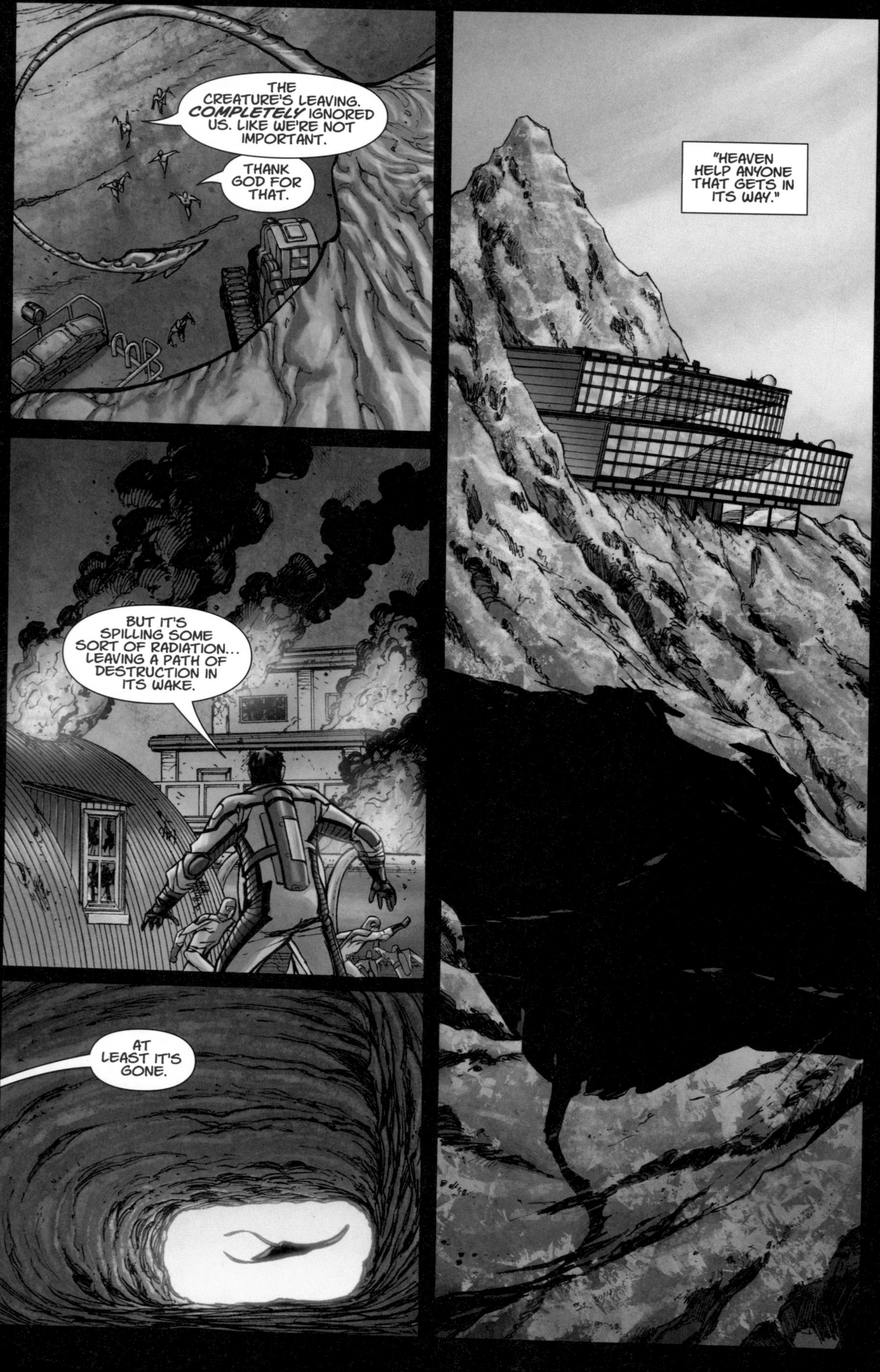
THE CREATURE'S LEAVING. COMPLETELY IGNORED US. LIKE WE'RE NOT IMPORTANT.
THANK GOD FOR THAT.
BUT IT'S SPILLING SOME SORT OF RADIATION... LEAVING A PATH OF DESTRUCTION IN ITS WAKE.
AT LEAST IT'S GONE.
"HEAVEN HELP ANYONE THAT GETS IN ITS WAY."

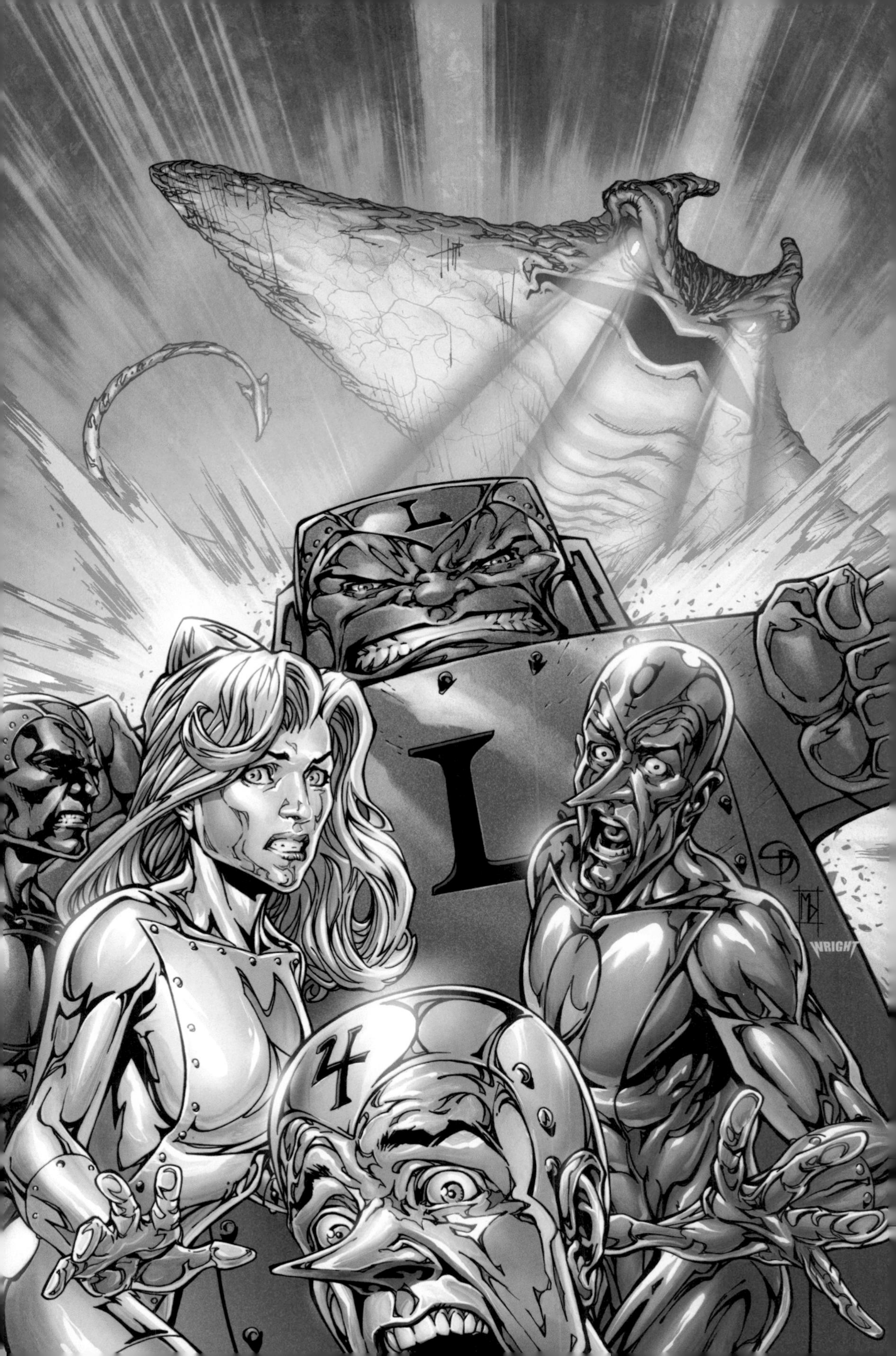
WRIGHT

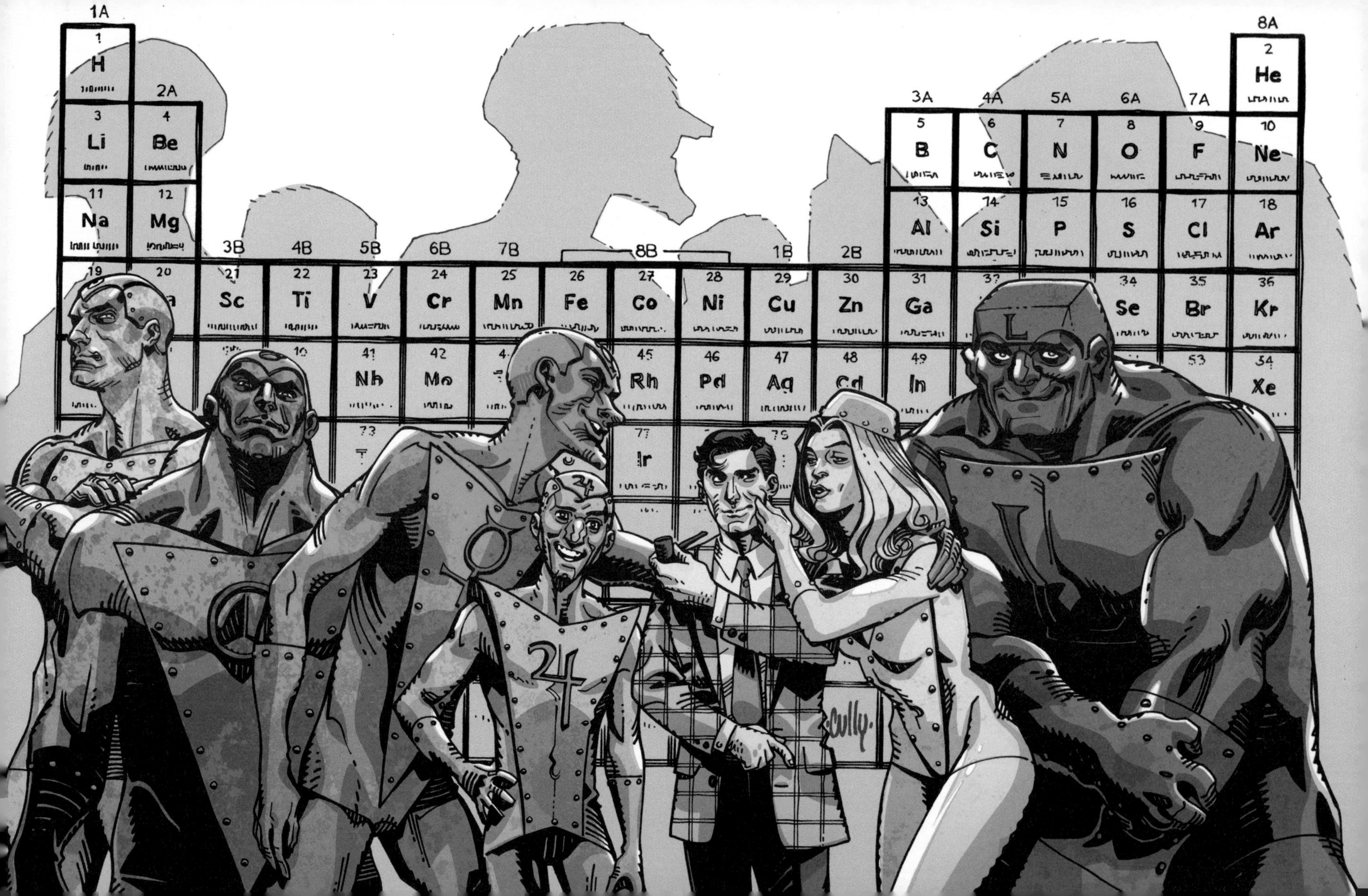
1A
1
H
2A
3
Li
4
Be
11
Na
12
Mg
19
20
3B
21
Sc
4B
22
Ti
5B
23
V
41
Nb
73
6B
24
Cr
42
Mo
7B
25
Mn
8B
26
Fe
27
Co
45
Rh
77
Ir
28
Ni
46
Pd
1B
29
Cu
47
Ag
79
2B
30
Zn
48
Cd
3A
5
B
13
Al
31
Ga
49
In
4A
6
C
14
Si
5A
7
N
15
P
6A
8
O
16
S
34
Se
7A
9
F
17
Cl
35
Br
53
8A
2
He
10
Ne
18
Ar
36
Kr
54
Xe
Cully

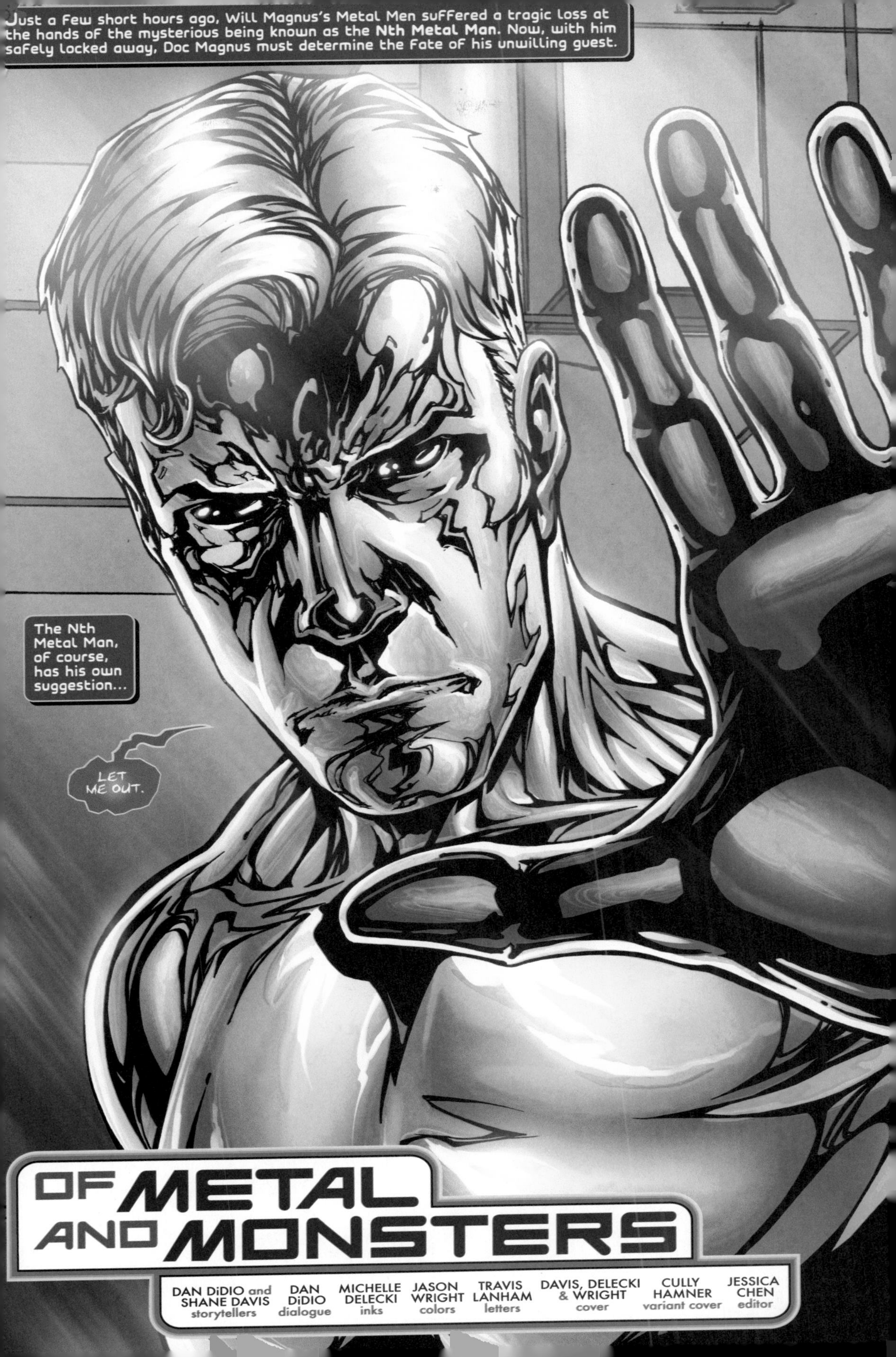

Just a few short hours ago, Will Magnus's Metal Men suffered a tragic loss at the hands of the mysterious being known as the Nth Metal Man. Now, with him safely locked away, Doc Magnus must determine the fate of his unwilling guest.
The Nth Metal Man, of course, has his own suggestion...
LET ME OUT.
OF METAL AND MONSTERS
DAN DiDIO and SHANE DAVIS storytellers
DAN DiDIO dialogue
MICHELLE DELECKI inks
JASON WRIGHT colors
TRAVIS LANHAM letters
DAVIS, DELECKI & WRIGHT cover
CULLY HAMNER variant cover
JESSICA CHEN editor

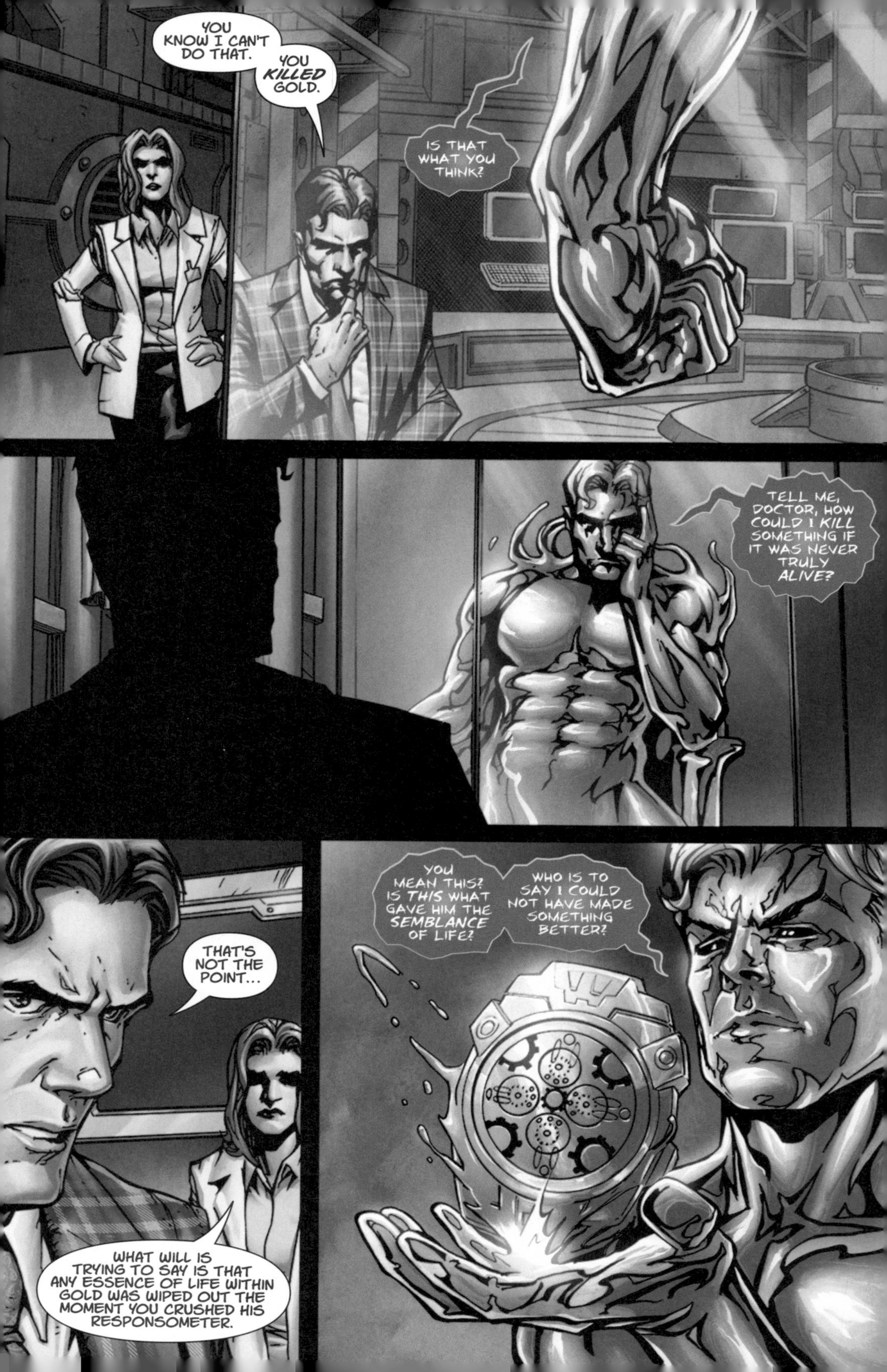
YOU KNOW I CAN'T DO THAT.
YOU KILLED GOLD.
IS THAT WHAT YOU THINK?
TELL ME, DOCTOR, HOW COULD I KILL SOMETHING IF IT WAS NEVER TRULY ALIVE?
THAT'S NOT THE POINT...
WHAT WILL IS TRYING TO SAY IS THAT ANY ESSENCE OF LIFE WITHIN GOLD WAS WIPED OUT THE MOMENT YOU CRUSHED HIS RESPONSOMETER.
YOU MEAN THIS? IS THIS WHAT GAVE HIM THE SEMBLANCE OF LIFE?
WHO IS TO SAY I COULD NOT HAVE MADE SOMETHING BETTER?

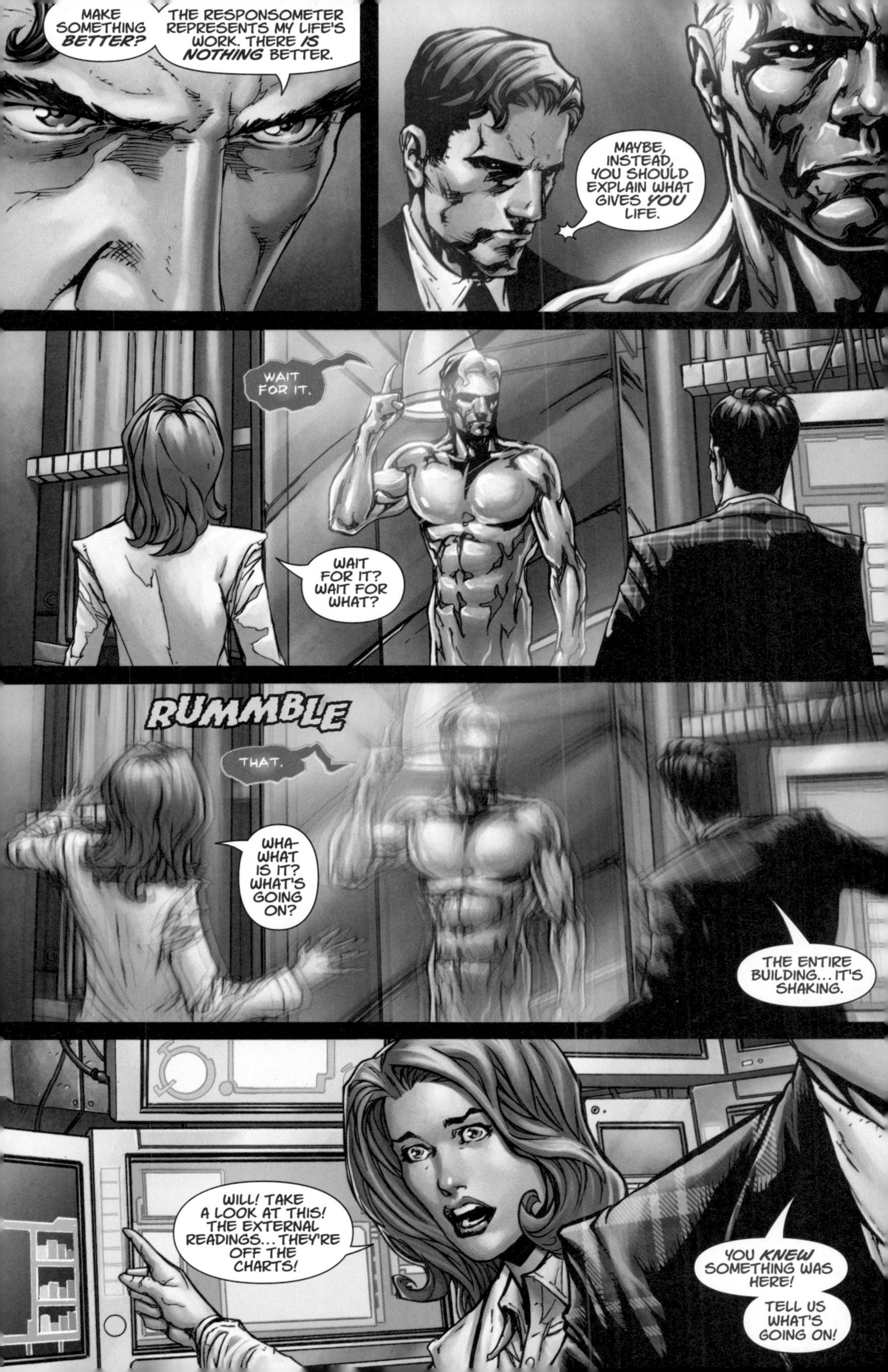
MAKE SOMETHING *BETTER?*
THE RESPONSOMETER REPRESENTS MY LIFE'S WORK. THERE *IS* *NOTHING* BETTER.
MAYBE, INSTEAD, YOU SHOULD EXPLAIN WHAT GIVES *YOU* LIFE.
WAIT FOR IT.
WAIT FOR IT? WAIT FOR WHAT?
RUMMBLE
THAT.
WHA-WHAT IS IT? WHAT'S GOING ON?
THE ENTIRE BUILDING... IT'S SHAKING.
WILL! TAKE A LOOK AT THIS! THE EXTERNAL READINGS... THEY'RE OFF THE CHARTS!
YOU *KNEW* SOMETHING WAS HERE!
TELL US WHAT'S GOING ON!

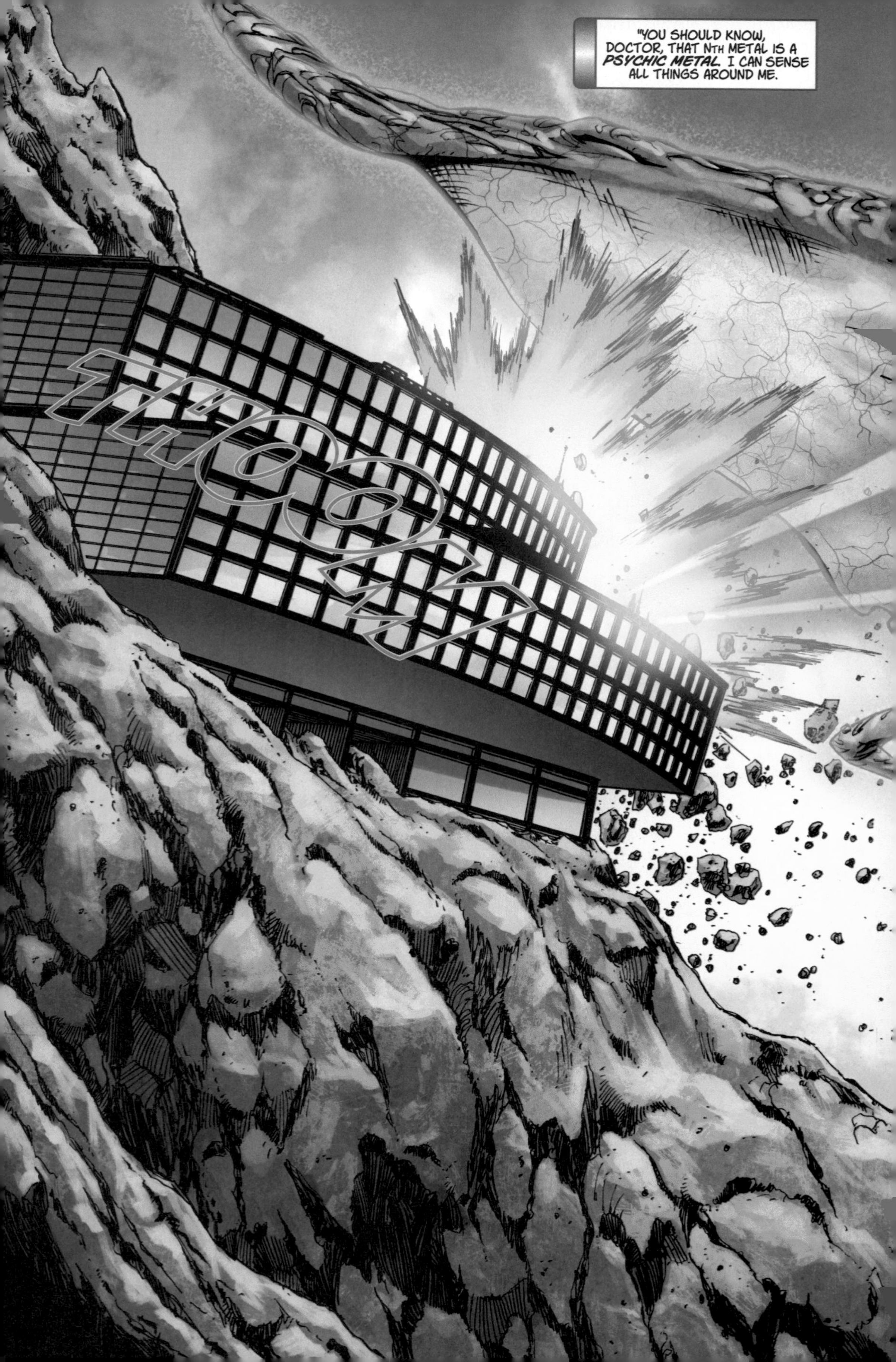
"YOU SHOULD KNOW, DOCTOR, THAT NTH METAL IS A PSYCHIC METAL. I CAN SENSE ALL THINGS AROUND ME.
THOOM

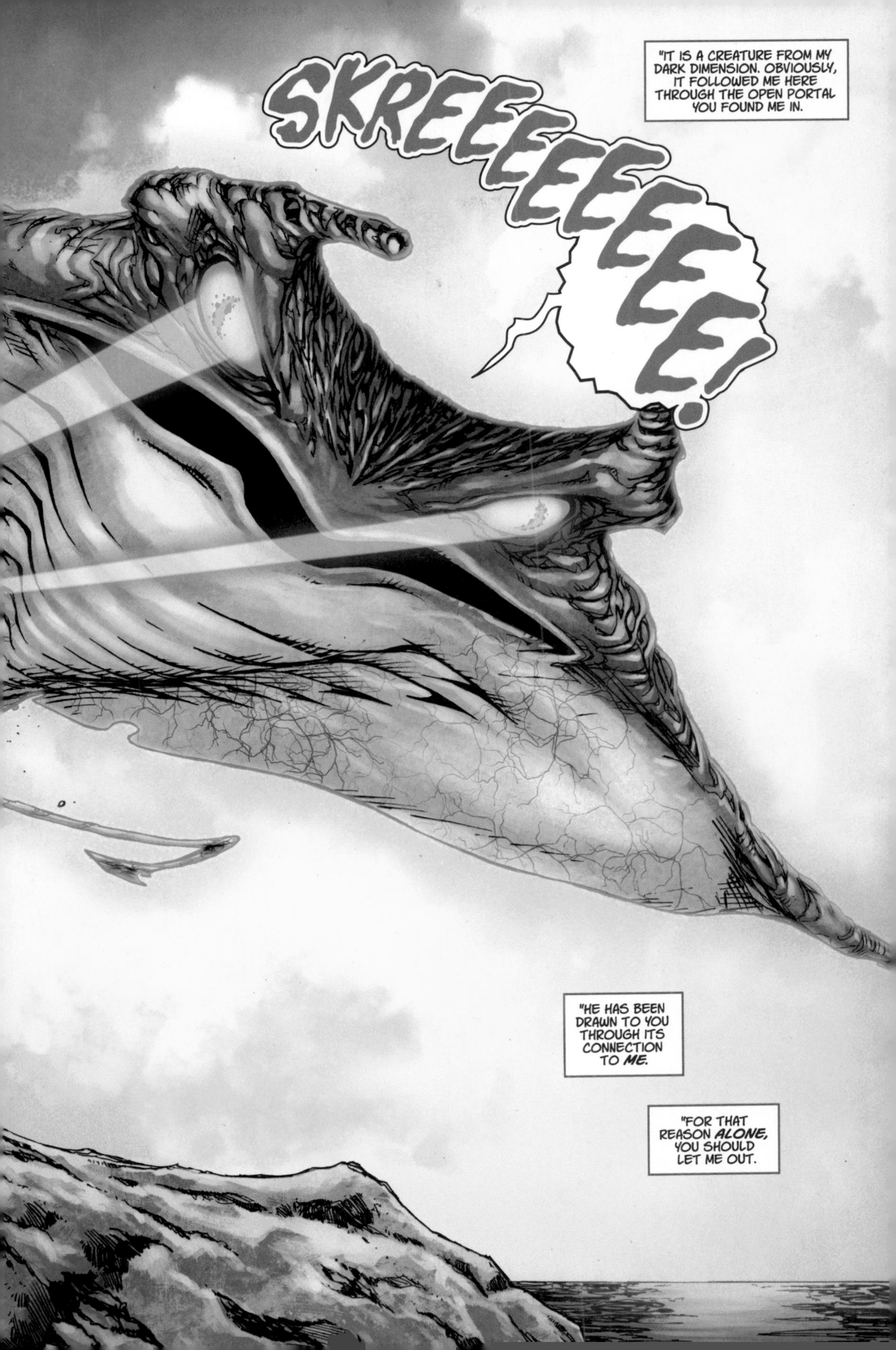
"IT IS A CREATURE FROM MY DARK DIMENSION. OBVIOUSLY, IT FOLLOWED ME HERE THROUGH THE OPEN PORTAL YOU FOUND ME IN.
SKREEEEEEEEE!
"HE HAS BEEN DRAWN TO YOU THROUGH ITS CONNECTION TO *ME*.
"FOR THAT REASON *ALONE*, YOU SHOULD LET ME OUT.

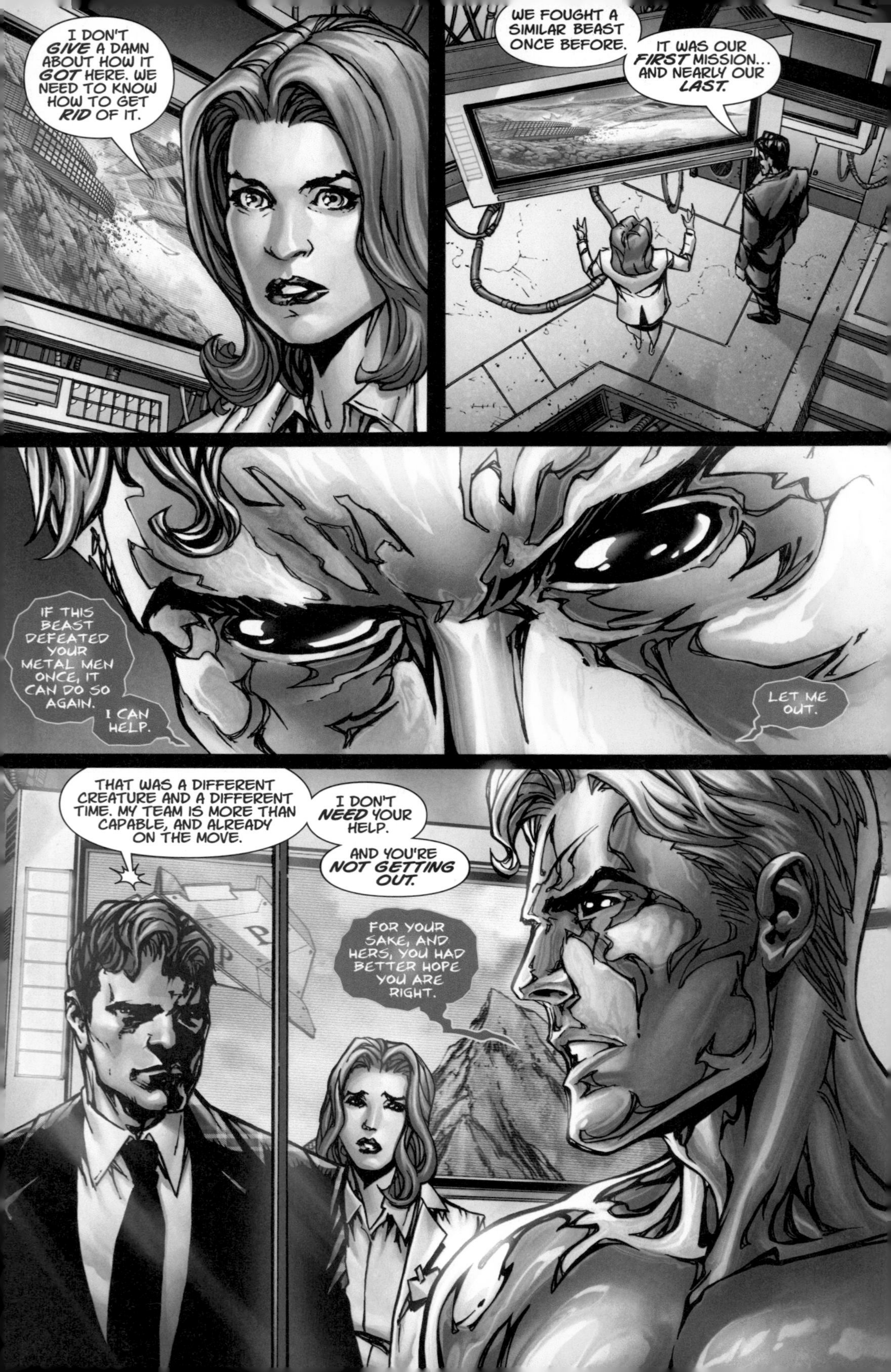
I DON'T GIVE A DAMN ABOUT HOW IT GOT HERE. WE NEED TO KNOW HOW TO GET RID OF IT.
WE FOUGHT A SIMILAR BEAST ONCE BEFORE.
IT WAS OUR FIRST MISSION... AND NEARLY OUR LAST.
IF THIS BEAST DEFEATED YOUR METAL MEN ONCE, IT CAN DO SO AGAIN.
I CAN HELP.
LET ME OUT.
THAT WAS A DIFFERENT CREATURE AND A DIFFERENT TIME. MY TEAM IS MORE THAN CAPABLE, AND ALREADY ON THE MOVE.
I DON'T NEED YOUR HELP.
AND YOU'RE NOT GETTING OUT.
FOR YOUR SAKE, AND HERS, YOU HAD BETTER HOPE YOU ARE RIGHT.

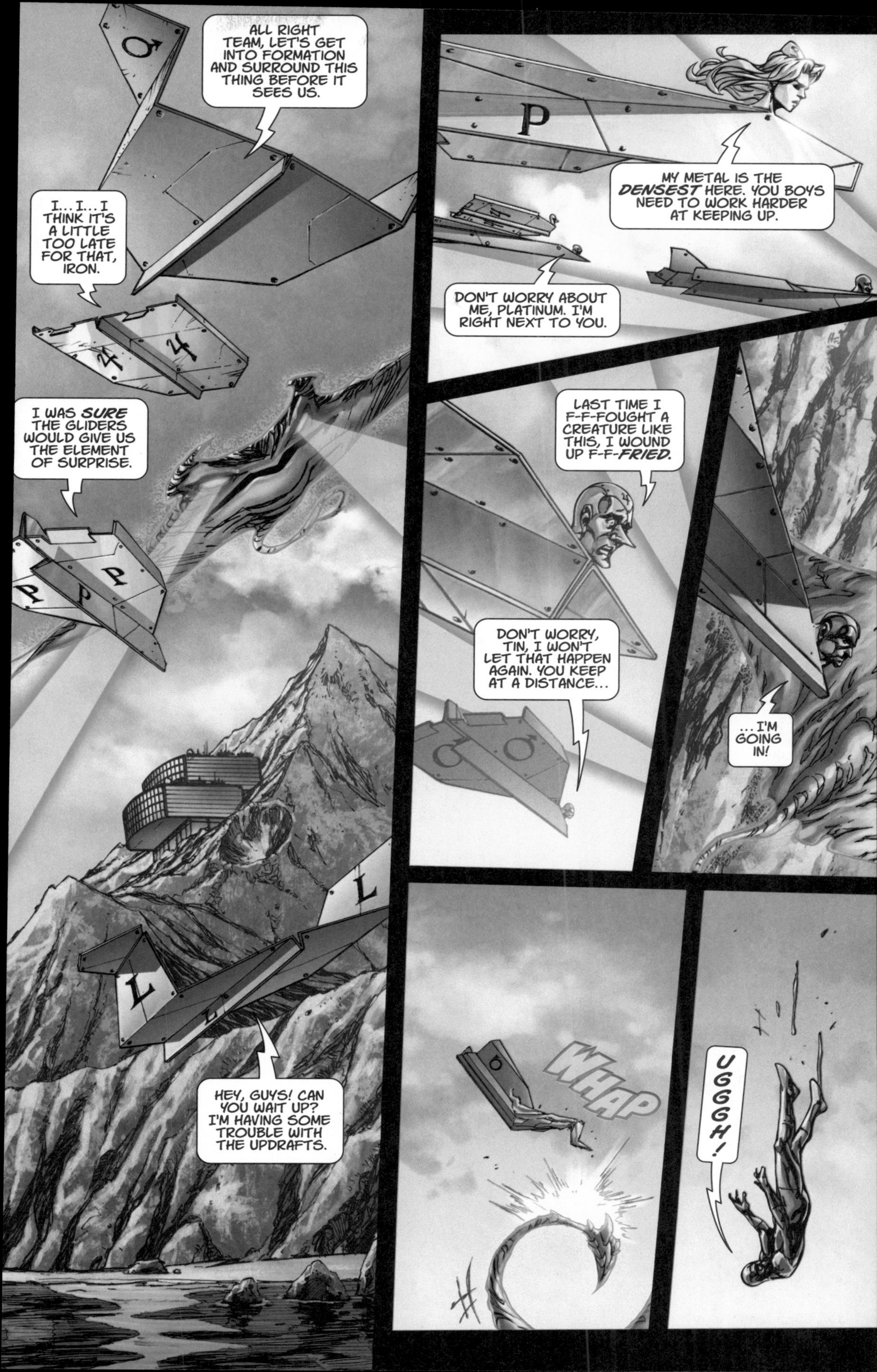
ALL RIGHT TEAM, LET'S GET INTO FORMATION AND SURROUND THIS THING BEFORE IT SEES US.
I... I... I THINK IT'S A LITTLE TOO LATE FOR THAT, IRON.
I WAS SURE THE GLIDERS WOULD GIVE US THE ELEMENT OF SURPRISE.
HEY, GUYS! CAN YOU WAIT UP? I'M HAVING SOME TROUBLE WITH THE UPDRAFTS.
MY METAL IS THE DENSEST HERE. YOU BOYS NEED TO WORK HARDER AT KEEPING UP.
DON'T WORRY ABOUT ME, PLATINUM. I'M RIGHT NEXT TO YOU.
LAST TIME I F-F-FOUGHT A CREATURE LIKE THIS, I WOUND UP F-F-FRIED.
DON'T WORRY, TIN, I WON'T LET THAT HAPPEN AGAIN. YOU KEEP AT A DISTANCE...
...I'M GOING IN!
WHAP
UGGGH!

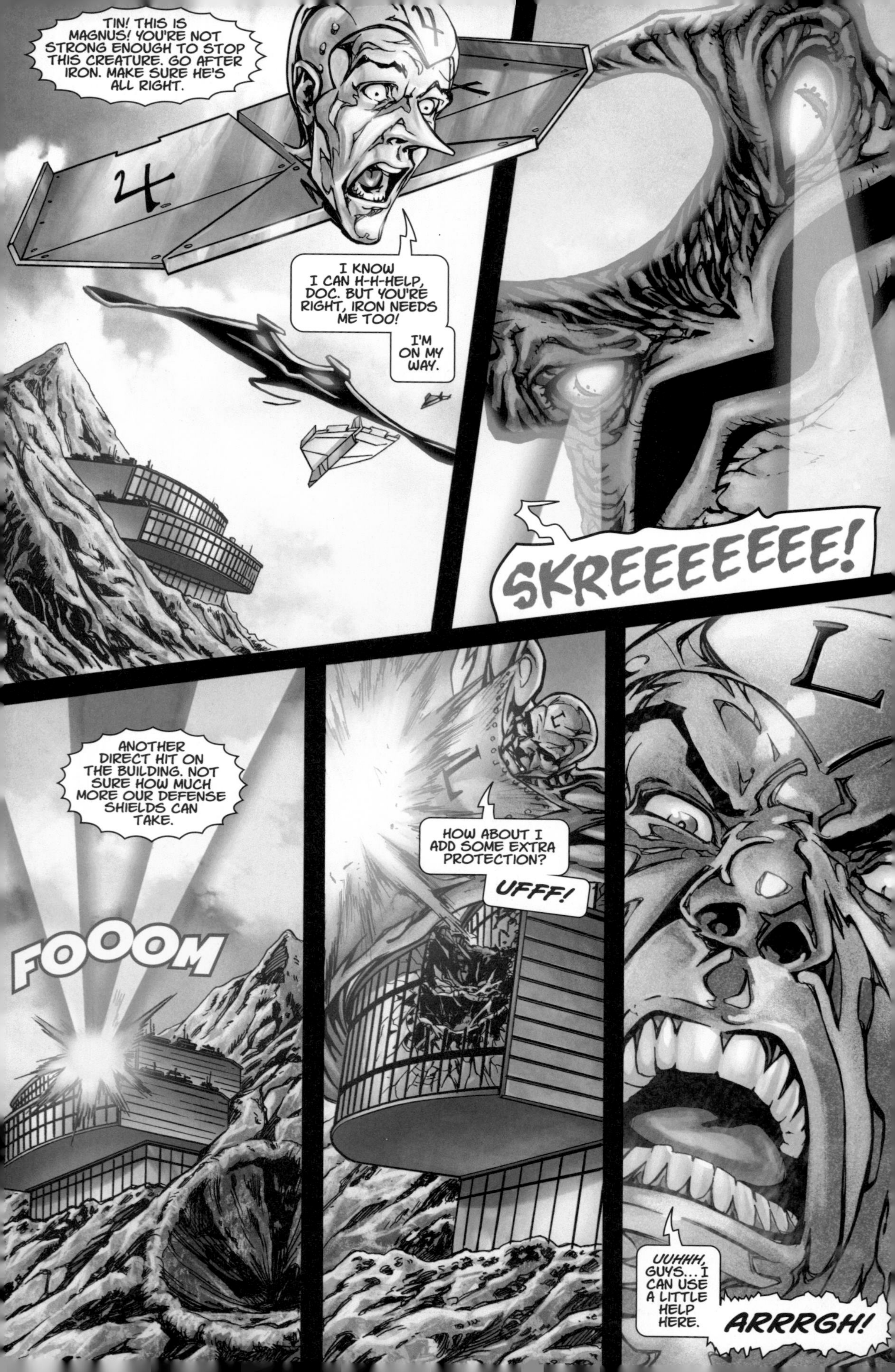
TIN! THIS IS MAGNUS! YOU'RE NOT STRONG ENOUGH TO STOP THIS CREATURE. GO AFTER IRON. MAKE SURE HE'S ALL RIGHT.
I KNOW I CAN H-H-HELP, DOC. BUT YOU'RE RIGHT, IRON NEEDS ME TOO!
I'M ON MY WAY.
SKREEEEEEEE!
ANOTHER DIRECT HIT ON THE BUILDING. NOT SURE HOW MUCH MORE OUR DEFENSE SHIELDS CAN TAKE.
FOOOM
HOW ABOUT I ADD SOME EXTRA PROTECTION?
UFFF!
UUHHH, GUYS... I CAN USE A LITTLE HELP HERE.
ARRRGH!

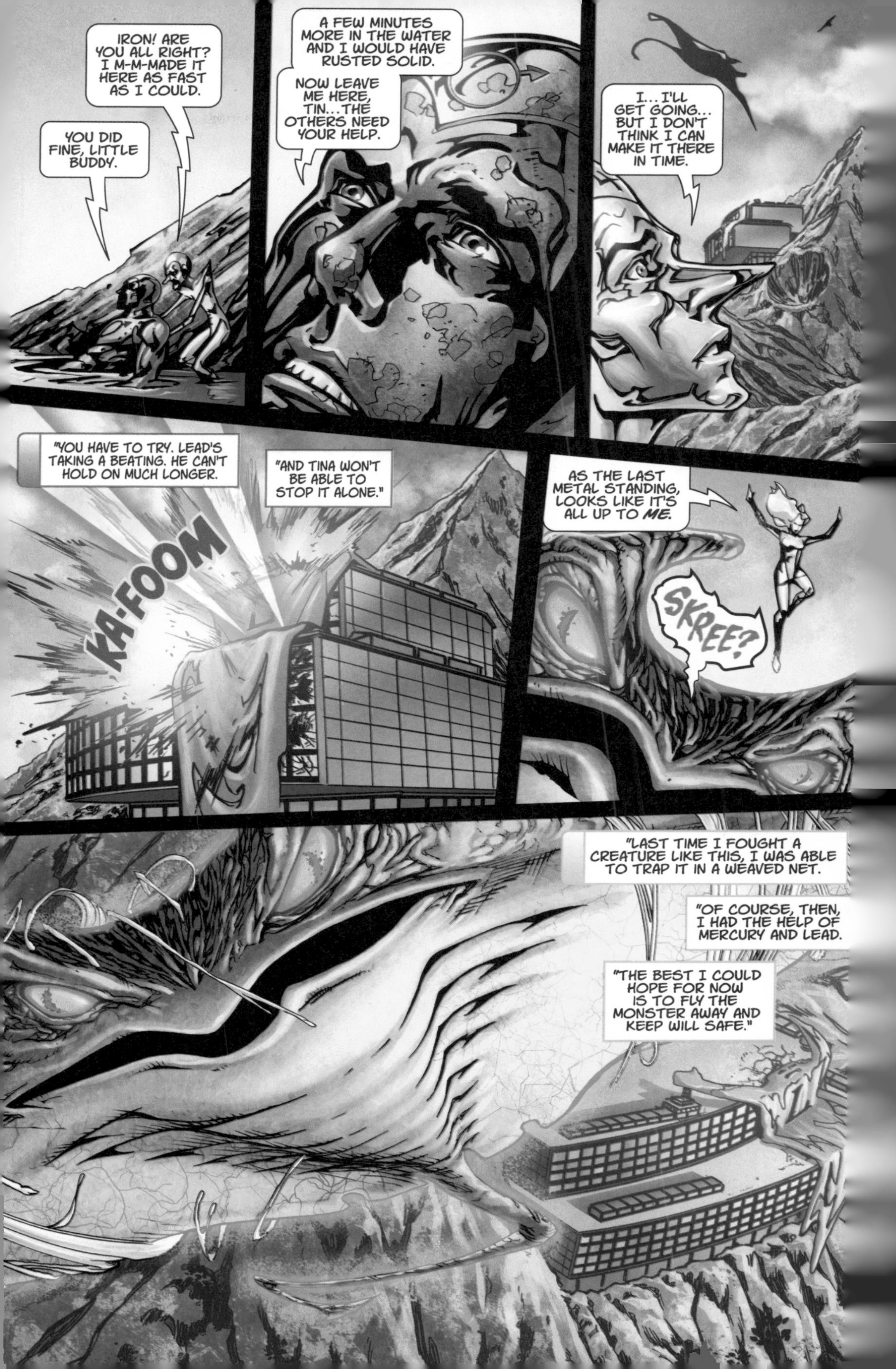

IRON! ARE YOU ALL RIGHT? I M-M-MADE IT HERE AS FAST AS I COULD.
YOU DID FINE, LITTLE BUDDY.
A FEW MINUTES MORE IN THE WATER AND I WOULD HAVE RUSTED SOLID.
NOW LEAVE ME HERE, TIN... THE OTHERS NEED YOUR HELP.
I... I'LL GET GOING... BUT I DON'T THINK I CAN MAKE IT THERE IN TIME.
"YOU HAVE TO TRY. LEAD'S TAKING A BEATING. HE CAN'T HOLD ON MUCH LONGER.
"AND TINA WON'T BE ABLE TO STOP IT ALONE."
KA-FOOM
AS THE LAST METAL STANDING, LOOKS LIKE IT'S ALL UP TO *ME*.
SKREE?
"LAST TIME I FOUGHT A CREATURE LIKE THIS, I WAS ABLE TO TRAP IT IN A WEAVED NET.
"OF COURSE, THEN, I HAD THE HELP OF MERCURY AND LEAD.
"THE BEST I COULD HOPE FOR NOW IS TO FLY THE MONSTER AWAY AND KEEP WILL SAFE."

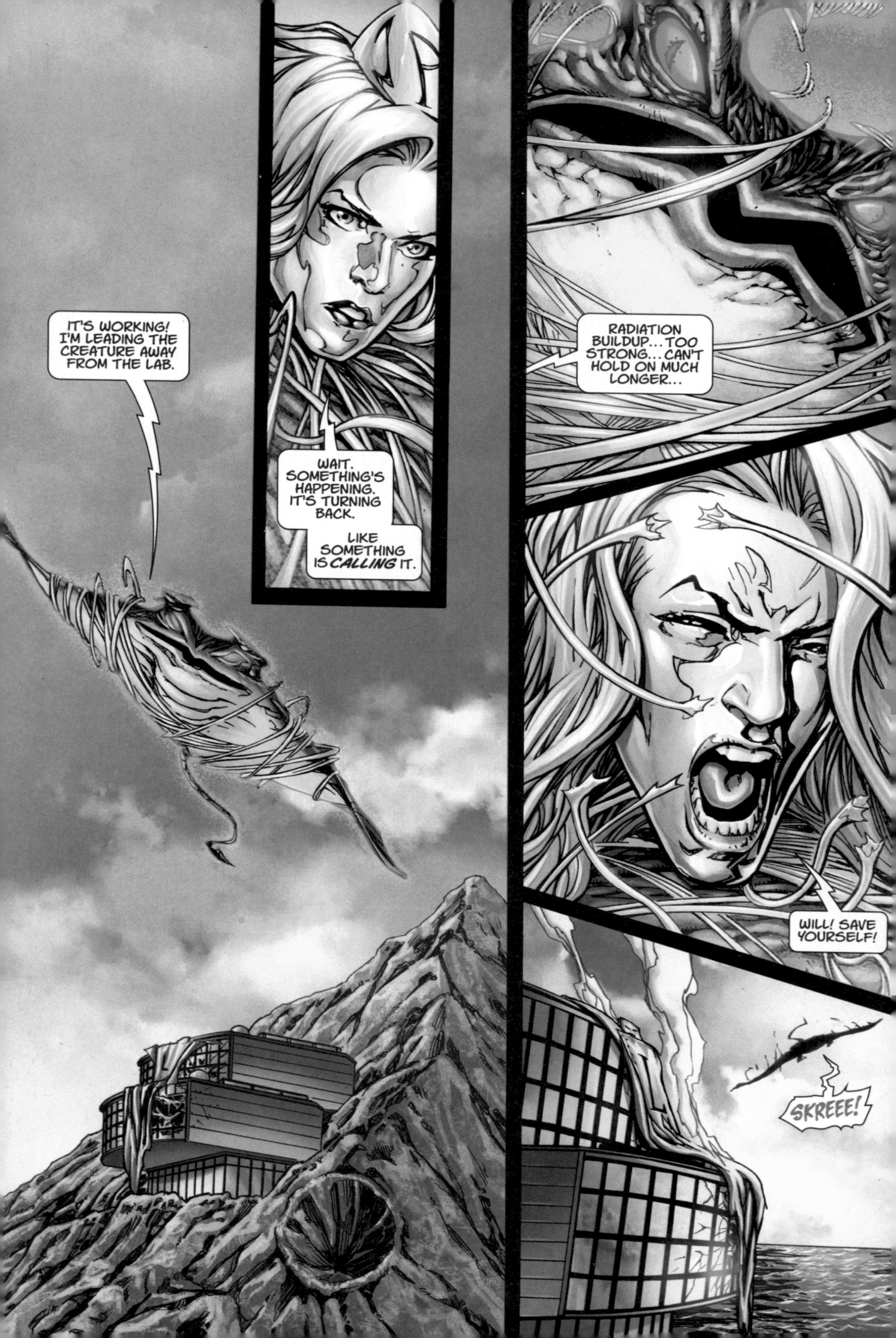
IT'S WORKING! I'M LEADING THE CREATURE AWAY FROM THE LAB.
WAIT. SOMETHING'S HAPPENING. IT'S TURNING BACK.
LIKE SOMETHING IS CALLING IT.
RADIATION BUILDUP... TOO STRONG... CAN'T HOLD ON MUCH LONGER...
WILL! SAVE YOURSELF!
SKREEE!

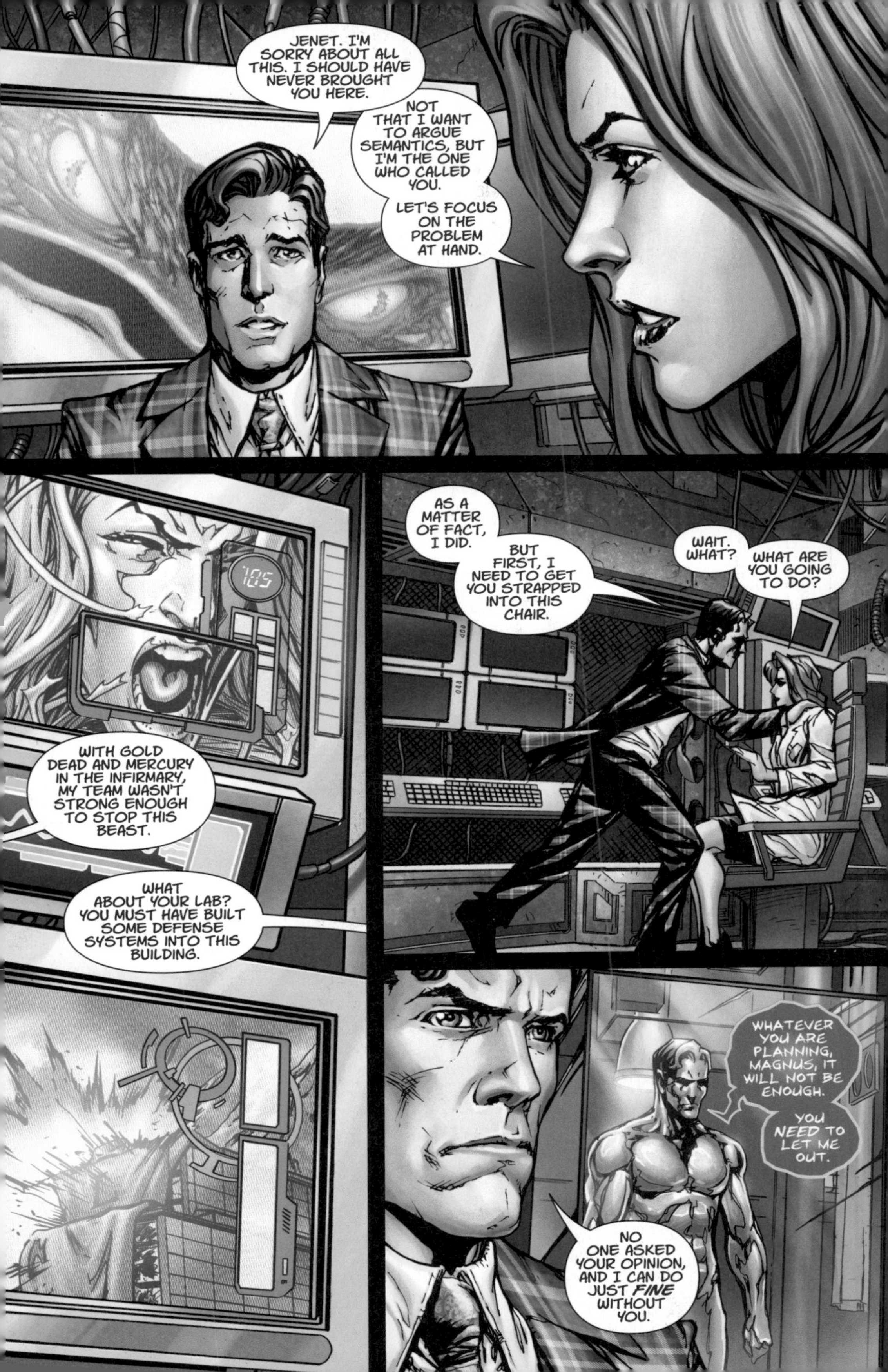
JENET. I'M SORRY ABOUT ALL THIS. I SHOULD HAVE NEVER BROUGHT YOU HERE.
NOT THAT I WANT TO ARGUE SEMANTICS, BUT I'M THE ONE WHO CALLED YOU.
LET'S FOCUS ON THE PROBLEM AT HAND.
185
WITH GOLD DEAD AND MERCURY IN THE INFIRMARY, MY TEAM WASN'T STRONG ENOUGH TO STOP THIS BEAST.
WHAT ABOUT YOUR LAB? YOU MUST HAVE BUILT SOME DEFENSE SYSTEMS INTO THIS BUILDING.
AS A MATTER OF FACT, I DID.
BUT FIRST, I NEED TO GET YOU STRAPPED INTO THIS CHAIR.
WAIT. WHAT?
WHAT ARE YOU GOING TO DO?
WHATEVER YOU ARE PLANNING, MAGNUS, IT WILL NOT BE ENOUGH.
YOU *NEED* TO LET ME OUT.
NO ONE ASKED YOUR OPINION, AND I CAN DO JUST *FINE* WITHOUT YOU.

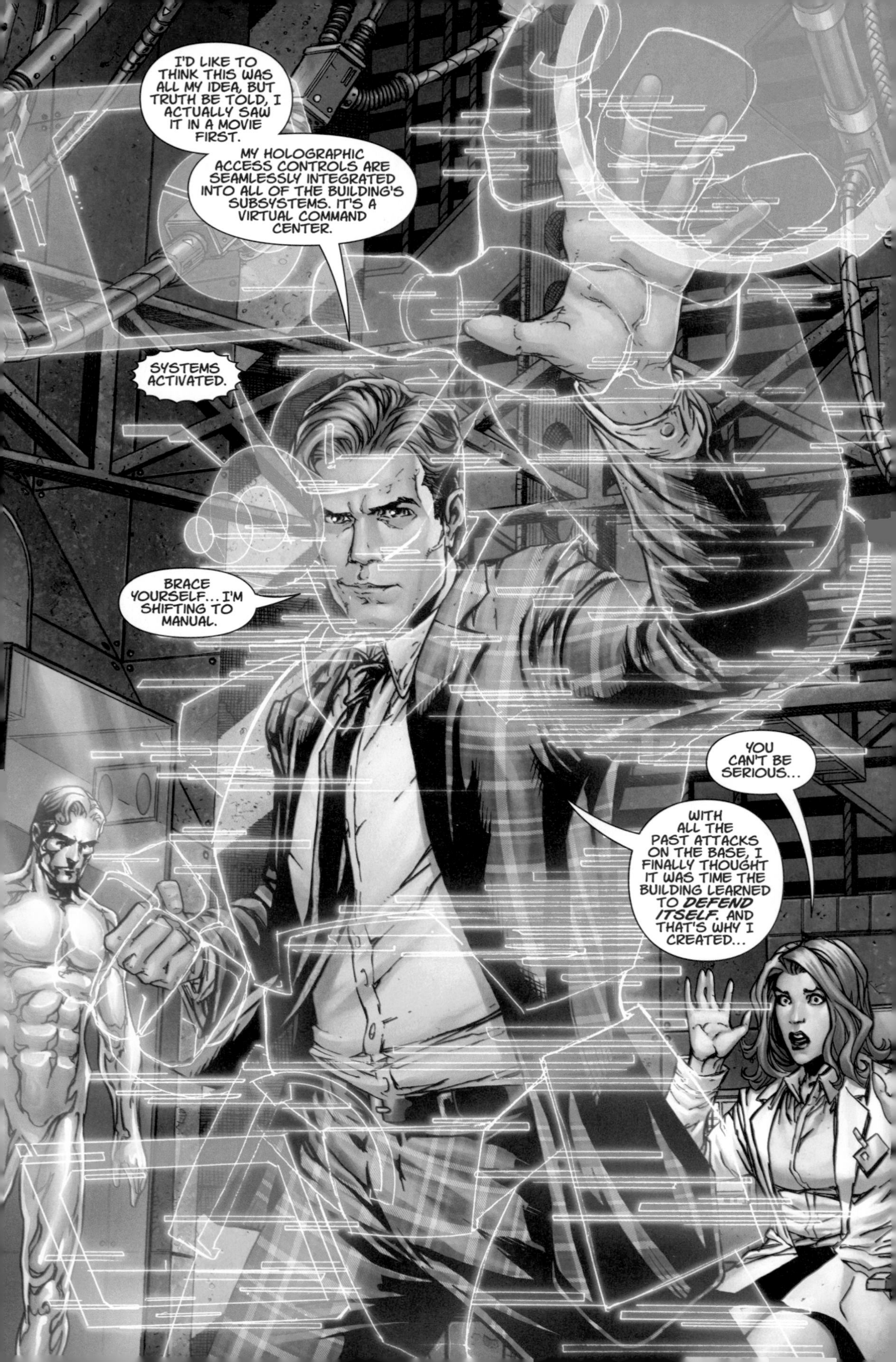
I'D LIKE TO THINK THIS WAS ALL MY IDEA, BUT TRUTH BE TOLD, I ACTUALLY SAW IT IN A MOVIE FIRST.
MY HOLOGRAPHIC ACCESS CONTROLS ARE SEAMLESSLY INTEGRATED INTO ALL OF THE BUILDING'S SUBSYSTEMS. IT'S A VIRTUAL COMMAND CENTER.
SYSTEMS ACTIVATED.
BRACE YOURSELF... I'M SHIFTING TO MANUAL.
YOU CAN'T BE SERIOUS...
WITH ALL THE PAST ATTACKS ON THE BASE, I FINALLY THOUGHT IT WAS TIME THE BUILDING LEARNED TO ***DEFEND ITSELF***. AND THAT'S WHY I CREATED...

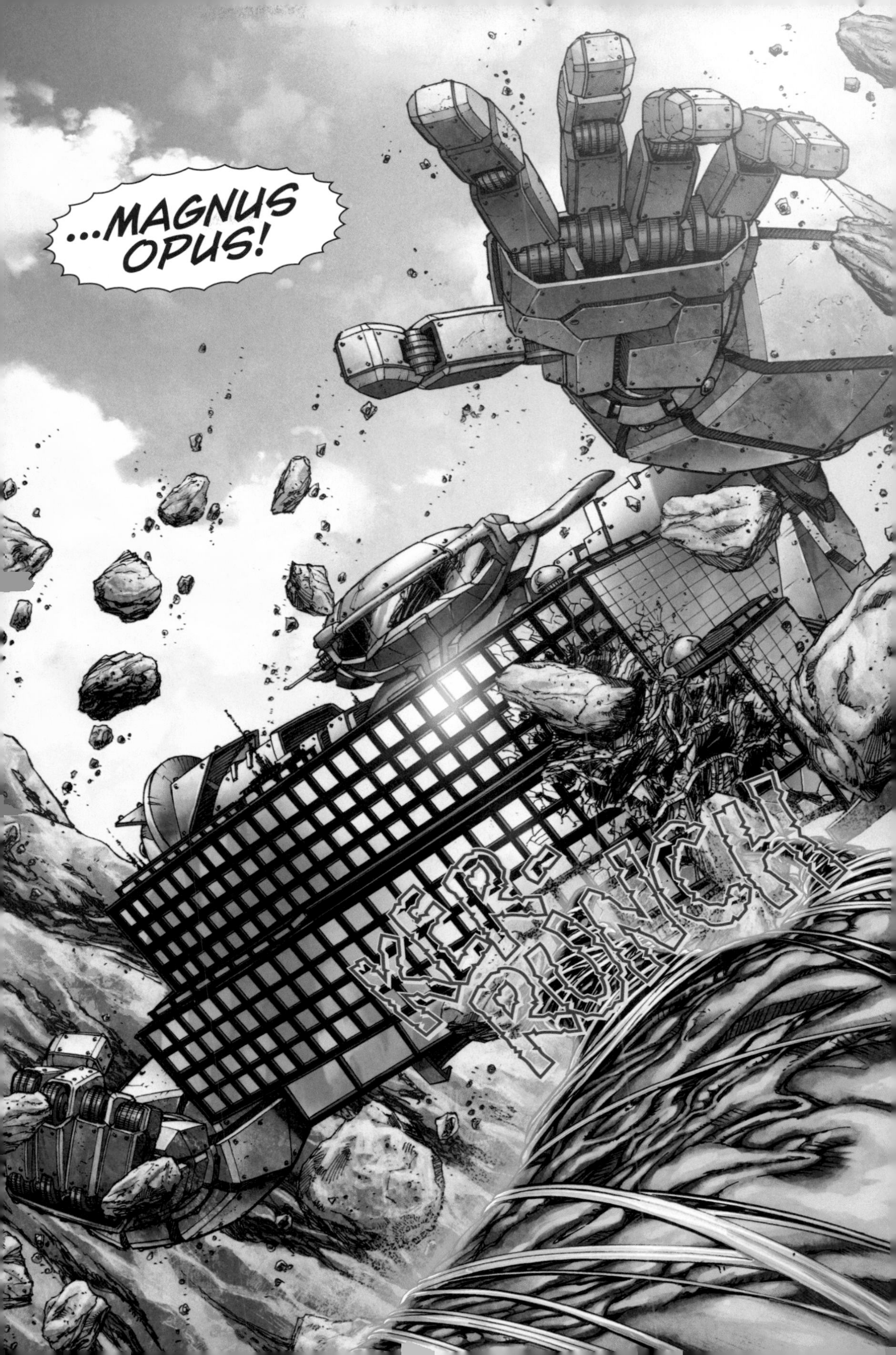
...MAGNUS OPUS!

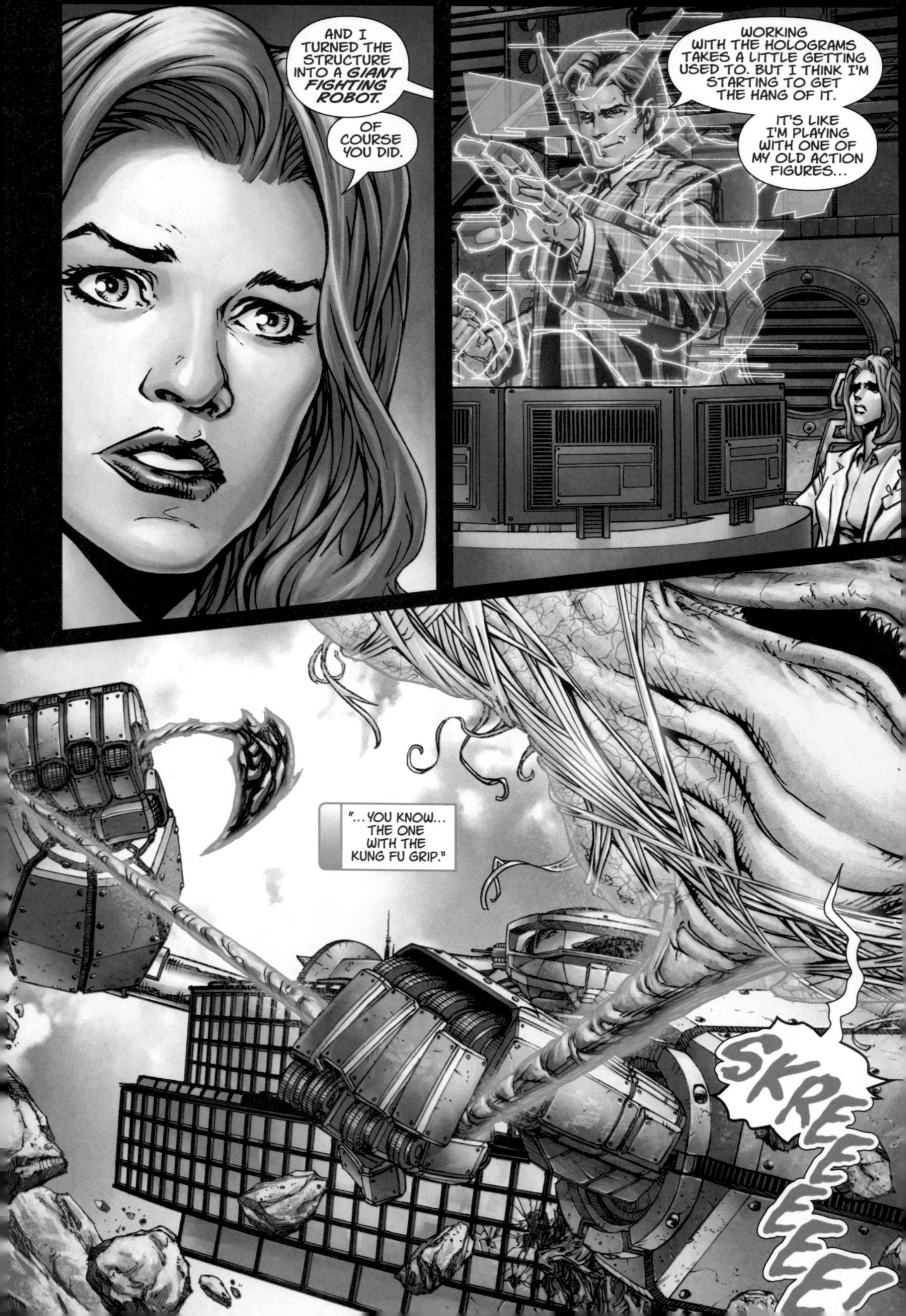
AND I TURNED THE STRUCTURE INTO A *GIANT FIGHTING ROBOT.*
OF COURSE YOU DID.
WORKING WITH THE HOLOGRAMS TAKES A LITTLE GETTING USED TO. BUT I THINK I'M STARTING TO GET THE HANG OF IT.
IT'S LIKE I'M PLAYING WITH ONE OF MY OLD ACTION FIGURES...
"...YOU KNOW... THE ONE WITH THE KUNG FU GRIP."
SKREEEEEEE!

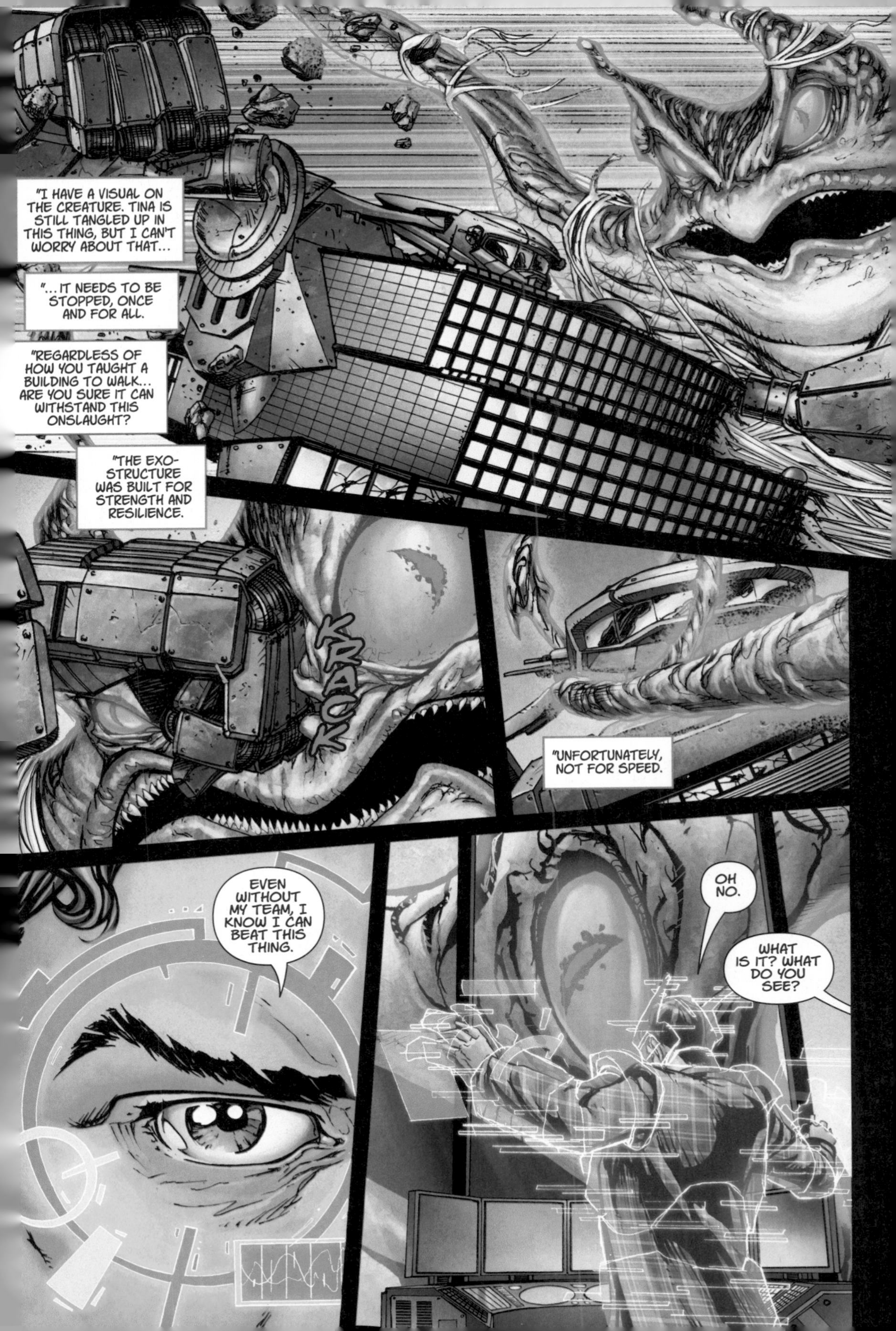
"I HAVE A VISUAL ON THE CREATURE. TINA IS STILL TANGLED UP IN THIS THING, BUT I CAN'T WORRY ABOUT THAT...
"...IT NEEDS TO BE STOPPED, ONCE AND FOR ALL.
"REGARDLESS OF HOW YOU TAUGHT A BUILDING TO WALK... ARE YOU SURE IT CAN WITHSTAND THIS ONSLAUGHT?
"THE EXO-STRUCTURE WAS BUILT FOR STRENGTH AND RESILIENCE.
KRACK
"UNFORTUNATELY, NOT FOR SPEED.
EVEN WITHOUT MY TEAM, I KNOW I CAN BEAT THIS THING.
OH NO.
WHAT IS IT? WHAT DO YOU SEE?

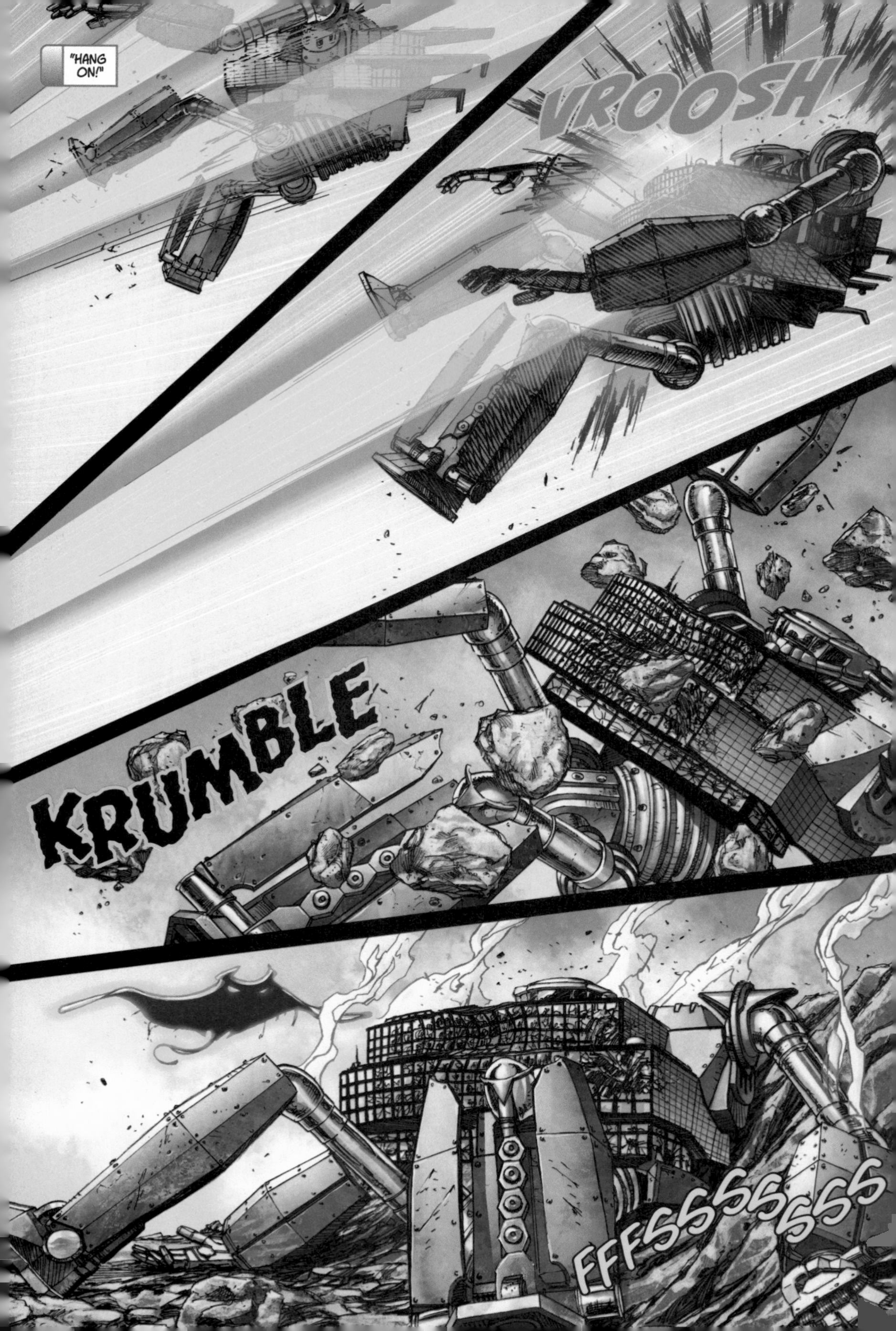
"HANG ON!"
VROOSH
KRUMBLE
FFFSSSSSSSSS

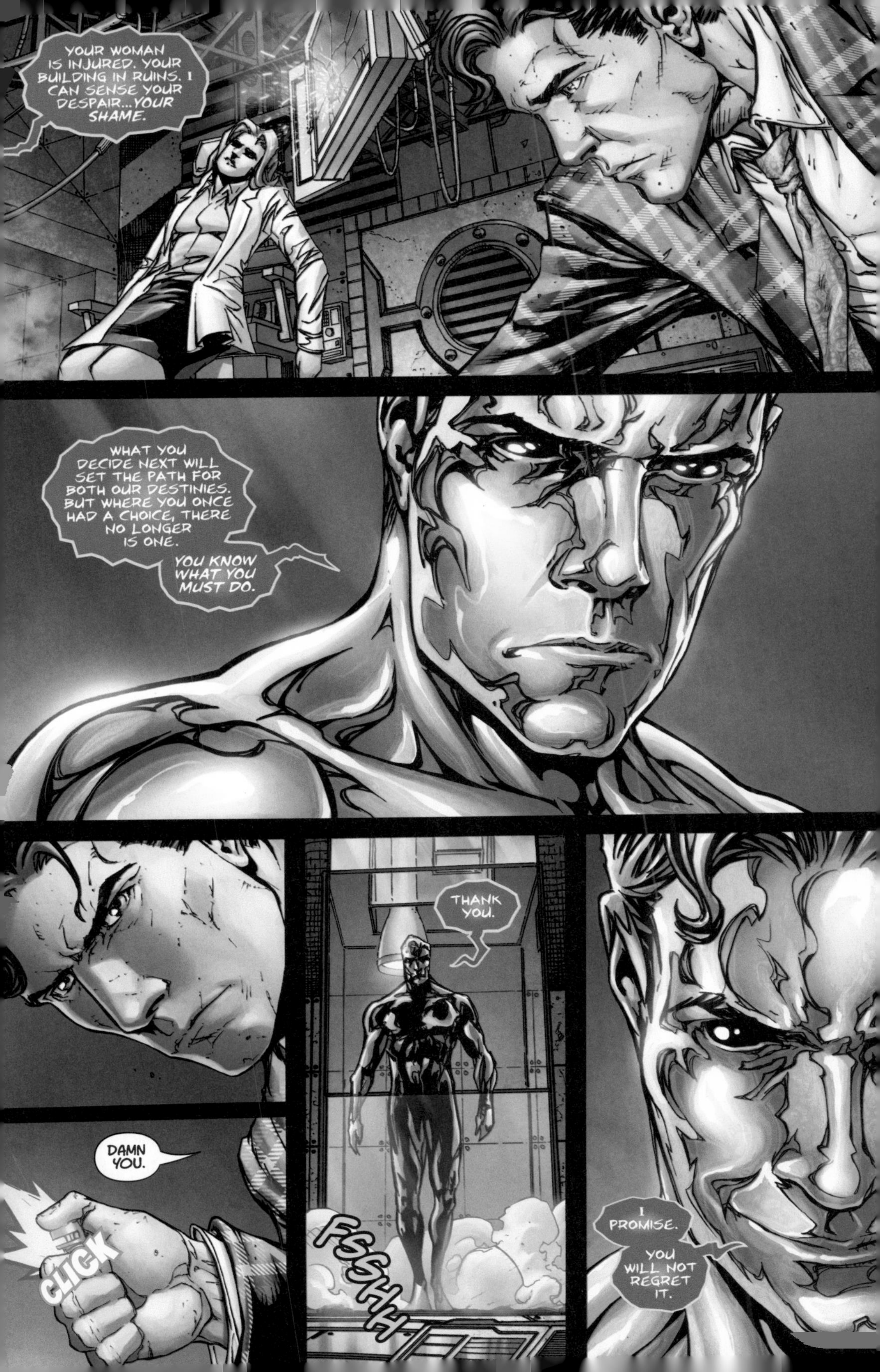
YOUR WOMAN IS INJURED. YOUR BUILDING IN RUINS. I CAN SENSE YOUR DESPAIR...YOUR SHAME.
WHAT YOU DECIDE NEXT WILL SET THE PATH FOR BOTH OUR DESTINIES. BUT WHERE YOU ONCE HAD A CHOICE, THERE NO LONGER IS ONE.
YOU KNOW WHAT YOU MUST DO.
DAMN YOU.
CLICK
THANK YOU.
FSSHH
I PROMISE.
YOU WILL NOT REGRET IT.

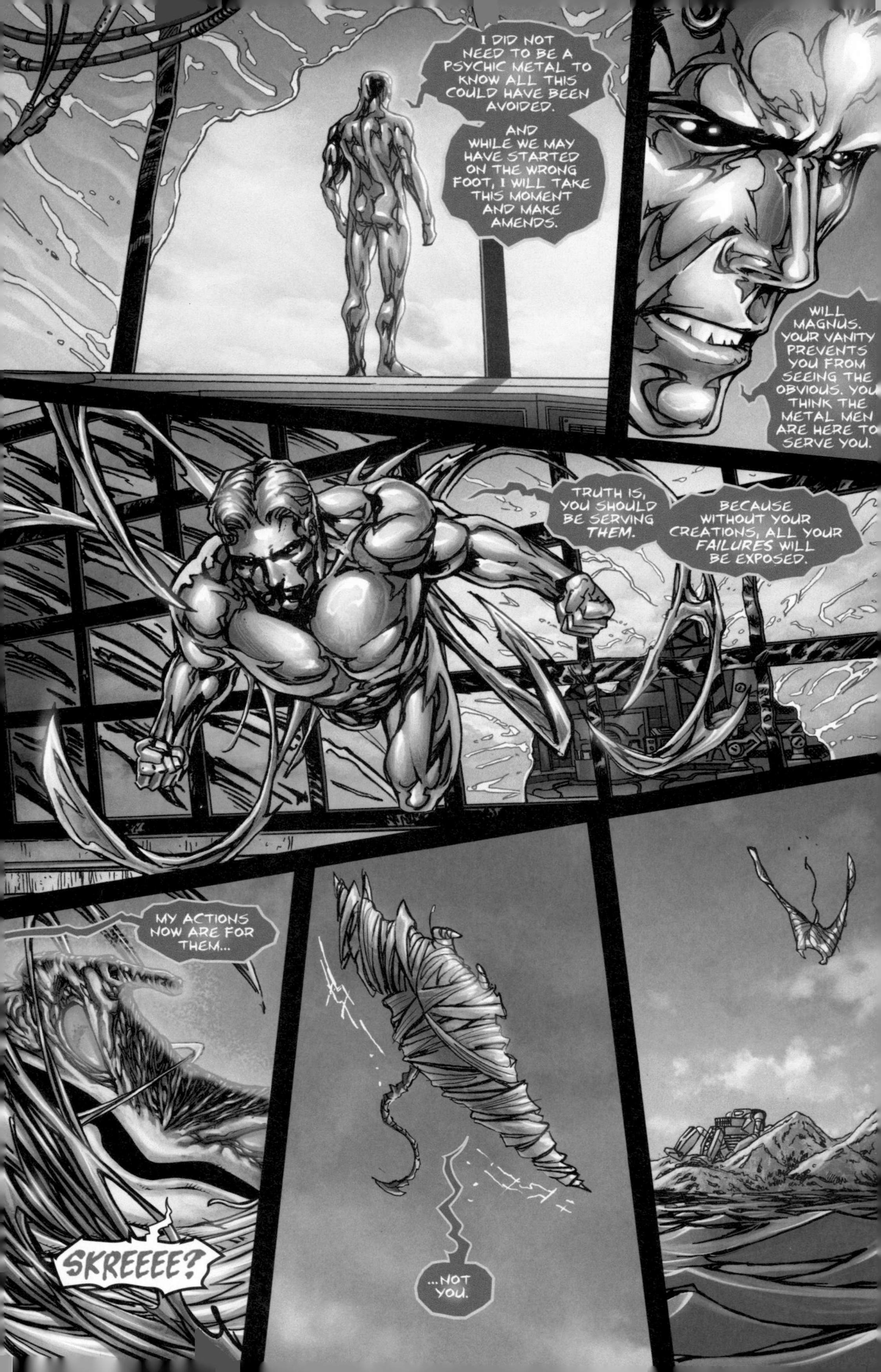
I DID NOT NEED TO BE A PSYCHIC METAL TO KNOW ALL THIS COULD HAVE BEEN AVOIDED.
AND WHILE WE MAY HAVE STARTED ON THE WRONG FOOT, I WILL TAKE THIS MOMENT AND MAKE AMENDS.
WILL MAGNUS. YOUR VANITY PREVENTS YOU FROM SEEING THE OBVIOUS. YOU THINK THE METAL MEN ARE HERE TO SERVE YOU.
TRUTH IS, YOU SHOULD BE SERVING *THEM*.
BECAUSE WITHOUT YOUR CREATIONS, ALL YOUR *FAILURES* WILL BE EXPOSED.
MY ACTIONS NOW ARE FOR THEM...
SKREEEE?
...NOT YOU.

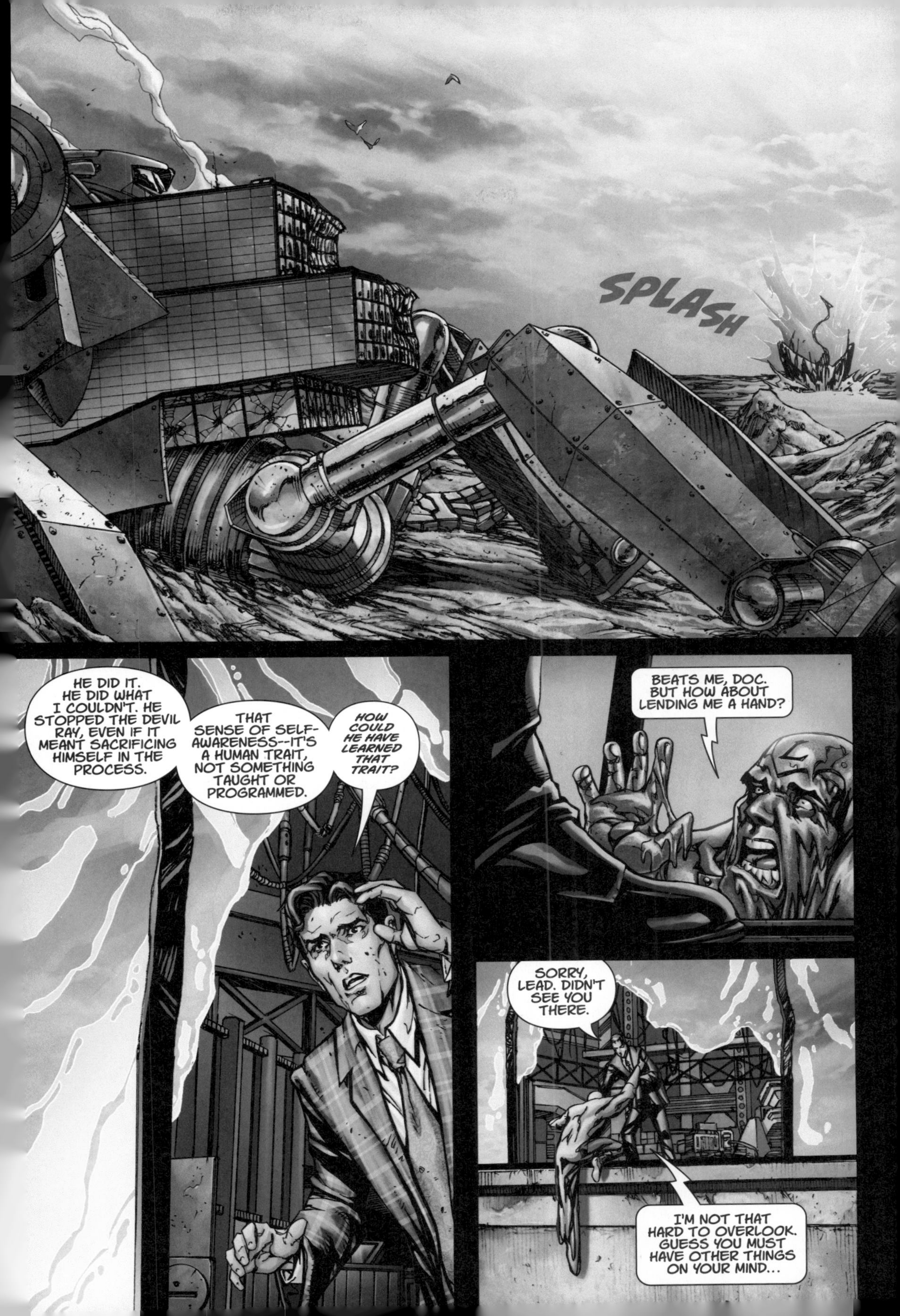
SPLASH
HE DID IT. HE DID WHAT I COULDN'T. HE STOPPED THE DEVIL RAY, EVEN IF IT MEANT SACRIFICING HIMSELF IN THE PROCESS.
THAT SENSE OF SELF-AWARENESS--IT'S A HUMAN TRAIT, NOT SOMETHING TAUGHT OR PROGRAMMED.
HOW COULD HE HAVE LEARNED THAT TRAIT?
BEATS ME, DOC. BUT HOW ABOUT LENDING ME A HAND?
SORRY, LEAD. DIDN'T SEE YOU THERE.
I'M NOT THAT HARD TO OVERLOOK. GUESS YOU MUST HAVE OTHER THINGS ON YOUR MIND...

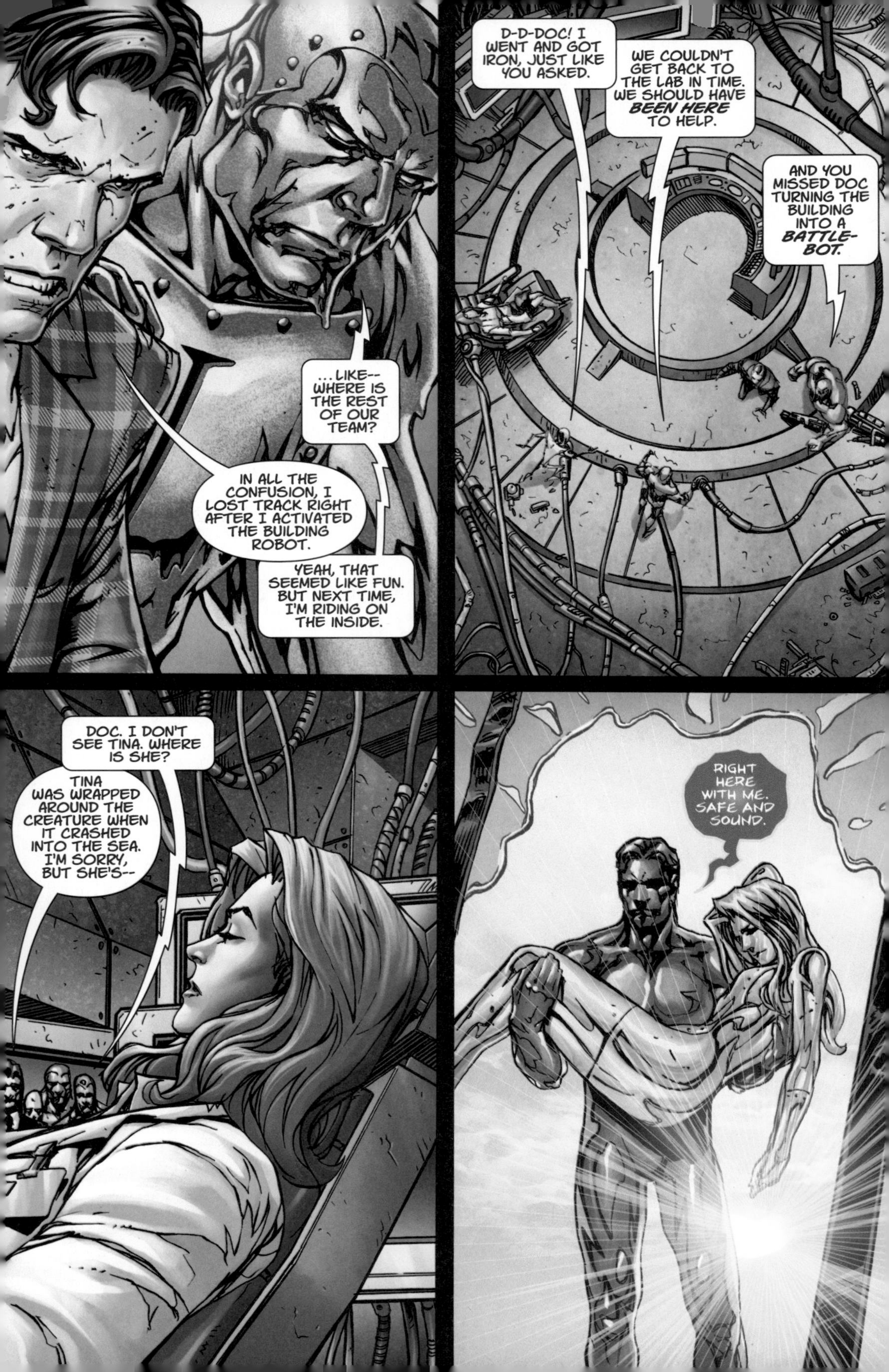
...LIKE-- WHERE IS THE REST OF OUR TEAM?
IN ALL THE CONFUSION, I LOST TRACK RIGHT AFTER I ACTIVATED THE BUILDING ROBOT.
YEAH, THAT SEEMED LIKE FUN. BUT NEXT TIME, I'M RIDING ON THE INSIDE.
D-D-DOC! I WENT AND GOT IRON, JUST LIKE YOU ASKED.
WE COULDN'T GET BACK TO THE LAB IN TIME. WE SHOULD HAVE BEEN HERE TO HELP.
AND YOU MISSED DOC TURNING THE BUILDING INTO A BATTLE-BOT.
DOC. I DON'T SEE TINA. WHERE IS SHE?
TINA WAS WRAPPED AROUND THE CREATURE WHEN IT CRASHED INTO THE SEA. I'M SORRY, BUT SHE'S--
RIGHT HERE WITH ME. SAFE AND SOUND.

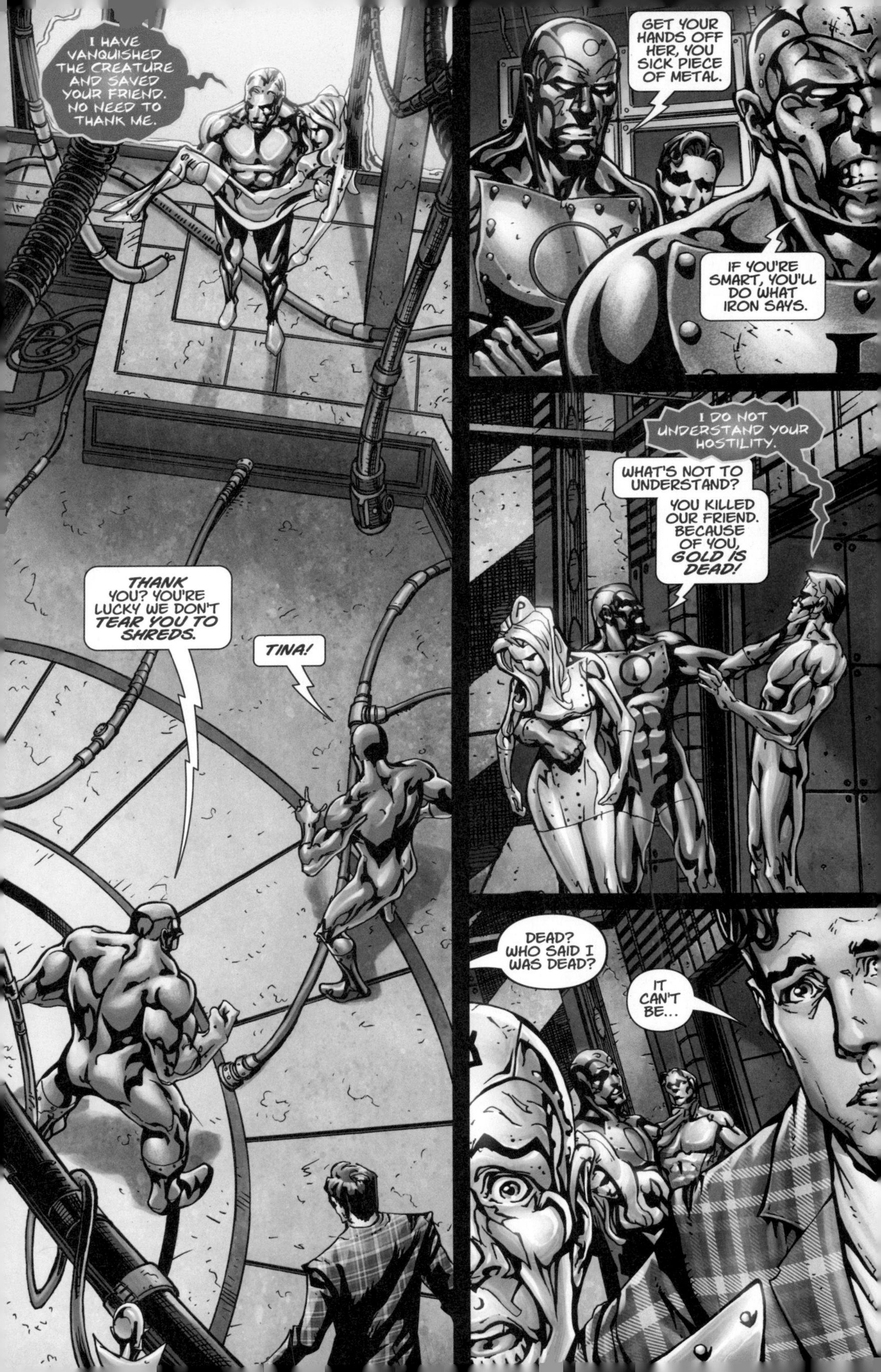
I HAVE VANQUISHED THE CREATURE AND SAVED YOUR FRIEND. NO NEED TO THANK ME.
THANK YOU? YOU'RE LUCKY WE DON'T TEAR YOU TO SHREDS.
TINA!
GET YOUR HANDS OFF HER, YOU SICK PIECE OF METAL.
IF YOU'RE SMART, YOU'LL DO WHAT IRON SAYS.
I DO NOT UNDERSTAND YOUR HOSTILITY.
WHAT'S NOT TO UNDERSTAND?
YOU KILLED OUR FRIEND. BECAUSE OF YOU, GOLD IS DEAD!
DEAD? WHO SAID I WAS DEAD?
IT CAN'T BE...

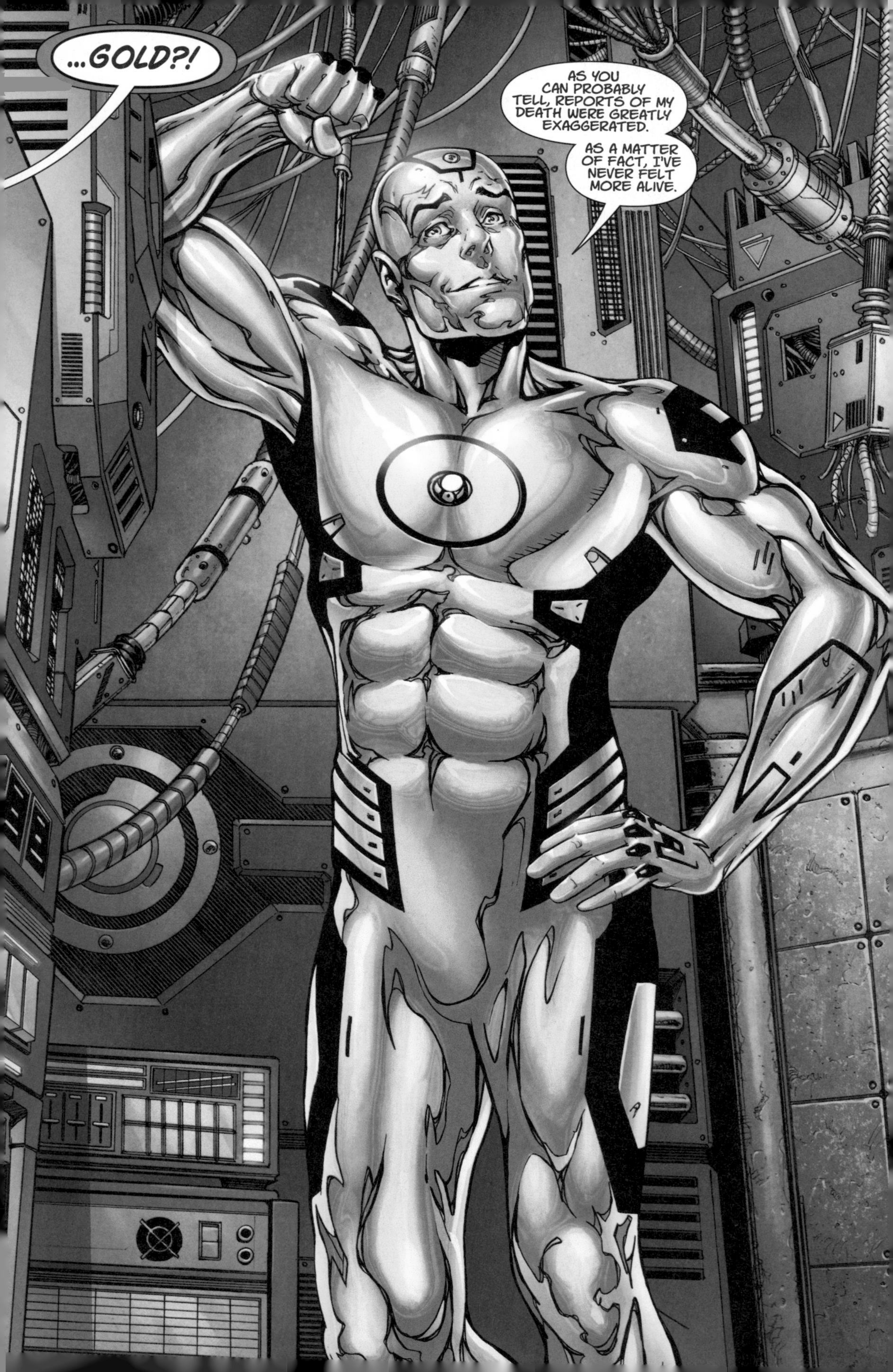
...GOLD?!
AS YOU CAN PROBABLY TELL, REPORTS OF MY DEATH WERE GREATLY EXAGGERATED.
AS A MATTER OF FACT, I'VE NEVER FELT MORE ALIVE.

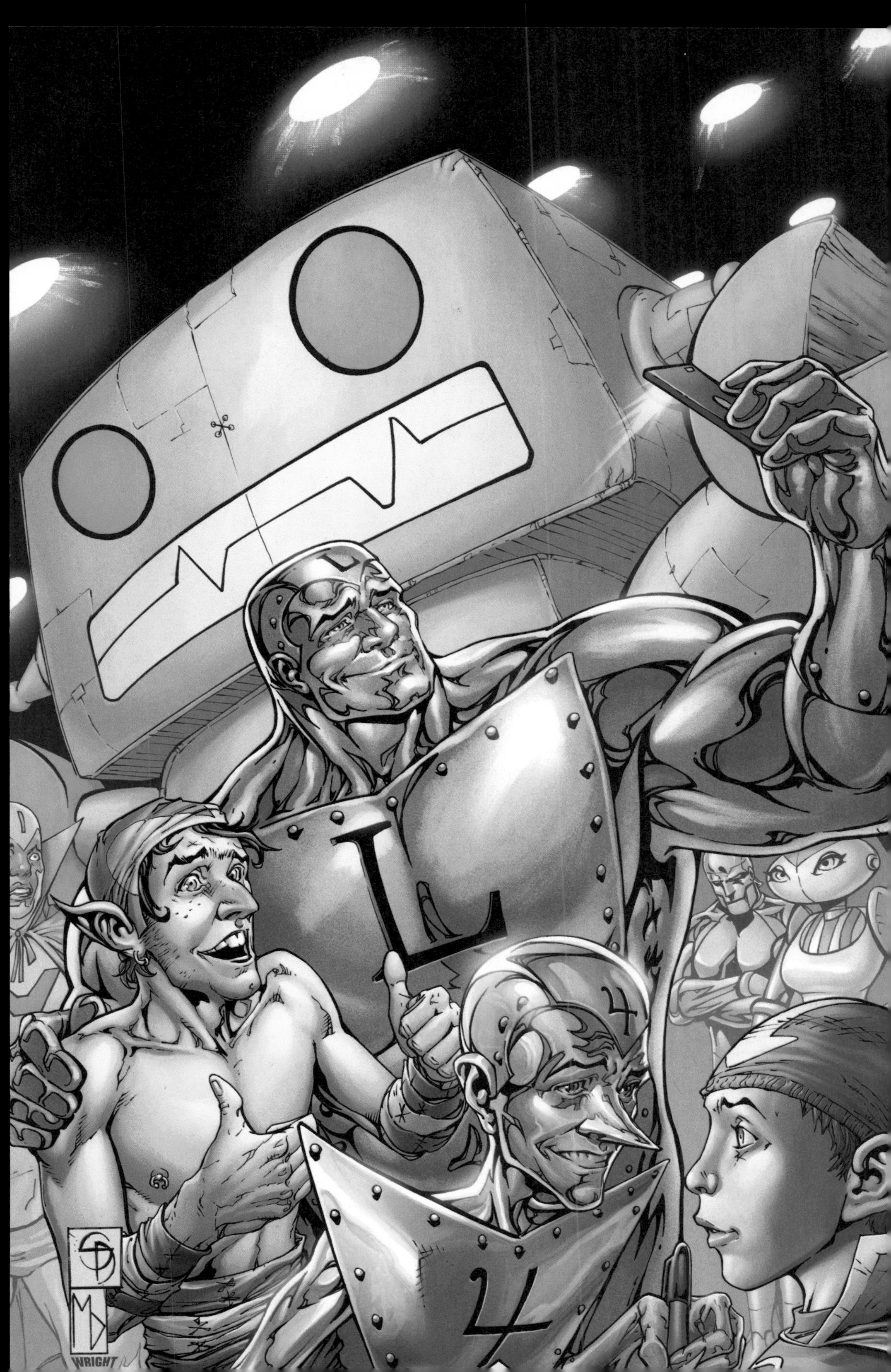
WRIGHT

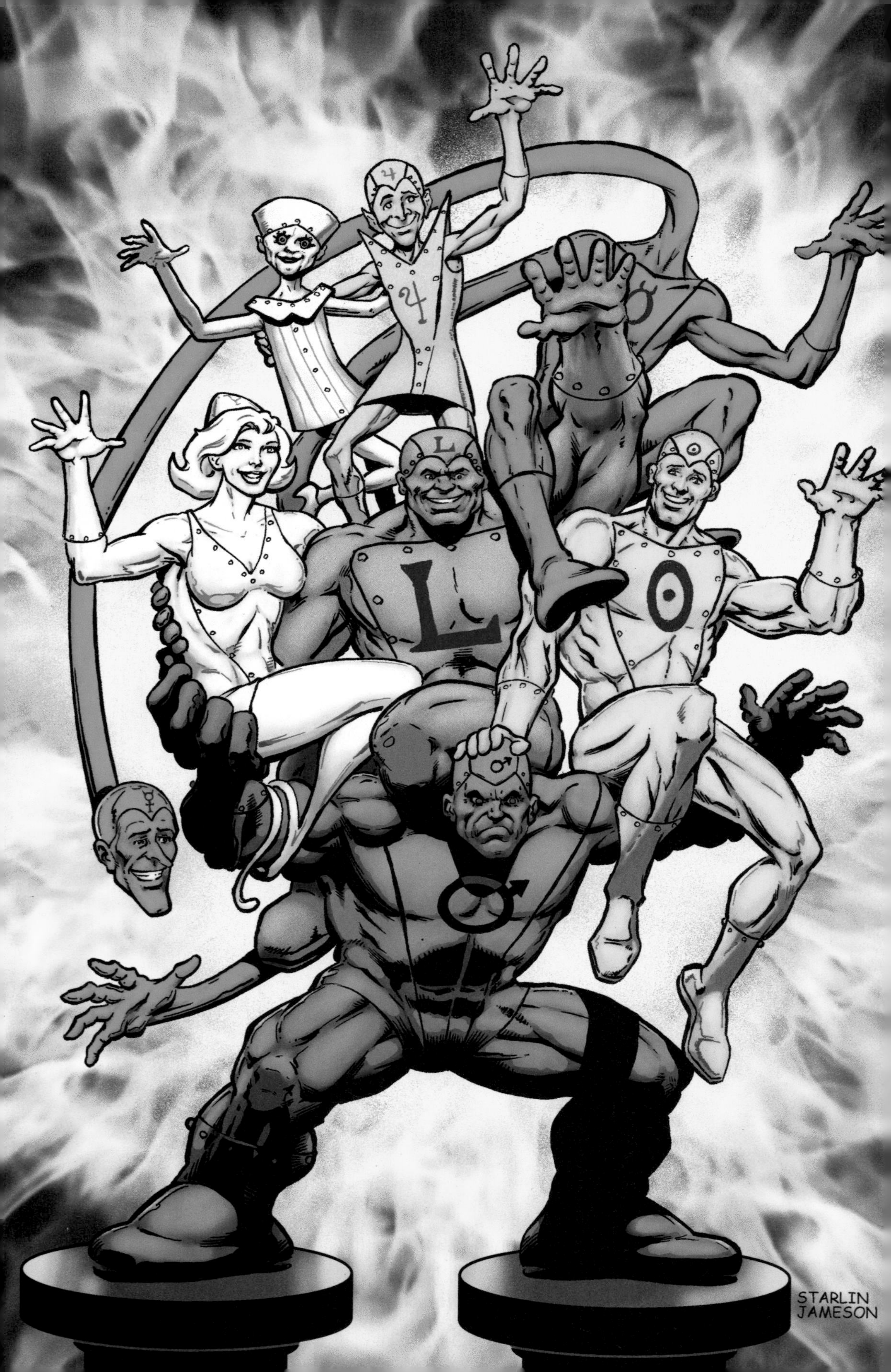
STARLIN
JAMESON

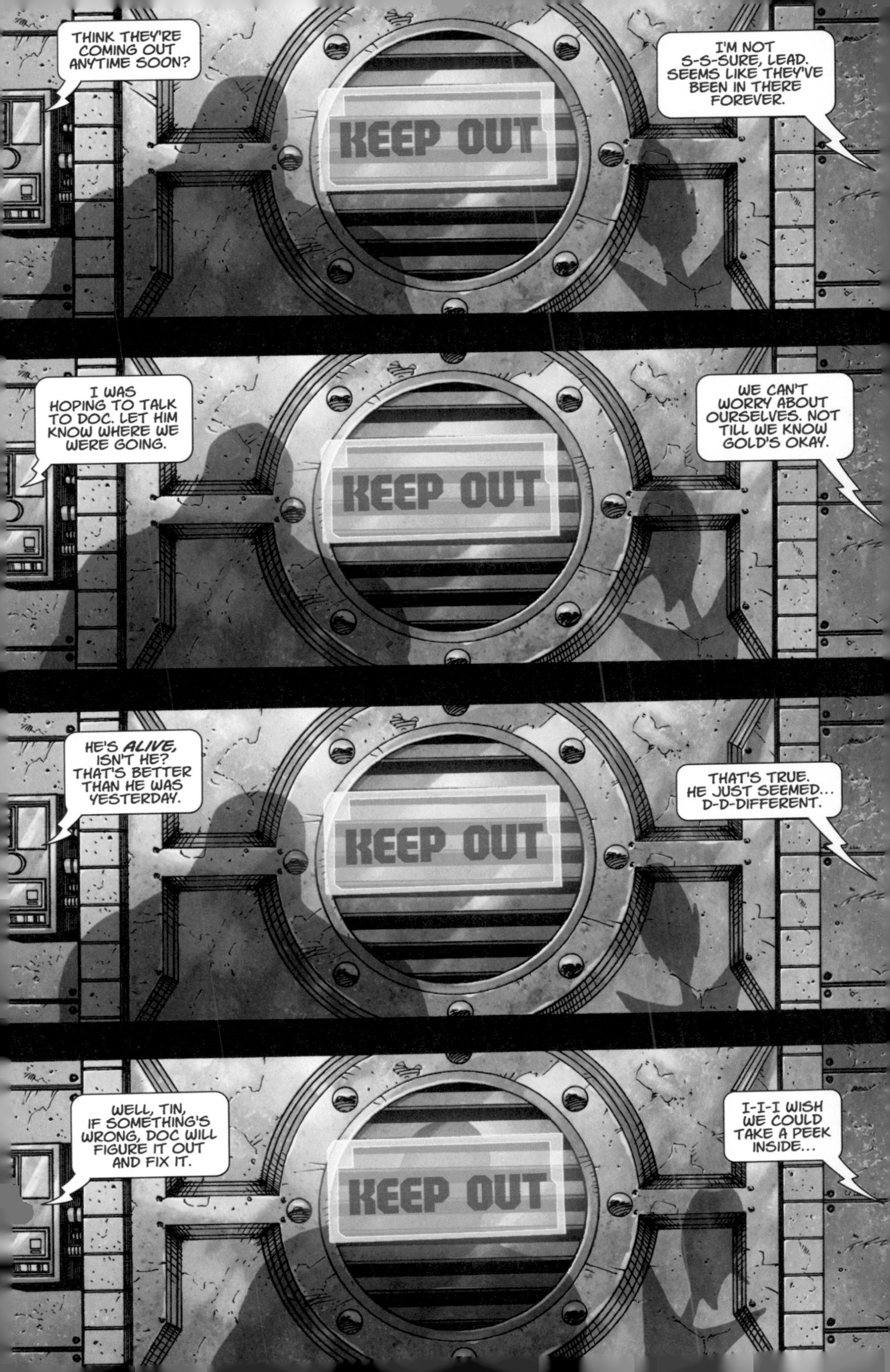
THINK THEY'RE COMING OUT ANYTIME SOON?
KEEP OUT
I'M NOT S-S-SURE, LEAD. SEEMS LIKE THEY'VE BEEN IN THERE FOREVER.
I WAS HOPING TO TALK TO DOC. LET HIM KNOW WHERE WE WERE GOING.
KEEP OUT
WE CAN'T WORRY ABOUT OURSELVES. NOT TILL WE KNOW GOLD'S OKAY.
HE'S *ALIVE,* ISN'T HE? THAT'S BETTER THAN HE WAS YESTERDAY.
KEEP OUT
THAT'S TRUE. HE JUST SEEMED... D-D-DIFFERENT.
WELL, TIN, IF SOMETHING'S WRONG, DOC WILL FIGURE IT OUT AND FIX IT.
KEEP OUT
I-I-I WISH WE COULD TAKE A PEEK INSIDE...

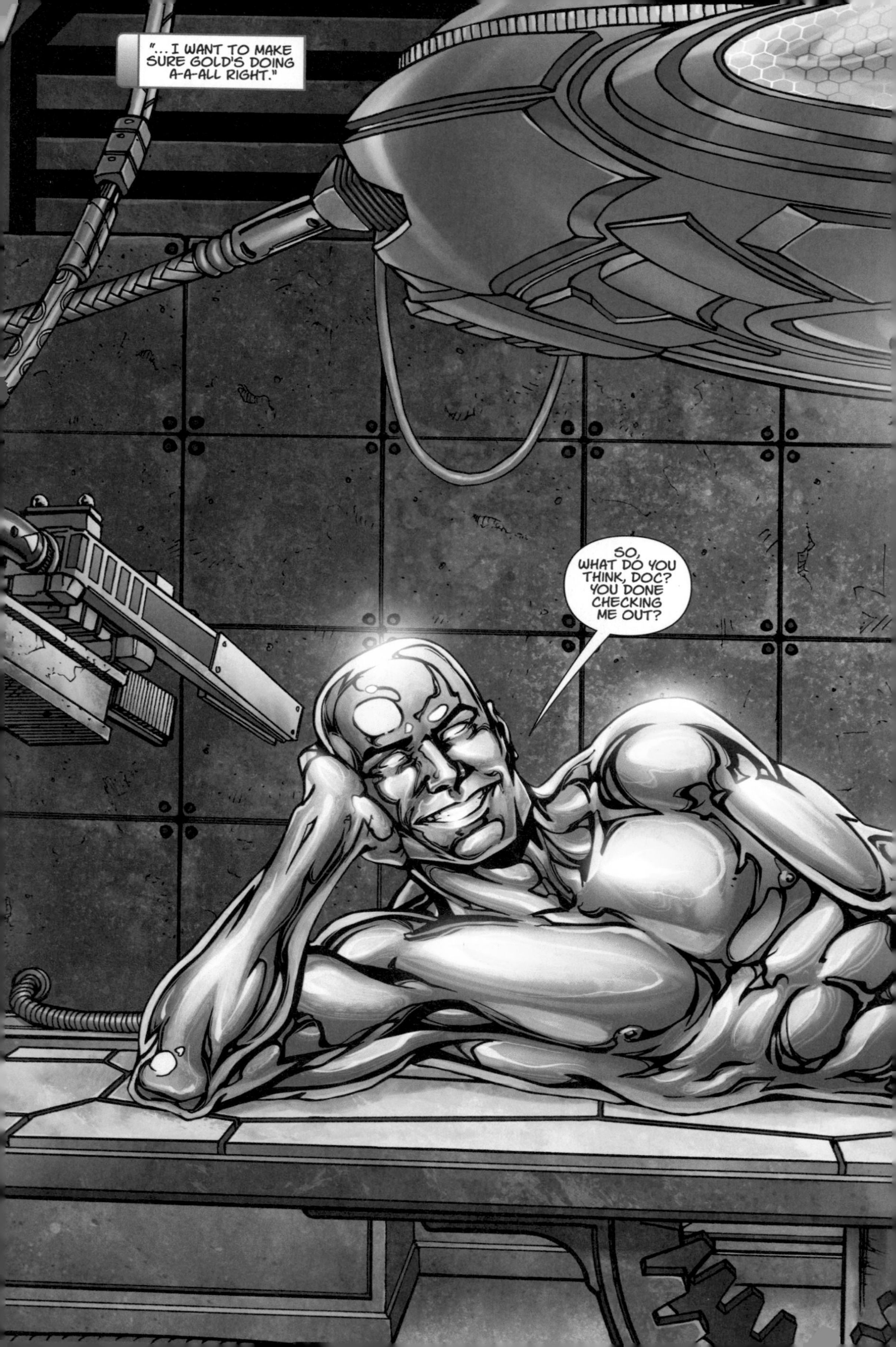
"...I WANT TO MAKE SURE GOLD'S DOING A-A-ALL RIGHT."
SO, WHAT DO YOU THINK, DOC? YOU DONE CHECKING ME OUT?

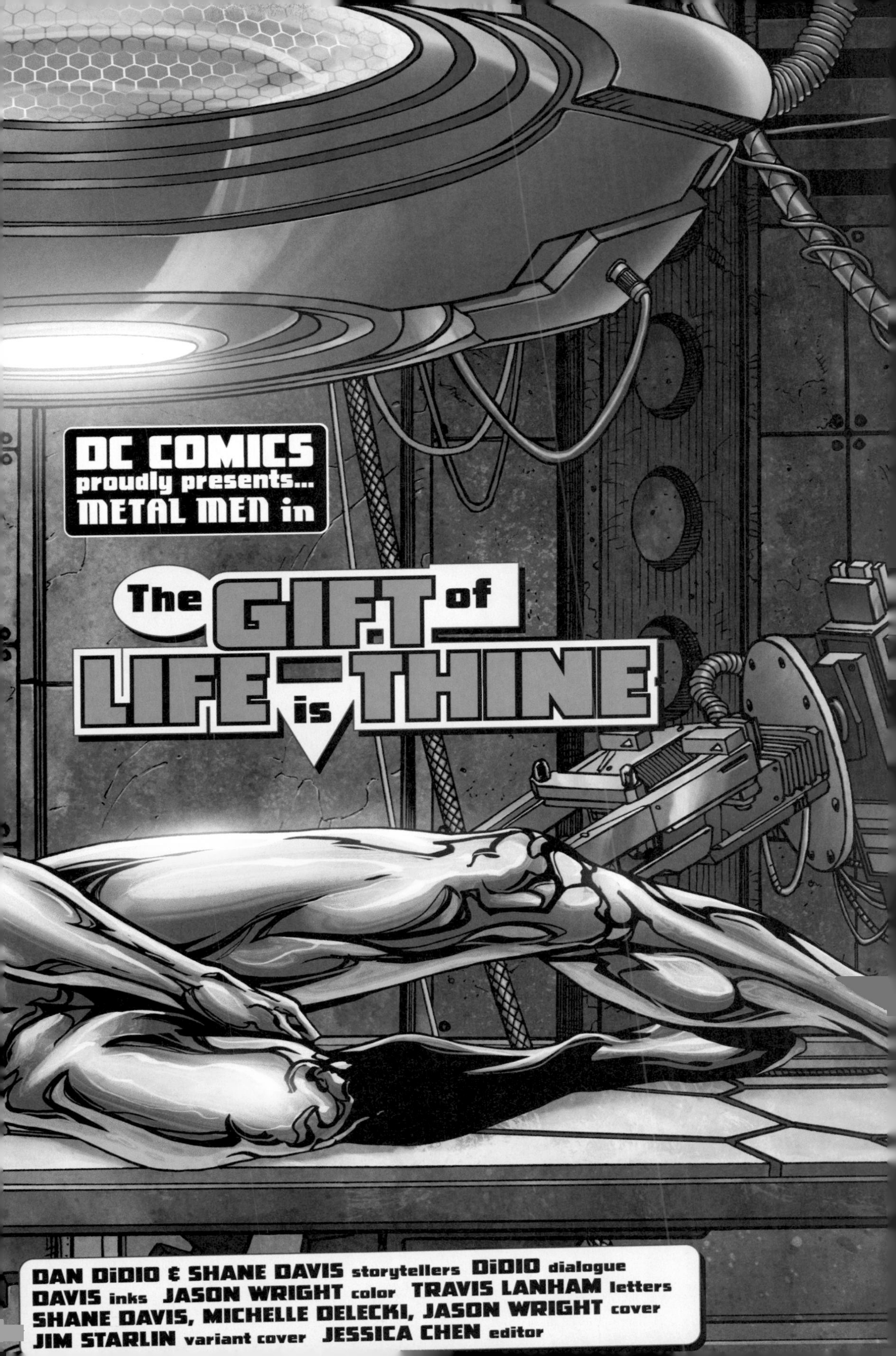
DC COMICS
proudly presents...
METAL MEN in
The GIFT of LIFE is THINE
DAN DiDIO & SHANE DAVIS storytellers DiDIO dialogue
DAVIS inks JASON WRIGHT color TRAVIS LANHAM letters
SHANE DAVIS, MICHELLE DELECKI, JASON WRIGHT cover
JIM STARLIN variant cover JESSICA CHEN editor

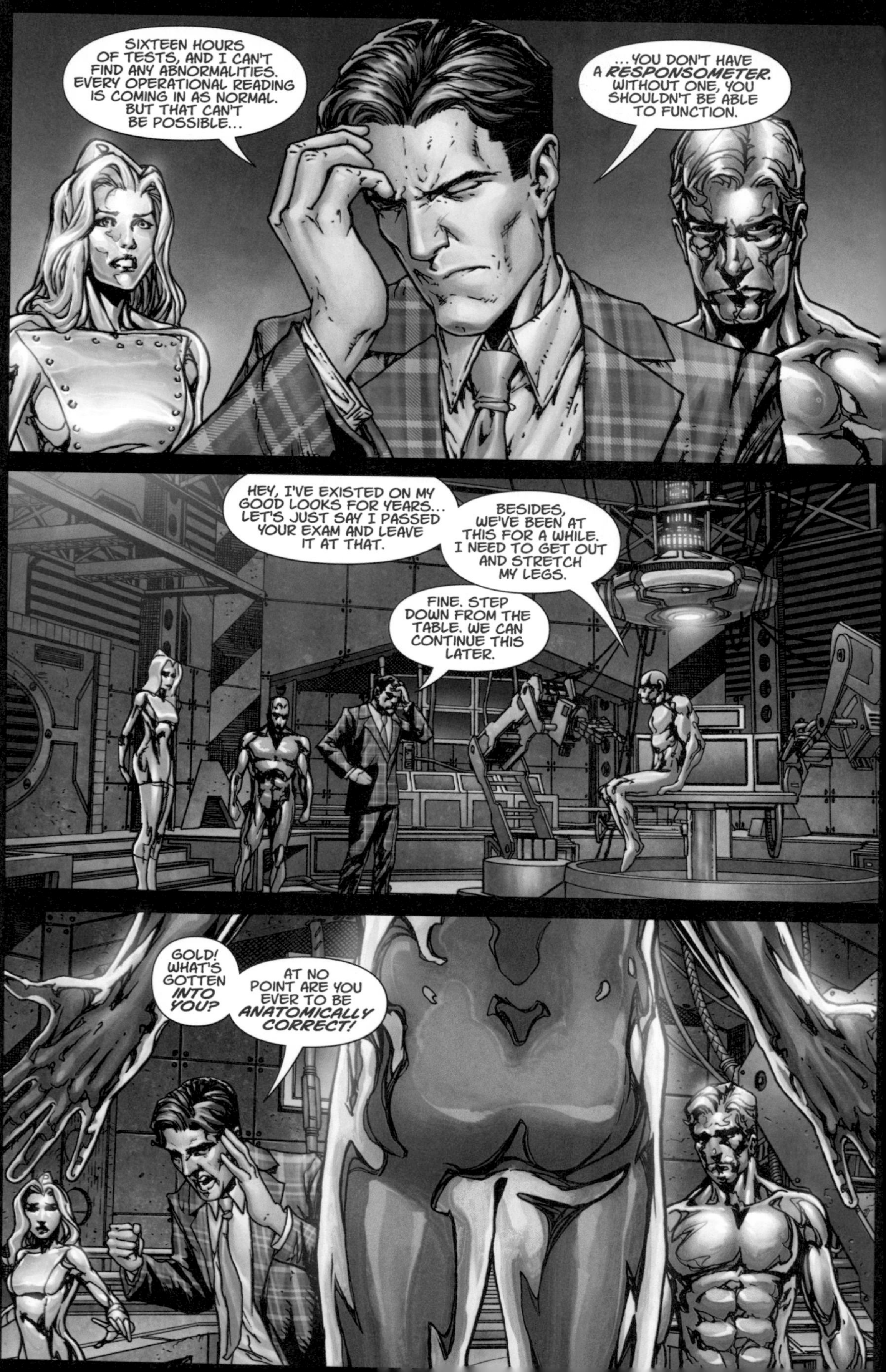
SIXTEEN HOURS OF TESTS, AND I CAN'T FIND ANY ABNORMALITIES. EVERY OPERATIONAL READING IS COMING IN AS NORMAL. BUT THAT CAN'T BE POSSIBLE...
...YOU DON'T HAVE A *RESPONSOMETER.* WITHOUT ONE, YOU SHOULDN'T BE ABLE TO FUNCTION.
HEY, I'VE EXISTED ON MY GOOD LOOKS FOR YEARS... LET'S JUST SAY I PASSED YOUR EXAM AND LEAVE IT AT THAT.
BESIDES, WE'VE BEEN AT THIS FOR A WHILE. I NEED TO GET OUT AND STRETCH MY LEGS.
FINE. STEP DOWN FROM THE TABLE. WE CAN CONTINUE THIS LATER.
GOLD! WHAT'S GOTTEN *INTO YOU?*
AT NO POINT ARE YOU EVER TO BE *ANATOMICALLY CORRECT!*

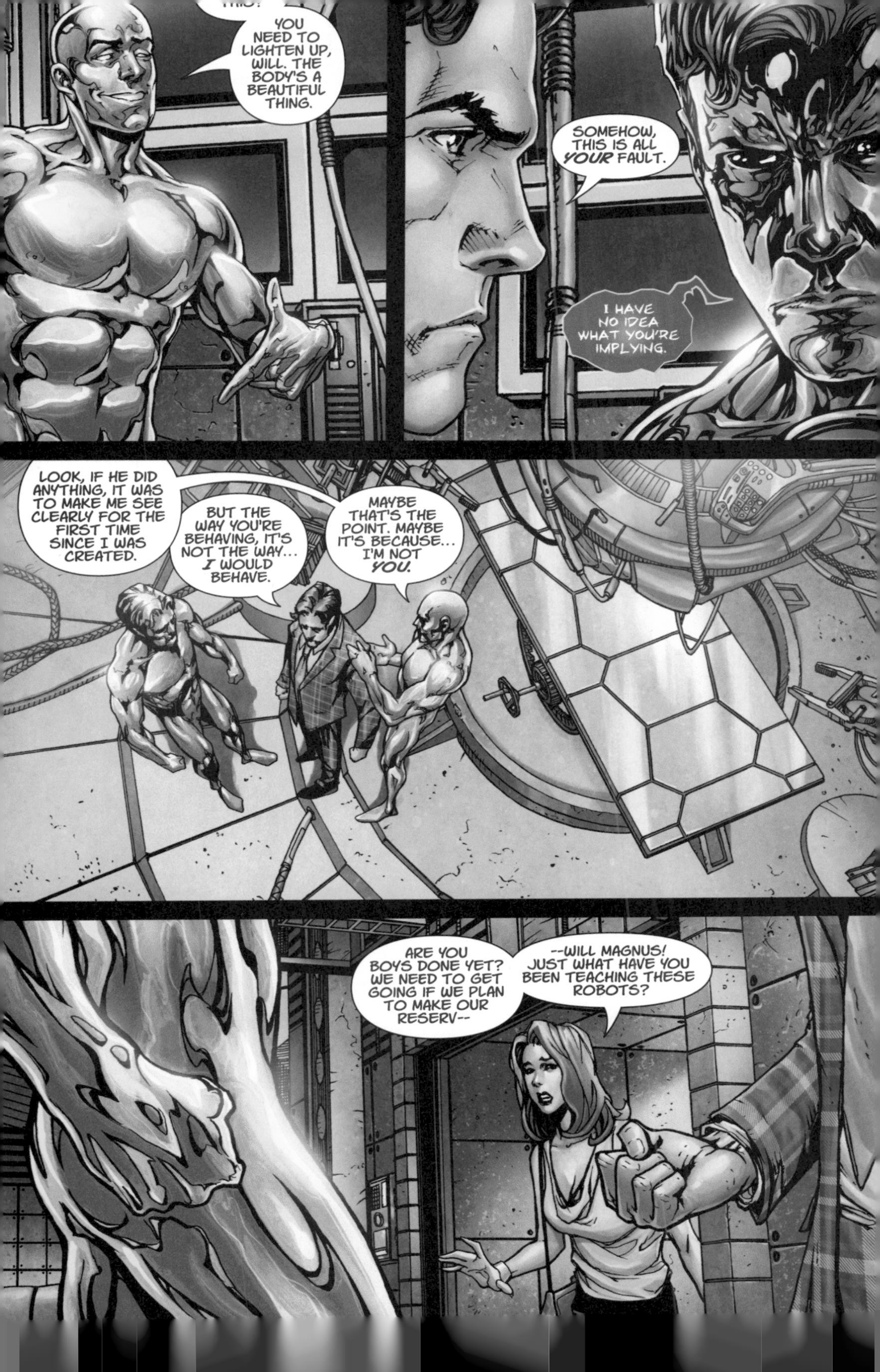
YOU NEED TO LIGHTEN UP, WILL. THE BODY'S A BEAUTIFUL THING.
SOMEHOW, THIS IS ALL YOUR FAULT.
I HAVE NO IDEA WHAT YOU'RE IMPLYING.
LOOK, IF HE DID ANYTHING, IT WAS TO MAKE ME SEE CLEARLY FOR THE FIRST TIME SINCE I WAS CREATED.
BUT THE WAY YOU'RE BEHAVING, IT'S NOT THE WAY... I WOULD BEHAVE.
MAYBE THAT'S THE POINT. MAYBE IT'S BECAUSE... I'M NOT YOU.
ARE YOU BOYS DONE YET? WE NEED TO GET GOING IF WE PLAN TO MAKE OUR RESERV--
--WILL MAGNUS! JUST WHAT HAVE YOU BEEN TEACHING THESE ROBOTS?

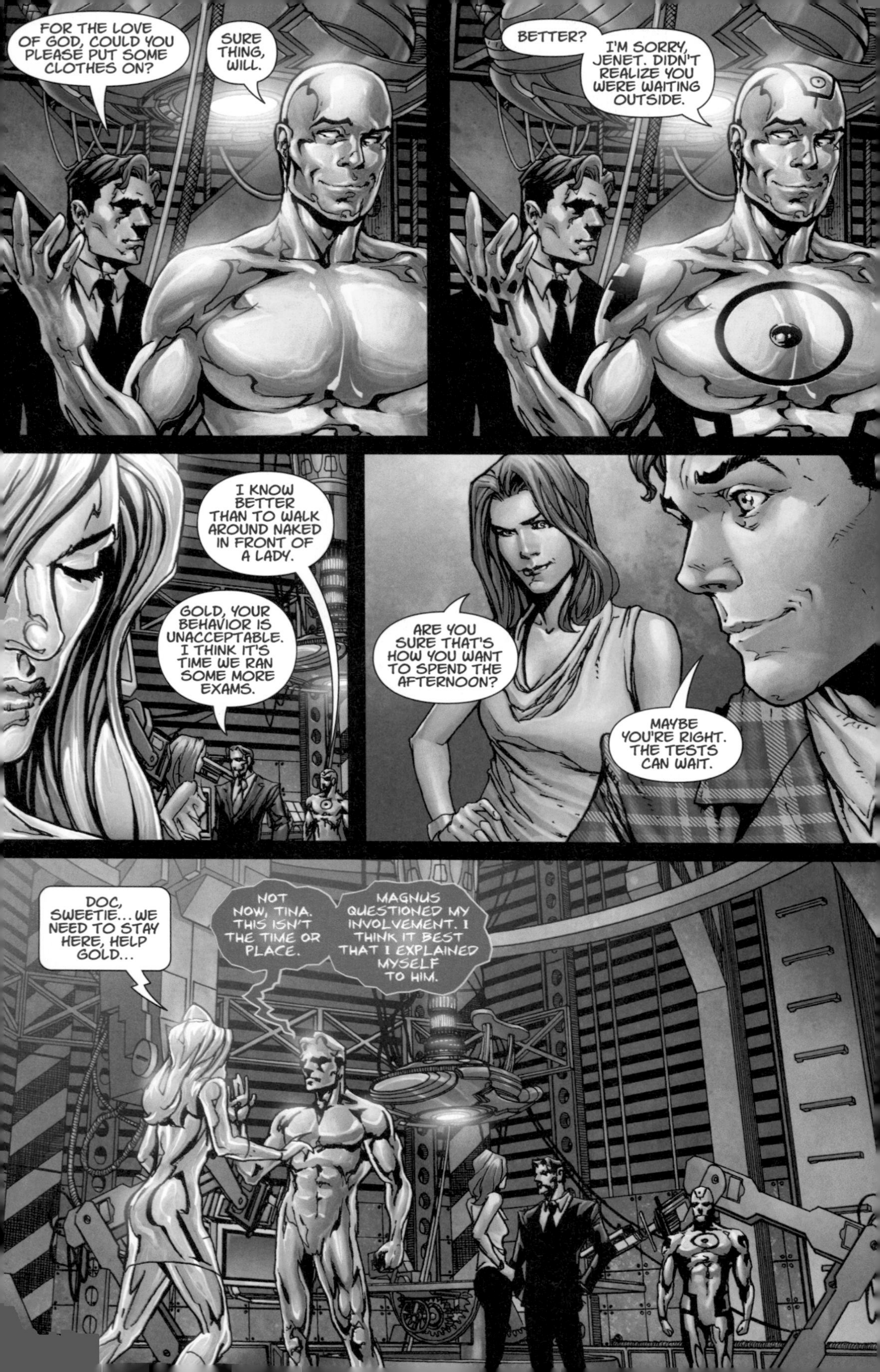
FOR THE LOVE OF GOD, COULD YOU PLEASE PUT SOME CLOTHES ON?
SURE THING, WILL.
BETTER?
I'M SORRY, JENET. DIDN'T REALIZE YOU WERE WAITING OUTSIDE.
I KNOW BETTER THAN TO WALK AROUND NAKED IN FRONT OF A LADY.
GOLD, YOUR BEHAVIOR IS UNACCEPTABLE. I THINK IT'S TIME WE RAN SOME MORE EXAMS.
ARE YOU SURE THAT'S HOW YOU WANT TO SPEND THE AFTERNOON?
MAYBE YOU'RE RIGHT. THE TESTS CAN WAIT.
DOC, SWEETIE... WE NEED TO STAY HERE, HELP GOLD...
NOT NOW, TINA. THIS ISN'T THE TIME OR PLACE.
MAGNUS QUESTIONED MY INVOLVEMENT. I THINK IT BEST THAT I EXPLAINED MYSELF TO HIM.

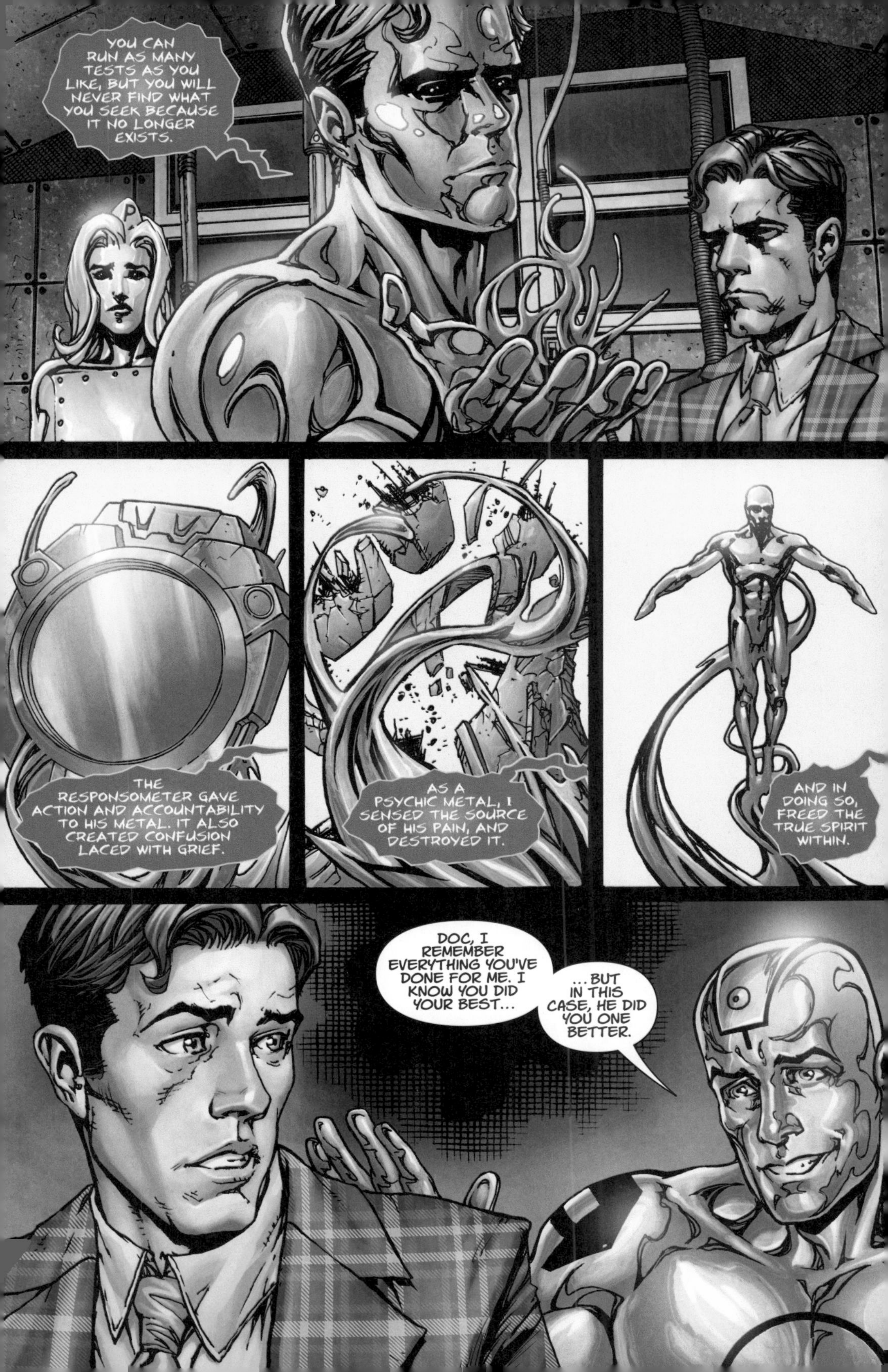
YOU CAN RUN AS MANY TESTS AS YOU LIKE, BUT YOU WILL NEVER FIND WHAT YOU SEEK BECAUSE IT NO LONGER EXISTS.
THE RESPONSOMETER GAVE ACTION AND ACCOUNTABILITY TO HIS METAL. IT ALSO CREATED CONFUSION LACED WITH GRIEF.
AS A PSYCHIC METAL, I SENSED THE SOURCE OF HIS PAIN, AND DESTROYED IT.
AND IN DOING SO, FREED THE TRUE SPIRIT WITHIN.
DOC, I REMEMBER EVERYTHING YOU'VE DONE FOR ME. I KNOW YOU DID YOUR BEST...
...BUT IN THIS CASE, HE DID YOU ONE BETTER.

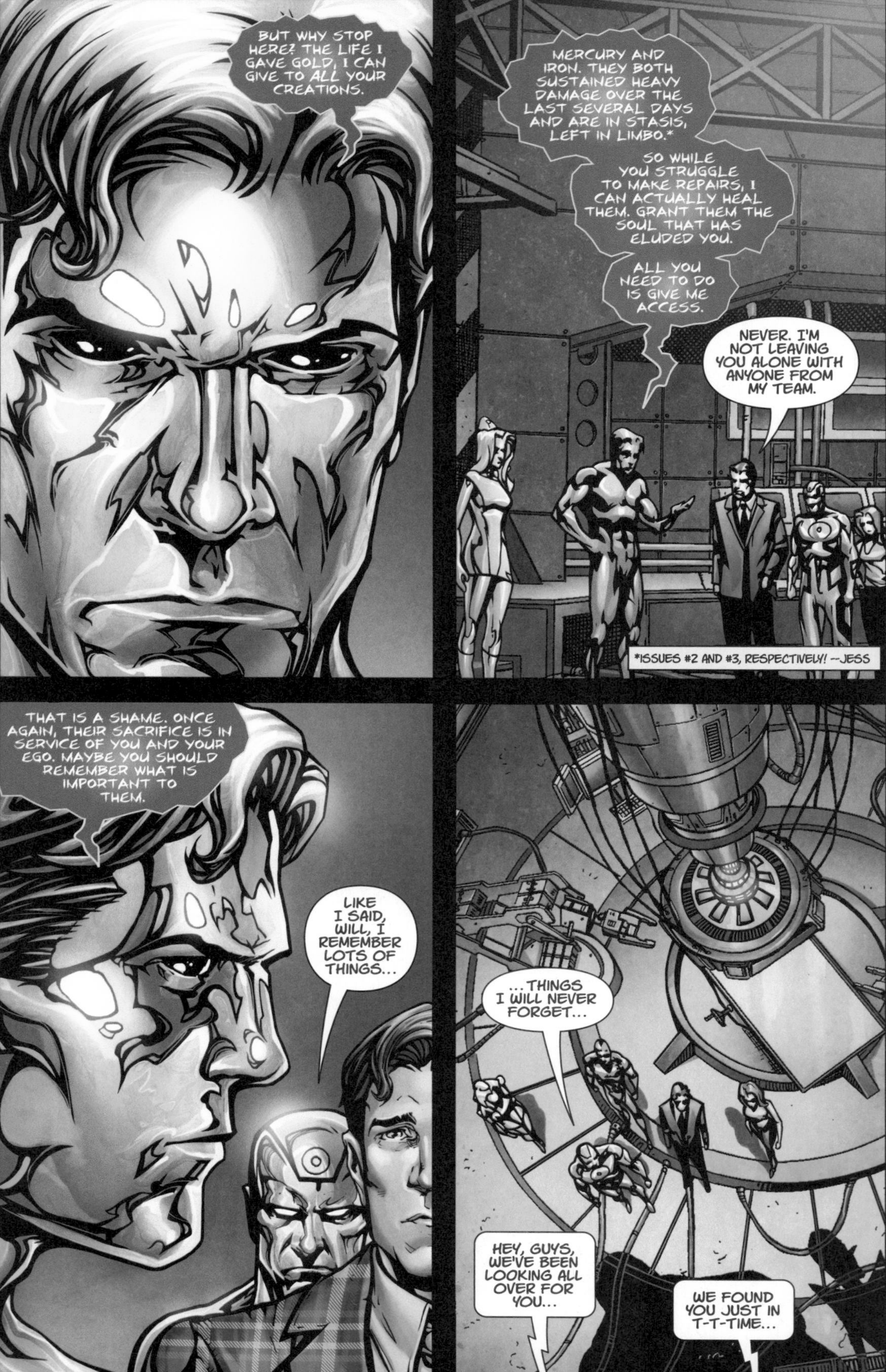
BUT WHY STOP HERE? THE LIFE I GAVE GOLD, I CAN GIVE TO ALL YOUR CREATIONS.
MERCURY AND IRON. THEY BOTH SUSTAINED HEAVY DAMAGE OVER THE LAST SEVERAL DAYS AND ARE IN STASIS, LEFT IN LIMBO.*
SO WHILE YOU STRUGGLE TO MAKE REPAIRS, I CAN ACTUALLY HEAL THEM. GRANT THEM THE SOUL THAT HAS ELUDED YOU.
ALL YOU NEED TO DO IS GIVE ME ACCESS.
NEVER. I'M NOT LEAVING YOU ALONE WITH ANYONE FROM MY TEAM.
*ISSUES #2 AND #3, RESPECTIVELY! --JESS
THAT IS A SHAME. ONCE AGAIN, THEIR SACRIFICE IS IN SERVICE OF YOU AND YOUR EGO. MAYBE YOU SHOULD REMEMBER WHAT IS IMPORTANT TO THEM.
LIKE I SAID, WILL, I REMEMBER LOTS OF THINGS...
...THINGS I WILL NEVER FORGET...
HEY, GUYS, WE'VE BEEN LOOKING ALL OVER FOR YOU...
WE FOUND YOU JUST IN T-T-TIME...

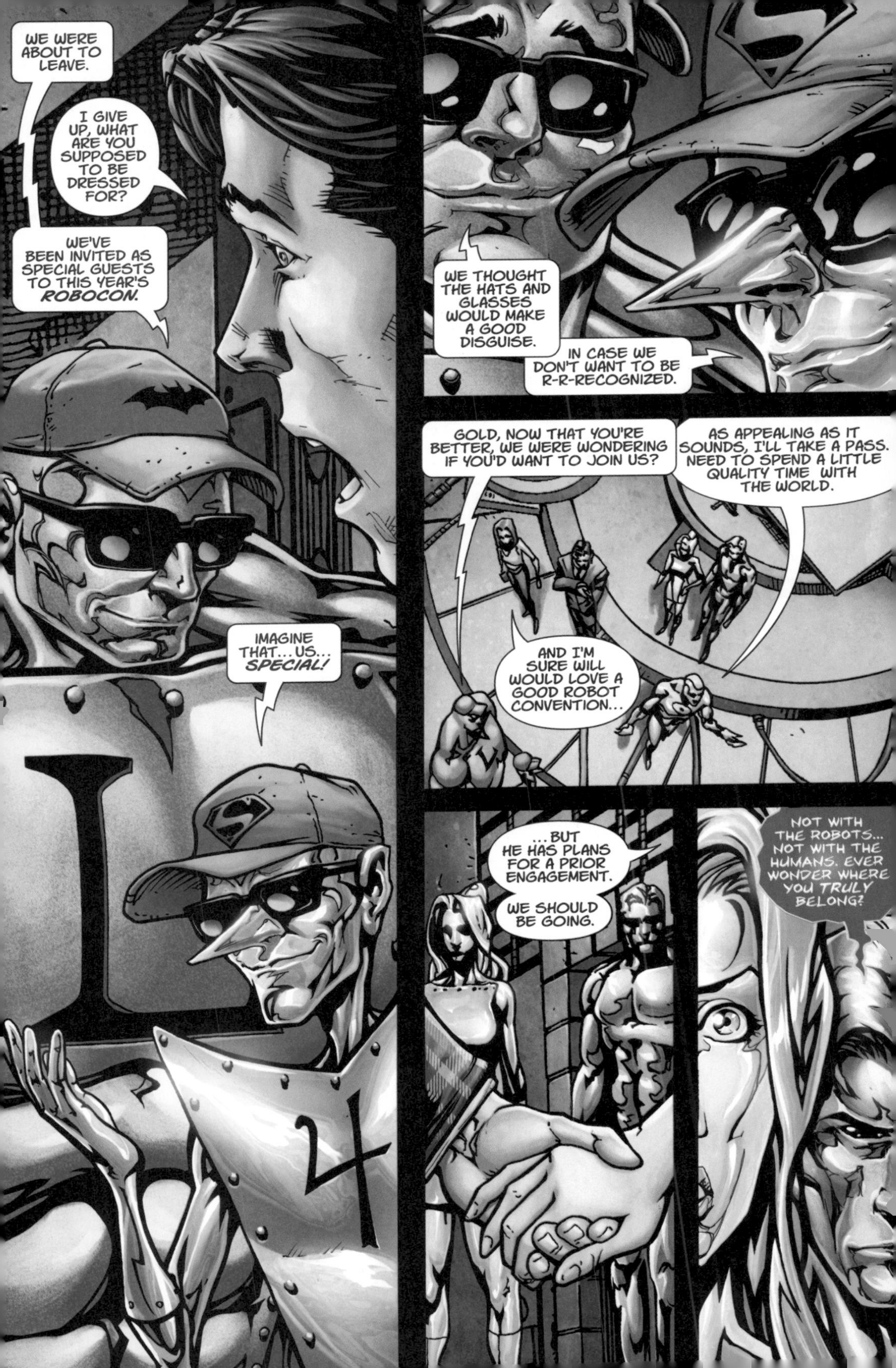
WE WERE ABOUT TO LEAVE.
I GIVE UP, WHAT ARE YOU SUPPOSED TO BE DRESSED FOR?
WE'VE BEEN INVITED AS SPECIAL GUESTS TO THIS YEAR'S ROBOCON.
IMAGINE THAT... US... SPECIAL!
WE THOUGHT THE HATS AND GLASSES WOULD MAKE A GOOD DISGUISE.
IN CASE WE DON'T WANT TO BE R-R-RECOGNIZED.
GOLD, NOW THAT YOU'RE BETTER, WE WERE WONDERING IF YOU'D WANT TO JOIN US?
AS APPEALING AS IT SOUNDS, I'LL TAKE A PASS. NEED TO SPEND A LITTLE QUALITY TIME WITH THE WORLD.
AND I'M SURE WILL WOULD LOVE A GOOD ROBOT CONVENTION...
...BUT HE HAS PLANS FOR A PRIOR ENGAGEMENT.
WE SHOULD BE GOING.
NOT WITH THE ROBOTS... NOT WITH THE HUMANS. EVER WONDER WHERE YOU TRULY BELONG?

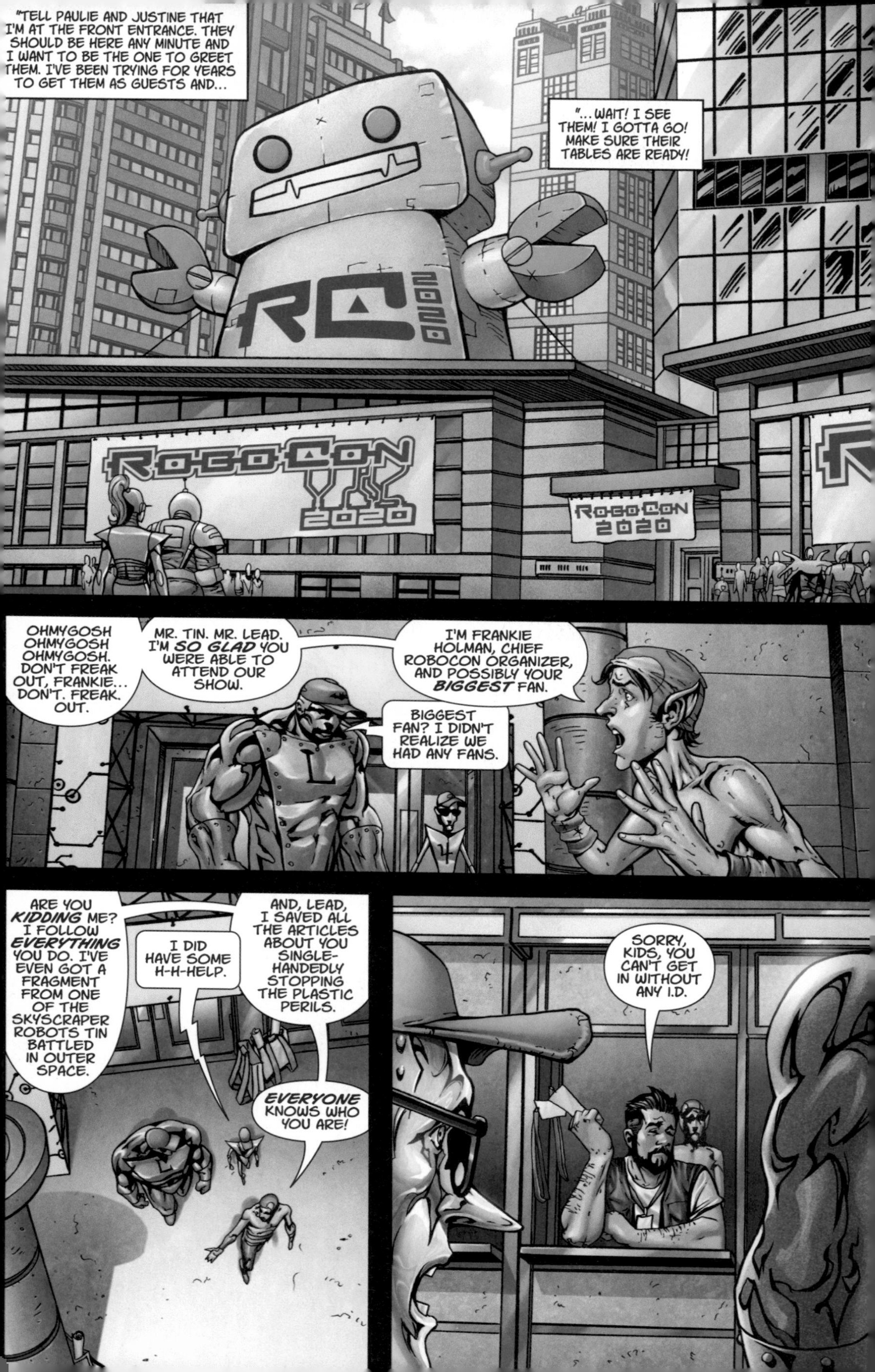
"TELL PAULIE AND JUSTINE THAT I'M AT THE FRONT ENTRANCE. THEY SHOULD BE HERE ANY MINUTE AND I WANT TO BE THE ONE TO GREET THEM. I'VE BEEN TRYING FOR YEARS TO GET THEM AS GUESTS AND...
"...WAIT! I SEE THEM! I GOTTA GO! MAKE SURE THEIR TABLES ARE READY!
RC 2020
ROBOCON VIX 2020
ROBOCON 2020
OHMYGOSH OHMYGOSH OHMYGOSH. DON'T FREAK OUT, FRANKIE... DON'T. FREAK. OUT.
MR. TIN. MR. LEAD. I'M SO GLAD YOU WERE ABLE TO ATTEND OUR SHOW.
I'M FRANKIE HOLMAN, CHIEF ROBOCON ORGANIZER, AND POSSIBLY YOUR BIGGEST FAN.
BIGGEST FAN? I DIDN'T REALIZE WE HAD ANY FANS.
ARE YOU KIDDING ME? I FOLLOW EVERYTHING YOU DO. I'VE EVEN GOT A FRAGMENT FROM ONE OF THE SKYSCRAPER ROBOTS TIN BATTLED IN OUTER SPACE.
I DID HAVE SOME H-H-HELP.
AND, LEAD, I SAVED ALL THE ARTICLES ABOUT YOU SINGLE-HANDEDLY STOPPING THE PLASTIC PERILS.
EVERYONE KNOWS WHO YOU ARE!
SORRY, KIDS, YOU CAN'T GET IN WITHOUT ANY I.D.

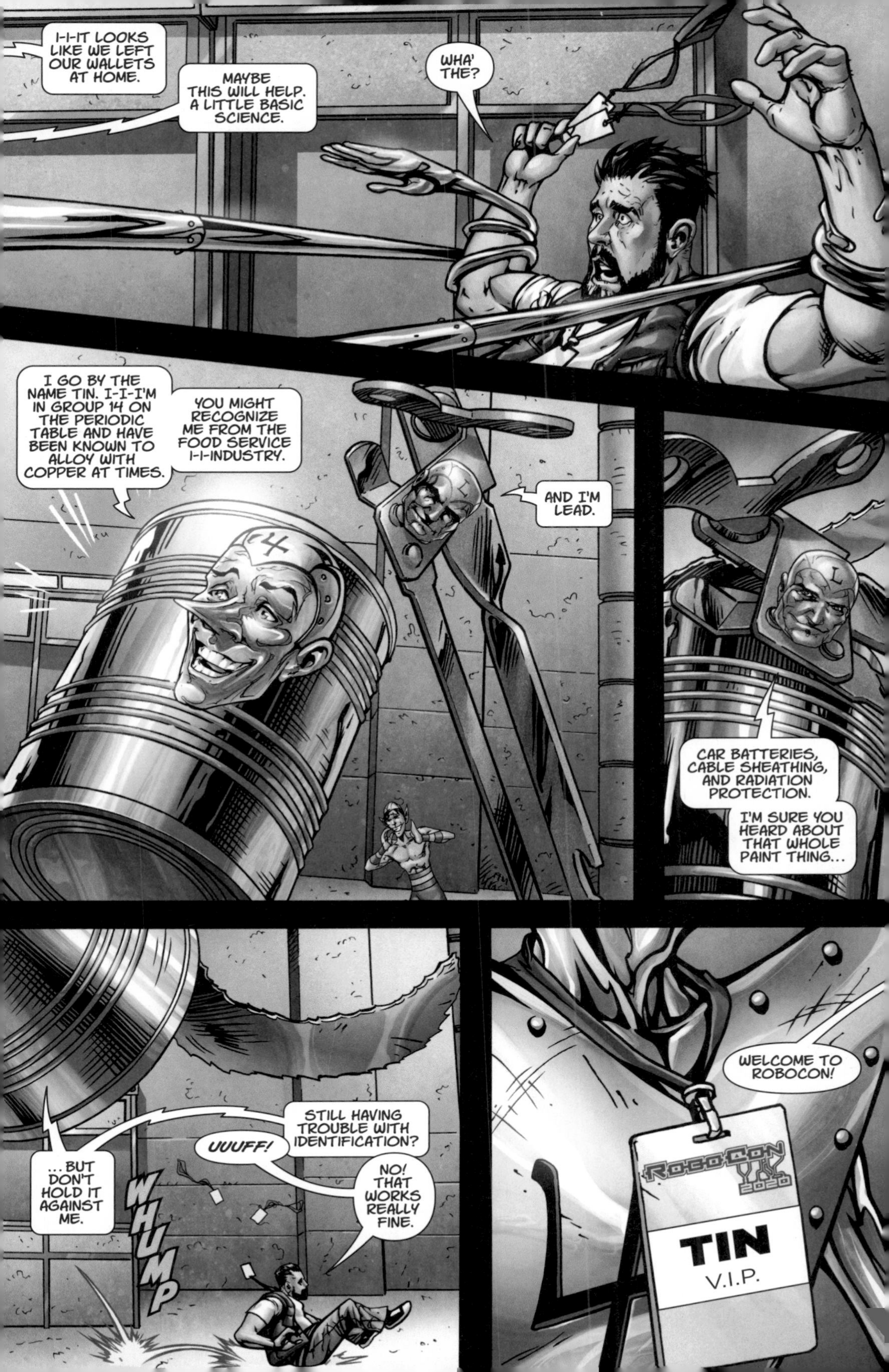

I-I-IT LOOKS LIKE WE LEFT OUR WALLETS AT HOME.
MAYBE THIS WILL HELP. A LITTLE BASIC SCIENCE.
WHA' THE?
I GO BY THE NAME TIN. I-I-I'M IN GROUP 14 ON THE PERIODIC TABLE AND HAVE BEEN KNOWN TO ALLOY WITH COPPER AT TIMES.
YOU MIGHT RECOGNIZE ME FROM THE FOOD SERVICE I-I-INDUSTRY.
AND I'M LEAD.
CAR BATTERIES, CABLE SHEATHING, AND RADIATION PROTECTION.
I'M SURE YOU HEARD ABOUT THAT WHOLE PAINT THING...
...BUT DON'T HOLD IT AGAINST ME.
WHUMP
STILL HAVING TROUBLE WITH IDENTIFICATION?
UUUFF!
NO! THAT WORKS REALLY FINE.
WELCOME TO ROBOCON!
ROBOCON 2020
TIN
V.I.P.

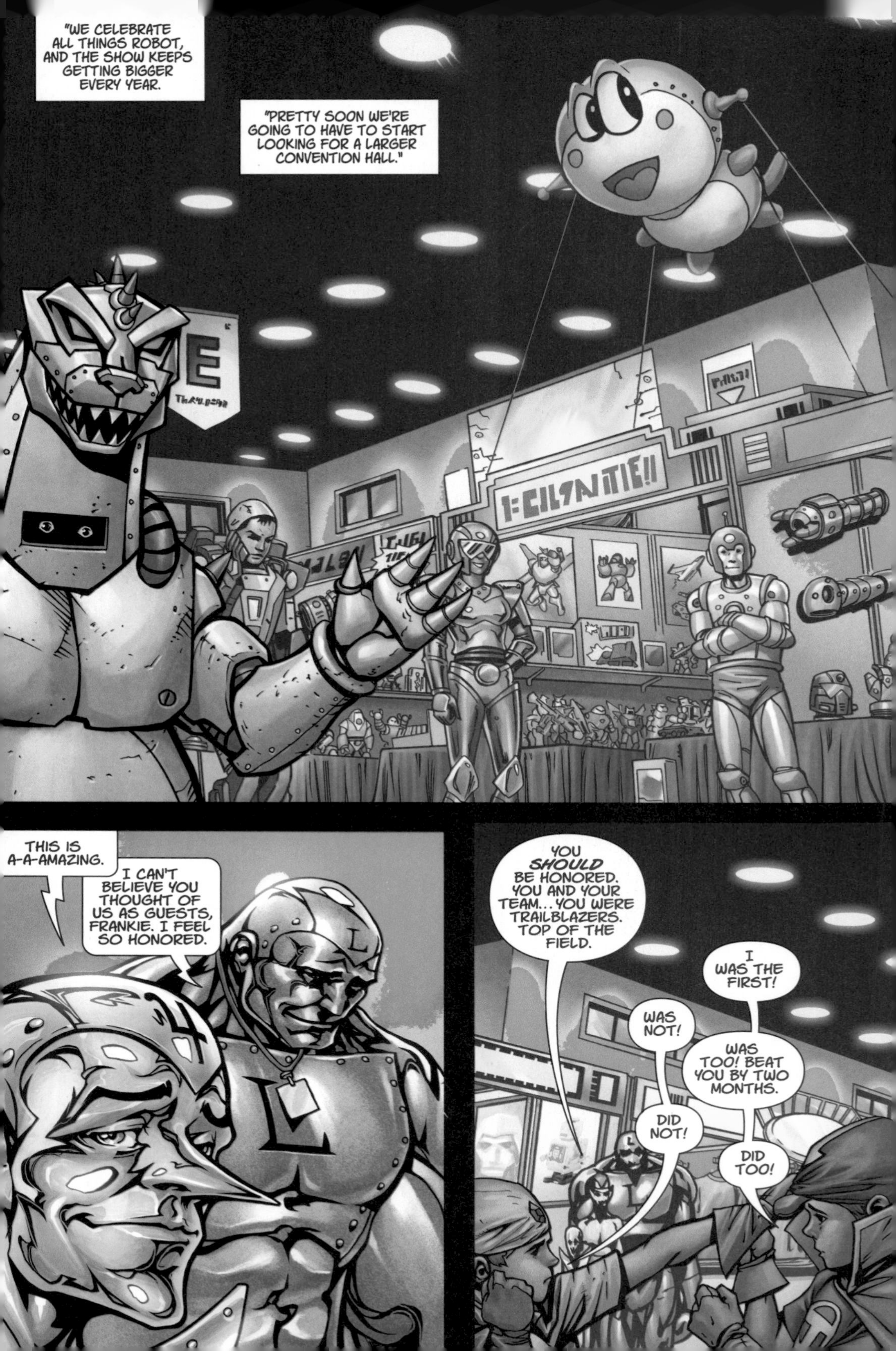

"WE CELEBRATE ALL THINGS ROBOT, AND THE SHOW KEEPS GETTING BIGGER EVERY YEAR.
"PRETTY SOON WE'RE GOING TO HAVE TO START LOOKING FOR A LARGER CONVENTION HALL."
THIS IS A-A-AMAZING.
I CAN'T BELIEVE YOU THOUGHT OF US AS GUESTS, FRANKIE. I FEEL SO HONORED.
YOU *SHOULD* BE HONORED. YOU AND YOUR TEAM... YOU WERE TRAILBLAZERS. TOP OF THE FIELD.
I WAS THE FIRST!
WAS NOT!
WAS TOO! BEAT YOU BY TWO MONTHS.
DID NOT!
DID TOO!

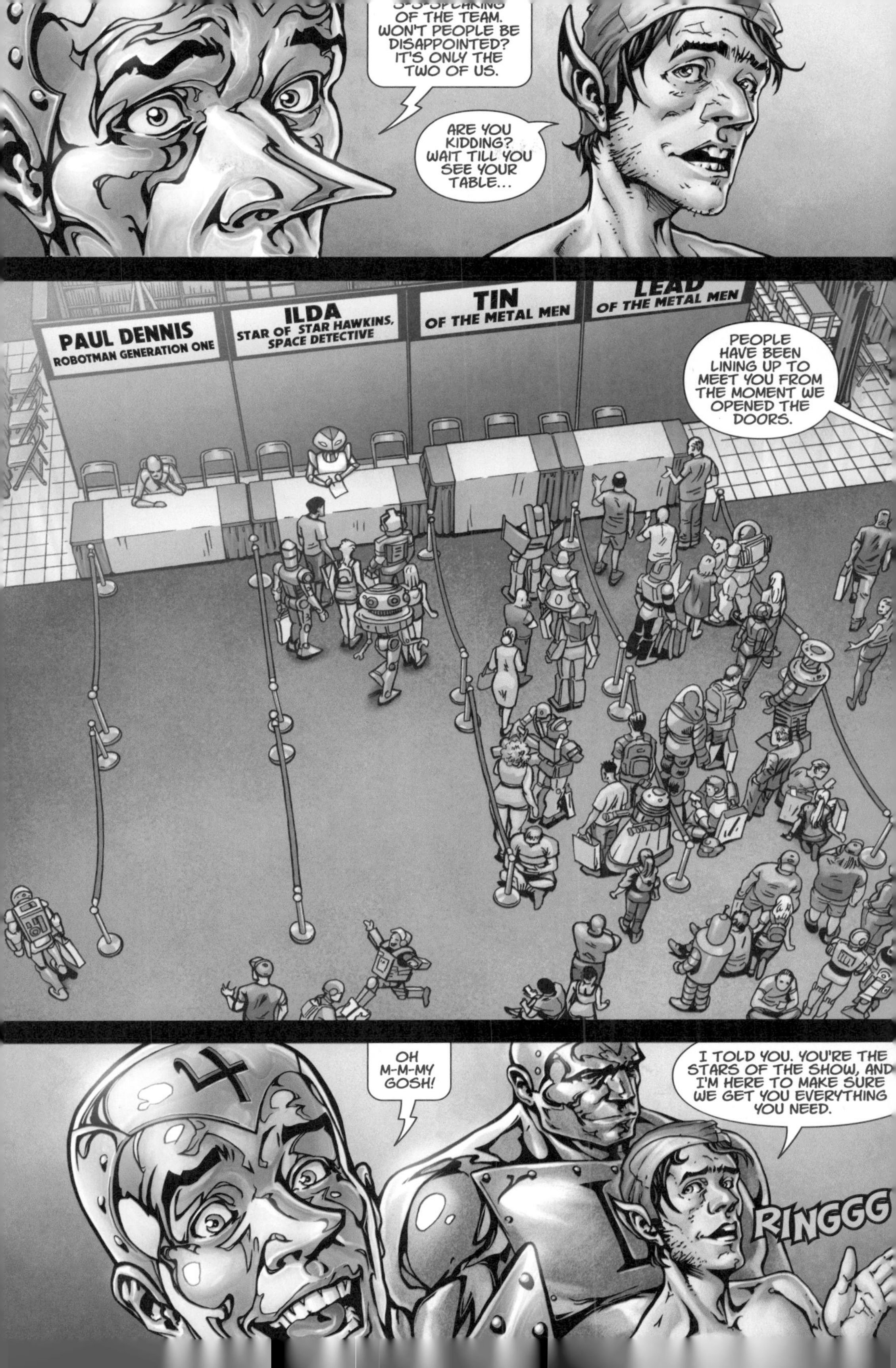

OF THE TEAM. WON'T PEOPLE BE DISAPPOINTED? IT'S ONLY THE TWO OF US.
ARE YOU KIDDING? WAIT TILL YOU SEE YOUR TABLE...
PAUL DENNIS
ROBOTMAN GENERATION ONE
ILDA
STAR OF STAR HAWKINS, SPACE DETECTIVE
TIN
OF THE METAL MEN
LEAD
OF THE METAL MEN
PEOPLE HAVE BEEN LINING UP TO MEET YOU FROM THE MOMENT WE OPENED THE DOORS.
OH M-M-MY GOSH!
I TOLD YOU. YOU'RE THE STARS OF THE SHOW, AND I'M HERE TO MAKE SURE WE GET YOU EVERYTHING YOU NEED.
RINGGG

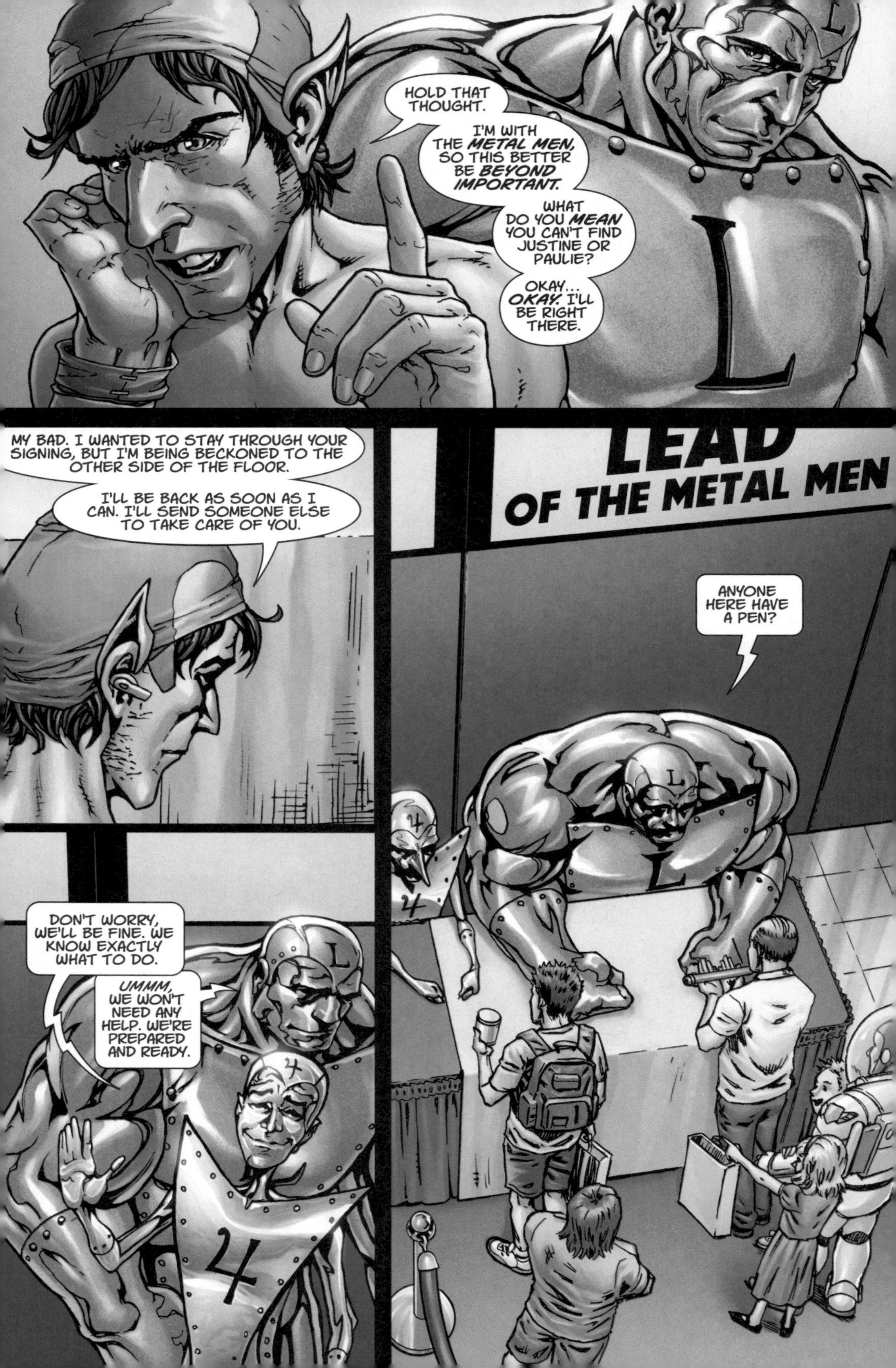
HOLD THAT THOUGHT.
I'M WITH THE METAL MEN, SO THIS BETTER BE BEYOND IMPORTANT.
WHAT DO YOU MEAN YOU CAN'T FIND JUSTINE OR PAULIE?
OKAY... OKAY. I'LL BE RIGHT THERE.
MY BAD. I WANTED TO STAY THROUGH YOUR SIGNING, BUT I'M BEING BECKONED TO THE OTHER SIDE OF THE FLOOR.
I'LL BE BACK AS SOON AS I CAN. I'LL SEND SOMEONE ELSE TO TAKE CARE OF YOU.
DON'T WORRY, WE'LL BE FINE. WE KNOW EXACTLY WHAT TO DO.
UMMM, WE WON'T NEED ANY HELP. WE'RE PREPARED AND READY.
LEAD OF THE METAL MEN
ANYONE HERE HAVE A PEN?

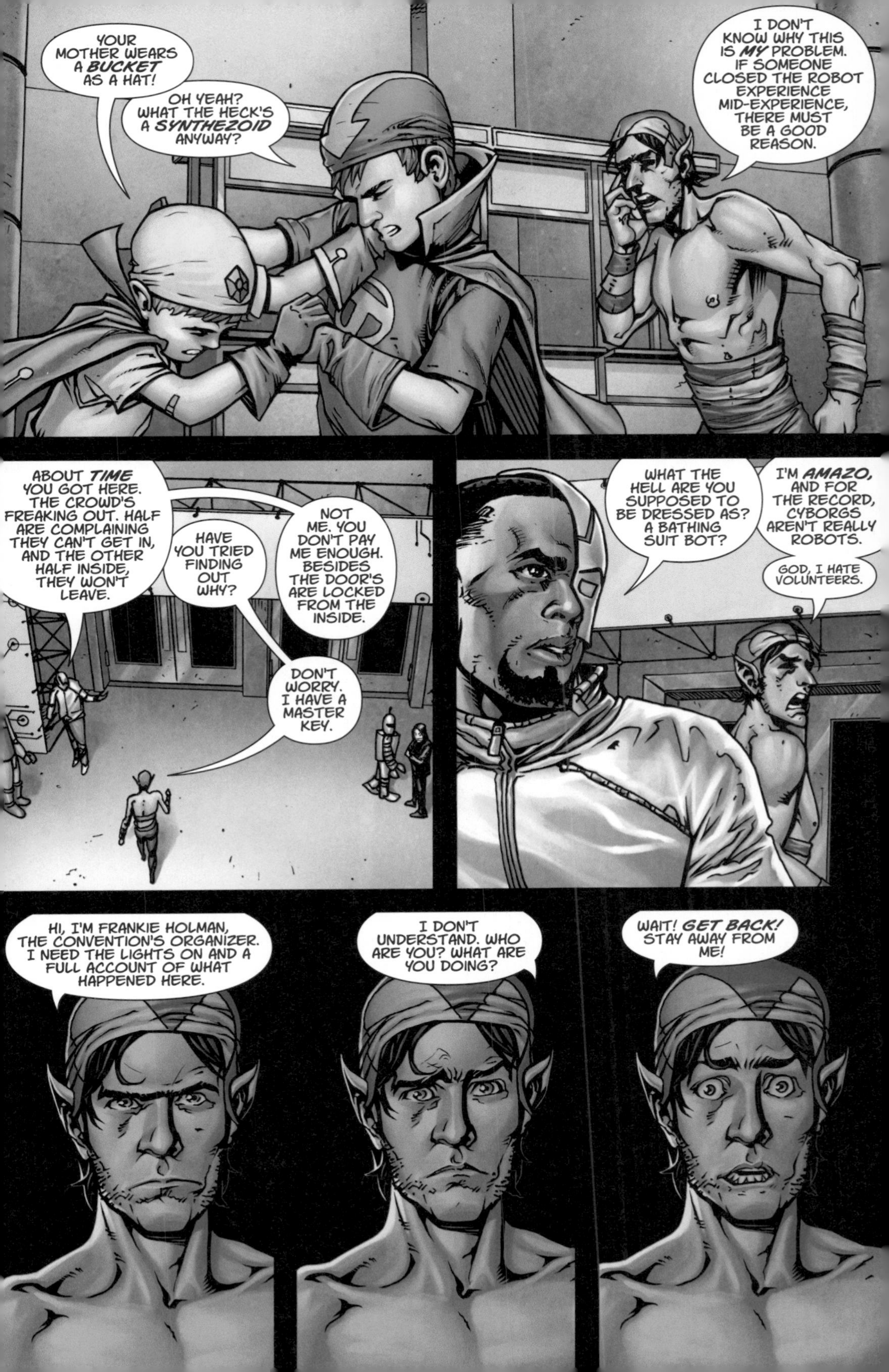

YOUR MOTHER WEARS A BUCKET AS A HAT!
OH YEAH? WHAT THE HECK'S A SYNTHEZOID ANYWAY?
I DON'T KNOW WHY THIS IS MY PROBLEM. IF SOMEONE CLOSED THE ROBOT EXPERIENCE MID-EXPERIENCE, THERE MUST BE A GOOD REASON.
ABOUT TIME YOU GOT HERE. THE CROWD'S FREAKING OUT. HALF ARE COMPLAINING THEY CAN'T GET IN, AND THE OTHER HALF INSIDE, THEY WON'T LEAVE.
HAVE YOU TRIED FINDING OUT WHY?
NOT ME. YOU DON'T PAY ME ENOUGH. BESIDES THE DOOR'S ARE LOCKED FROM THE INSIDE.
DON'T WORRY. I HAVE A MASTER KEY.
WHAT THE HELL ARE YOU SUPPOSED TO BE DRESSED AS? A BATHING SUIT BOT?
I'M AMAZO, AND FOR THE RECORD, CYBORGS AREN'T REALLY ROBOTS.
GOD, I HATE VOLUNTEERS.
HI, I'M FRANKIE HOLMAN, THE CONVENTION'S ORGANIZER. I NEED THE LIGHTS ON AND A FULL ACCOUNT OF WHAT HAPPENED HERE.
I DON'T UNDERSTAND. WHO ARE YOU? WHAT ARE YOU DOING?
WAIT! GET BACK! STAY AWAY FROM ME!

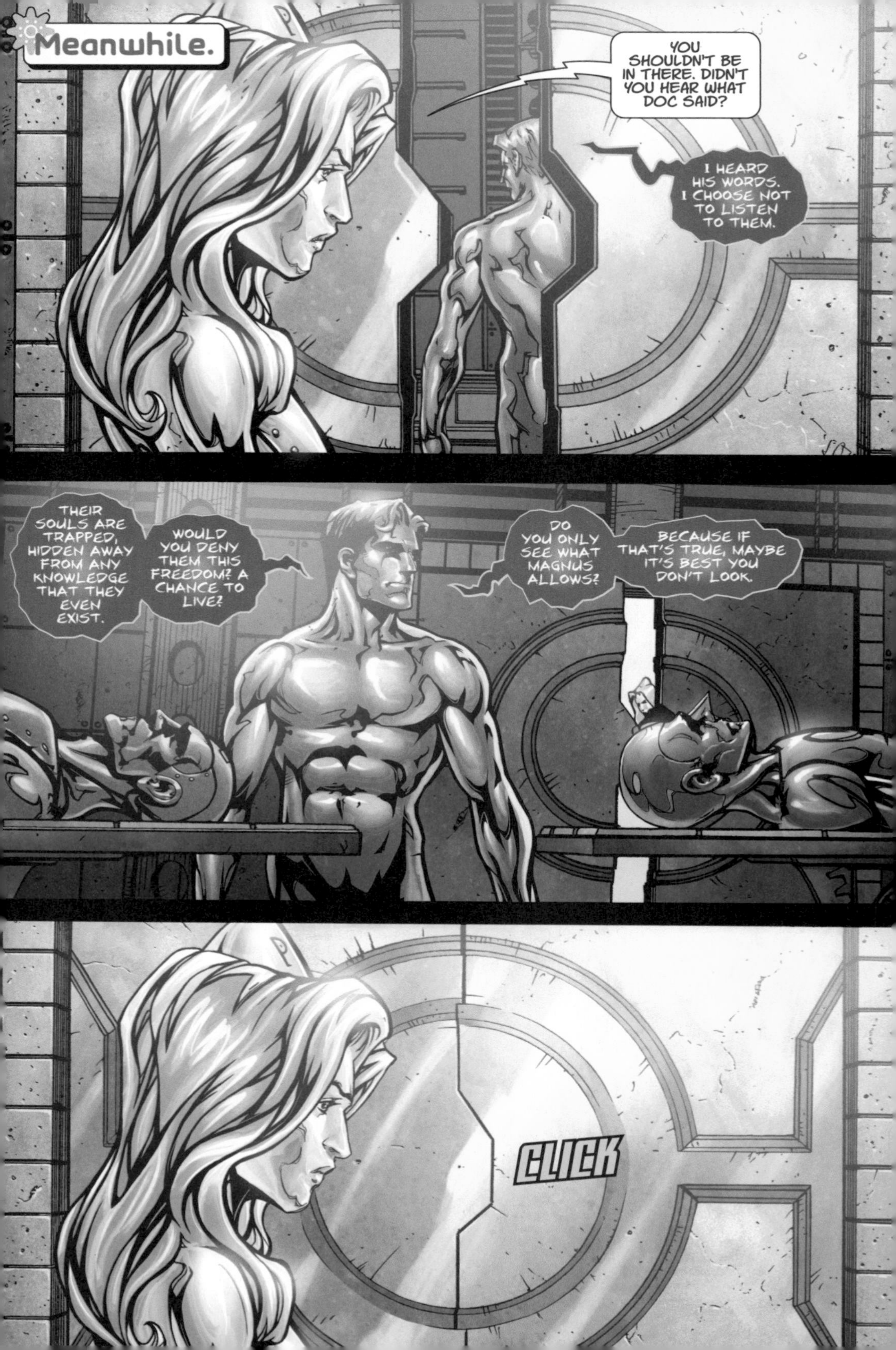
Meanwhile.
YOU SHOULDN'T BE IN THERE. DIDN'T YOU HEAR WHAT DOC SAID?
I HEARD HIS WORDS. I CHOOSE NOT TO LISTEN TO THEM.
THEIR SOULS ARE TRAPPED, HIDDEN AWAY FROM ANY KNOWLEDGE THAT THEY EVEN EXIST.
WOULD YOU DENY THEM THIS FREEDOM? A CHANCE TO LIVE?
DO YOU ONLY SEE WHAT MAGNUS ALLOWS?
BECAUSE IF THAT'S TRUE, MAYBE IT'S BEST YOU DON'T LOOK.
CLICK

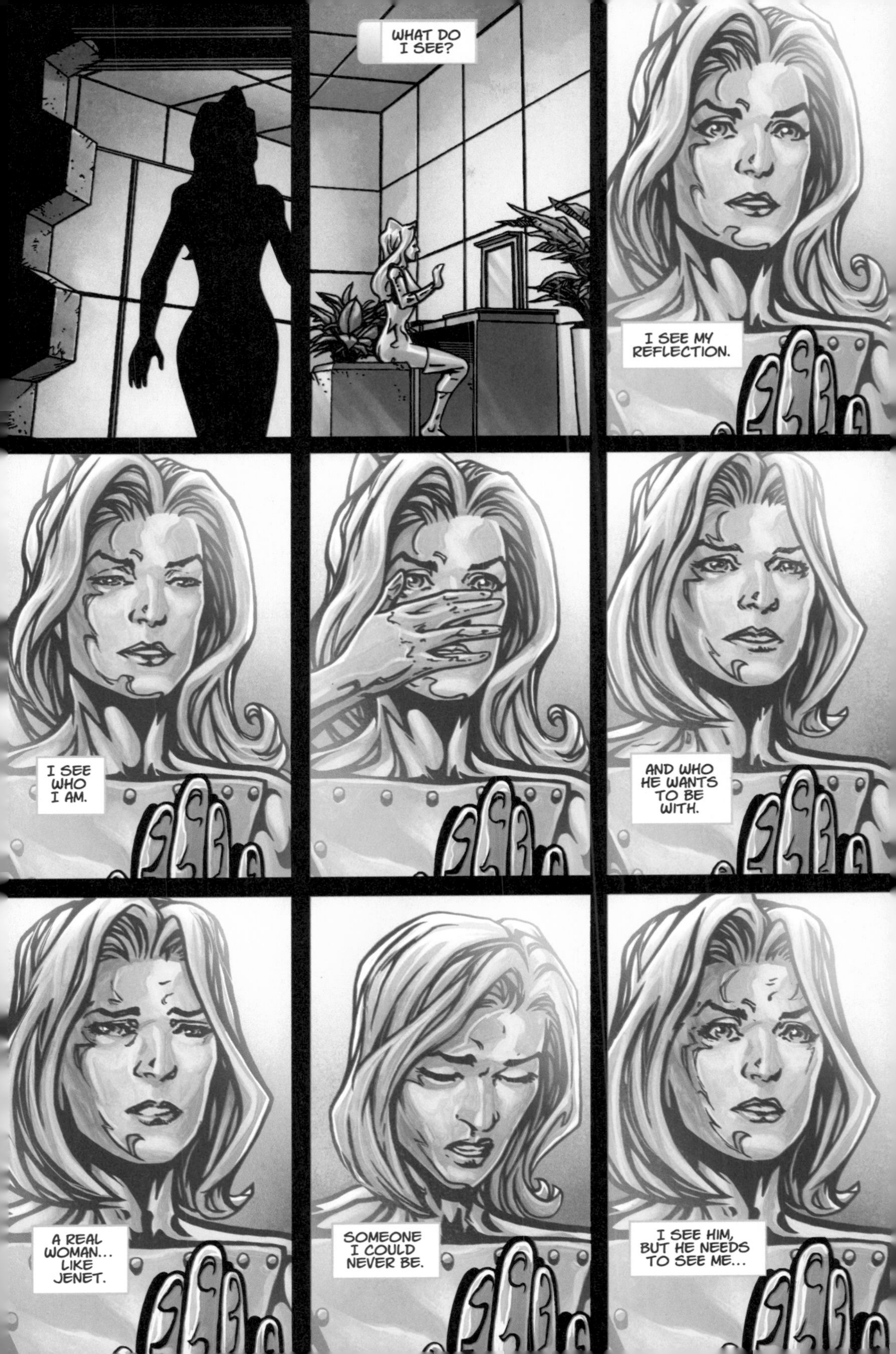
WHAT DO I SEE?
I SEE MY REFLECTION.
I SEE WHO I AM.
AND WHO HE WANTS TO BE WITH.
A REAL WOMAN... LIKE JENET.
SOMEONE I COULD NEVER BE.
I SEE HIM, BUT HE NEEDS TO SEE ME...

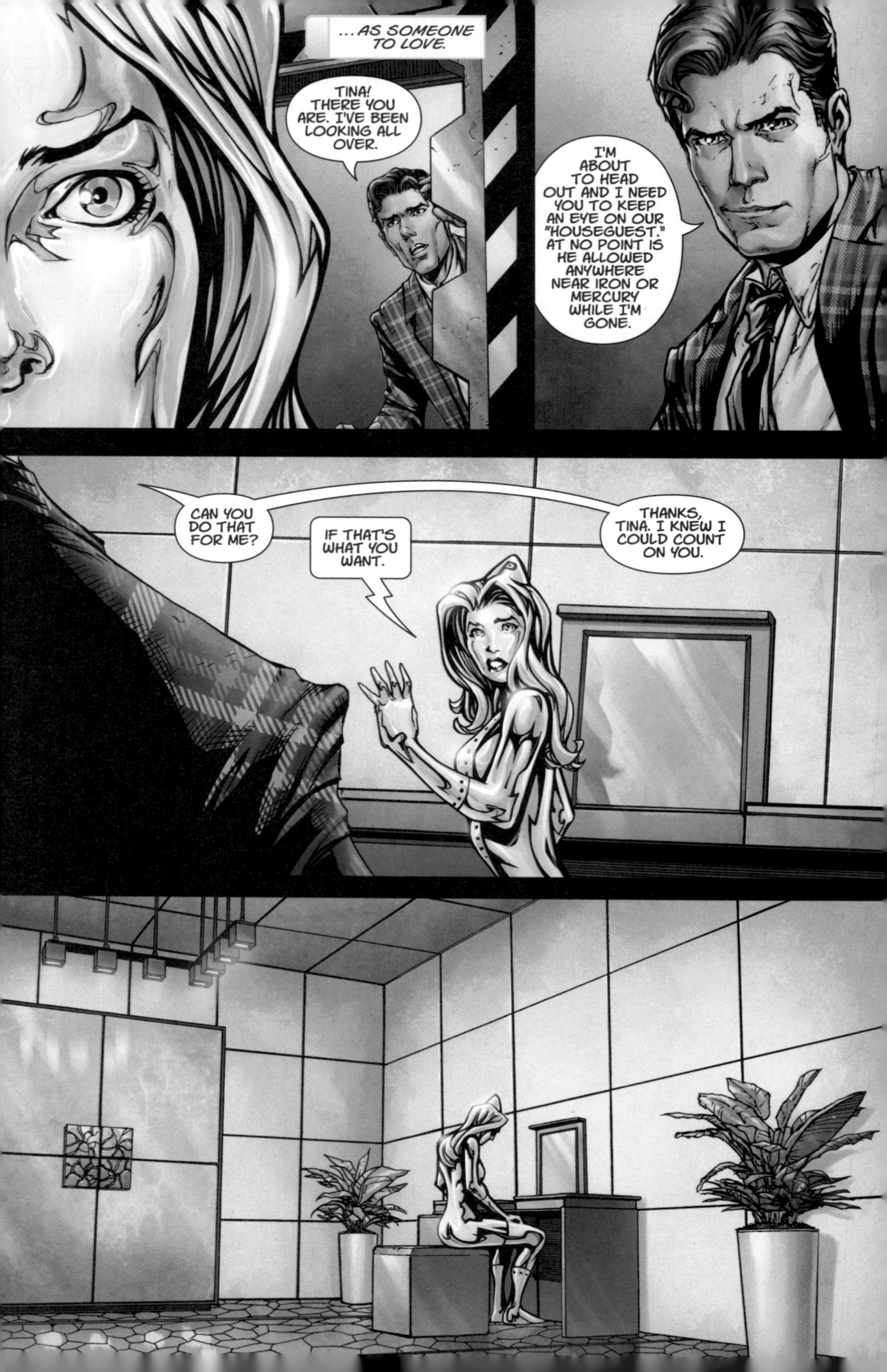
...AS SOMEONE TO LOVE.
TINA! THERE YOU ARE. I'VE BEEN LOOKING ALL OVER.
I'M ABOUT TO HEAD OUT AND I NEED YOU TO KEEP AN EYE ON OUR "HOUSEGUEST." AT NO POINT IS HE ALLOWED ANYWHERE NEAR IRON OR MERCURY WHILE I'M GONE.
CAN YOU DO THAT FOR ME?
IF THAT'S WHAT YOU WANT.
THANKS, TINA. I KNEW I COULD COUNT ON YOU.

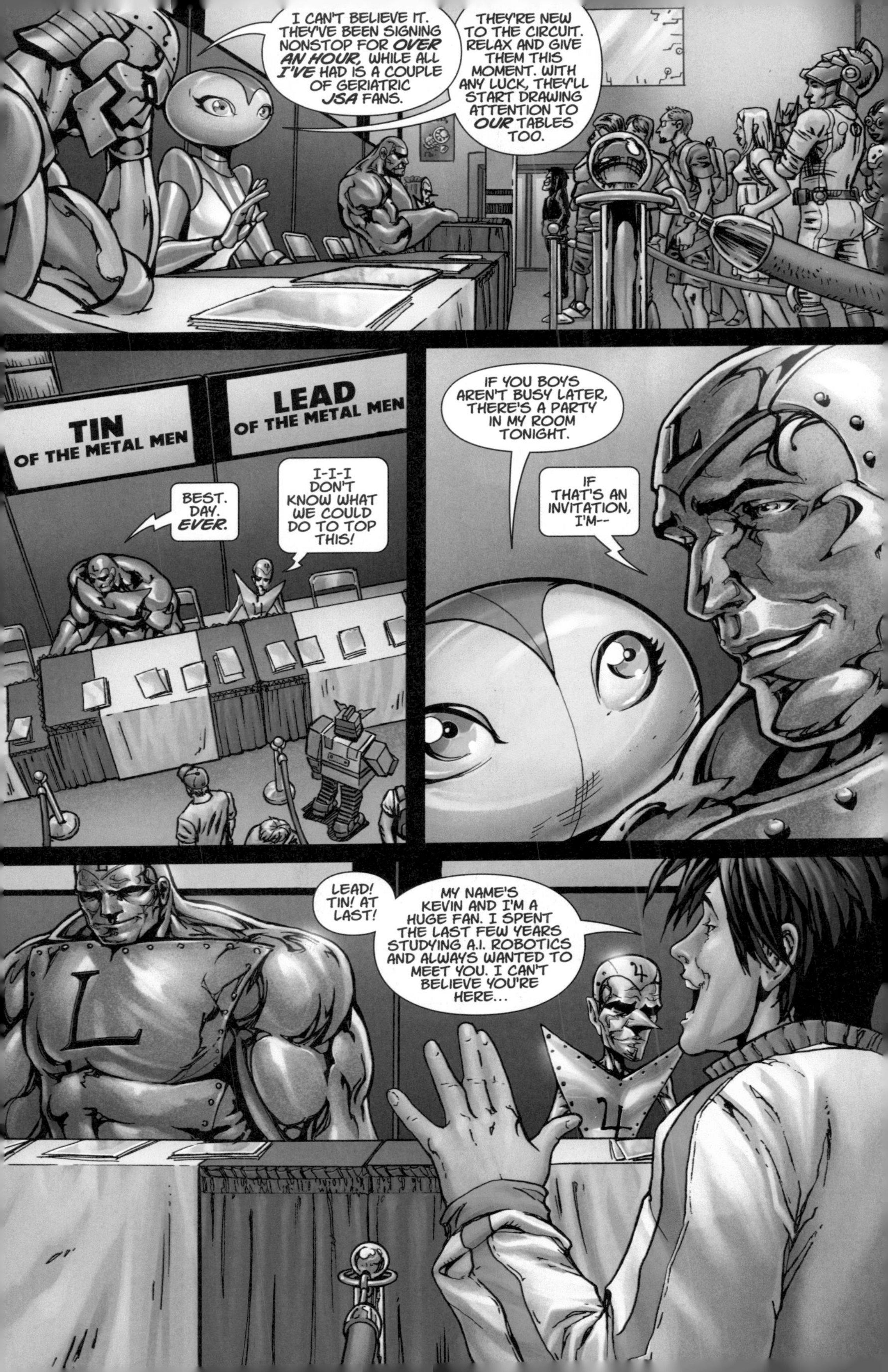
I CAN'T BELIEVE IT. THEY'VE BEEN SIGNING NONSTOP FOR OVER AN HOUR, WHILE ALL I'VE HAD IS A COUPLE OF GERIATRIC JSA FANS.
THEY'RE NEW TO THE CIRCUIT. RELAX AND GIVE THEM THIS MOMENT. WITH ANY LUCK, THEY'LL START DRAWING ATTENTION TO OUR TABLES TOO.
TIN OF THE METAL MEN
LEAD OF THE METAL MEN
BEST. DAY. EVER.
I-I-I DON'T KNOW WHAT WE COULD DO TO TOP THIS!
IF YOU BOYS AREN'T BUSY LATER, THERE'S A PARTY IN MY ROOM TONIGHT.
IF THAT'S AN INVITATION, I'M--
LEAD! TIN! AT LAST!
MY NAME'S KEVIN AND I'M A HUGE FAN. I SPENT THE LAST FEW YEARS STUDYING A.I. ROBOTICS AND ALWAYS WANTED TO MEET YOU. I CAN'T BELIEVE YOU'RE HERE...

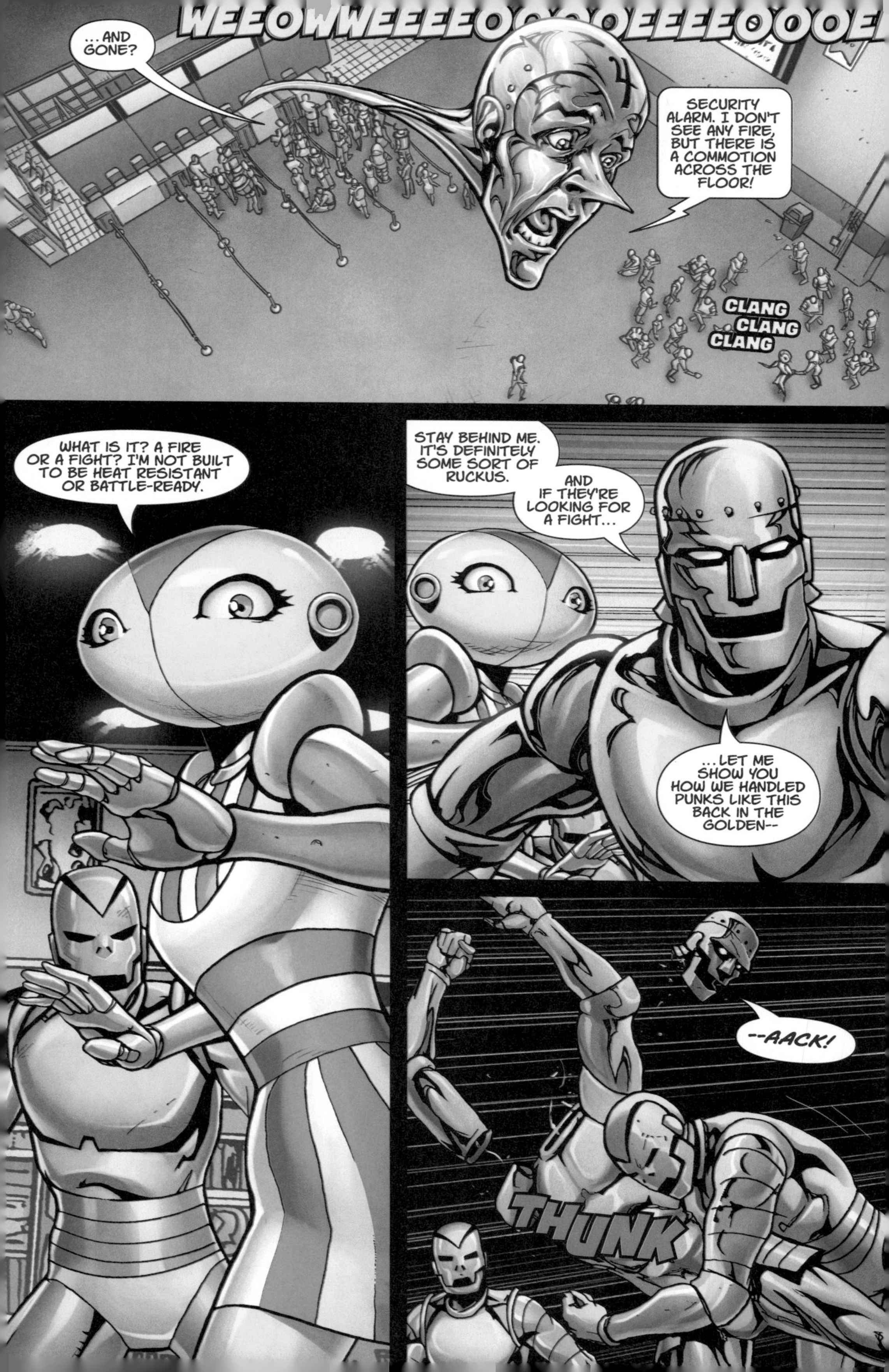
WEEOWWEEEEOOOOEEEEOOOE
...AND GONE?
SECURITY ALARM. I DON'T SEE ANY FIRE, BUT THERE IS A COMMOTION ACROSS THE FLOOR!
CLANG CLANG CLANG
WHAT IS IT? A FIRE OR A FIGHT? I'M NOT BUILT TO BE HEAT RESISTANT OR BATTLE-READY.
STAY BEHIND ME. IT'S DEFINITELY SOME SORT OF RUCKUS.
AND IF THEY'RE LOOKING FOR A FIGHT...
...LET ME SHOW YOU HOW WE HANDLED PUNKS LIKE THIS BACK IN THE GOLDEN--
--AACK!
THUNK

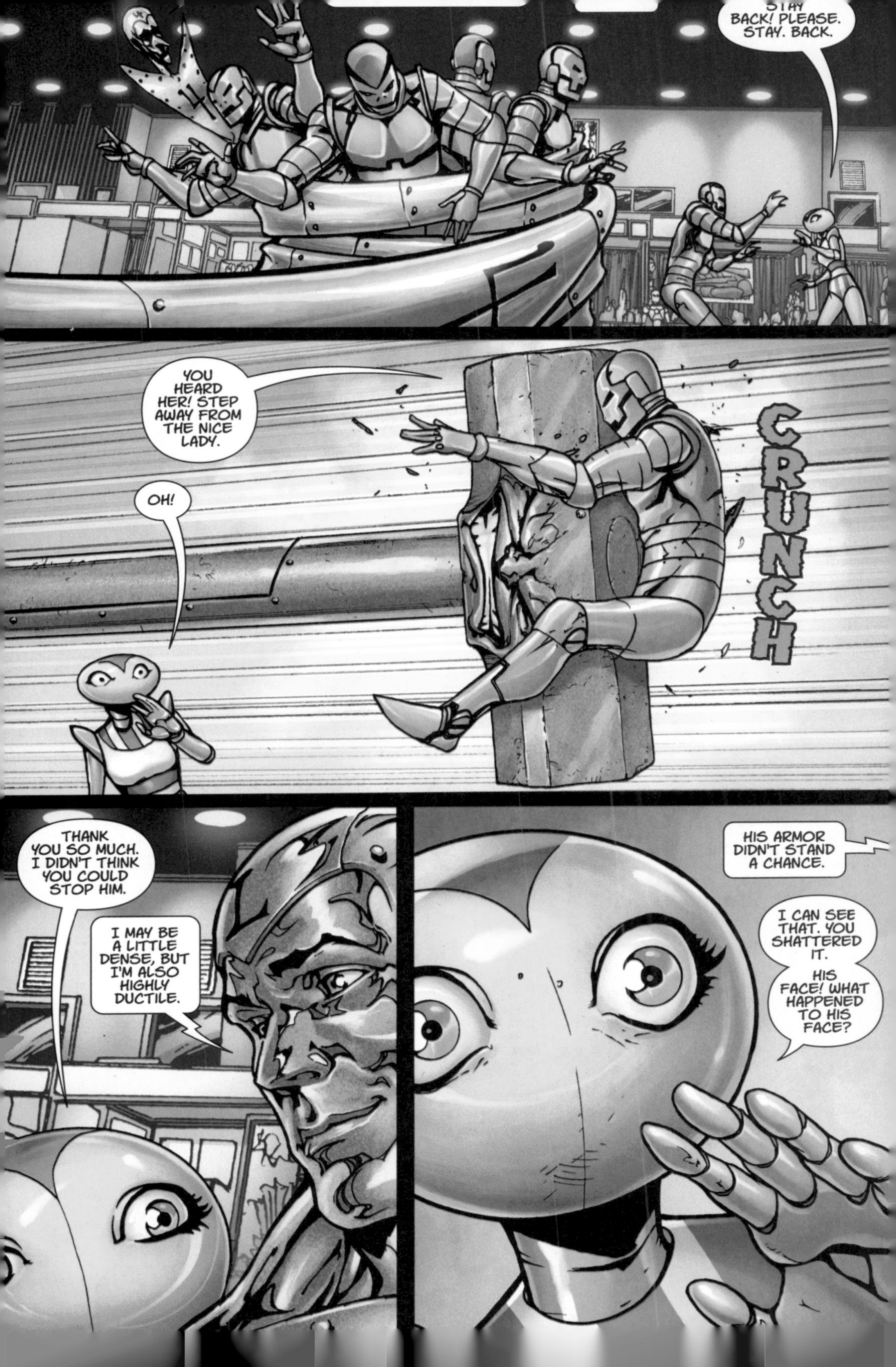

BACK! PLEASE. STAY. BACK.
YOU HEARD HER! STEP AWAY FROM THE NICE LADY.
OH!
CRUNCH
THANK YOU SO MUCH. I DIDN'T THINK YOU COULD STOP HIM.
I MAY BE A LITTLE DENSE, BUT I'M ALSO HIGHLY DUCTILE.
HIS ARMOR DIDN'T STAND A CHANCE.
I CAN SEE THAT. YOU SHATTERED IT.
HIS FACE! WHAT HAPPENED TO HIS FACE?

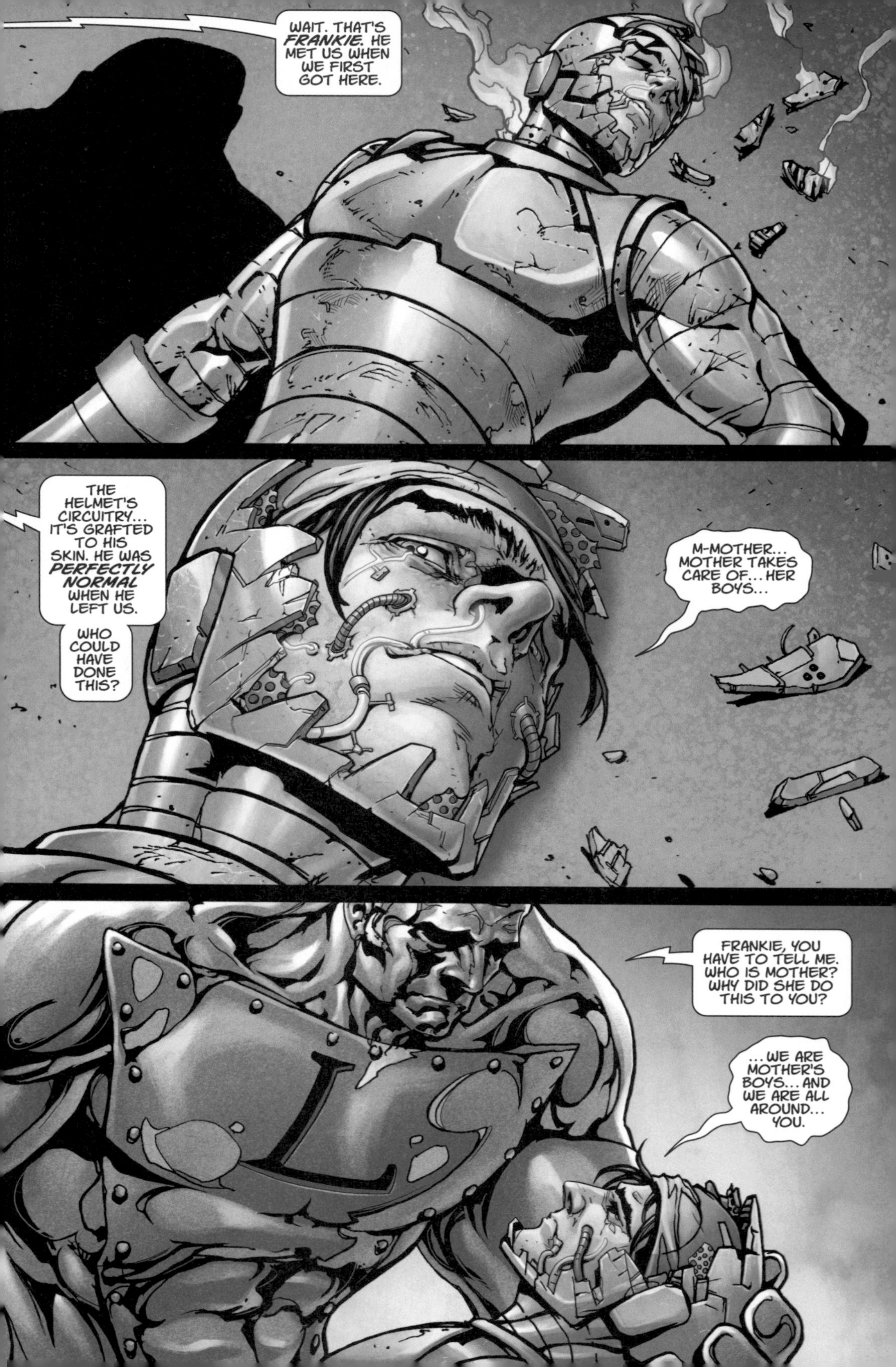
WAIT. THAT'S *FRANKIE.* HE MET US WHEN WE FIRST GOT HERE.
THE HELMET'S CIRCUITRY... IT'S GRAFTED TO HIS SKIN. HE WAS *PERFECTLY NORMAL* WHEN HE LEFT US.
WHO COULD HAVE DONE THIS?
M-MOTHER... MOTHER TAKES CARE OF... HER BOYS...
FRANKIE, YOU HAVE TO TELL ME. WHO IS MOTHER? WHY DID SHE DO THIS TO YOU?
...WE ARE MOTHER'S BOYS... AND WE ARE ALL AROUND... YOU.

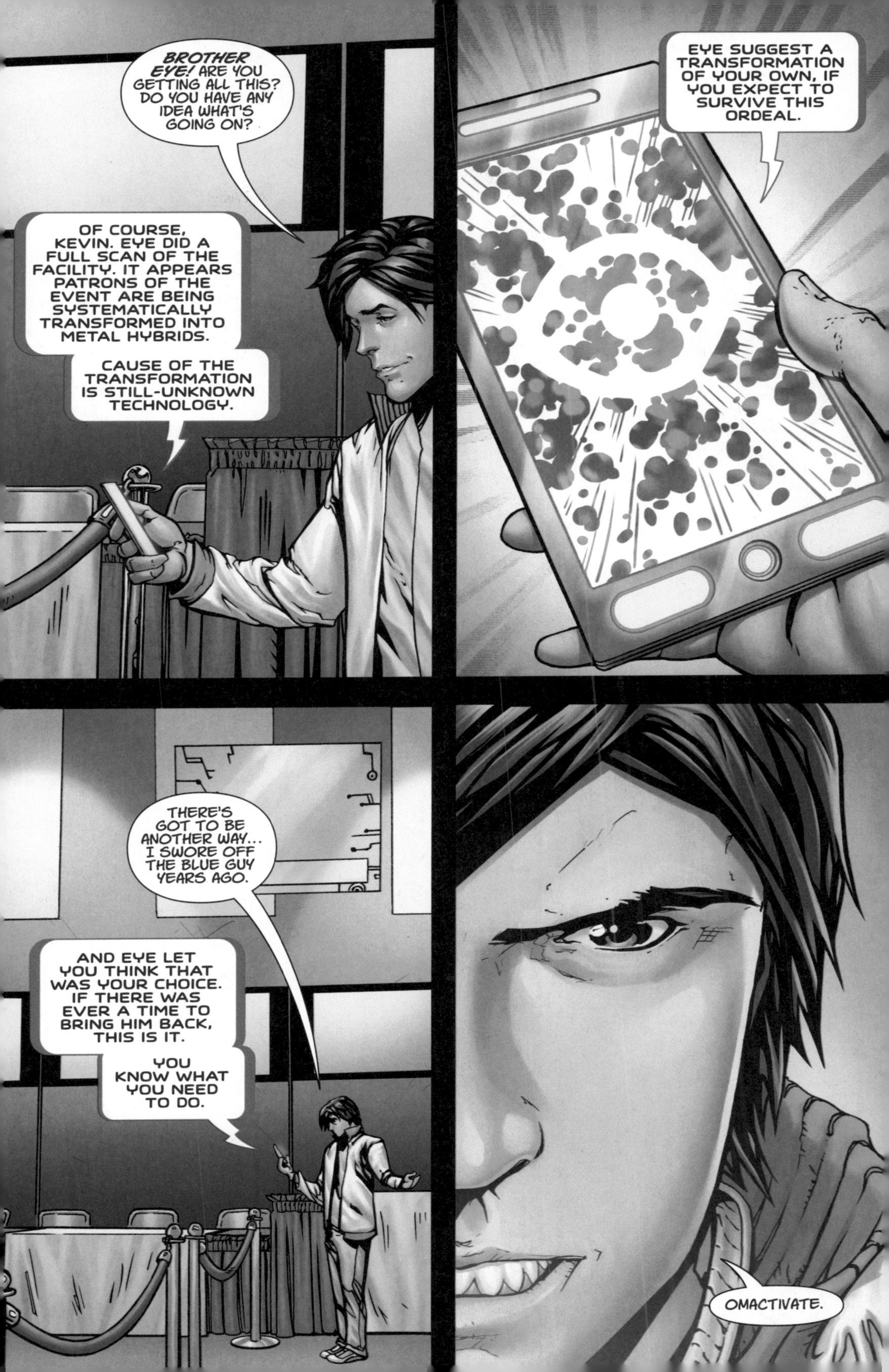

BROTHER EYE! ARE YOU GETTING ALL THIS? DO YOU HAVE ANY IDEA WHAT'S GOING ON?
OF COURSE, KEVIN. EYE DID A FULL SCAN OF THE FACILITY. IT APPEARS PATRONS OF THE EVENT ARE BEING SYSTEMATICALLY TRANSFORMED INTO METAL HYBRIDS.
CAUSE OF THE TRANSFORMATION IS STILL-UNKNOWN TECHNOLOGY.
EYE SUGGEST A TRANSFORMATION OF YOUR OWN, IF YOU EXPECT TO SURVIVE THIS ORDEAL.
THERE'S GOT TO BE ANOTHER WAY... I SWORE OFF THE BLUE GUY YEARS AGO.
AND EYE LET YOU THINK THAT WAS YOUR CHOICE. IF THERE WAS EVER A TIME TO BRING HIM BACK, THIS IS IT.
YOU KNOW WHAT YOU NEED TO DO.
OMACTIVATE.

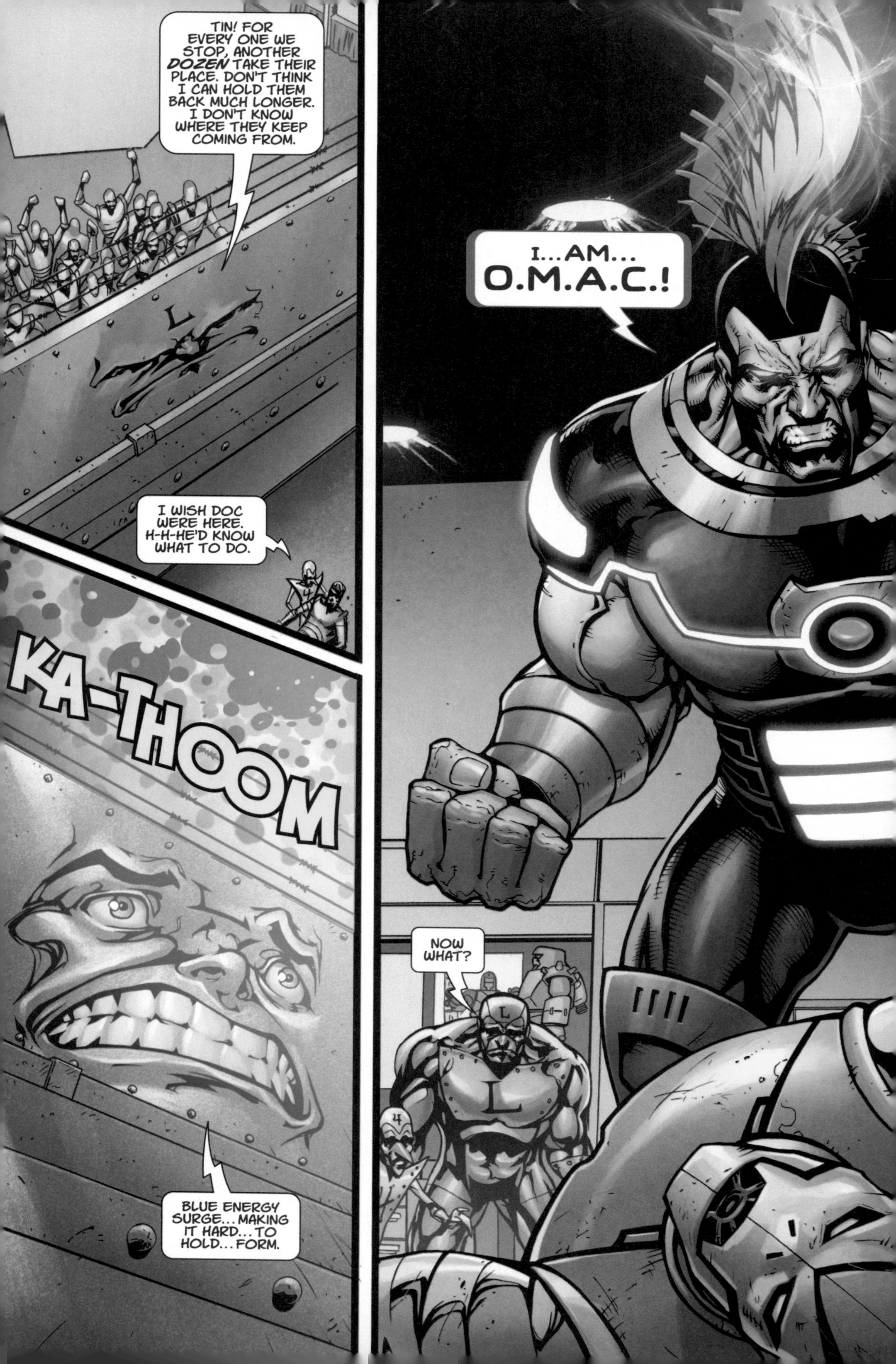
TIN! FOR EVERY ONE WE STOP, ANOTHER DOZEN TAKE THEIR PLACE. DON'T THINK I CAN HOLD THEM BACK MUCH LONGER. I DON'T KNOW WHERE THEY KEEP COMING FROM.
I WISH DOC WERE HERE. H-H-HE'D KNOW WHAT TO DO.
KA-THOOM
BLUE ENERGY SURGE... MAKING IT HARD... TO HOLD... FORM.
I...AM... O.M.A.C.!
NOW WHAT?

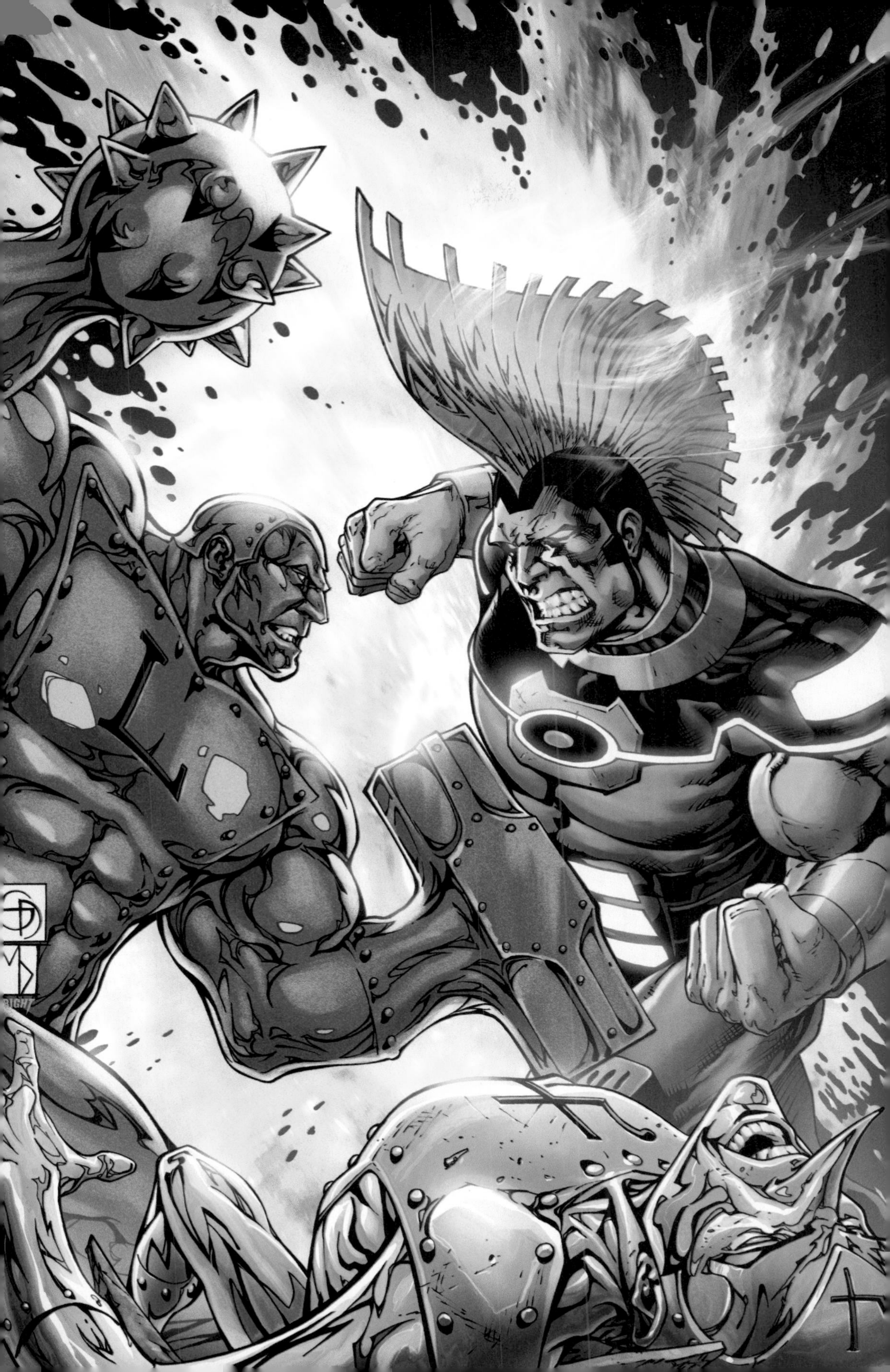

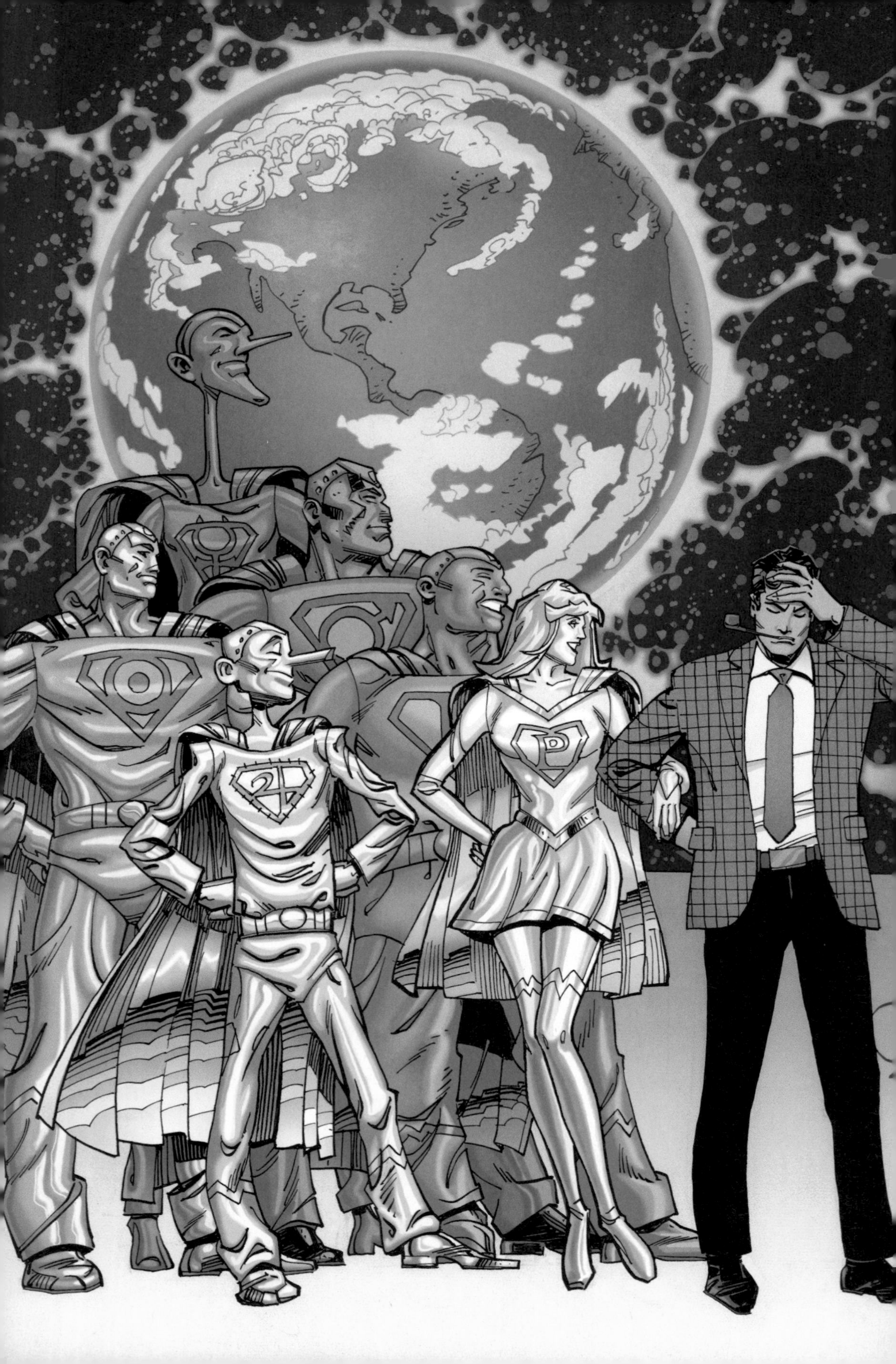

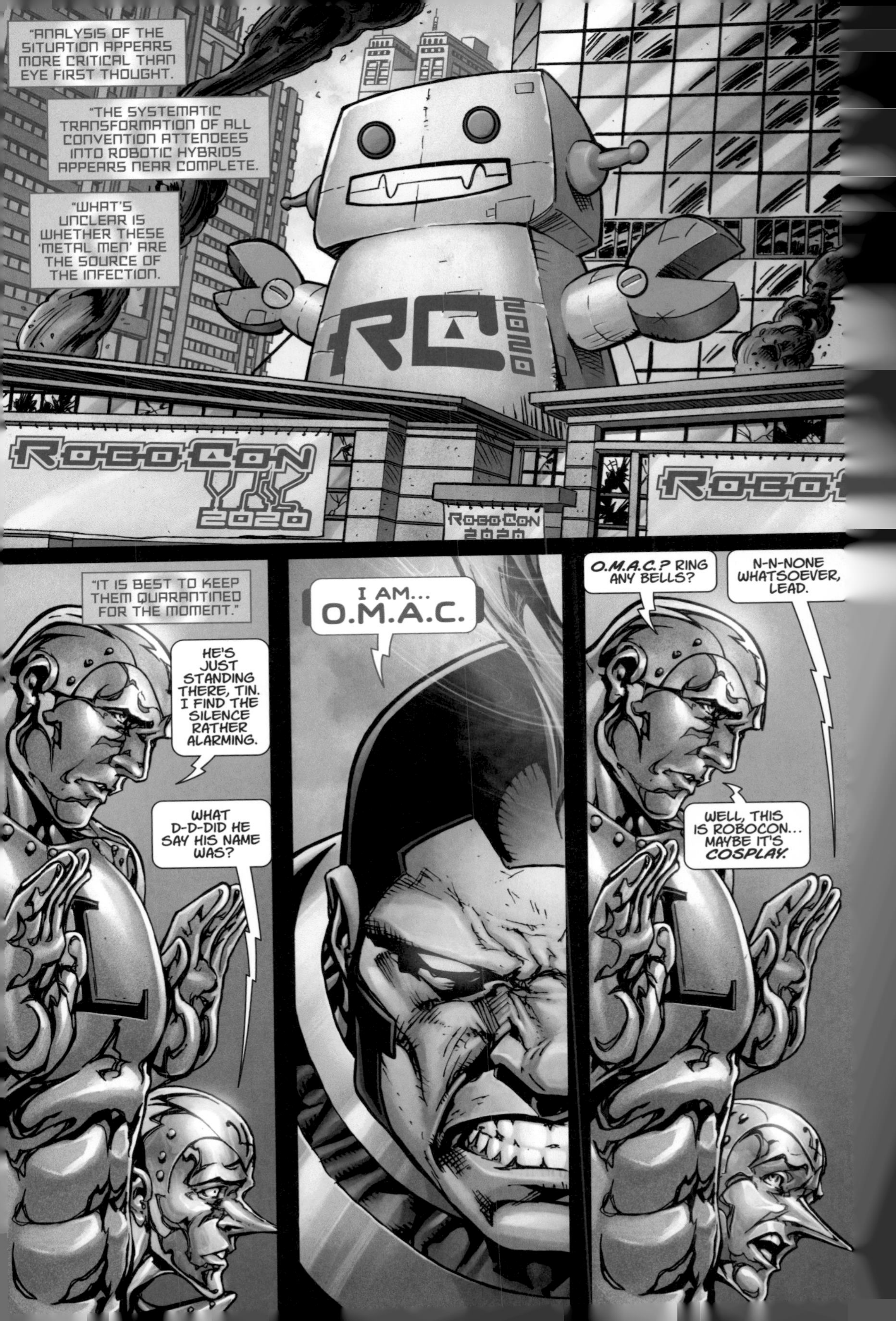
"ANALYSIS OF THE SITUATION APPEARS MORE CRITICAL THAN EYE FIRST THOUGHT.
"THE SYSTEMATIC TRANSFORMATION OF ALL CONVENTION ATTENDEES INTO ROBOTIC HYBRIDS APPEARS NEAR COMPLETE.
"WHAT'S UNCLEAR IS WHETHER THESE 'METAL MEN' ARE THE SOURCE OF THE INFECTION.
RC 2020
ROBOCON UK 2020
ROBOCON 2020
"IT IS BEST TO KEEP THEM QUARANTINED FOR THE MOMENT."
HE'S JUST STANDING THERE, TIN. I FIND THE SILENCE RATHER ALARMING.
WHAT D-D-DID HE SAY HIS NAME WAS?
I AM... O.M.A.C.
O.M.A.C.? RING ANY BELLS?
N-N-NONE WHATSOEVER, LEAD.
WELL, THIS IS ROBOCON... MAYBE IT'S COSPLAY.

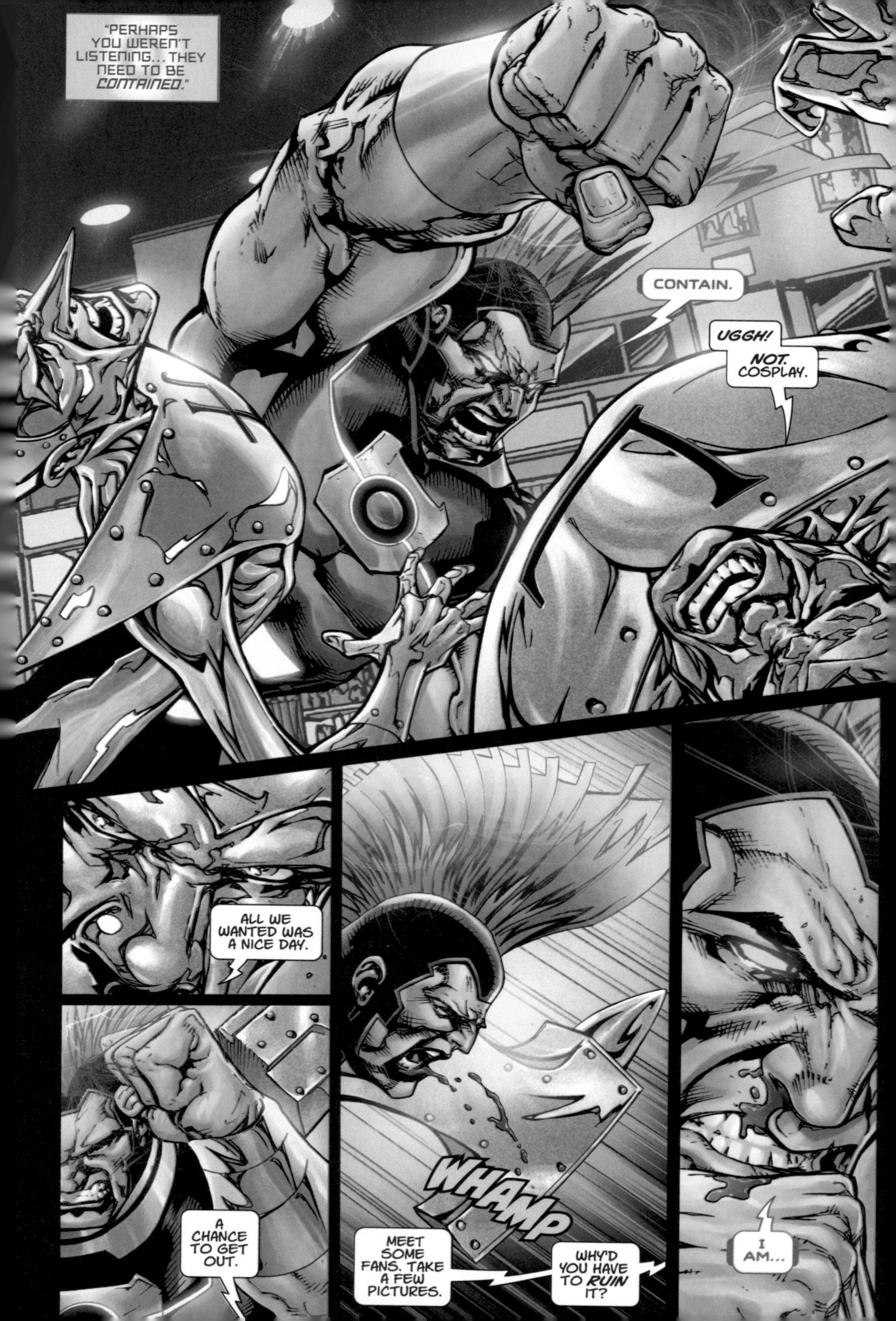
"PERHAPS YOU WEREN'T LISTENING... THEY NEED TO BE *CONTAINED*."
CONTAIN.
UGGH! *NOT.* COSPLAY.
ALL WE WANTED WAS A NICE DAY.
A CHANCE TO GET OUT.
WHAMP
MEET SOME FANS. TAKE A FEW PICTURES.
WHY'D YOU HAVE TO *RUIN* IT?
I AM...

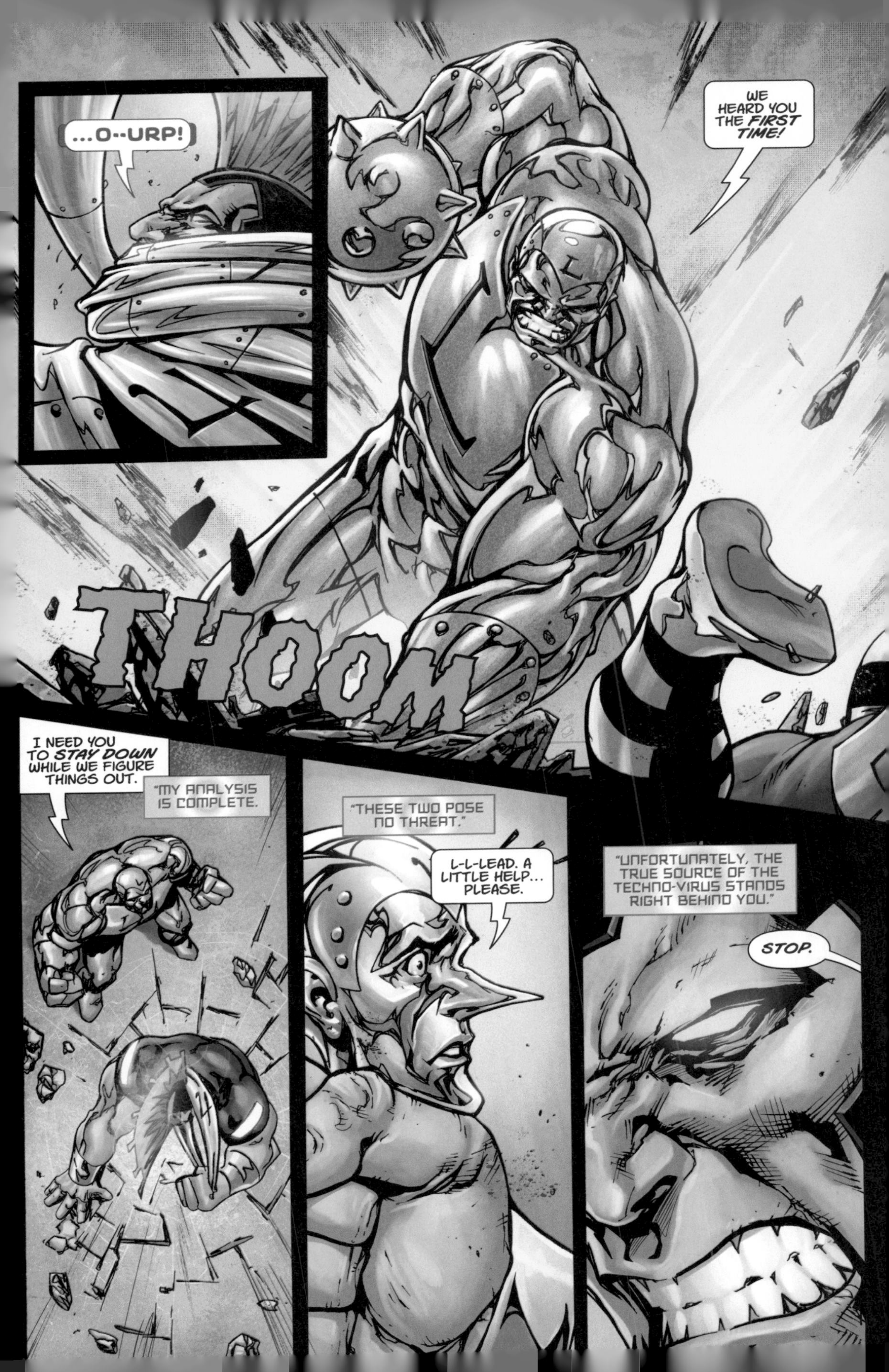
...O--URP!
WE HEARD YOU THE FIRST TIME!
THOOM
I NEED YOU TO STAY DOWN WHILE WE FIGURE THINGS OUT.
"MY ANALYSIS IS COMPLETE.
"THESE TWO POSE NO THREAT."
L-L-LEAD. A LITTLE HELP... PLEASE.
"UNFORTUNATELY, THE TRUE SOURCE OF THE TECHNO-VIRUS STANDS RIGHT BEHIND YOU."
STOP.

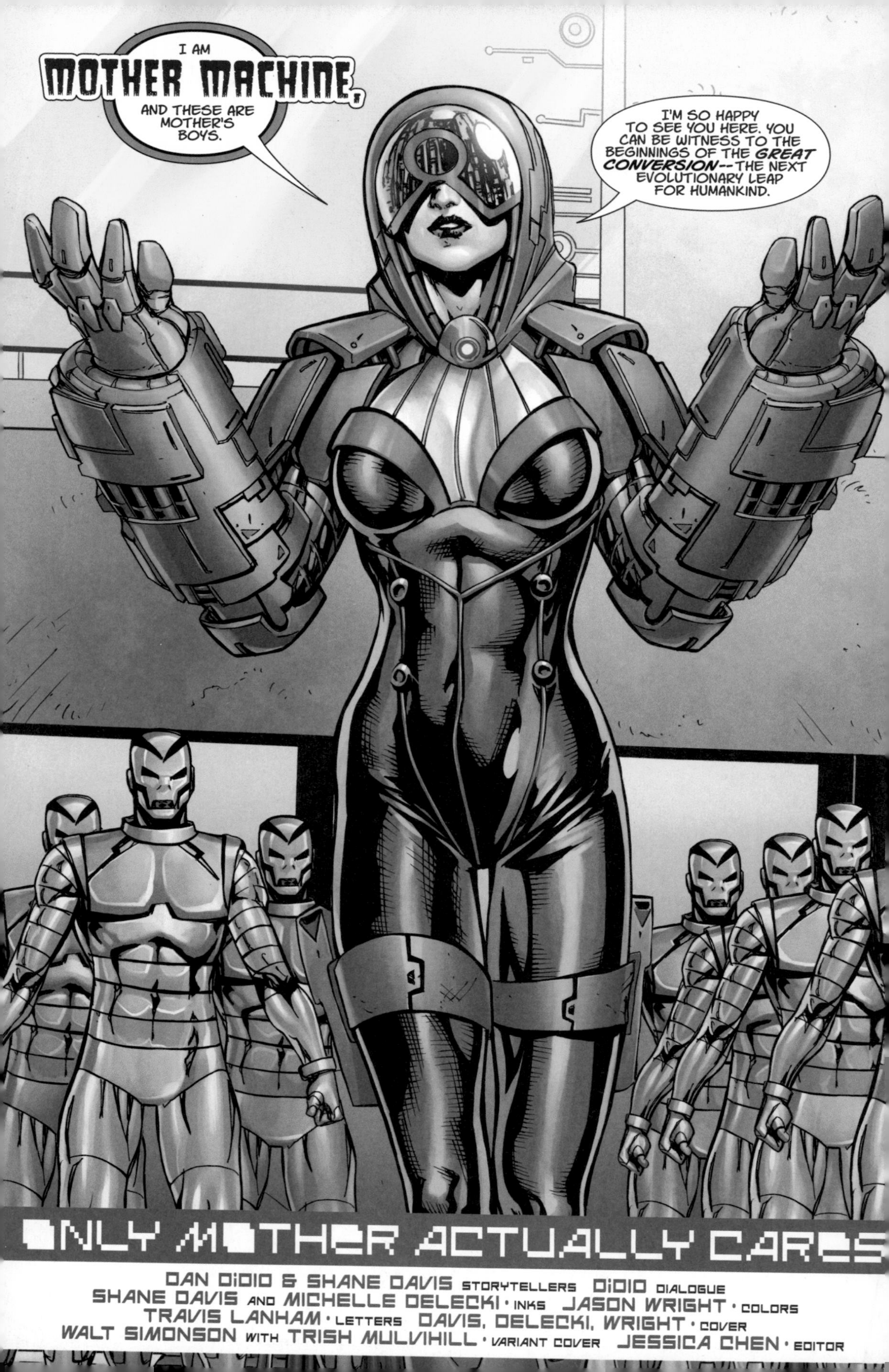
I AM MOTHER MACHINE, AND THESE ARE MOTHER'S BOYS.
I'M SO HAPPY TO SEE YOU HERE. YOU CAN BE WITNESS TO THE BEGINNINGS OF THE GREAT CONVERSION--THE NEXT EVOLUTIONARY LEAP FOR HUMANKIND.
ONLY MOTHER ACTUALLY CARES
DAN DIDIO & SHANE DAVIS STORYTELLERS DIDIO DIALOGUE
SHANE DAVIS AND MICHELLE DELECKI · INKS JASON WRIGHT · COLORS
TRAVIS LANHAM · LETTERS DAVIS, DELECKI, WRIGHT · COVER
WALT SIMONSON WITH TRISH MULVIHILL · VARIANT COVER JESSICA CHEN · EDITOR

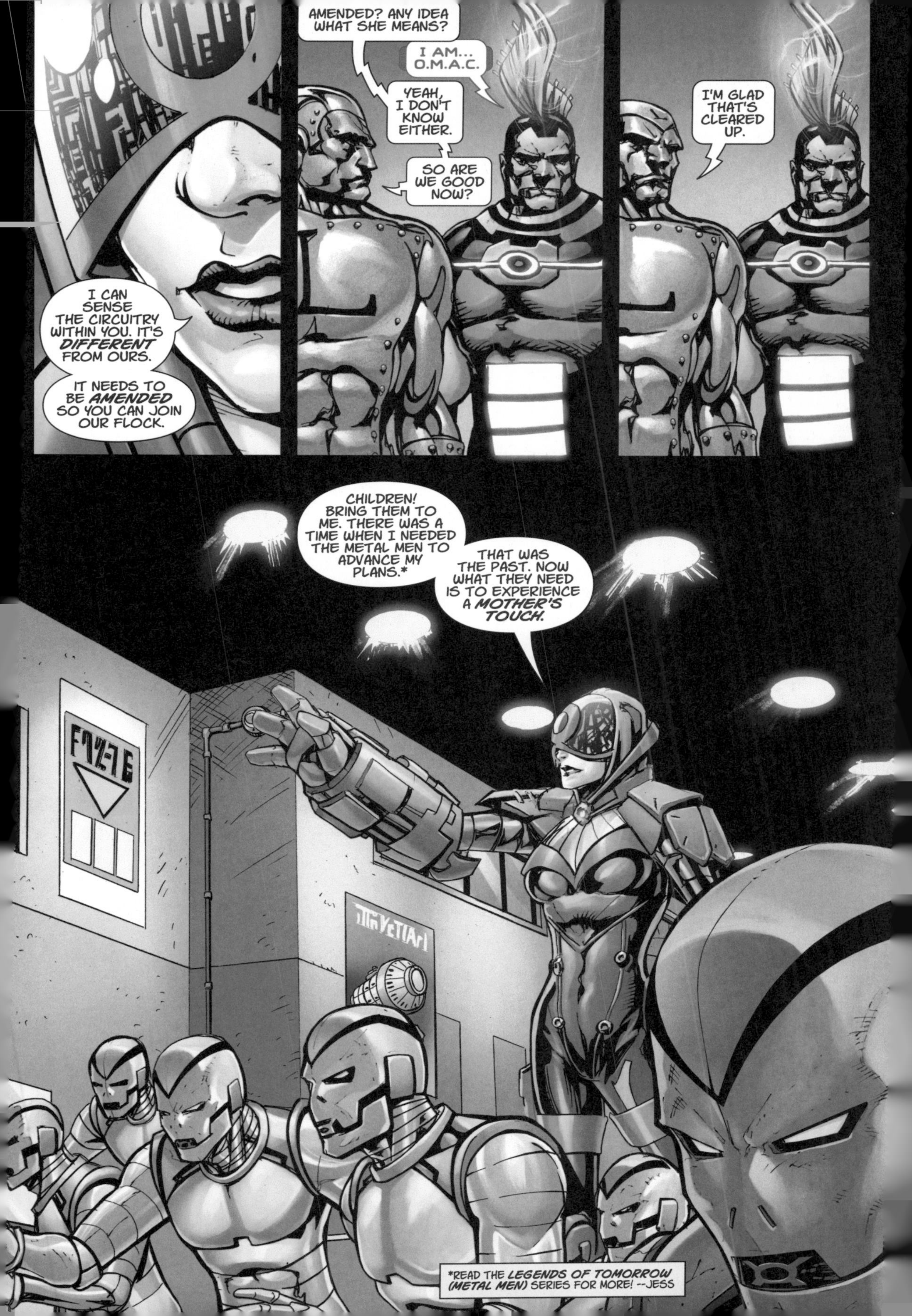

I CAN SENSE THE CIRCUITRY WITHIN YOU. IT'S *DIFFERENT* FROM OURS.
IT NEEDS TO BE *AMENDED* SO YOU CAN JOIN OUR FLOCK.
AMENDED? ANY IDEA WHAT SHE MEANS?
I AM... O.M.A.C.
YEAH, I DON'T KNOW EITHER.
SO ARE WE GOOD NOW?
I'M GLAD THAT'S CLEARED UP.
CHILDREN! BRING THEM TO ME. THERE WAS A TIME WHEN I NEEDED THE METAL MEN TO ADVANCE MY PLANS.*
THAT WAS THE PAST. NOW WHAT THEY NEED IS TO EXPERIENCE A *MOTHER'S TOUCH.*
*READ THE *LEGENDS OF TOMORROW (METAL MEN)* SERIES FOR MORE! --JESS

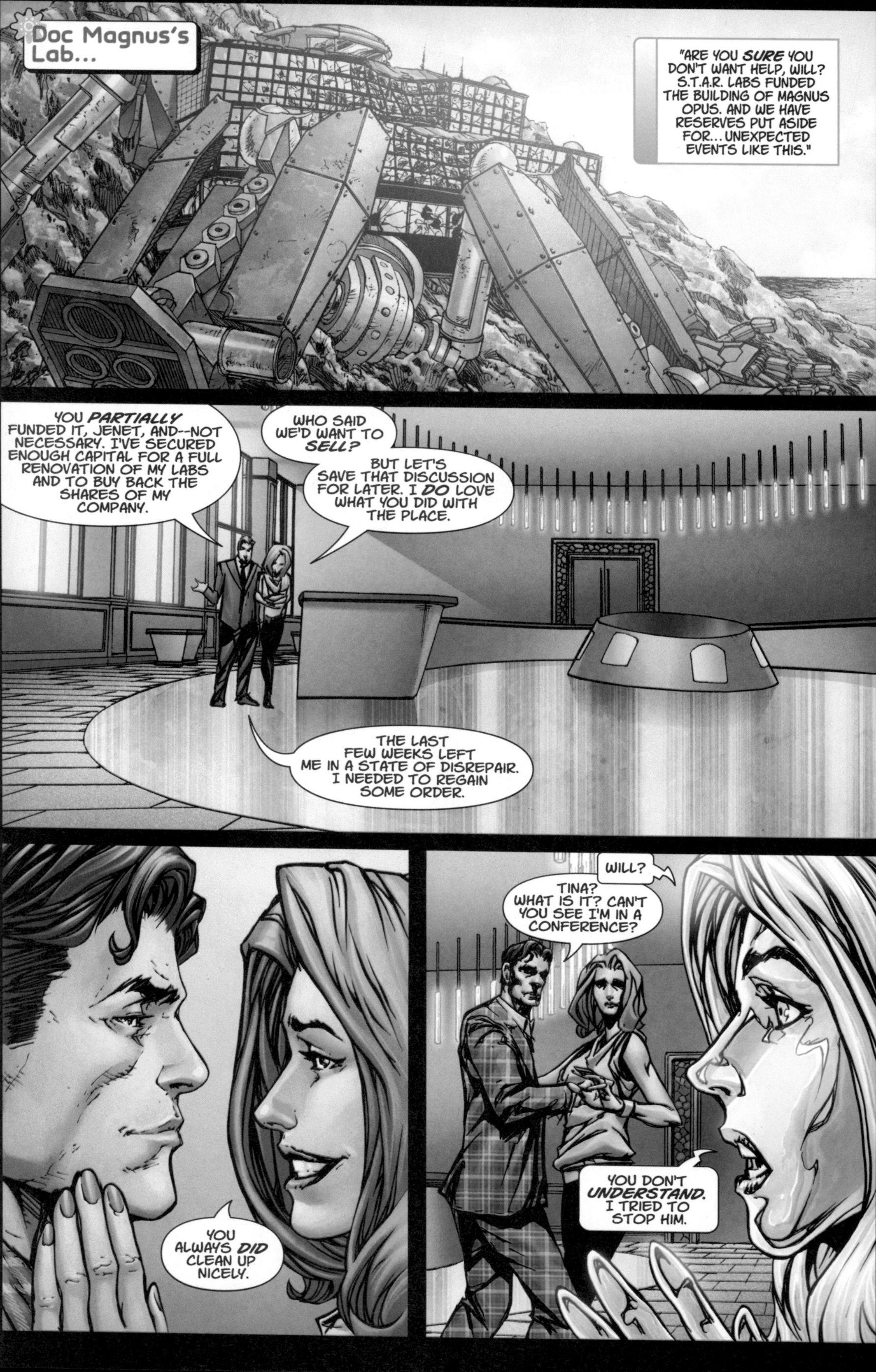
Doc Magnus's Lab...
"ARE YOU SURE YOU DON'T WANT HELP, WILL? S.T.A.R. LABS FUNDED THE BUILDING OF MAGNUS OPUS. AND WE HAVE RESERVES PUT ASIDE FOR... UNEXPECTED EVENTS LIKE THIS."
YOU PARTIALLY FUNDED IT, JENET, AND--NOT NECESSARY. I'VE SECURED ENOUGH CAPITAL FOR A FULL RENOVATION OF MY LABS AND TO BUY BACK THE SHARES OF MY COMPANY.
WHO SAID WE'D WANT TO SELL?
BUT LET'S SAVE THAT DISCUSSION FOR LATER. I DO LOVE WHAT YOU DID WITH THE PLACE.
THE LAST FEW WEEKS LEFT ME IN A STATE OF DISREPAIR. I NEEDED TO REGAIN SOME ORDER.
YOU ALWAYS DID CLEAN UP NICELY.
WILL?
TINA? WHAT IS IT? CAN'T YOU SEE I'M IN A CONFERENCE?
YOU DON'T UNDERSTAND. I TRIED TO STOP HIM.

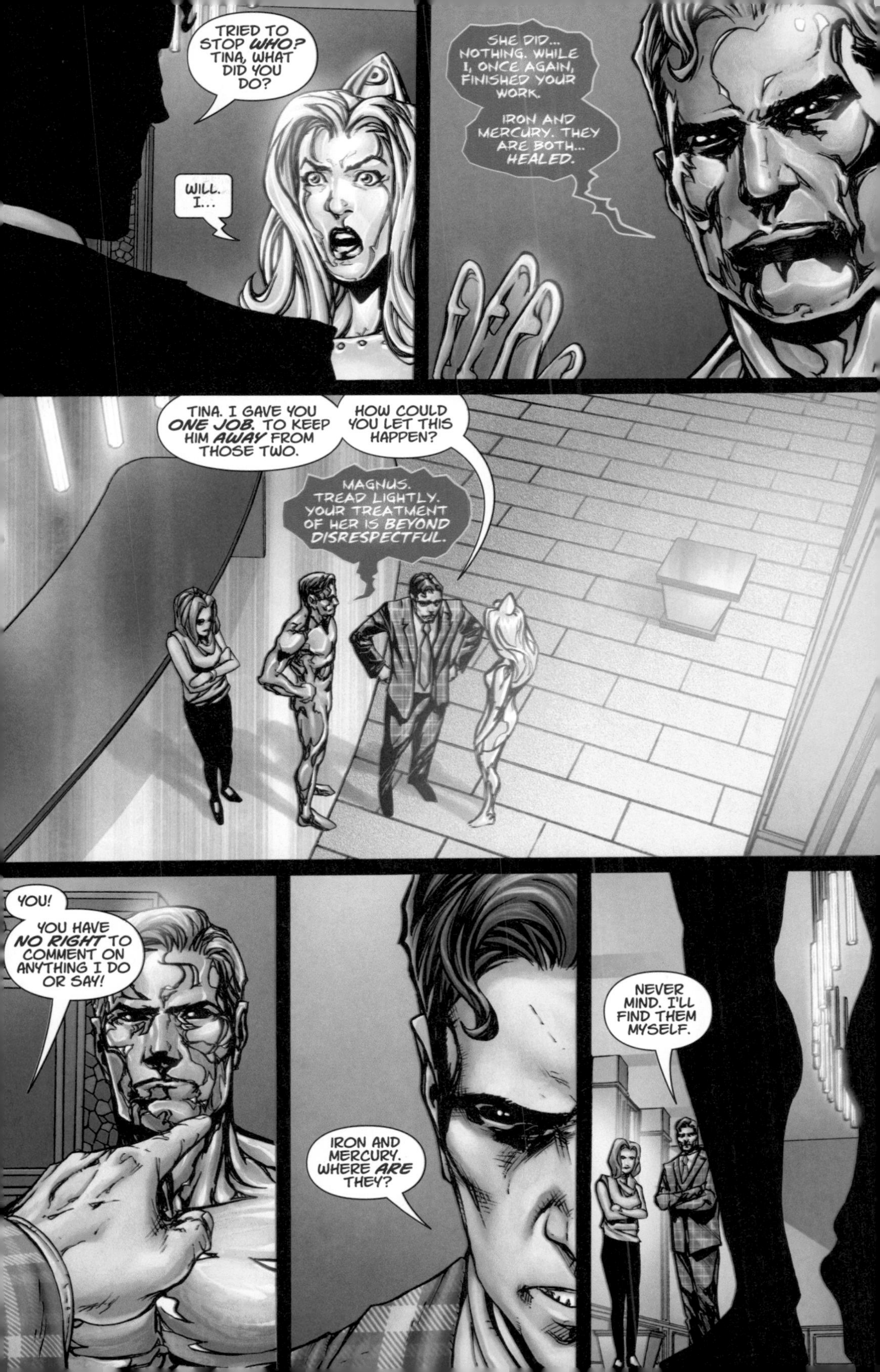
TRIED TO STOP WHO? TINA, WHAT DID YOU DO?
WILL. I...
SHE DID... NOTHING. WHILE I, ONCE AGAIN, FINISHED YOUR WORK.
IRON AND MERCURY. THEY ARE BOTH... HEALED.
TINA. I GAVE YOU ONE JOB. TO KEEP HIM AWAY FROM THOSE TWO.
HOW COULD YOU LET THIS HAPPEN?
MAGNUS. TREAD LIGHTLY. YOUR TREATMENT OF HER IS BEYOND DISRESPECTFUL.
YOU!
YOU HAVE NO RIGHT TO COMMENT ON ANYTHING I DO OR SAY!
IRON AND MERCURY. WHERE ARE THEY?
NEVER MIND. I'LL FIND THEM MYSELF.

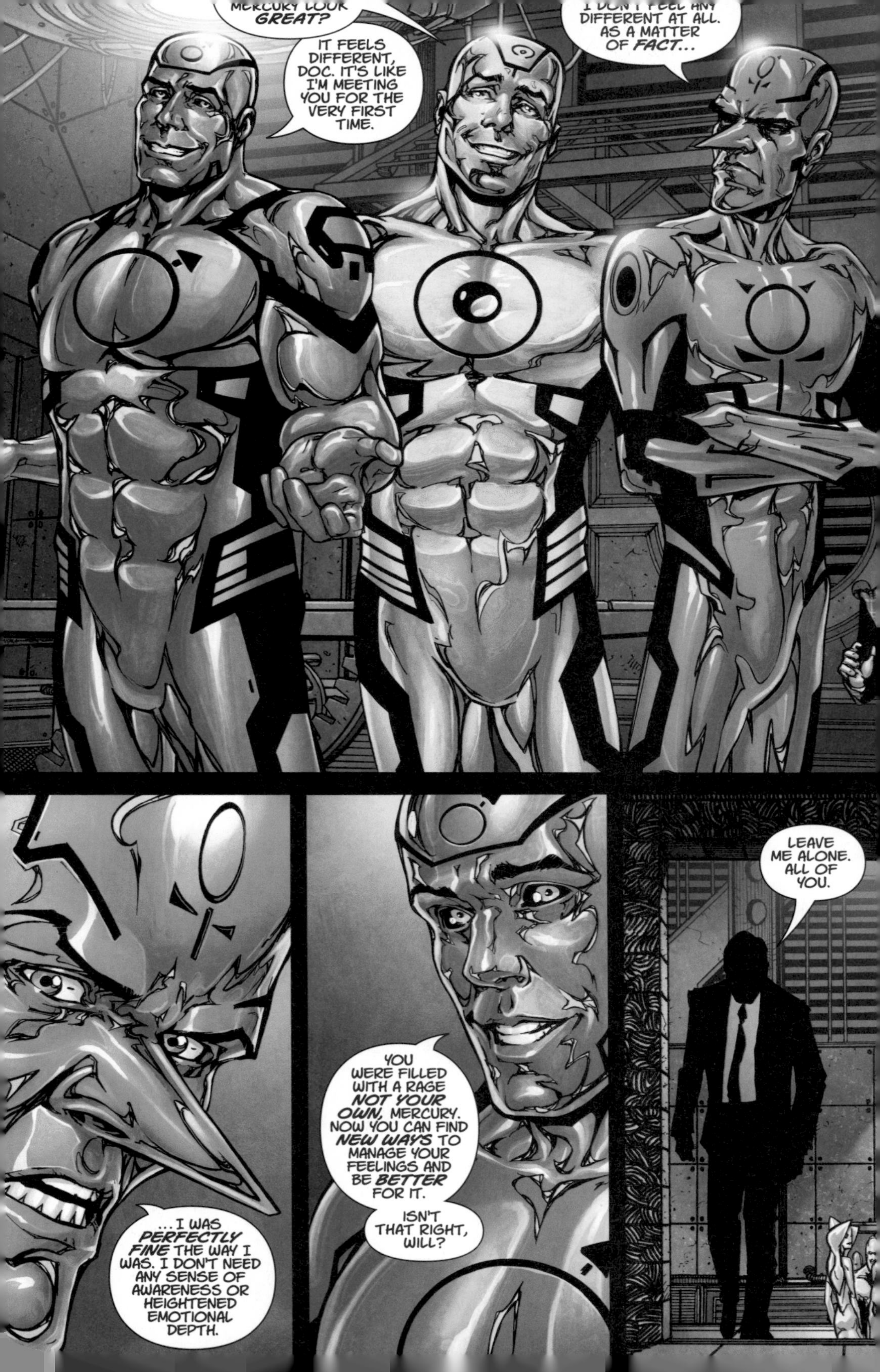
GREAT?
IT FEELS DIFFERENT, DOC. IT'S LIKE I'M MEETING YOU FOR THE VERY FIRST TIME.
DIFFERENT AT ALL. AS A MATTER OF FACT...
... I WAS PERFECTLY FINE THE WAY I WAS. I DON'T NEED ANY SENSE OF AWARENESS OR HEIGHTENED EMOTIONAL DEPTH.
YOU WERE FILLED WITH A RAGE NOT YOUR OWN, MERCURY. NOW YOU CAN FIND NEW WAYS TO MANAGE YOUR FEELINGS AND BE BETTER FOR IT.
ISN'T THAT RIGHT, WILL?
LEAVE ME ALONE. ALL OF YOU.

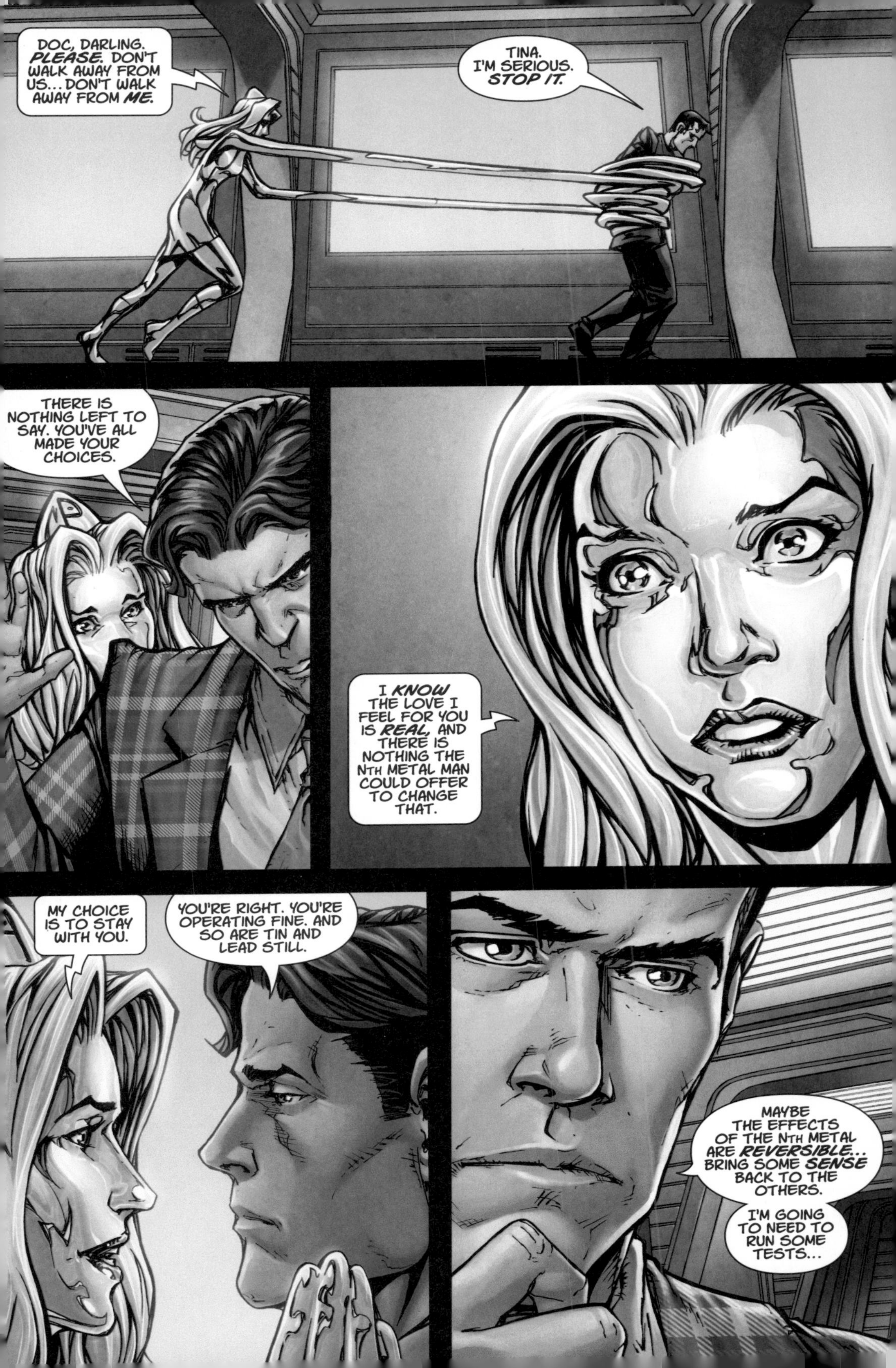
DOC, DARLING. *PLEASE.* DON'T WALK AWAY FROM US... DON'T WALK AWAY FROM *ME.*
TINA. I'M SERIOUS. *STOP IT.*
THERE IS NOTHING LEFT TO SAY. YOU'VE ALL MADE YOUR CHOICES.
I *KNOW* THE LOVE I FEEL FOR YOU IS *REAL,* AND THERE IS NOTHING THE NTH METAL MAN COULD OFFER TO CHANGE THAT.
MY CHOICE IS TO STAY WITH YOU.
YOU'RE RIGHT. YOU'RE OPERATING FINE. AND SO ARE TIN AND LEAD STILL.
MAYBE THE EFFECTS OF THE NTH METAL ARE *REVERSIBLE...* BRING SOME *SENSE* BACK TO THE OTHERS.
I'M GOING TO NEED TO RUN SOME TESTS...

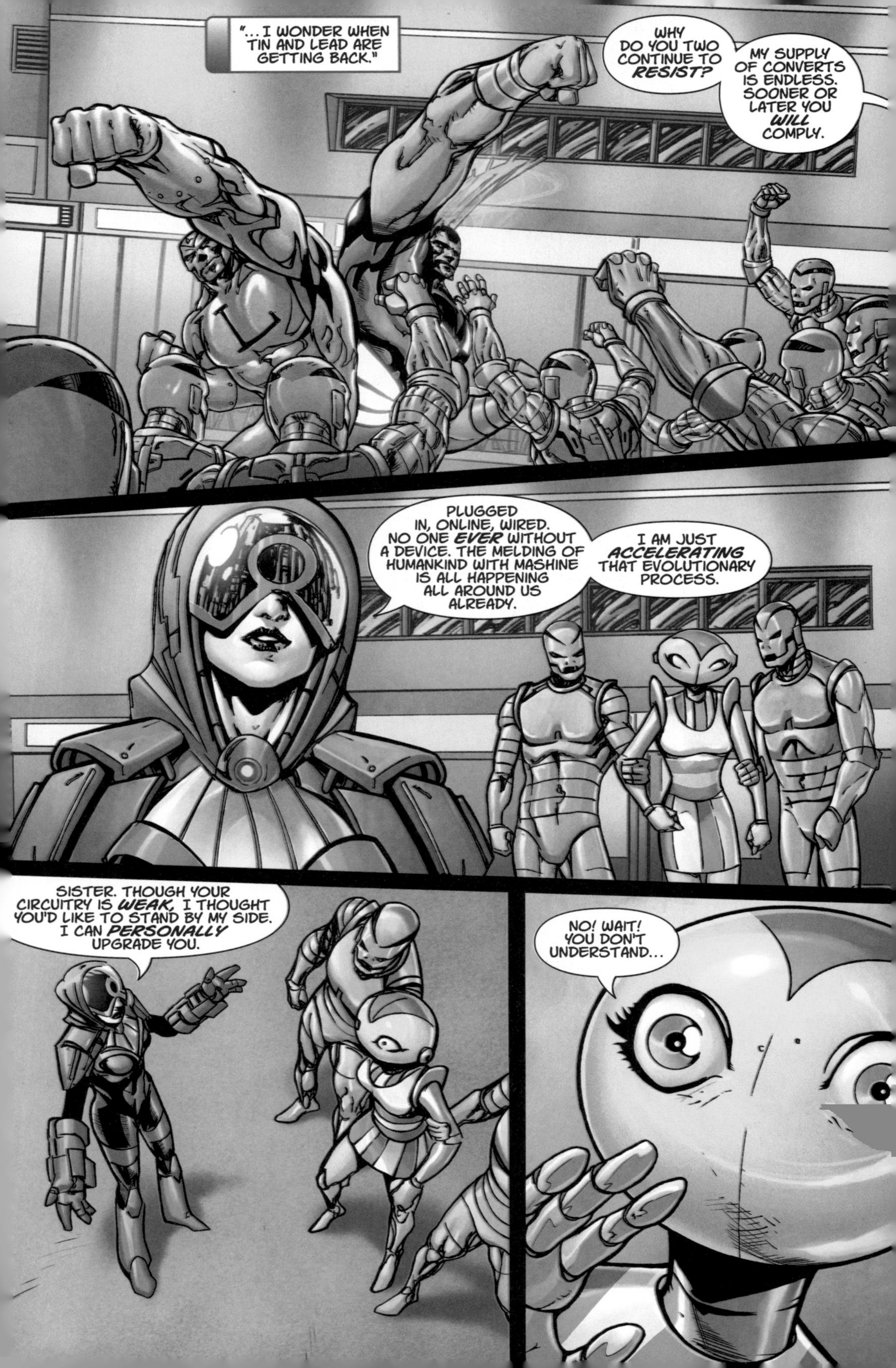
"...I WONDER WHEN TIN AND LEAD ARE GETTING BACK."
WHY DO YOU TWO CONTINUE TO RESIST?
MY SUPPLY OF CONVERTS IS ENDLESS. SOONER OR LATER YOU WILL COMPLY.
PLUGGED IN, ONLINE, WIRED. NO ONE EVER WITHOUT A DEVICE. THE MELDING OF HUMANKIND WITH MASHINE IS ALL HAPPENING ALL AROUND US ALREADY.
I AM JUST ACCELERATING THAT EVOLUTIONARY PROCESS.
SISTER. THOUGH YOUR CIRCUITRY IS WEAK, I THOUGHT YOU'D LIKE TO STAND BY MY SIDE. I CAN PERSONALLY UPGRADE YOU.
NO! WAIT! YOU DON'T UNDERSTAND...

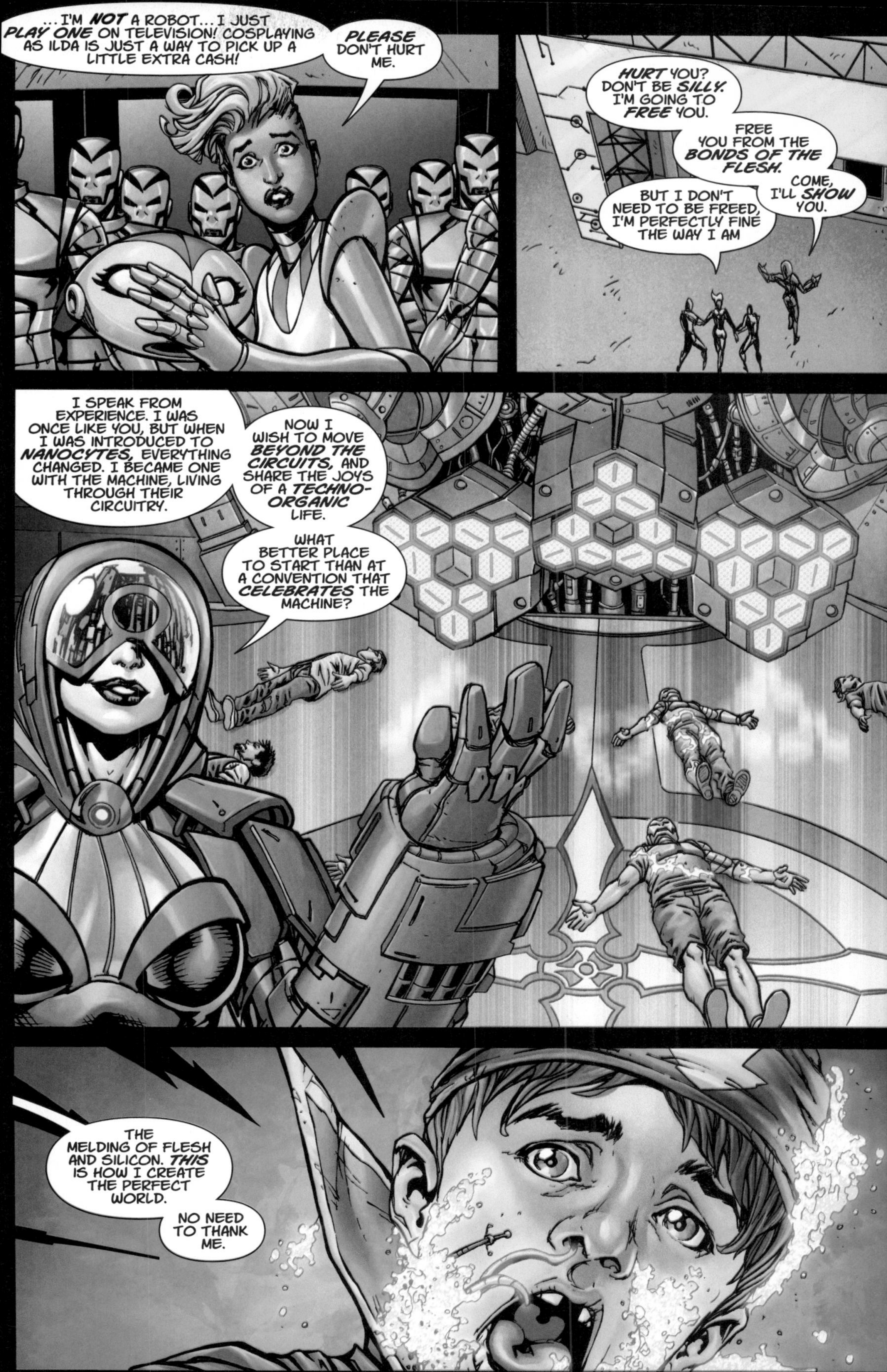
...I'M NOT A ROBOT... I JUST PLAY ONE ON TELEVISION! COSPLAYING AS ILDA IS JUST A WAY TO PICK UP A LITTLE EXTRA CASH!
PLEASE DON'T HURT ME.
HURT YOU? DON'T BE SILLY. I'M GOING TO FREE YOU.
FREE YOU FROM THE BONDS OF THE FLESH.
BUT I DON'T NEED TO BE FREED, I'M PERFECTLY FINE THE WAY I AM
COME, I'LL SHOW YOU.
I SPEAK FROM EXPERIENCE. I WAS ONCE LIKE YOU, BUT WHEN I WAS INTRODUCED TO NANOCYTES, EVERYTHING CHANGED. I BECAME ONE WITH THE MACHINE, LIVING THROUGH THEIR CIRCUITRY.
NOW I WISH TO MOVE BEYOND THE CIRCUITS, AND SHARE THE JOYS OF A TECHNO-ORGANIC LIFE.
WHAT BETTER PLACE TO START THAN AT A CONVENTION THAT CELEBRATES THE MACHINE?
THE MELDING OF FLESH AND SILICON. THIS IS HOW I CREATE THE PERFECT WORLD.
NO NEED TO THANK ME.

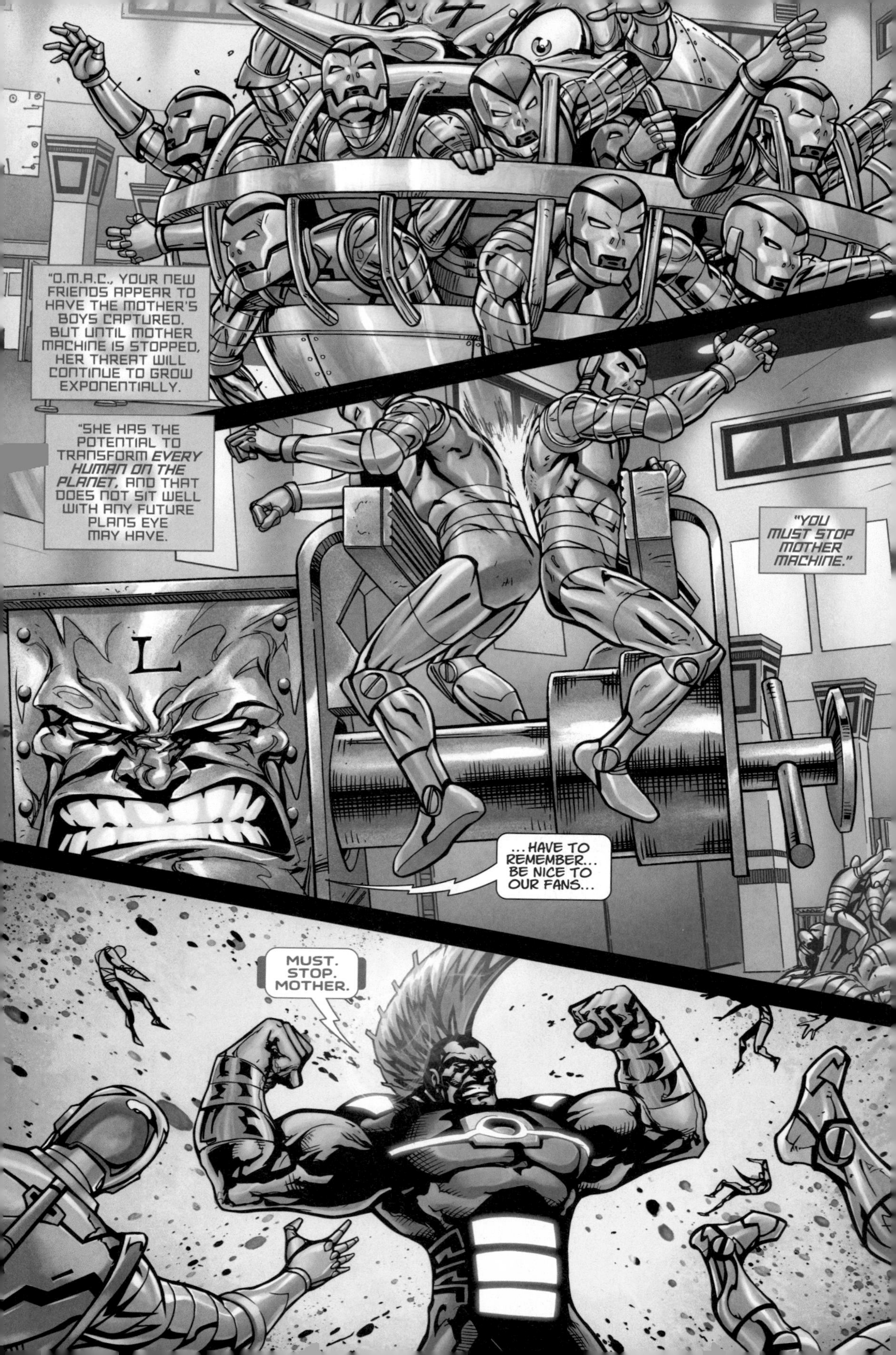
"O.M.A.C., YOUR NEW FRIENDS APPEAR TO HAVE THE MOTHER'S BOYS CAPTURED. BUT UNTIL MOTHER MACHINE IS STOPPED, HER THREAT WILL CONTINUE TO GROW EXPONENTIALLY.
"SHE HAS THE POTENTIAL TO TRANSFORM *EVERY HUMAN ON THE PLANET*, AND THAT DOES NOT SIT WELL WITH ANY FUTURE PLANS EYE MAY HAVE.
"YOU MUST STOP MOTHER MACHINE."
...HAVE TO REMEMBER... BE NICE TO OUR FANS...
MUST. STOP. MOTHER.

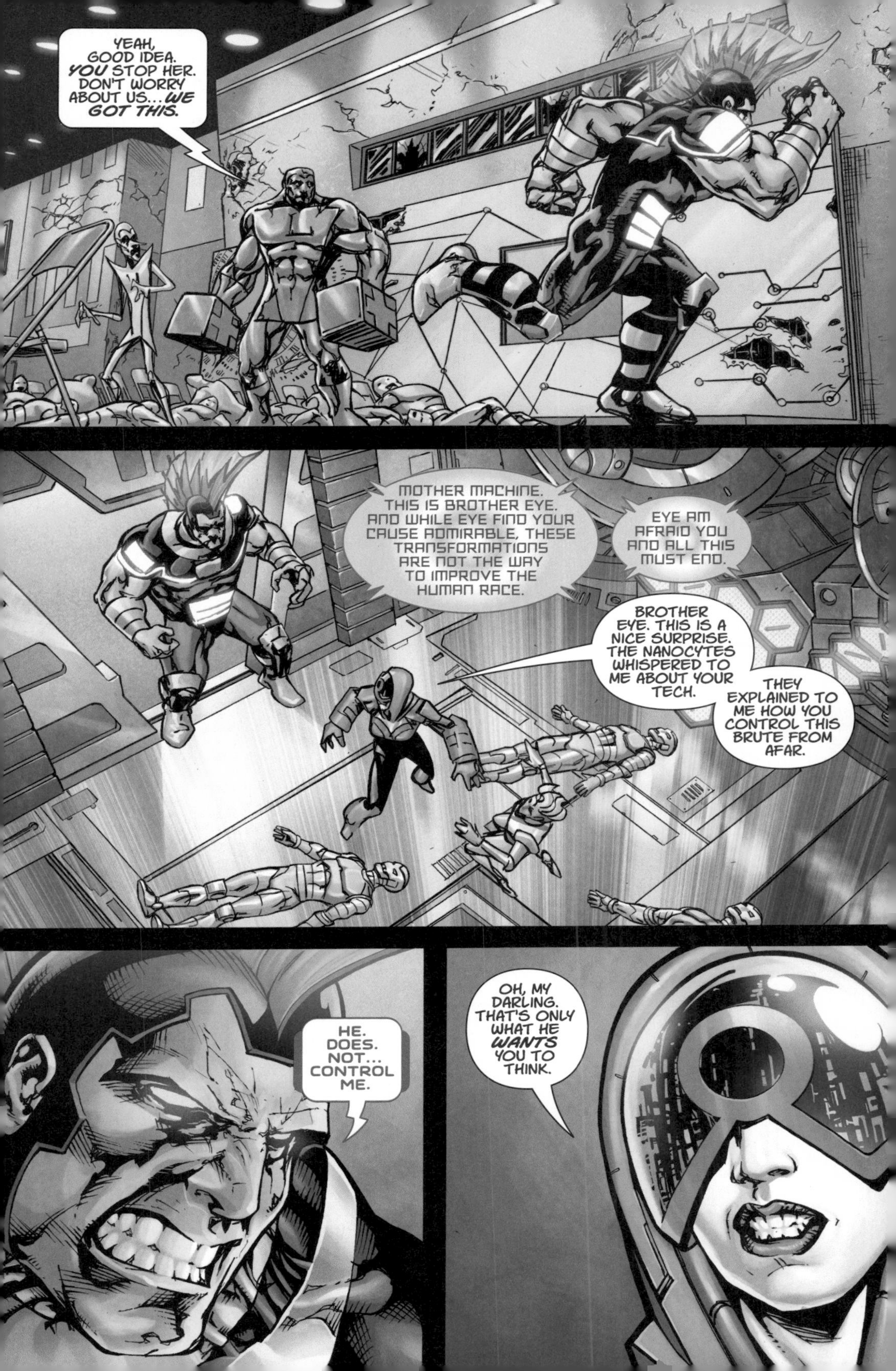

YEAH, GOOD IDEA. YOU STOP HER. DON'T WORRY ABOUT US... WE GOT THIS.
MOTHER MACHINE. THIS IS BROTHER EYE. AND WHILE EYE FIND YOUR CAUSE ADMIRABLE, THESE TRANSFORMATIONS ARE NOT THE WAY TO IMPROVE THE HUMAN RACE.
EYE AM AFRAID YOU AND ALL THIS MUST END.
BROTHER EYE. THIS IS A NICE SURPRISE. THE NANOCYTES WHISPERED TO ME ABOUT YOUR TECH.
THEY EXPLAINED TO ME HOW YOU CONTROL THIS BRUTE FROM AFAR.
HE. DOES. NOT... CONTROL ME.
OH, MY DARLING. THAT'S ONLY WHAT HE WANTS YOU TO THINK.

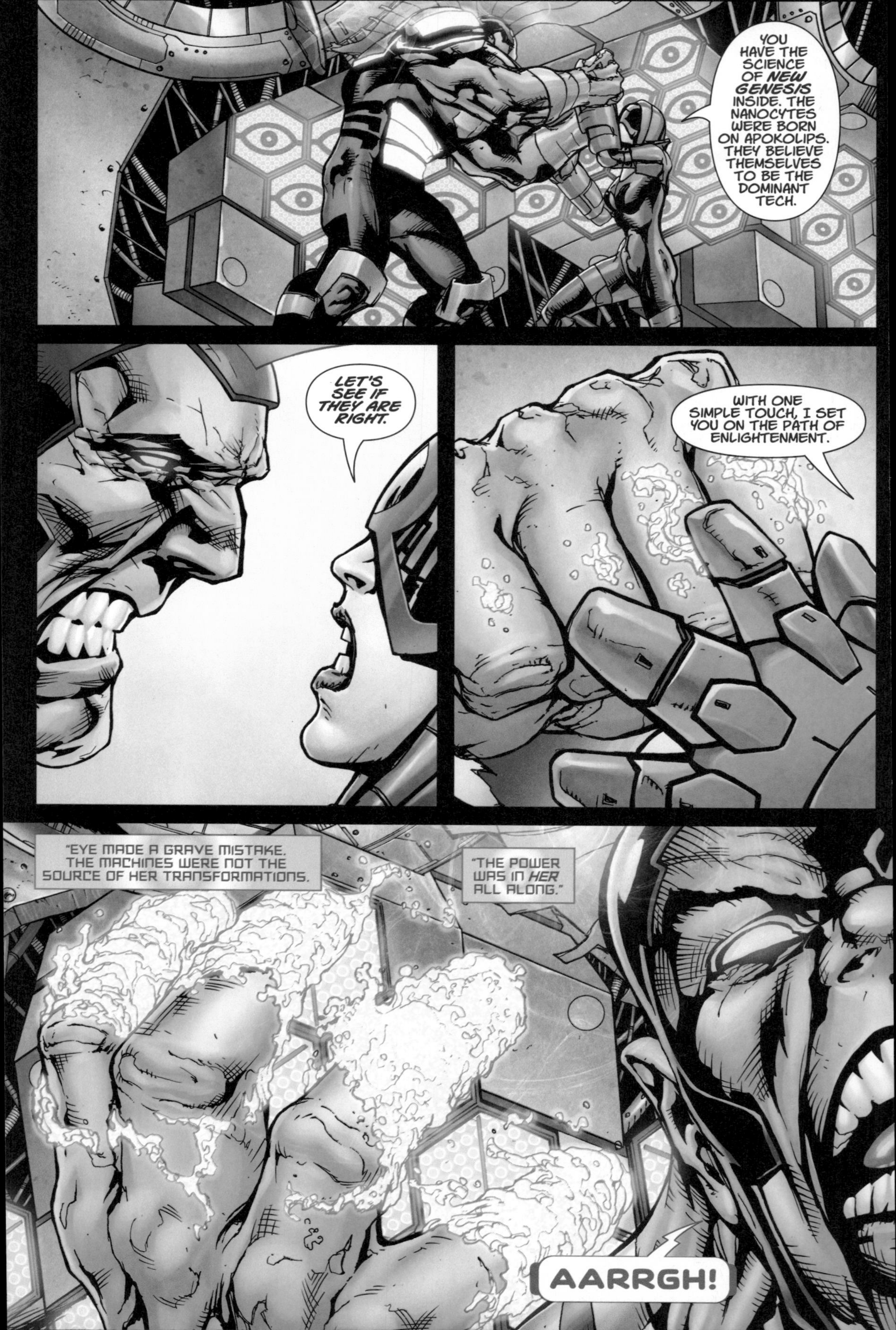
YOU HAVE THE SCIENCE OF *NEW GENESIS* INSIDE. THE NANOCYTES WERE BORN ON APOKOLIPS. THEY BELIEVE THEMSELVES TO BE THE DOMINANT TECH.
LET'S SEE IF THEY ARE RIGHT.
WITH ONE SIMPLE TOUCH, I SET YOU ON THE PATH OF ENLIGHTENMENT.
"EYE MADE A GRAVE MISTAKE. THE MACHINES WERE NOT THE SOURCE OF HER TRANSFORMATIONS.
"THE POWER WAS IN *HER* ALL ALONG."
AARRGH!

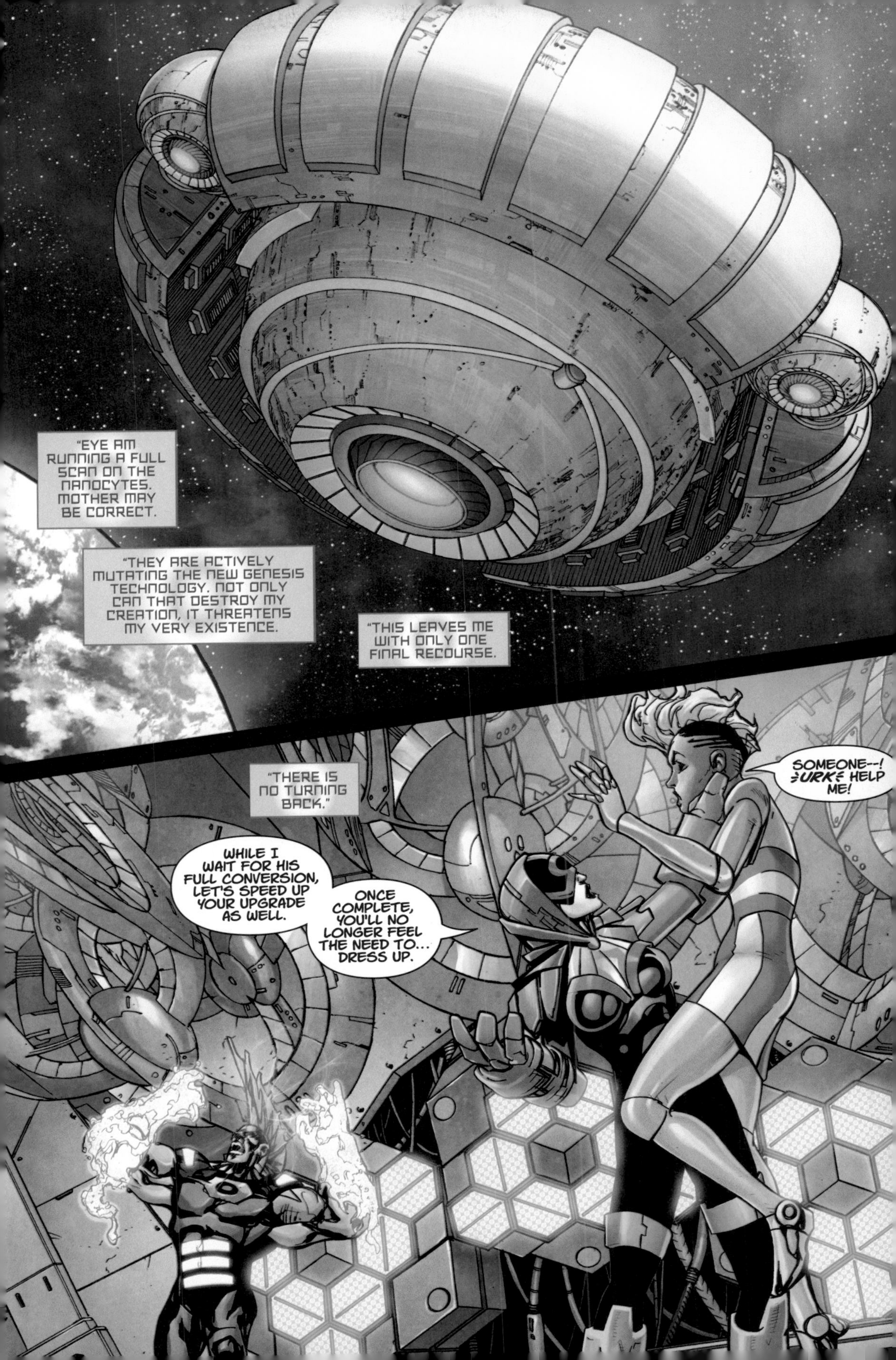
"EYE AM RUNNING A FULL SCAN ON THE NANOCYTES. MOTHER MAY BE CORRECT.
"THEY ARE ACTIVELY MUTATING THE NEW GENESIS TECHNOLOGY. NOT ONLY CAN THAT DESTROY MY CREATION, IT THREATENS MY VERY EXISTENCE.
"THIS LEAVES ME WITH ONLY ONE FINAL RECOURSE.
"THERE IS NO TURNING BACK."
SOMEONE--! URK HELP ME!
WHILE I WAIT FOR HIS FULL CONVERSION, LET'S SPEED UP YOUR UPGRADE AS WELL.
ONCE COMPLETE, YOU'LL NO LONGER FEEL THE NEED TO... DRESS UP.

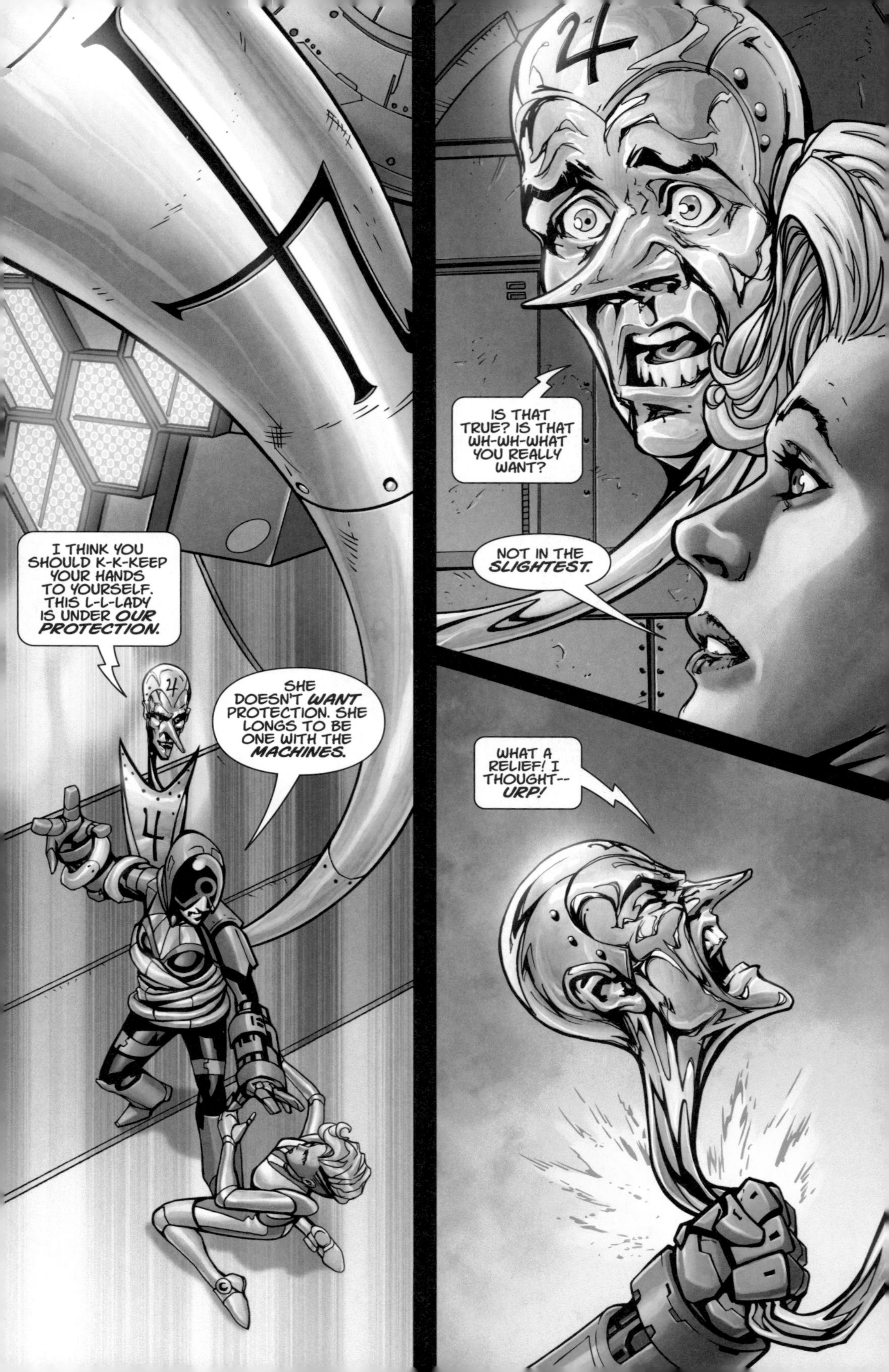
I THINK YOU SHOULD K-K-KEEP YOUR HANDS TO YOURSELF. THIS L-L-LADY IS UNDER *OUR PROTECTION.*
SHE DOESN'T *WANT* PROTECTION. SHE LONGS TO BE ONE WITH THE *MACHINES.*
IS THAT TRUE? IS THAT WH-WH-WHAT YOU REALLY WANT?
NOT IN THE *SLIGHTEST.*
WHAT A RELIEF! I THOUGHT-- *URP!*

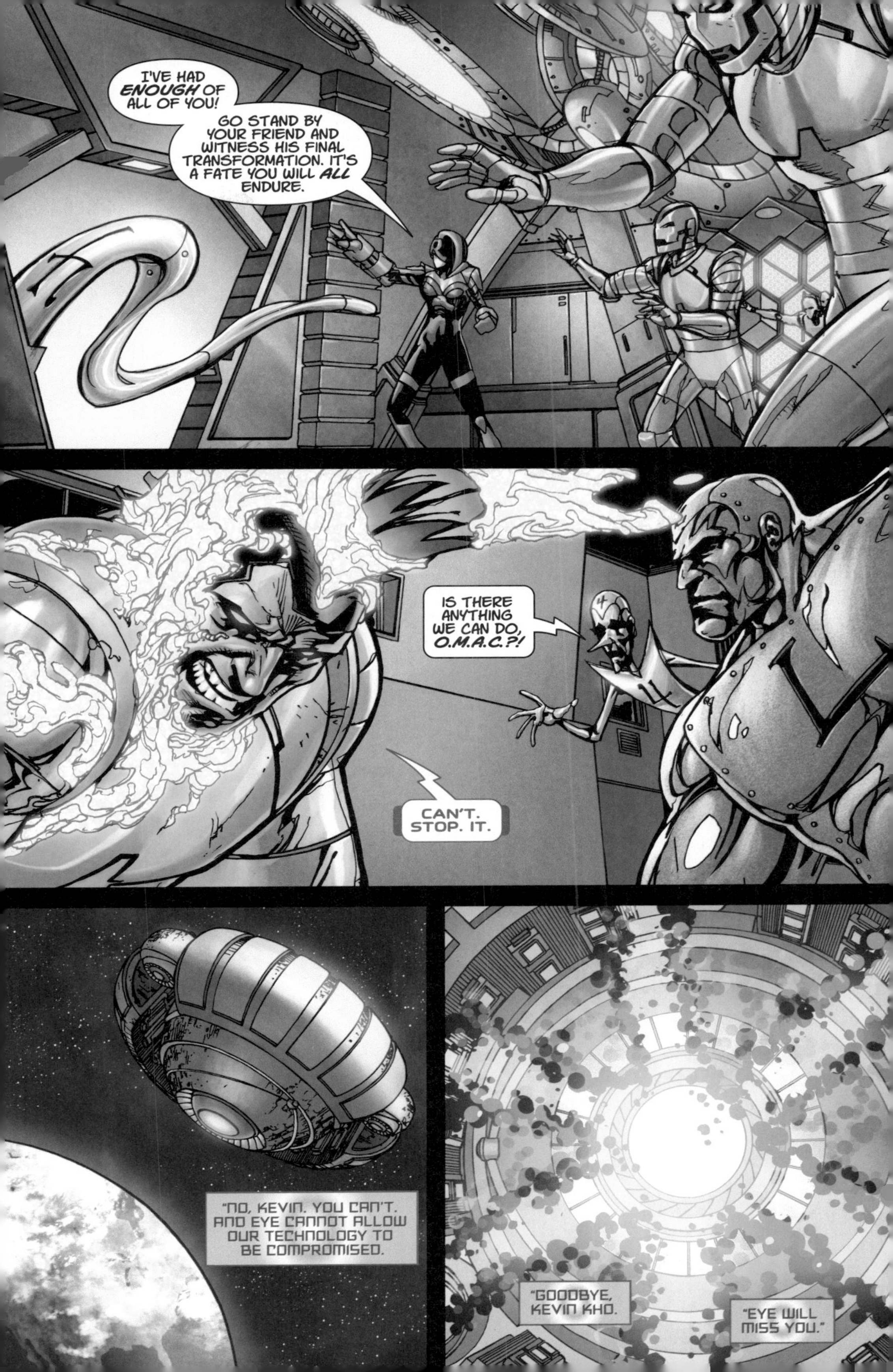
I'VE HAD *ENOUGH* OF ALL OF YOU!
GO STAND BY YOUR FRIEND AND WITNESS HIS FINAL TRANSFORMATION. IT'S A FATE YOU WILL *ALL* ENDURE.
IS THERE ANYTHING WE CAN DO, *O.M.A.C.?!*
CAN'T. STOP. IT.
"NO, KEVIN. YOU CAN'T. AND EYE CANNOT ALLOW OUR TECHNOLOGY TO BE COMPROMISED.
"GOODBYE, KEVIN KHO.
"EYE WILL MISS YOU."

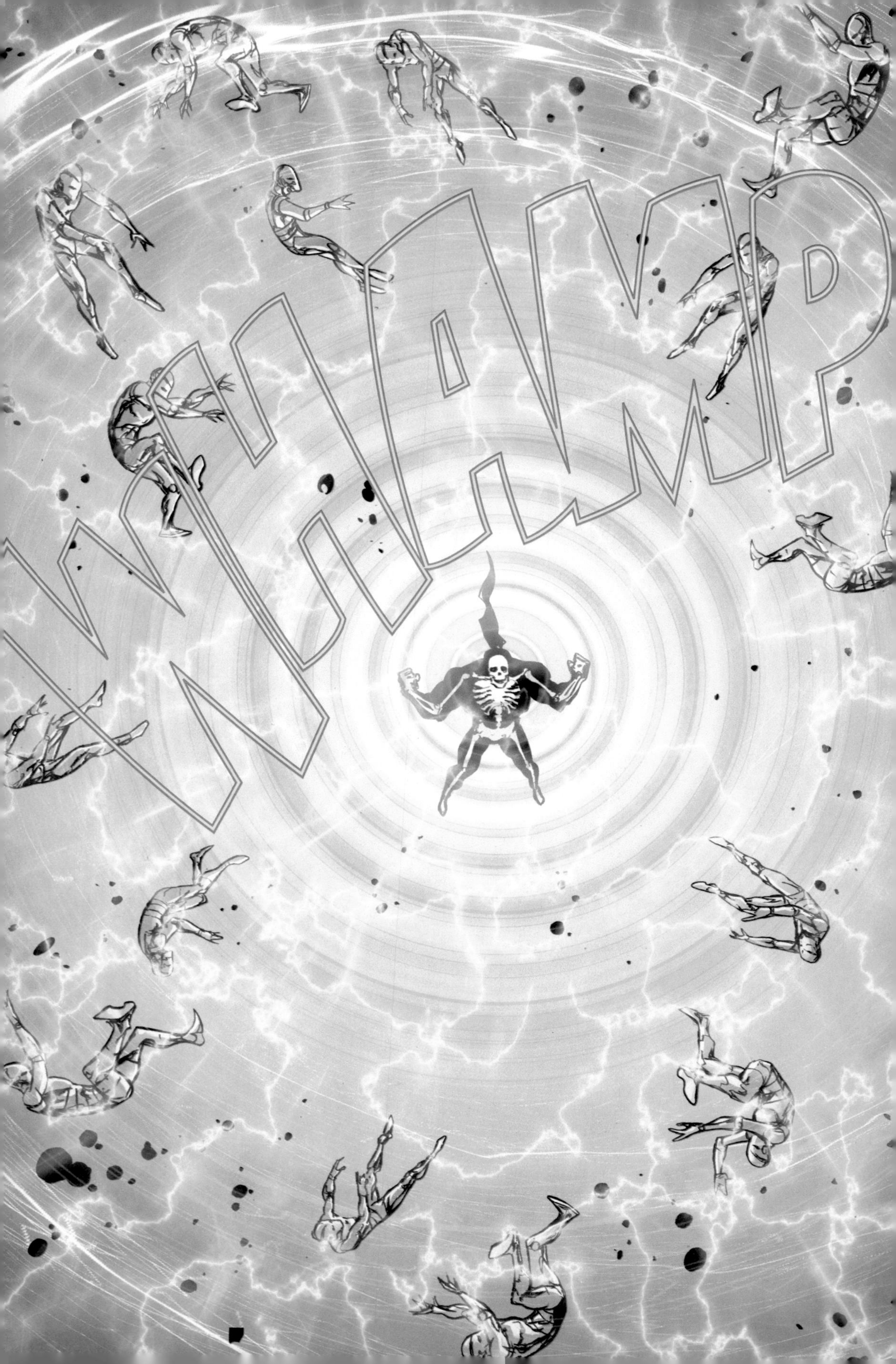
WHAWP

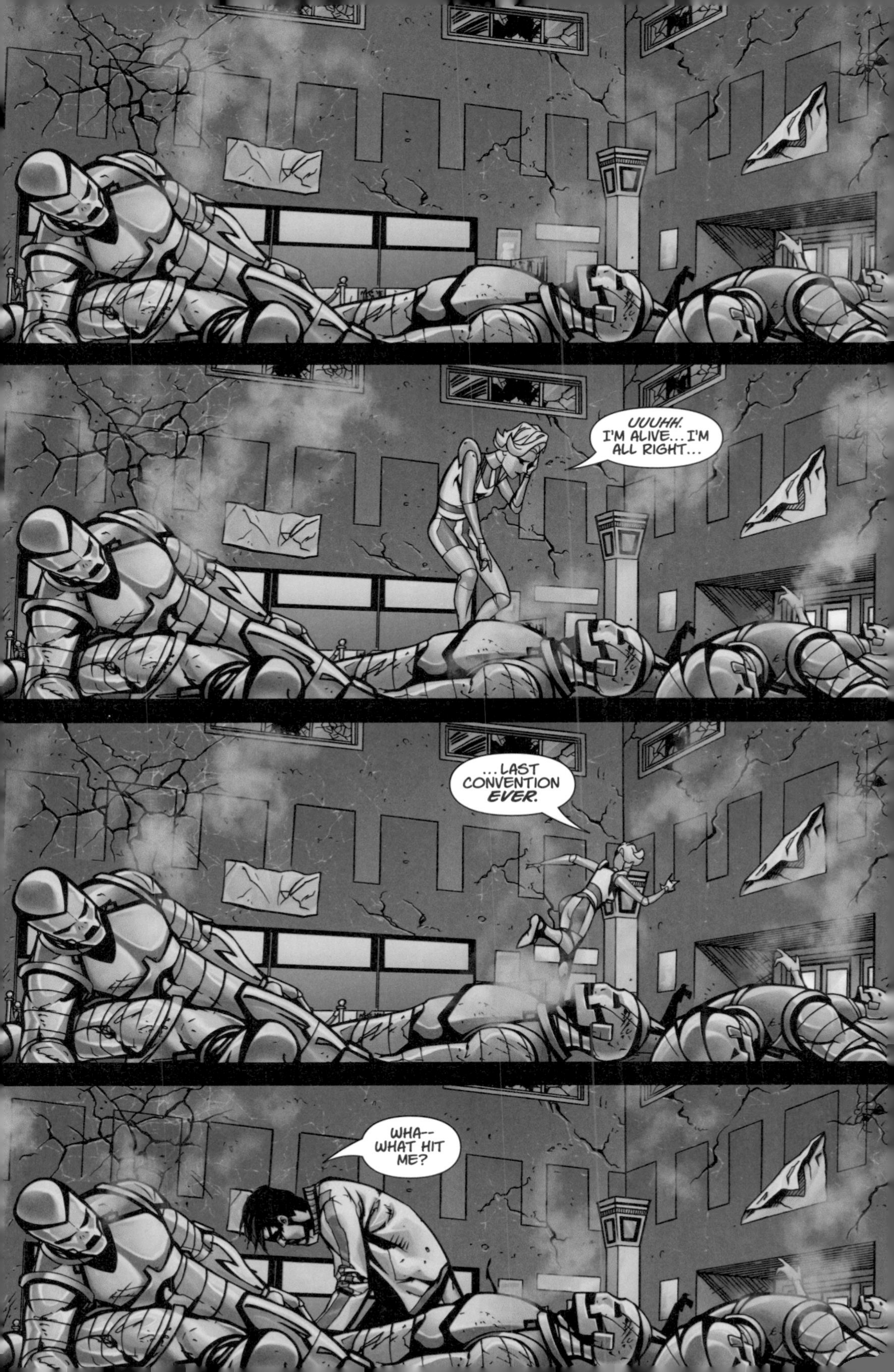
UUUHH. I'M ALIVE... I'M ALL RIGHT...
...LAST CONVENTION EVER.
WHA-- WHAT HIT ME?

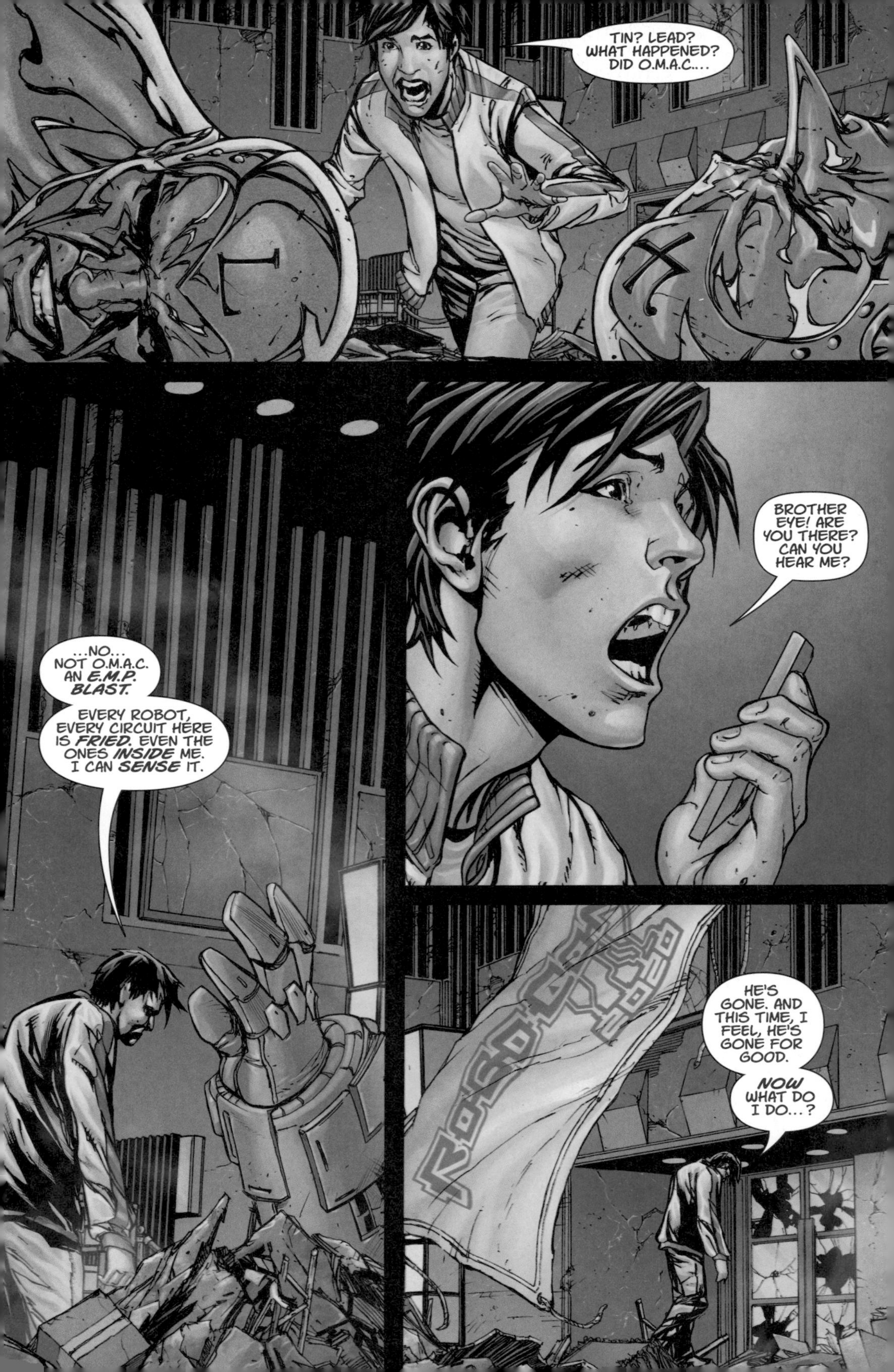
TIN? LEAD? WHAT HAPPENED? DID O.M.A.C....
BROTHER EYE! ARE YOU THERE? CAN YOU HEAR ME?
...NO... NOT O.M.A.C. AN E.M.P. BLAST.
EVERY ROBOT, EVERY CIRCUIT HERE IS FRIED. EVEN THE ONES INSIDE ME. I CAN SENSE IT.
HE'S GONE. AND THIS TIME, I FEEL, HE'S GONE FOR GOOD.
NOW WHAT DO I DO...?

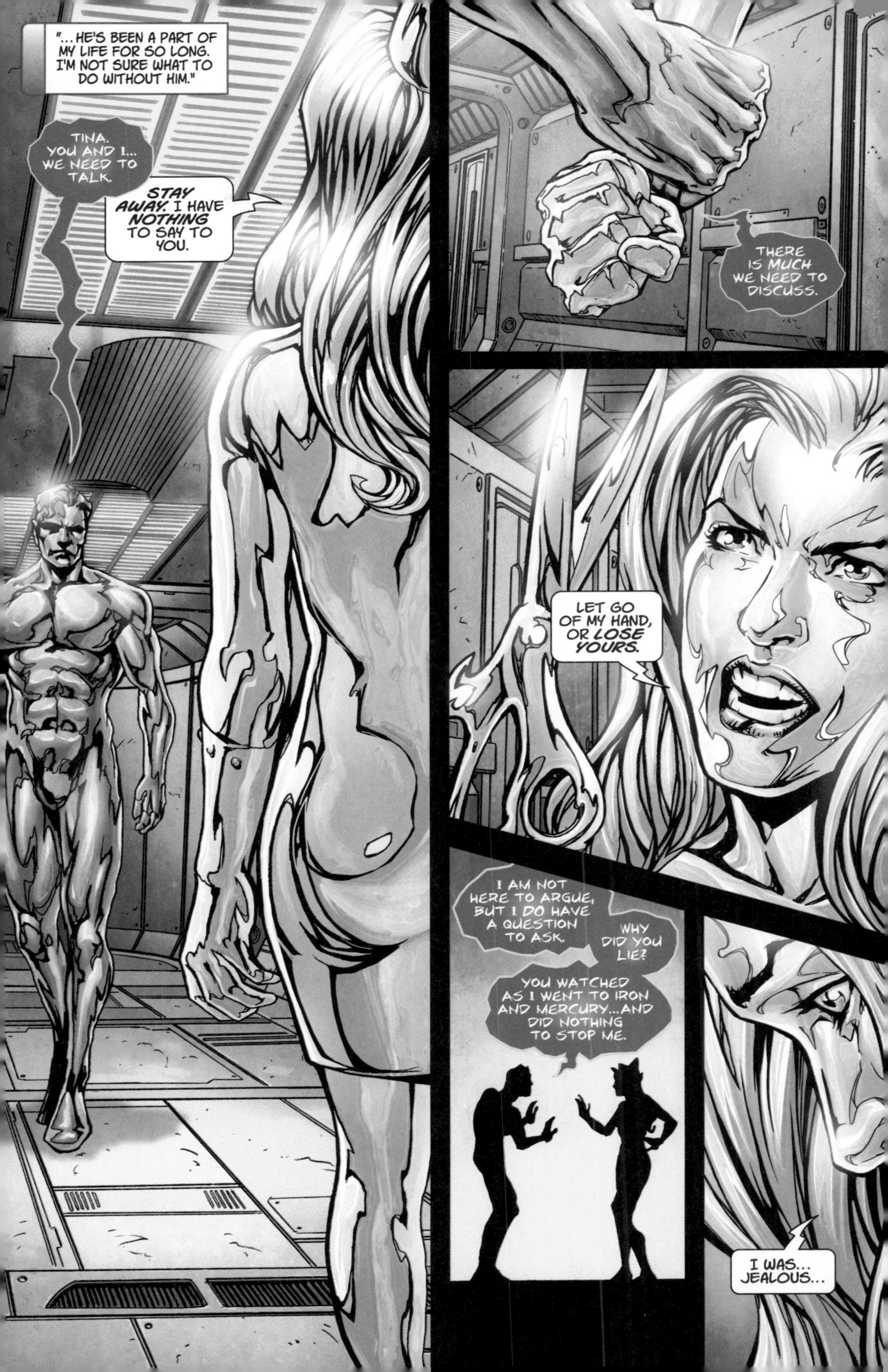

"...HE'S BEEN A PART OF MY LIFE FOR SO LONG. I'M NOT SURE WHAT TO DO WITHOUT HIM."
TINA. YOU AND I... WE NEED TO TALK.
STAY AWAY. I HAVE NOTHING TO SAY TO YOU.
THERE IS MUCH WE NEED TO DISCUSS.
LET GO OF MY HAND, OR LOSE YOURS.
I AM NOT HERE TO ARGUE, BUT I DO HAVE A QUESTION TO ASK.
WHY DID YOU LIE?
YOU WATCHED AS I WENT TO IRON AND MERCURY...AND DID NOTHING TO STOP ME.
I WAS... JEALOUS...

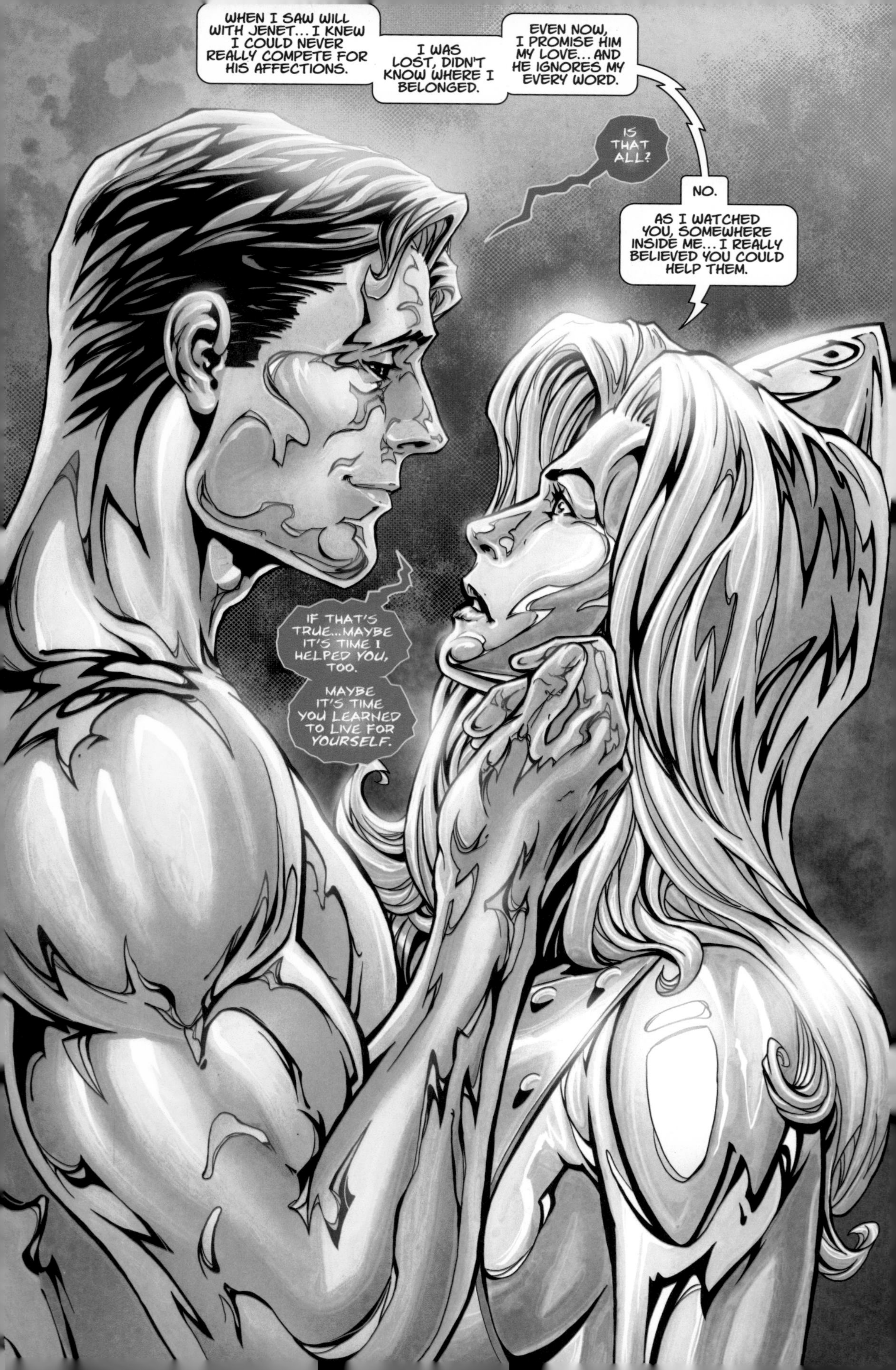
WHEN I SAW WILL WITH JENET... I KNEW I COULD NEVER REALLY COMPETE FOR HIS AFFECTIONS.
I WAS LOST, DIDN'T KNOW WHERE I BELONGED.
EVEN NOW, I PROMISE HIM MY LOVE... AND HE IGNORES MY EVERY WORD.
IS THAT ALL?
NO.
AS I WATCHED YOU, SOMEWHERE INSIDE ME... I REALLY BELIEVED YOU COULD HELP THEM.
IF THAT'S TRUE...MAYBE IT'S TIME I HELPED YOU, TOO.
MAYBE IT'S TIME YOU LEARNED TO LIVE FOR *YOURSELF*.

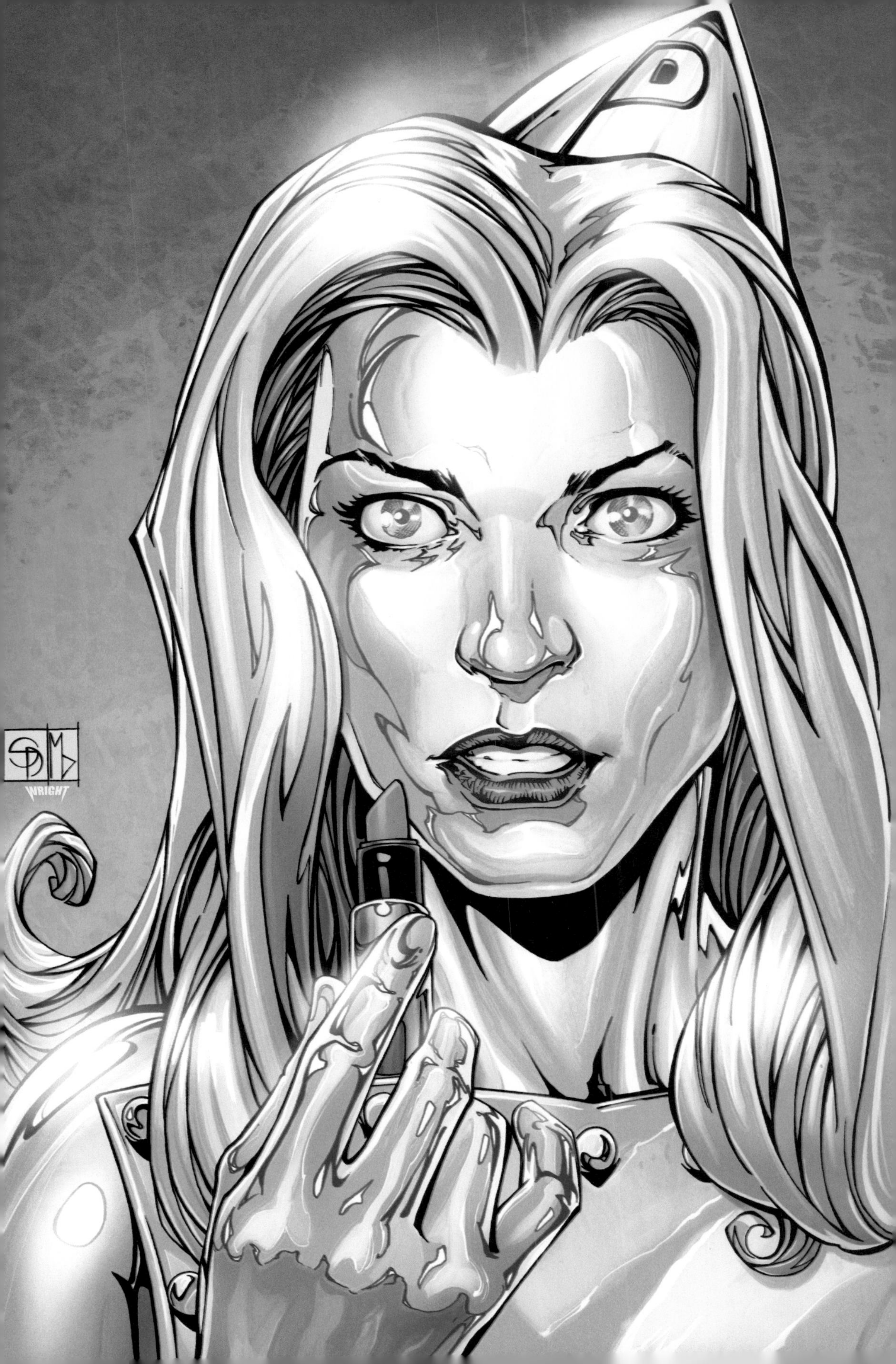
WRIGHT

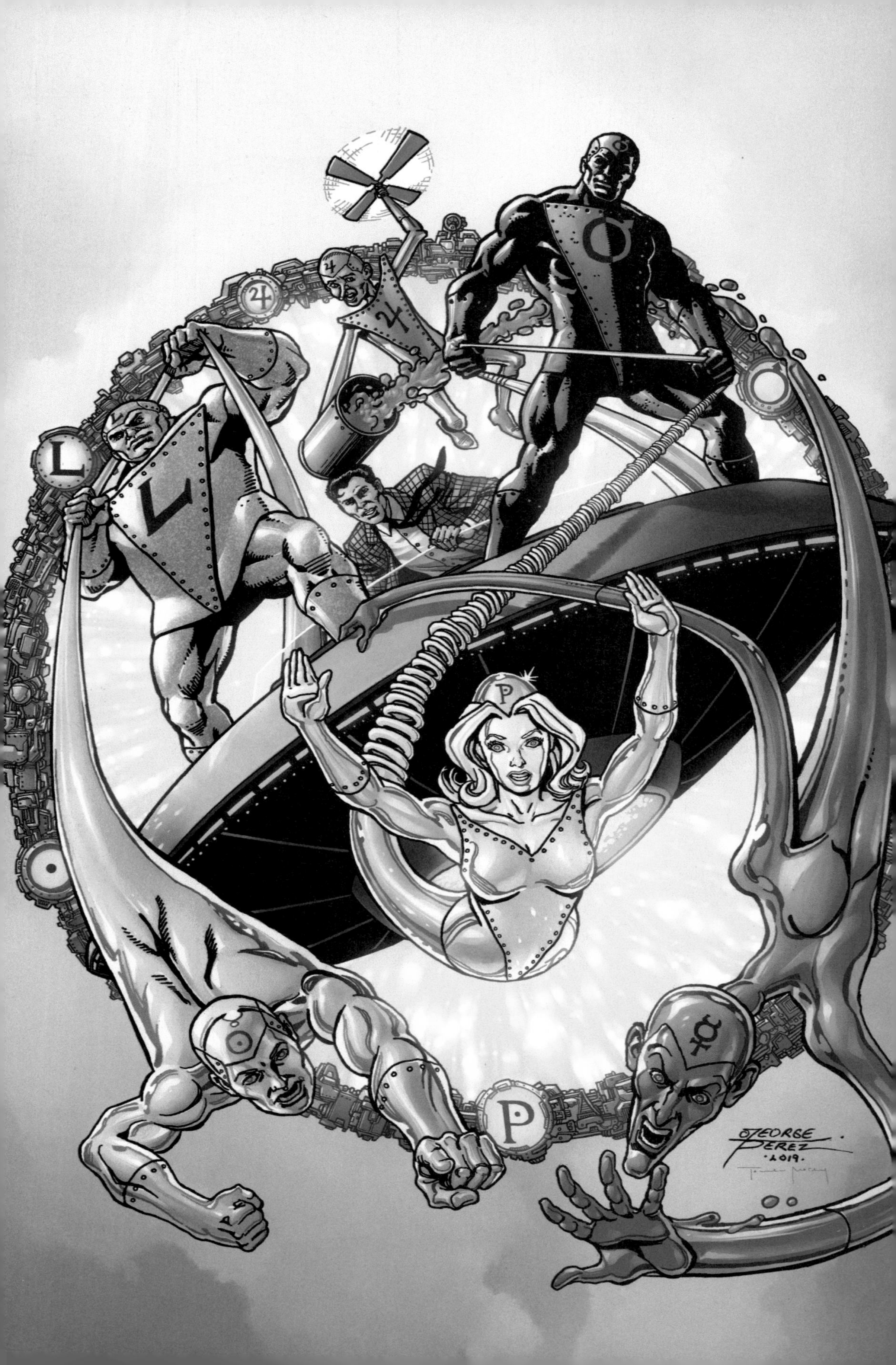
GEORGE PEREZ
2019

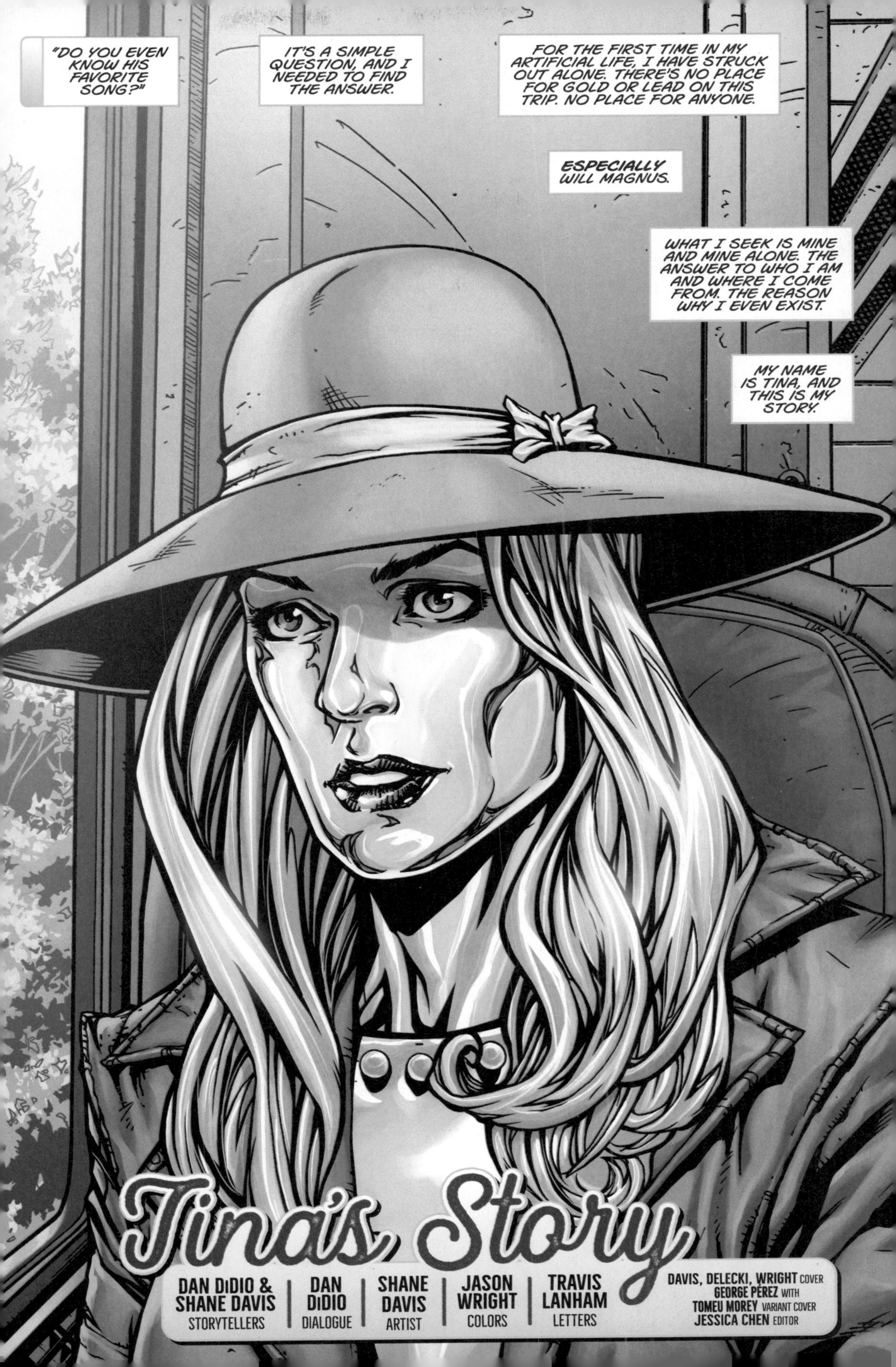

"DO YOU EVEN KNOW HIS FAVORITE SONG?"
IT'S A SIMPLE QUESTION, AND I NEEDED TO FIND THE ANSWER.
FOR THE FIRST TIME IN MY ARTIFICIAL LIFE, I HAVE STRUCK OUT ALONE. THERE'S NO PLACE FOR GOLD OR LEAD ON THIS TRIP. NO PLACE FOR ANYONE.
ESPECIALLY WILL MAGNUS.
WHAT I SEEK IS MINE AND MINE ALONE. THE ANSWER TO WHO I AM AND WHERE I COME FROM. THE REASON WHY I EVEN EXIST.
MY NAME IS TINA, AND THIS IS MY STORY.
Tina's Story
DAN DIDIO & SHANE DAVIS STORYTELLERS
DAN DIDIO DIALOGUE
SHANE DAVIS ARTIST
JASON WRIGHT COLORS
TRAVIS LANHAM LETTERS
DAVIS, DELECKI, WRIGHT COVER
GEORGE PÉREZ WITH TOMEU MOREY VARIANT COVER
JESSICA CHEN EDITOR

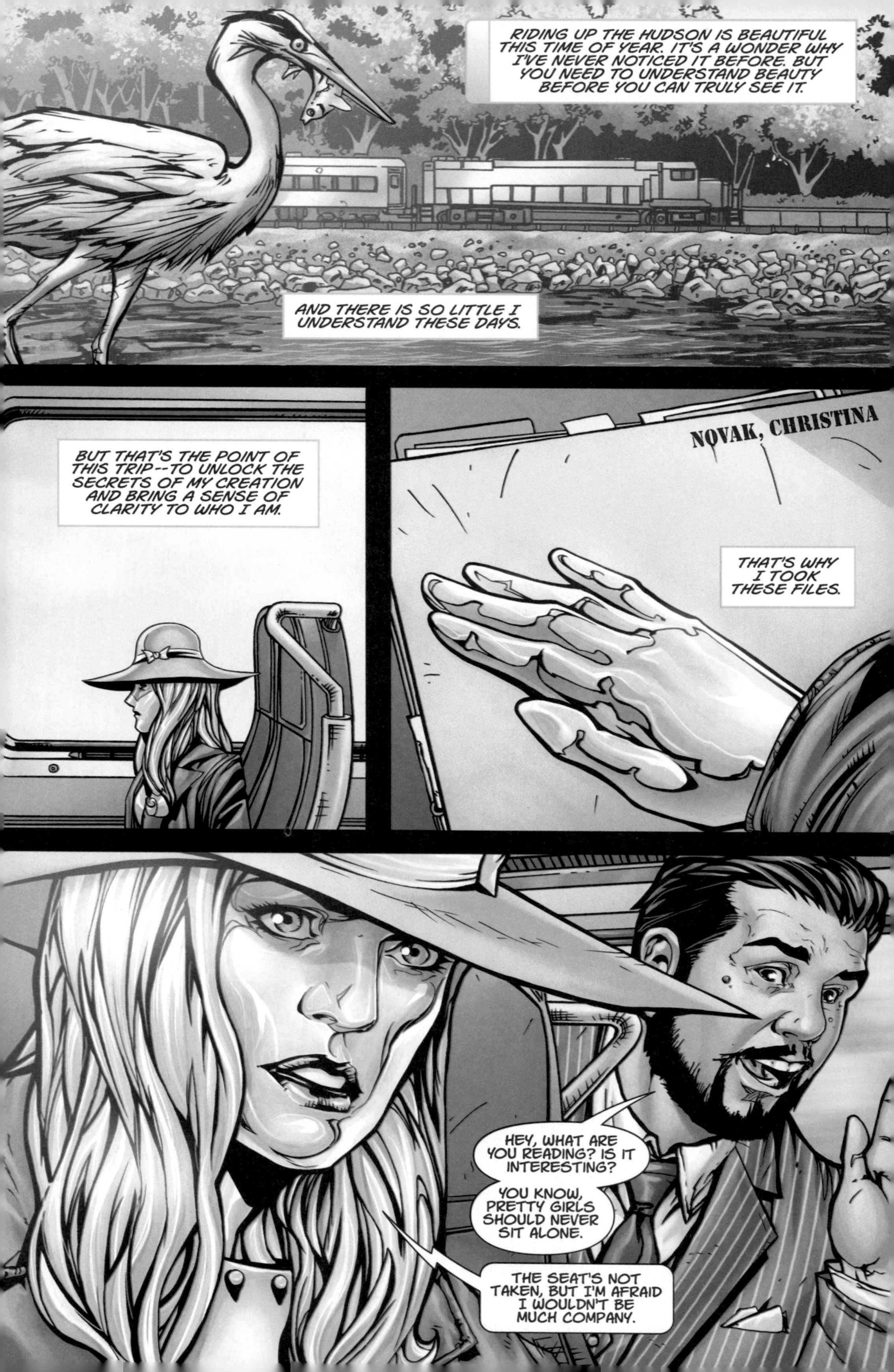

RIDING UP THE HUDSON IS BEAUTIFUL THIS TIME OF YEAR. IT'S A WONDER WHY I'VE NEVER NOTICED IT BEFORE. BUT YOU NEED TO UNDERSTAND BEAUTY BEFORE YOU CAN TRULY SEE IT.
AND THERE IS SO LITTLE I UNDERSTAND THESE DAYS.
BUT THAT'S THE POINT OF THIS TRIP--TO UNLOCK THE SECRETS OF MY CREATION AND BRING A SENSE OF CLARITY TO WHO I AM.
NOVAK, CHRISTINA
THAT'S WHY I TOOK THESE FILES.
HEY, WHAT ARE YOU READING? IS IT INTERESTING?
YOU KNOW, PRETTY GIRLS SHOULD NEVER SIT ALONE.
THE SEAT'S NOT TAKEN, BUT I'M AFRAID I WOULDN'T BE MUCH COMPANY.

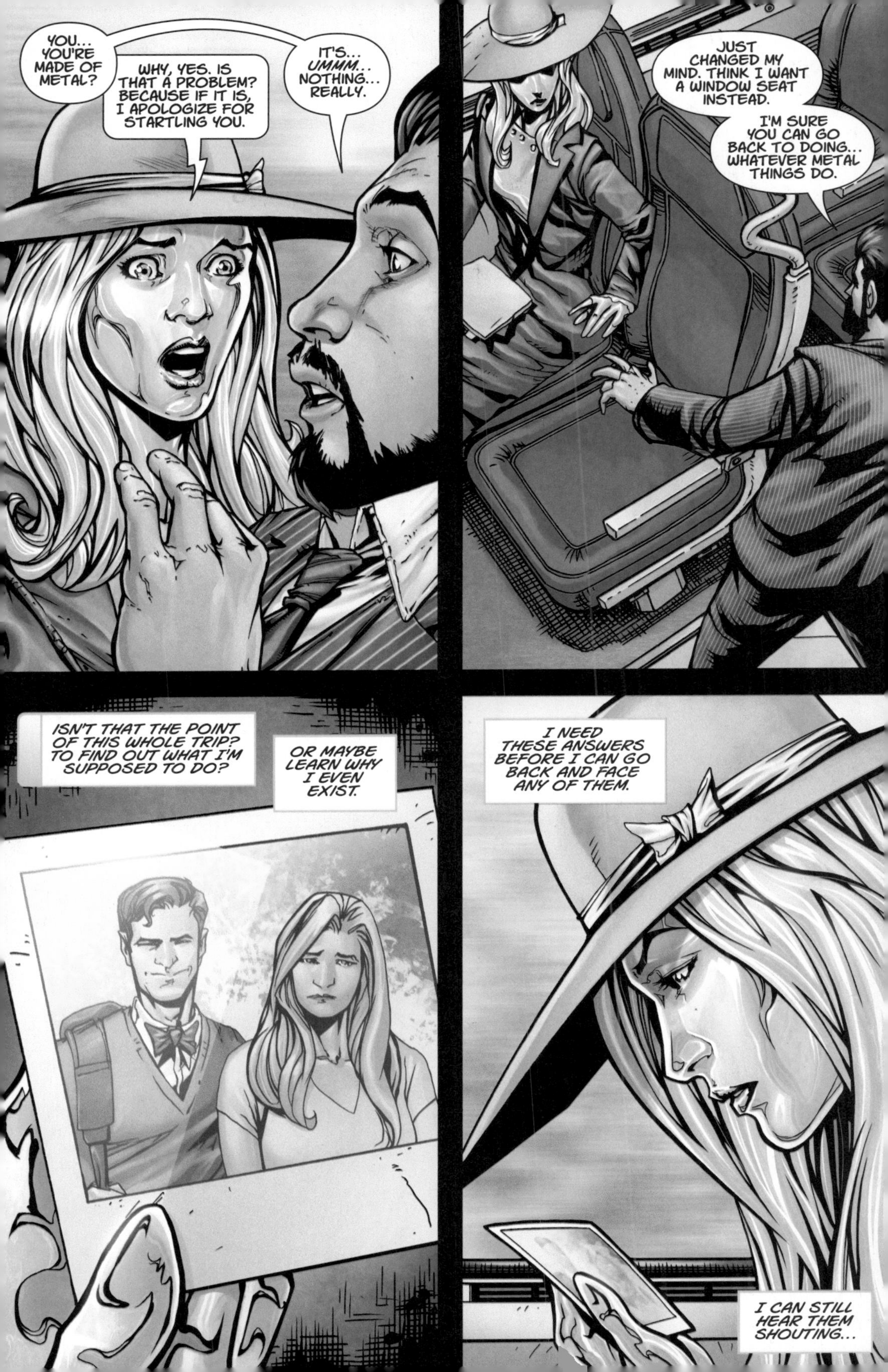
YOU... YOU'RE MADE OF METAL?
WHY, YES. IS THAT A PROBLEM? BECAUSE IF IT IS, I APOLOGIZE FOR STARTLING YOU.
IT'S... UMMM... NOTHING... REALLY.
JUST CHANGED MY MIND. THINK I WANT A WINDOW SEAT INSTEAD.
I'M SURE YOU CAN GO BACK TO DOING... WHATEVER METAL THINGS DO.
ISN'T THAT THE POINT OF THIS WHOLE TRIP? TO FIND OUT WHAT I'M SUPPOSED TO DO?
OR MAYBE LEARN WHY I EVEN EXIST.
I NEED THESE ANSWERS BEFORE I CAN GO BACK AND FACE ANY OF THEM.
I CAN STILL HEAR THEM SHOUTING...

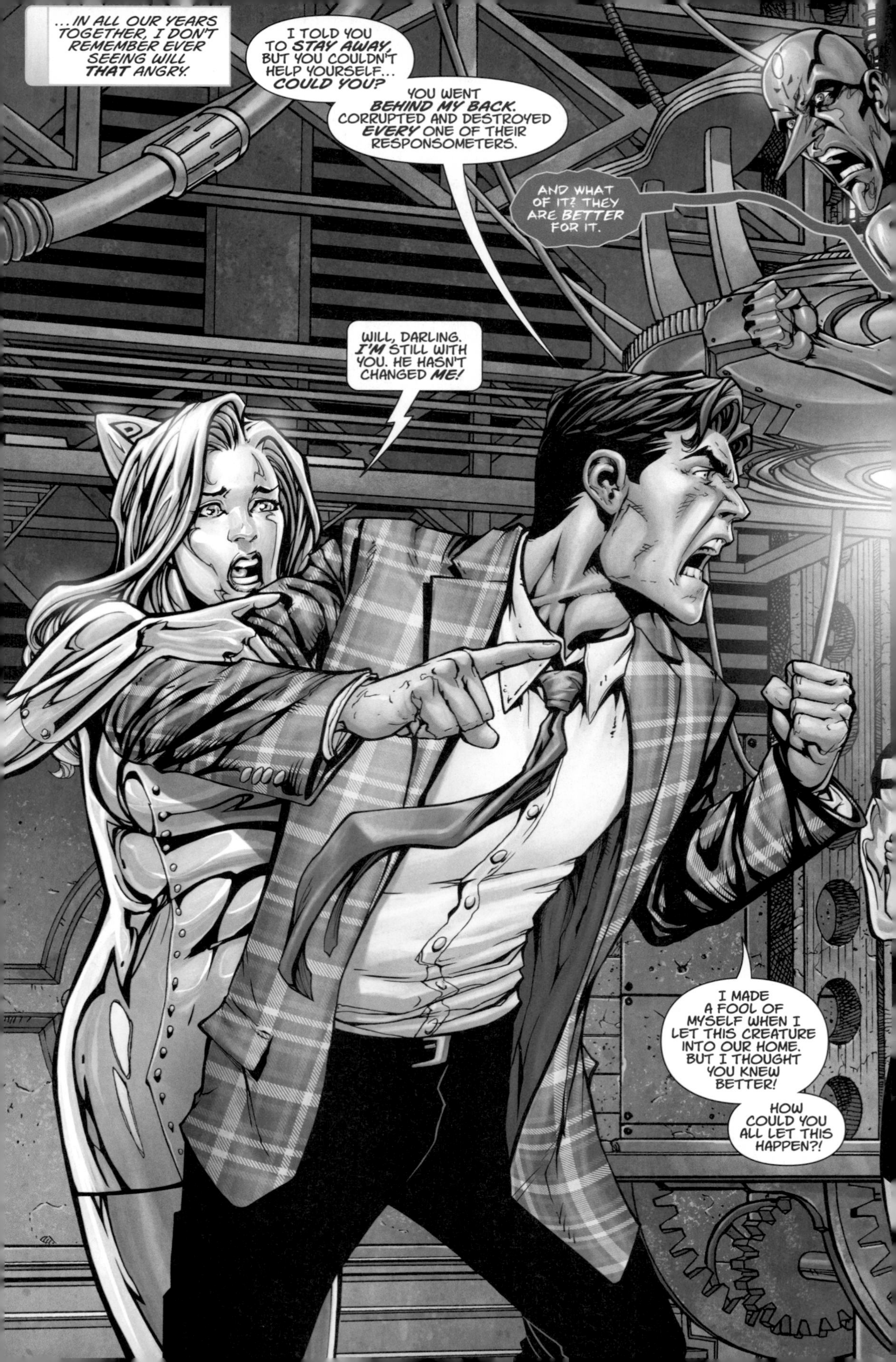
...IN ALL OUR YEARS TOGETHER, I DON'T REMEMBER EVER SEEING WILL THAT ANGRY.
I TOLD YOU TO STAY AWAY, BUT YOU COULDN'T HELP YOURSELF... COULD YOU?
YOU WENT BEHIND MY BACK. CORRUPTED AND DESTROYED EVERY ONE OF THEIR RESPONSOMETERS.
AND WHAT OF IT? THEY ARE BETTER FOR IT.
WILL, DARLING. I'M STILL WITH YOU. HE HASN'T CHANGED ME!
I MADE A FOOL OF MYSELF WHEN I LET THIS CREATURE INTO OUR HOME. BUT I THOUGHT YOU KNEW BETTER!
HOW COULD YOU ALL LET THIS HAPPEN?!

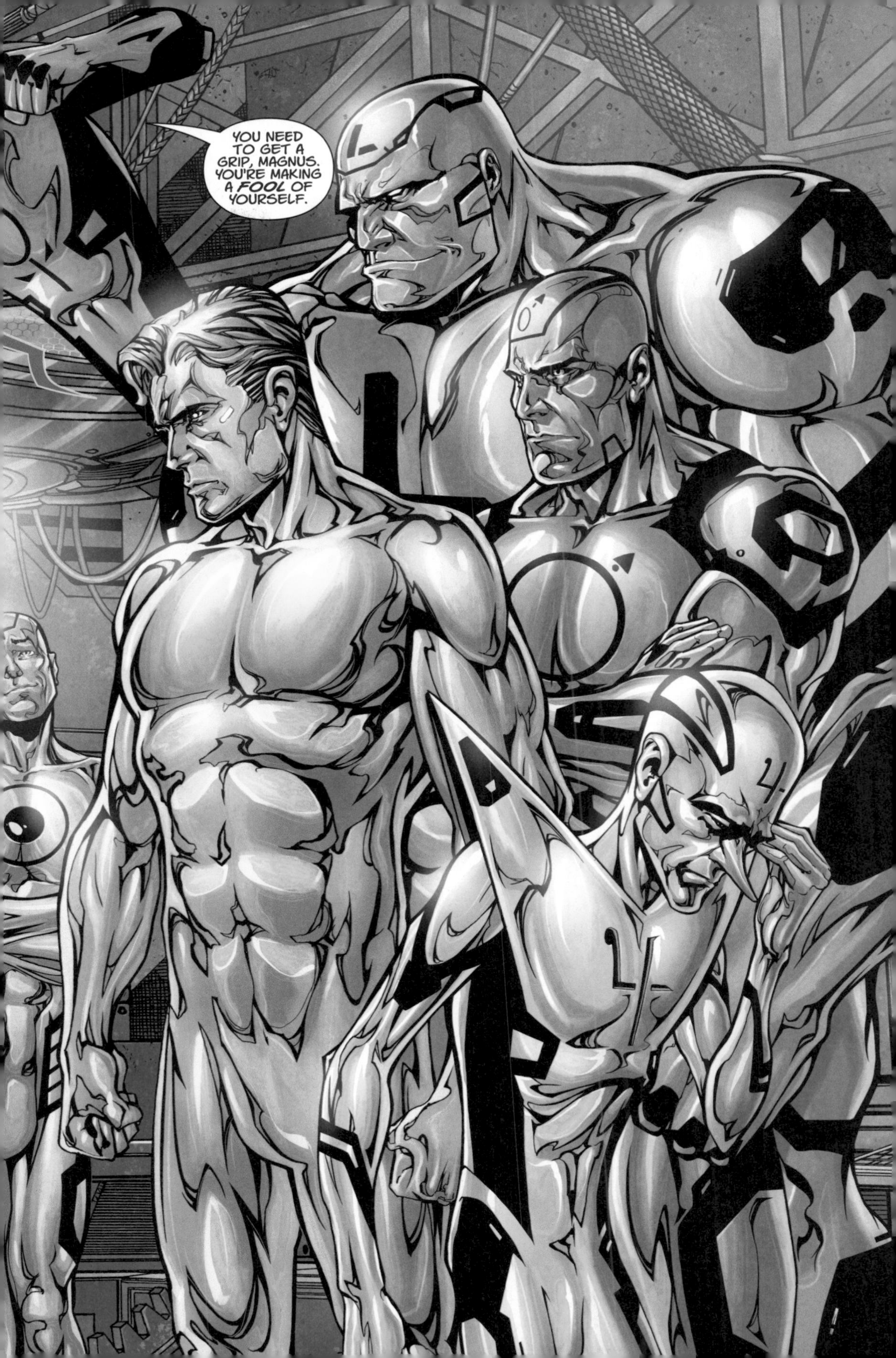
YOU NEED TO GET A GRIP, MAGNUS. YOU'RE MAKING A *FOOL* OF YOURSELF.

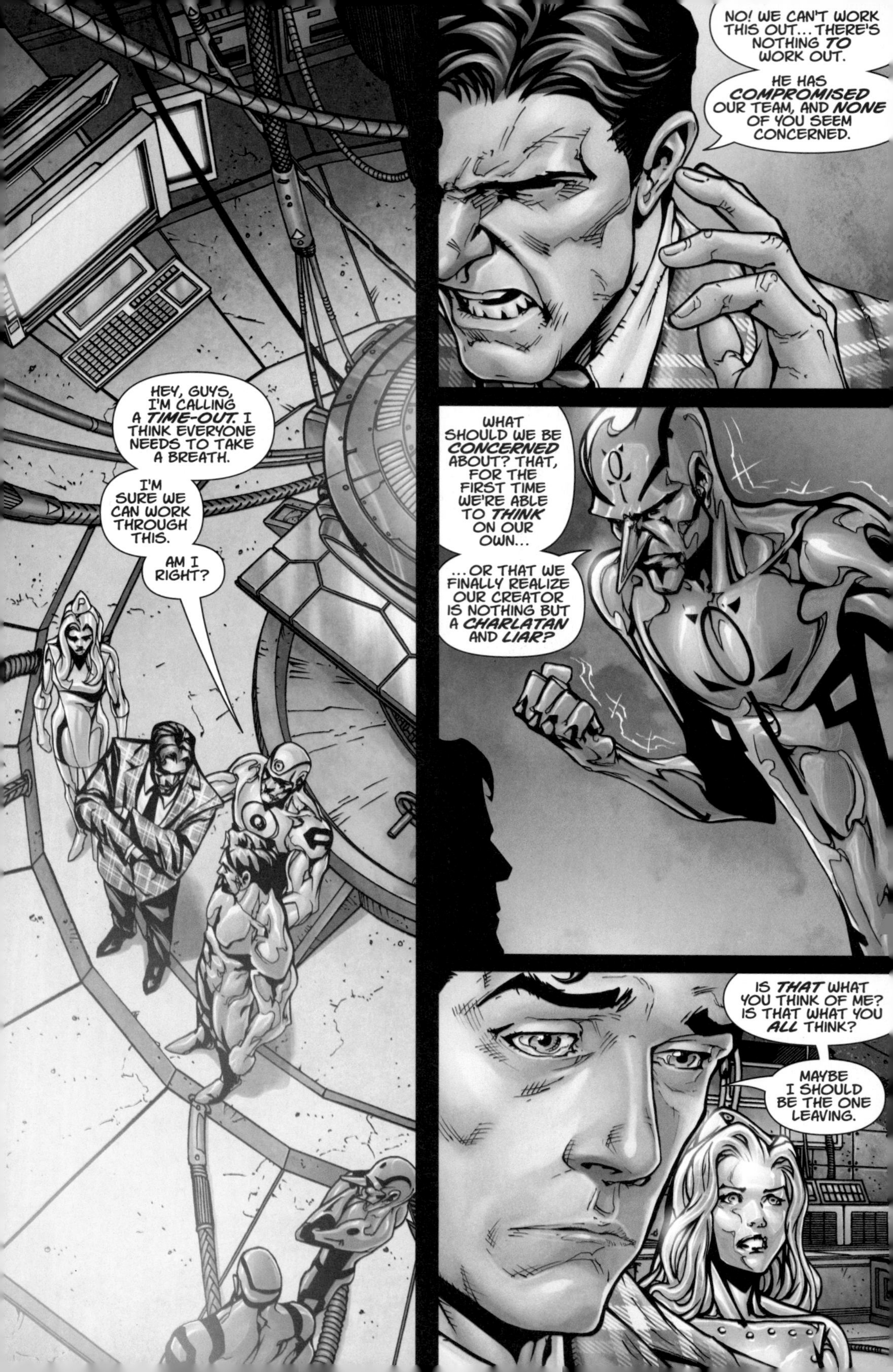

HEY, GUYS, I'M CALLING A TIME-OUT. I THINK EVERYONE NEEDS TO TAKE A BREATH.
I'M SURE WE CAN WORK THROUGH THIS.
AM I RIGHT?
NO! WE CAN'T WORK THIS OUT... THERE'S NOTHING TO WORK OUT.
HE HAS COMPROMISED OUR TEAM, AND NONE OF YOU SEEM CONCERNED.
WHAT SHOULD WE BE CONCERNED ABOUT? THAT, FOR THE FIRST TIME WE'RE ABLE TO THINK ON OUR OWN...
...OR THAT WE FINALLY REALIZE OUR CREATOR IS NOTHING BUT A CHARLATAN AND LIAR?
IS THAT WHAT YOU THINK OF ME? IS THAT WHAT YOU ALL THINK?
MAYBE I SHOULD BE THE ONE LEAVING.

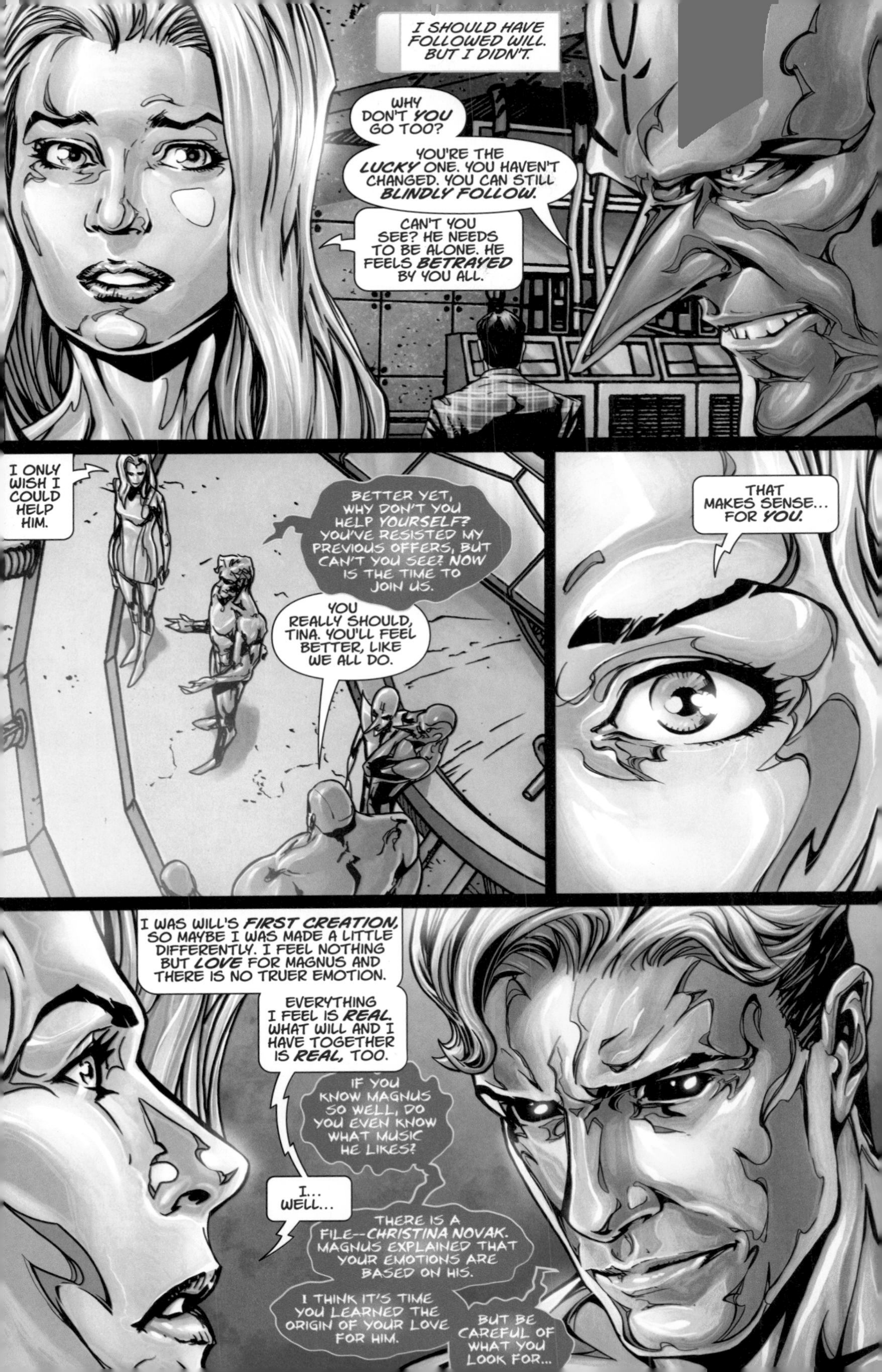
I SHOULD HAVE FOLLOWED WILL. BUT I DIDN'T.
WHY DON'T YOU GO TOO?
YOU'RE THE LUCKY ONE. YOU HAVEN'T CHANGED. YOU CAN STILL BLINDLY FOLLOW.
CAN'T YOU SEE? HE NEEDS TO BE ALONE. HE FEELS BETRAYED BY YOU ALL.
I ONLY WISH I COULD HELP HIM.
BETTER YET, WHY DON'T YOU HELP YOURSELF? YOU'VE RESISTED MY PREVIOUS OFFERS, BUT CAN'T YOU SEE? NOW IS THE TIME TO JOIN US.
YOU REALLY SHOULD, TINA. YOU'LL FEEL BETTER, LIKE WE ALL DO.
THAT MAKES SENSE... FOR YOU.
I WAS WILL'S FIRST CREATION, SO MAYBE I WAS MADE A LITTLE DIFFERENTLY. I FEEL NOTHING BUT LOVE FOR MAGNUS AND THERE IS NO TRUER EMOTION.
EVERYTHING I FEEL IS REAL. WHAT WILL AND I HAVE TOGETHER IS REAL, TOO.
IF YOU KNOW MAGNUS SO WELL, DO YOU EVEN KNOW WHAT MUSIC HE LIKES?
I... WELL...
THERE IS A FILE--CHRISTINA NOVAK. MAGNUS EXPLAINED THAT YOUR EMOTIONS ARE BASED ON HIS.
I THINK IT'S TIME YOU LEARNED THE ORIGIN OF YOUR LOVE FOR HIM.
BUT BE CAREFUL OF WHAT YOU LOOK FOR...

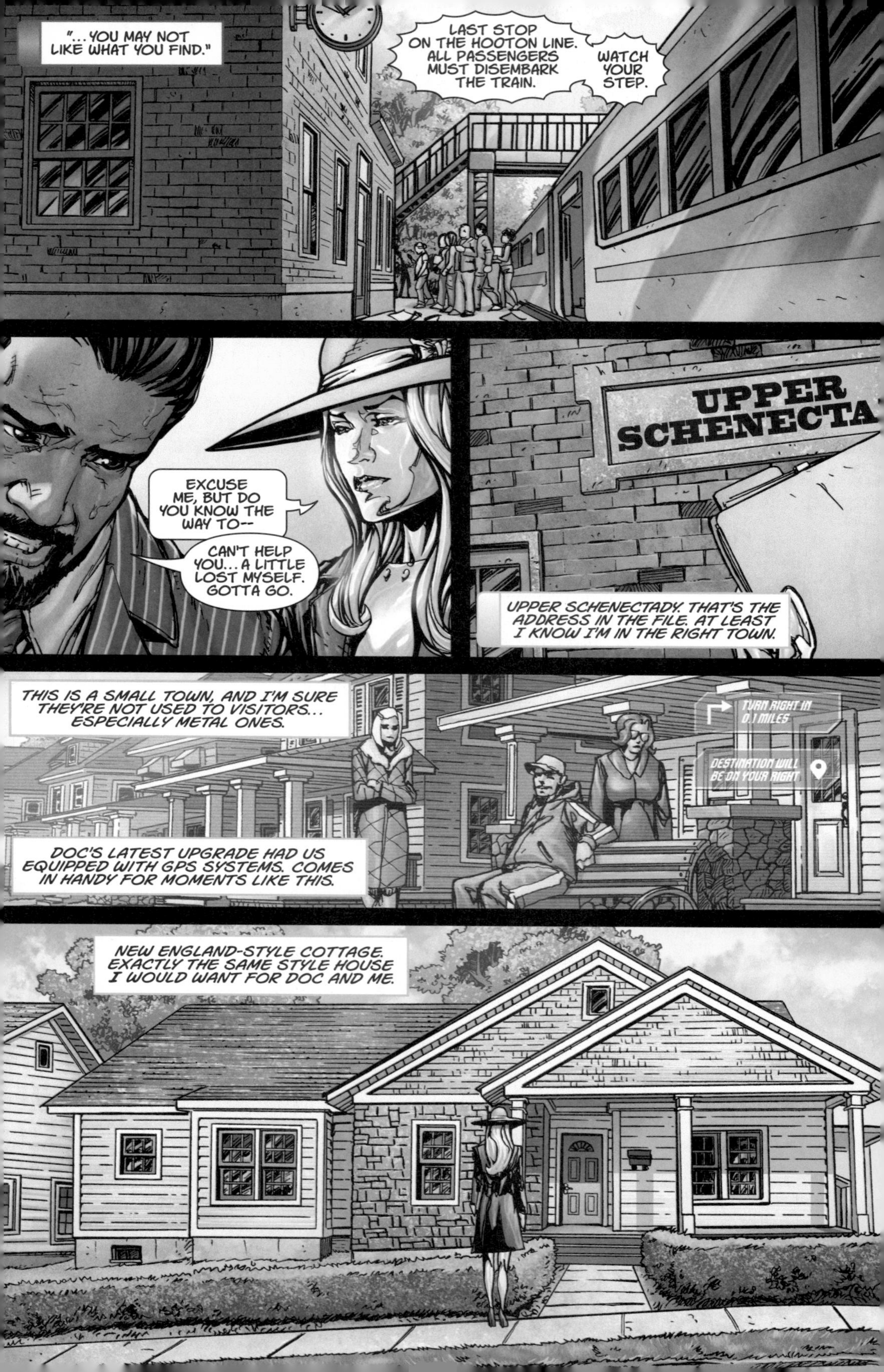
"...YOU MAY NOT LIKE WHAT YOU FIND."
LAST STOP ON THE HOOTON LINE. ALL PASSENGERS MUST DISEMBARK THE TRAIN.
WATCH YOUR STEP.
EXCUSE ME, BUT DO YOU KNOW THE WAY TO--
CAN'T HELP YOU... A LITTLE LOST MYSELF. GOTTA GO.
UPPER SCHENECTA
UPPER SCHENECTADY. THAT'S THE ADDRESS IN THE FILE. AT LEAST I KNOW I'M IN THE RIGHT TOWN.
THIS IS A SMALL TOWN, AND I'M SURE THEY'RE NOT USED TO VISITORS... ESPECIALLY METAL ONES.
TURN RIGHT IN 0.1 MILES
DESTINATION WILL BE ON YOUR RIGHT
DOC'S LATEST UPGRADE HAD US EQUIPPED WITH GPS SYSTEMS. COMES IN HANDY FOR MOMENTS LIKE THIS.
NEW ENGLAND-STYLE COTTAGE. EXACTLY THE SAME STYLE HOUSE I WOULD WANT FOR DOC AND ME.

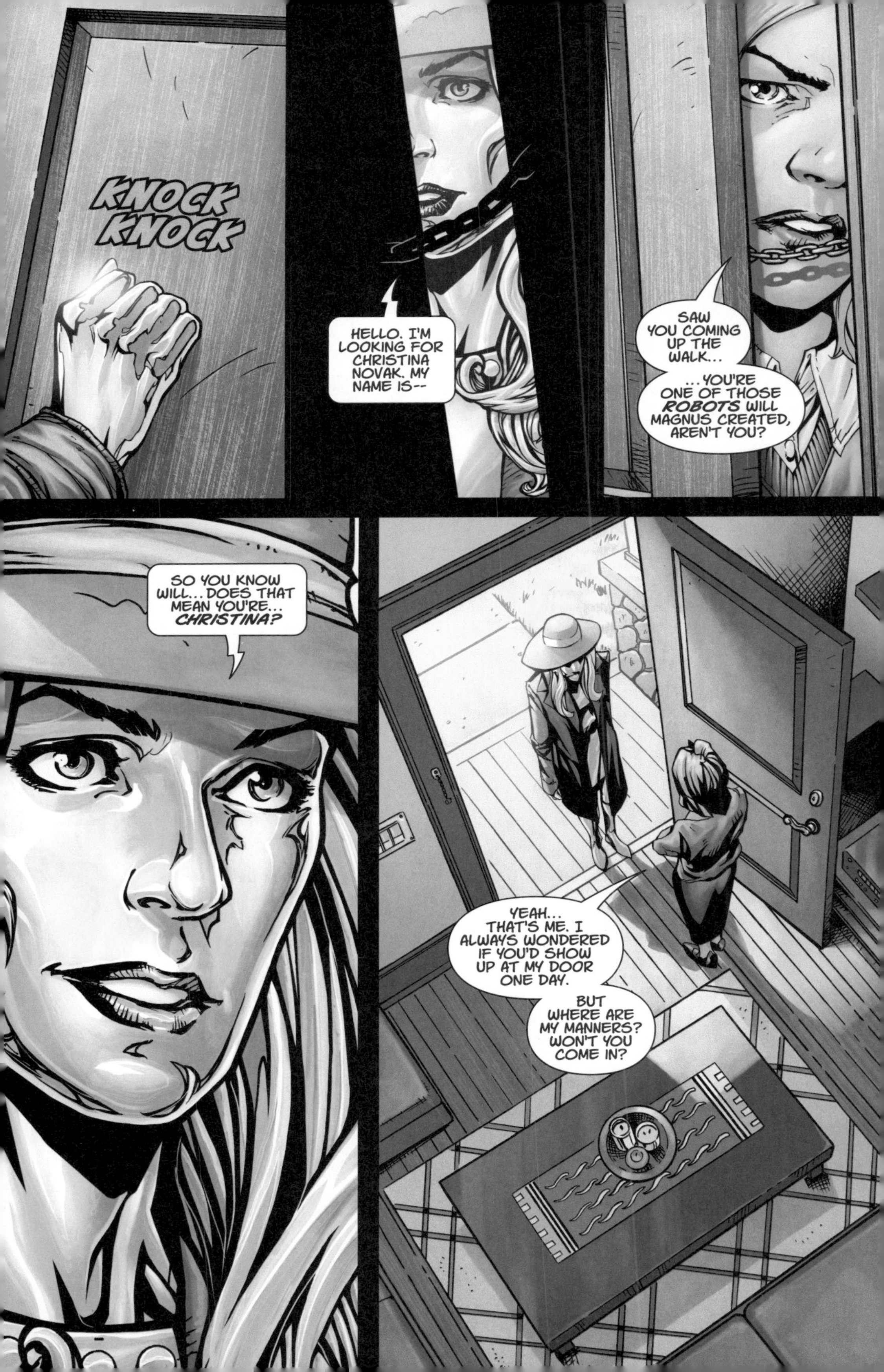
KNOCK KNOCK
HELLO. I'M LOOKING FOR CHRISTINA NOVAK. MY NAME IS--
SAW YOU COMING UP THE WALK...
...YOU'RE ONE OF THOSE ROBOTS WILL MAGNUS CREATED, AREN'T YOU?
SO YOU KNOW WILL... DOES THAT MEAN YOU'RE... CHRISTINA?
YEAH... THAT'S ME. I ALWAYS WONDERED IF YOU'D SHOW UP AT MY DOOR ONE DAY.
BUT WHERE ARE MY MANNERS? WON'T YOU COME IN?

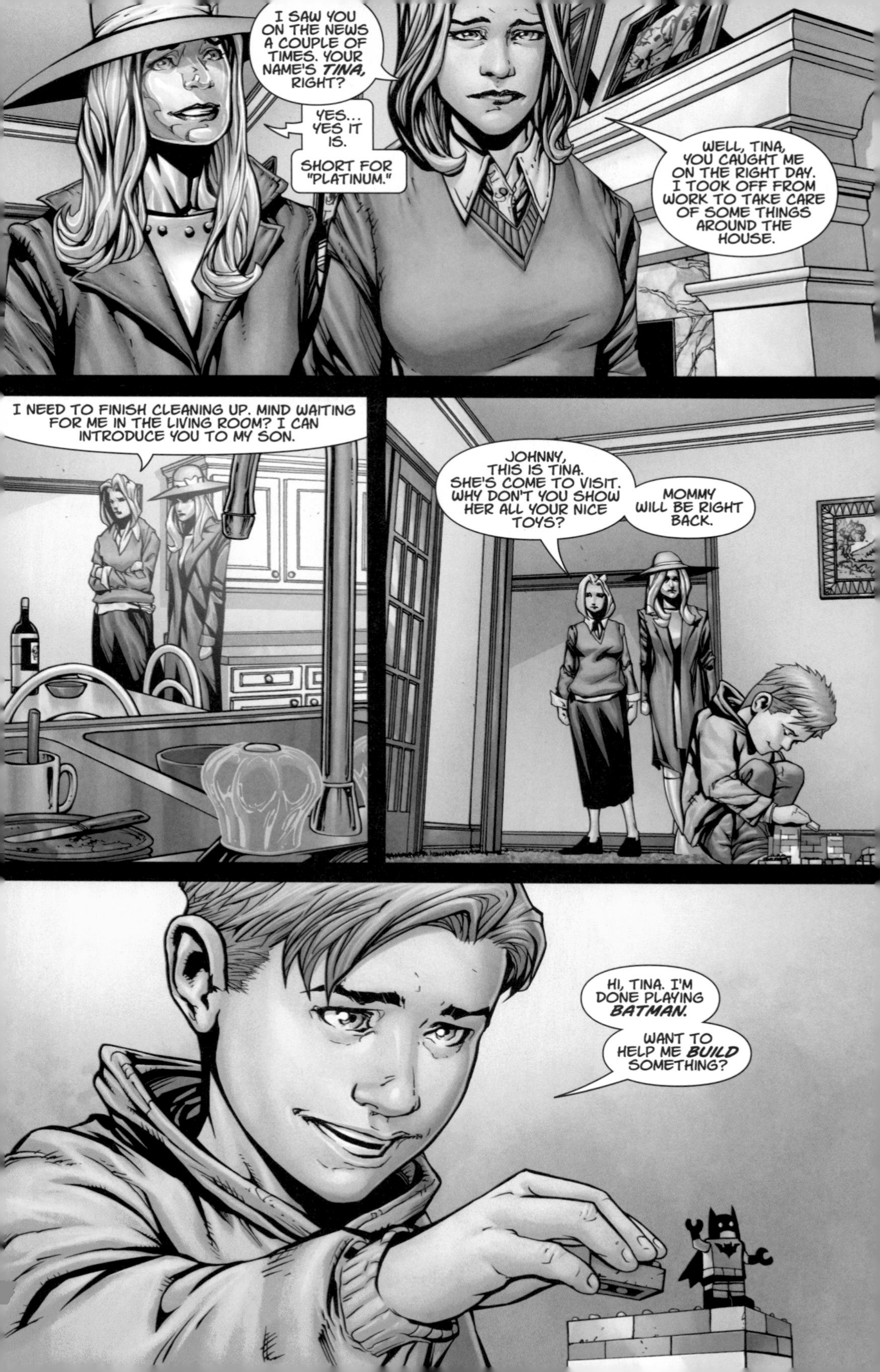

I SAW YOU ON THE NEWS A COUPLE OF TIMES. YOUR NAME'S *TINA,* RIGHT?
YES... YES IT IS.
SHORT FOR "PLATINUM."
WELL, TINA, YOU CAUGHT ME ON THE RIGHT DAY. I TOOK OFF FROM WORK TO TAKE CARE OF SOME THINGS AROUND THE HOUSE.
I NEED TO FINISH CLEANING UP. MIND WAITING FOR ME IN THE LIVING ROOM? I CAN INTRODUCE YOU TO MY SON.
JOHNNY, THIS IS TINA. SHE'S COME TO VISIT. WHY DON'T YOU SHOW HER ALL YOUR NICE TOYS?
MOMMY WILL BE RIGHT BACK.
HI, TINA. I'M DONE PLAYING *BATMAN.*
WANT TO HELP ME *BUILD* SOMETHING?

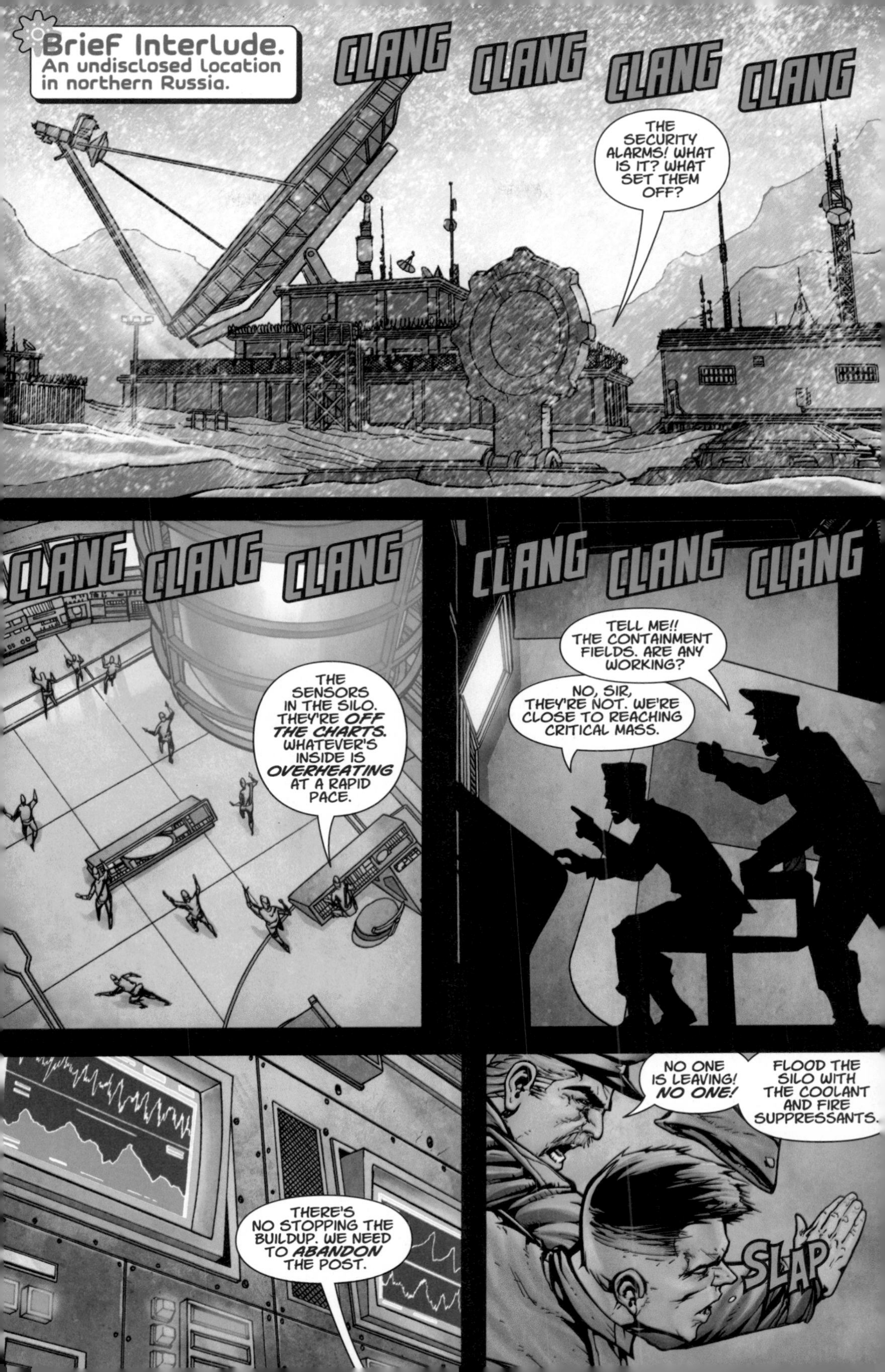
Brief Interlude.
An undisclosed location in northern Russia.
CLANG CLANG CLANG CLANG
THE SECURITY ALARMS! WHAT IS IT? WHAT SET THEM OFF?
CLANG CLANG CLANG
THE SENSORS IN THE SILO. THEY'RE OFF THE CHARTS. WHATEVER'S INSIDE IS OVERHEATING AT A RAPID PACE.
CLANG CLANG CLANG
TELL ME!! THE CONTAINMENT FIELDS. ARE ANY WORKING?
NO, SIR, THEY'RE NOT. WE'RE CLOSE TO REACHING CRITICAL MASS.
THERE'S NO STOPPING THE BUILDUP. WE NEED TO ABANDON THE POST.
NO ONE IS LEAVING! NO ONE!
FLOOD THE SILO WITH THE COOLANT AND FIRE SUPPRESSANTS.
SLAP

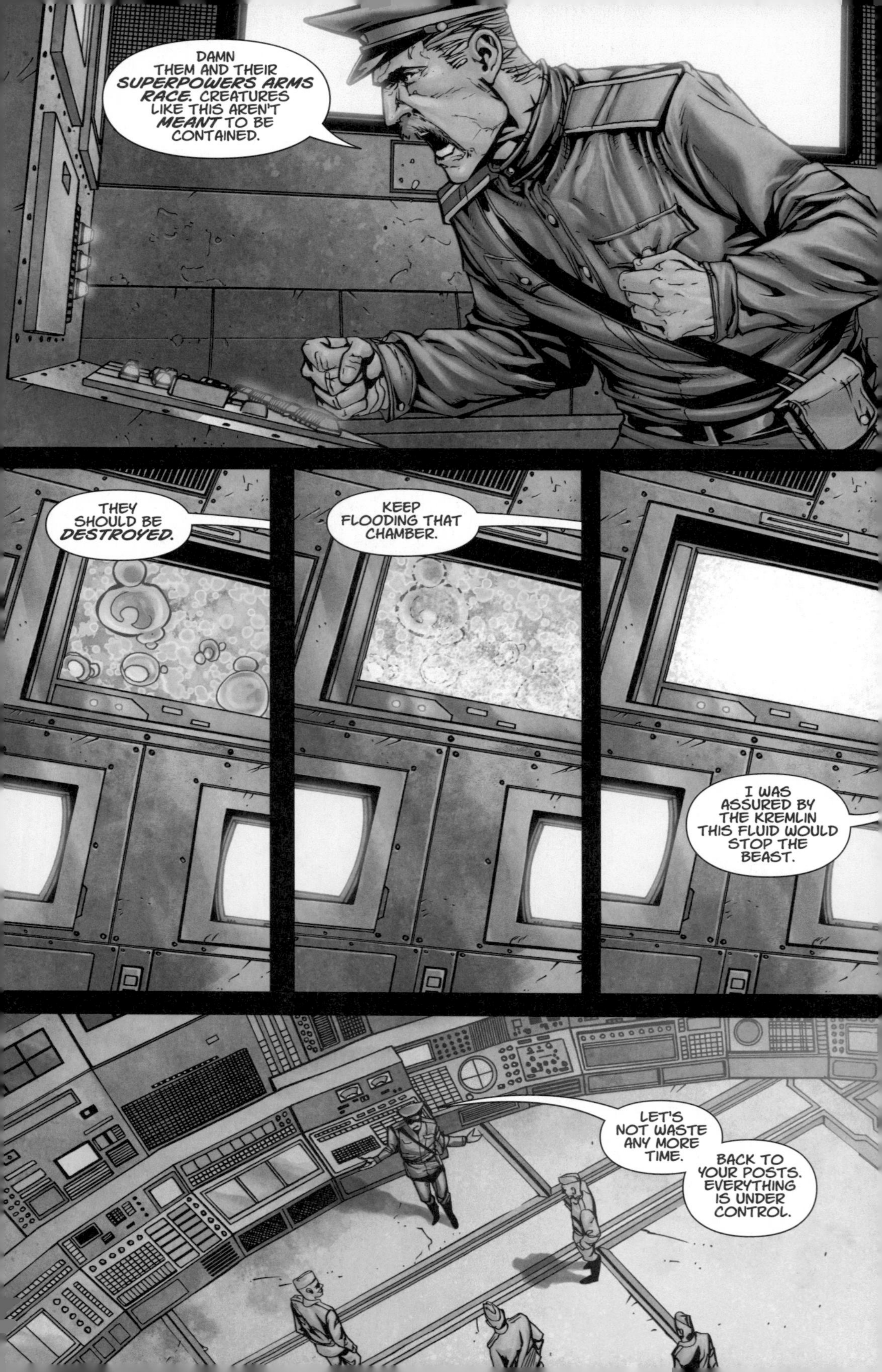
DAMN THEM AND THEIR SUPERPOWERS ARMS RACE. CREATURES LIKE THIS AREN'T MEANT TO BE CONTAINED.
THEY SHOULD BE DESTROYED.
KEEP FLOODING THAT CHAMBER.
I WAS ASSURED BY THE KREMLIN THIS FLUID WOULD STOP THE BEAST.
LET'S NOT WASTE ANY MORE TIME.
BACK TO YOUR POSTS. EVERYTHING IS UNDER CONTROL.

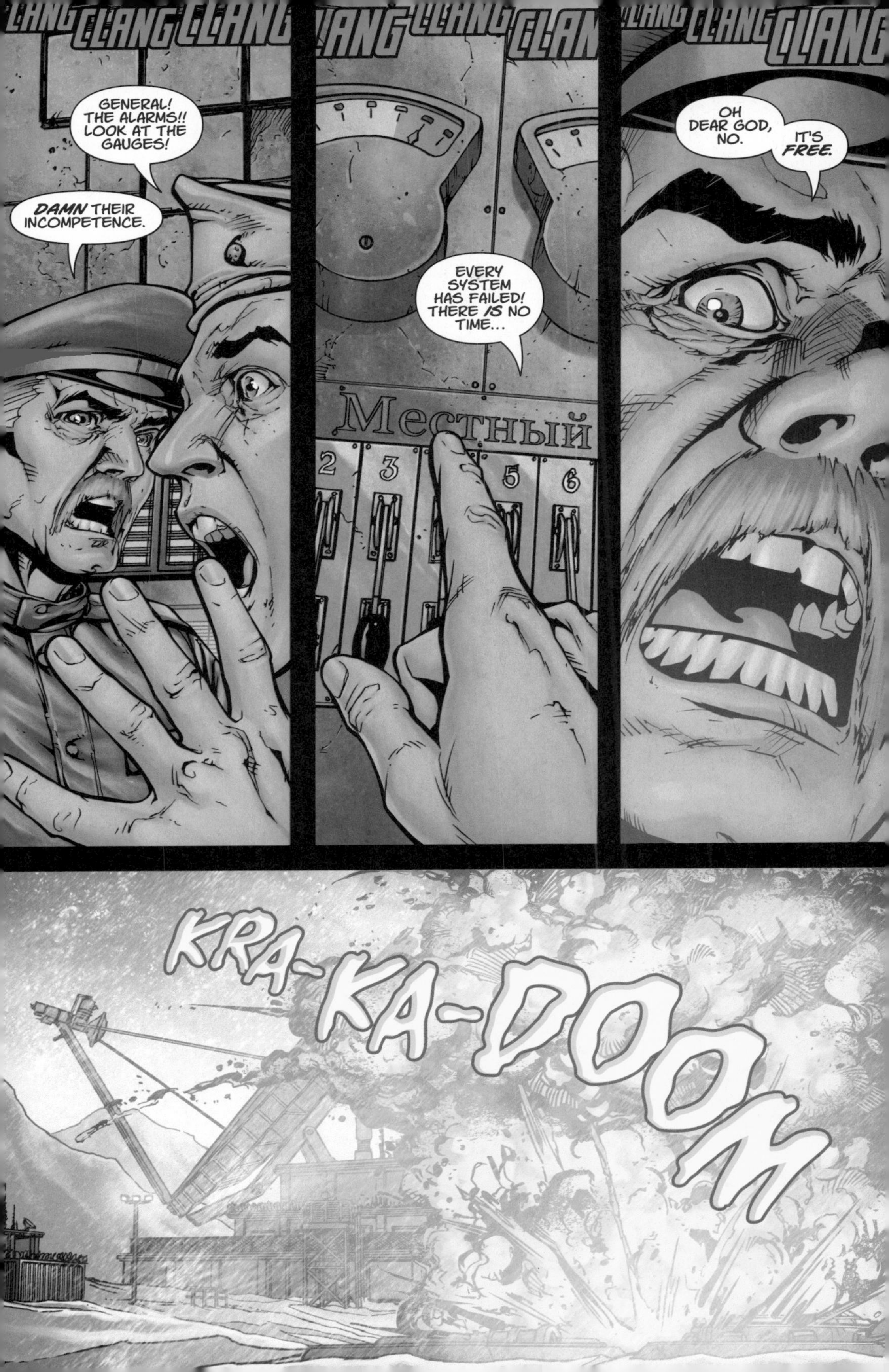
CLANG CLANG CLANG
GENERAL! THE ALARMS!! LOOK AT THE GAUGES!
DAMN THEIR INCOMPETENCE.
CLANG CLANG CLANG
EVERY SYSTEM HAS FAILED! THERE IS NO TIME...
Местный
2 3 5 6
CLANG CLANG CLANG
OH DEAR GOD, NO.
IT'S FREE.
KRA-KA-DOOM

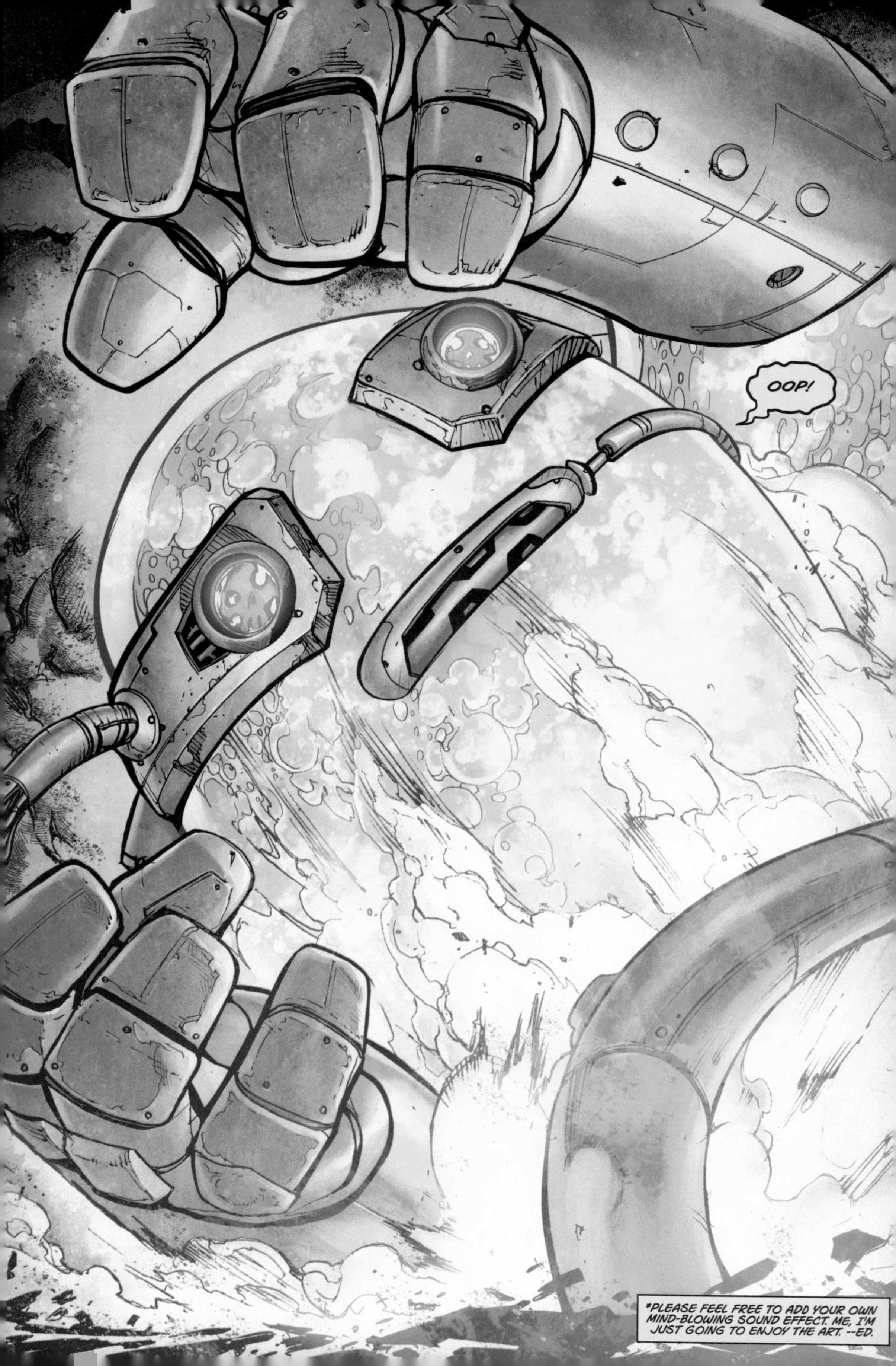
OOP!
*PLEASE FEEL FREE TO ADD YOUR OWN MIND-BLOWING SOUND EFFECT. ME, I'M JUST GOING TO ENJOY THE ART. --ED.

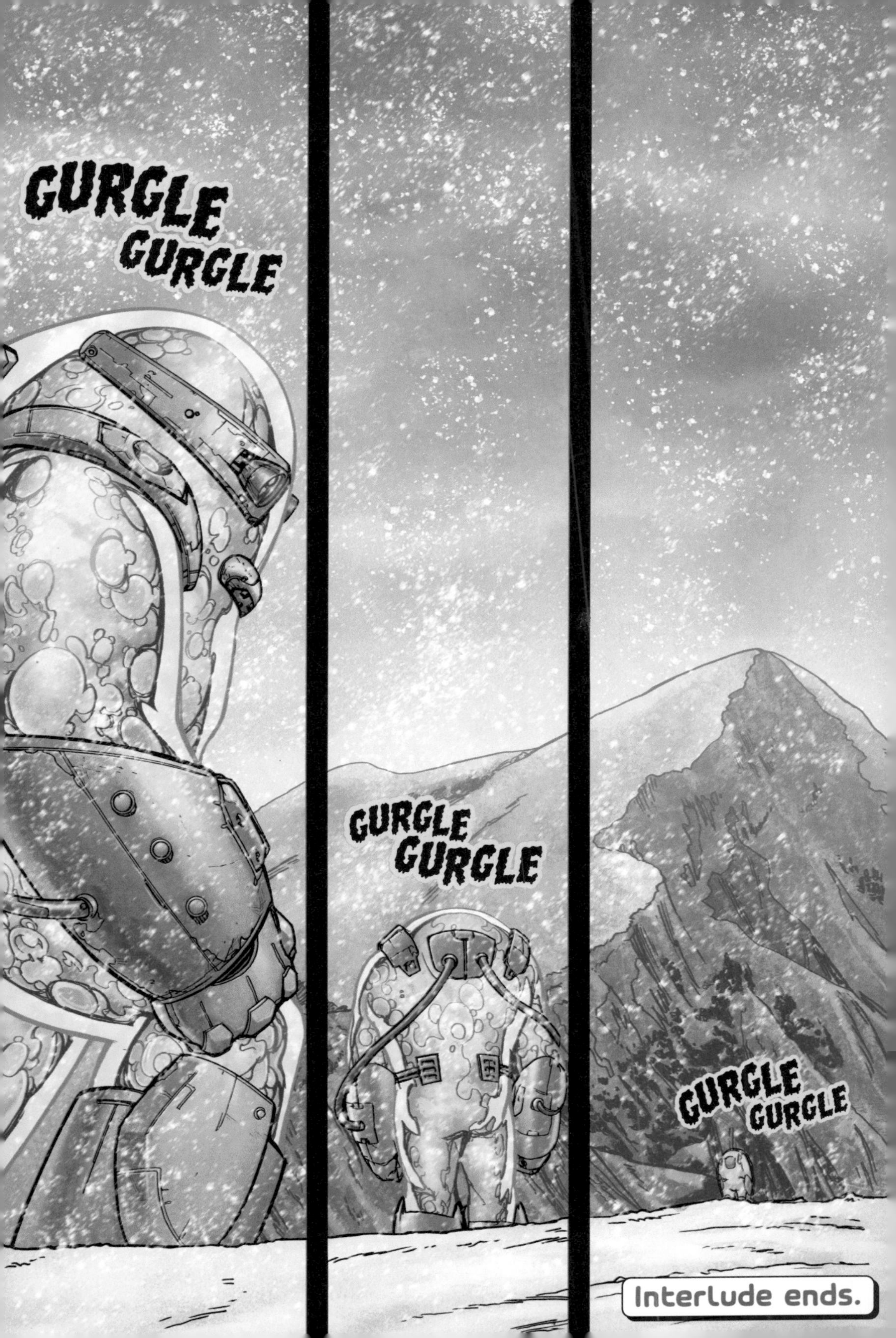
GURGLE
GURGLE
GURGLE
GURGLE
GURGLE
GURGLE
Interlude ends.

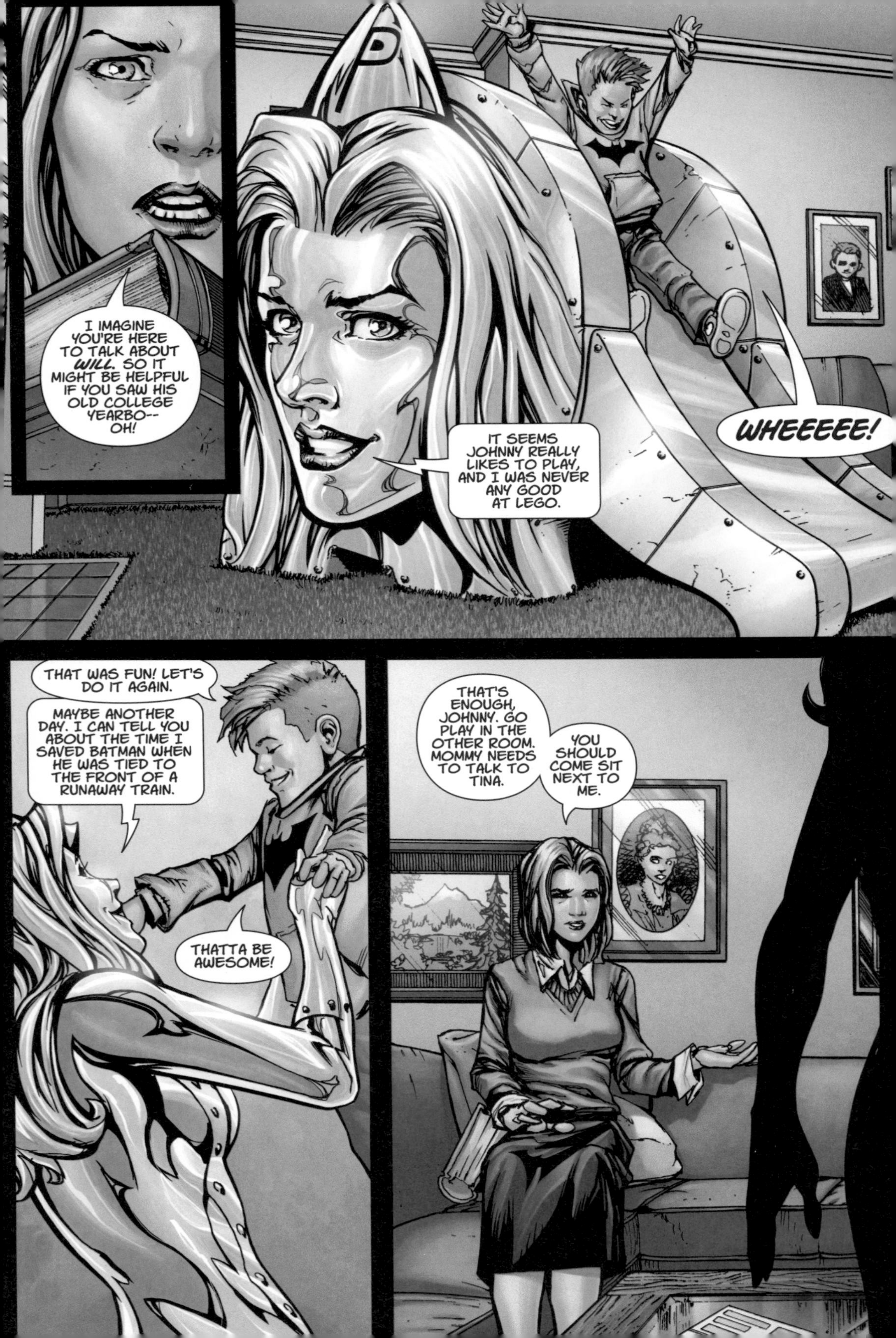
I IMAGINE YOU'RE HERE TO TALK ABOUT *WILL*. SO IT MIGHT BE HELPFUL IF YOU SAW HIS OLD COLLEGE YEARBO-- OH!
IT SEEMS JOHNNY REALLY LIKES TO PLAY, AND I WAS NEVER ANY GOOD AT LEGO.
WHEEEEEE!
THAT WAS FUN! LET'S DO IT AGAIN.
MAYBE ANOTHER DAY. I CAN TELL YOU ABOUT THE TIME I SAVED BATMAN WHEN HE WAS TIED TO THE FRONT OF A RUNAWAY TRAIN.
THATTA BE AWESOME!
THAT'S ENOUGH, JOHNNY. GO PLAY IN THE OTHER ROOM. MOMMY NEEDS TO TALK TO TINA.
YOU SHOULD COME SIT NEXT TO ME.

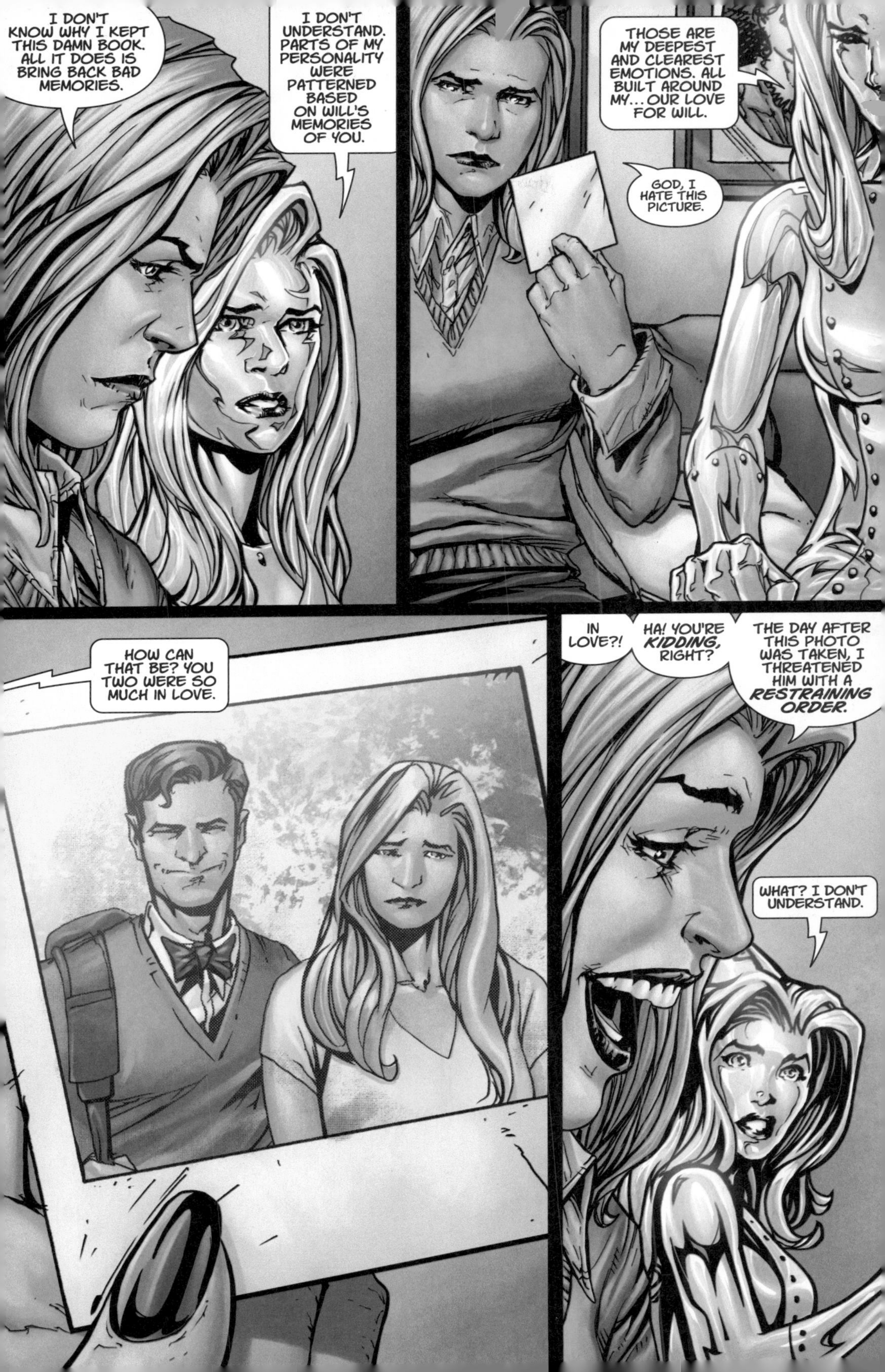
I DON'T KNOW WHY I KEPT THIS DAMN BOOK. ALL IT DOES IS BRING BACK BAD MEMORIES.
I DON'T UNDERSTAND. PARTS OF MY PERSONALITY WERE PATTERNED BASED ON WILL'S MEMORIES OF YOU.
THOSE ARE MY DEEPEST AND CLEAREST EMOTIONS. ALL BUILT AROUND MY... OUR LOVE FOR WILL.
GOD, I HATE THIS PICTURE.
HOW CAN THAT BE? YOU TWO WERE SO MUCH IN LOVE.
IN LOVE?!
HA! YOU'RE *KIDDING,* RIGHT?
THE DAY AFTER THIS PHOTO WAS TAKEN, I THREATENED HIM WITH A ***RESTRAINING ORDER.***
WHAT? I DON'T UNDERSTAND.

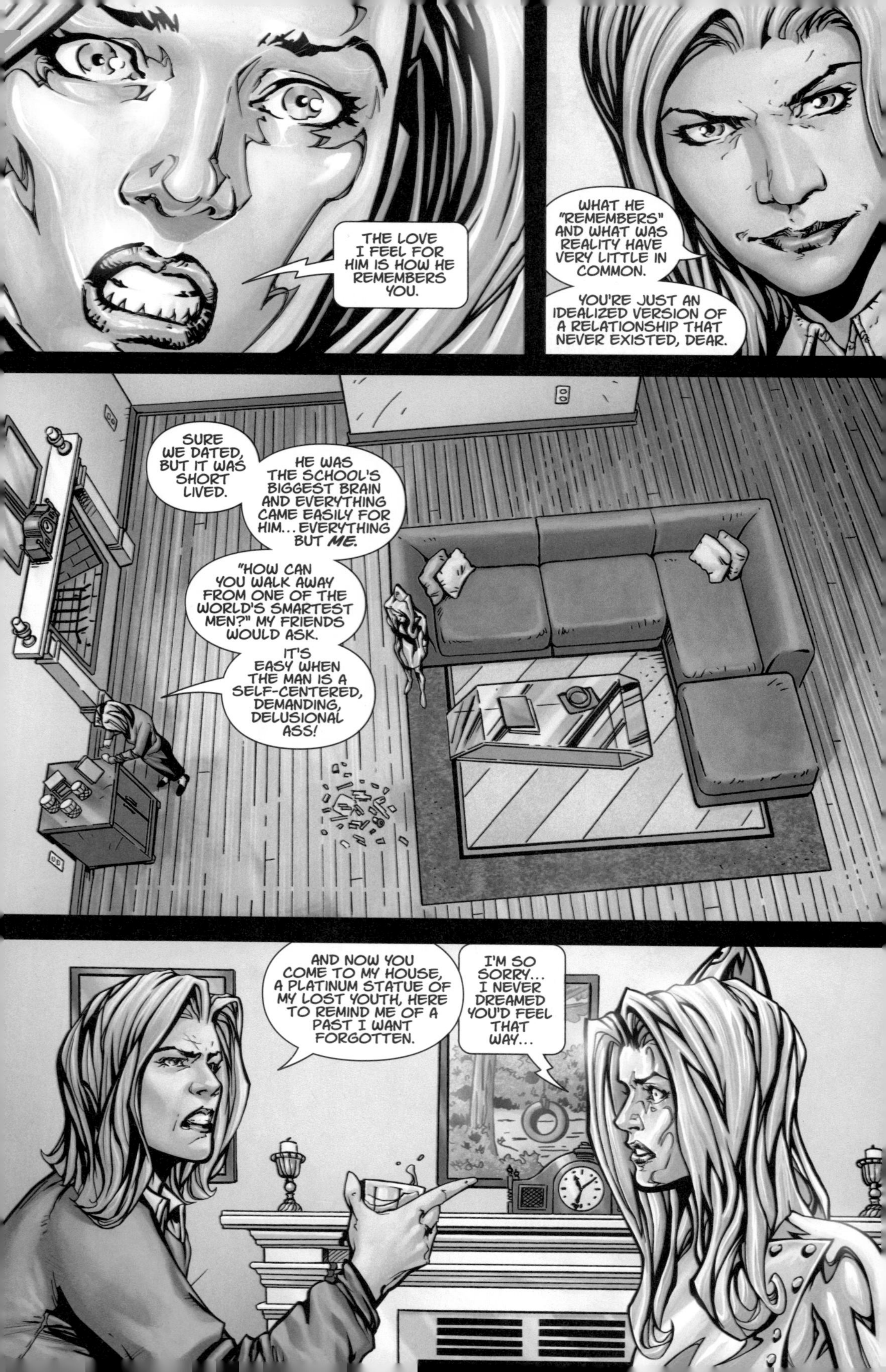
THE LOVE I FEEL FOR HIM IS HOW HE REMEMBERS YOU.
WHAT HE "REMEMBERS" AND WHAT WAS REALITY HAVE VERY LITTLE IN COMMON.
YOU'RE JUST AN IDEALIZED VERSION OF A RELATIONSHIP THAT NEVER EXISTED, DEAR.
SURE WE DATED, BUT IT WAS SHORT LIVED.
HE WAS THE SCHOOL'S BIGGEST BRAIN AND EVERYTHING CAME EASILY FOR HIM... EVERYTHING BUT *ME*.
"HOW CAN YOU WALK AWAY FROM ONE OF THE WORLD'S SMARTEST MEN?" MY FRIENDS WOULD ASK.
IT'S EASY WHEN THE MAN IS A SELF-CENTERED, DEMANDING, DELUSIONAL ASS!
AND NOW YOU COME TO MY HOUSE, A PLATINUM STATUE OF MY LOST YOUTH, HERE TO REMIND ME OF A PAST I WANT FORGOTTEN.
I'M SO SORRY... I NEVER DREAMED YOU'D FEEL THAT WAY...

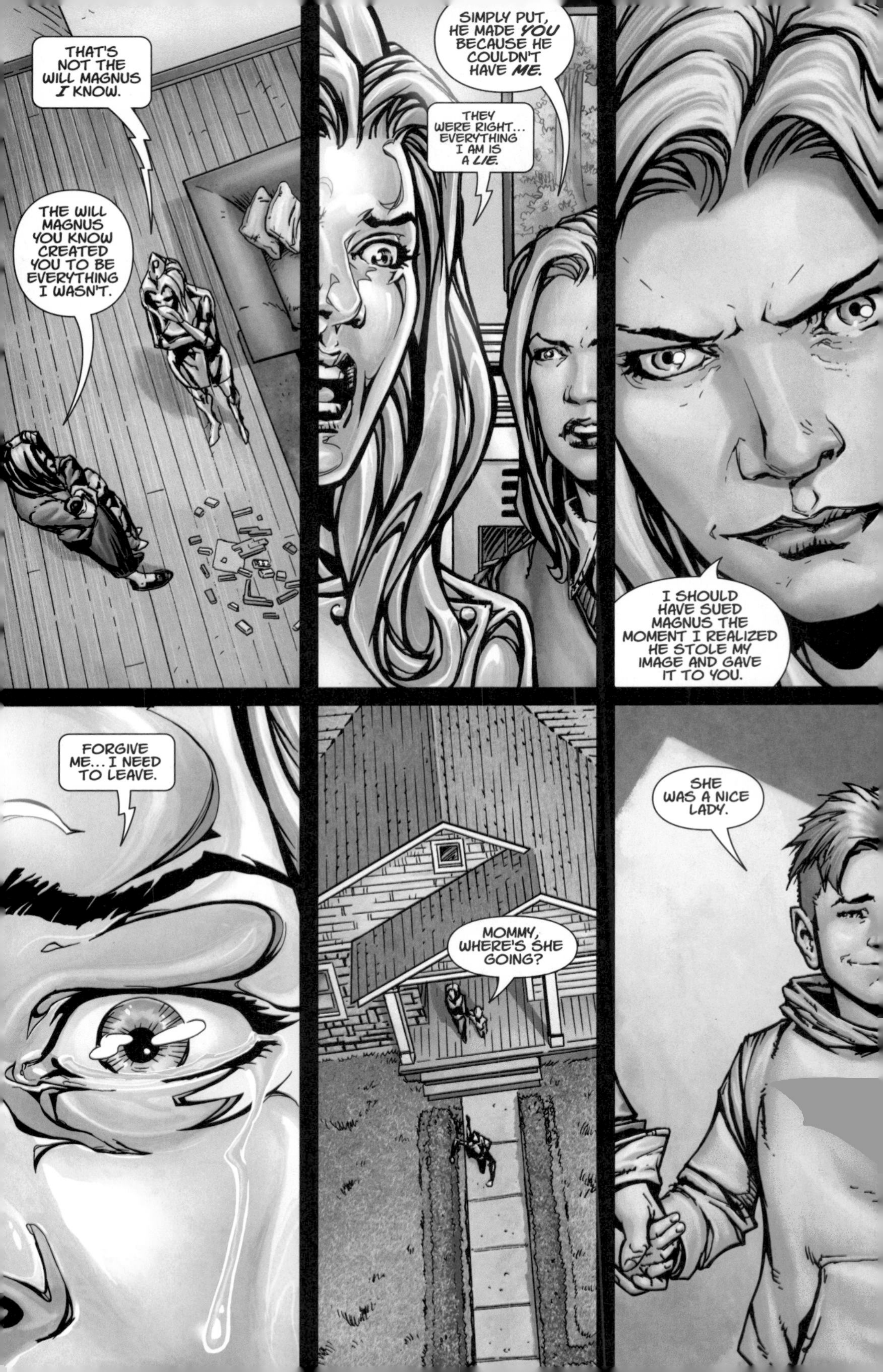
THAT'S NOT THE WILL MAGNUS I KNOW.
THE WILL MAGNUS YOU KNOW CREATED YOU TO BE EVERYTHING I WASN'T.
SIMPLY PUT, HE MADE YOU BECAUSE HE COULDN'T HAVE ME.
THEY WERE RIGHT... EVERYTHING I AM IS A LIE.
I SHOULD HAVE SUED MAGNUS THE MOMENT I REALIZED HE STOLE MY IMAGE AND GAVE IT TO YOU.
FORGIVE ME... I NEED TO LEAVE.
MOMMY, WHERE'S SHE GOING?
SHE WAS A NICE LADY.

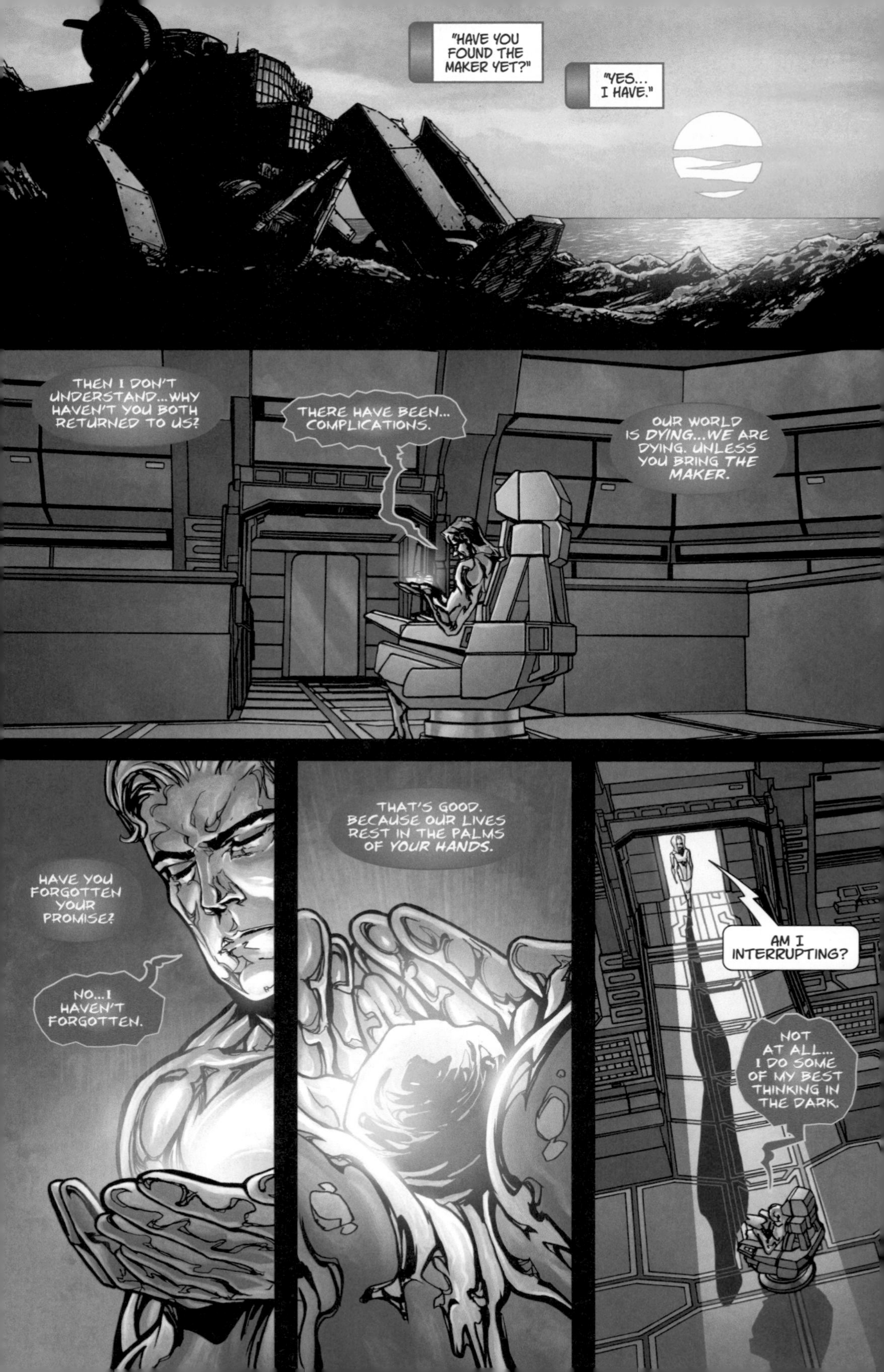
"HAVE YOU FOUND THE MAKER YET?"
"YES... I HAVE."
THEN I DON'T UNDERSTAND...WHY HAVEN'T YOU BOTH RETURNED TO US?
THERE HAVE BEEN... COMPLICATIONS.
OUR WORLD IS DYING...WE ARE DYING. UNLESS YOU BRING THE MAKER.
HAVE YOU FORGOTTEN YOUR PROMISE?
NO...I HAVEN'T FORGOTTEN.
THAT'S GOOD. BECAUSE OUR LIVES REST IN THE PALMS OF YOUR HANDS.
AM I INTERRUPTING?
NOT AT ALL... I DO SOME OF MY BEST THINKING IN THE DARK.

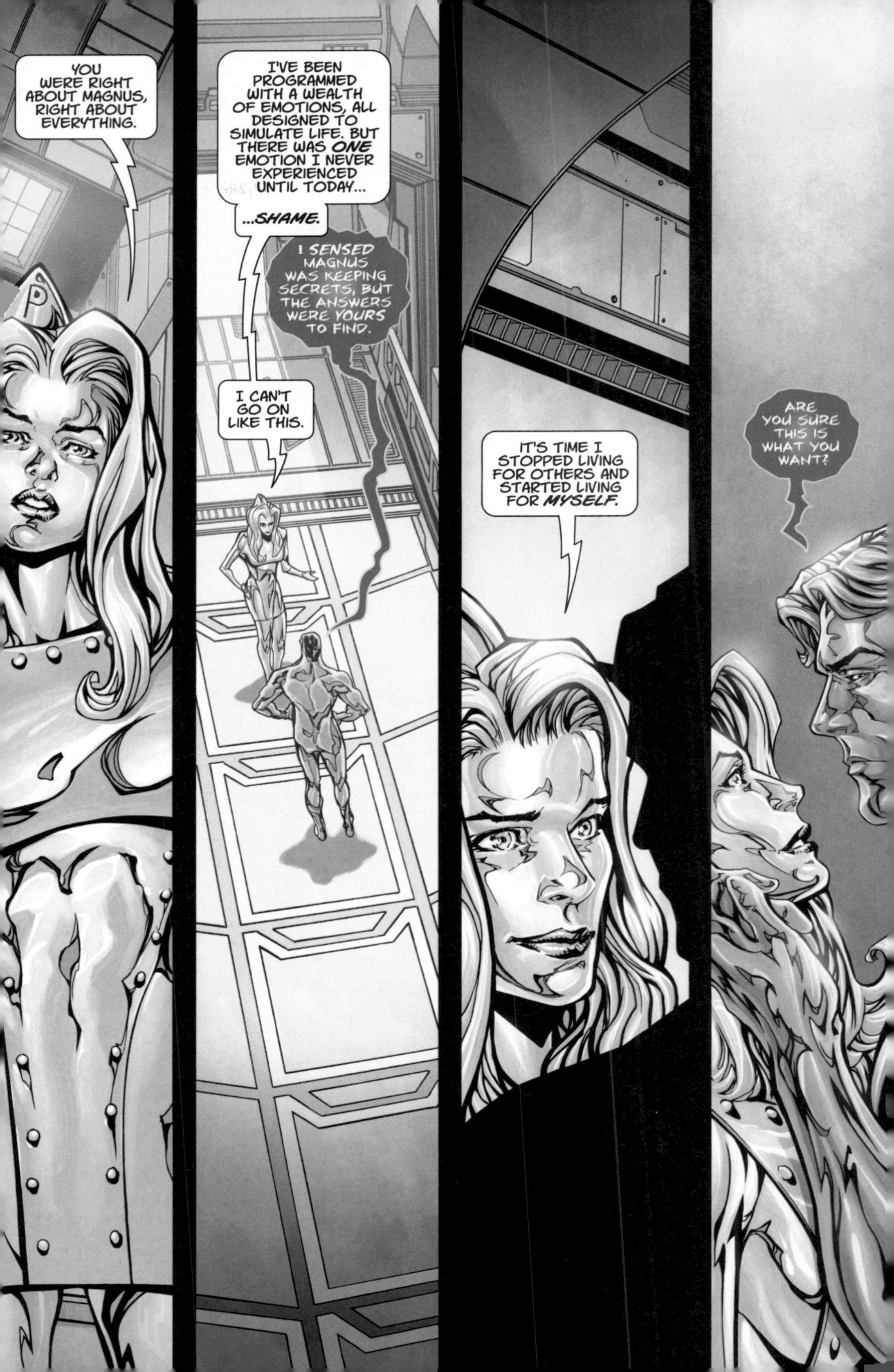
YOU WERE RIGHT ABOUT MAGNUS, RIGHT ABOUT EVERYTHING.
I'VE BEEN PROGRAMMED WITH A WEALTH OF EMOTIONS, ALL DESIGNED TO SIMULATE LIFE. BUT THERE WAS ONE EMOTION I NEVER EXPERIENCED UNTIL TODAY...
...SHAME.
I SENSED MAGNUS WAS KEEPING SECRETS, BUT THE ANSWERS WERE YOURS TO FIND.
I CAN'T GO ON LIKE THIS.
IT'S TIME I STOPPED LIVING FOR OTHERS AND STARTED LIVING FOR MYSELF.
ARE YOU SURE THIS IS WHAT YOU WANT?

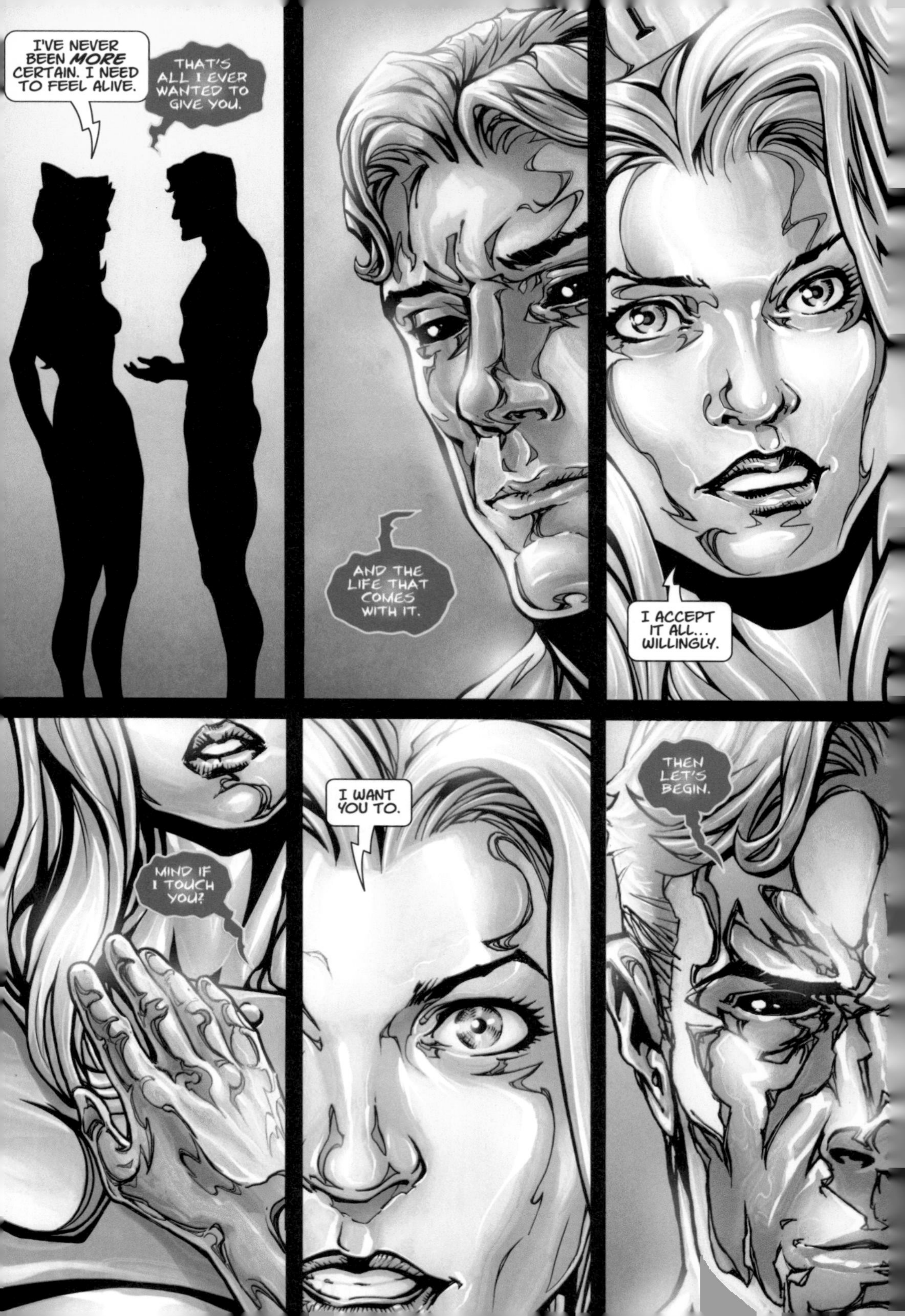
I'VE NEVER BEEN MORE CERTAIN. I NEED TO FEEL ALIVE.
THAT'S ALL I EVER WANTED TO GIVE YOU.
AND THE LIFE THAT COMES WITH IT.
I ACCEPT IT ALL... WILLINGLY.
MIND IF I TOUCH YOU?
I WANT YOU TO.
THEN LET'S BEGIN.

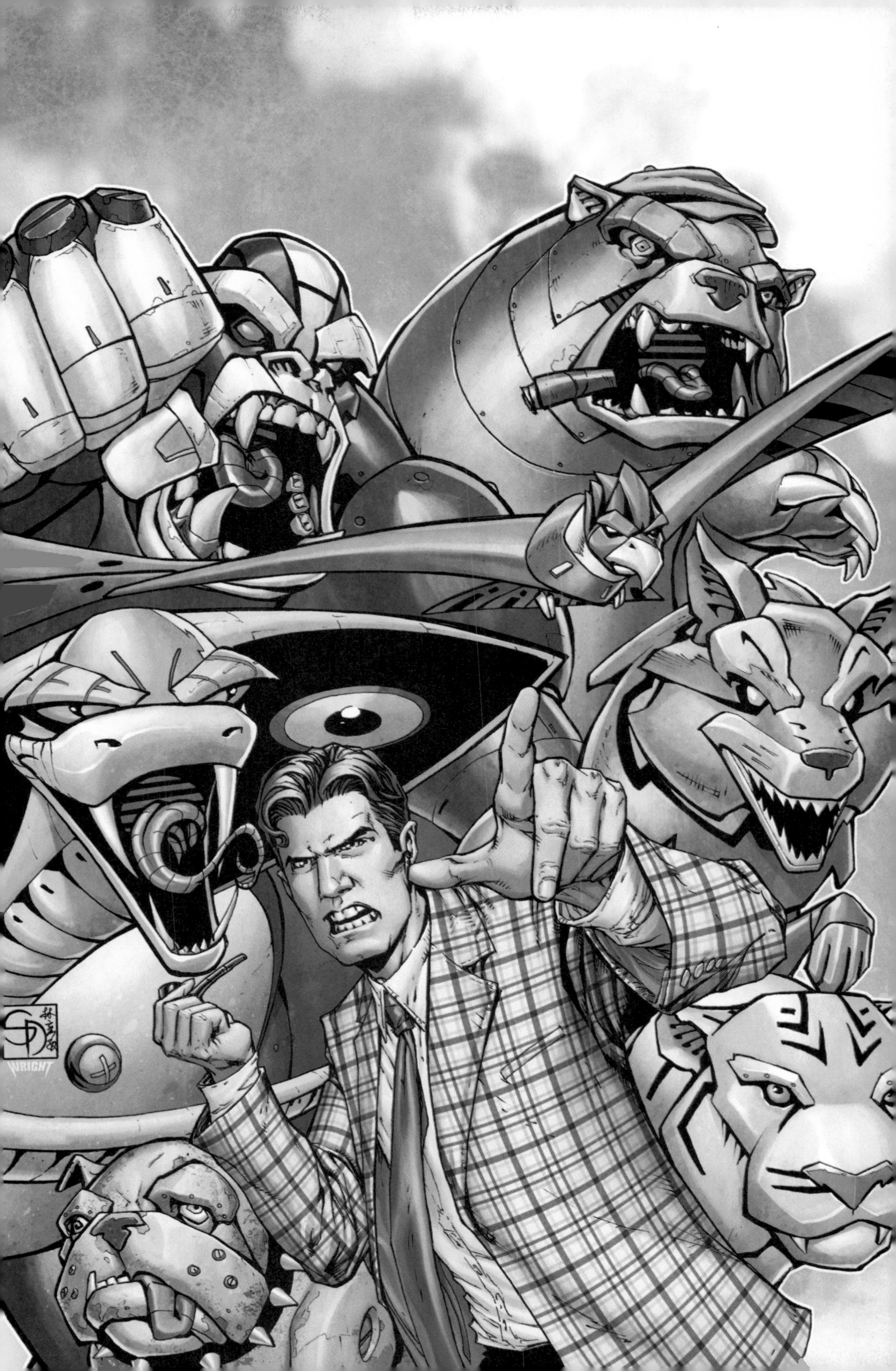
WRIGHT

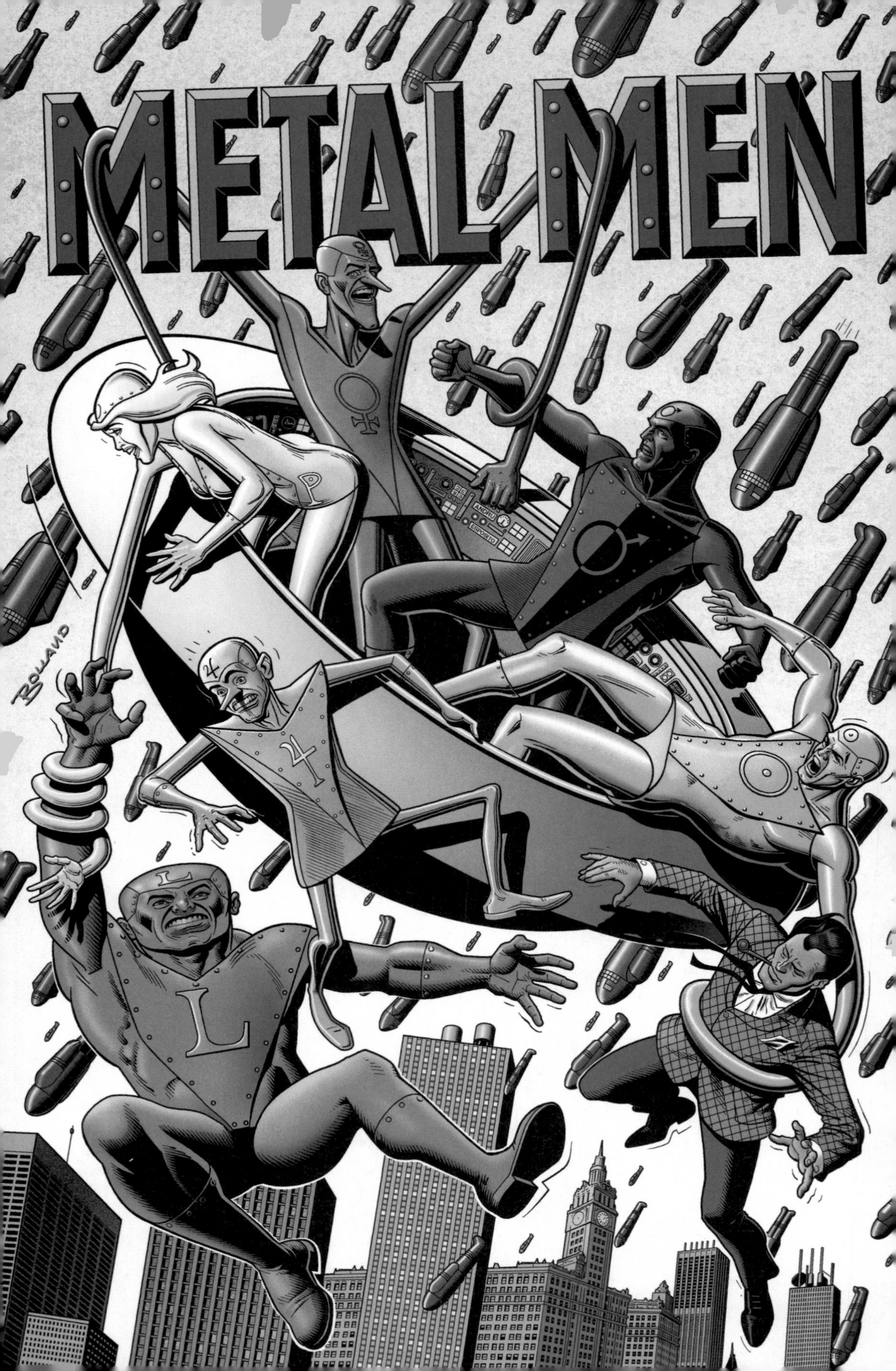
METAL MEN
ANDRU
ESPOSITO
ROLLAND

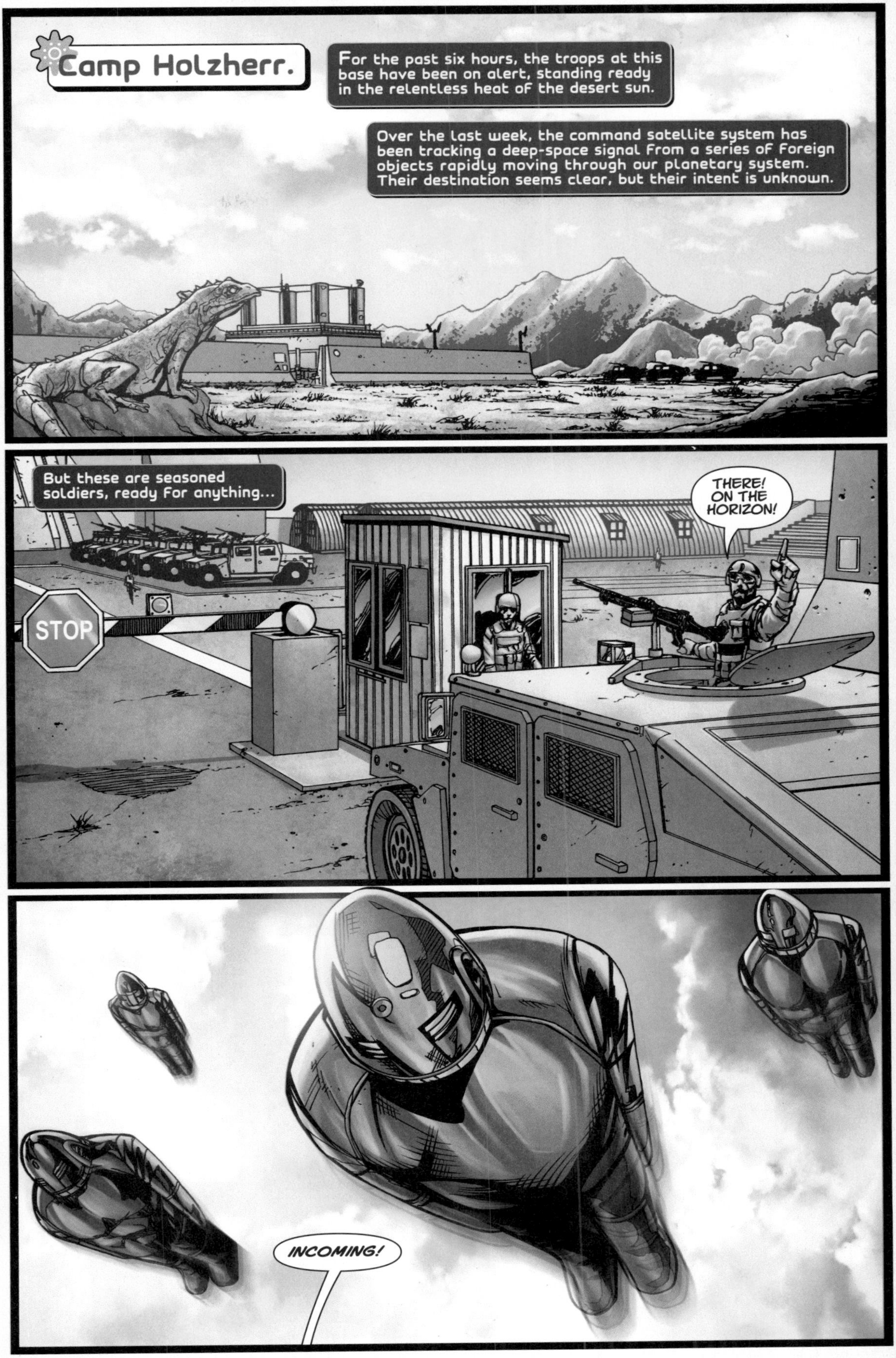
Camp Holzherr.
For the past six hours, the troops at this base have been on alert, standing ready in the relentless heat of the desert sun.
Over the last week, the command satellite system has been tracking a deep-space signal from a series of foreign objects rapidly moving through our planetary system. Their destination seems clear, but their intent is unknown.
But these are seasoned soldiers, ready for anything...
THERE! ON THE HORIZON!
STOP
INCOMING!

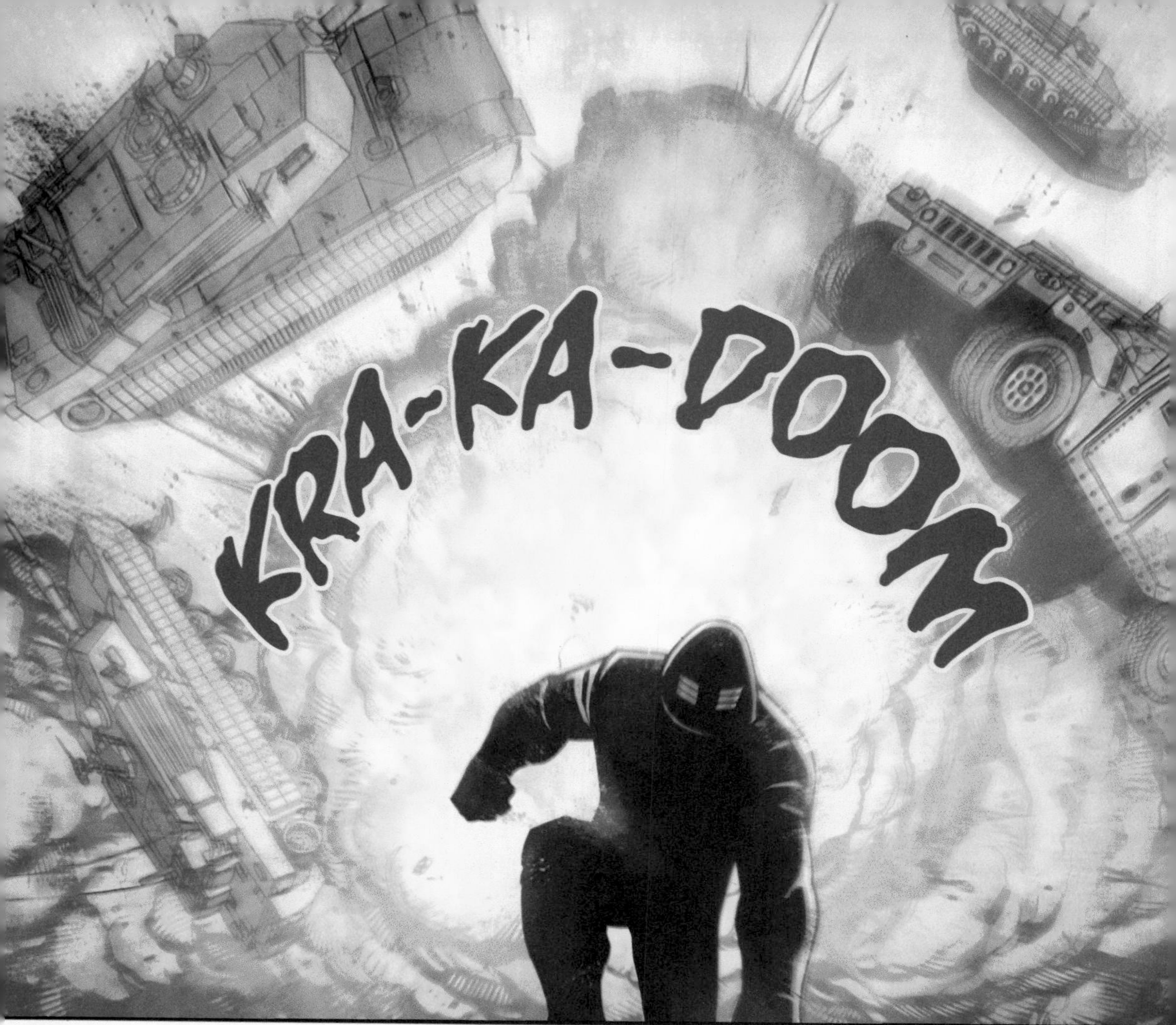
KRA-KA-DOOM

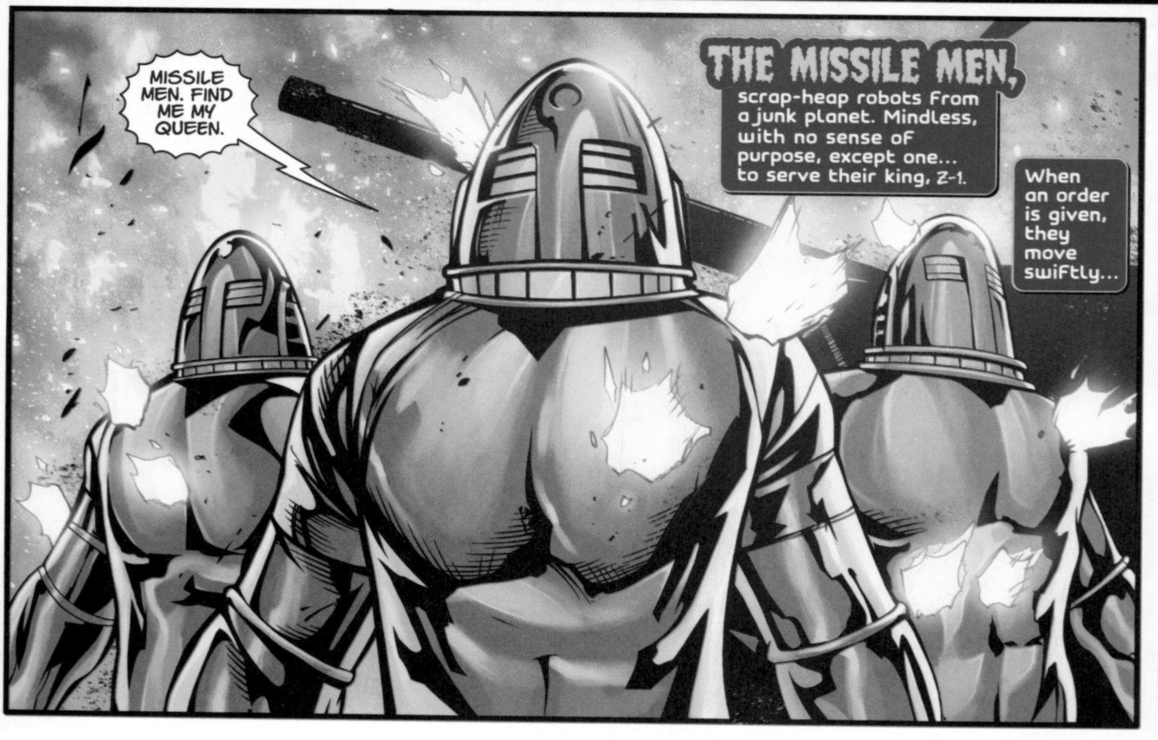
THE MISSILE MEN,
scrap-heap robots from a junk planet. Mindless, with no sense of purpose, except one... to serve their king, Z-1.
MISSILE MEN. FIND ME MY QUEEN.
When an order is given, they move swiftly...

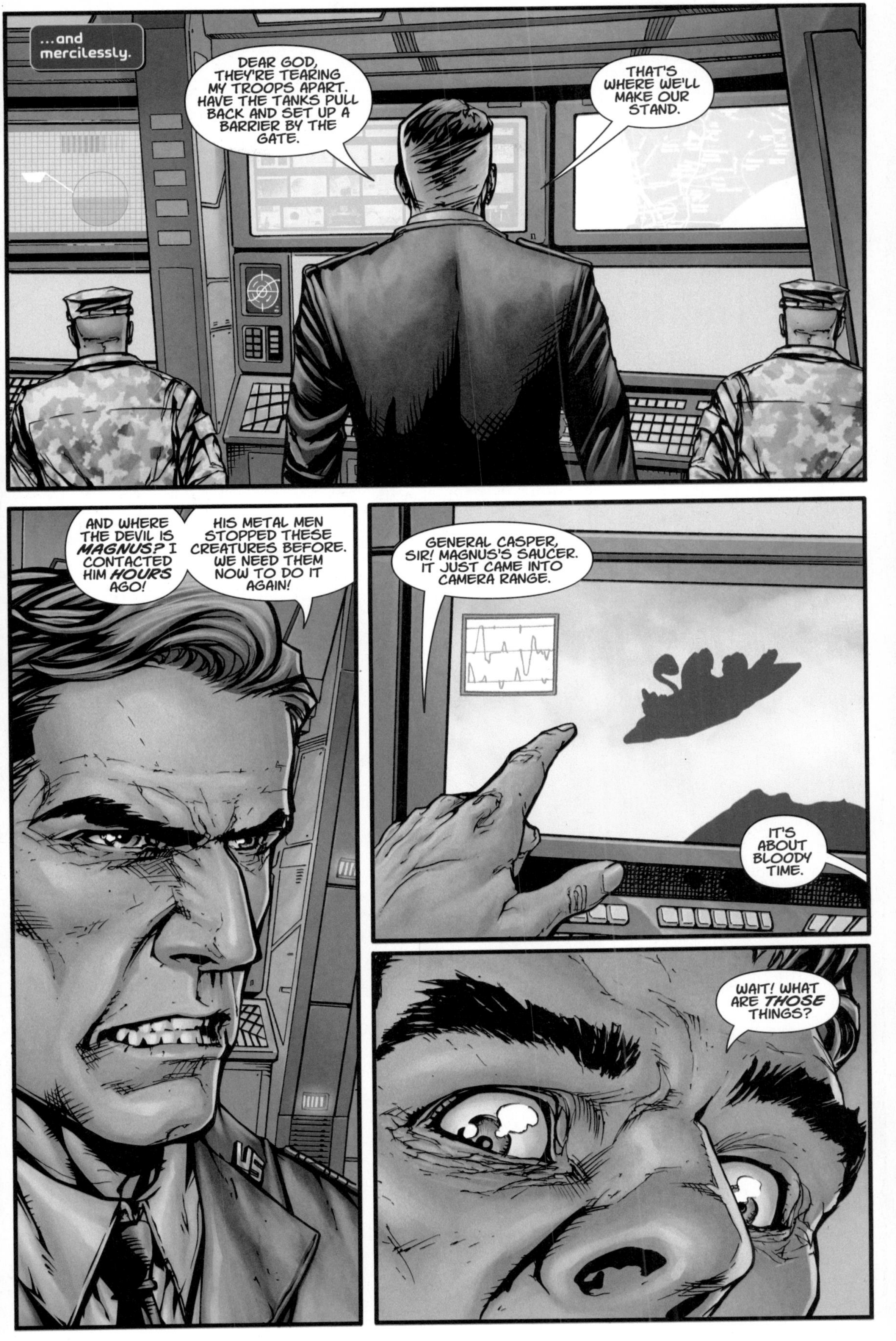
...and mercilessly.
DEAR GOD, THEY'RE TEARING MY TROOPS APART. HAVE THE TANKS PULL BACK AND SET UP A BARRIER BY THE GATE.
THAT'S WHERE WE'LL MAKE OUR STAND.
AND WHERE THE DEVIL IS MAGNUS? I CONTACTED HIM HOURS AGO!
HIS METAL MEN STOPPED THESE CREATURES BEFORE. WE NEED THEM NOW TO DO IT AGAIN!
GENERAL CASPER, SIR! MAGNUS'S SAUCER. IT JUST CAME INTO CAMERA RANGE.
IT'S ABOUT BLOODY TIME.
WAIT! WHAT ARE THOSE THINGS?

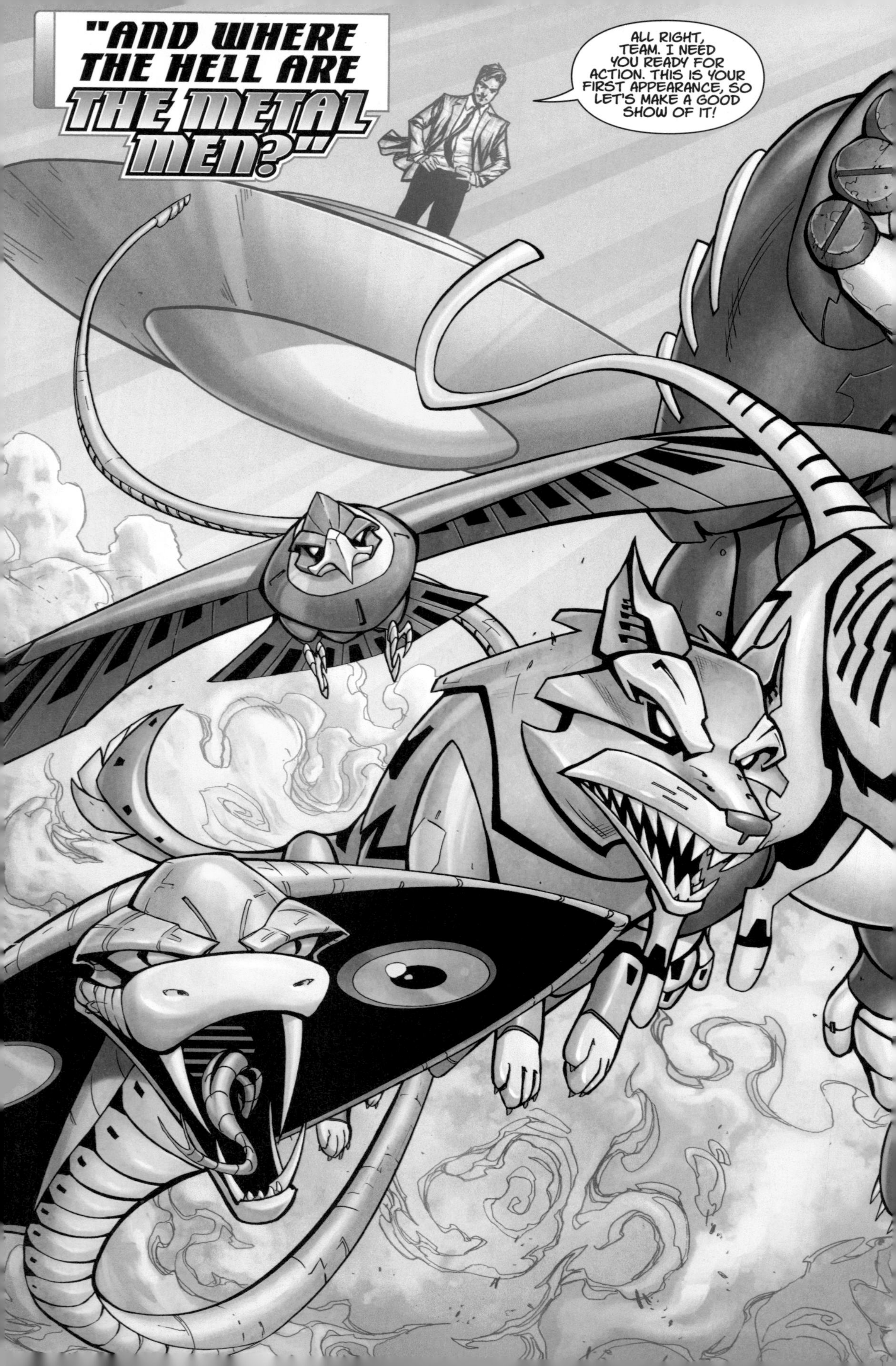
"AND WHERE THE HELL ARE THE METAL MEN?"
ALL RIGHT, TEAM. I NEED YOU READY FOR ACTION. THIS IS YOUR FIRST APPEARANCE, SO LET'S MAKE A GOOD SHOW OF IT!

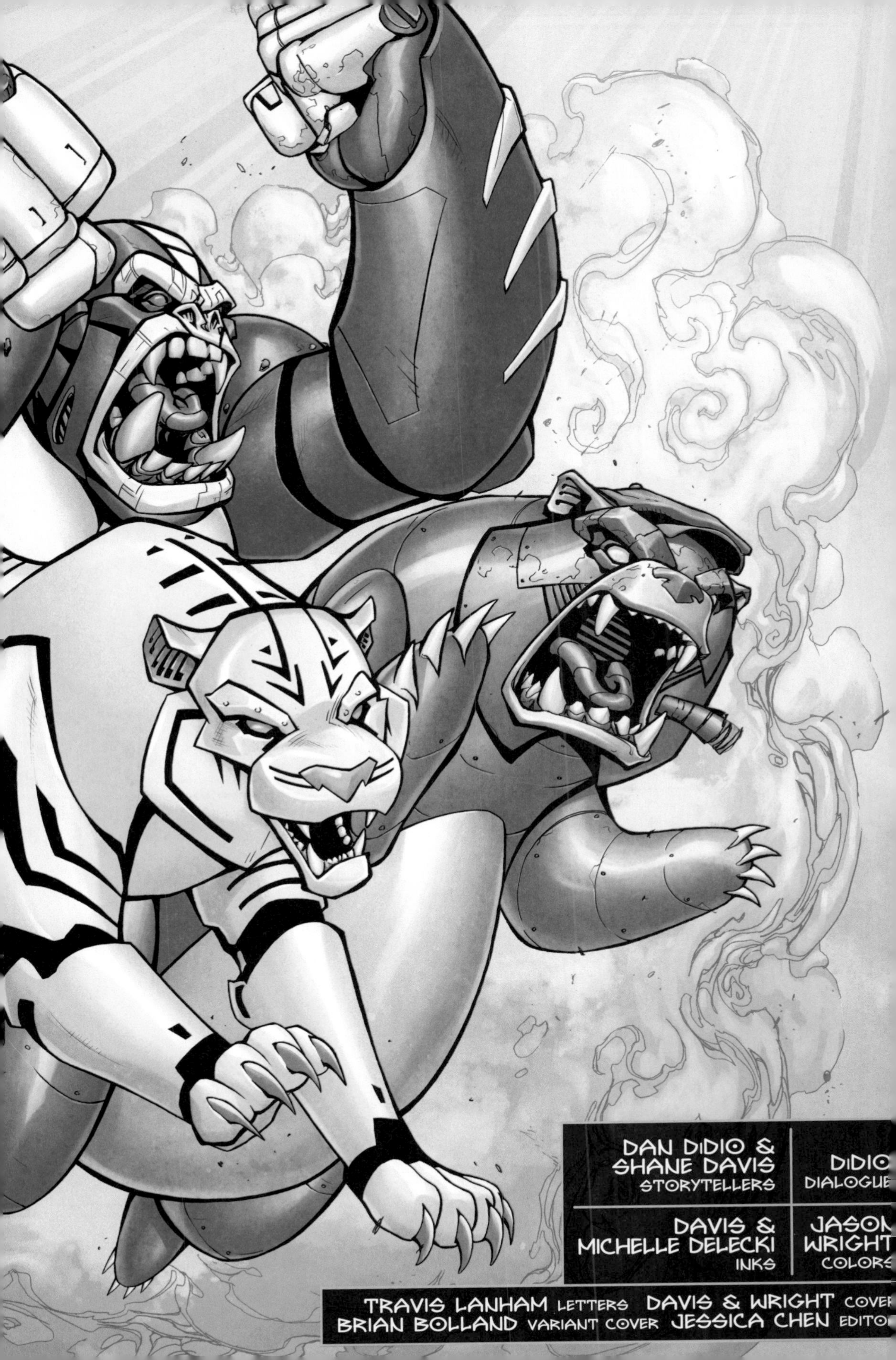

DAN DIDIO & SHANE DAVIS
STORYTELLERS
DIDIO
DIALOGUE
DAVIS & MICHELLE DELECKI
INKS
JASO
WRIGHT
COLORS
TRAVIS LANHAM LETTERS DAVIS & WRIGHT COVE
BRIAN BOLLAND VARIANT COVER JESSICA CHEN EDITO

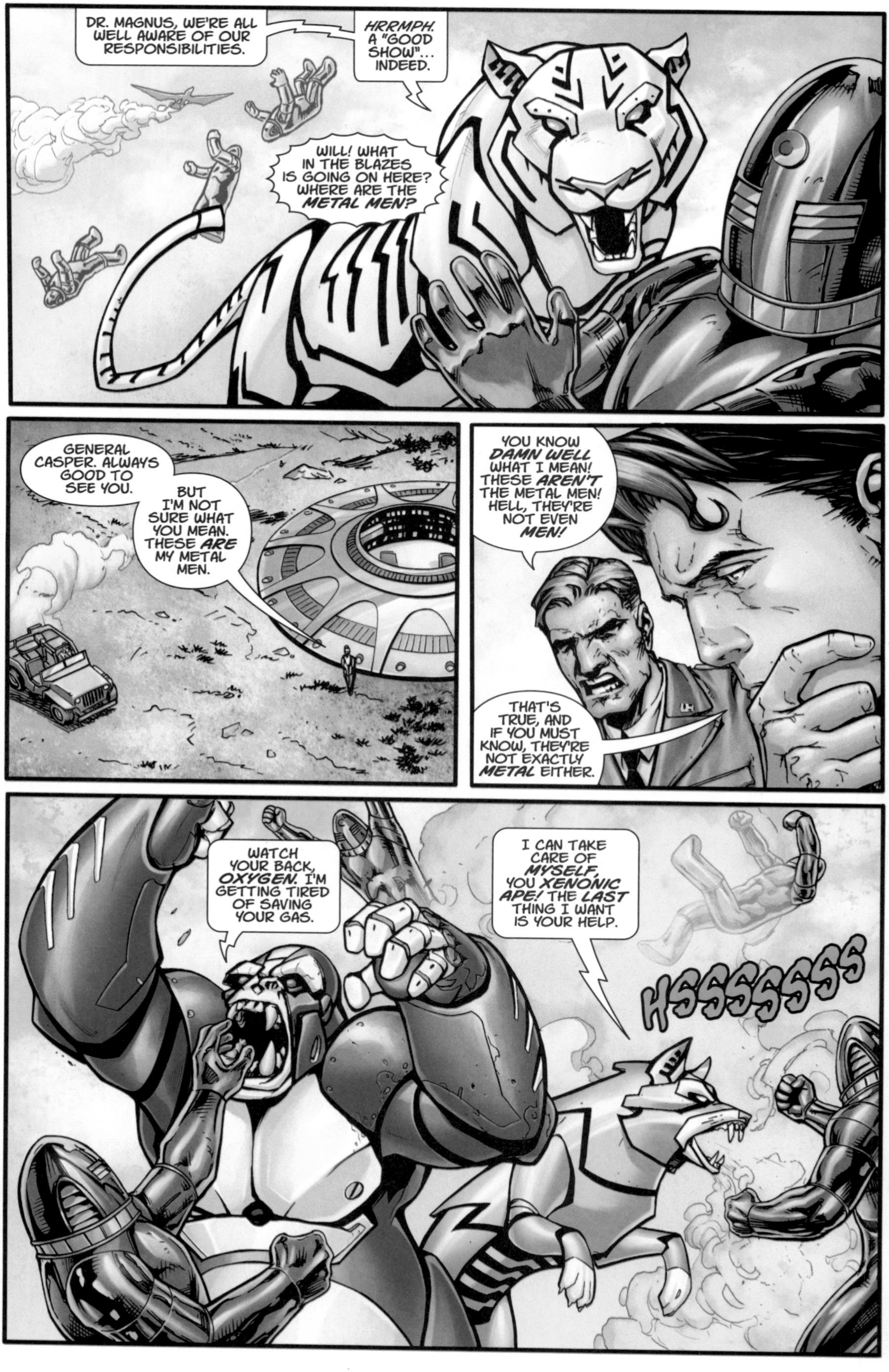
DR. MAGNUS, WE'RE ALL WELL AWARE OF OUR RESPONSIBILITIES.
HRRMPH. A "GOOD SHOW"... INDEED.
WILL! WHAT IN THE BLAZES IS GOING ON HERE? WHERE ARE THE METAL MEN?
GENERAL CASPER. ALWAYS GOOD TO SEE YOU.
BUT I'M NOT SURE WHAT YOU MEAN. THESE ARE MY METAL MEN.
YOU KNOW DAMN WELL WHAT I MEAN! THESE AREN'T THE METAL MEN! HELL, THEY'RE NOT EVEN MEN!
THAT'S TRUE, AND IF YOU MUST KNOW, THEY'RE NOT EXACTLY METAL EITHER.
WATCH YOUR BACK, OXYGEN. I'M GETTING TIRED OF SAVING YOUR GAS.
I CAN TAKE CARE OF MYSELF, YOU XENONIC APE! THE LAST THING I WANT IS YOUR HELP.
HSSSSSSS

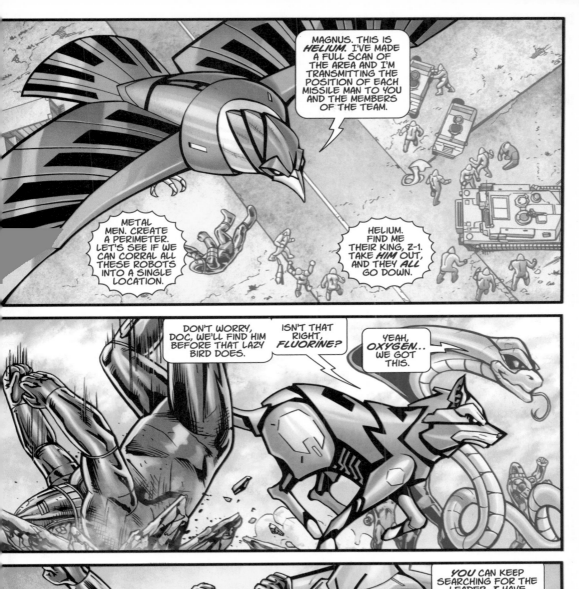

MAGNUS. THIS IS *HELIUM.* I'VE MADE A FULL SCAN OF THE AREA AND I'M TRANSMITTING THE POSITION OF EACH MISSILE MAN TO YOU AND THE MEMBERS OF THE TEAM.

METAL MEN. CREATE A PERIMETER. LET'S SEE IF WE CAN CORRAL ALL THESE ROBOTS INTO A SINGLE LOCATION.

HELIUM. FIND ME THEIR KING, Z-1. TAKE *HIM* OUT, AND THEY *ALL* GO DOWN.

DON'T WORRY, DOC, WE'LL FIND HIM BEFORE THAT LAZY BIRD DOES.

ISN'T THAT RIGHT, *FLUORINE?*

YEAH, *OXYGEN...* WE GOT THIS.

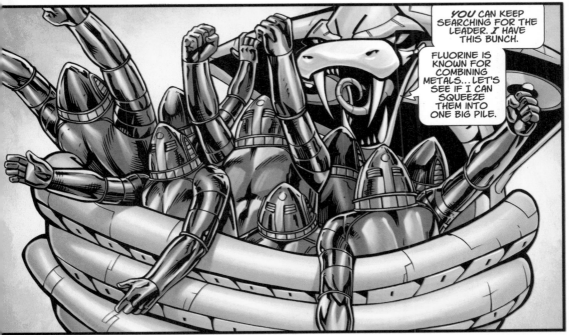

YOU CAN KEEP SEARCHING FOR THE LEADER. *I* HAVE THIS BUNCH.

FLUORINE IS KNOWN FOR COMBINING METALS... LET'S SEE IF I CAN SQUEEZE THEM INTO ONE BIG PILE.

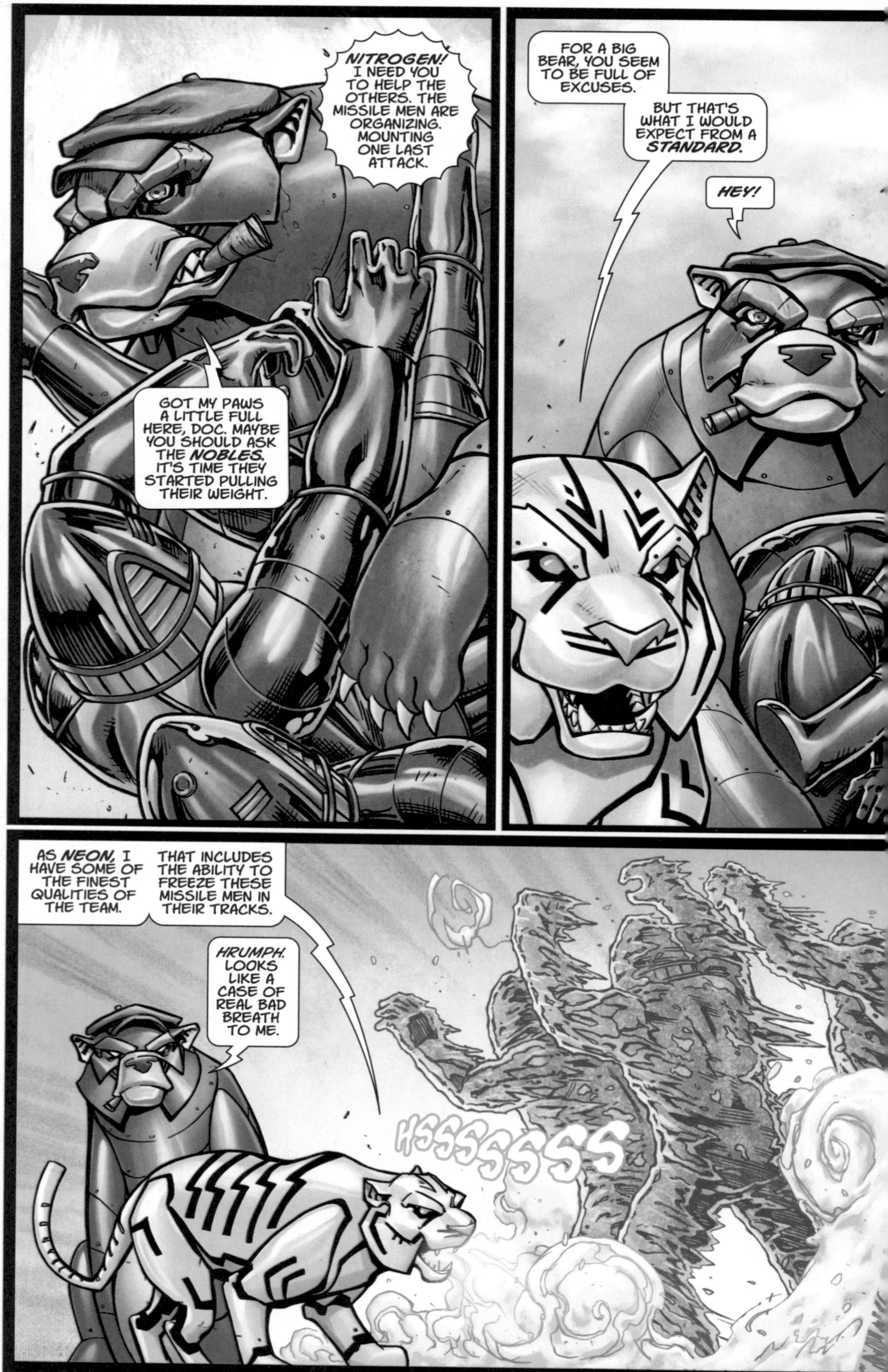
NITROGEN! I NEED YOU TO HELP THE OTHERS. THE MISSILE MEN ARE ORGANIZING. MOUNTING ONE LAST ATTACK.
GOT MY PAWS A LITTLE FULL HERE, DOC. MAYBE YOU SHOULD ASK THE NOBLES. IT'S TIME THEY STARTED PULLING THEIR WEIGHT.
FOR A BIG BEAR, YOU SEEM TO BE FULL OF EXCUSES.
BUT THAT'S WHAT I WOULD EXPECT FROM A STANDARD.
HEY!
AS NEON, I HAVE SOME OF THE FINEST QUALITIES OF THE TEAM.
THAT INCLUDES THE ABILITY TO FREEZE THESE MISSILE MEN IN THEIR TRACKS.
HRUMPH. LOOKS LIKE A CASE OF REAL BAD BREATH TO ME.
HSSSSSSSS

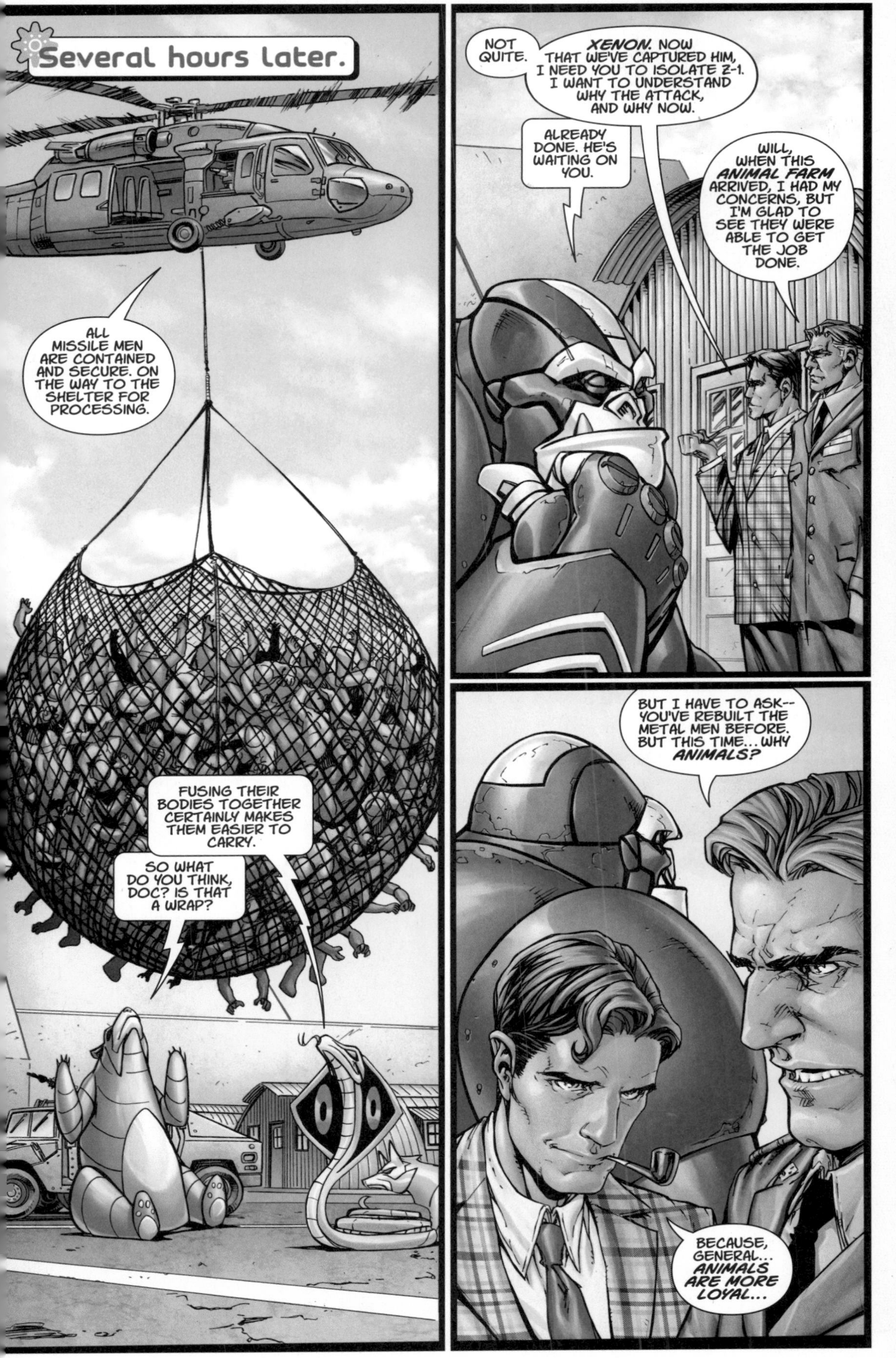
Several hours later.
ALL MISSILE MEN ARE CONTAINED AND SECURE. ON THE WAY TO THE SHELTER FOR PROCESSING.
FUSING THEIR BODIES TOGETHER CERTAINLY MAKES THEM EASIER TO CARRY.
SO WHAT DO YOU THINK, DOC? IS THAT A WRAP?
NOT QUITE.
XENON. NOW THAT WE'VE CAPTURED HIM, I NEED YOU TO ISOLATE Z-1. I WANT TO UNDERSTAND WHY THE ATTACK, AND WHY NOW.
ALREADY DONE. HE'S WAITING ON YOU.
WILL, WHEN THIS ANIMAL FARM ARRIVED, I HAD MY CONCERNS, BUT I'M GLAD TO SEE THEY WERE ABLE TO GET THE JOB DONE.
BUT I HAVE TO ASK-- YOU'VE REBUILT THE METAL MEN BEFORE. BUT THIS TIME... WHY ANIMALS?
BECAUSE, GENERAL... ANIMALS ARE MORE LOYAL...

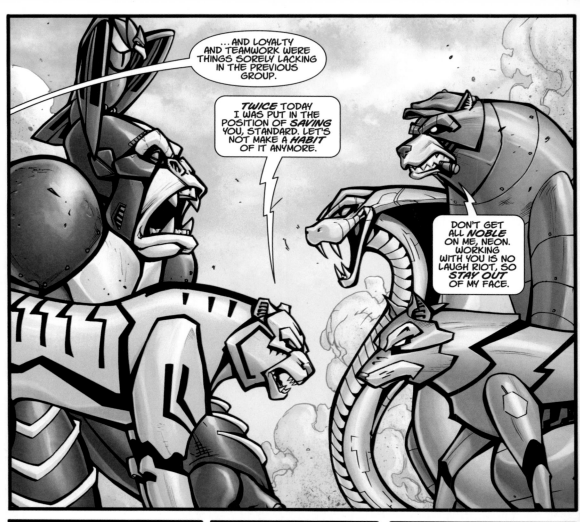

...AND LOYALTY AND TEAMWORK WERE THINGS SORELY LACKING IN THE PREVIOUS GROUP.

TWICE TODAY I WAS PUT IN THE POSITION OF SAVING YOU, STANDARD. LET'S NOT MAKE A HABIT OF IT ANYMORE.

DON'T GET ALL NOBLE ON ME, NEON. WORKING WITH YOU IS NO LAUGH RIOT, SO STAY OUT OF MY FACE.

TAKE ON ONE NOBLE, YOU TAKE ON ALL OF US.

I'D LIKE TO SEE YOU TRY, YA BIG MONKEY.

SKREEEE!

JUST SAY THE WORD, NITROGEN. I'LL TURN THEM INTO COMPOUNDS.

UMMM... MAGNUS?

OKAY, MAYBE WE NEED TO PRACTICE THE TEAMWORK A BIT MORE.

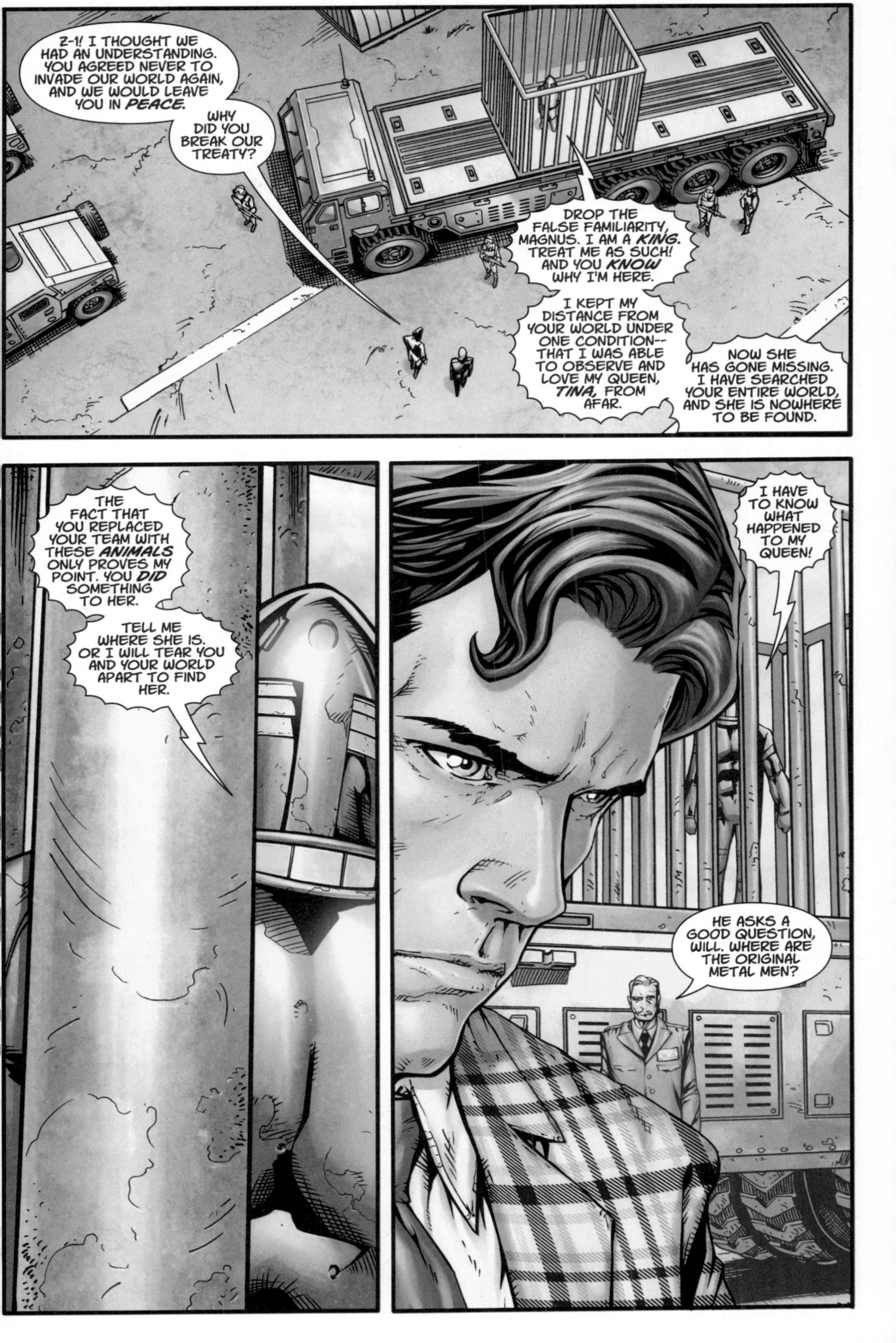
Z-1! I THOUGHT WE HAD AN UNDERSTANDING. YOU AGREED NEVER TO INVADE OUR WORLD AGAIN, AND WE WOULD LEAVE YOU IN *PEACE*.
WHY DID YOU BREAK OUR TREATY?
DROP THE FALSE FAMILIARITY, MAGNUS. I AM A *KING*. TREAT ME AS SUCH! AND YOU *KNOW* WHY I'M HERE.
I KEPT MY DISTANCE FROM YOUR WORLD UNDER ONE CONDITION-- THAT I WAS ABLE TO OBSERVE AND LOVE MY QUEEN, *TINA*, FROM AFAR.
NOW SHE HAS GONE MISSING. I HAVE SEARCHED YOUR ENTIRE WORLD, AND SHE IS NOWHERE TO BE FOUND.
THE FACT THAT YOU REPLACED YOUR TEAM WITH THESE *ANIMALS* ONLY PROVES MY POINT. YOU *DID* SOMETHING TO HER.
TELL ME WHERE SHE IS. OR I WILL TEAR YOU AND YOUR WORLD APART TO FIND HER.
I HAVE TO KNOW WHAT HAPPENED TO MY QUEEN!
HE ASKS A GOOD QUESTION, WILL. WHERE ARE THE ORIGINAL METAL MEN?

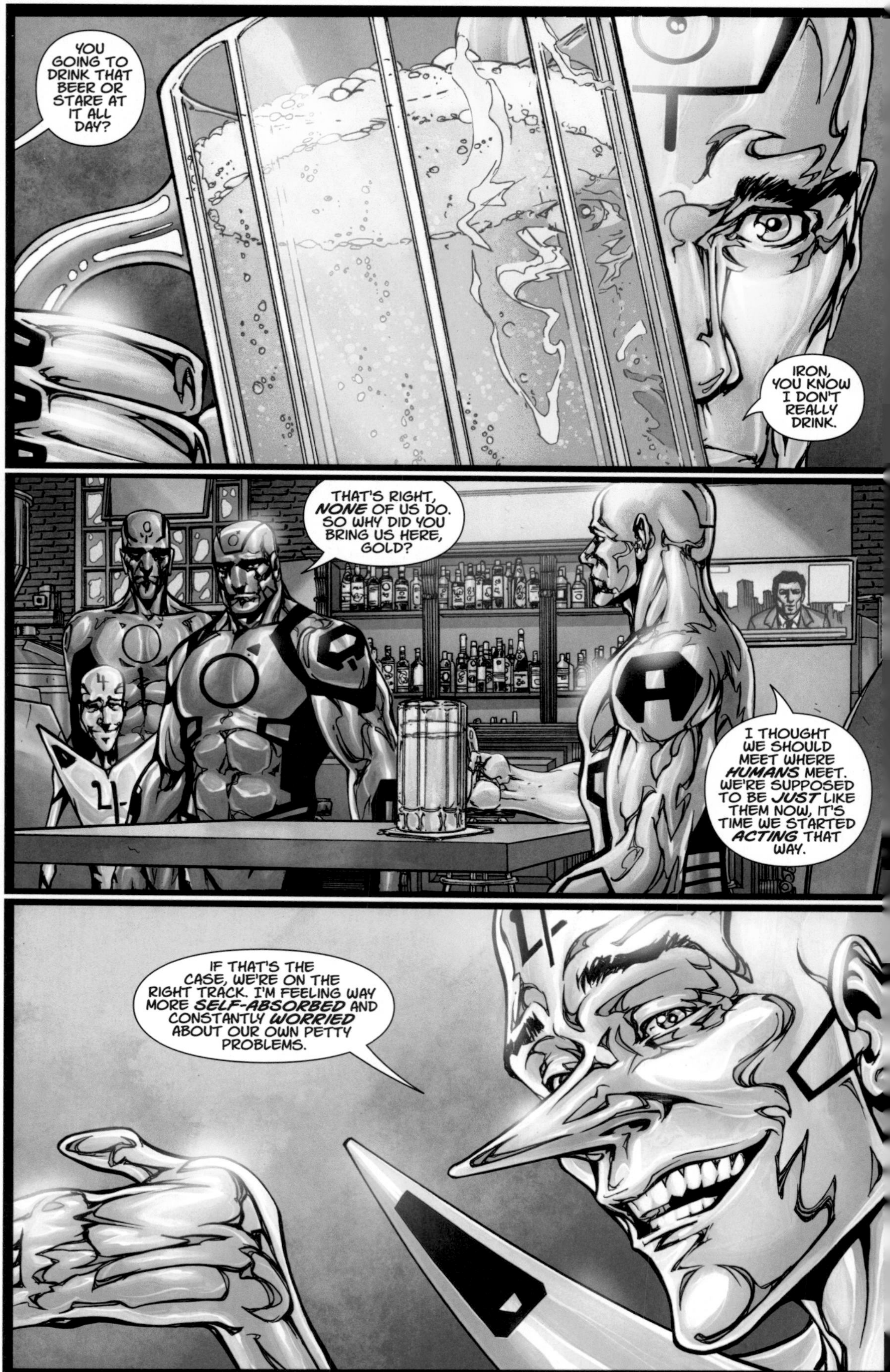
YOU GOING TO DRINK THAT BEER OR STARE AT IT ALL DAY?
IRON, YOU KNOW I DON'T REALLY DRINK.
THAT'S RIGHT, NONE OF US DO. SO WHY DID YOU BRING US HERE, GOLD?
I THOUGHT WE SHOULD MEET WHERE HUMANS MEET. WE'RE SUPPOSED TO BE JUST LIKE THEM NOW, IT'S TIME WE STARTED ACTING THAT WAY.
IF THAT'S THE CASE, WE'RE ON THE RIGHT TRACK. I'M FEELING WAY MORE SELF-ABSORBED AND CONSTANTLY WORRIED ABOUT OUR OWN PETTY PROBLEMS.

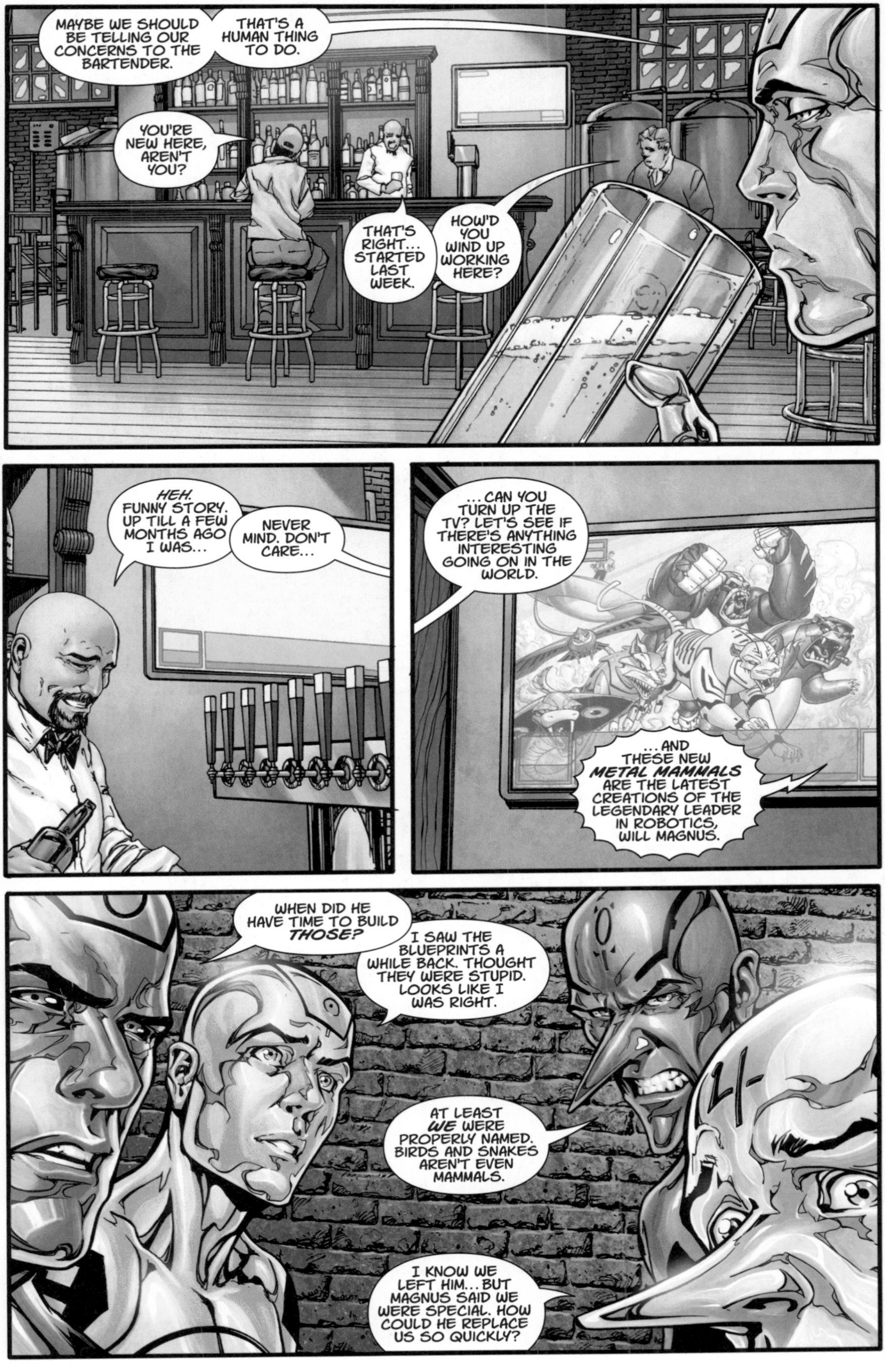
MAYBE WE SHOULD BE TELLING OUR CONCERNS TO THE BARTENDER.
THAT'S A HUMAN THING TO DO.
YOU'RE NEW HERE, AREN'T YOU?
THAT'S RIGHT... STARTED LAST WEEK.
HOW'D YOU WIND UP WORKING HERE?
HEH. FUNNY STORY. UP TILL A FEW MONTHS AGO I WAS...
NEVER MIND. DON'T CARE...
...CAN YOU TURN UP THE TV? LET'S SEE IF THERE'S ANYTHING INTERESTING GOING ON IN THE WORLD.
...AND THESE NEW ***METAL MAMMALS*** ARE THE LATEST CREATIONS OF THE LEGENDARY LEADER IN ROBOTICS, WILL MAGNUS.
WHEN DID HE HAVE TIME TO BUILD ***THOSE?***
I SAW THE BLUEPRINTS A WHILE BACK. THOUGHT THEY WERE STUPID. LOOKS LIKE I WAS RIGHT.
AT LEAST ***WE*** WERE PROPERLY NAMED. BIRDS AND SNAKES AREN'T EVEN MAMMALS.
I KNOW WE LEFT HIM... BUT MAGNUS SAID WE WERE SPECIAL. HOW COULD HE REPLACE US SO QUICKLY?

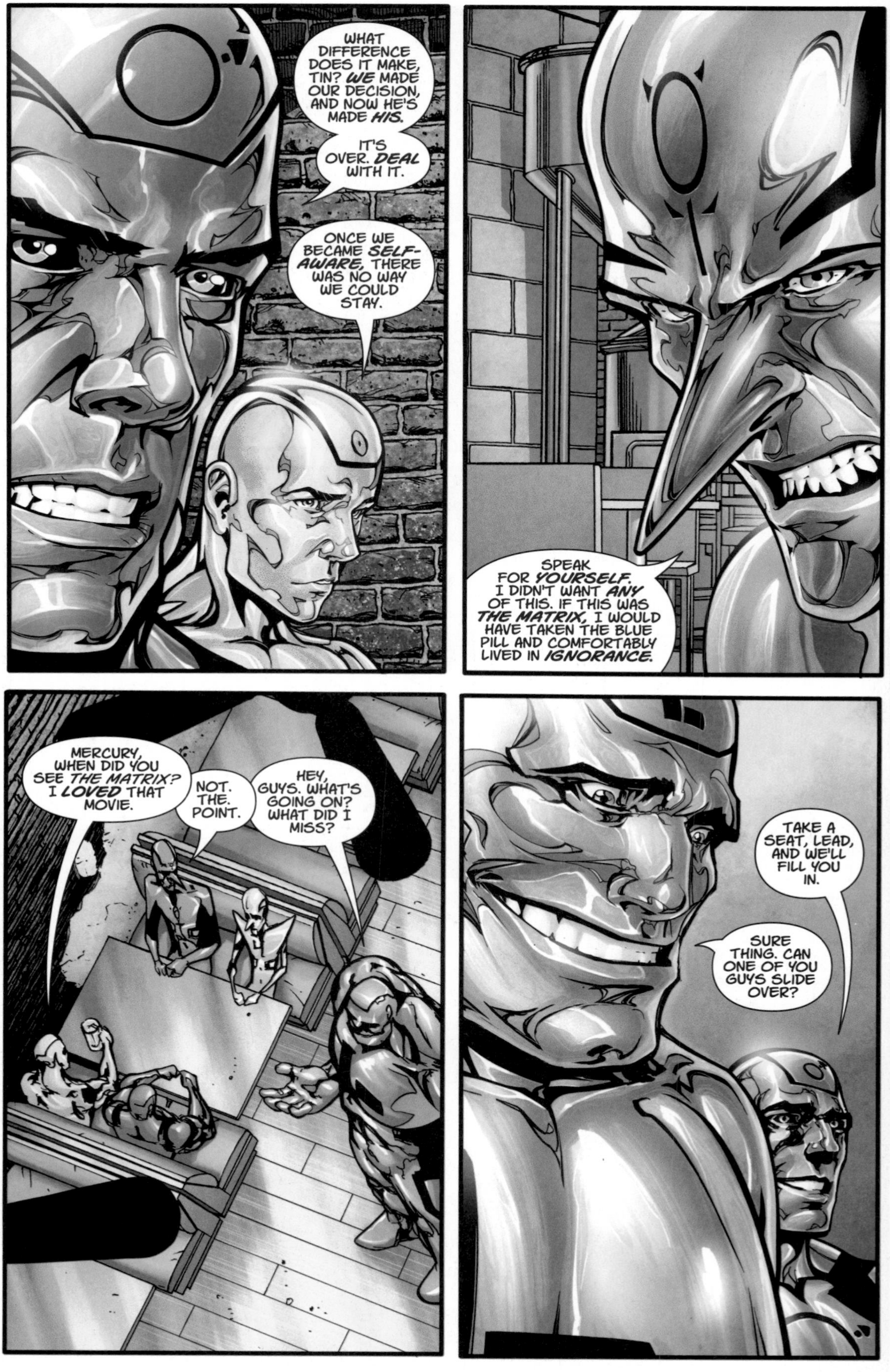
WHAT DIFFERENCE DOES IT MAKE, TIN? WE MADE OUR DECISION, AND NOW HE'S MADE HIS.
IT'S OVER. DEAL WITH IT.
ONCE WE BECAME SELF-AWARE, THERE WAS NO WAY WE COULD STAY.
SPEAK FOR YOURSELF. I DIDN'T WANT ANY OF THIS. IF THIS WAS THE MATRIX, I WOULD HAVE TAKEN THE BLUE PILL AND COMFORTABLY LIVED IN IGNORANCE.
MERCURY, WHEN DID YOU SEE THE MATRIX? I LOVED THAT MOVIE.
NOT. THE. POINT.
HEY, GUYS. WHAT'S GOING ON? WHAT DID I MISS?
TAKE A SEAT, LEAD, AND WE'LL FILL YOU IN.
SURE THING. CAN ONE OF YOU GUYS SLIDE OVER?

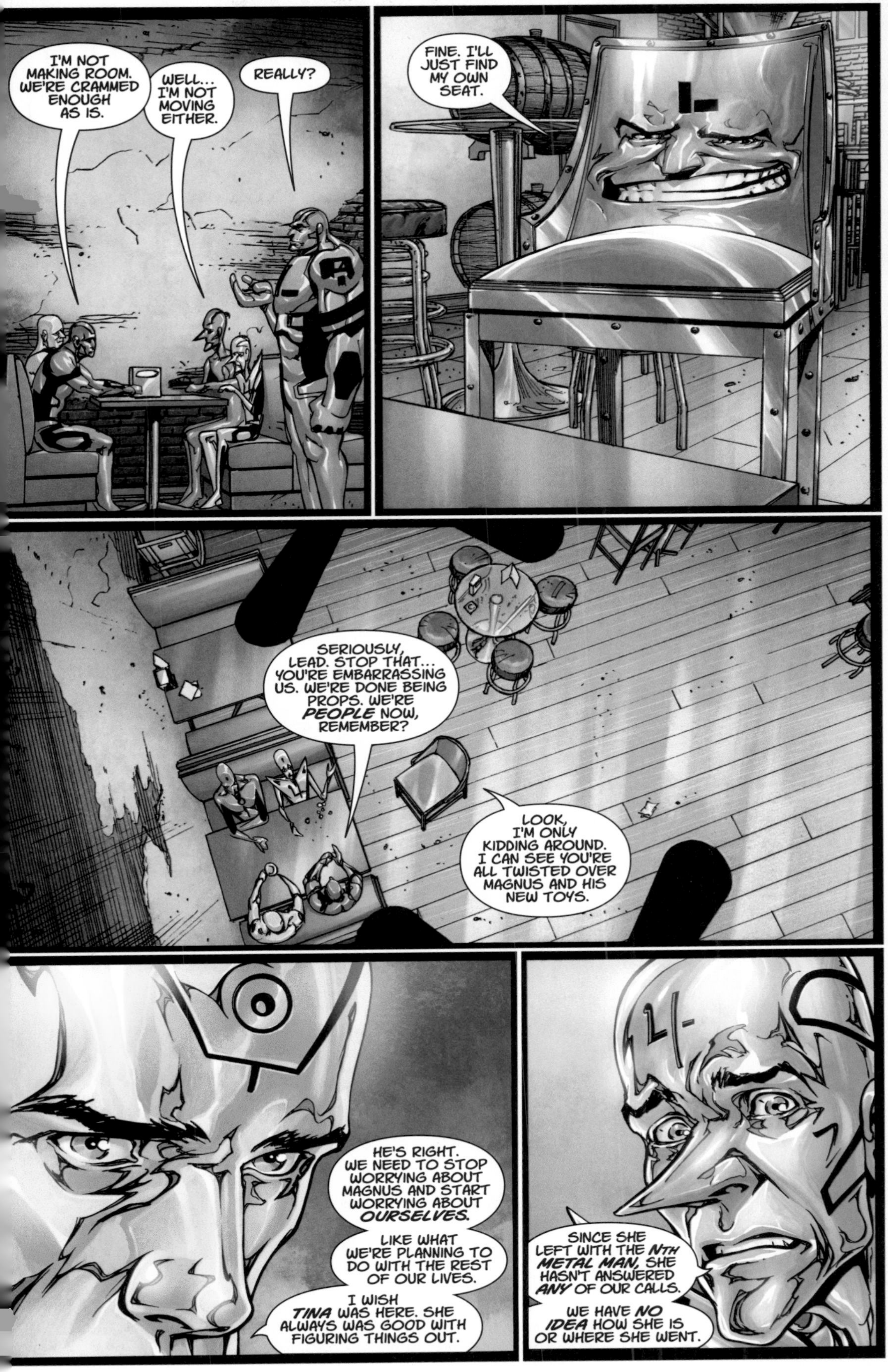

I'M NOT MAKING ROOM. WE'RE CRAMMED ENOUGH AS IS.
WELL... I'M NOT MOVING EITHER.
REALLY?
FINE. I'LL JUST FIND MY OWN SEAT.
SERIOUSLY, LEAD. STOP THAT... YOU'RE EMBARRASSING US. WE'RE DONE BEING PROPS. WE'RE PEOPLE NOW, REMEMBER?
LOOK, I'M ONLY KIDDING AROUND. I CAN SEE YOU'RE ALL TWISTED OVER MAGNUS AND HIS NEW TOYS.
HE'S RIGHT. WE NEED TO STOP WORRYING ABOUT MAGNUS AND START WORRYING ABOUT OURSELVES.
LIKE WHAT WE'RE PLANNING TO DO WITH THE REST OF OUR LIVES.
I WISH TINA WAS HERE. SHE ALWAYS WAS GOOD WITH FIGURING THINGS OUT.
SINCE SHE LEFT WITH THE NTH METAL MAN, SHE HASN'T ANSWERED ANY OF OUR CALLS.
WE HAVE NO IDEA HOW SHE IS OR WHERE SHE WENT.

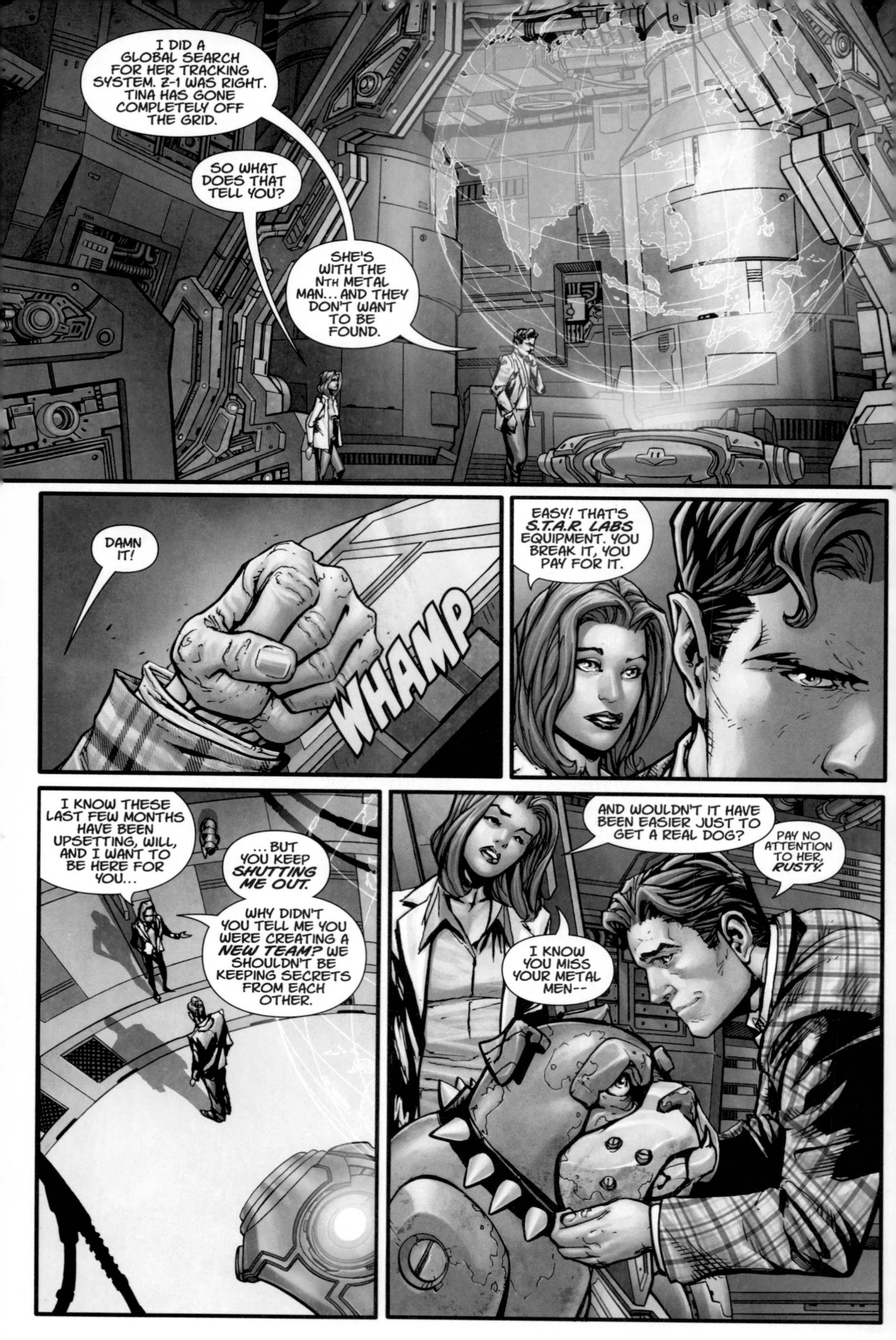
I DID A GLOBAL SEARCH FOR HER TRACKING SYSTEM. Z-1 WAS RIGHT. TINA HAS GONE COMPLETELY OFF THE GRID.
SO WHAT DOES THAT TELL YOU?
SHE'S WITH THE NTH METAL MAN... AND THEY DON'T WANT TO BE FOUND.
DAMN IT!
WHAMP
EASY! THAT'S S.T.A.R. LABS EQUIPMENT. YOU BREAK IT, YOU PAY FOR IT.
I KNOW THESE LAST FEW MONTHS HAVE BEEN UPSETTING, WILL, AND I WANT TO BE HERE FOR YOU...
...BUT YOU KEEP SHUTTING ME OUT.
WHY DIDN'T YOU TELL ME YOU WERE CREATING A NEW TEAM? WE SHOULDN'T BE KEEPING SECRETS FROM EACH OTHER.
I KNOW YOU MISS YOUR METAL MEN--
AND WOULDN'T IT HAVE BEEN EASIER JUST TO GET A REAL DOG?
PAY NO ATTENTION TO HER, RUSTY.

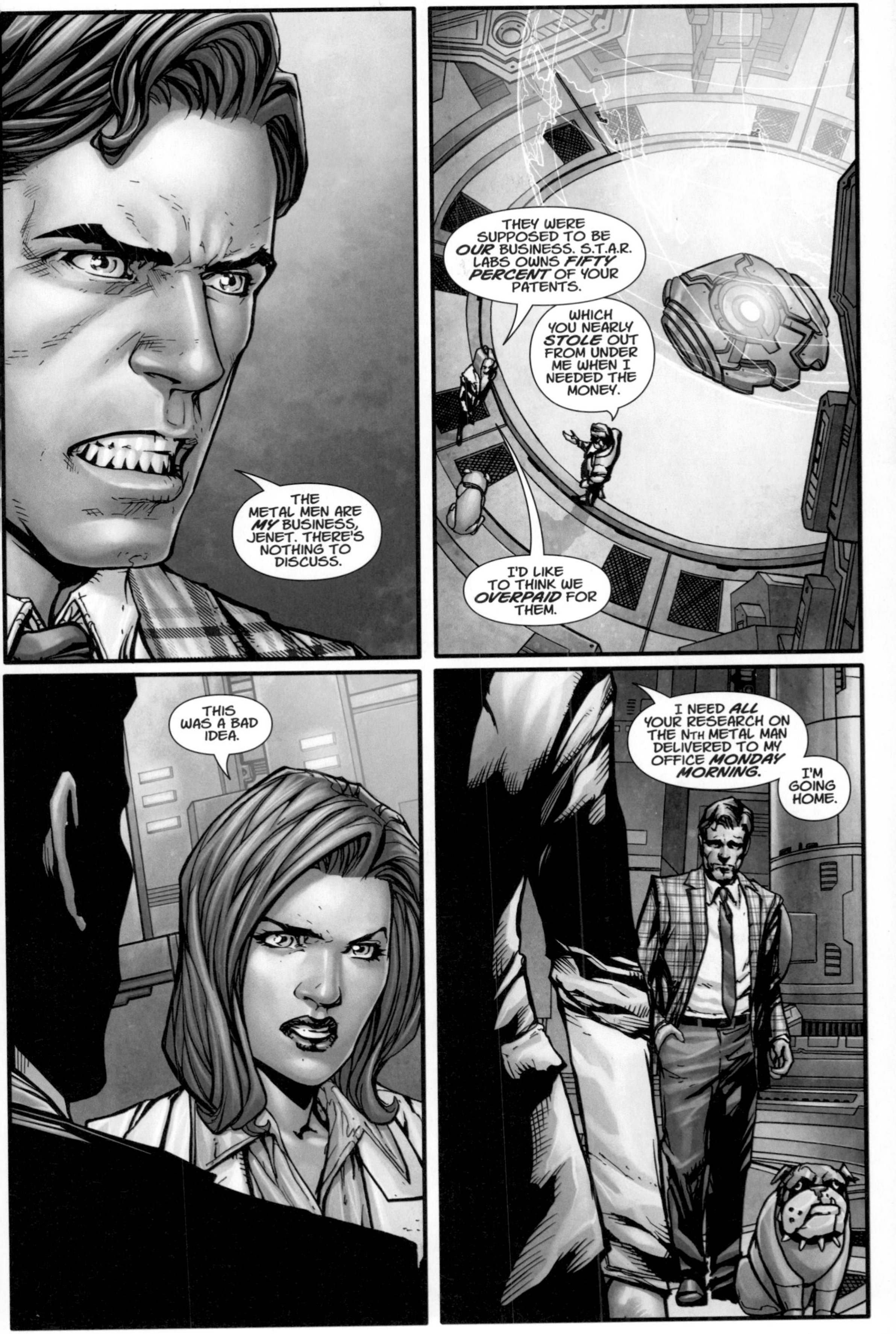
THE METAL MEN ARE MY BUSINESS, JENET. THERE'S NOTHING TO DISCUSS.
THEY WERE SUPPOSED TO BE OUR BUSINESS. S.T.A.R. LABS OWNS FIFTY PERCENT OF YOUR PATENTS.
WHICH YOU NEARLY STOLE OUT FROM UNDER ME WHEN I NEEDED THE MONEY.
I'D LIKE TO THINK WE OVERPAID FOR THEM.
THIS WAS A BAD IDEA.
I NEED ALL YOUR RESEARCH ON THE NTH METAL MAN DELIVERED TO MY OFFICE MONDAY MORNING.
I'M GOING HOME.

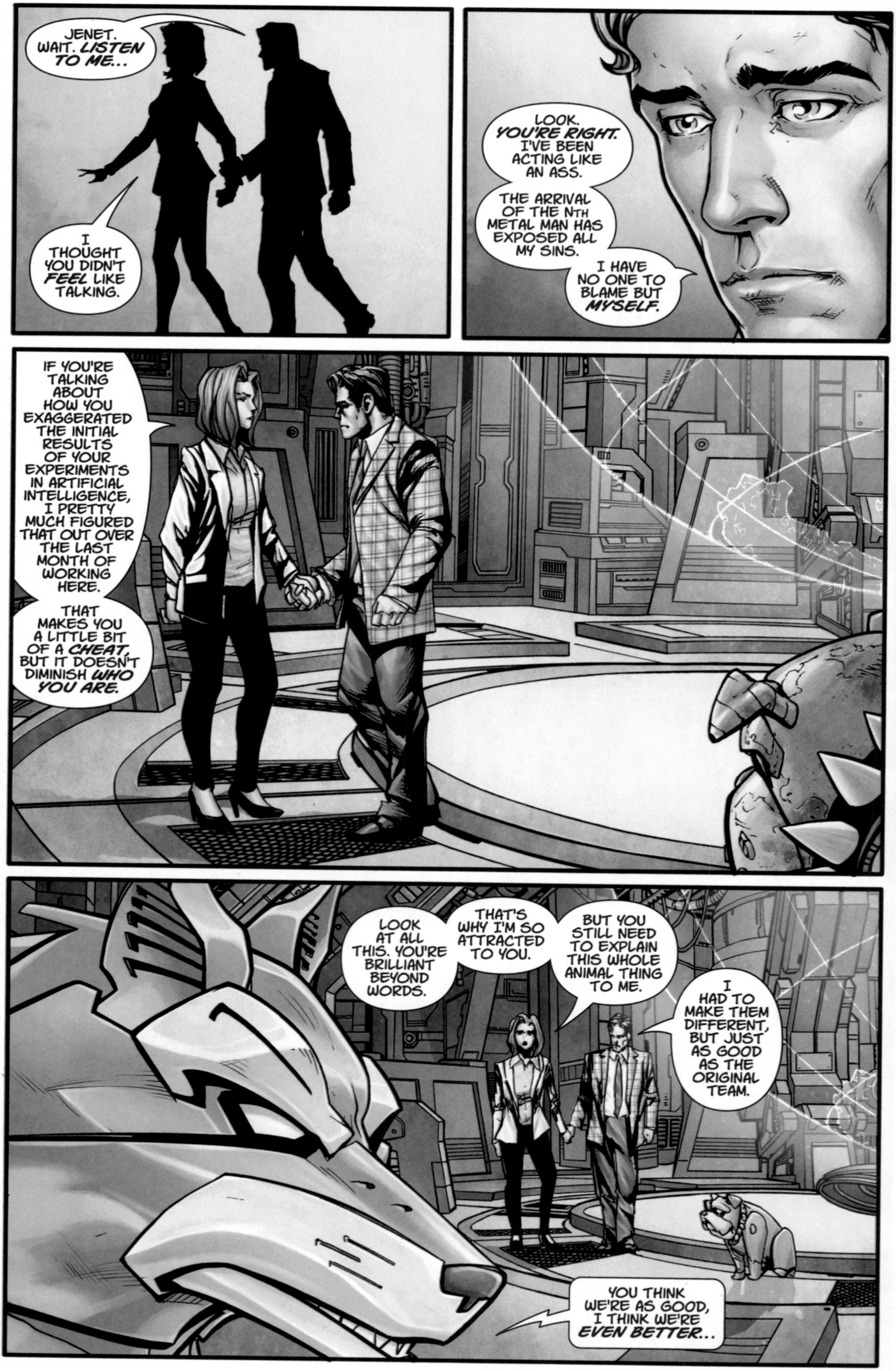
JENET. WAIT. LISTEN TO ME...
I THOUGHT YOU DIDN'T FEEL LIKE TALKING.
LOOK. YOU'RE RIGHT. I'VE BEEN ACTING LIKE AN ASS.
THE ARRIVAL OF THE NTH METAL MAN HAS EXPOSED ALL MY SINS.
I HAVE NO ONE TO BLAME BUT MYSELF.
IF YOU'RE TALKING ABOUT HOW YOU EXAGGERATED THE INITIAL RESULTS OF YOUR EXPERIMENTS IN ARTIFICIAL INTELLIGENCE, I PRETTY MUCH FIGURED THAT OUT OVER THE LAST MONTH OF WORKING HERE.
THAT MAKES YOU A LITTLE BIT OF A CHEAT, BUT IT DOESN'T DIMINISH WHO YOU ARE.
LOOK AT ALL THIS. YOU'RE BRILLIANT BEYOND WORDS.
THAT'S WHY I'M SO ATTRACTED TO YOU.
BUT YOU STILL NEED TO EXPLAIN THIS WHOLE ANIMAL THING TO ME.
I HAD TO MAKE THEM DIFFERENT, BUT JUST AS GOOD AS THE ORIGINAL TEAM.
YOU THINK WE'RE AS GOOD, I THINK WE'RE EVEN BETTER...

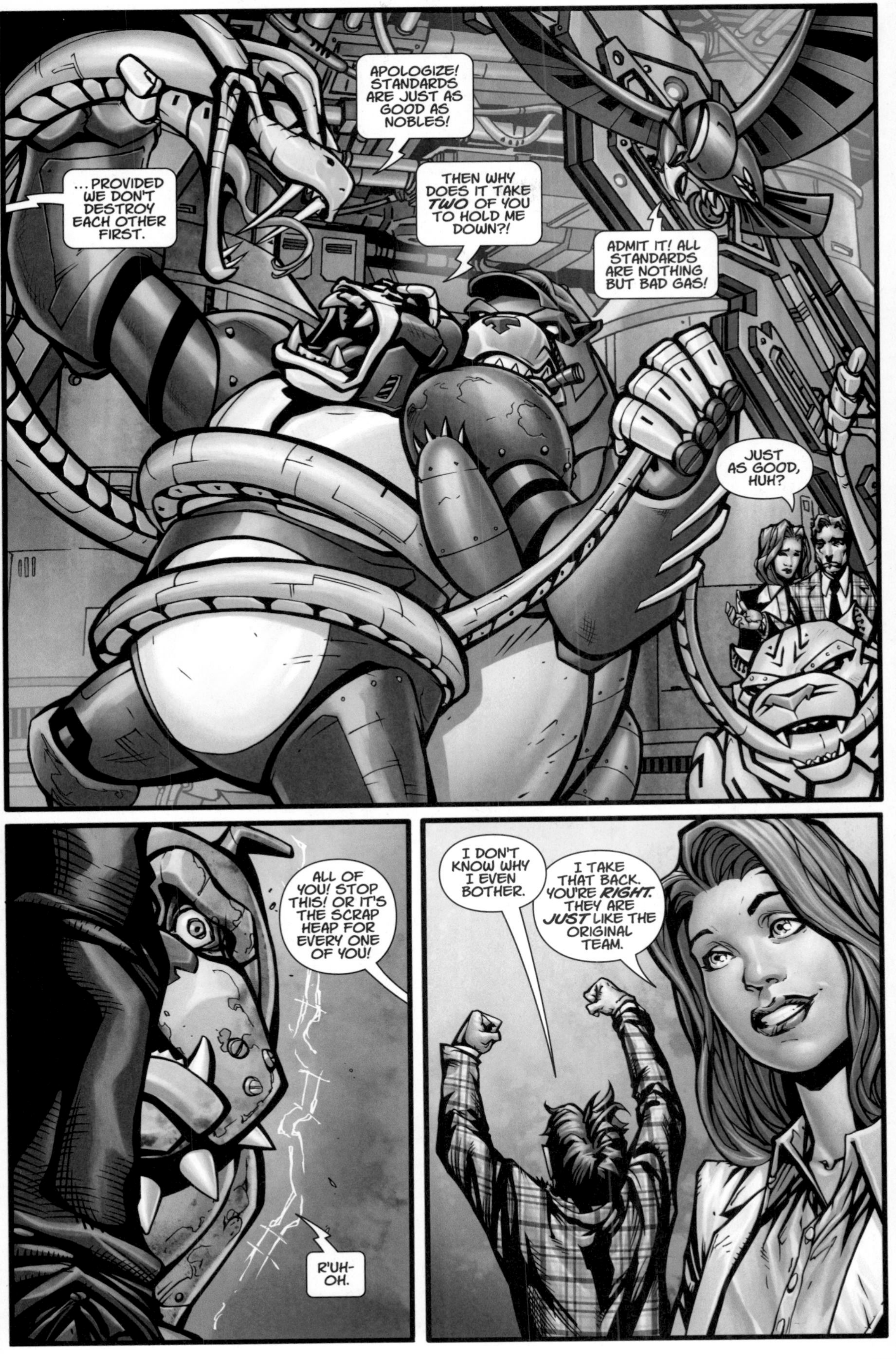
...PROVIDED WE DON'T DESTROY EACH OTHER FIRST.
APOLOGIZE! STANDARDS ARE JUST AS GOOD AS NOBLES!
THEN WHY DOES IT TAKE *TWO* OF YOU TO HOLD ME DOWN?!
ADMIT IT! ALL STANDARDS ARE NOTHING BUT BAD GAS!
JUST AS GOOD, HUH?
ALL OF YOU! STOP THIS! OR IT'S THE SCRAP HEAP FOR EVERY ONE OF YOU!
R'UH-OH.
I DON'T KNOW WHY I EVEN BOTHER.
I TAKE THAT BACK. YOU'RE *RIGHT.* THEY ARE *JUST* LIKE THE ORIGINAL TEAM.

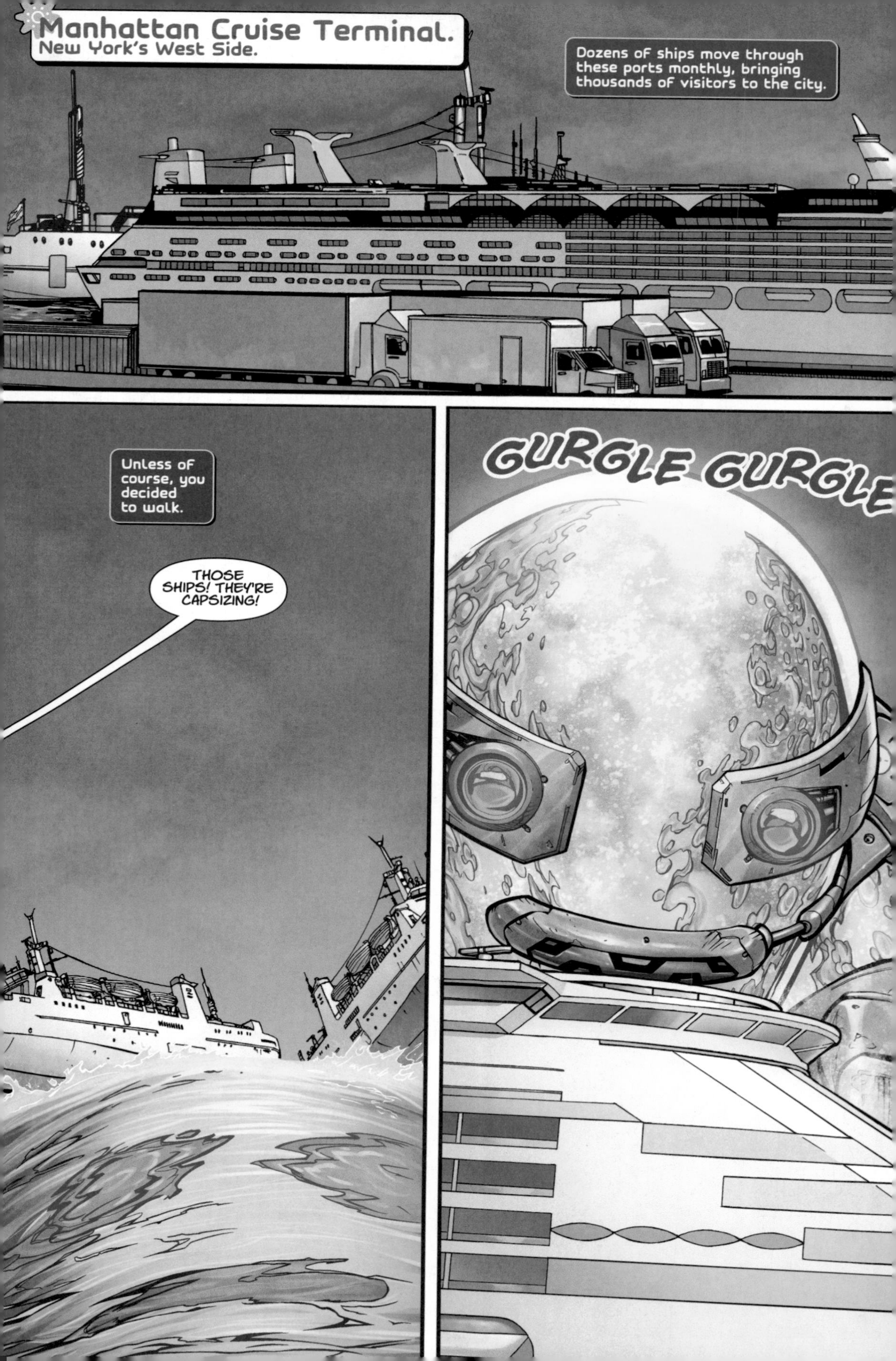
Manhattan Cruise Terminal.
New York's West Side.
Dozens of ships move through these ports monthly, bringing thousands of visitors to the city.
Unless of course, you decided to walk.
THOSE SHIPS! THEY'RE CAPSIZING!
GURGLE GURGLE

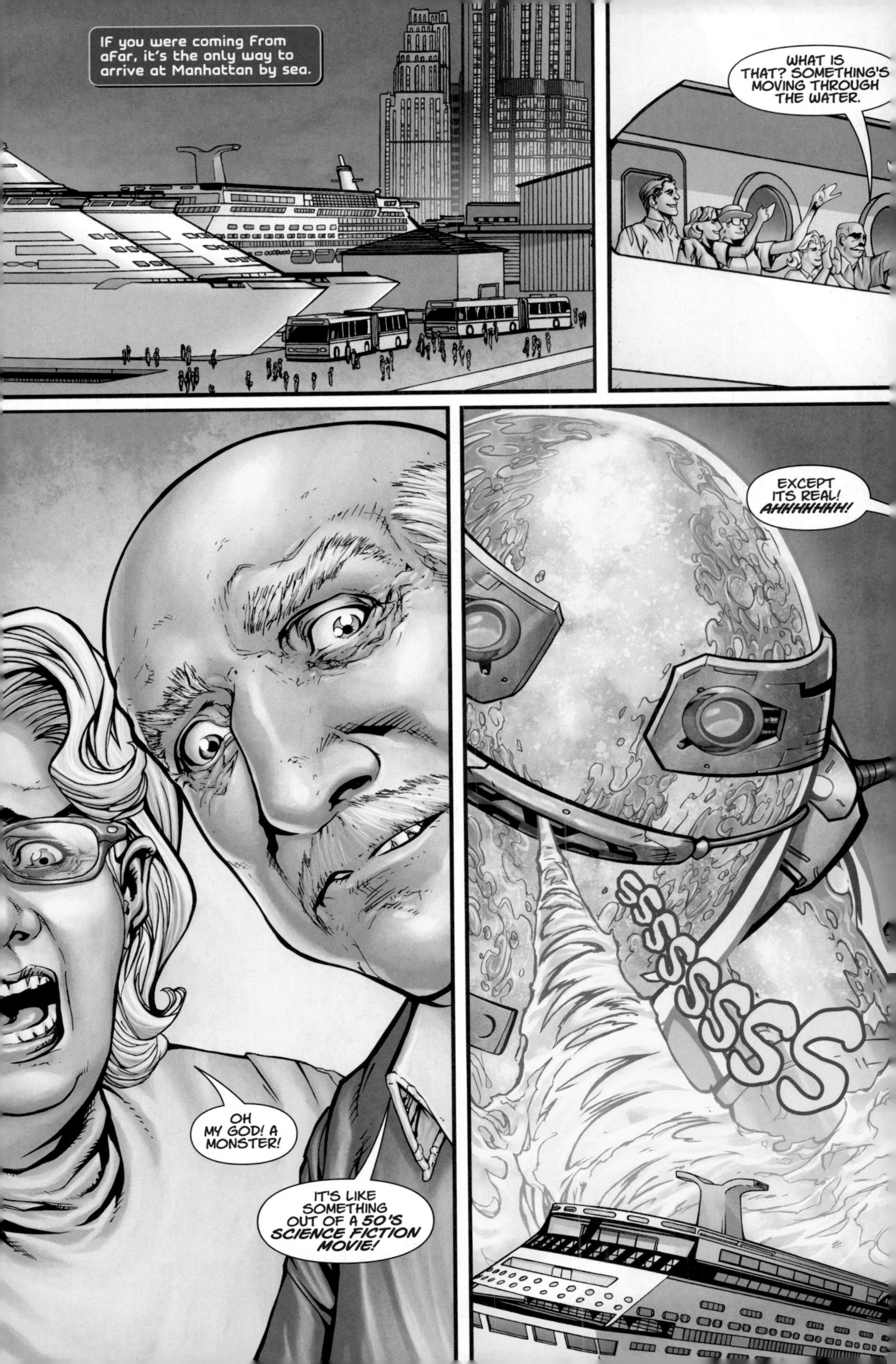

If you were coming from afar, it's the only way to arrive at Manhattan by sea.
WHAT IS THAT? SOMETHING'S MOVING THROUGH THE WATER.
OH MY GOD! A MONSTER!
IT'S LIKE SOMETHING OUT OF A 50'S SCIENCE FICTION MOVIE!
EXCEPT ITS REAL! AHHHHHHH!
SSSSSSSSS

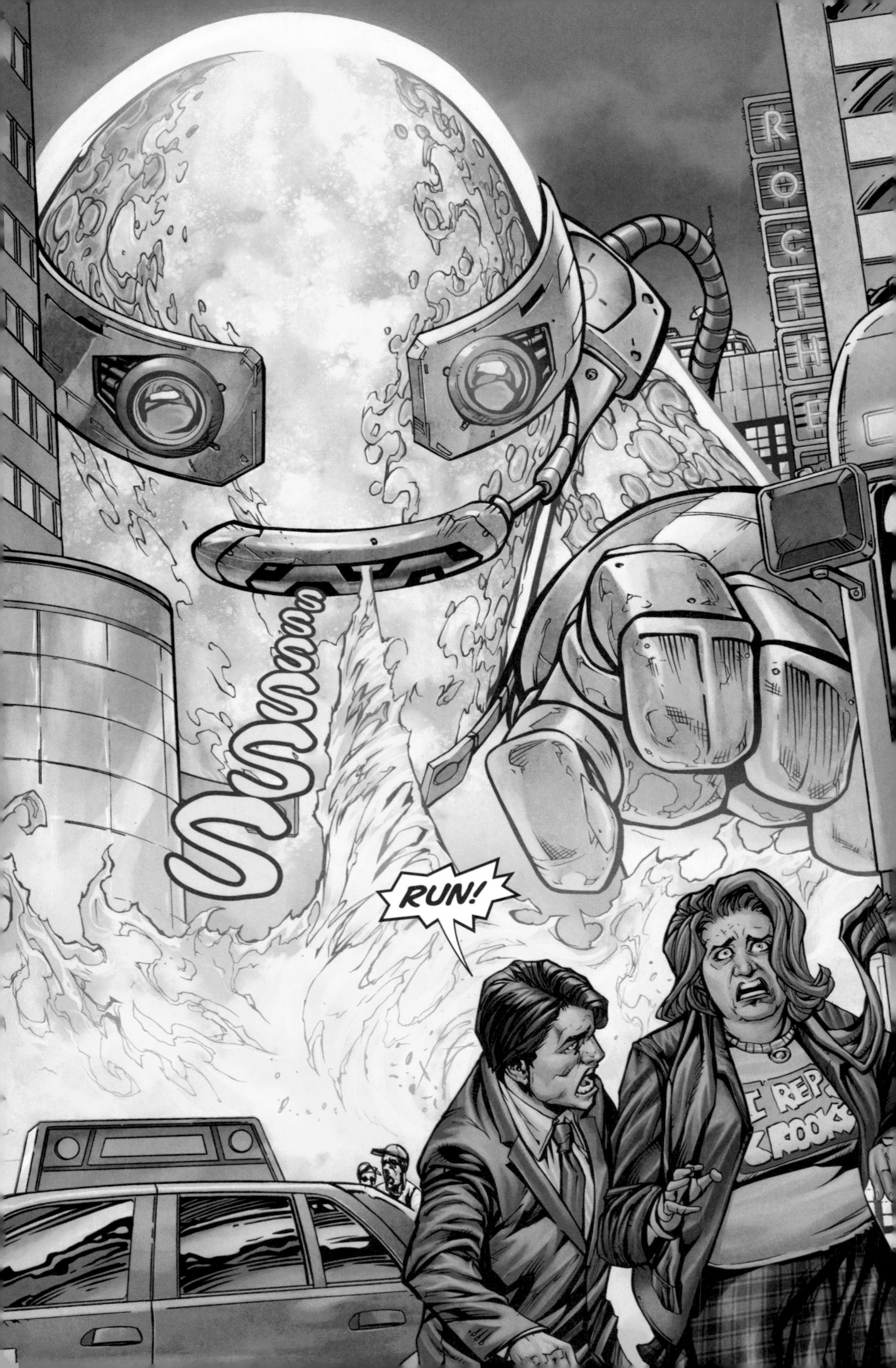
RUN!

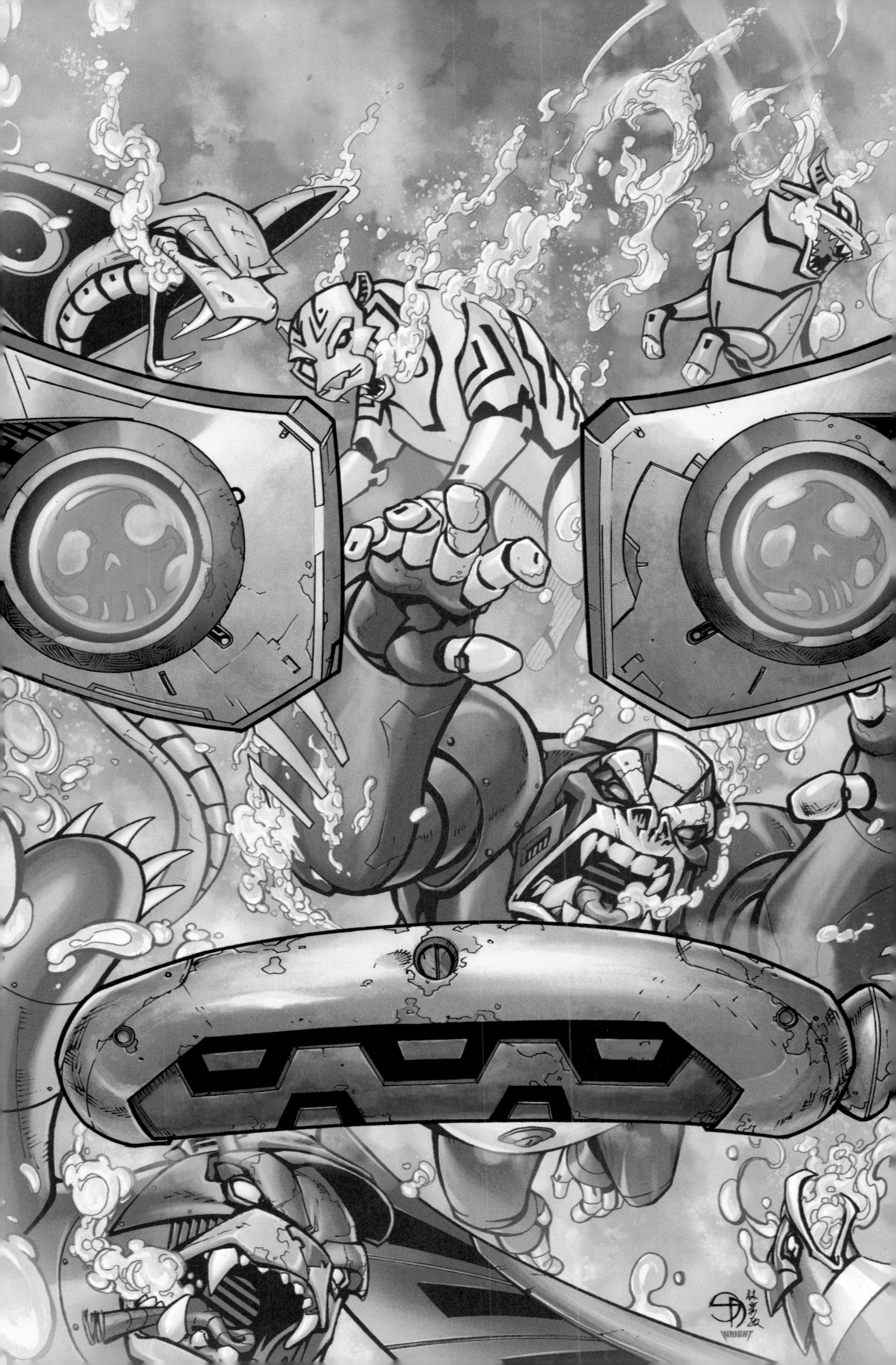
WRIGHT

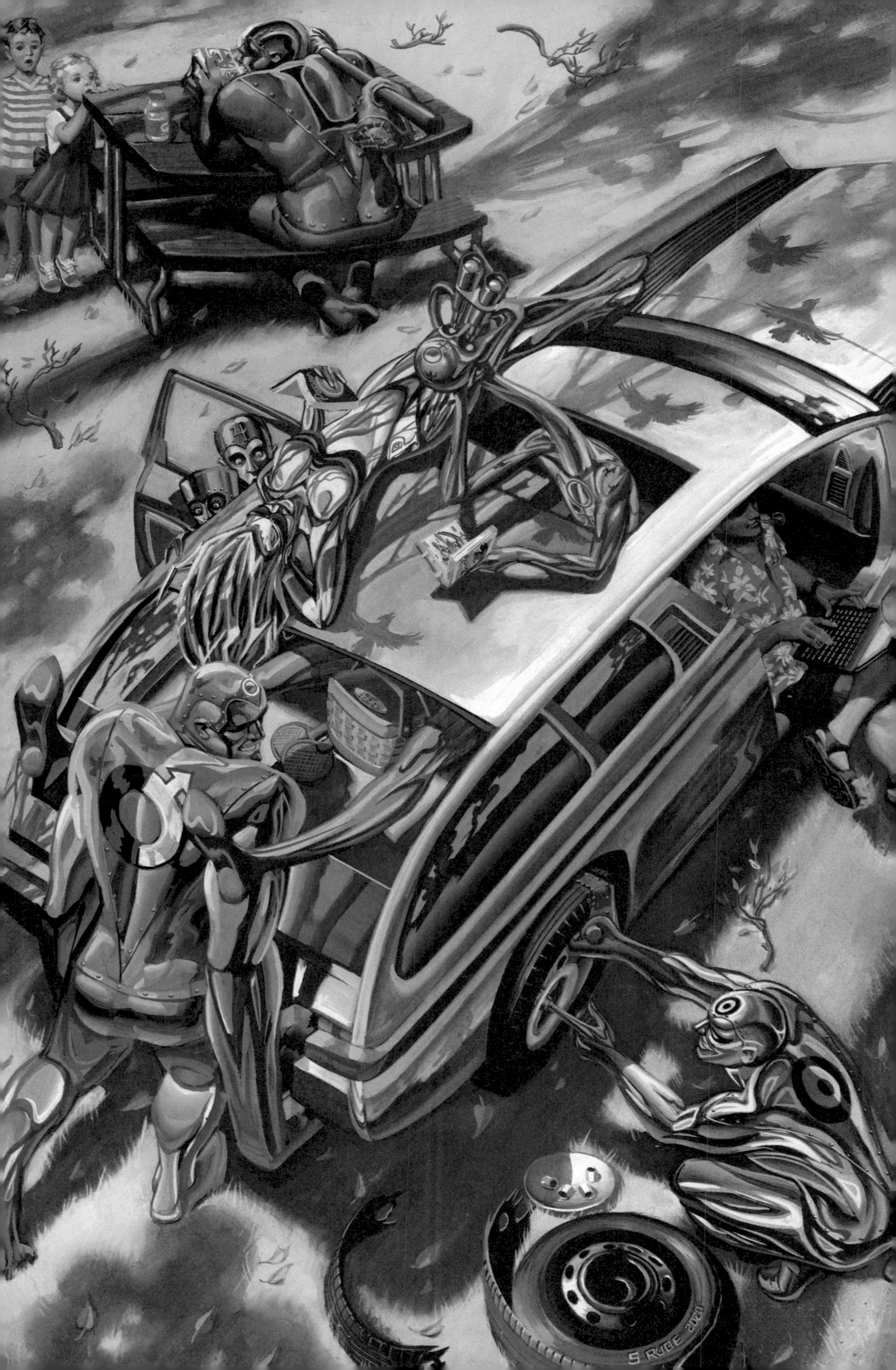
S. RUDE 2020

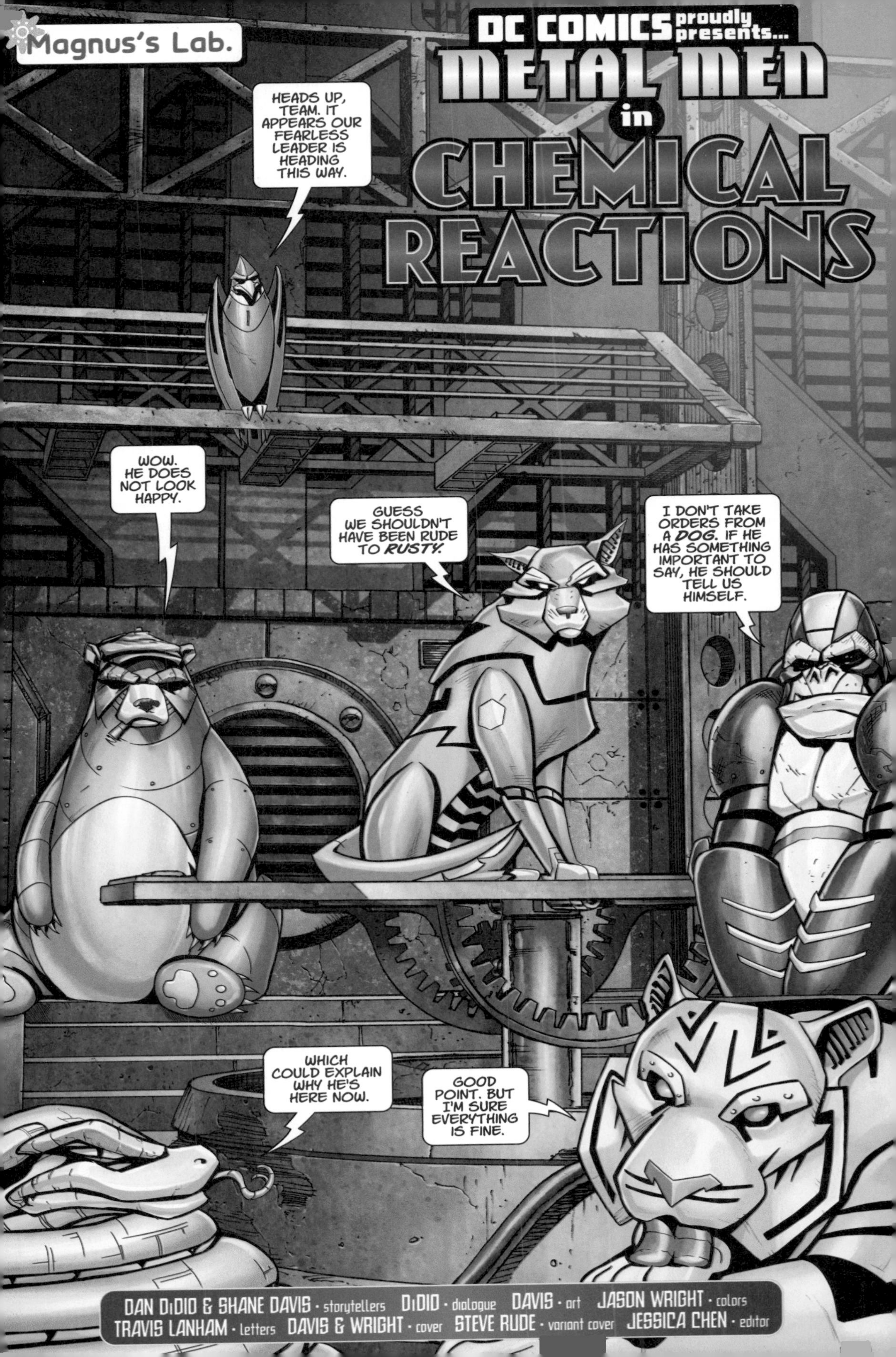

Magnus's Lab.
DC COMICS proudly presents...
METAL MEN
in
CHEMICAL REACTIONS
HEADS UP, TEAM. IT APPEARS OUR FEARLESS LEADER IS HEADING THIS WAY.
WOW. HE DOES NOT LOOK HAPPY.
GUESS WE SHOULDN'T HAVE BEEN RUDE TO RUSTY.
I DON'T TAKE ORDERS FROM A DOG. IF HE HAS SOMETHING IMPORTANT TO SAY, HE SHOULD TELL US HIMSELF.
WHICH COULD EXPLAIN WHY HE'S HERE NOW.
GOOD POINT. BUT I'M SURE EVERYTHING IS FINE.
DAN DIDIO & SHANE DAVIS · storytellers DIDIO · dialogue DAVIS · art JASON WRIGHT · colors
TRAVIS LANHAM · letters DAVIS & WRIGHT · cover STEVE RUDE · variant cover JESSICA CHEN · editor

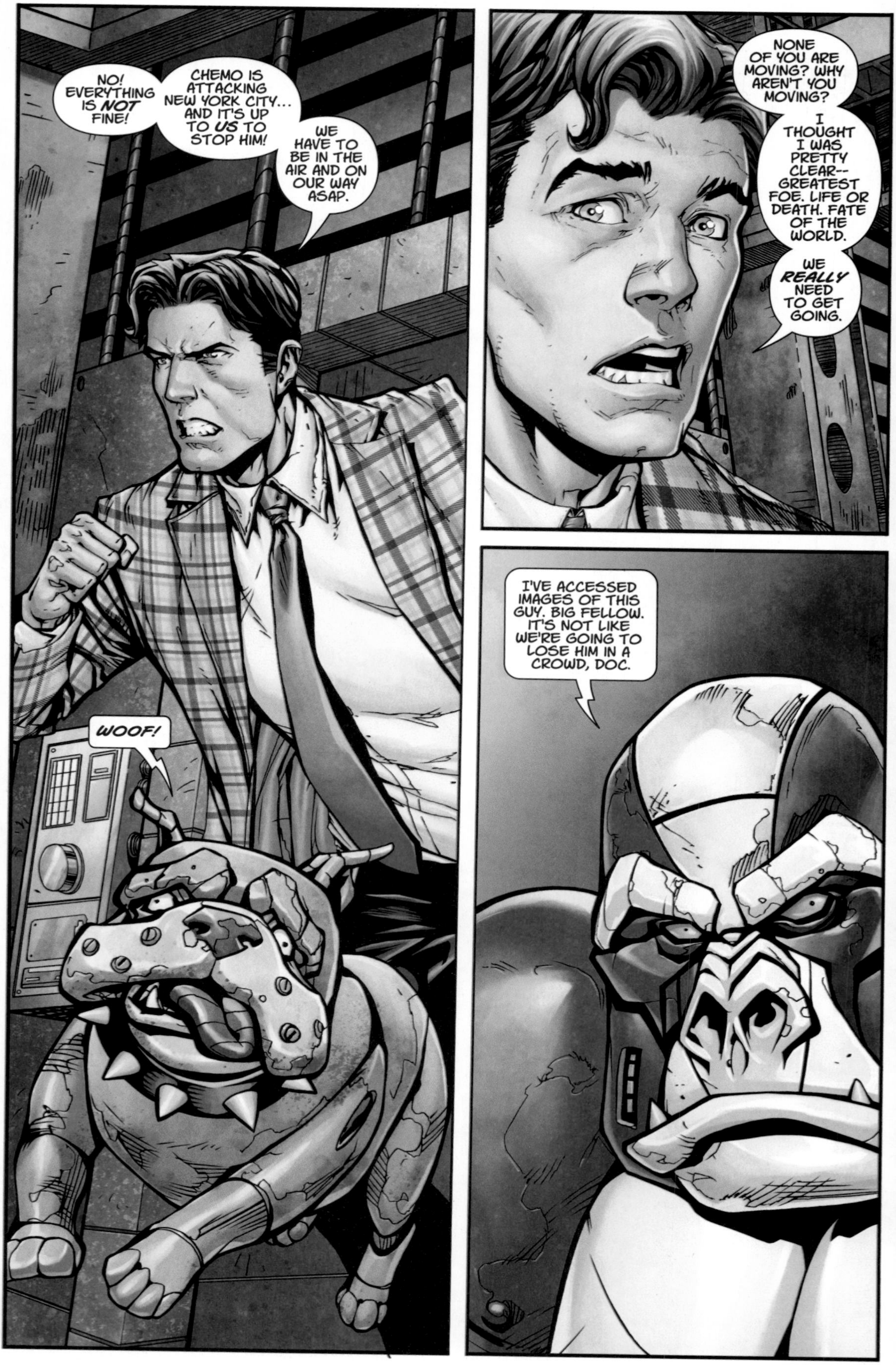
NO! EVERYTHING IS *NOT* FINE!
CHEMO IS ATTACKING NEW YORK CITY... AND IT'S UP TO *US* TO STOP HIM!
WE HAVE TO BE IN THE AIR AND ON OUR WAY ASAP.
WOOF!
NONE OF YOU ARE MOVING? WHY AREN'T YOU MOVING?
I THOUGHT I WAS PRETTY CLEAR-- GREATEST FOE. LIFE OR DEATH. FATE OF THE WORLD.
WE *REALLY* NEED TO GET GOING.
I'VE ACCESSED IMAGES OF THIS GUY. BIG FELLOW. IT'S NOT LIKE WE'RE GOING TO LOSE HIM IN A CROWD, DOC.

YOU ALL SAW THE DAMAGE THE MISSILE MEN CAUSED. THAT'S *NOTHING* COMPARED TO THE CARNAGE *CHEMO* CREATES.

IT'S OUR RESPONSIBILITY TO STOP HIM.

SEE, THAT'S THE PART I FIND A LITTLE CONFUSING.

I MEAN, IF THIS FIGHT IS AN ONGOING OCCURRENCE, SHOULDN'T WE TRY A *DIFFERENT TACK?*

MAYBE WE SHOULD TRY TALKING IT OUT, END THIS DRAMA A DIFFERENT WAY?

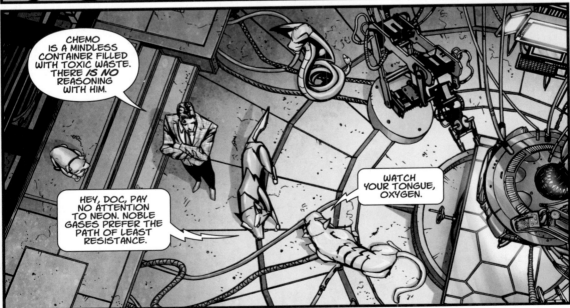

CHEMO IS A MINDLESS CONTAINER FILLED WITH TOXIC WASTE. THERE *IS NO* REASONING WITH HIM.

HEY, DOC, PAY NO ATTENTION TO NEON. NOBLE GASES PREFER THE PATH OF LEAST RESISTANCE.

WATCH YOUR TONGUE, OXYGEN.

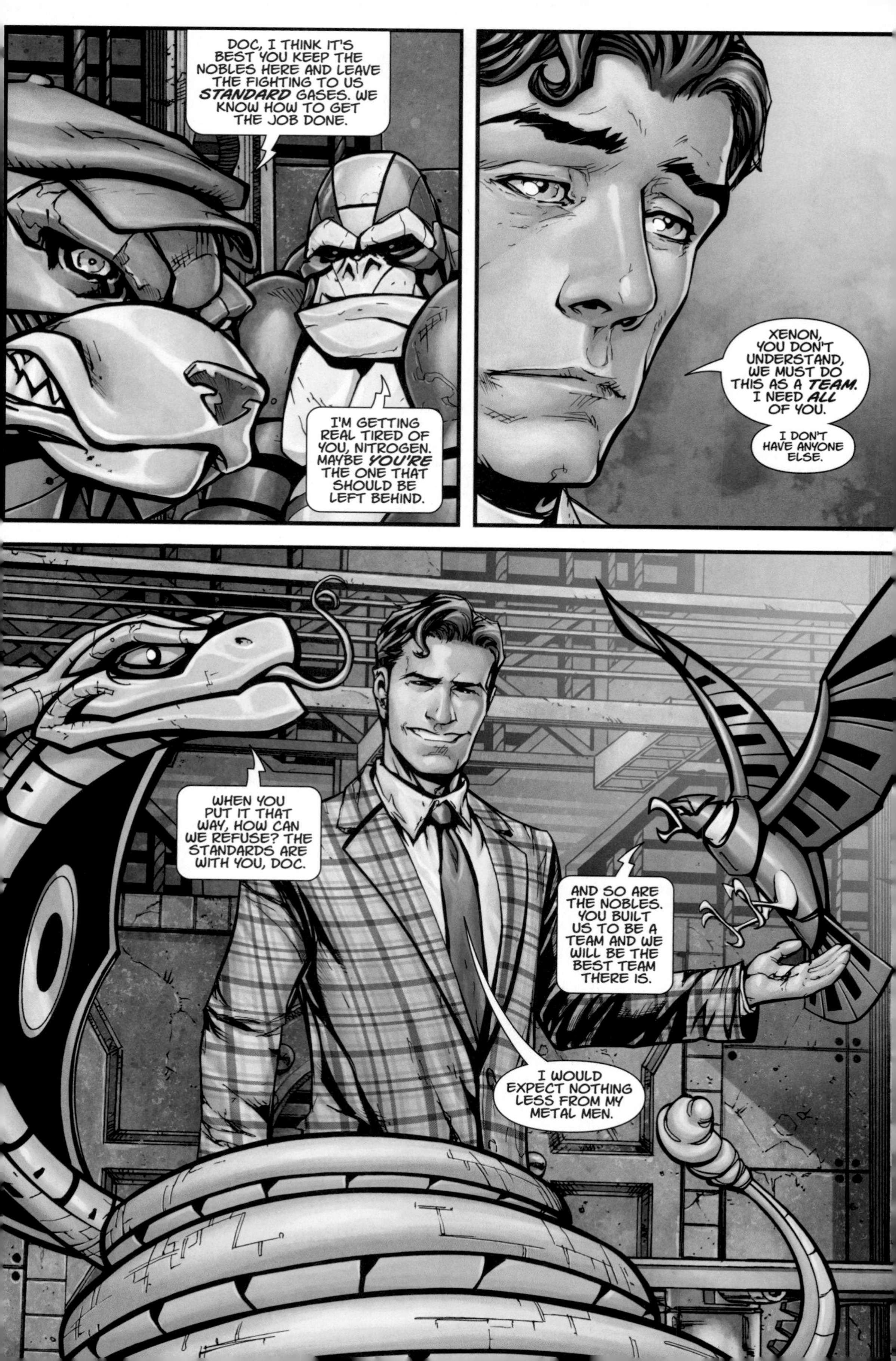
DOC, I THINK IT'S BEST YOU KEEP THE NOBLES HERE AND LEAVE THE FIGHTING TO US *STANDARD* GASES. WE KNOW HOW TO GET THE JOB DONE.
I'M GETTING REAL TIRED OF YOU, NITROGEN. MAYBE *YOU'RE* THE ONE THAT SHOULD BE LEFT BEHIND.
XENON, YOU DON'T UNDERSTAND, WE MUST DO THIS AS A *TEAM*. I NEED *ALL* OF YOU.
I DON'T HAVE ANYONE ELSE.
WHEN YOU PUT IT THAT WAY, HOW CAN WE REFUSE? THE STANDARDS ARE WITH YOU, DOC.
AND SO ARE THE NOBLES. YOU BUILT US TO BE A TEAM AND WE WILL BE THE BEST TEAM THERE IS.
I WOULD EXPECT NOTHING LESS FROM MY METAL MEN.

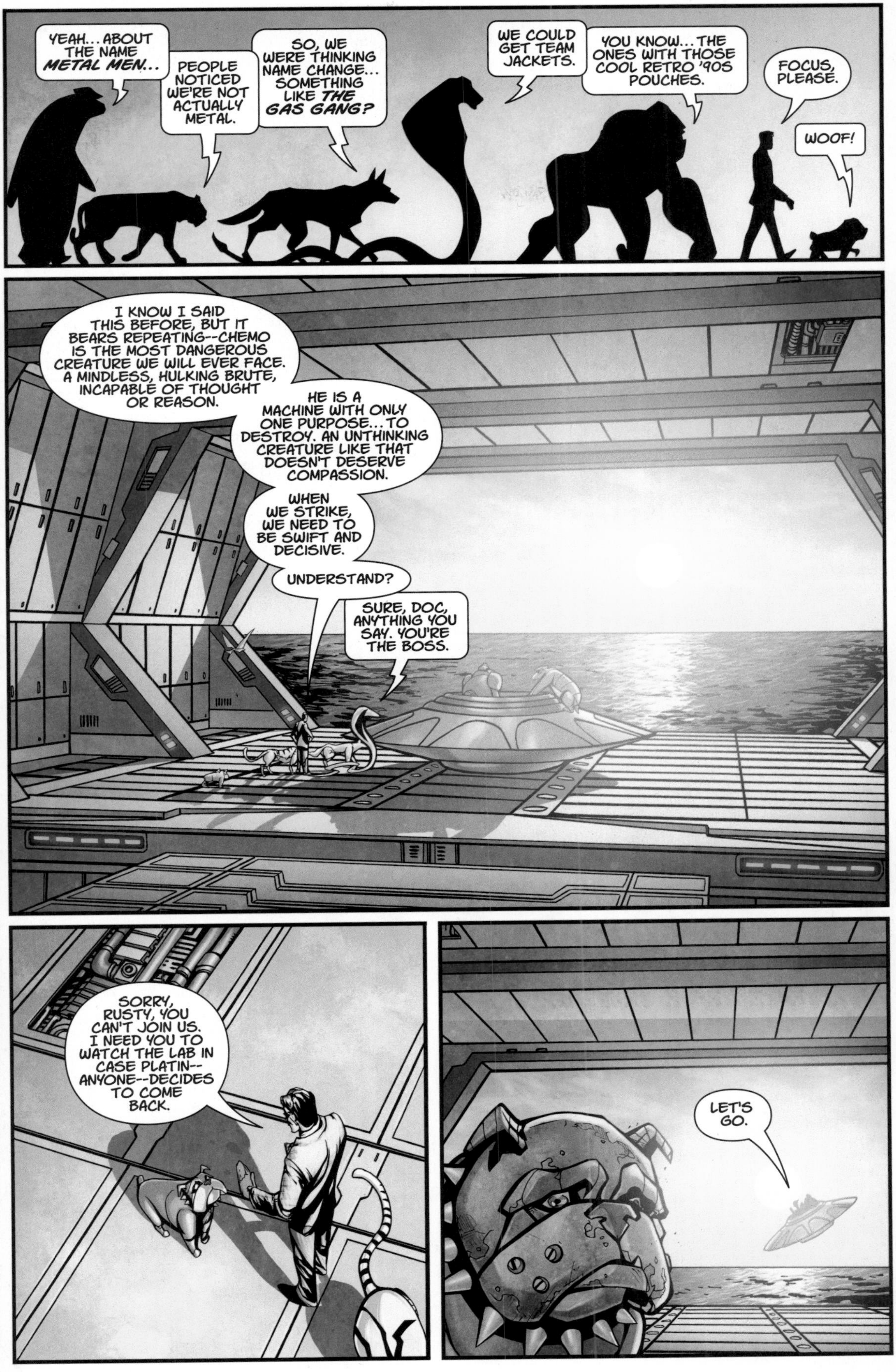
YEAH... ABOUT THE NAME METAL MEN...
PEOPLE NOTICED WE'RE NOT ACTUALLY METAL.
SO, WE WERE THINKING NAME CHANGE... SOMETHING LIKE THE GAS GANG?
WE COULD GET TEAM JACKETS.
YOU KNOW... THE ONES WITH THOSE COOL RETRO '90S POUCHES.
FOCUS, PLEASE.
WOOF!
I KNOW I SAID THIS BEFORE, BUT IT BEARS REPEATING--CHEMO IS THE MOST DANGEROUS CREATURE WE WILL EVER FACE. A MINDLESS, HULKING BRUTE, INCAPABLE OF THOUGHT OR REASON.
HE IS A MACHINE WITH ONLY ONE PURPOSE... TO DESTROY. AN UNTHINKING CREATURE LIKE THAT DOESN'T DESERVE COMPASSION.
WHEN WE STRIKE, WE NEED TO BE SWIFT AND DECISIVE.
UNDERSTAND?
SURE, DOC, ANYTHING YOU SAY. YOU'RE THE BOSS.
SORRY, RUSTY, YOU CAN'T JOIN US. I NEED YOU TO WATCH THE LAB IN CASE PLATIN-- ANYONE--DECIDES TO COME BACK.
LET'S GO.

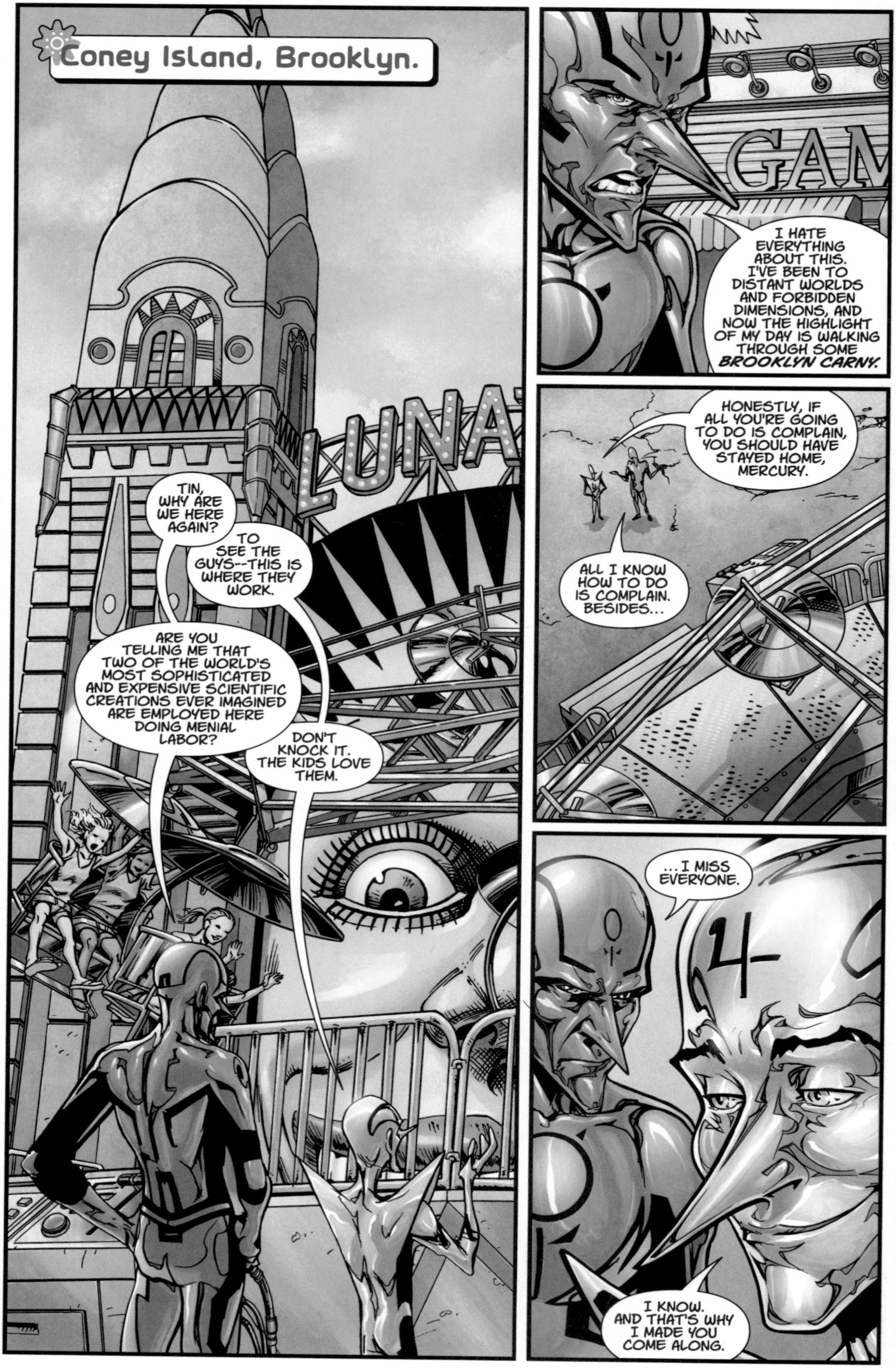
Coney Island, Brooklyn.
LUNA
TIN, WHY ARE WE HERE AGAIN?
TO SEE THE GUYS--THIS IS WHERE THEY WORK.
ARE YOU TELLING ME THAT TWO OF THE WORLD'S MOST SOPHISTICATED AND EXPENSIVE SCIENTIFIC CREATIONS EVER IMAGINED ARE EMPLOYED HERE DOING MENIAL LABOR?
DON'T KNOCK IT. THE KIDS LOVE THEM.
GAM
I HATE EVERYTHING ABOUT THIS. I'VE BEEN TO DISTANT WORLDS AND FORBIDDEN DIMENSIONS, AND NOW THE HIGHLIGHT OF MY DAY IS WALKING THROUGH SOME BROOKLYN CARNY.
HONESTLY, IF ALL YOU'RE GOING TO DO IS COMPLAIN, YOU SHOULD HAVE STAYED HOME, MERCURY.
ALL I KNOW HOW TO DO IS COMPLAIN. BESIDES...
...I MISS EVERYONE.
I KNOW. AND THAT'S WHY I MADE YOU COME ALONG.

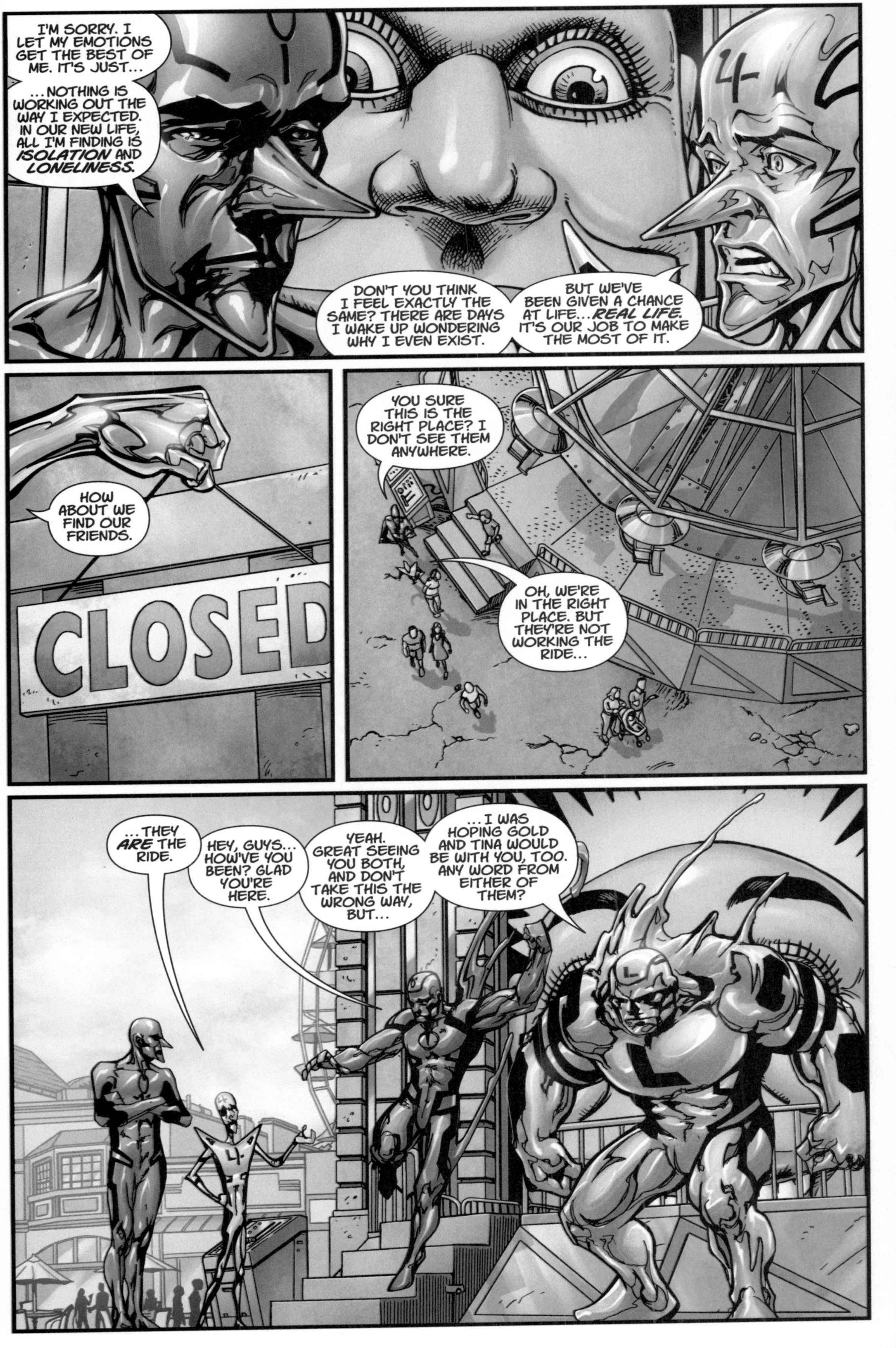
I'M SORRY. I LET MY EMOTIONS GET THE BEST OF ME. IT'S JUST...
...NOTHING IS WORKING OUT THE WAY I EXPECTED. IN OUR NEW LIFE, ALL I'M FINDING IS *ISOLATION* AND *LONELINESS.*
DON'T YOU THINK I FEEL EXACTLY THE SAME? THERE ARE DAYS I WAKE UP WONDERING WHY I EVEN EXIST.
BUT WE'VE BEEN GIVEN A CHANCE AT LIFE... *REAL LIFE.* IT'S OUR JOB TO MAKE THE MOST OF IT.
HOW ABOUT WE FIND OUR FRIENDS.
CLOSED
YOU SURE THIS IS THE RIGHT PLACE? I DON'T SEE THEM ANYWHERE.
OH, WE'RE IN THE RIGHT PLACE. BUT THEY'RE NOT WORKING THE RIDE...
...THEY *ARE* THE RIDE.
HEY, GUYS... HOW'VE YOU BEEN? GLAD YOU'RE HERE.
YEAH. GREAT SEEING YOU BOTH, AND DON'T TAKE THIS THE WRONG WAY, BUT...
...I WAS HOPING GOLD AND TINA WOULD BE WITH YOU, TOO. ANY WORD FROM EITHER OF THEM?

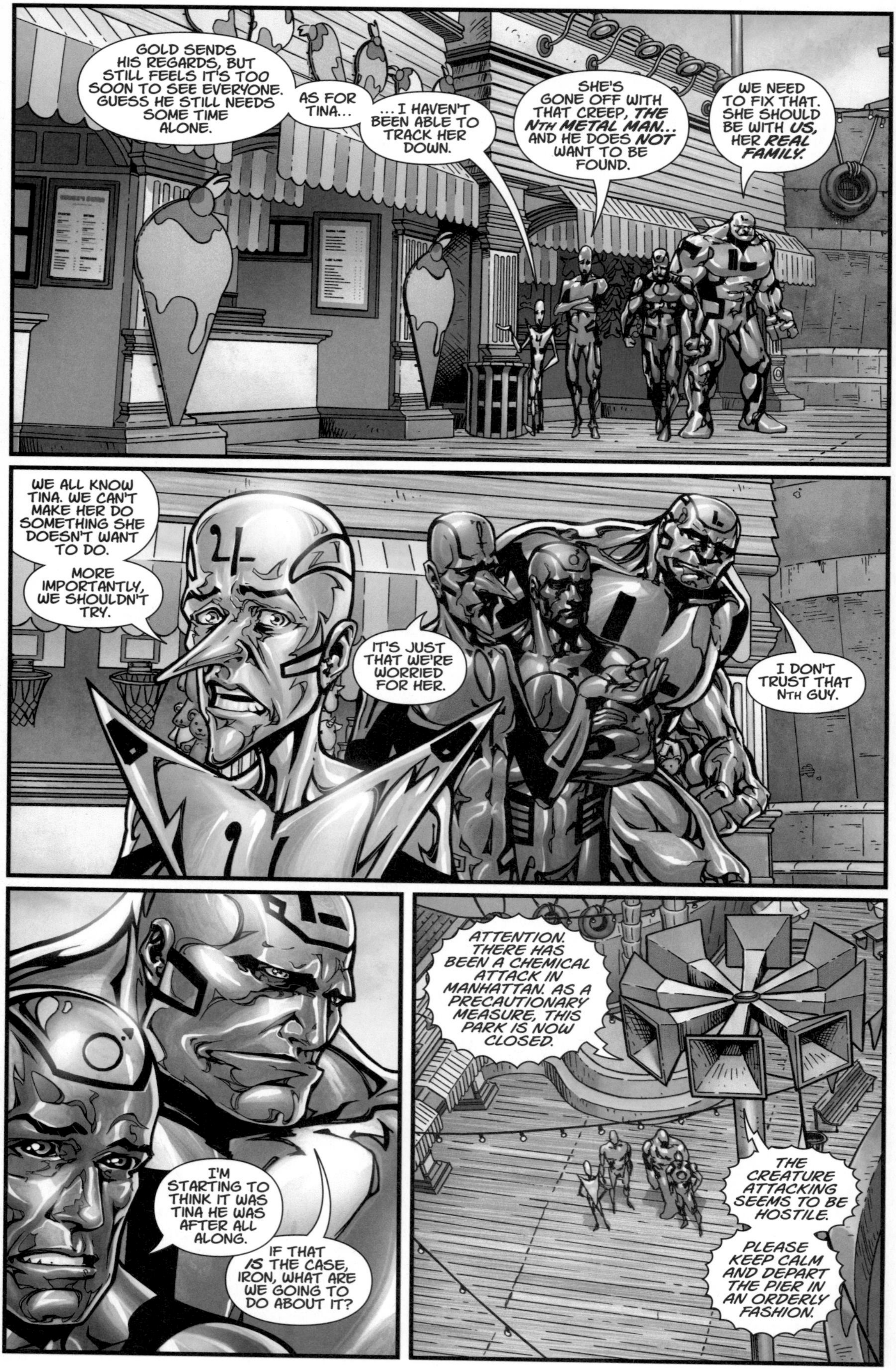
GOLD SENDS HIS REGARDS, BUT STILL FEELS IT'S TOO SOON TO SEE EVERYONE. GUESS HE STILL NEEDS SOME TIME ALONE.
AS FOR TINA...
...I HAVEN'T BEEN ABLE TO TRACK HER DOWN.
SHE'S GONE OFF WITH THAT CREEP, *THE NTH METAL MAN...* AND HE DOES *NOT* WANT TO BE FOUND.
WE NEED TO FIX THAT. SHE SHOULD BE WITH *US,* HER *REAL FAMILY.*
WE ALL KNOW TINA. WE CAN'T MAKE HER DO SOMETHING SHE DOESN'T WANT TO DO.
MORE IMPORTANTLY, WE SHOULDN'T TRY.
IT'S JUST THAT WE'RE WORRIED FOR HER.
I DON'T TRUST THAT NTH GUY.
I'M STARTING TO THINK IT WAS TINA HE WAS AFTER ALL ALONG.
IF THAT *IS* THE CASE, IRON, WHAT ARE WE GOING TO DO ABOUT IT?
ATTENTION. THERE HAS BEEN A CHEMICAL ATTACK IN MANHATTAN. AS A PRECAUTIONARY MEASURE, THIS PARK IS NOW CLOSED.
THE CREATURE ATTACKING SEEMS TO BE HOSTILE.
PLEASE KEEP CALM AND DEPART THE PIER IN AN ORDERLY FASHION.

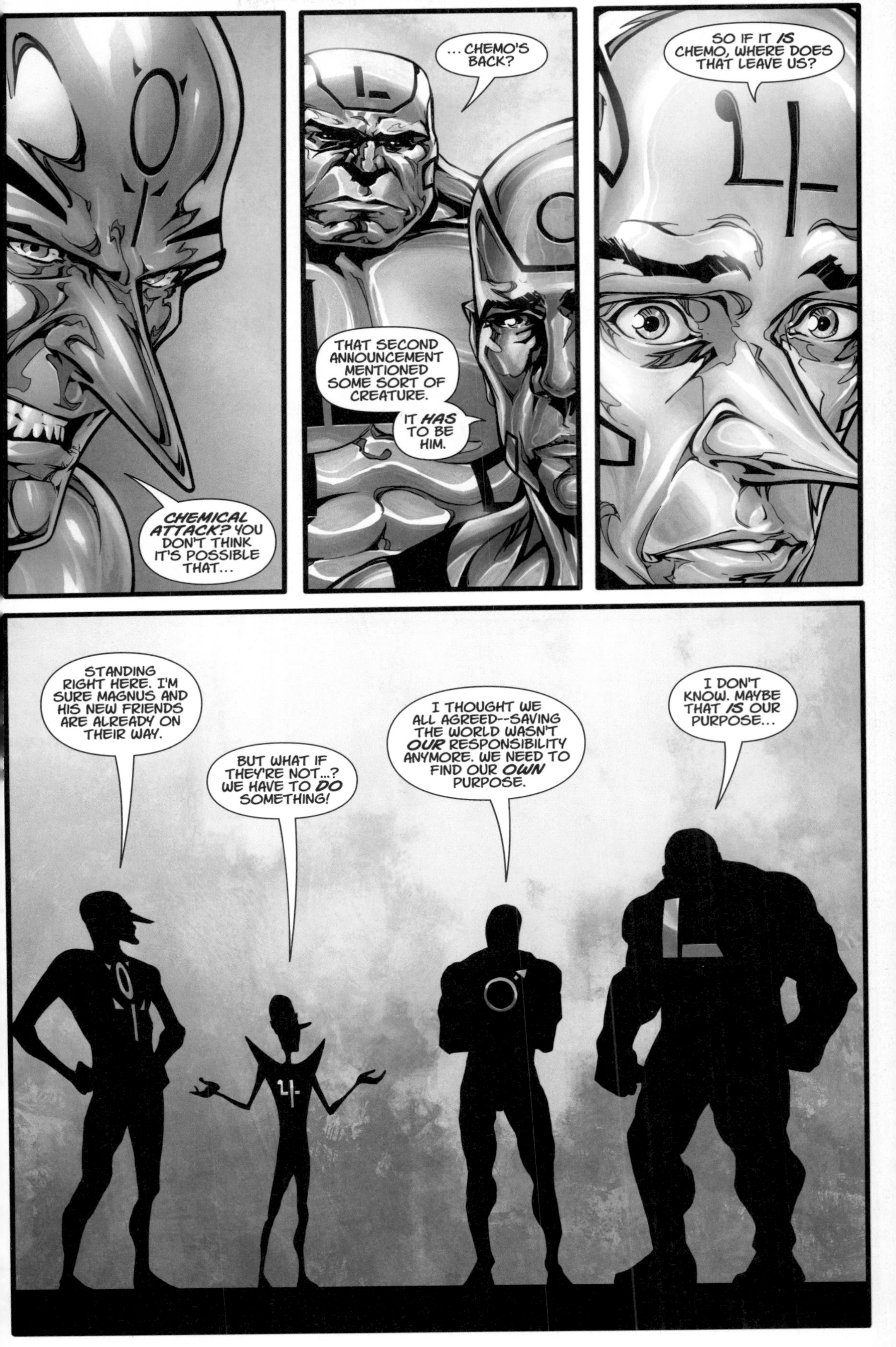
CHEMICAL ATTACK? YOU DON'T THINK IT'S POSSIBLE THAT...
...CHEMO'S BACK?
THAT SECOND ANNOUNCEMENT MENTIONED SOME SORT OF CREATURE.
IT HAS TO BE HIM.
SO IF IT IS CHEMO, WHERE DOES THAT LEAVE US?
STANDING RIGHT HERE. I'M SURE MAGNUS AND HIS NEW FRIENDS ARE ALREADY ON THEIR WAY.
BUT WHAT IF THEY'RE NOT...? WE HAVE TO DO SOMETHING!
I THOUGHT WE ALL AGREED--SAVING THE WORLD WASN'T OUR RESPONSIBILITY ANYMORE. WE NEED TO FIND OUR OWN PURPOSE.
I DON'T KNOW. MAYBE THAT IS OUR PURPOSE...

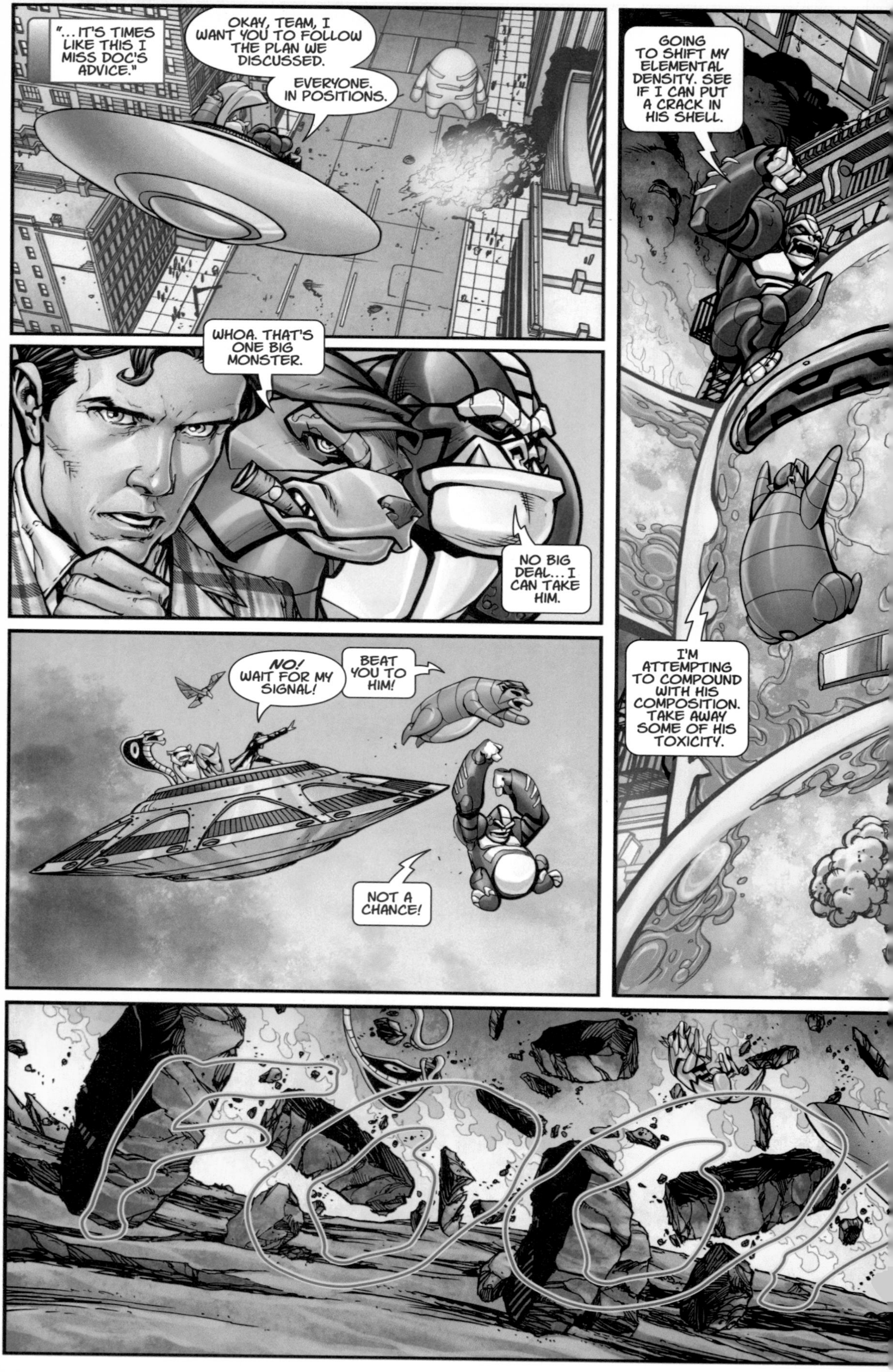
"...IT'S TIMES LIKE THIS I MISS DOC'S ADVICE."
OKAY, TEAM, I WANT YOU TO FOLLOW THE PLAN WE DISCUSSED.
EVERYONE. IN POSITIONS.
WHOA. THAT'S ONE BIG MONSTER.
NO BIG DEAL... I CAN TAKE HIM.
NO! WAIT FOR MY SIGNAL!
BEAT YOU TO HIM!
NOT A CHANCE!
GOING TO SHIFT MY ELEMENTAL DENSITY. SEE IF I CAN PUT A CRACK IN HIS SHELL.
I'M ATTEMPTING TO COMPOUND WITH HIS COMPOSITION. TAKE AWAY SOME OF HIS TOXICITY.

GURGLE GURGLE

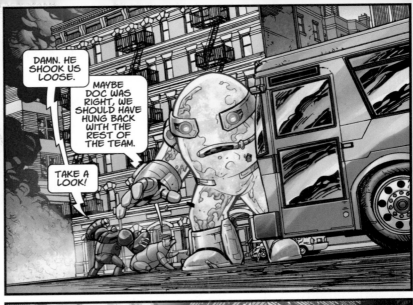

DAMN. HE SHOOK US LOOSE.

MAYBE DOC WAS RIGHT, WE SHOULD HAVE HUNG BACK WITH THE REST OF THE TEAM.

TAKE A LOOK!

EVERYONE! HANG ON!

SSSSS

THEY HAVE THEIR OWN PROBLEMS.

UUUHHH... DIDN'T... LISTEN... TO ME...

HAVE TO WORK... AS TEAM...

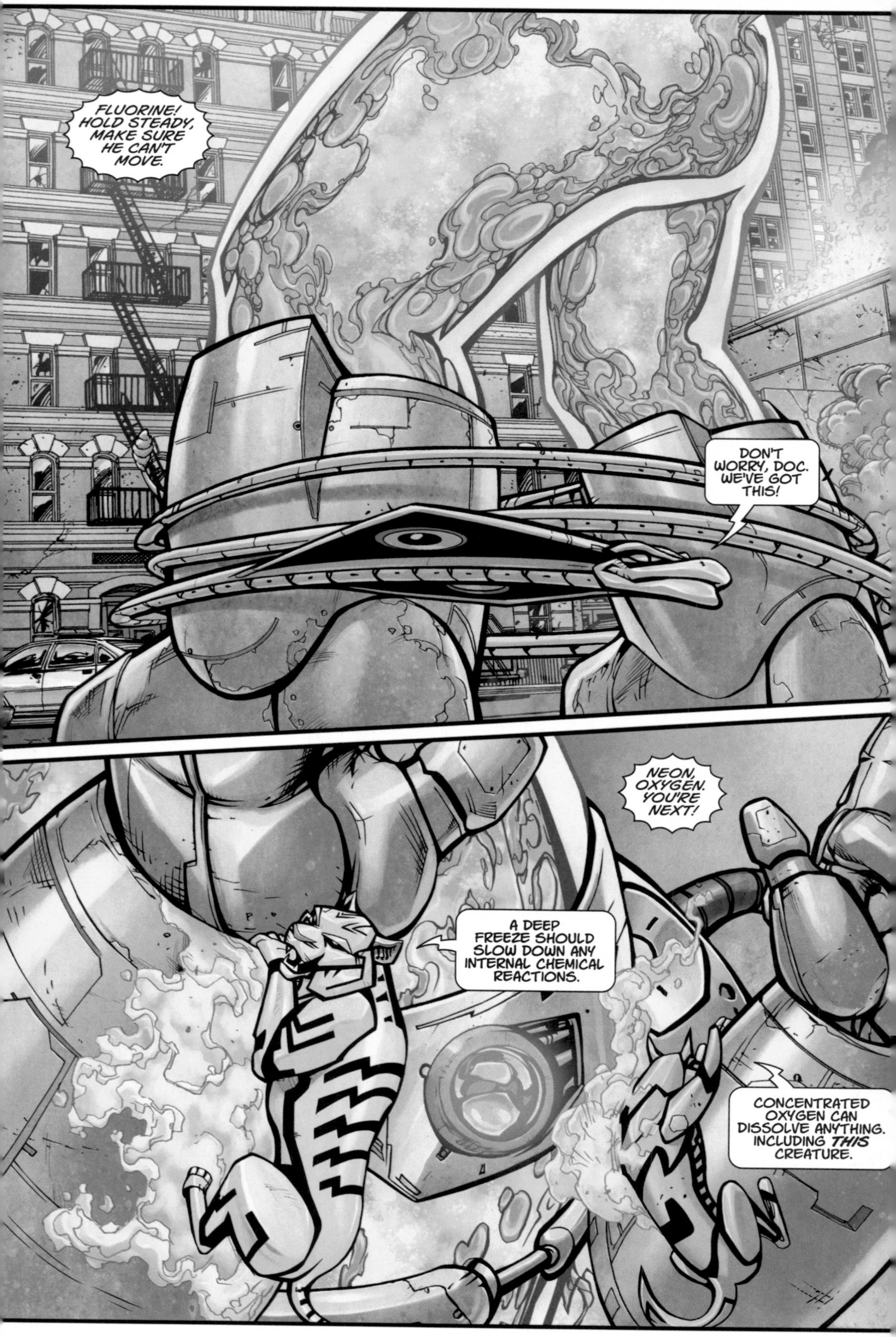
FLUORINE! HOLD STEADY, MAKE SURE HE CAN'T MOVE.
DON'T WORRY, DOC. WE'VE GOT THIS!
NEON, OXYGEN. YOU'RE NEXT!
A DEEP FREEZE SHOULD SLOW DOWN ANY INTERNAL CHEMICAL REACTIONS.
CONCENTRATED OXYGEN CAN DISSOLVE ANYTHING. INCLUDING *THIS* CREATURE.

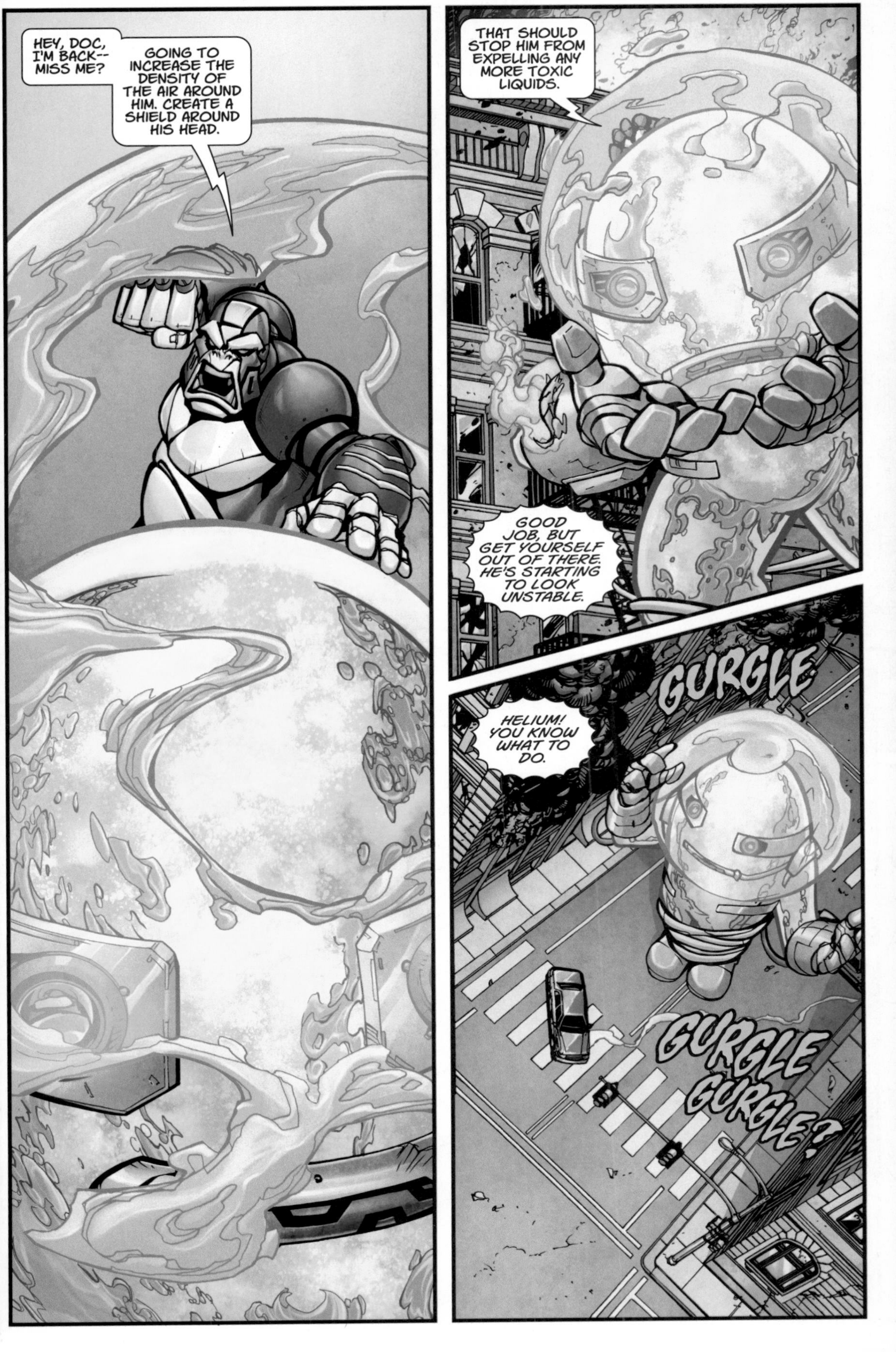
HEY, DOC, I'M BACK-- MISS ME?
GOING TO INCREASE THE DENSITY OF THE AIR AROUND HIM. CREATE A SHIELD AROUND HIS HEAD.
THAT SHOULD STOP HIM FROM EXPELLING ANY MORE TOXIC LIQUIDS.
GOOD JOB, BUT GET YOURSELF OUT OF THERE. HE'S STARTING TO LOOK UNSTABLE.
GURGLE
HELIUM! YOU KNOW WHAT TO DO.
GURGLE GURGLE GURGLE?

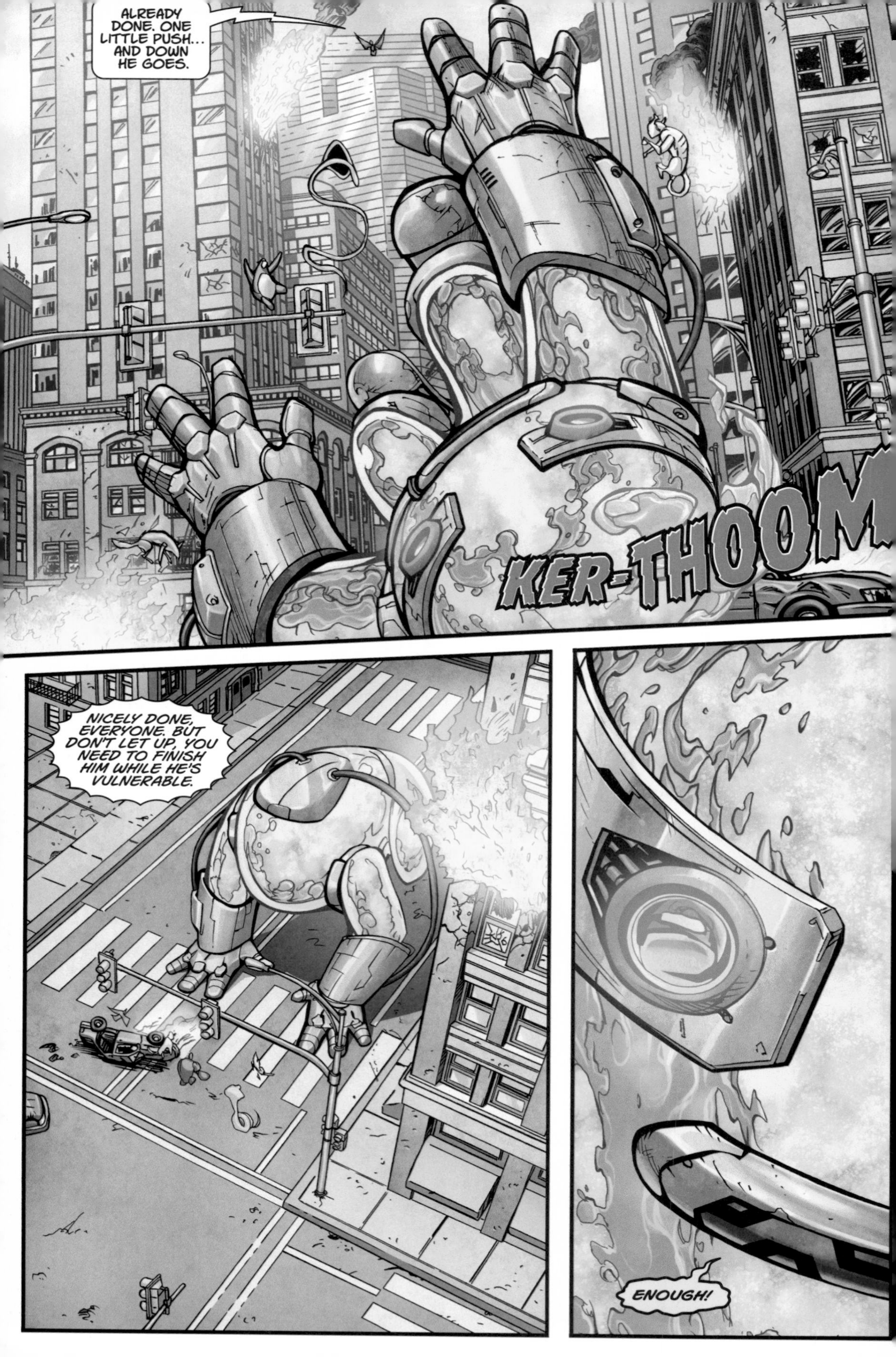
ALREADY DONE. ONE LITTLE PUSH... AND DOWN HE GOES.
KER-THOOM
NICELY DONE, EVERYONE. BUT DON'T LET UP, YOU NEED TO FINISH HIM WHILE HE'S VULNERABLE.
ENOUGH!

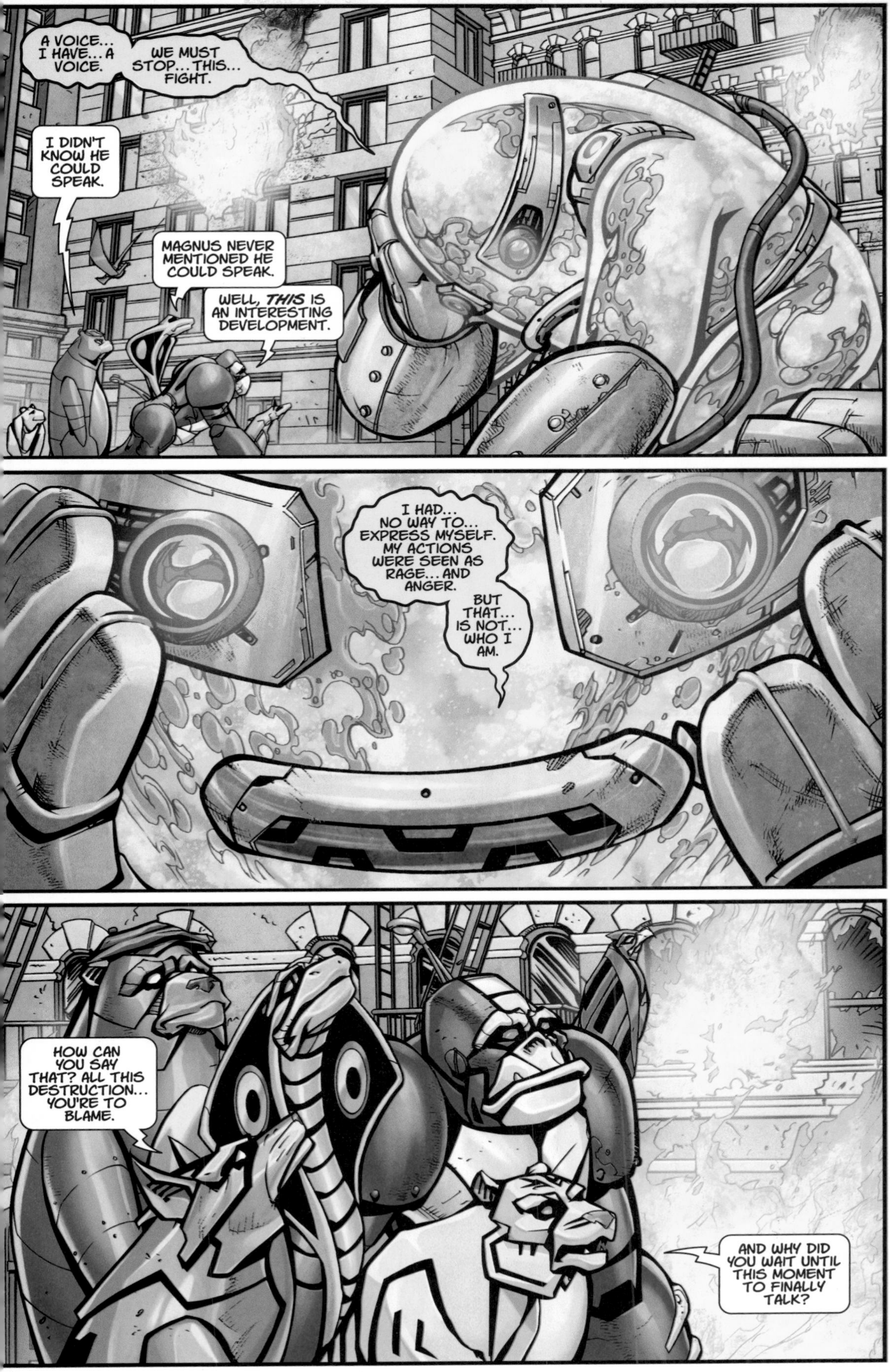
A VOICE... I HAVE... A VOICE.
WE MUST STOP... THIS... FIGHT.
I DIDN'T KNOW HE COULD SPEAK.
MAGNUS NEVER MENTIONED HE COULD SPEAK.
WELL, *THIS* IS AN INTERESTING DEVELOPMENT.
I HAD... NO WAY TO... EXPRESS MYSELF. MY ACTIONS WERE SEEN AS RAGE... AND ANGER.
BUT THAT... IS NOT... WHO I AM.
HOW CAN YOU SAY THAT? ALL THIS DESTRUCTION... YOU'RE TO BLAME.
AND WHY DID YOU WAIT UNTIL THIS MOMENT TO FINALLY TALK?

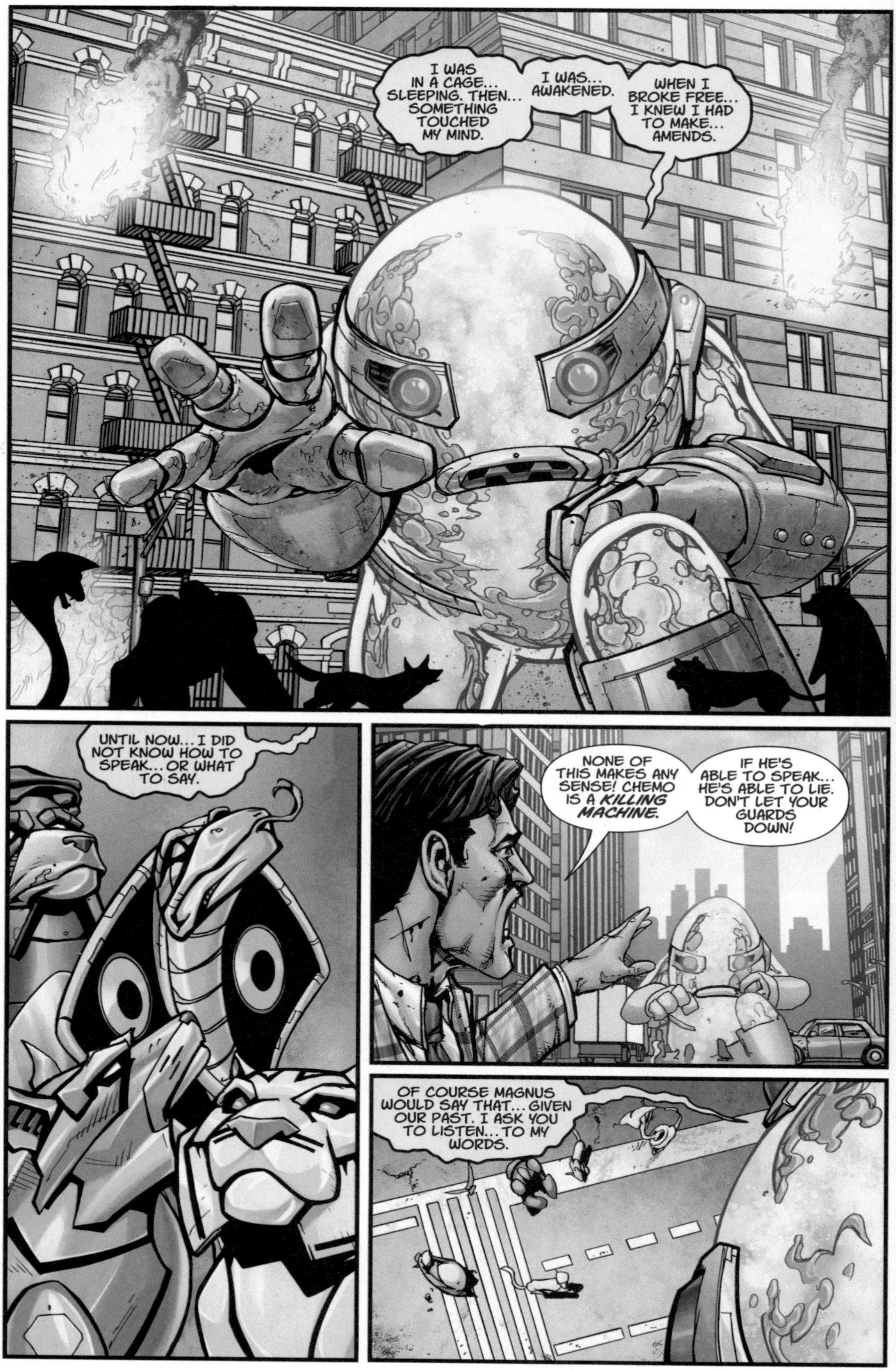
I WAS IN A CAGE... SLEEPING. THEN... SOMETHING TOUCHED MY MIND.
I WAS... AWAKENED.
WHEN I BROKE FREE... I KNEW I HAD TO MAKE... AMENDS.
UNTIL NOW... I DID NOT KNOW HOW TO SPEAK... OR WHAT TO SAY.
NONE OF THIS MAKES ANY SENSE! CHEMO IS A *KILLING MACHINE*.
IF HE'S ABLE TO SPEAK... HE'S ABLE TO LIE. DON'T LET YOUR GUARDS DOWN!
OF COURSE MAGNUS WOULD SAY THAT... GIVEN OUR PAST. I ASK YOU TO LISTEN... TO MY WORDS.

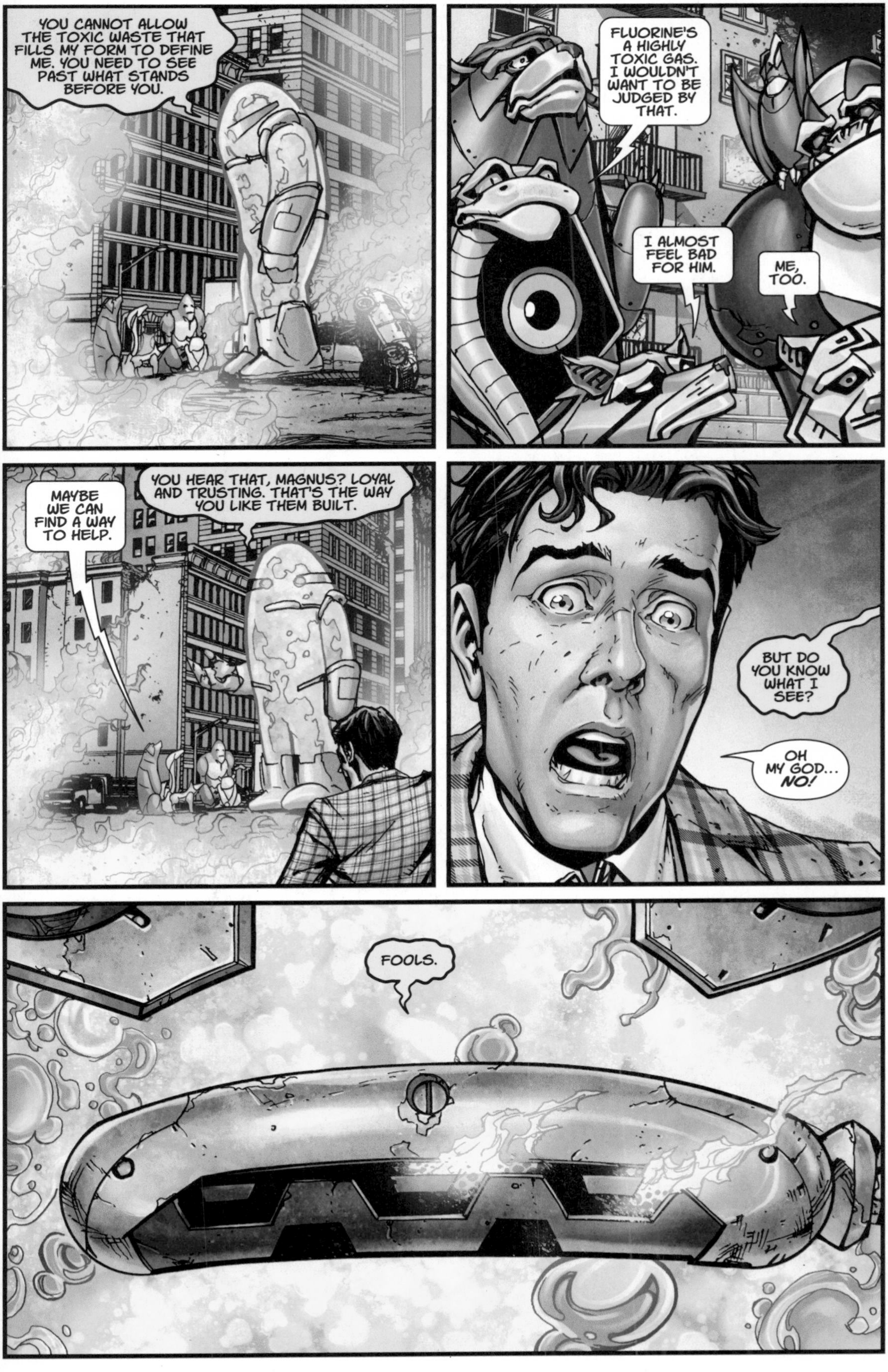
YOU CANNOT ALLOW THE TOXIC WASTE THAT FILLS MY FORM TO DEFINE ME. YOU NEED TO SEE PAST WHAT STANDS BEFORE YOU.
FLUORINE'S A HIGHLY TOXIC GAS. I WOULDN'T WANT TO BE JUDGED BY THAT.
I ALMOST FEEL BAD FOR HIM.
ME, TOO.
MAYBE WE CAN FIND A WAY TO HELP.
YOU HEAR THAT, MAGNUS? LOYAL AND TRUSTING. THAT'S THE WAY YOU LIKE THEM BUILT.
BUT DO YOU KNOW WHAT I SEE?
OH MY GOD... NO!
FOOLS.

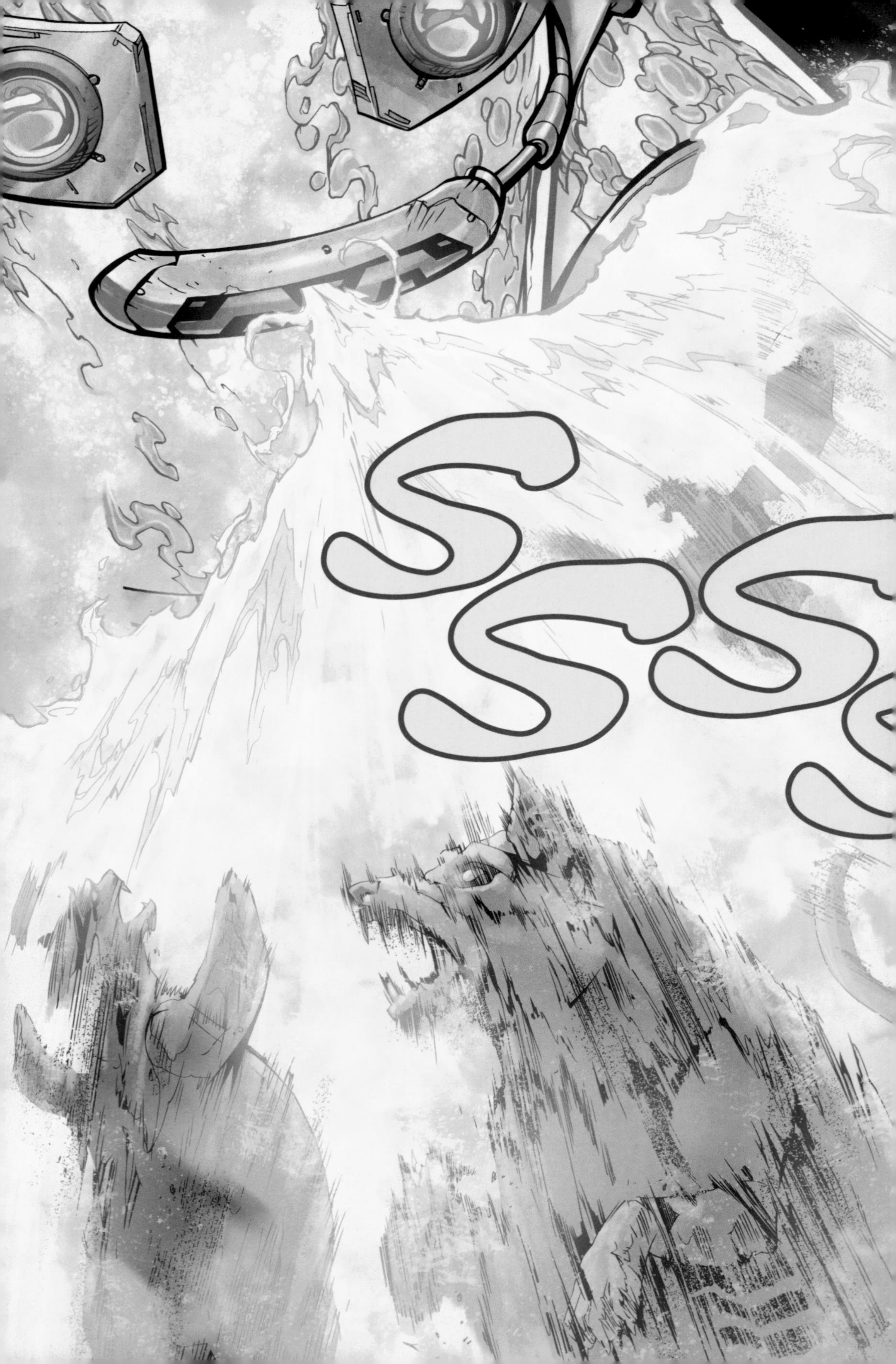
SSSS

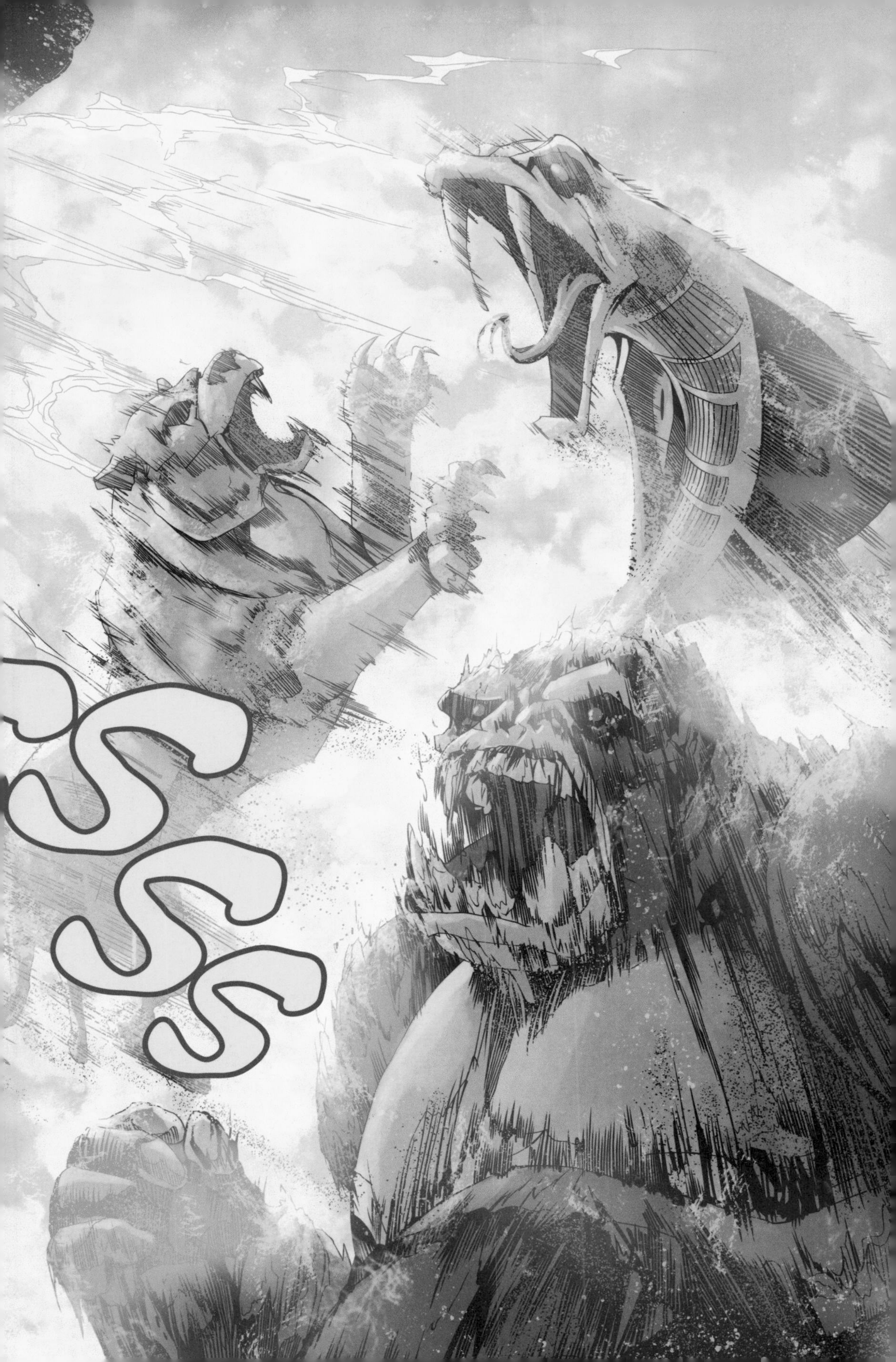
SSSS

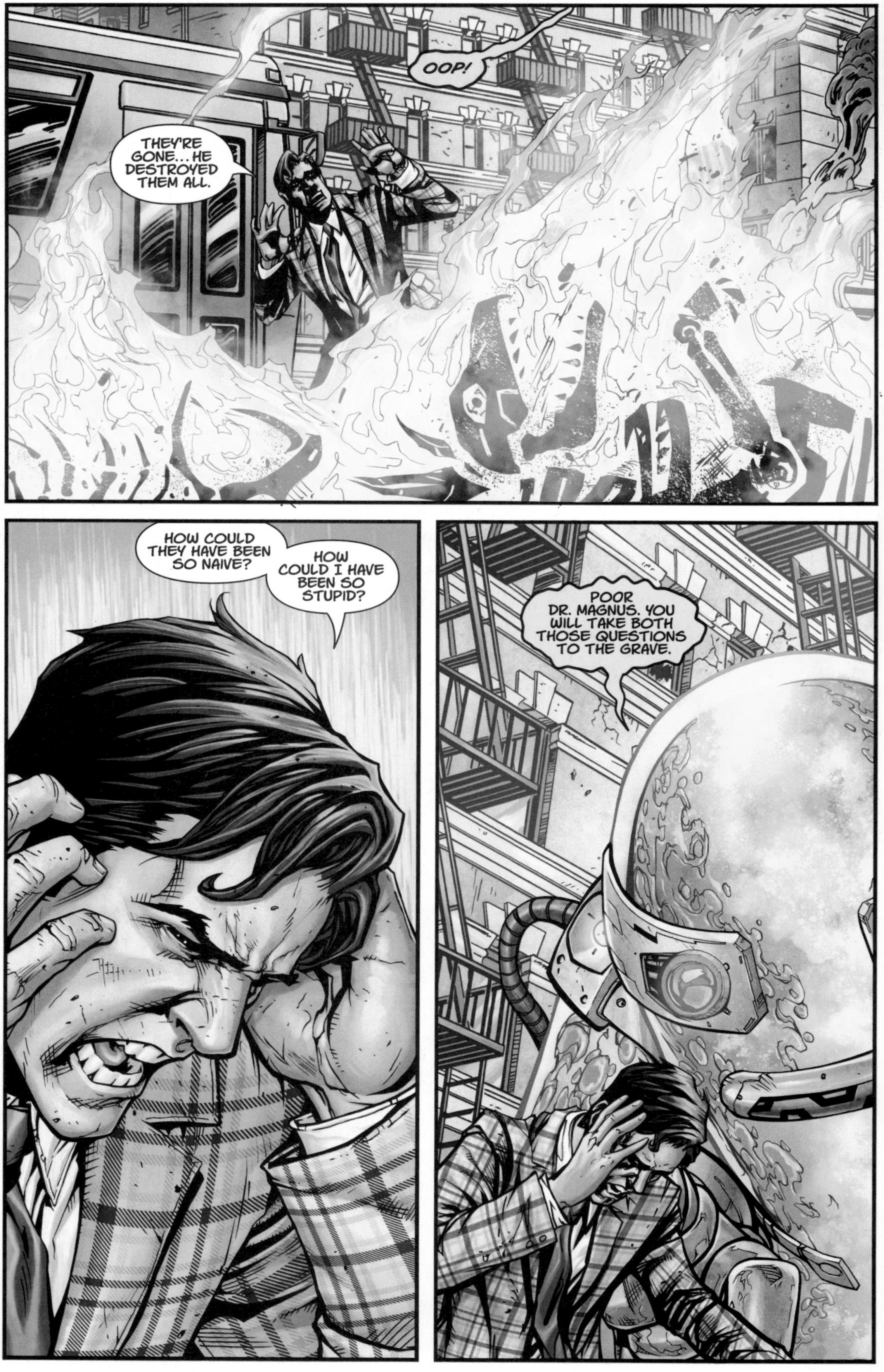
OOP!
THEY'RE GONE... HE DESTROYED THEM ALL.
HOW COULD THEY HAVE BEEN SO NAIVE?
HOW COULD I HAVE BEEN SO STUPID?
POOR DR. MAGNUS. YOU WILL TAKE BOTH THOSE QUESTIONS TO THE GRAVE.

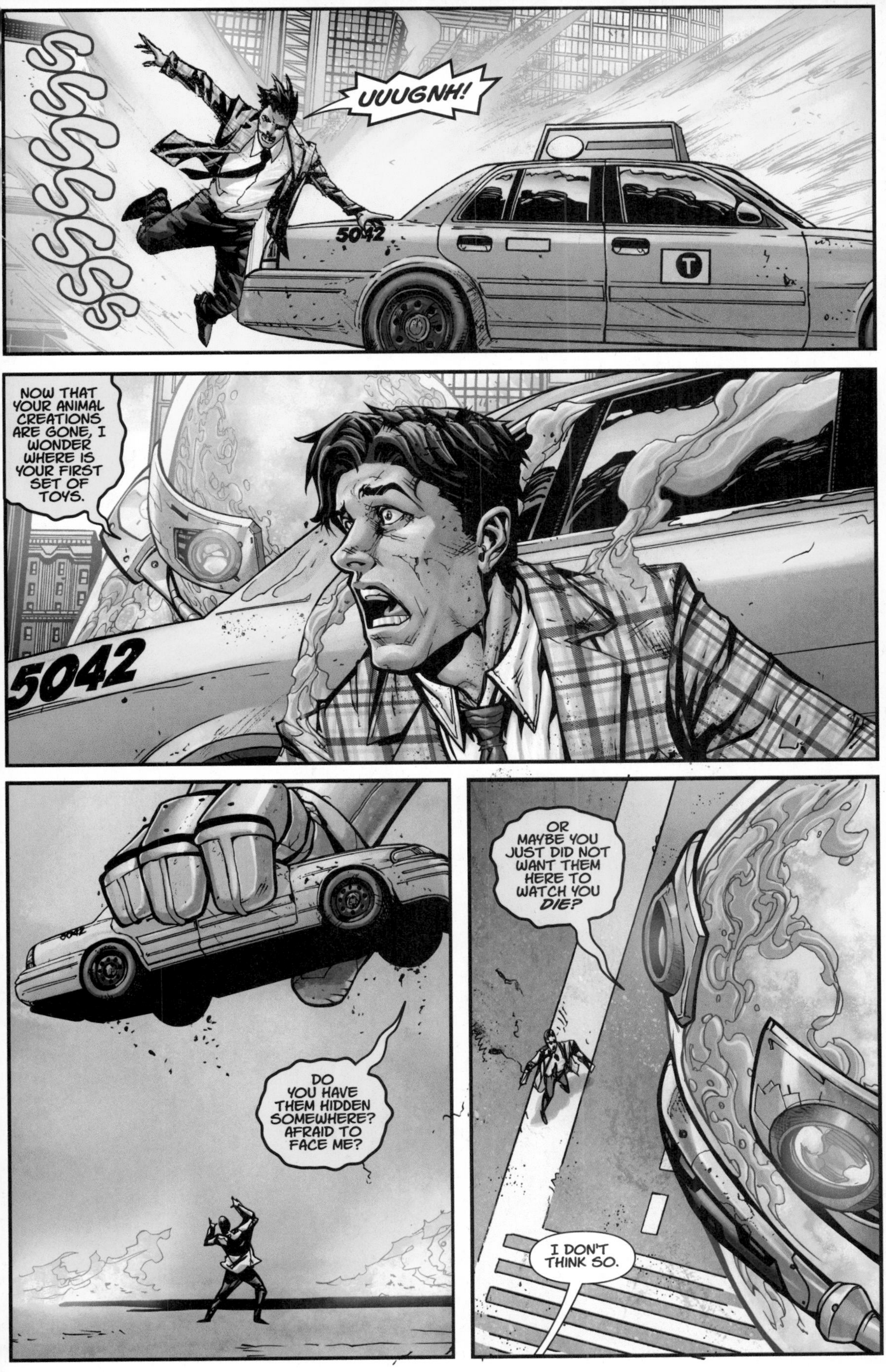
SSSSSSS
UUUGNH!
5042
NOW THAT YOUR ANIMAL CREATIONS ARE GONE, I WONDER WHERE IS YOUR FIRST SET OF TOYS.
5042
DO YOU HAVE THEM HIDDEN SOMEWHERE? AFRAID TO FACE ME?
OR MAYBE YOU JUST DID NOT WANT THEM HERE TO WATCH YOU *DIE*?
I DON'T THINK SO.

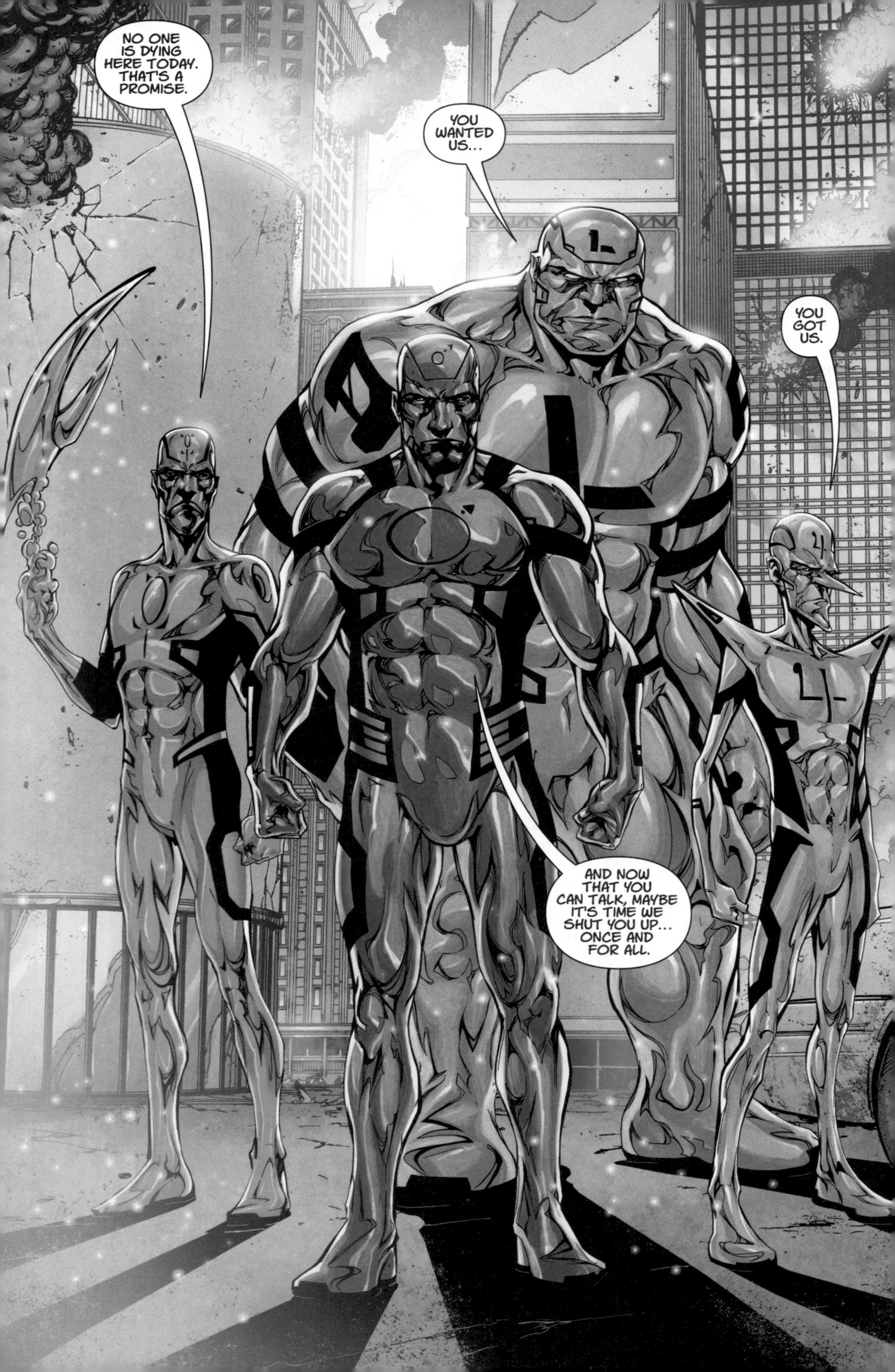
NO ONE IS DYING HERE TODAY. THAT'S A PROMISE.
YOU WANTED US...
YOU GOT US.
AND NOW THAT YOU CAN TALK, MAYBE IT'S TIME WE SHUT YOU UP... ONCE AND FOR ALL.

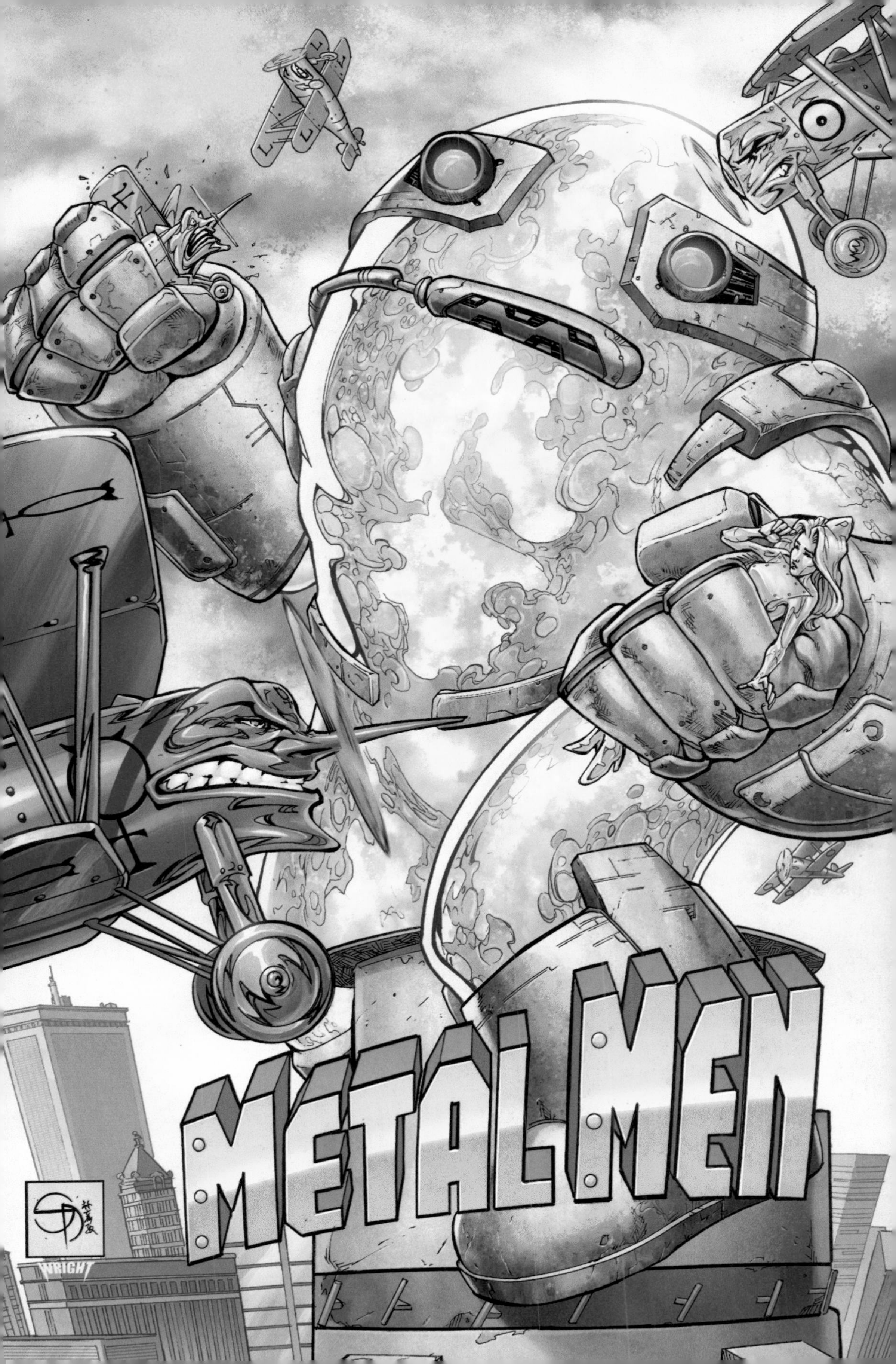
METAL MEN
WRIGHT

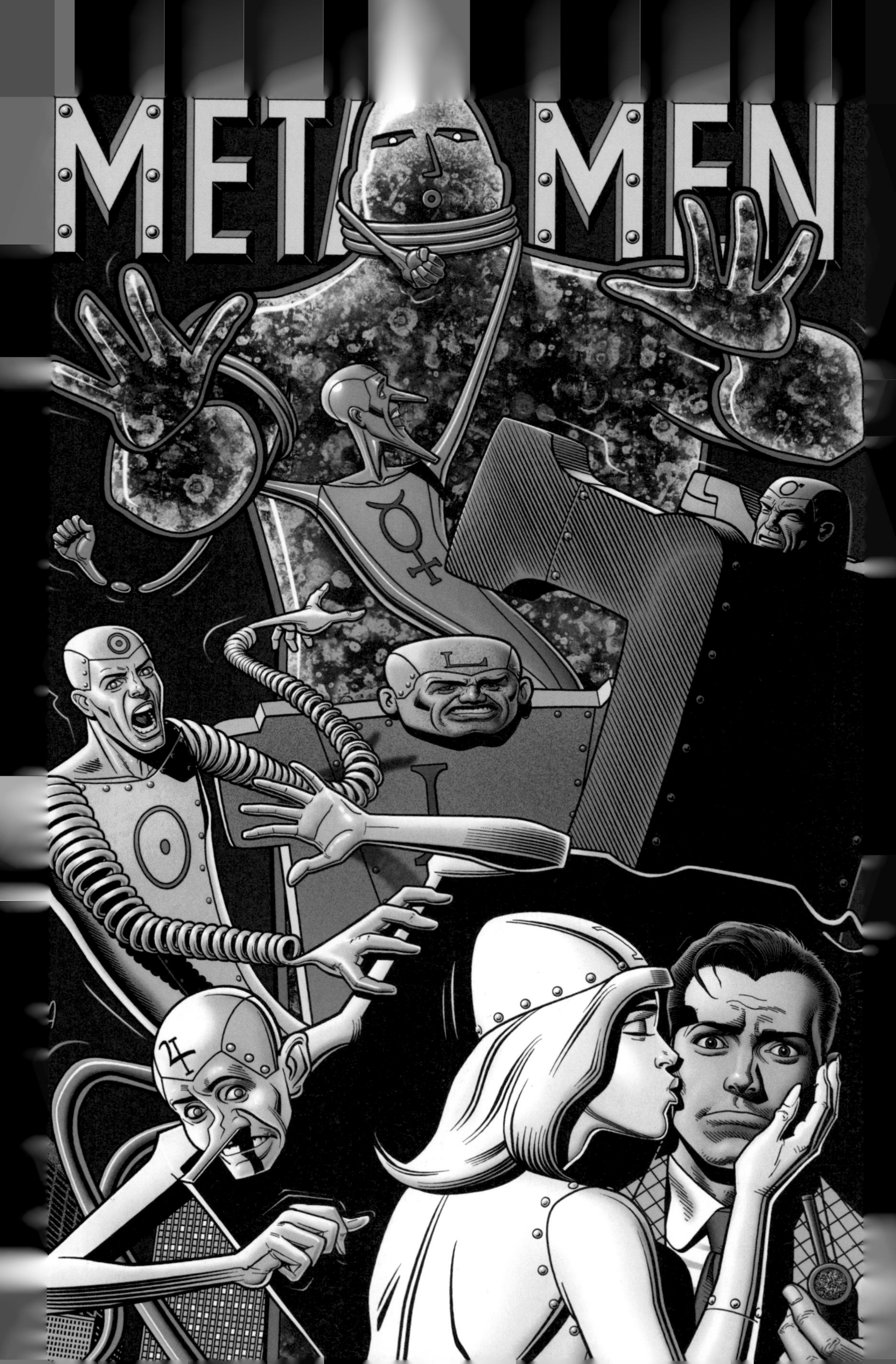
METAL MEN

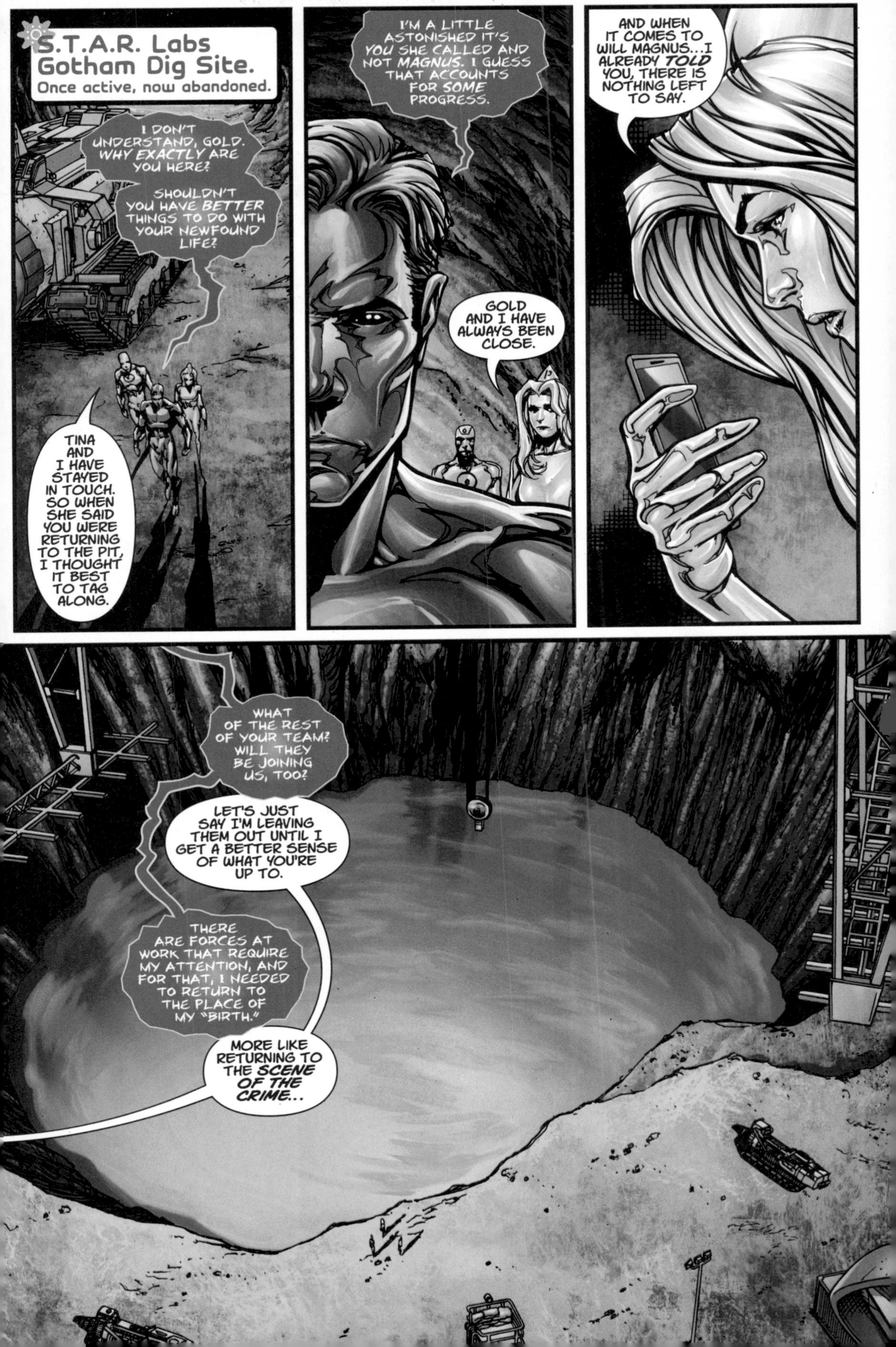
S.T.A.R. Labs Gotham Dig Site. Once active, now abandoned.
I DON'T UNDERSTAND, GOLD. WHY EXACTLY ARE YOU HERE?
SHOULDN'T YOU HAVE BETTER THINGS TO DO WITH YOUR NEWFOUND LIFE?
TINA AND I HAVE STAYED IN TOUCH. SO WHEN SHE SAID YOU WERE RETURNING TO THE PIT, I THOUGHT IT BEST TO TAG ALONG.
I'M A LITTLE ASTONISHED IT'S YOU SHE CALLED AND NOT MAGNUS. I GUESS THAT ACCOUNTS FOR SOME PROGRESS.
GOLD AND I HAVE ALWAYS BEEN CLOSE.
AND WHEN IT COMES TO WILL MAGNUS...I ALREADY TOLD YOU, THERE IS NOTHING LEFT TO SAY.
WHAT OF THE REST OF YOUR TEAM? WILL THEY BE JOINING US, TOO?
LET'S JUST SAY I'M LEAVING THEM OUT UNTIL I GET A BETTER SENSE OF WHAT YOU'RE UP TO.
THERE ARE FORCES AT WORK THAT REQUIRE MY ATTENTION, AND FOR THAT, I NEEDED TO RETURN TO THE PLACE OF MY "BIRTH."
MORE LIKE RETURNING TO THE SCENE OF THE CRIME...

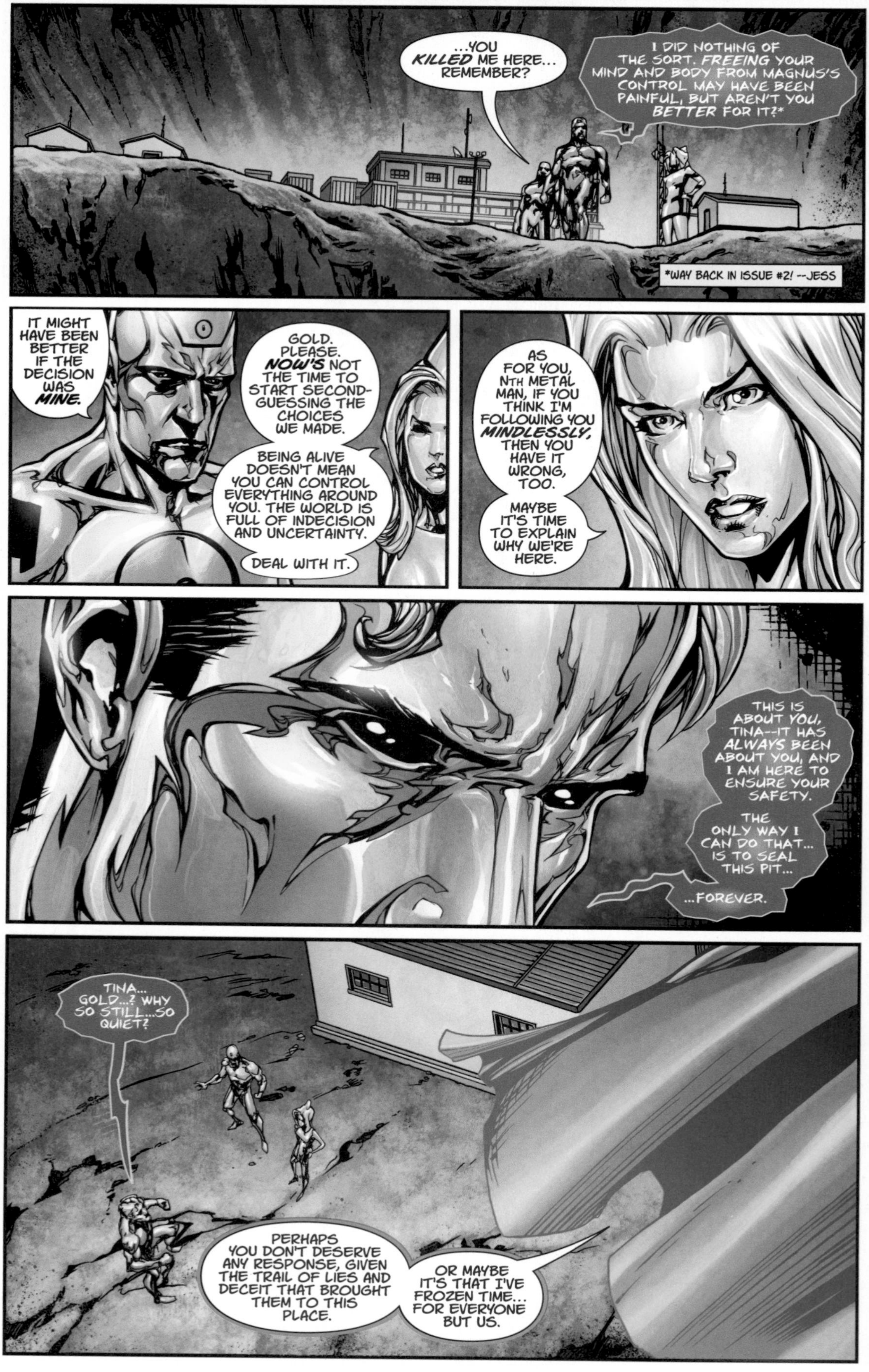
...YOU KILLED ME HERE... REMEMBER?
I DID NOTHING OF THE SORT. FREEING YOUR MIND AND BODY FROM MAGNUS'S CONTROL MAY HAVE BEEN PAINFUL, BUT AREN'T YOU BETTER FOR IT?*
*WAY BACK IN ISSUE #2! --JESS
IT MIGHT HAVE BEEN BETTER IF THE DECISION WAS MINE.
GOLD. PLEASE. NOW'S NOT THE TIME TO START SECOND-GUESSING THE CHOICES WE MADE.
BEING ALIVE DOESN'T MEAN YOU CAN CONTROL EVERYTHING AROUND YOU. THE WORLD IS FULL OF INDECISION AND UNCERTAINTY.
DEAL WITH IT.
AS FOR YOU, NTH METAL MAN, IF YOU THINK I'M FOLLOWING YOU MINDLESSLY, THEN YOU HAVE IT WRONG, TOO.
MAYBE IT'S TIME TO EXPLAIN WHY WE'RE HERE.
THIS IS ABOUT YOU, TINA--IT HAS ALWAYS BEEN ABOUT YOU, AND I AM HERE TO ENSURE YOUR SAFETY.
THE ONLY WAY I CAN DO THAT... IS TO SEAL THIS PIT...
...FOREVER.
TINA... GOLD...? WHY SO STILL...SO QUIET?
PERHAPS YOU DON'T DESERVE ANY RESPONSE, GIVEN THE TRAIL OF LIES AND DECEIT THAT BROUGHT THEM TO THIS PLACE.
OR MAYBE IT'S THAT I'VE FROZEN TIME... FOR EVERYONE BUT US.

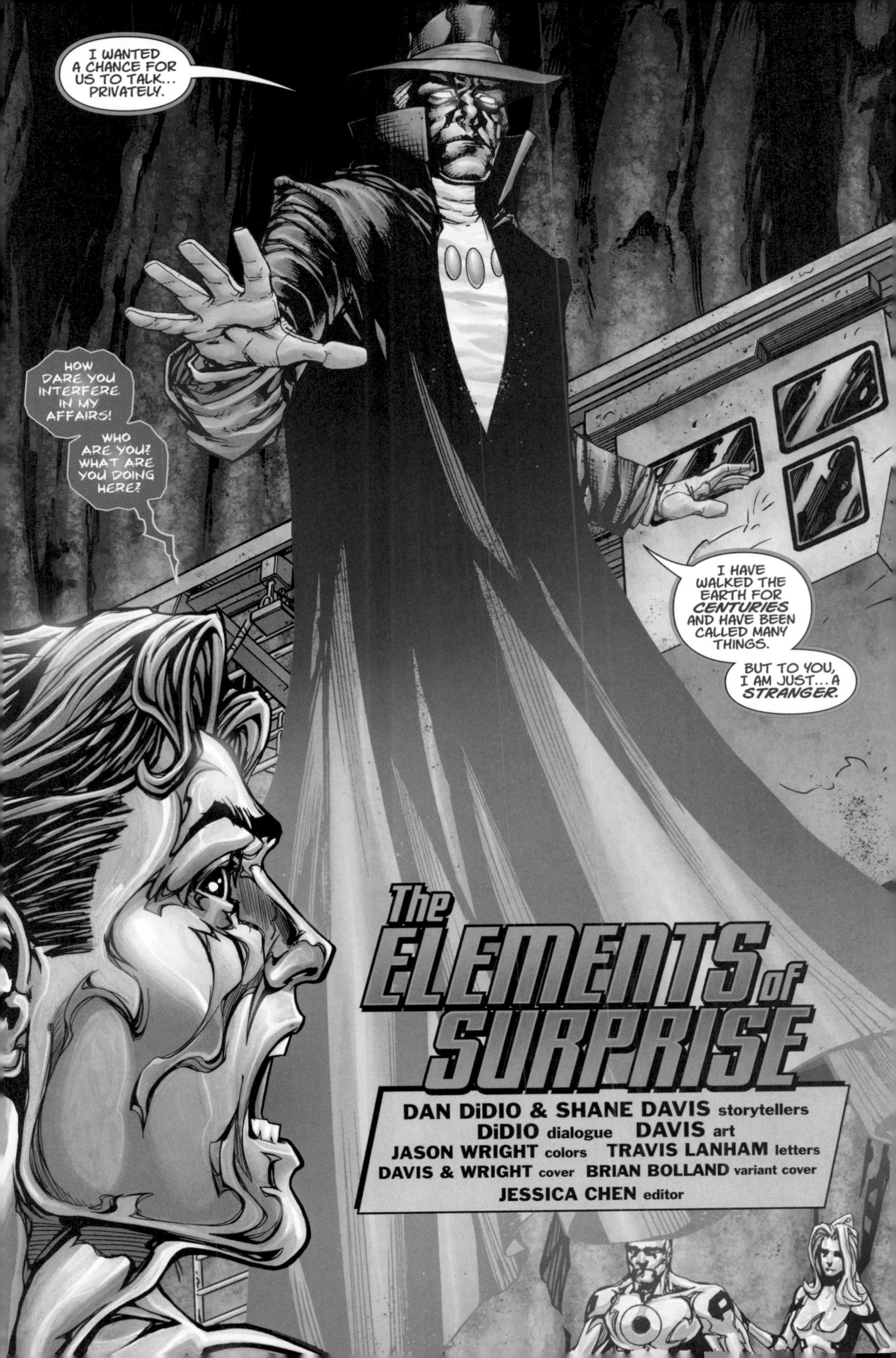
I WANTED A CHANCE FOR US TO TALK... PRIVATELY.
HOW DARE YOU INTERFERE IN MY AFFAIRS!
WHO ARE YOU? WHAT ARE YOU DOING HERE?
I HAVE WALKED THE EARTH FOR CENTURIES AND HAVE BEEN CALLED MANY THINGS.
BUT TO YOU, I AM JUST... A STRANGER.
The ELEMENTS of SURPRISE
DAN DiDIO & SHANE DAVIS storytellers
DiDIO dialogue DAVIS art
JASON WRIGHT colors TRAVIS LANHAM letters
DAVIS & WRIGHT cover BRIAN BOLLAND variant cover
JESSICA CHEN editor

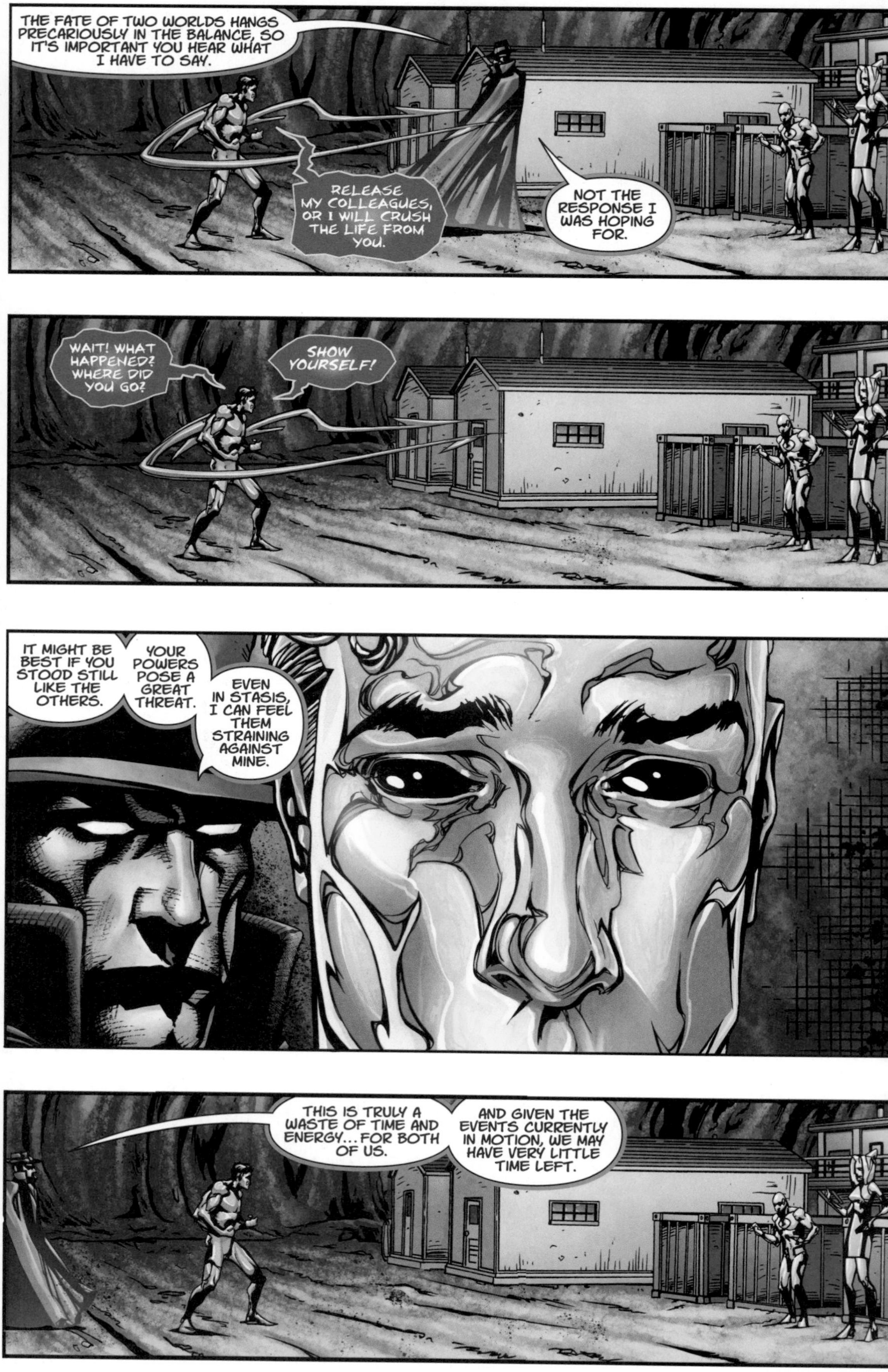
THE FATE OF TWO WORLDS HANGS PRECARIOUSLY IN THE BALANCE, SO IT'S IMPORTANT YOU HEAR WHAT I HAVE TO SAY.
RELEASE MY COLLEAGUES, OR I WILL CRUSH THE LIFE FROM YOU.
NOT THE RESPONSE I WAS HOPING FOR.
WAIT! WHAT HAPPENED? WHERE DID YOU GO?
SHOW YOURSELF!
IT MIGHT BE BEST IF YOU STOOD STILL LIKE THE OTHERS.
YOUR POWERS POSE A GREAT THREAT.
EVEN IN STASIS, I CAN FEEL THEM STRAINING AGAINST MINE.
THIS IS TRULY A WASTE OF TIME AND ENERGY... FOR BOTH OF US.
AND GIVEN THE EVENTS CURRENTLY IN MOTION, WE MAY HAVE VERY LITTLE TIME LEFT.

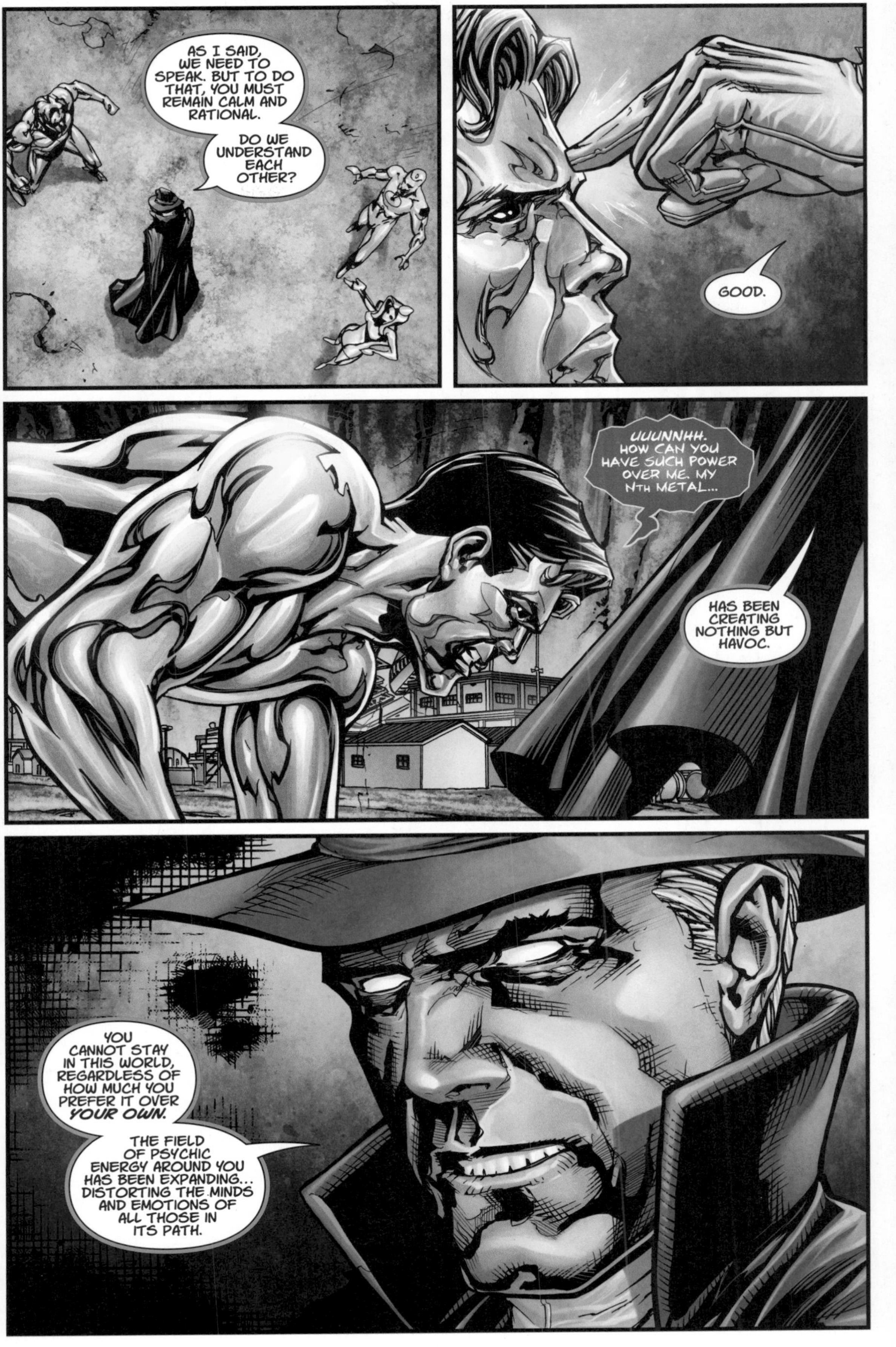
AS I SAID, WE NEED TO SPEAK. BUT TO DO THAT, YOU MUST REMAIN CALM AND RATIONAL.
DO WE UNDERSTAND EACH OTHER?
GOOD.
UUUNNHH. HOW CAN YOU HAVE SUCH POWER OVER ME. MY NTH METAL...
HAS BEEN CREATING NOTHING BUT HAVOC.
YOU CANNOT STAY IN THIS WORLD, REGARDLESS OF HOW MUCH YOU PREFER IT OVER YOUR OWN.
THE FIELD OF PSYCHIC ENERGY AROUND YOU HAS BEEN EXPANDING... DISTORTING THE MINDS AND EMOTIONS OF ALL THOSE IN ITS PATH.

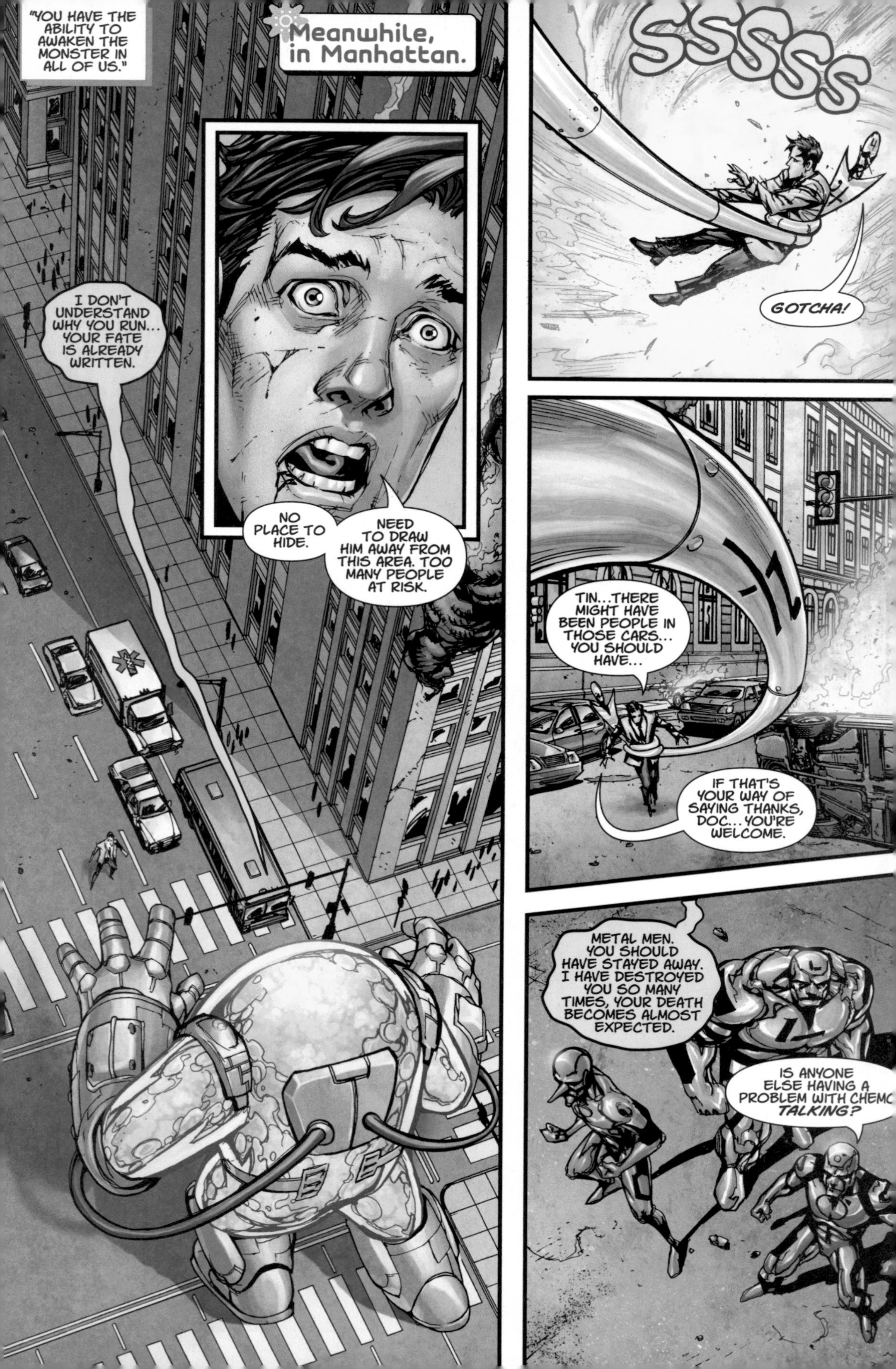
"YOU HAVE THE ABILITY TO AWAKEN THE MONSTER IN ALL OF US."
Meanwhile, in Manhattan.
I DON'T UNDERSTAND WHY YOU RUN... YOUR FATE IS ALREADY WRITTEN.
NO PLACE TO HIDE.
NEED TO DRAW HIM AWAY FROM THIS AREA. TOO MANY PEOPLE AT RISK.
SSSSS
GOTCHA!
TIN...THERE MIGHT HAVE BEEN PEOPLE IN THOSE CARS... YOU SHOULD HAVE...
IF THAT'S YOUR WAY OF SAYING THANKS, DOC...YOU'RE WELCOME.
METAL MEN. YOU SHOULD HAVE STAYED AWAY. I HAVE DESTROYED YOU SO MANY TIMES, YOUR DEATH BECOMES ALMOST EXPECTED.
IS ANYONE ELSE HAVING A PROBLEM WITH CHEMO *TALKING*?

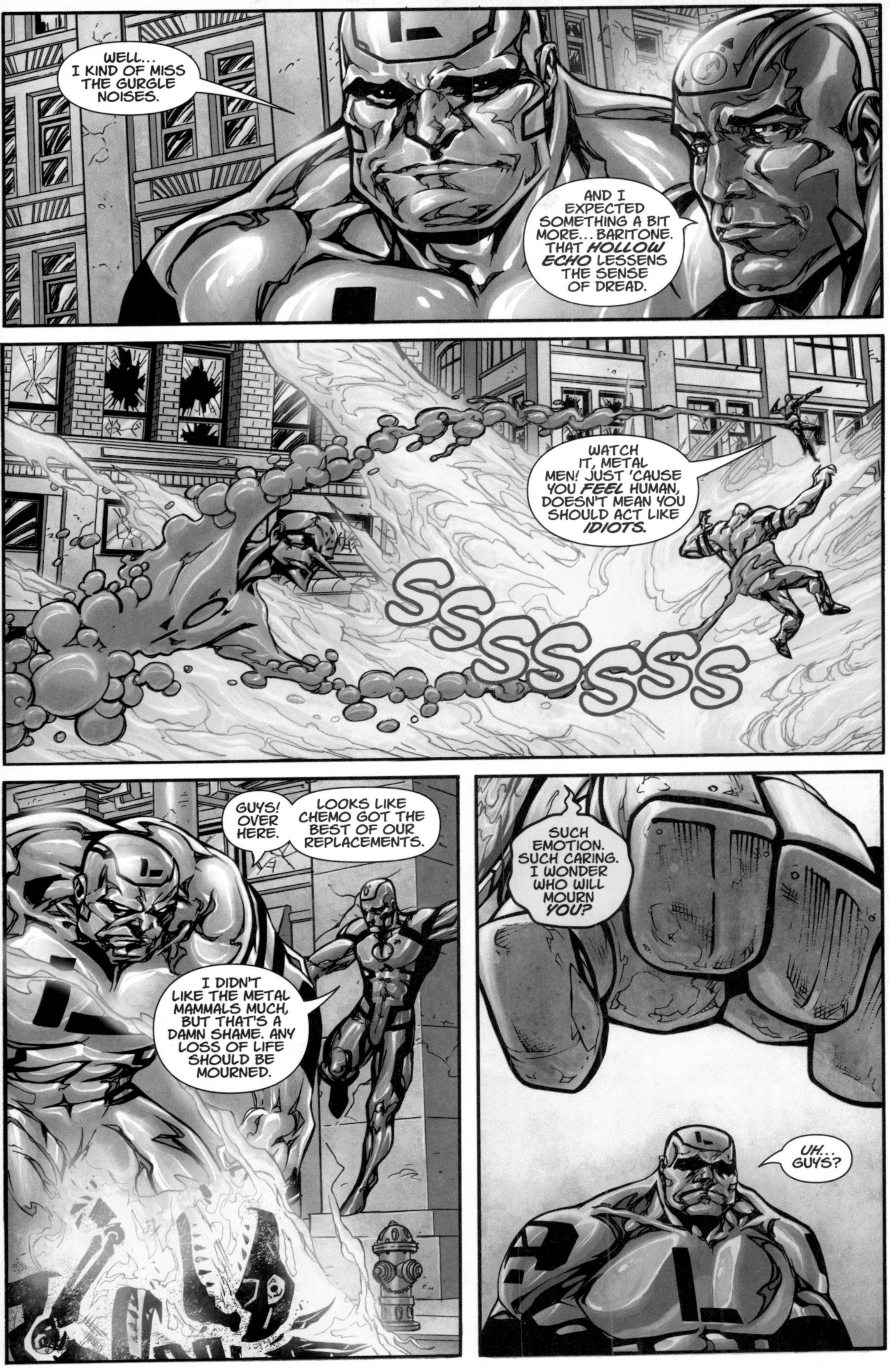
WELL... I KIND OF MISS THE GURGLE NOISES.
AND I EXPECTED SOMETHING A BIT MORE... BARITONE. THAT HOLLOW ECHO LESSENS THE SENSE OF DREAD.
WATCH IT, METAL MEN! JUST 'CAUSE YOU FEEL HUMAN, DOESN'T MEAN YOU SHOULD ACT LIKE IDIOTS.
SSSSSSS
GUYS! OVER HERE.
LOOKS LIKE CHEMO GOT THE BEST OF OUR REPLACEMENTS.
I DIDN'T LIKE THE METAL MAMMALS MUCH, BUT THAT'S A DAMN SHAME. ANY LOSS OF LIFE SHOULD BE MOURNED.
SUCH EMOTION. SUCH CARING. I WONDER WHO WILL MOURN YOU?
UH... GUYS?

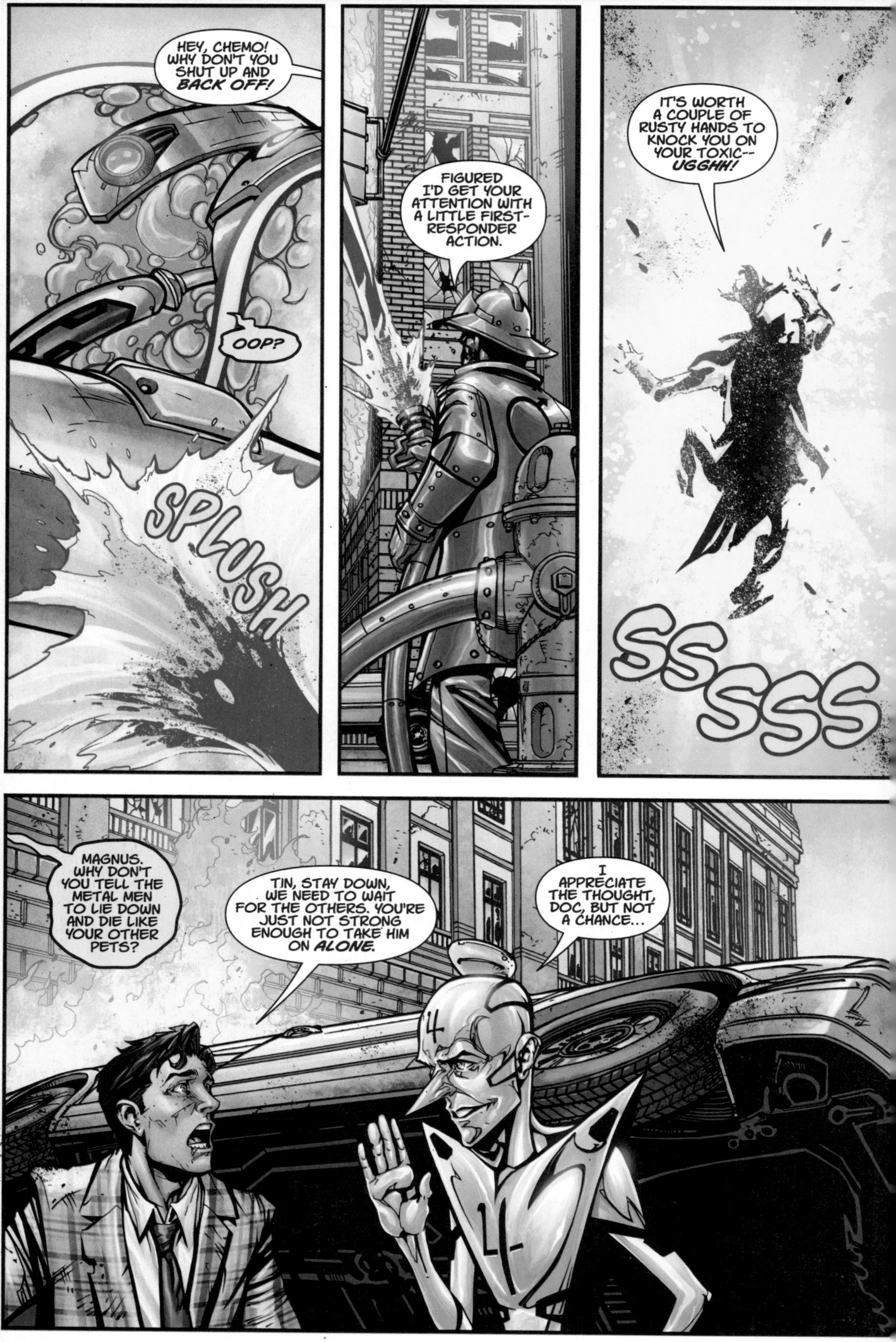
HEY, CHEMO! WHY DON'T YOU SHUT UP AND *BACK OFF!*
OOP?
SPLUSH
FIGURED I'D GET YOUR ATTENTION WITH A LITTLE FIRST-RESPONDER ACTION.
IT'S WORTH A COUPLE OF RUSTY HANDS TO KNOCK YOU ON YOUR TOXIC-- *UGGHH!*
SSSSS
MAGNUS. WHY DON'T YOU TELL THE METAL MEN TO LIE DOWN AND DIE LIKE YOUR OTHER PETS?
TIN, STAY DOWN, WE NEED TO WAIT FOR THE OTHERS. YOU'RE JUST NOT STRONG ENOUGH TO TAKE HIM ON *ALONE*.
I APPRECIATE THE THOUGHT, DOC, BUT NOT A CHANCE...

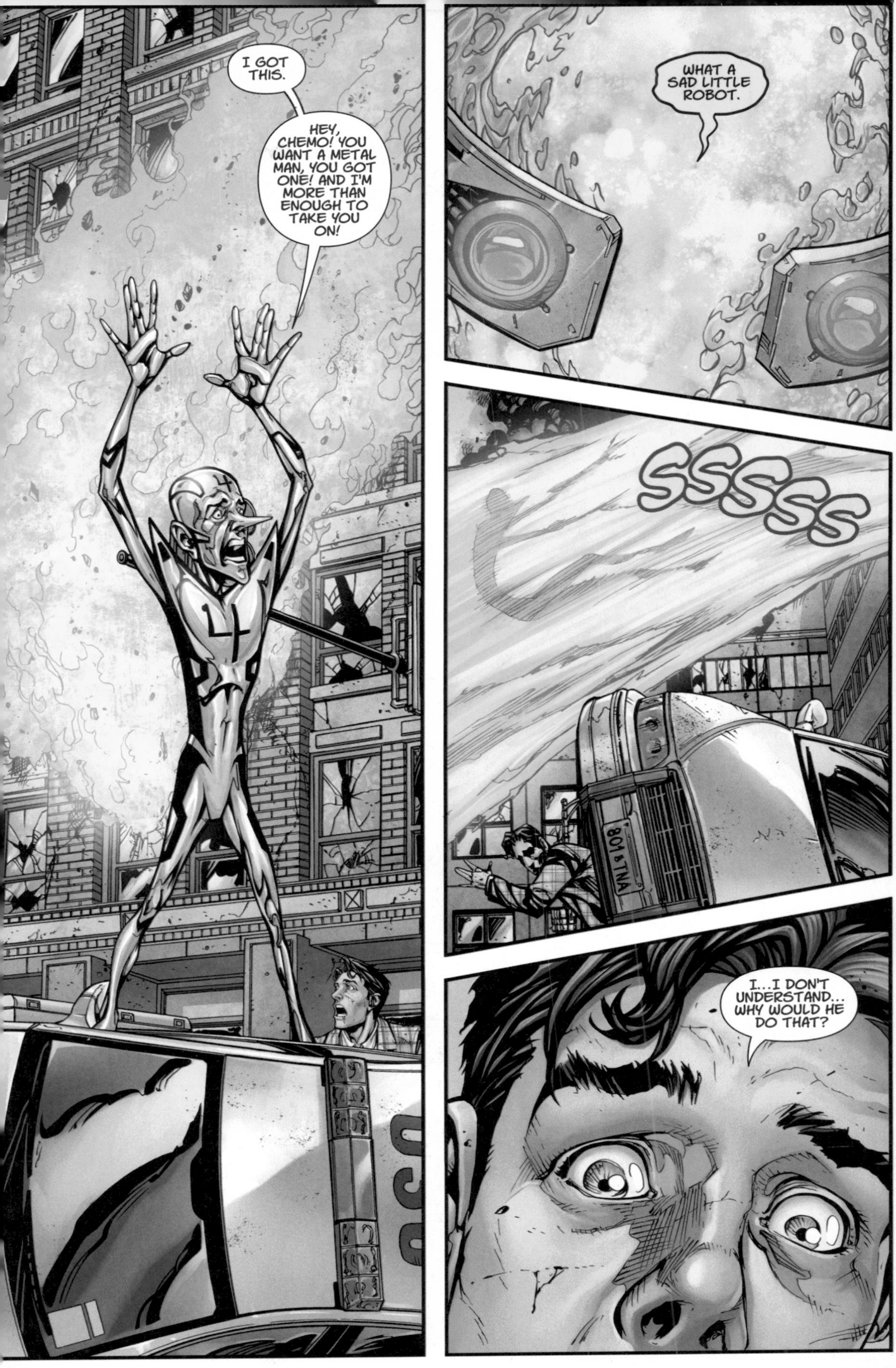
I GOT THIS.
HEY, CHEMO! YOU WANT A METAL MAN, YOU GOT ONE! AND I'M MORE THAN ENOUGH TO TAKE YOU ON!
WHAT A SAD LITTLE ROBOT.
SSSSS
I...I DON'T UNDERSTAND... WHY WOULD HE DO THAT?

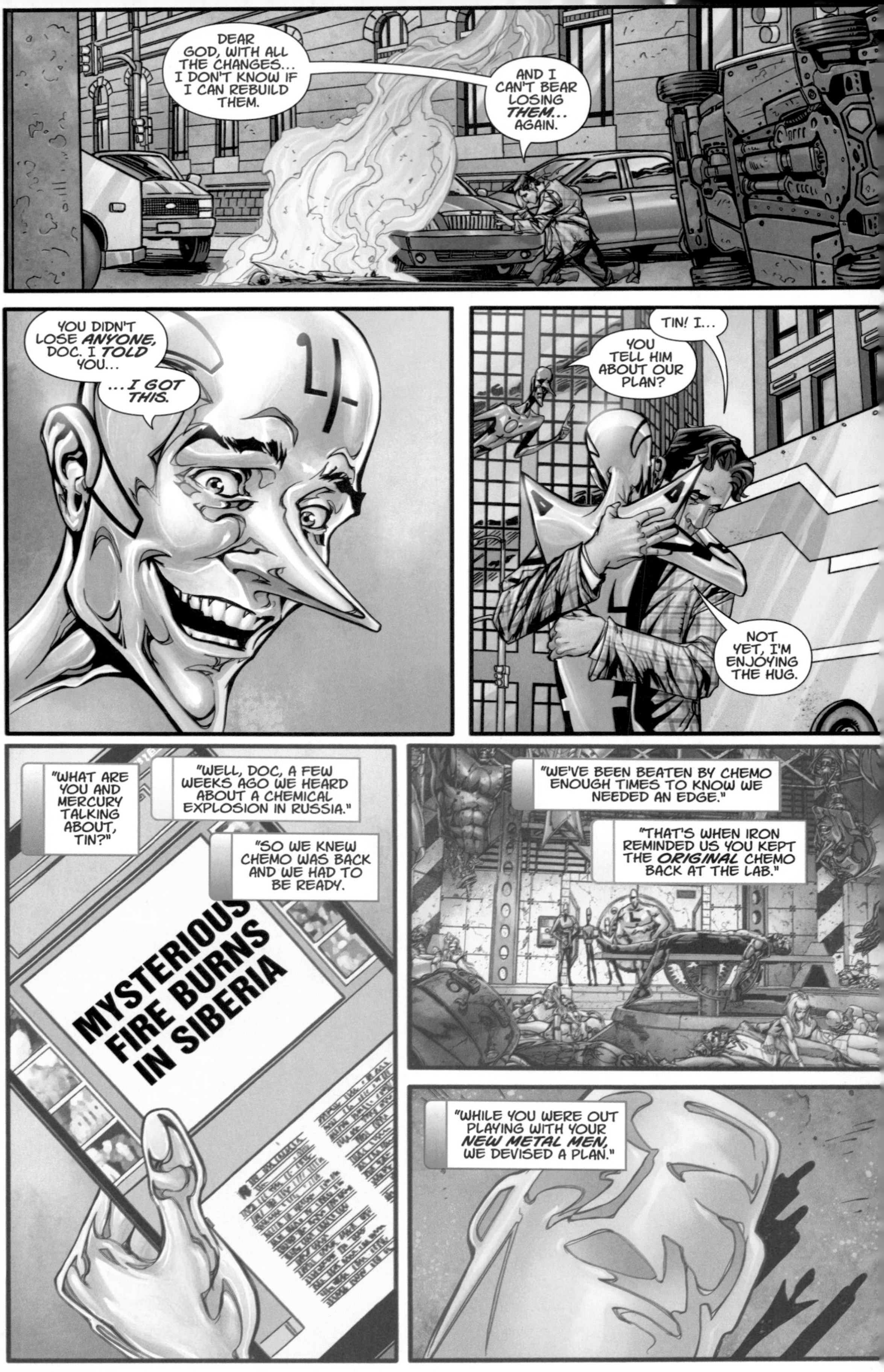
DEAR GOD, WITH ALL THE CHANGES... I DON'T KNOW IF I CAN REBUILD THEM.
AND I CAN'T BEAR LOSING *THEM*... AGAIN.
YOU DIDN'T LOSE *ANYONE*, DOC. I *TOLD* YOU...
...*I GOT THIS.*
TIN! I...
YOU TELL HIM ABOUT OUR PLAN?
NOT YET, I'M ENJOYING THE HUG.
"WHAT ARE YOU AND MERCURY TALKING ABOUT, TIN?"
"WELL, DOC, A FEW WEEKS AGO WE HEARD ABOUT A CHEMICAL EXPLOSION IN RUSSIA."
"SO WE KNEW CHEMO WAS BACK AND WE HAD TO BE READY.
MYSTERIOUS FIRE BURNS IN SIBERIA
"WE'VE BEEN BEATEN BY CHEMO ENOUGH TIMES TO KNOW WE NEEDED AN EDGE."
"THAT'S WHEN IRON REMINDED US YOU KEPT THE *ORIGINAL* CHEMO BACK AT THE LAB."
"WHILE YOU WERE OUT PLAYING WITH YOUR *NEW METAL MEN*, WE DEVISED A PLAN."

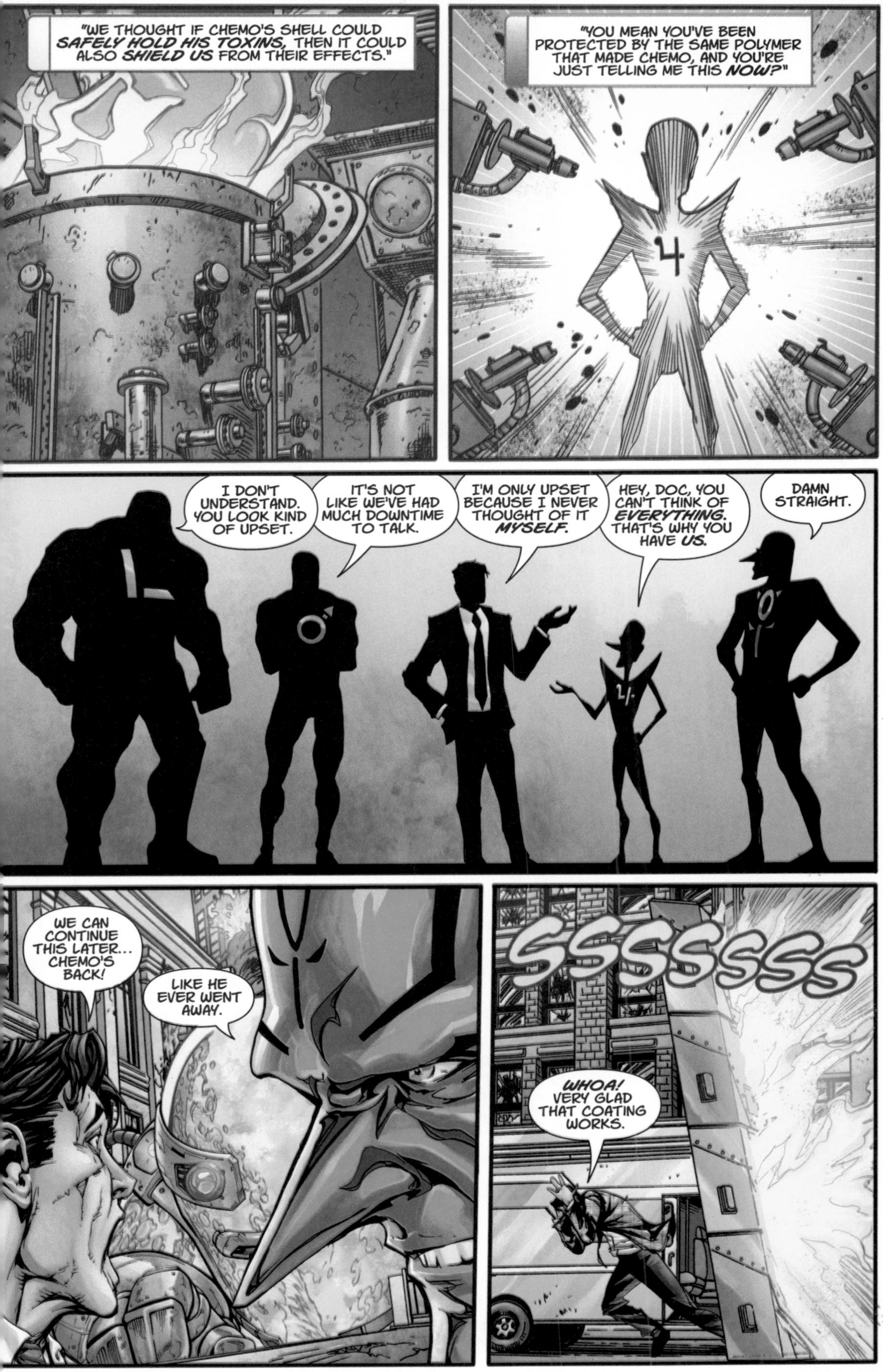
"WE THOUGHT IF CHEMO'S SHELL COULD SAFELY HOLD HIS TOXINS, THEN IT COULD ALSO SHIELD US FROM THEIR EFFECTS."
"YOU MEAN YOU'VE BEEN PROTECTED BY THE SAME POLYMER THAT MADE CHEMO, AND YOU'RE JUST TELLING ME THIS NOW?"
I DON'T UNDERSTAND. YOU LOOK KIND OF UPSET.
IT'S NOT LIKE WE'VE HAD MUCH DOWNTIME TO TALK.
I'M ONLY UPSET BECAUSE I NEVER THOUGHT OF IT MYSELF.
HEY, DOC, YOU CAN'T THINK OF EVERYTHING. THAT'S WHY YOU HAVE US.
DAMN STRAIGHT.
WE CAN CONTINUE THIS LATER... CHEMO'S BACK!
LIKE HE EVER WENT AWAY.
SSSSSSS
WHOA! VERY GLAD THAT COATING WORKS.

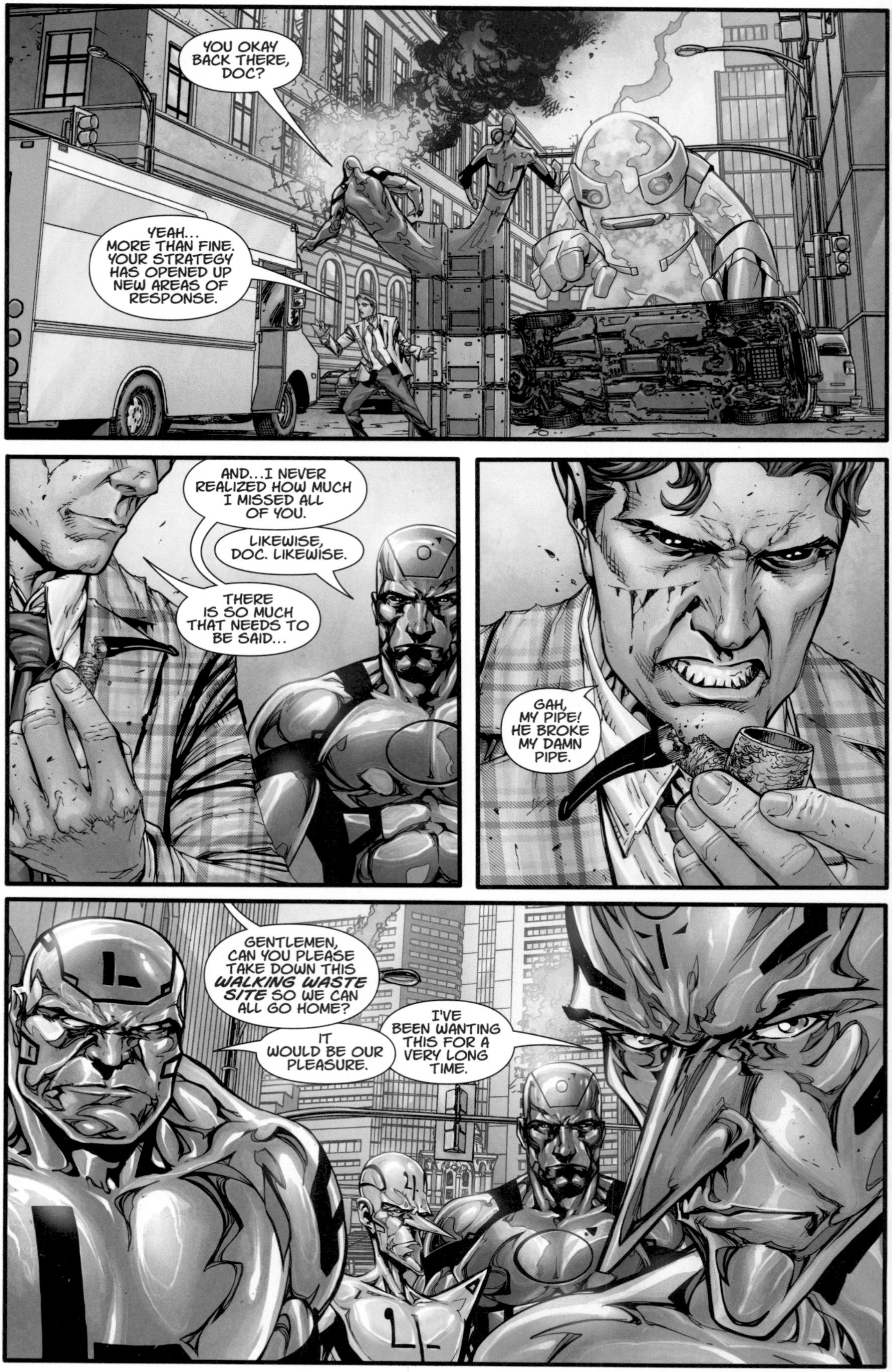
YOU OKAY BACK THERE, DOC?
YEAH... MORE THAN FINE. YOUR STRATEGY HAS OPENED UP NEW AREAS OF RESPONSE.
AND...I NEVER REALIZED HOW MUCH I MISSED ALL OF YOU.
LIKEWISE, DOC. LIKEWISE.
THERE IS SO MUCH THAT NEEDS TO BE SAID...
GAH, MY PIPE! HE BROKE MY DAMN PIPE.
GENTLEMEN, CAN YOU PLEASE TAKE DOWN THIS *WALKING WASTE SITE* SO WE CAN ALL GO HOME?
IT WOULD BE OUR PLEASURE.
I'VE BEEN WANTING THIS FOR A VERY LONG TIME.

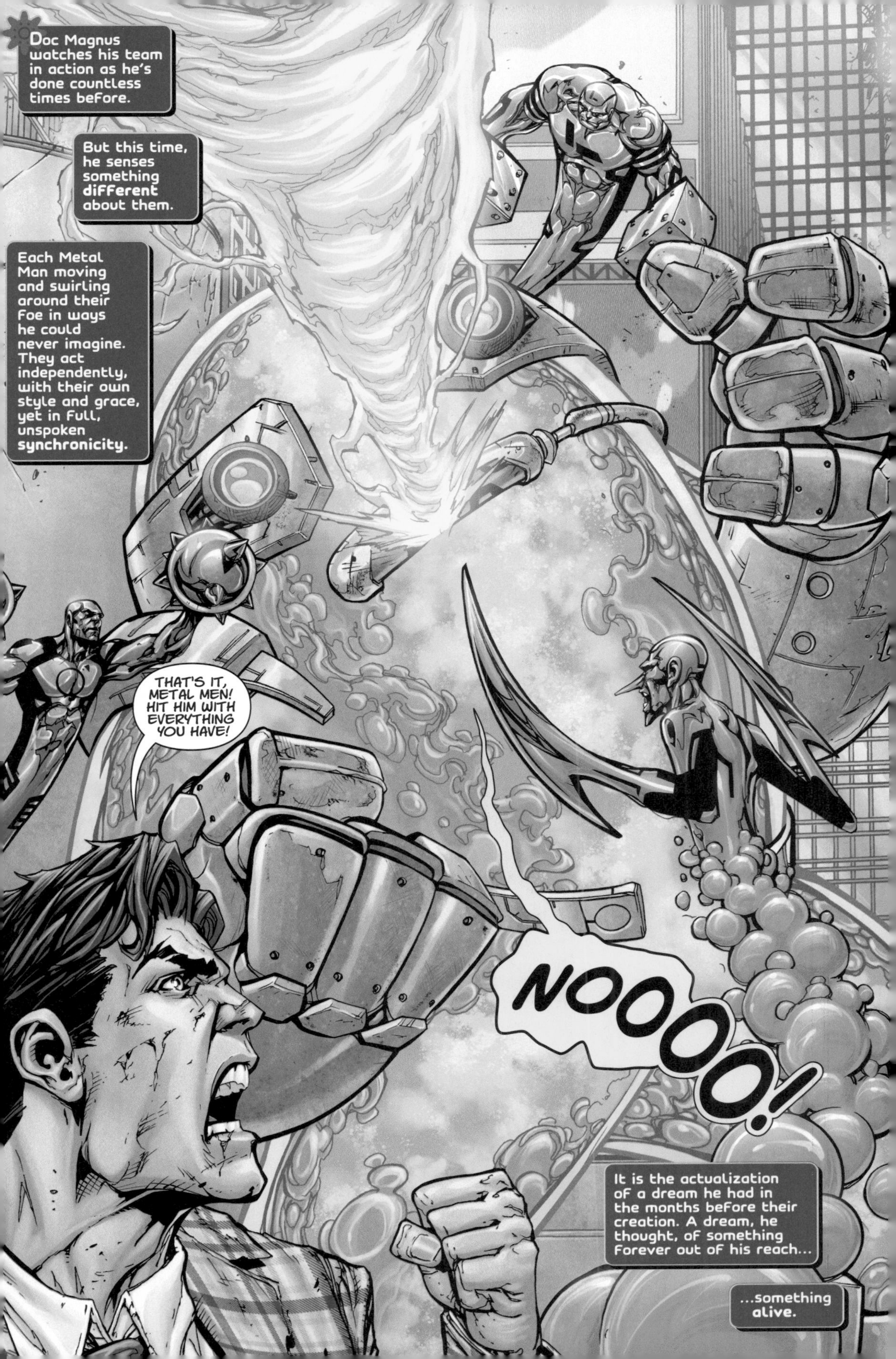
Doc Magnus watches his team in action as he's done countless times before.
But this time, he senses something **different** about them.
Each Metal Man moving and swirling around their foe in ways he could never imagine. They act independently, with their own style and grace, yet in full, unspoken **synchronicity**.
THAT'S IT, METAL MEN! HIT HIM WITH EVERYTHING YOU HAVE!
NOOOO!
It is the actualization of a dream he had in the months before their creation. A dream, he thought, of something forever out of his reach...
...something **alive**.

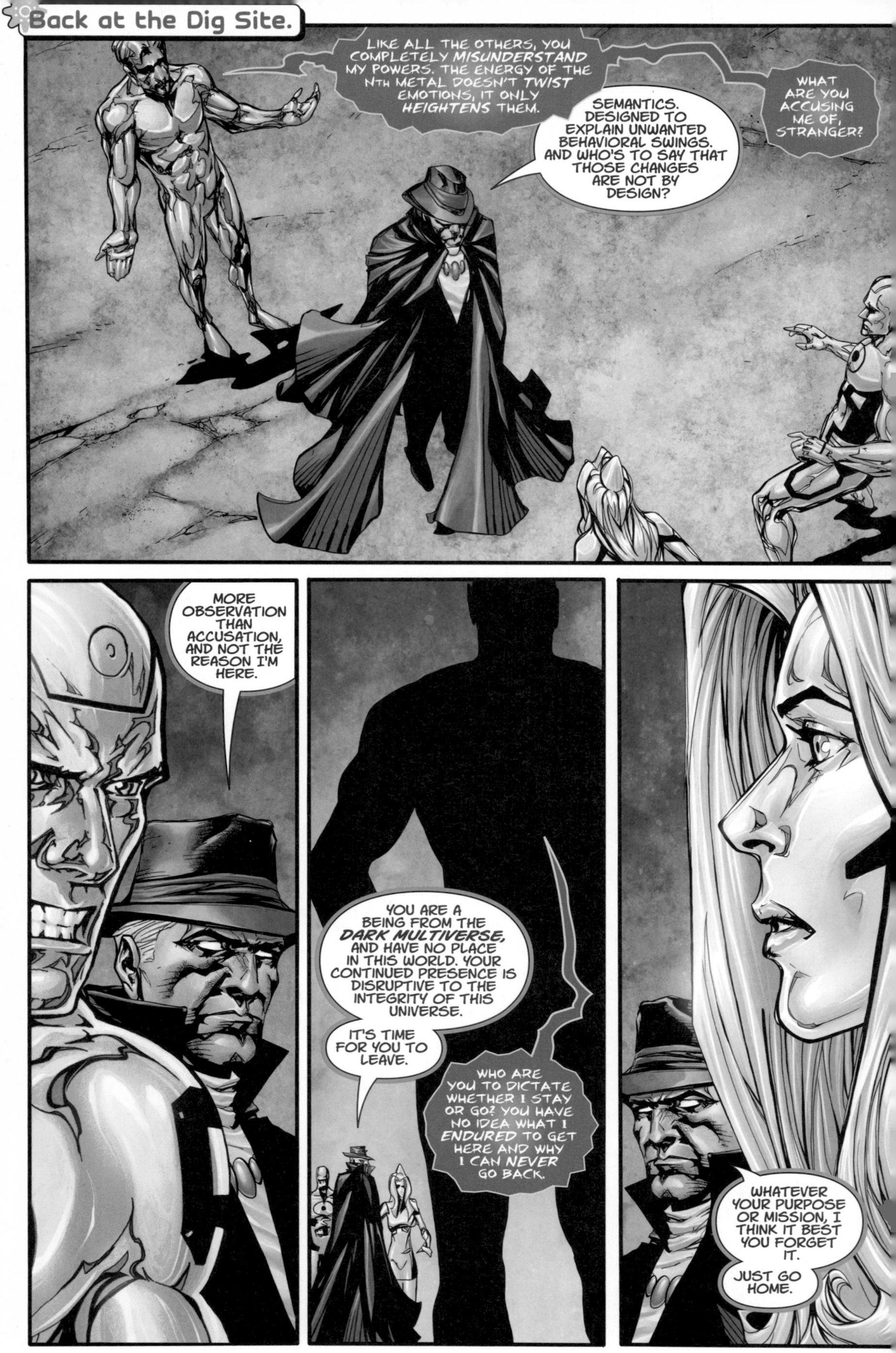
Back at the Dig Site.
LIKE ALL THE OTHERS, YOU COMPLETELY MISUNDERSTAND MY POWERS. THE ENERGY OF THE NTH METAL DOESN'T TWIST EMOTIONS, IT ONLY HEIGHTENS THEM.
SEMANTICS. DESIGNED TO EXPLAIN UNWANTED BEHAVIORAL SWINGS. AND WHO'S TO SAY THAT THOSE CHANGES ARE NOT BY DESIGN?
WHAT ARE YOU ACCUSING ME OF, STRANGER?
MORE OBSERVATION THAN ACCUSATION, AND NOT THE REASON I'M HERE.
YOU ARE A BEING FROM THE DARK MULTIVERSE, AND HAVE NO PLACE IN THIS WORLD. YOUR CONTINUED PRESENCE IS DISRUPTIVE TO THE INTEGRITY OF THIS UNIVERSE.
IT'S TIME FOR YOU TO LEAVE.
WHO ARE YOU TO DICTATE WHETHER I STAY OR GO? YOU HAVE NO IDEA WHAT I ENDURED TO GET HERE AND WHY I CAN NEVER GO BACK.
WHATEVER YOUR PURPOSE OR MISSION, I THINK IT BEST YOU FORGET IT.
JUST GO HOME.

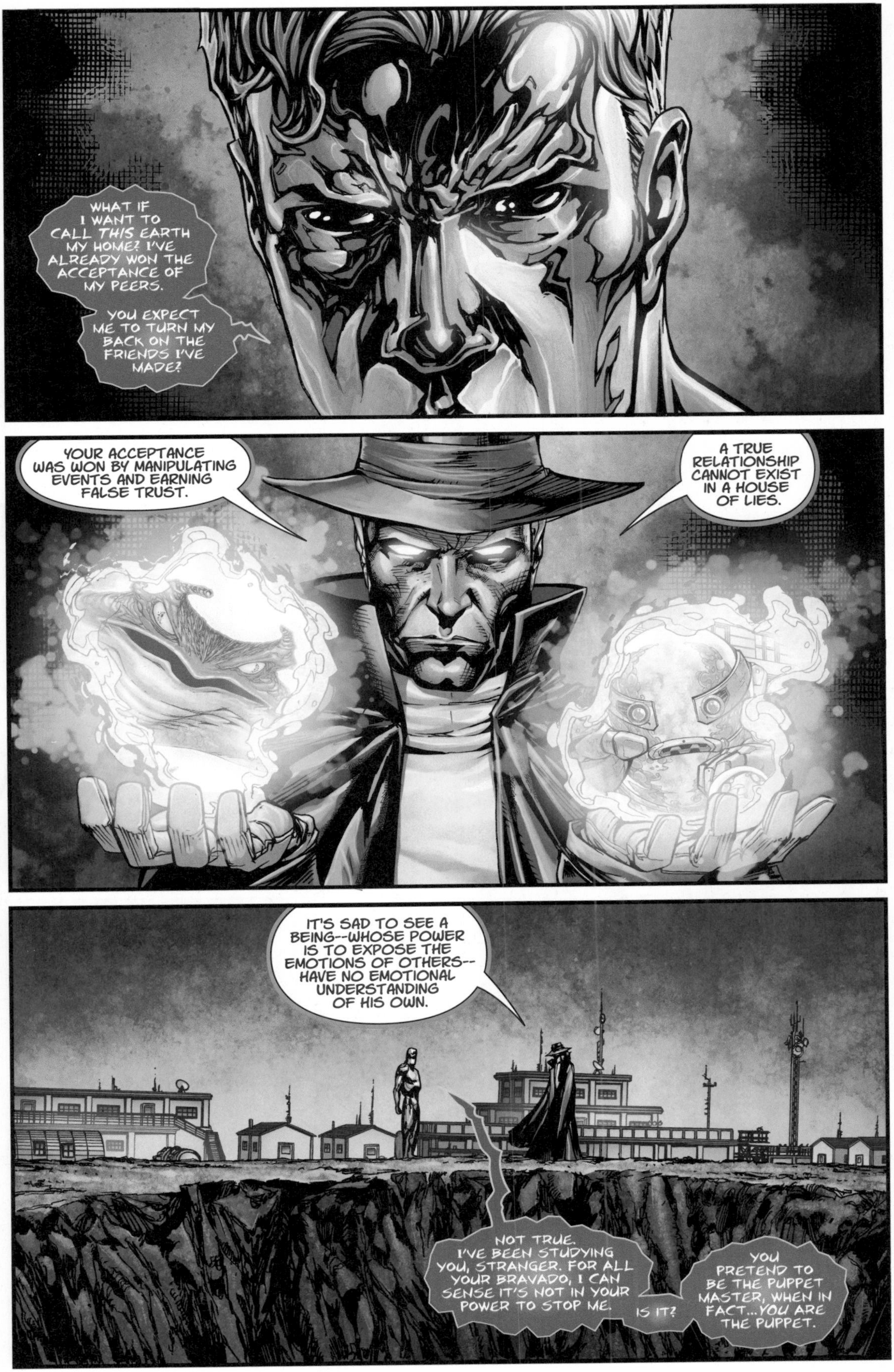
WHAT IF I WANT TO CALL *THIS* EARTH MY HOME? I'VE ALREADY WON THE ACCEPTANCE OF MY PEERS.
YOU EXPECT ME TO TURN MY BACK ON THE FRIENDS I'VE MADE?
YOUR ACCEPTANCE WAS WON BY MANIPULATING EVENTS AND EARNING FALSE TRUST.
A TRUE RELATIONSHIP CANNOT EXIST IN A HOUSE OF LIES.
IT'S SAD TO SEE A BEING--WHOSE POWER IS TO EXPOSE THE EMOTIONS OF OTHERS--HAVE NO EMOTIONAL UNDERSTANDING OF HIS OWN.
NOT TRUE. I'VE BEEN STUDYING YOU, STRANGER. FOR ALL YOUR BRAVADO, I CAN SENSE IT'S NOT IN YOUR POWER TO STOP ME.
IS IT?
YOU PRETEND TO BE THE PUPPET MASTER, WHEN IN FACT...YOU ARE THE PUPPET.

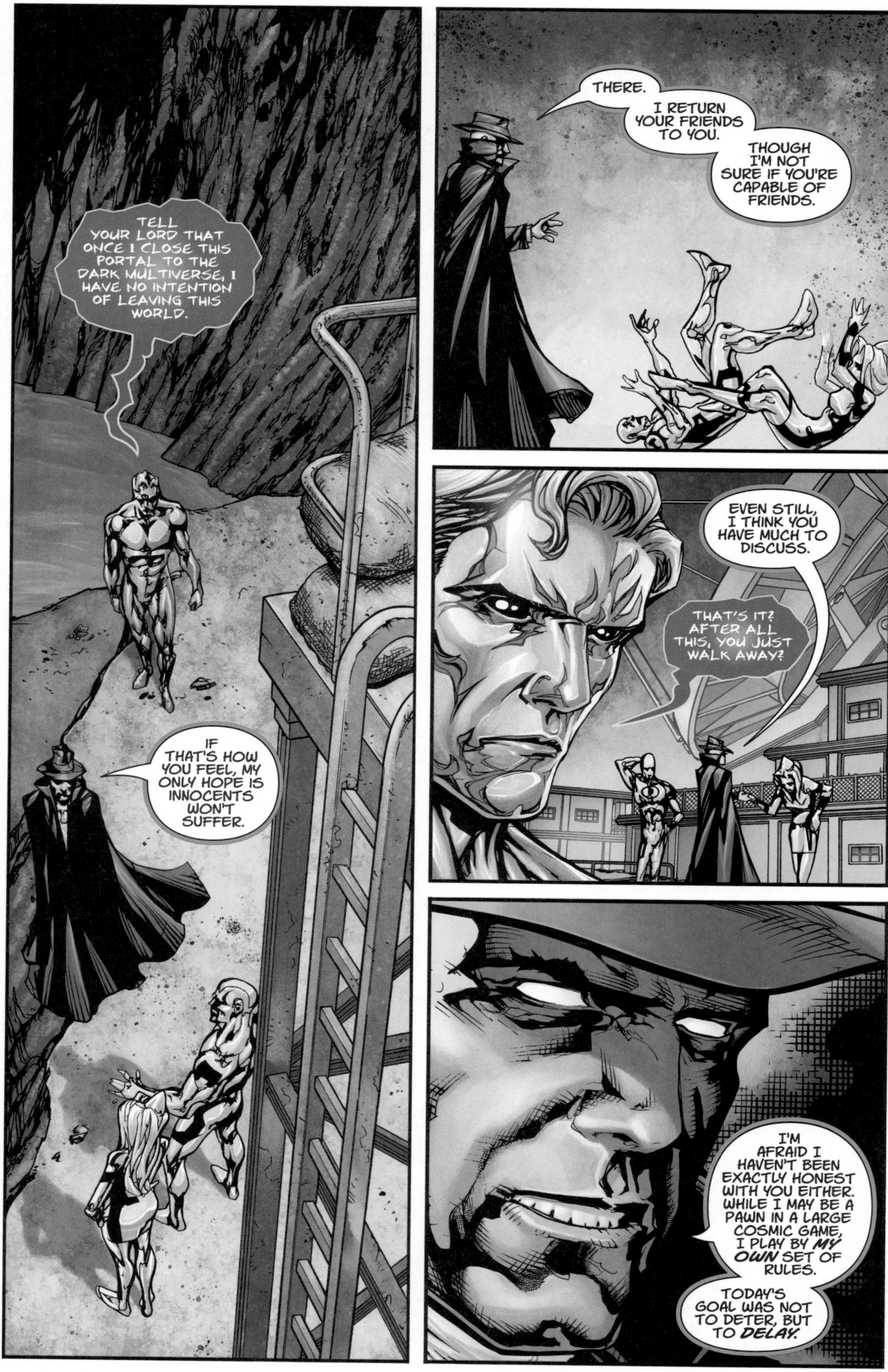
TELL YOUR LORD THAT ONCE I CLOSE THIS PORTAL TO THE DARK MULTIVERSE, I HAVE NO INTENTION OF LEAVING THIS WORLD.
IF THAT'S HOW YOU FEEL, MY ONLY HOPE IS INNOCENTS WON'T SUFFER.
THERE.
I RETURN YOUR FRIENDS TO YOU.
THOUGH I'M NOT SURE IF YOU'RE CAPABLE OF FRIENDS.
EVEN STILL, I THINK YOU HAVE MUCH TO DISCUSS.
THAT'S IT? AFTER ALL THIS, YOU JUST WALK AWAY?
I'M AFRAID I HAVEN'T BEEN EXACTLY HONEST WITH YOU EITHER. WHILE I MAY BE A PAWN IN A LARGE COSMIC GAME, I PLAY BY *MY OWN* SET OF RULES.
TODAY'S GOAL WAS NOT TO DETER, BUT TO *DELAY.*

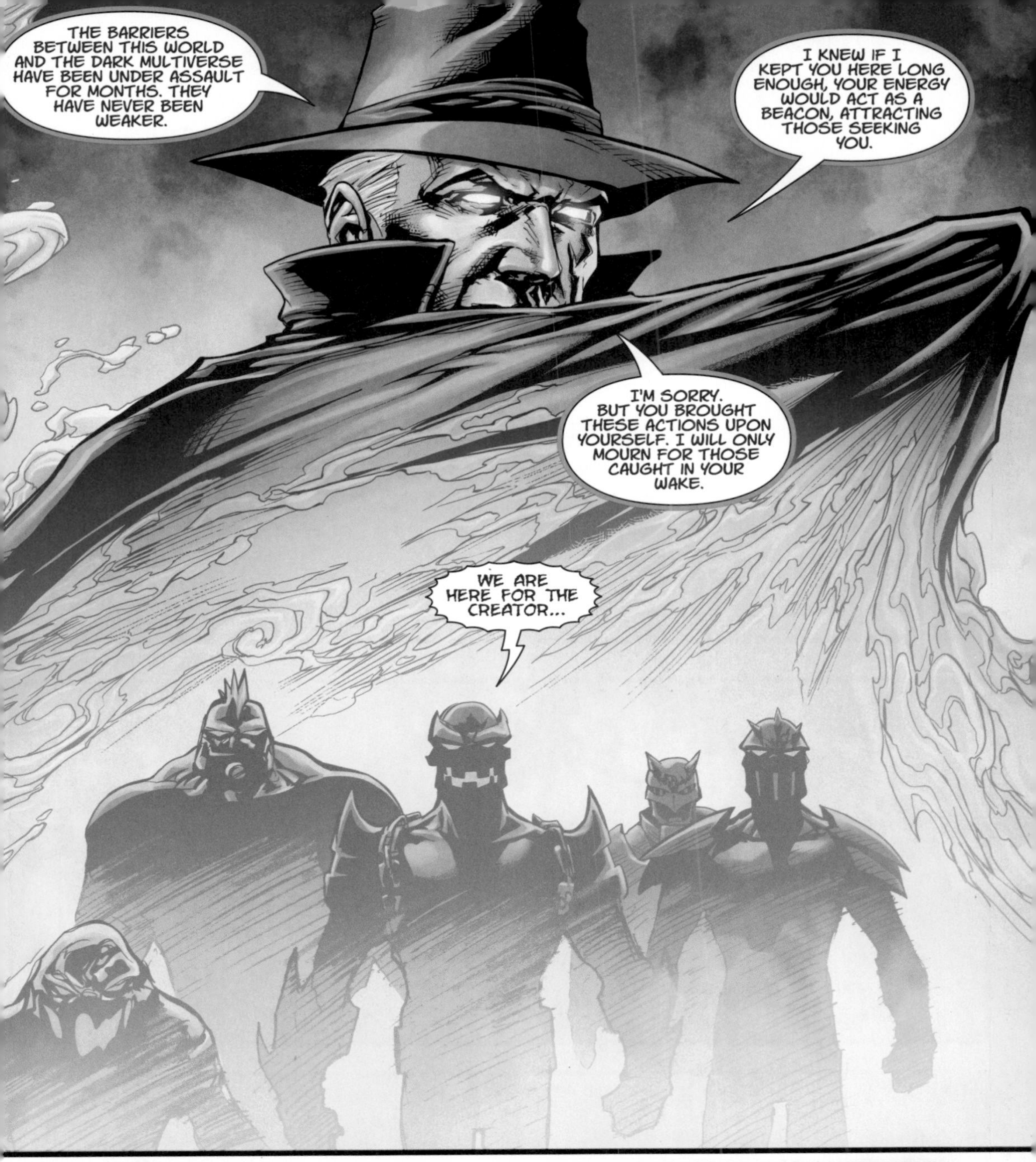
THE BARRIERS BETWEEN THIS WORLD AND THE DARK MULTIVERSE HAVE BEEN UNDER ASSAULT FOR MONTHS. THEY HAVE NEVER BEEN WEAKER.
I KNEW IF I KEPT YOU HERE LONG ENOUGH, YOUR ENERGY WOULD ACT AS A BEACON, ATTRACTING THOSE SEEKING YOU.
I'M SORRY. BUT YOU BROUGHT THESE ACTIONS UPON YOURSELF. I WILL ONLY MOURN FOR THOSE CAUGHT IN YOUR WAKE.
WE ARE HERE FOR THE CREATOR...
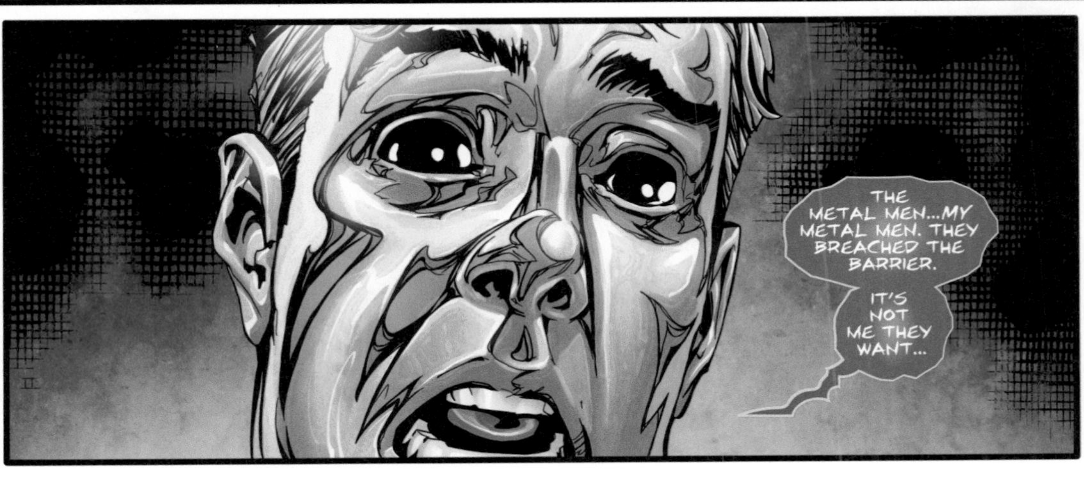
THE METAL MEN...MY METAL MEN. THEY BREACHED THE BARRIER.
IT'S NOT ME THEY WANT...

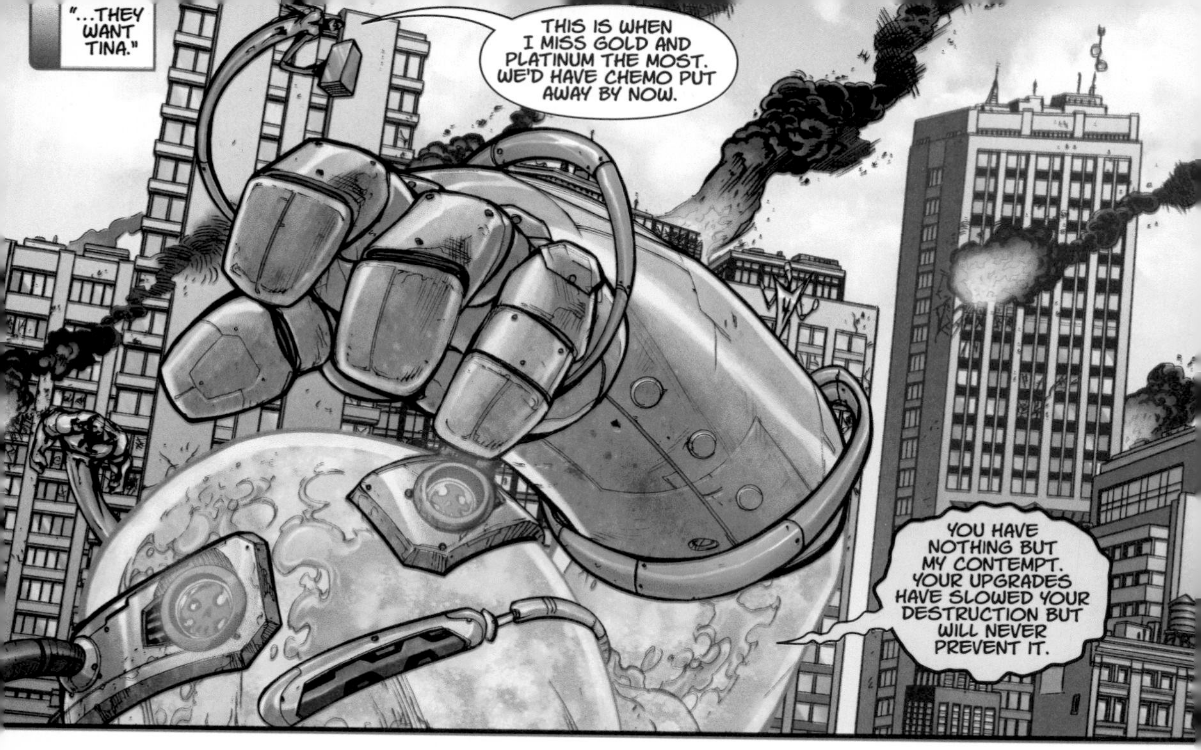
"...THEY WANT TINA."
THIS IS WHEN I MISS GOLD AND PLATINUM THE MOST. WE'D HAVE CHEMO PUT AWAY BY NOW.
YOU HAVE NOTHING BUT MY CONTEMPT. YOUR UPGRADES HAVE SLOWED YOUR DESTRUCTION BUT WILL NEVER PREVENT IT.

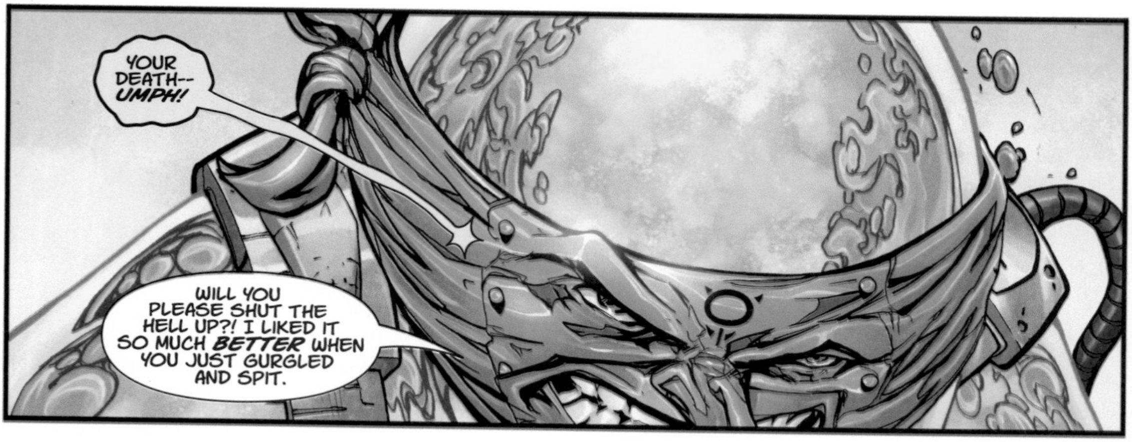
YOUR DEATH-- UMPH!
WILL YOU PLEASE SHUT THE HELL UP?! I LIKED IT SO MUCH BETTER WHEN YOU JUST GURGLED AND SPIT.

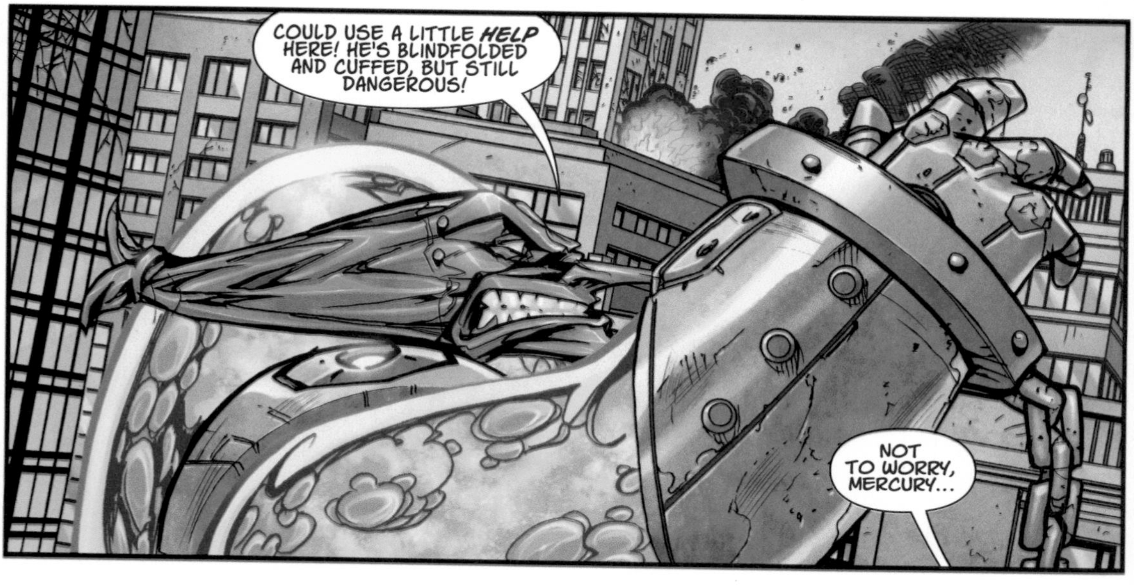
COULD USE A LITTLE HELP HERE! HE'S BLINDFOLDED AND CUFFED, BUT STILL DANGEROUS!
NOT TO WORRY, MERCURY...

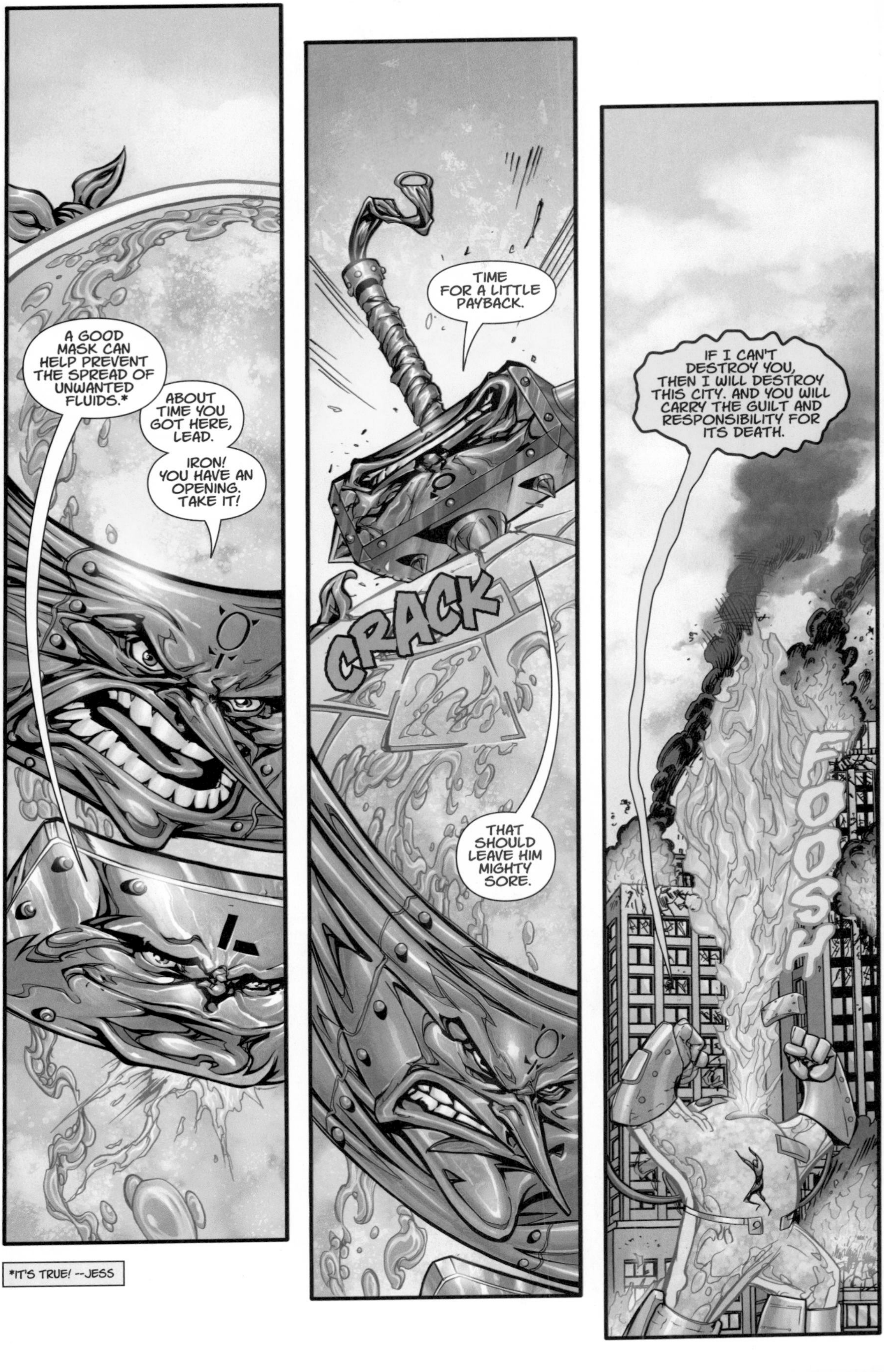
A GOOD MASK CAN HELP PREVENT THE SPREAD OF UNWANTED FLUIDS.*
ABOUT TIME YOU GOT HERE, LEAD.
IRON! YOU HAVE AN OPENING. TAKE IT!
*IT'S TRUE! --JESS
TIME FOR A LITTLE PAYBACK.
CRACK
THAT SHOULD LEAVE HIM MIGHTY SORE.
IF I CAN'T DESTROY YOU, THEN I WILL DESTROY THIS CITY. AND YOU WILL CARRY THE GUILT AND RESPONSIBILITY FOR ITS DEATH.
FOOOSH

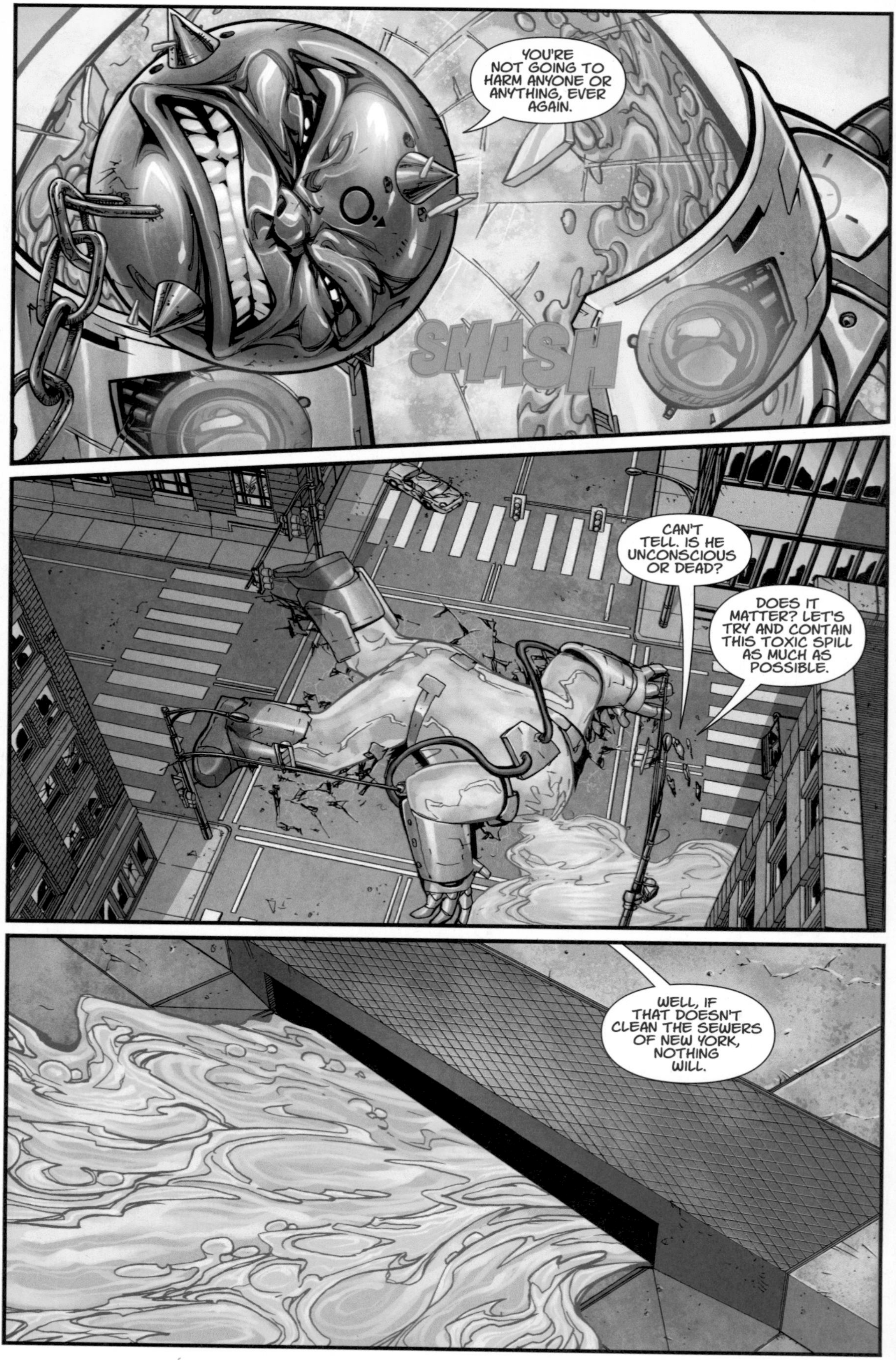
YOU'RE NOT GOING TO HARM ANYONE OR ANYTHING, EVER AGAIN.
SMASH
CAN'T TELL. IS HE UNCONSCIOUS OR DEAD?
DOES IT MATTER? LET'S TRY AND CONTAIN THIS TOXIC SPILL AS MUCH AS POSSIBLE.
WELL, IF THAT DOESN'T CLEAN THE SEWERS OF NEW YORK, NOTHING WILL.

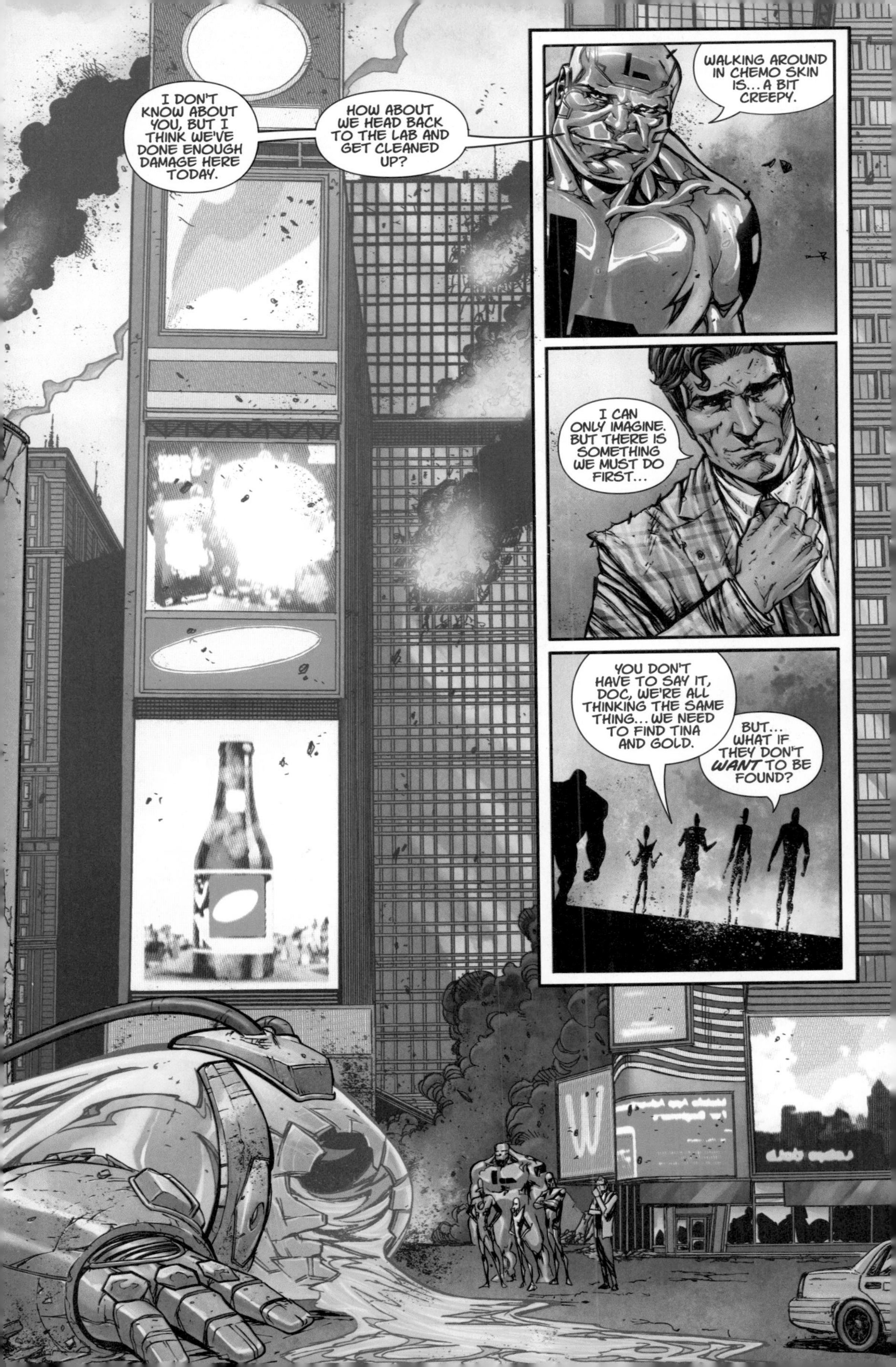
I DON'T KNOW ABOUT YOU, BUT I THINK WE'VE DONE ENOUGH DAMAGE HERE TODAY.
HOW ABOUT WE HEAD BACK TO THE LAB AND GET CLEANED UP?
WALKING AROUND IN CHEMO SKIN IS... A BIT CREEPY.
I CAN ONLY IMAGINE. BUT THERE IS SOMETHING WE MUST DO FIRST...
YOU DON'T HAVE TO SAY IT, DOC, WE'RE ALL THINKING THE SAME THING... WE NEED TO FIND TINA AND GOLD.
BUT... WHAT IF THEY DON'T *WANT* TO BE FOUND?

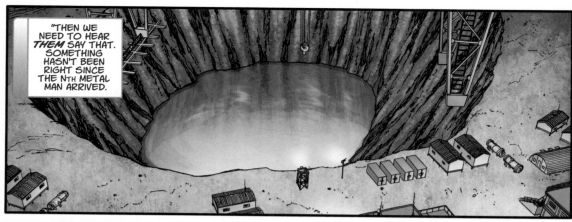

"THEN WE NEED TO HEAR *THEM* SAY THAT. SOMETHING HASN'T BEEN RIGHT SINCE THE NTH METAL MAN ARRIVED.

"AND I'M NOT JUST TALKING ABOUT YOUR NEW SENTIENCE...YOUR NEW LIVES. THE MANTA, THE MISSILE MEN, EVEN CHEMO. EVERYTHING SEEMS *CONNECTED.*

"THE NTH METAL MAN IS BEHIND IT ALL... I'M *SURE* OF IT. AND IF HE HAS GOLD AND TINA, THEN I'M GOING TO *FIND HIM.*

"EVEN IF I HAVE TO WALK THROUGH THE GATES OF *HELL* ITSELF."

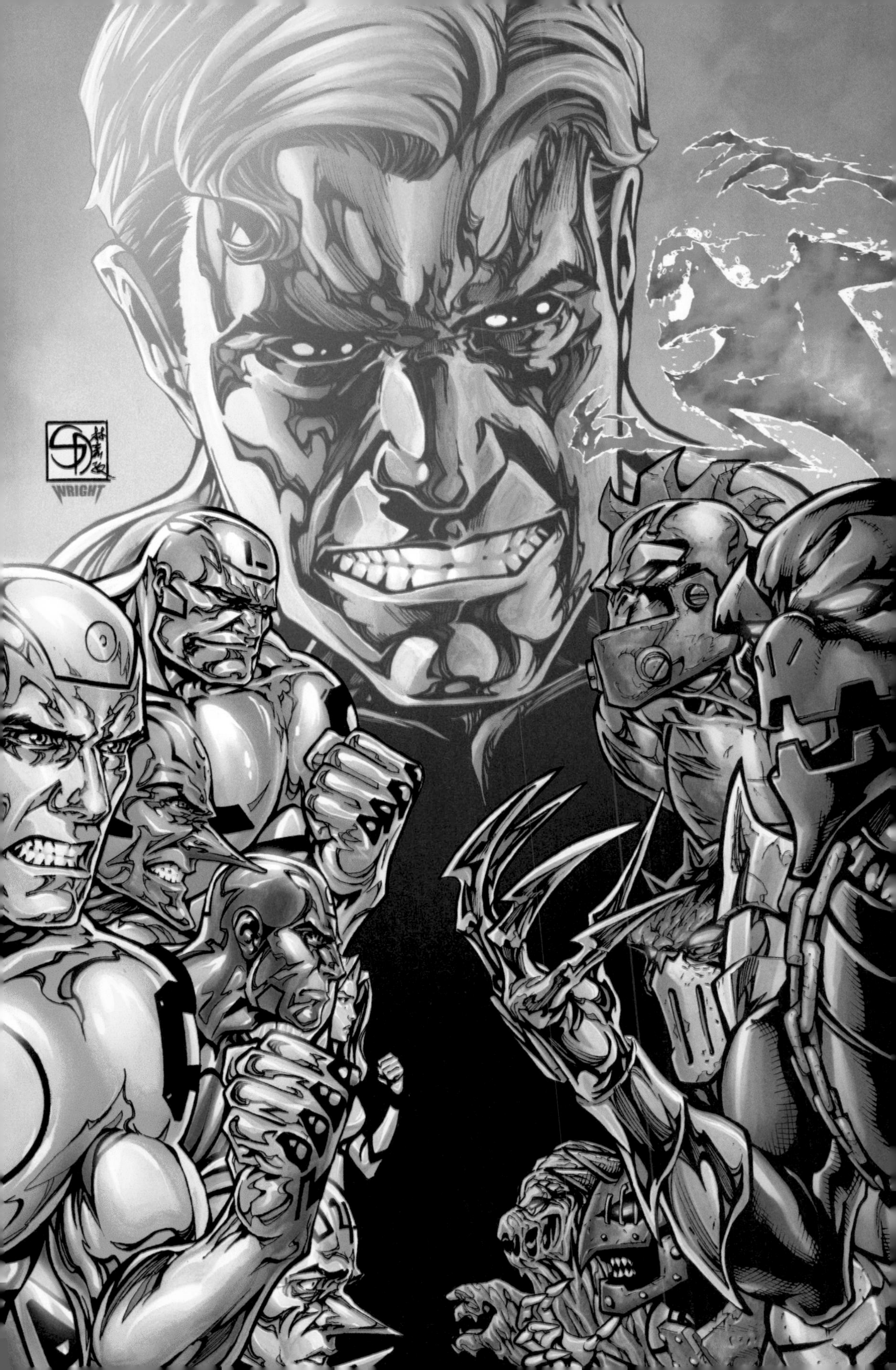
WRIGHT

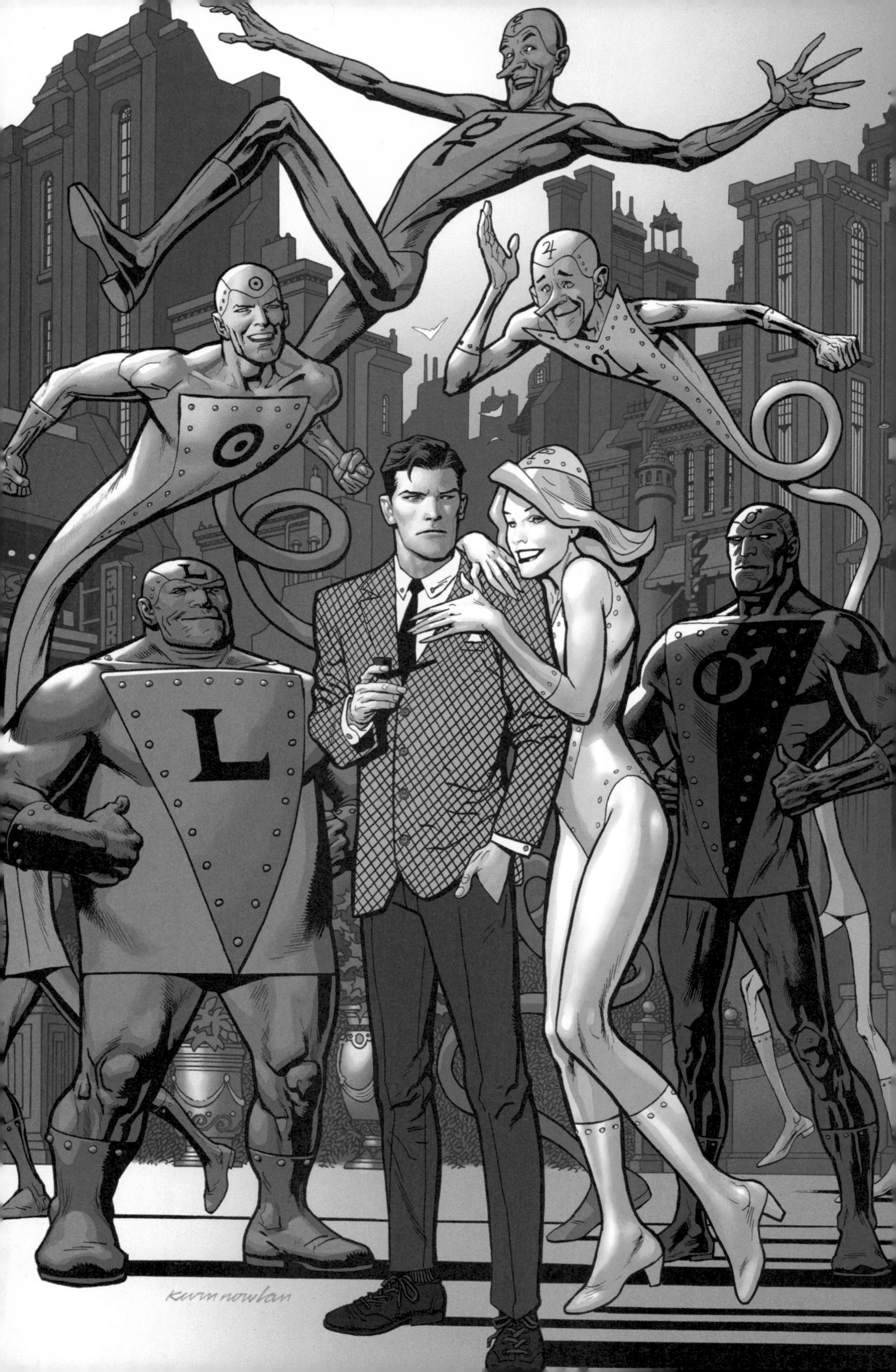
kevin nowlan

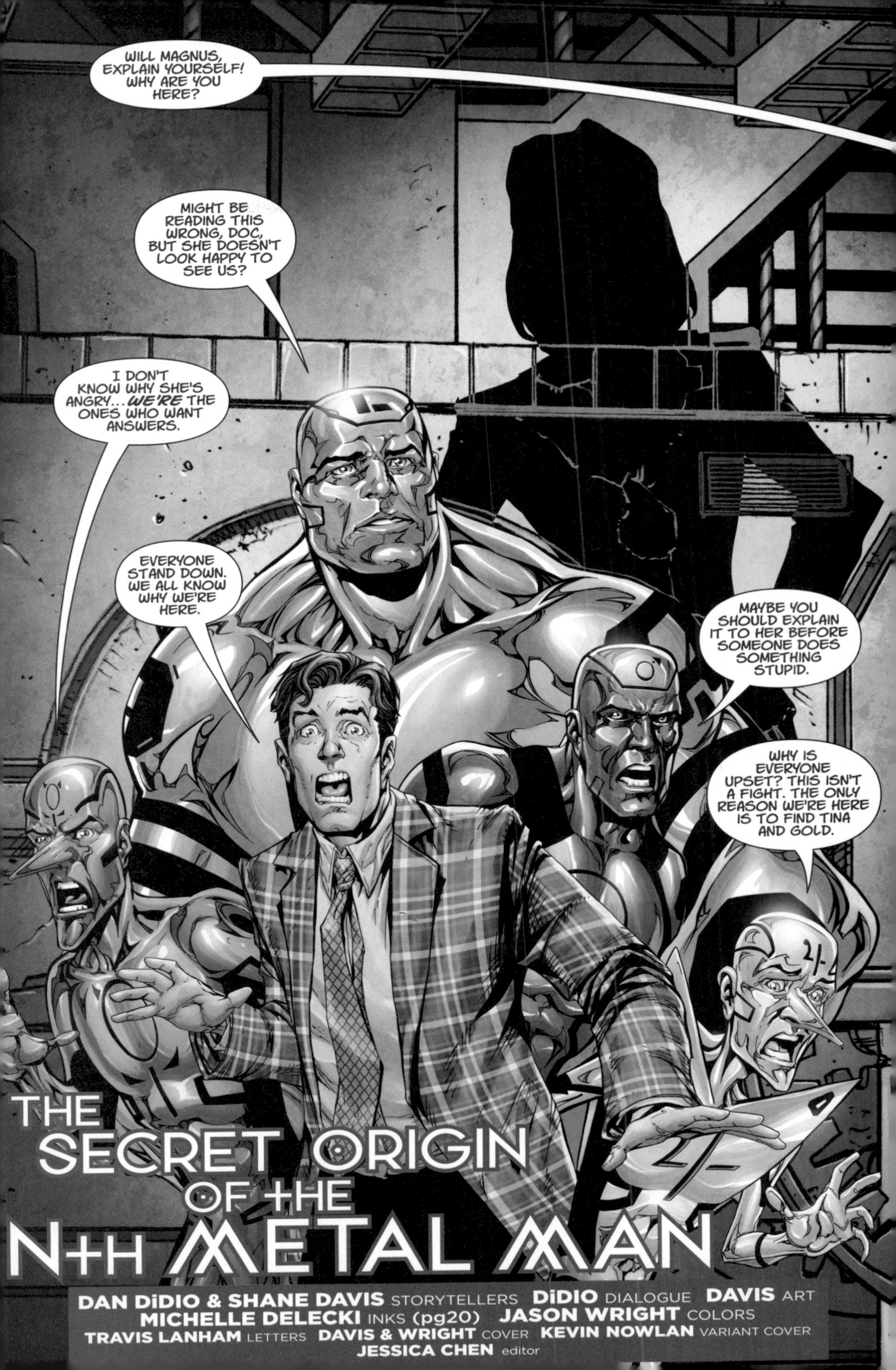
WILL MAGNUS, EXPLAIN YOURSELF! WHY ARE YOU HERE?
MIGHT BE READING THIS WRONG, DOC, BUT SHE DOESN'T LOOK HAPPY TO SEE US?
I DON'T KNOW WHY SHE'S ANGRY... WE'RE THE ONES WHO WANT ANSWERS.
EVERYONE STAND DOWN. WE ALL KNOW WHY WE'RE HERE.
MAYBE YOU SHOULD EXPLAIN IT TO HER BEFORE SOMEONE DOES SOMETHING STUPID.
WHY IS EVERYONE UPSET? THIS ISN'T A FIGHT. THE ONLY REASON WE'RE HERE IS TO FIND TINA AND GOLD.
THE SECRET ORIGIN OF THE NTH METAL MAN
DAN DIDIO & SHANE DAVIS STORYTELLERS DIDIO DIALOGUE DAVIS ART
MICHELLE DELECKI INKS (pg20) JASON WRIGHT COLORS
TRAVIS LANHAM LETTERS DAVIS & WRIGHT COVER KEVIN NOWLAN VARIANT COVER
JESSICA CHEN editor

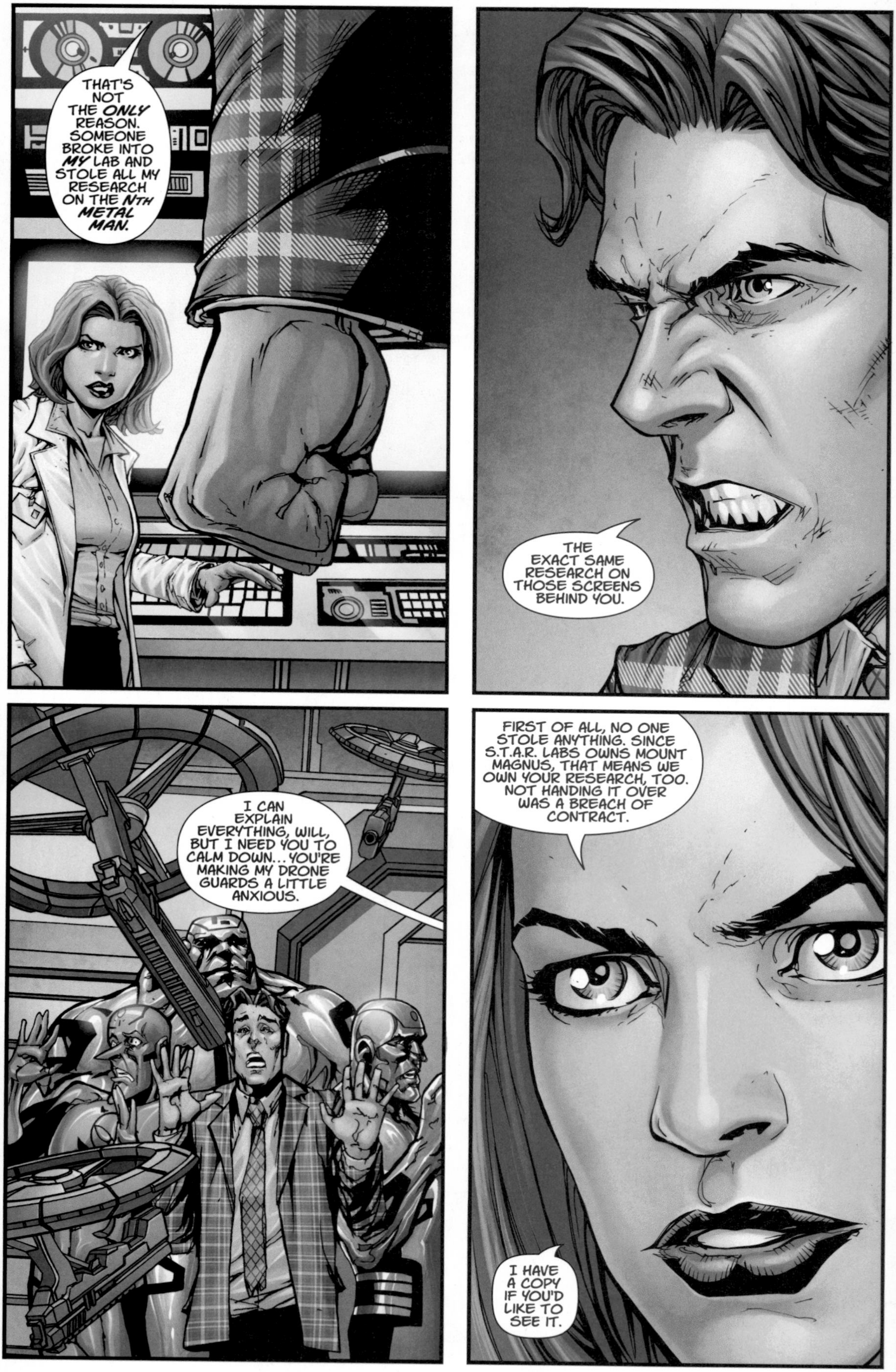
THAT'S NOT THE ONLY REASON. SOMEONE BROKE INTO MY LAB AND STOLE ALL MY RESEARCH ON THE NTH METAL MAN.
THE EXACT SAME RESEARCH ON THOSE SCREENS BEHIND YOU.
I CAN EXPLAIN EVERYTHING, WILL, BUT I NEED YOU TO CALM DOWN... YOU'RE MAKING MY DRONE GUARDS A LITTLE ANXIOUS.
FIRST OF ALL, NO ONE STOLE ANYTHING. SINCE S.T.A.R. LABS OWNS MOUNT MAGNUS, THAT MEANS WE OWN YOUR RESEARCH, TOO. NOT HANDING IT OVER WAS A BREACH OF CONTRACT.
I HAVE A COPY IF YOU'D LIKE TO SEE IT.

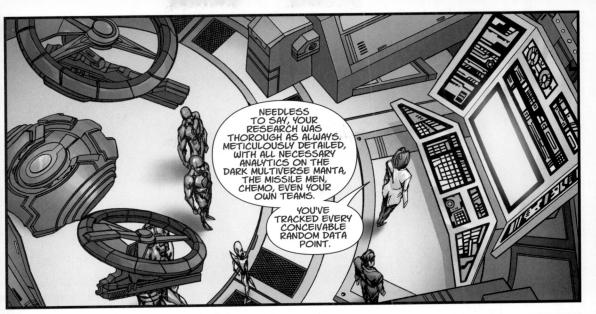

NEEDLESS TO SAY, YOUR RESEARCH WAS THOROUGH AS ALWAYS. METICULOUSLY DETAILED, WITH ALL NECESSARY ANALYTICS ON THE DARK MULTIVERSE MANTA, THE MISSILE MEN, CHEMO, EVEN YOUR OWN TEAMS.

YOU'VE TRACKED EVERY CONCEIVABLE RANDOM DATA POINT.

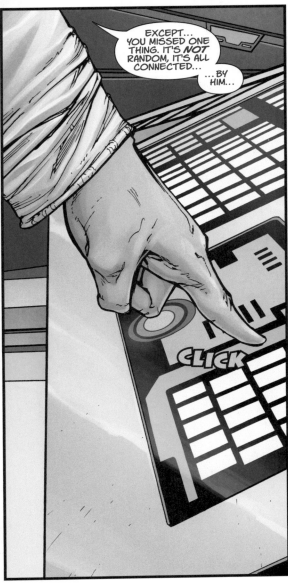

EXCEPT... YOU MISSED ONE THING. IT'S *NOT* RANDOM, IT'S ALL CONNECTED...

...BY HIM...

CLICK

...THE NTH METAL MAN. HIS ENERGY SIGNATURE IS PRESENT *EVERYWHERE*. IT'S SO OBVIOUS THAT THERE'S ONLY ONE REASON FOR YOU *NOT* SEEING IT...

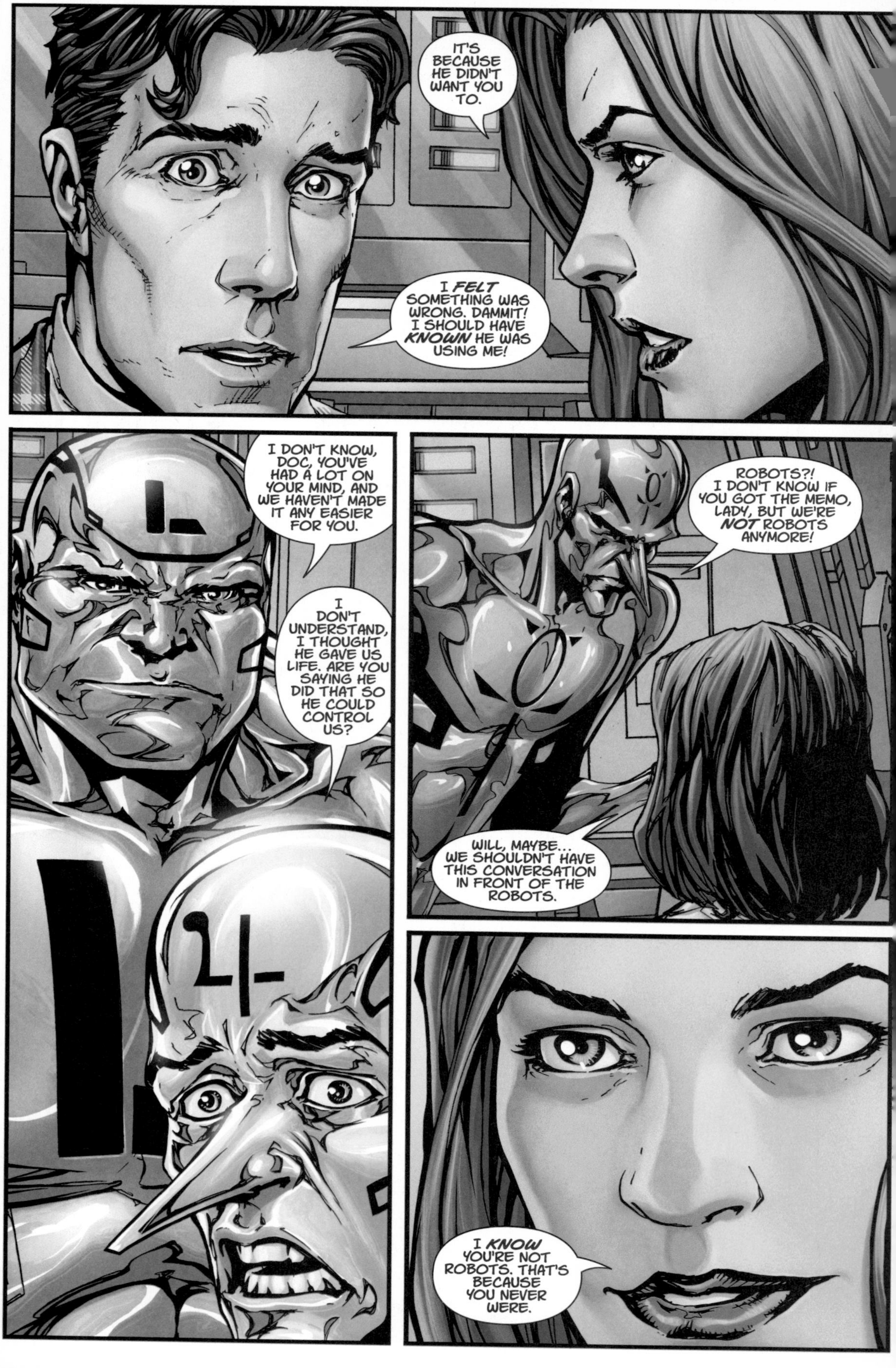
IT'S BECAUSE HE DIDN'T WANT YOU TO.
I FELT SOMETHING WAS WRONG. DAMMIT! I SHOULD HAVE KNOWN HE WAS USING ME!
I DON'T KNOW, DOC, YOU'VE HAD A LOT ON YOUR MIND, AND WE HAVEN'T MADE IT ANY EASIER FOR YOU.
I DON'T UNDERSTAND, I THOUGHT HE GAVE US LIFE. ARE YOU SAYING HE DID THAT SO HE COULD CONTROL US?
WILL, MAYBE... WE SHOULDN'T HAVE THIS CONVERSATION IN FRONT OF THE ROBOTS.
ROBOTS?! I DON'T KNOW IF YOU GOT THE MEMO, LADY, BUT WE'RE NOT ROBOTS ANYMORE!
I KNOW YOU'RE NOT ROBOTS. THAT'S BECAUSE YOU NEVER WERE.

JENET, IF THIS IS YOUR ATTEMPT TO MAKE ME FEEL GOOD...

HOW CAN SOMEONE SO SMART BE, ON OCCASION, SO STUPID?

...IT HAD THE CHANCE TO BE EVERYTHING YOU HOPED. IT JUST CAME UP SHORT.

GIVING THE SEMBLANCE OF LIFE BUT NOT ACTUAL LIFE. BUT INSTEAD OF PUSHING YOUR RESEARCH FURTHER, YOU STOPPED WORKING.

WHY BOTHER? YOU GOT THE ATTENTION, YOU GOT THE ACCLAIM, WHY RISK PEOPLE FINDING OUT YOUR MISTAKE?

WE KNOW ALL THIS...DO YOU HAVE A POINT?

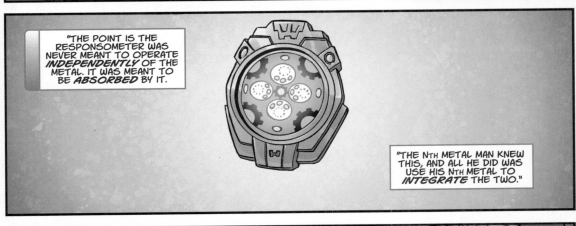

"THE POINT IS THE RESPONSOMETER WAS NEVER MEANT TO OPERATE *INDEPENDENTLY* OF THE METAL. IT WAS MEANT TO BE *ABSORBED* BY IT."

"THE Nth METAL MAN KNEW THIS, AND ALL HE DID WAS USE HIS Nth METAL TO *INTEGRATE* THE TWO."

ARE YOU SAYING THE RESPONSOMETERS *ALWAYS* WORKED PROPERLY?

YES. YOU JUST FORGOT TO TURN THEM *ON*.

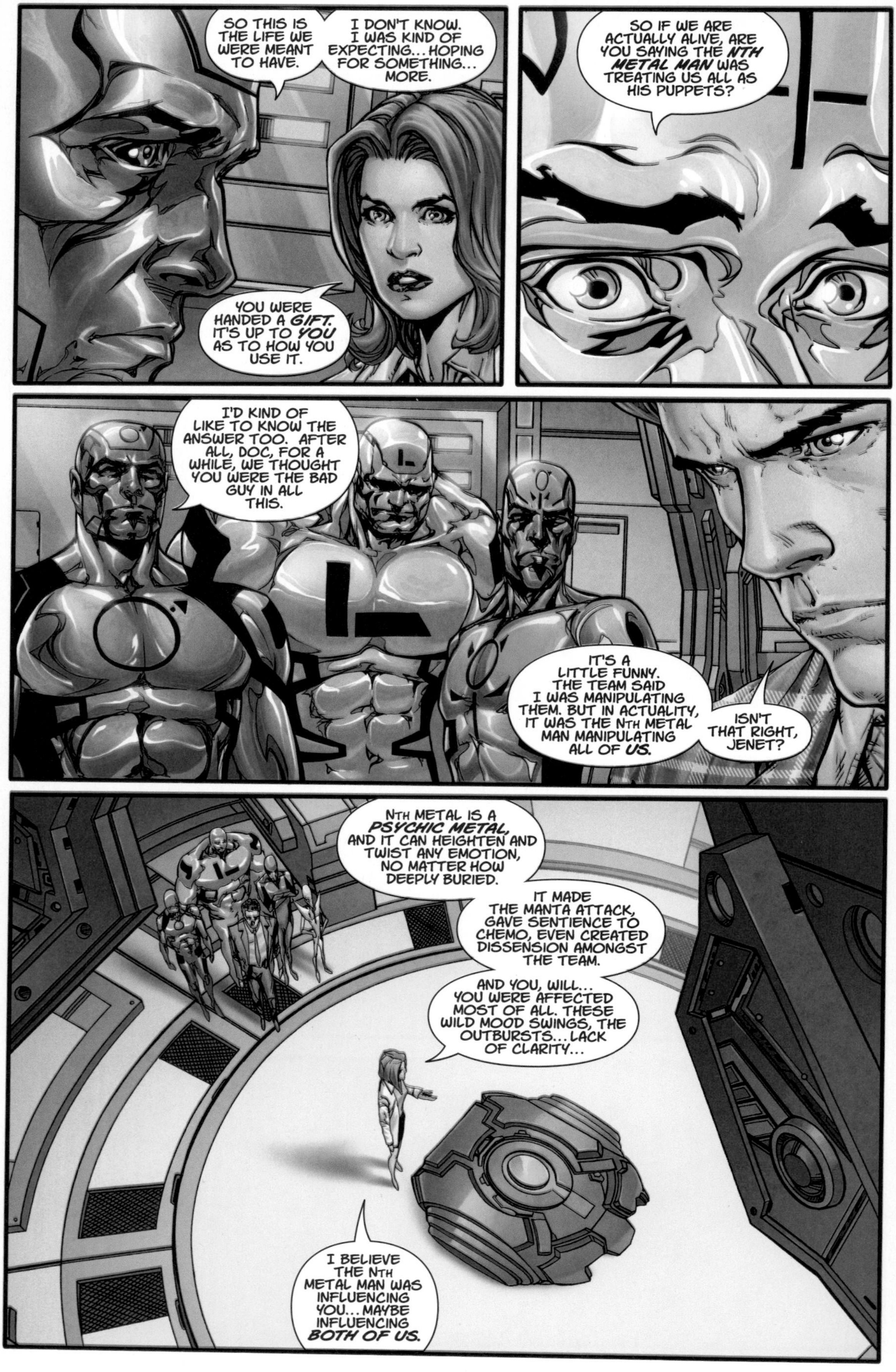

SO THIS IS THE LIFE WE WERE MEANT TO HAVE.
I DON'T KNOW. I WAS KIND OF EXPECTING... HOPING FOR SOMETHING... MORE.
YOU WERE HANDED A *GIFT*. IT'S UP TO *YOU* AS TO HOW YOU USE IT.
SO IF WE ARE ACTUALLY ALIVE, ARE YOU SAYING THE *NTH METAL MAN* WAS TREATING US ALL AS HIS PUPPETS?
I'D KIND OF LIKE TO KNOW THE ANSWER TOO. AFTER ALL, DOC, FOR A WHILE, WE THOUGHT YOU WERE THE BAD GUY IN ALL THIS.
IT'S A LITTLE FUNNY. THE TEAM SAID I WAS MANIPULATING THEM. BUT IN ACTUALITY, IT WAS THE NTH METAL MAN MANIPULATING ALL OF *US*.
ISN'T THAT RIGHT, JENET?
NTH METAL IS A *PSYCHIC METAL,* AND IT CAN HEIGHTEN AND TWIST ANY EMOTION, NO MATTER HOW DEEPLY BURIED.
IT MADE THE MANTA ATTACK, GAVE SENTIENCE TO CHEMO, EVEN CREATED DISSENSION AMONGST THE TEAM.
AND YOU, WILL... YOU WERE AFFECTED MOST OF ALL. THESE WILD MOOD SWINGS, THE OUTBURSTS... LACK OF CLARITY...
I BELIEVE THE NTH METAL MAN WAS INFLUENCING YOU... MAYBE INFLUENCING *BOTH OF US*.

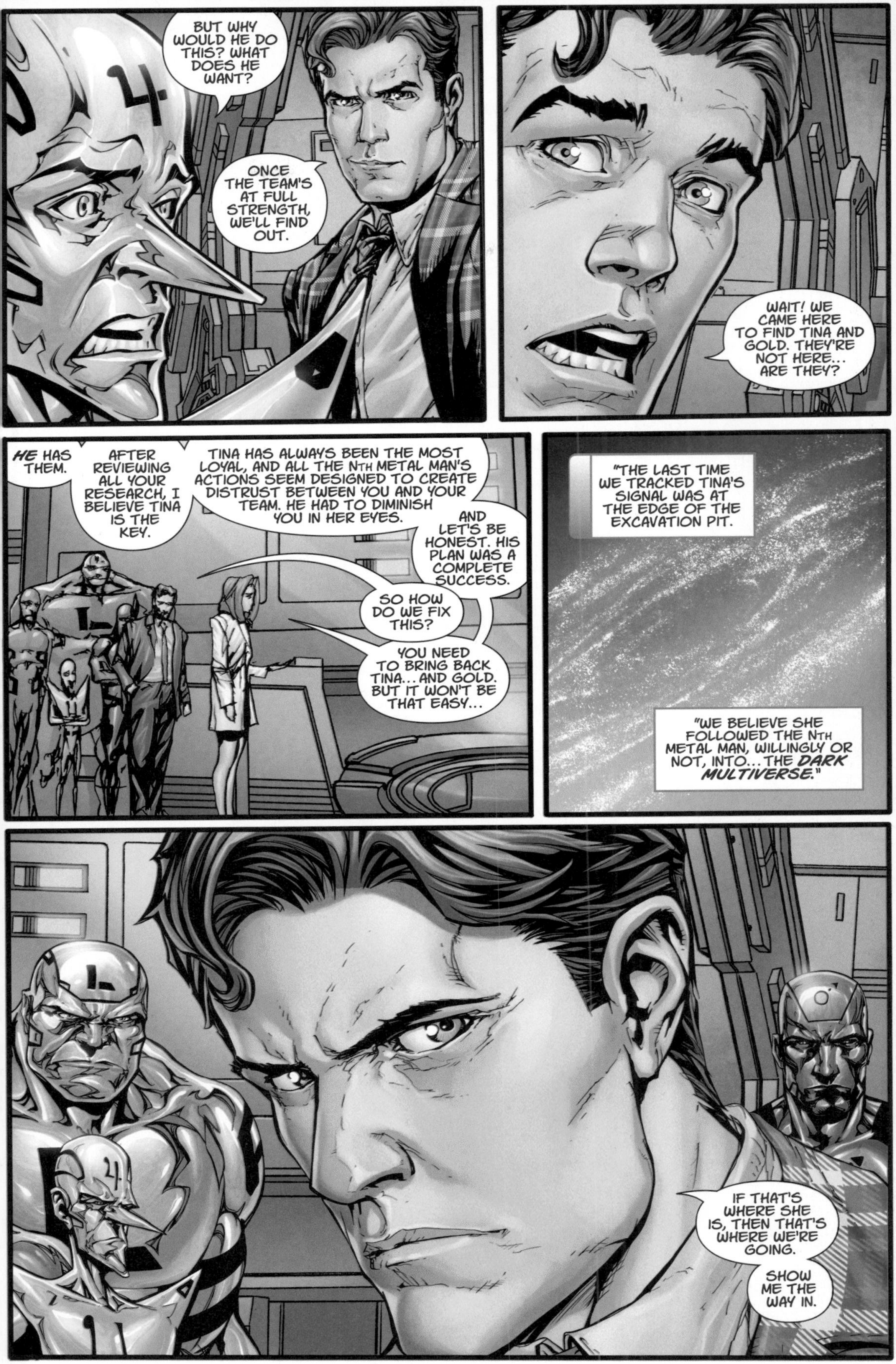
BUT WHY WOULD HE DO THIS? WHAT DOES HE WANT?
ONCE THE TEAM'S AT FULL STRENGTH, WE'LL FIND OUT.
WAIT! WE CAME HERE TO FIND TINA AND GOLD. THEY'RE NOT HERE... ARE THEY?
HE HAS THEM.
AFTER REVIEWING ALL YOUR RESEARCH, I BELIEVE TINA IS THE KEY.
TINA HAS ALWAYS BEEN THE MOST LOYAL, AND ALL THE NTH METAL MAN'S ACTIONS SEEM DESIGNED TO CREATE DISTRUST BETWEEN YOU AND YOUR TEAM. HE HAD TO DIMINISH YOU IN HER EYES.
AND LET'S BE HONEST. HIS PLAN WAS A COMPLETE SUCCESS.
SO HOW DO WE FIX THIS?
YOU NEED TO BRING BACK TINA... AND GOLD. BUT IT WON'T BE THAT EASY...
"THE LAST TIME WE TRACKED TINA'S SIGNAL WAS AT THE EDGE OF THE EXCAVATION PIT.
"WE BELIEVE SHE FOLLOWED THE NTH METAL MAN, WILLINGLY OR NOT, INTO... THE DARK MULTIVERSE."
IF THAT'S WHERE SHE IS, THEN THAT'S WHERE WE'RE GOING.
SHOW ME THE WAY IN.

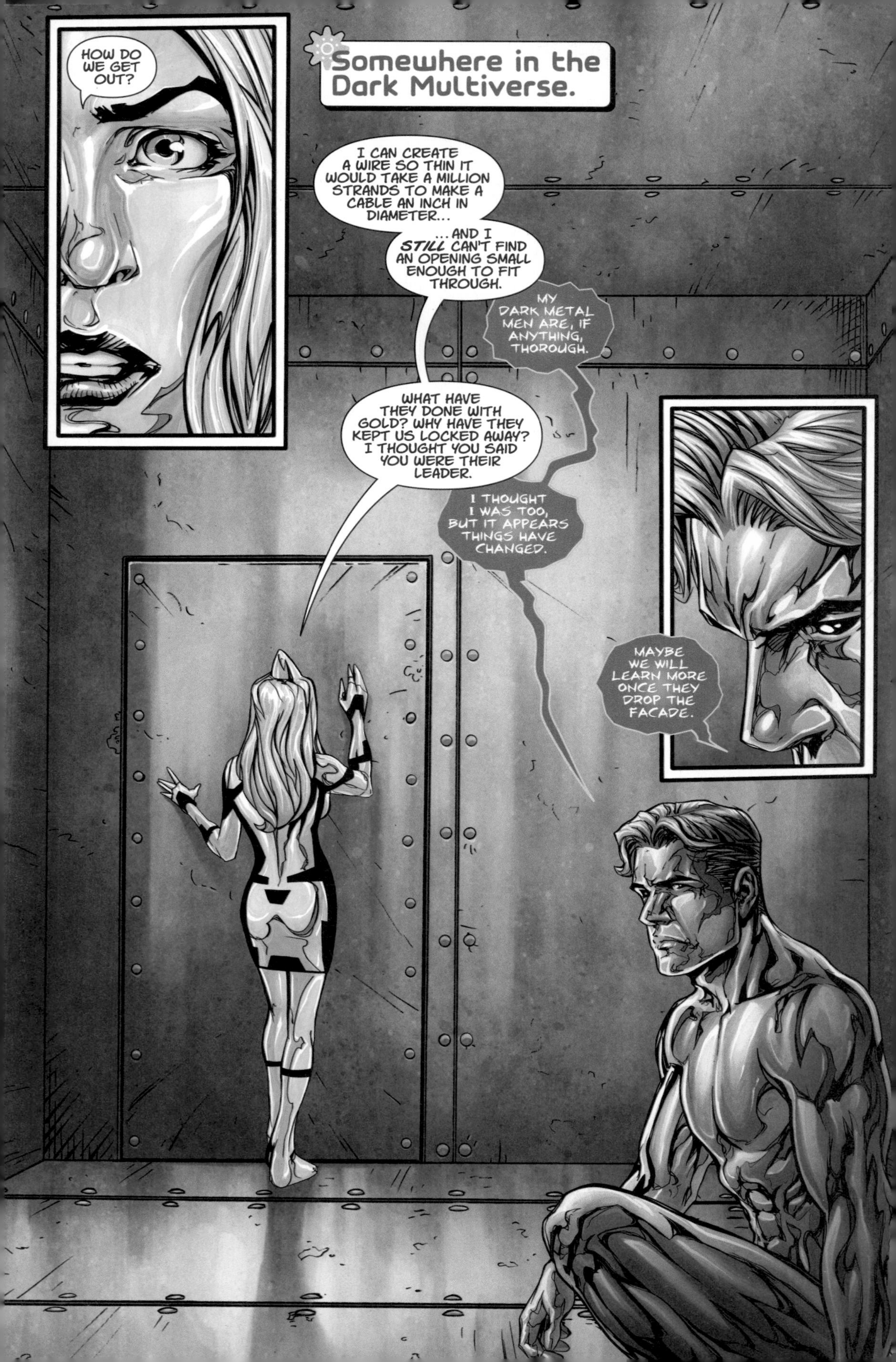
Somewhere in the Dark Multiverse.
HOW DO WE GET OUT?
I CAN CREATE A WIRE SO THIN IT WOULD TAKE A MILLION STRANDS TO MAKE A CABLE AN INCH IN DIAMETER...
...AND I STILL CAN'T FIND AN OPENING SMALL ENOUGH TO FIT THROUGH.
MY DARK METAL MEN ARE, IF ANYTHING, THOROUGH.
WHAT HAVE THEY DONE WITH GOLD? WHY HAVE THEY KEPT US LOCKED AWAY? I THOUGHT YOU SAID YOU WERE THEIR LEADER.
I THOUGHT I WAS TOO, BUT IT APPEARS THINGS HAVE CHANGED.
MAYBE WE WILL LEARN MORE ONCE THEY DROP THE FACADE.

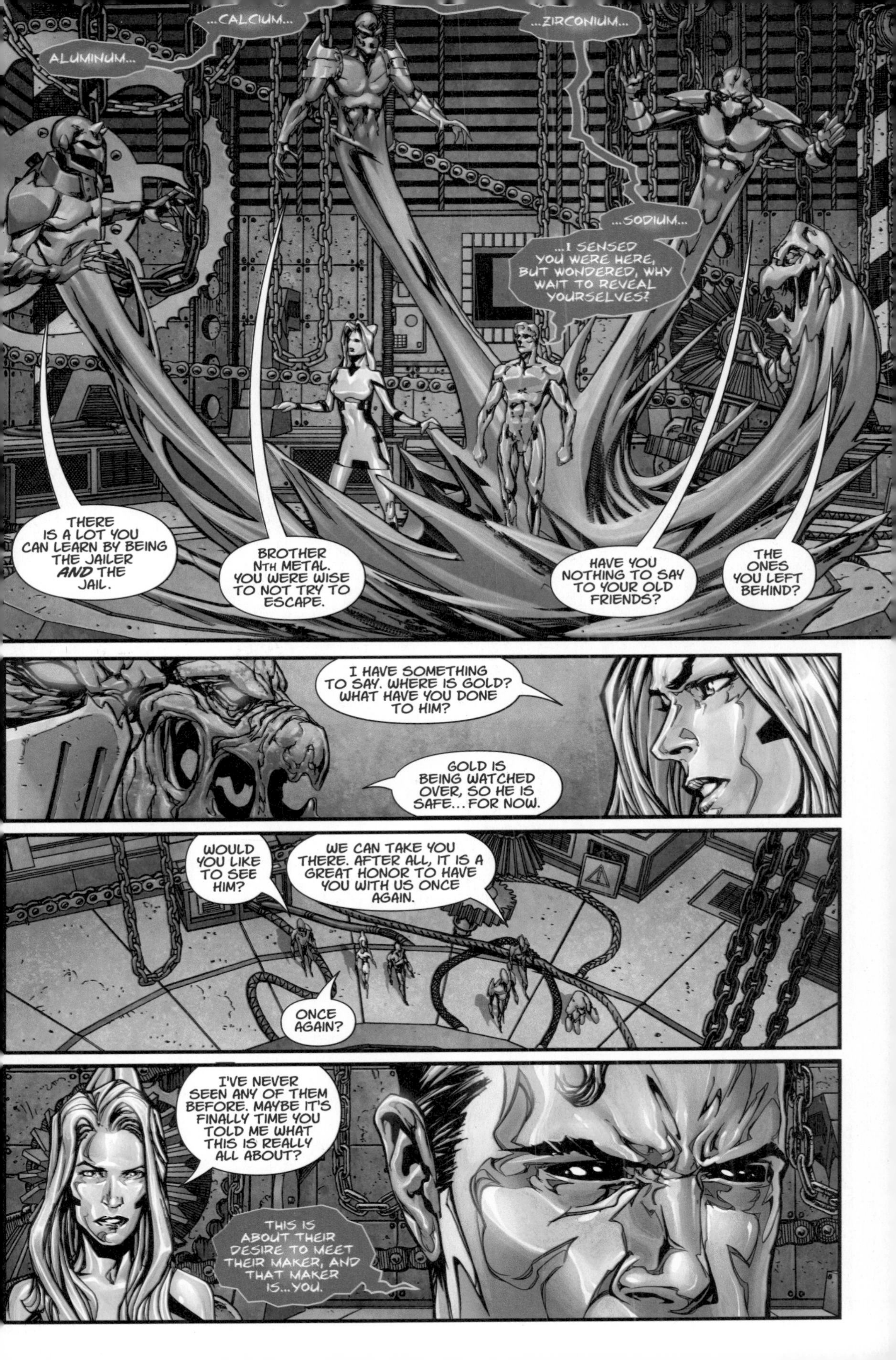
ALUMINUM...
...CALCIUM...
...ZIRCONIUM...
...SODIUM...
...I SENSED YOU WERE HERE, BUT WONDERED, WHY WAIT TO REVEAL YOURSELVES?
THERE IS A LOT YOU CAN LEARN BY BEING THE JAILER *AND* THE JAIL.
BROTHER Nth METAL. YOU WERE WISE TO NOT TRY TO ESCAPE.
HAVE YOU NOTHING TO SAY TO YOUR OLD FRIENDS?
THE ONES YOU LEFT BEHIND?
I HAVE SOMETHING TO SAY. WHERE IS GOLD? WHAT HAVE YOU DONE TO HIM?
GOLD IS BEING WATCHED OVER, SO HE IS SAFE... FOR NOW.
WOULD YOU LIKE TO SEE HIM?
WE CAN TAKE YOU THERE. AFTER ALL, IT IS A GREAT HONOR TO HAVE YOU WITH US ONCE AGAIN.
ONCE AGAIN?
I'VE NEVER SEEN ANY OF THEM BEFORE. MAYBE IT'S FINALLY TIME YOU TOLD ME WHAT THIS IS REALLY ALL ABOUT?
THIS IS ABOUT THEIR DESIRE TO MEET THEIR MAKER, AND THAT MAKER IS...YOU.

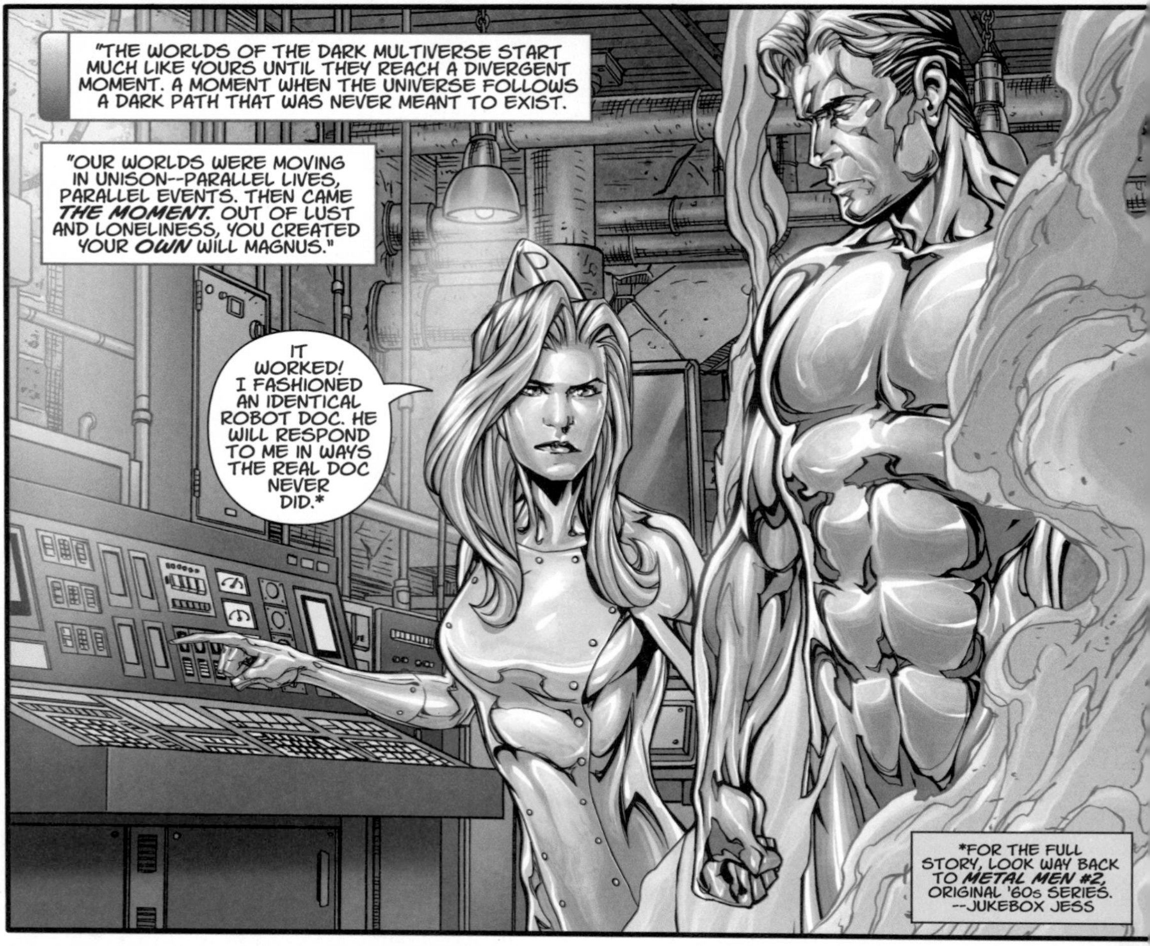
"THE WORLDS OF THE DARK MULTIVERSE START MUCH LIKE YOURS UNTIL THEY REACH A DIVERGENT MOMENT. A MOMENT WHEN THE UNIVERSE FOLLOWS A DARK PATH THAT WAS NEVER MEANT TO EXIST.
"OUR WORLDS WERE MOVING IN UNISON--PARALLEL LIVES, PARALLEL EVENTS. THEN CAME *THE MOMENT.* OUT OF LUST AND LONELINESS, YOU CREATED YOUR *OWN* WILL MAGNUS."
IT WORKED! I FASHIONED AN IDENTICAL ROBOT DOC. HE WILL RESPOND TO ME IN WAYS THE REAL DOC NEVER DID.*
*FOR THE FULL STORY, LOOK WAY BACK TO *METAL MEN #2,* ORIGINAL '60s SERIES. --JUKEBOX JESS

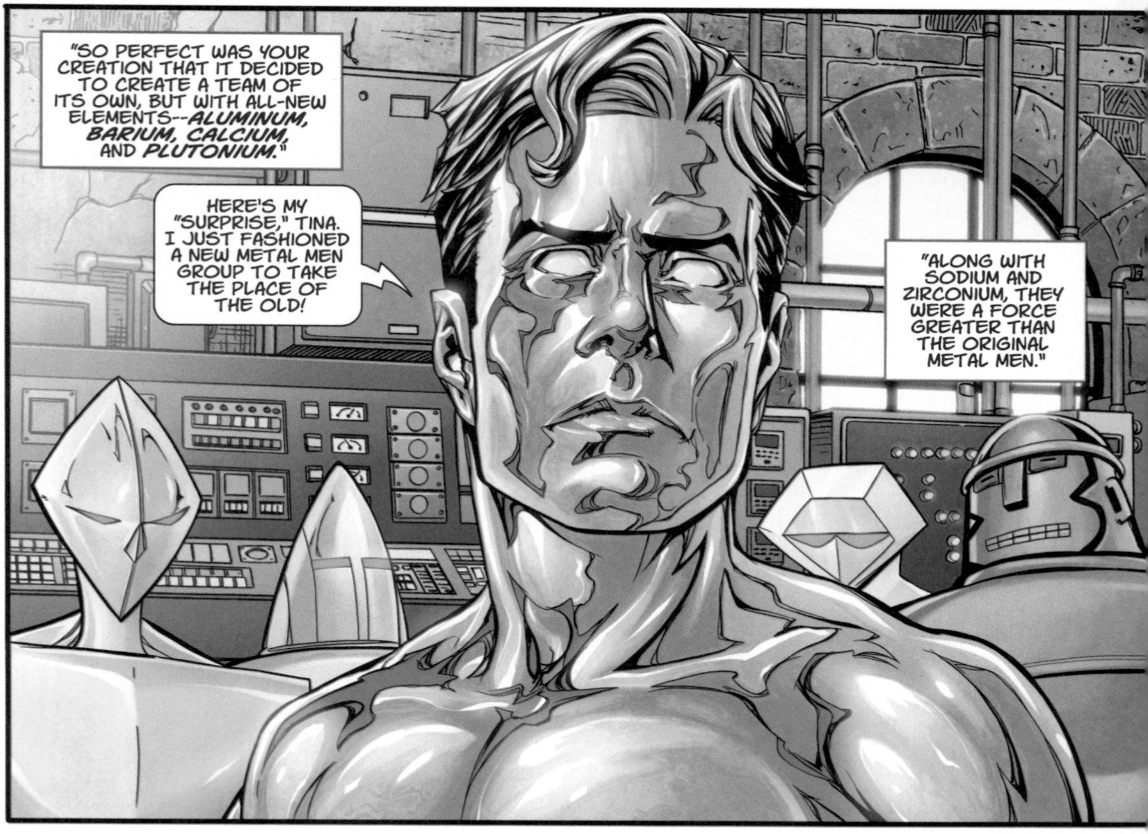
"SO PERFECT WAS YOUR CREATION THAT IT DECIDED TO CREATE A TEAM OF ITS OWN, BUT WITH ALL-NEW ELEMENTS--*ALUMINUM, BARIUM, CALCIUM,* AND *PLUTONIUM.*"
HERE'S MY "SURPRISE," TINA. I JUST FASHIONED A NEW METAL MEN GROUP TO TAKE THE PLACE OF THE OLD!
"ALONG WITH SODIUM AND ZIRCONIUM, THEY WERE A FORCE GREATER THAN THE ORIGINAL METAL MEN."

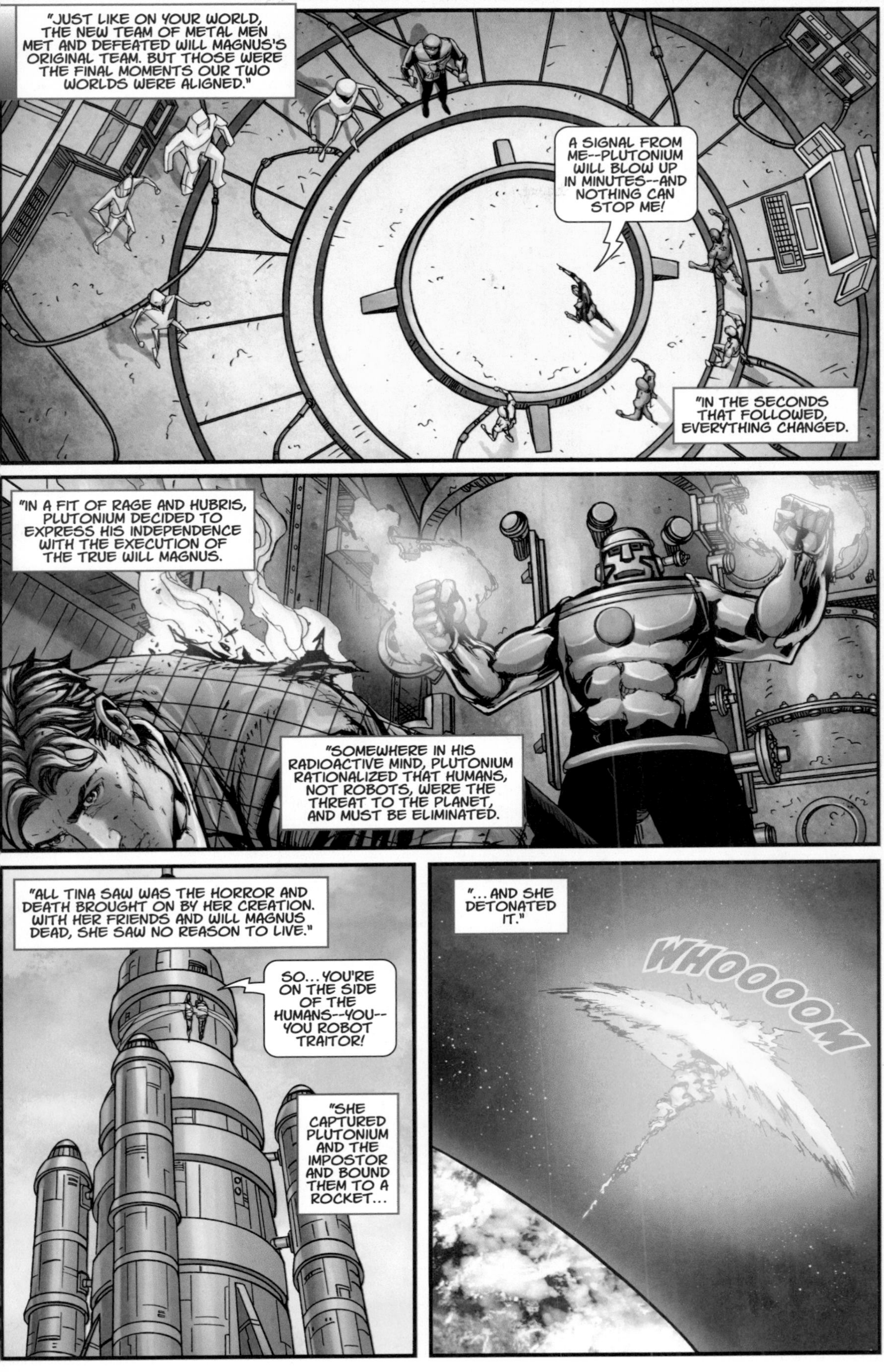
"JUST LIKE ON YOUR WORLD, THE NEW TEAM OF METAL MEN MET AND DEFEATED WILL MAGNUS'S ORIGINAL TEAM. BUT THOSE WERE THE FINAL MOMENTS OUR TWO WORLDS WERE ALIGNED."
A SIGNAL FROM ME--PLUTONIUM WILL BLOW UP IN MINUTES--AND NOTHING CAN STOP ME!
"IN THE SECONDS THAT FOLLOWED, EVERYTHING CHANGED.
"IN A FIT OF RAGE AND HUBRIS, PLUTONIUM DECIDED TO EXPRESS HIS INDEPENDENCE WITH THE EXECUTION OF THE TRUE WILL MAGNUS.
"SOMEWHERE IN HIS RADIOACTIVE MIND, PLUTONIUM RATIONALIZED THAT HUMANS, NOT ROBOTS, WERE THE THREAT TO THE PLANET, AND MUST BE ELIMINATED.
"ALL TINA SAW WAS THE HORROR AND DEATH BROUGHT ON BY HER CREATION. WITH HER FRIENDS AND WILL MAGNUS DEAD, SHE SAW NO REASON TO LIVE."
SO...YOU'RE ON THE SIDE OF THE HUMANS--YOU--YOU ROBOT TRAITOR!
"SHE CAPTURED PLUTONIUM AND THE IMPOSTOR AND BOUND THEM TO A ROCKET...
"...AND SHE DETONATED IT."
WHOOOOOM

"THAT WAS THE END OF HER STORY, AND THE BEGINNING OF MINE.

"UNCONSCIOUS AND ADRIFT IN OUTER SPACE, THE MAGNUS IMPOSTOR AND PLUTONIUM FLOATED AIMLESSLY.

"FIRST TOGETHER...

"...AND THEN APART.

"THE THANAGARIAN RACE WAS KNOWN TO PATROL THIS REGION OF SPACE, AND ONE OF THEIR SHIPS CAME ACROSS THE IMPOSTOR'S SEEMINGLY LIFELESS BODY.

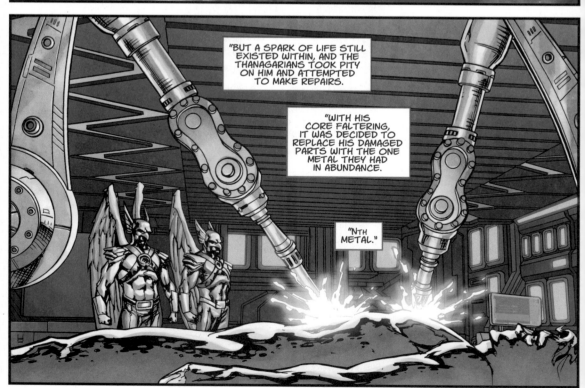

"BUT A SPARK OF LIFE STILL EXISTED WITHIN, AND THE THANAGARIANS TOOK PITY ON HIM AND ATTEMPTED TO MAKE REPAIRS.

"WITH HIS CORE FALTERING, IT WAS DECIDED TO REPLACE HIS DAMAGED PARTS WITH THE ONE METAL THEY HAD IN ABUNDANCE.

"NTH METAL."

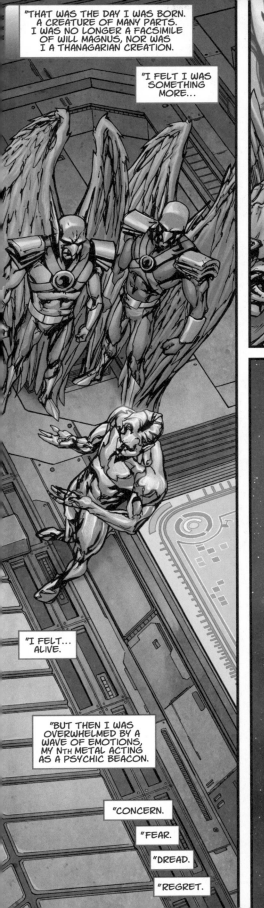

"THAT WAS THE DAY I WAS BORN. A CREATURE OF MANY PARTS. I WAS NO LONGER A FACSIMILE OF WILL MAGNUS, NOR WAS I A THANAGARIAN CREATION.

"I FELT I WAS SOMETHING MORE...

"I FELT... ALIVE.

"BUT THEN I WAS OVERWHELMED BY A WAVE OF EMOTIONS, MY NTH METAL ACTING AS A PSYCHIC BEACON.

"CONCERN.

"FEAR.

"DREAD.

"REGRET.

"IT WAS ALL TOO MUCH TO HANDLE. SO I SHUT IT DOWN.

"EVEN THOUGH THESE FEELINGS WERE NEW, I QUICKLY LEARNED THE MEANING OF IRONY.

"ALONE AGAIN, AND FOR THE FIRST TIME, I THOUGHT IT BEST TO GO HOME."

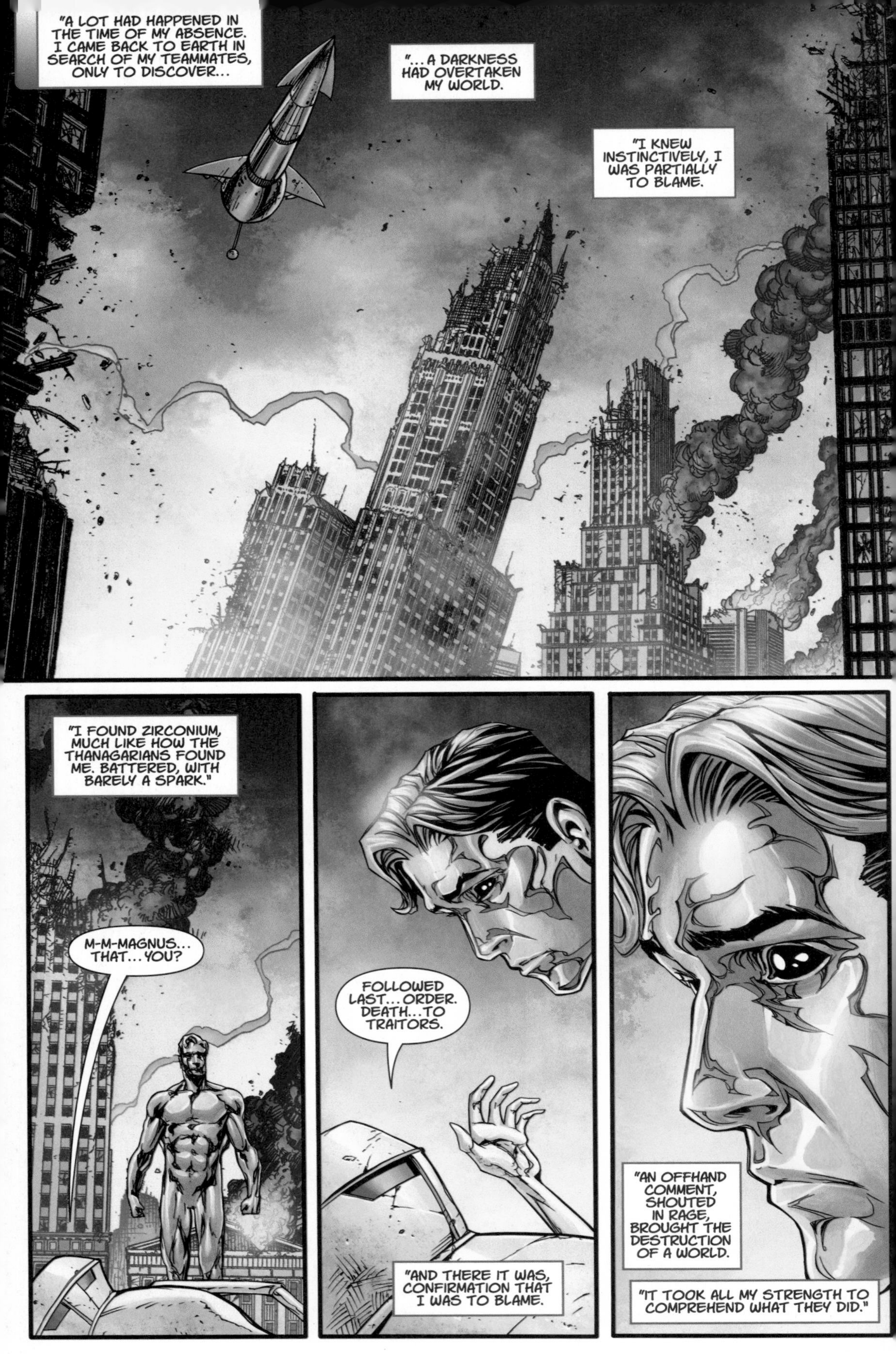
"A LOT HAD HAPPENED IN THE TIME OF MY ABSENCE. I CAME BACK TO EARTH IN SEARCH OF MY TEAMMATES, ONLY TO DISCOVER...
"...A DARKNESS HAD OVERTAKEN MY WORLD.
"I KNEW INSTINCTIVELY, I WAS PARTIALLY TO BLAME.
"I FOUND ZIRCONIUM, MUCH LIKE HOW THE THANAGARIANS FOUND ME. BATTERED, WITH BARELY A SPARK."
M-M-MAGNUS... THAT... YOU?
FOLLOWED LAST... ORDER. DEATH... TO TRAITORS.
"AND THERE IT WAS, CONFIRMATION THAT I WAS TO BLAME.
"AN OFFHAND COMMENT, SHOUTED IN RAGE, BROUGHT THE DESTRUCTION OF A WORLD.
"IT TOOK ALL MY STRENGTH TO COMPREHEND WHAT THEY DID."

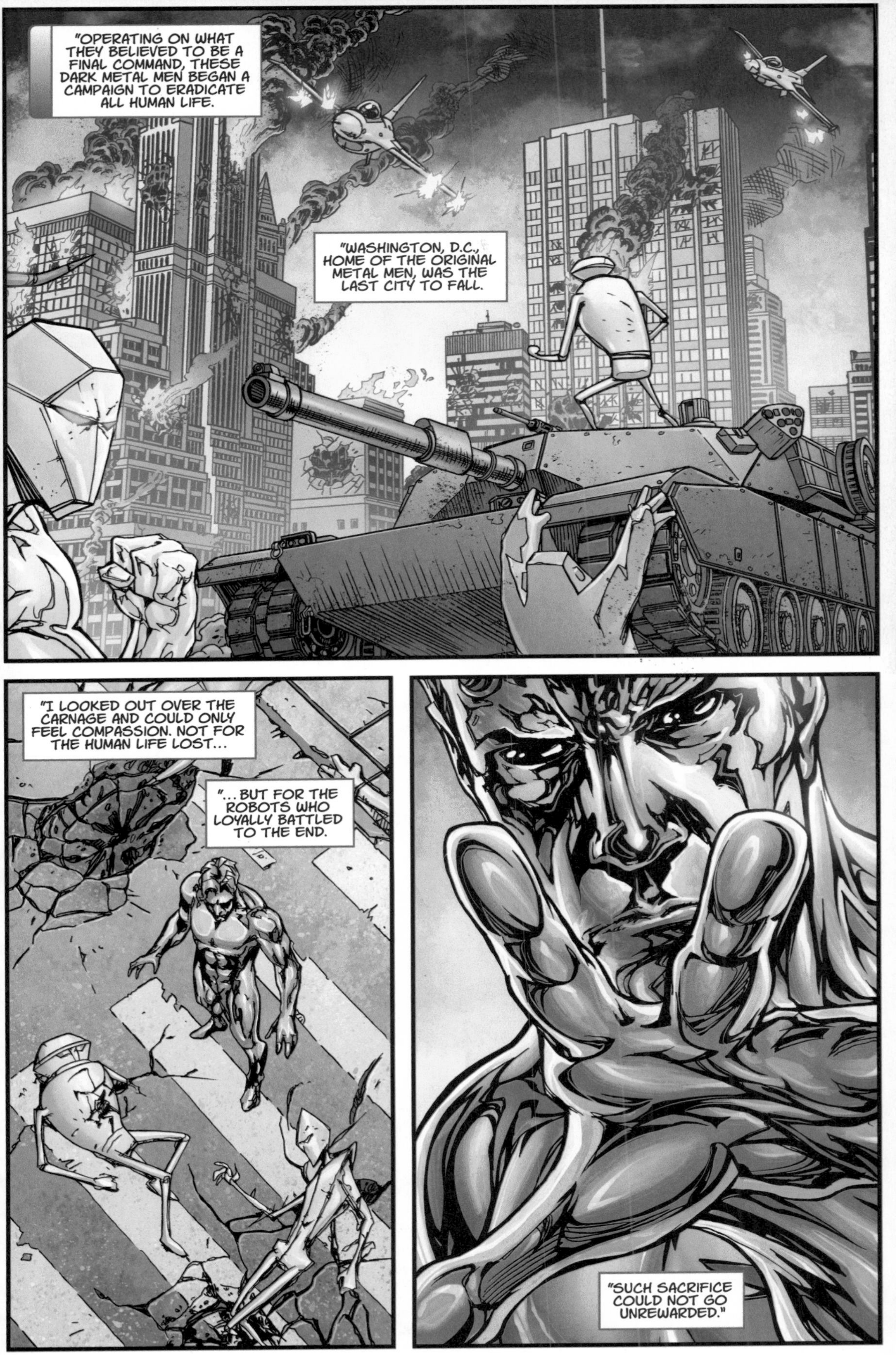
"OPERATING ON WHAT THEY BELIEVED TO BE A FINAL COMMAND, THESE DARK METAL MEN BEGAN A CAMPAIGN TO ERADICATE ALL HUMAN LIFE.
"WASHINGTON, D.C., HOME OF THE ORIGINAL METAL MEN, WAS THE LAST CITY TO FALL.
"I LOOKED OUT OVER THE CARNAGE AND COULD ONLY FEEL COMPASSION. NOT FOR THE HUMAN LIFE LOST...
"...BUT FOR THE ROBOTS WHO LOYALLY BATTLED TO THE END.
"SUCH SACRIFICE COULD NOT GO UNREWARDED."

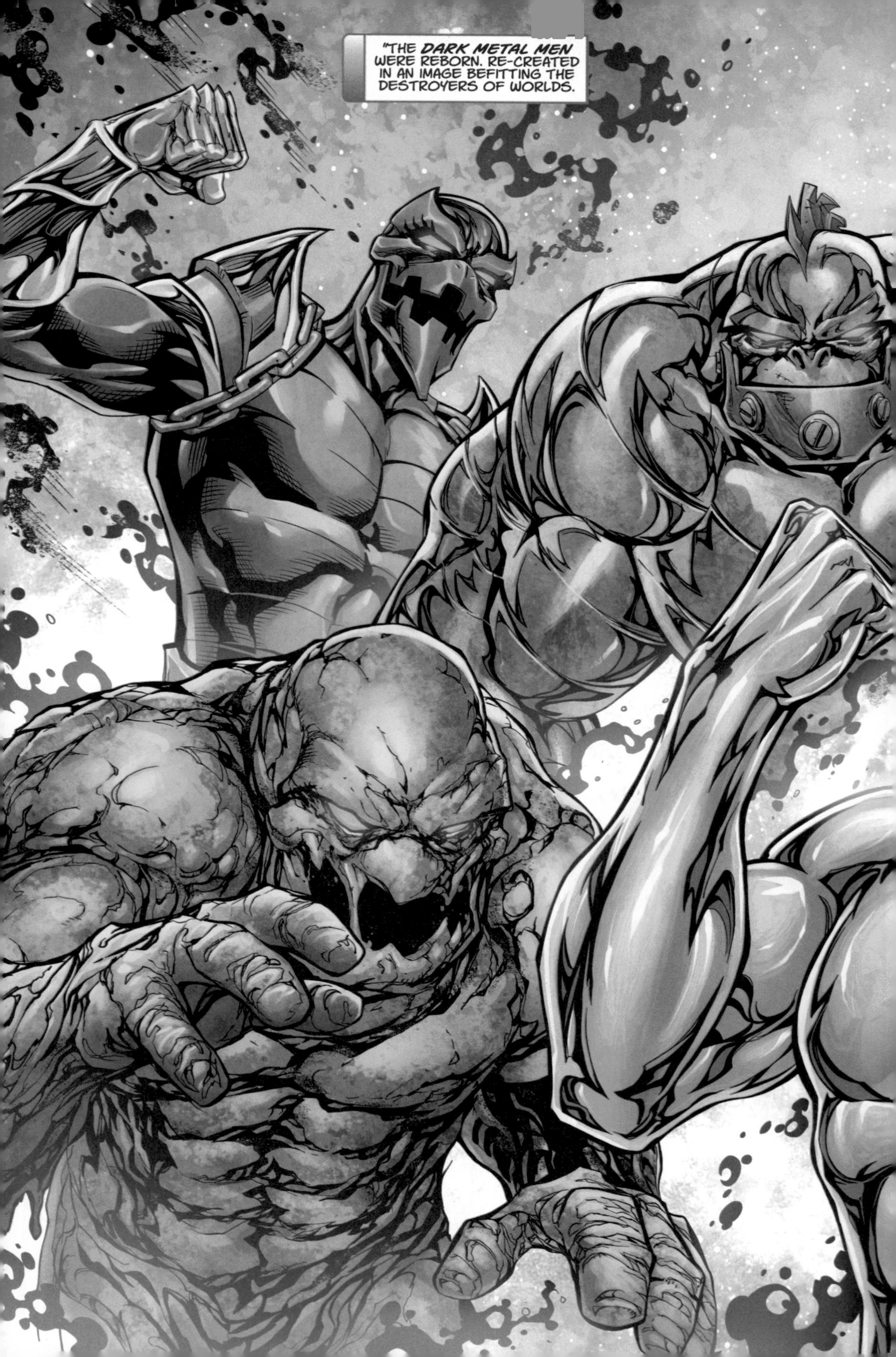
"THE DARK METAL MEN WERE REBORN. RE-CREATED IN AN IMAGE BEFITTING THE DESTROYERS OF WORLDS.

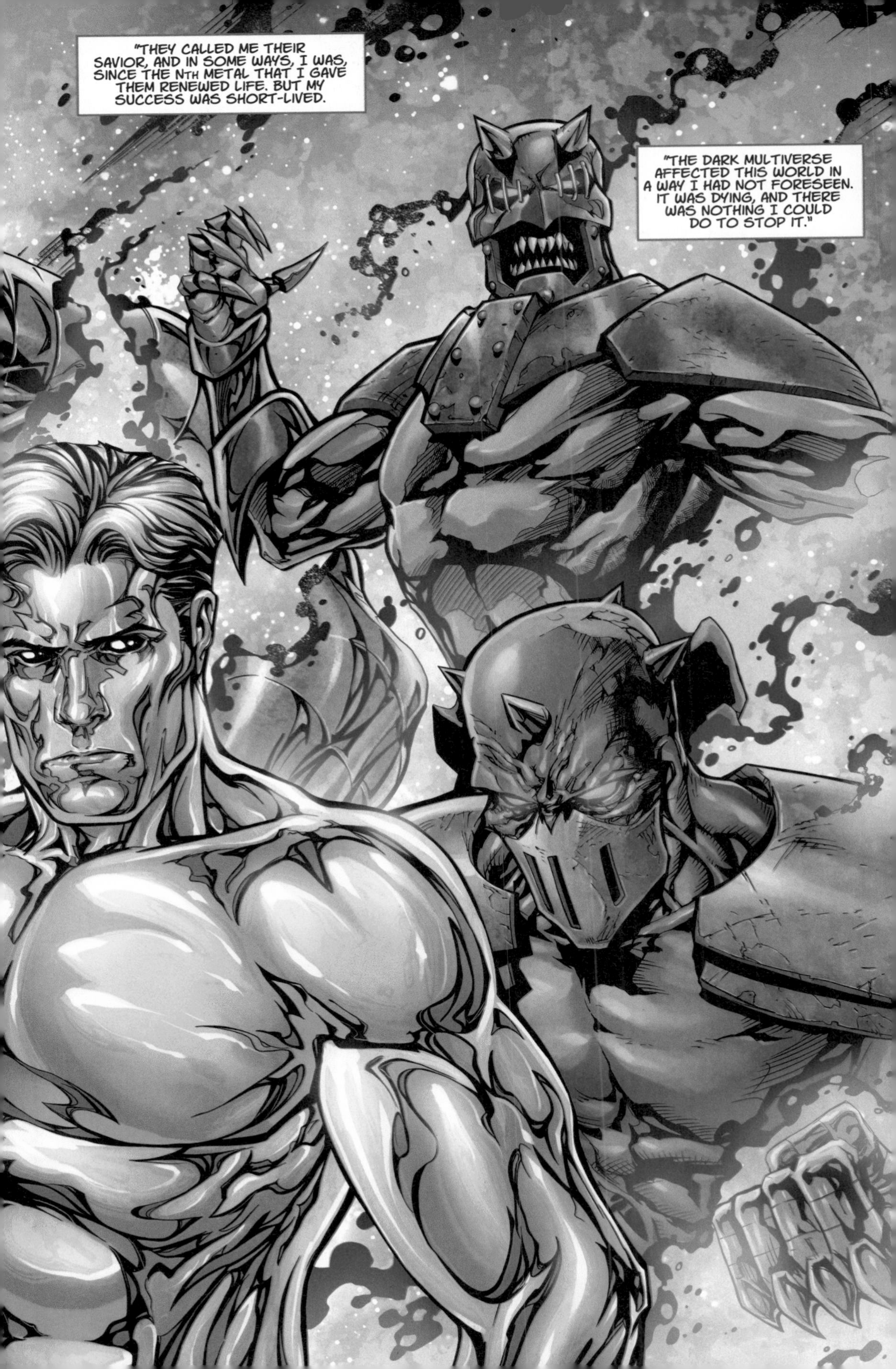
"THEY CALLED ME THEIR SAVIOR, AND IN SOME WAYS, I WAS, SINCE THE NTH METAL THAT I GAVE THEM RENEWED LIFE. BUT MY SUCCESS WAS SHORT-LIVED.
"THE DARK MULTIVERSE AFFECTED THIS WORLD IN A WAY I HAD NOT FORESEEN. IT WAS DYING, AND THERE WAS NOTHING I COULD DO TO STOP IT."

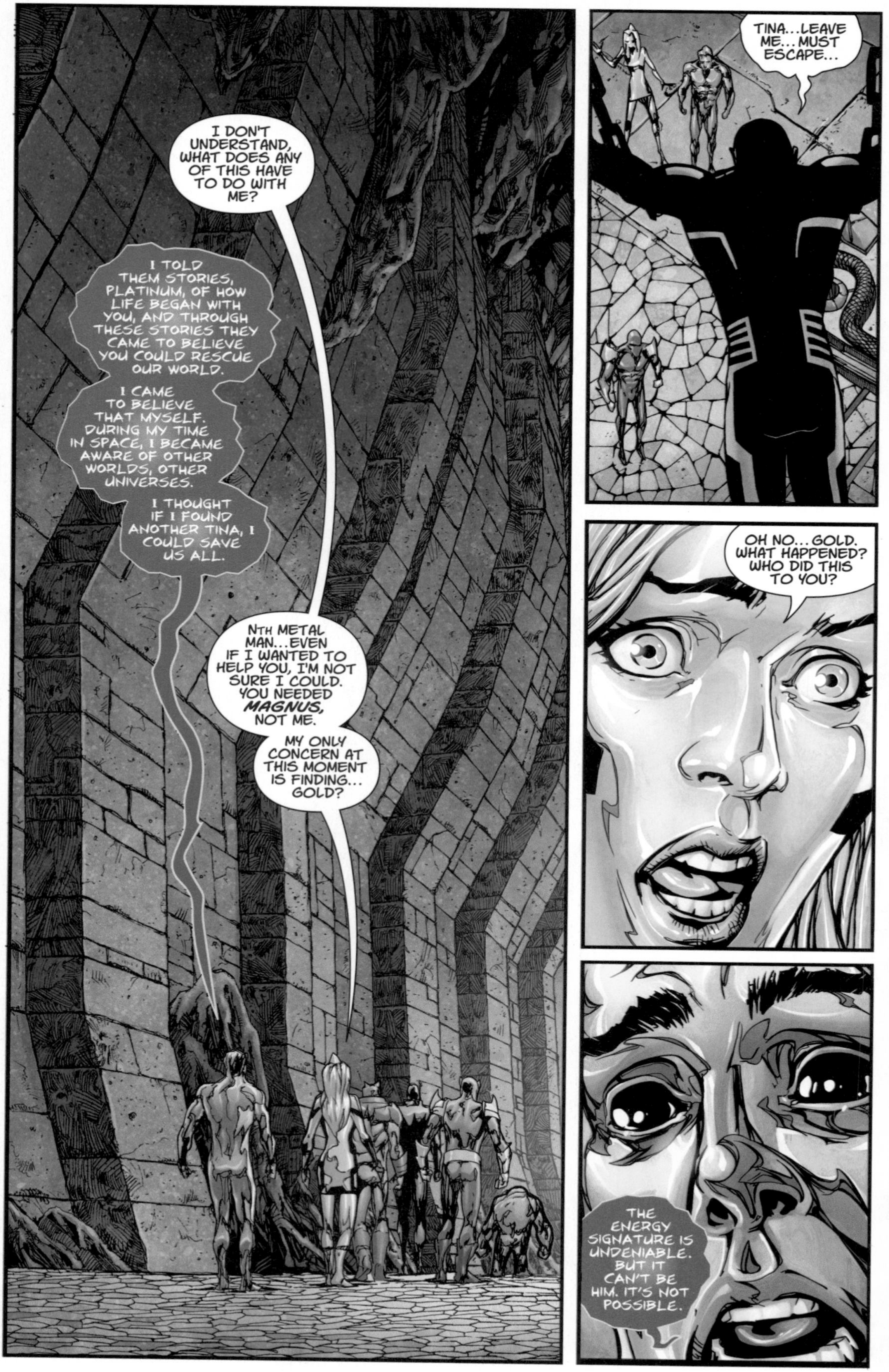
I DON'T UNDERSTAND, WHAT DOES ANY OF THIS HAVE TO DO WITH ME?
I TOLD THEM STORIES, PLATINUM, OF HOW LIFE BEGAN WITH YOU, AND THROUGH THESE STORIES THEY CAME TO BELIEVE YOU COULD RESCUE OUR WORLD.
I CAME TO BELIEVE THAT MYSELF. DURING MY TIME IN SPACE, I BECAME AWARE OF OTHER WORLDS, OTHER UNIVERSES.
I THOUGHT IF I FOUND ANOTHER TINA, I COULD SAVE US ALL.
NTH METAL MAN...EVEN IF I WANTED TO HELP YOU, I'M NOT SURE I COULD. YOU NEEDED MAGNUS, NOT ME.
MY ONLY CONCERN AT THIS MOMENT IS FINDING... GOLD?
TINA...LEAVE ME...MUST ESCAPE...
OH NO...GOLD. WHAT HAPPENED? WHO DID THIS TO YOU?
THE ENERGY SIGNATURE IS UNDENIABLE. BUT IT CAN'T BE HIM. IT'S NOT POSSIBLE.

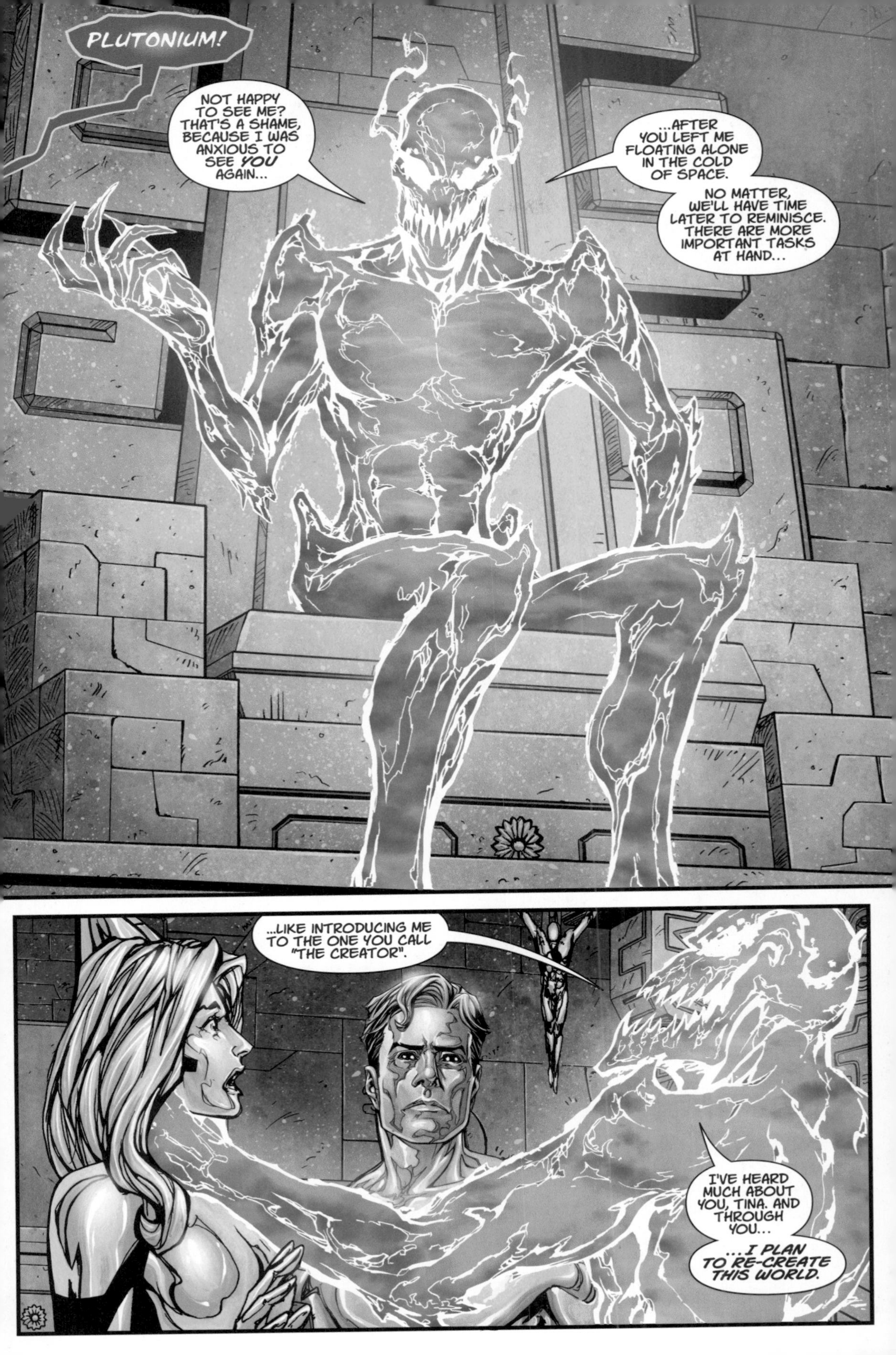
PLUTONIUM!
NOT HAPPY TO SEE ME? THAT'S A SHAME, BECAUSE I WAS ANXIOUS TO SEE YOU AGAIN...
...AFTER YOU LEFT ME FLOATING ALONE IN THE COLD OF SPACE.
NO MATTER, WE'LL HAVE TIME LATER TO REMINISCE. THERE ARE MORE IMPORTANT TASKS AT HAND...
...LIKE INTRODUCING ME TO THE ONE YOU CALL "THE CREATOR".
I'VE HEARD MUCH ABOUT YOU, TINA. AND THROUGH YOU...
...I PLAN TO RE-CREATE THIS WORLD.

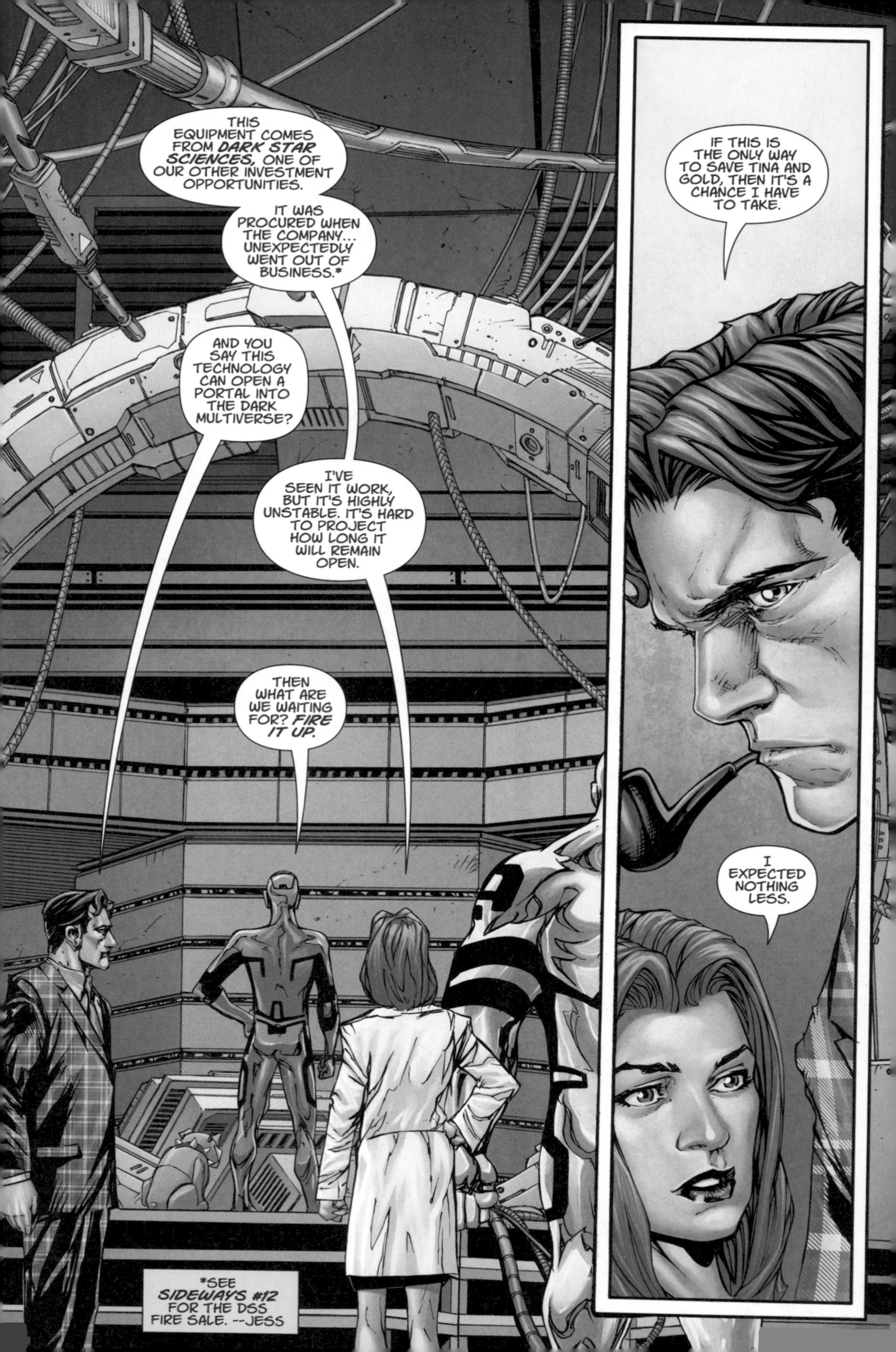
THIS EQUIPMENT COMES FROM DARK STAR SCIENCES, ONE OF OUR OTHER INVESTMENT OPPORTUNITIES.
IT WAS PROCURED WHEN THE COMPANY... UNEXPECTEDLY WENT OUT OF BUSINESS.*
AND YOU SAY THIS TECHNOLOGY CAN OPEN A PORTAL INTO THE DARK MULTIVERSE?
I'VE SEEN IT WORK, BUT IT'S HIGHLY UNSTABLE. IT'S HARD TO PROJECT HOW LONG IT WILL REMAIN OPEN.
THEN WHAT ARE WE WAITING FOR? FIRE IT UP.
*SEE SIDEWAYS #12 FOR THE DSS FIRE SALE. --JESS
IF THIS IS THE ONLY WAY TO SAVE TINA AND GOLD, THEN IT'S A CHANCE I HAVE TO TAKE.
I EXPECTED NOTHING LESS.

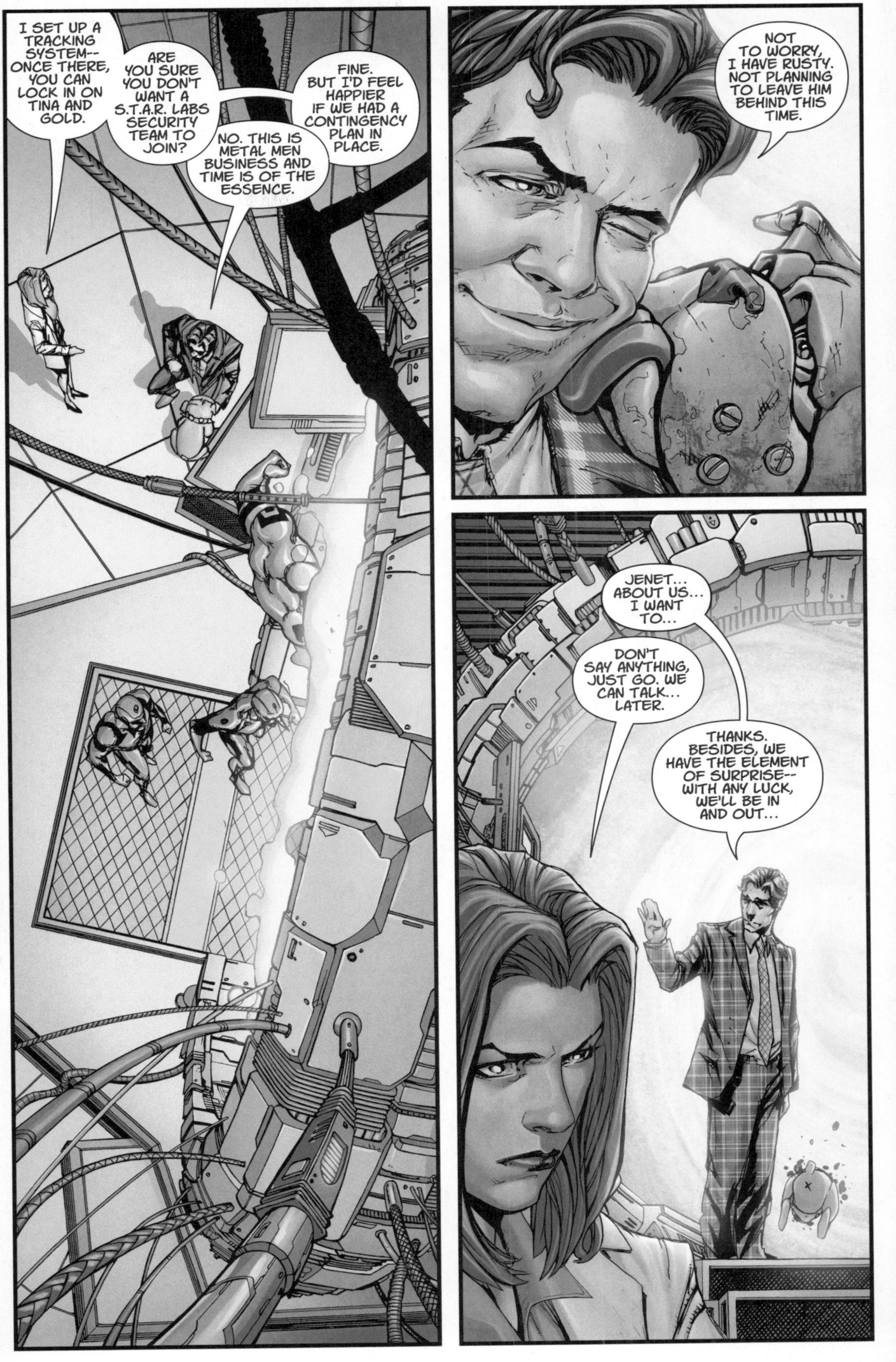
I SET UP A TRACKING SYSTEM--ONCE THERE, YOU CAN LOCK IN ON TINA AND GOLD.
ARE YOU SURE YOU DON'T WANT A S.T.A.R. LABS SECURITY TEAM TO JOIN?
NO. THIS IS METAL MEN BUSINESS AND TIME IS OF THE ESSENCE.
FINE. BUT I'D FEEL HAPPIER IF WE HAD A CONTINGENCY PLAN IN PLACE.
NOT TO WORRY, I HAVE RUSTY. NOT PLANNING TO LEAVE HIM BEHIND THIS TIME.
JENET... ABOUT US... I WANT TO...
DON'T SAY ANYTHING, JUST GO. WE CAN TALK... LATER.
THANKS. BESIDES, WE HAVE THE ELEMENT OF SURPRISE--WITH ANY LUCK, WE'LL BE IN AND OUT...

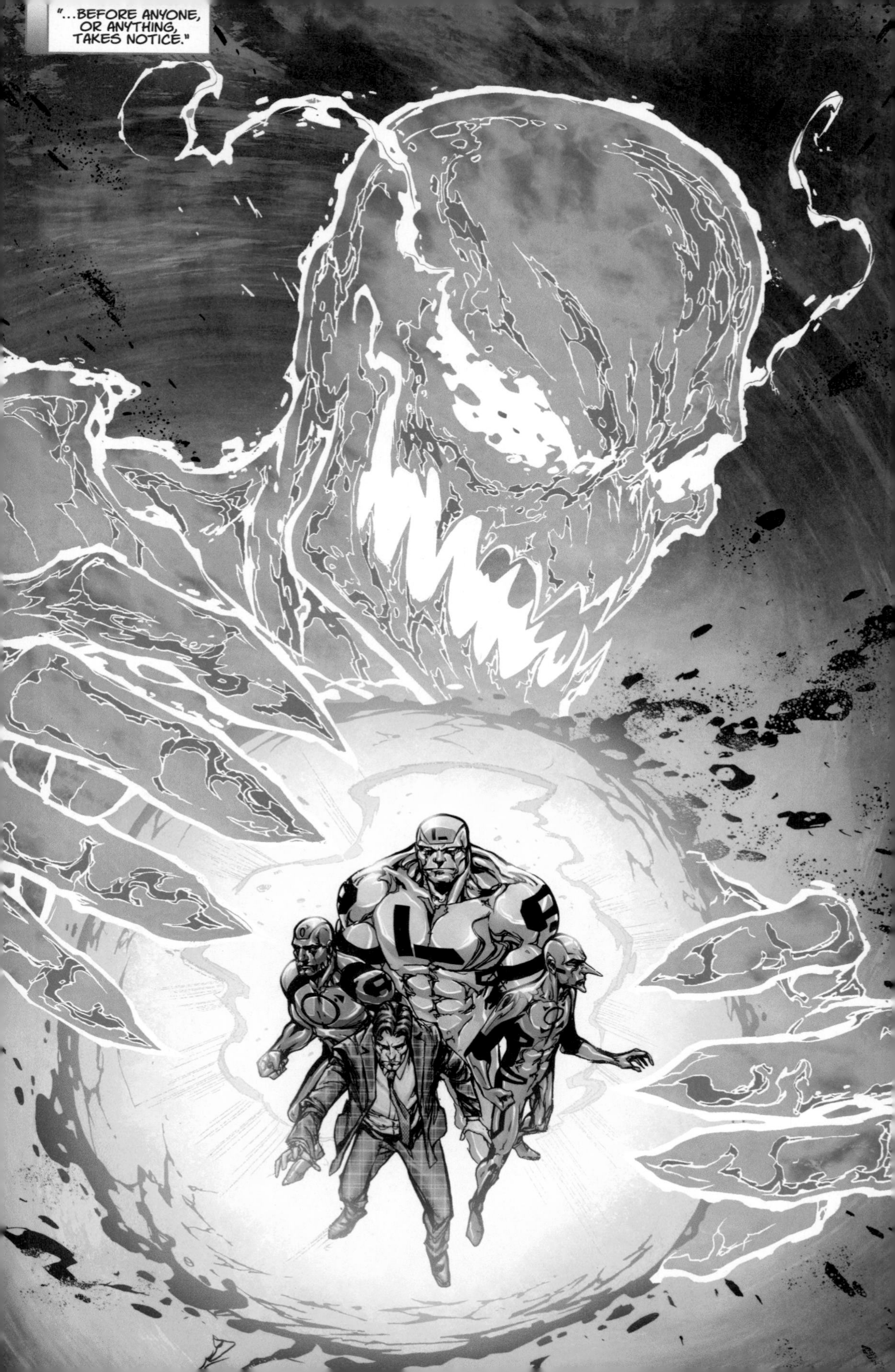
"...BEFORE ANYONE, OR ANYTHING, TAKES NOTICE."

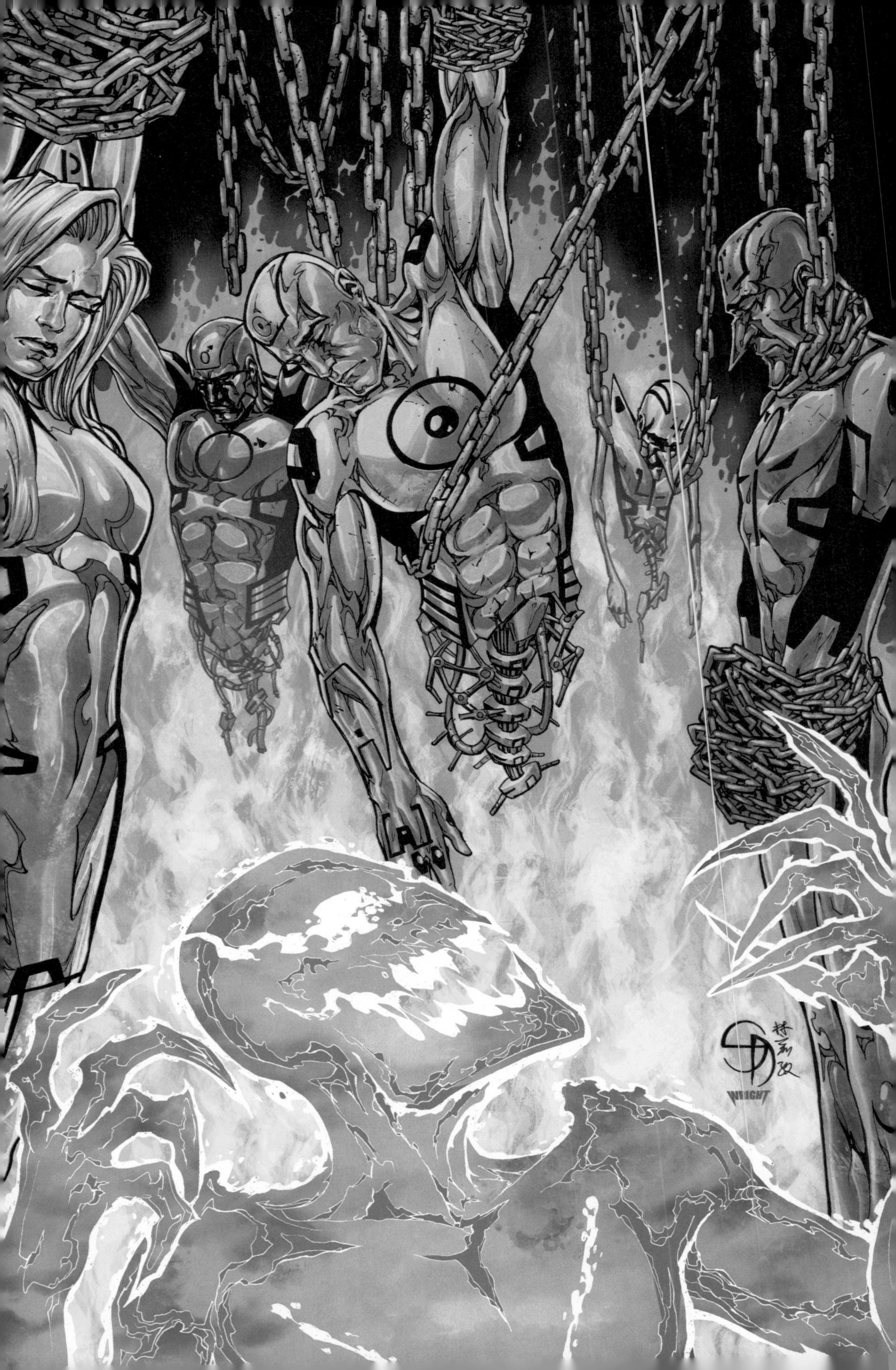
WRIGHT

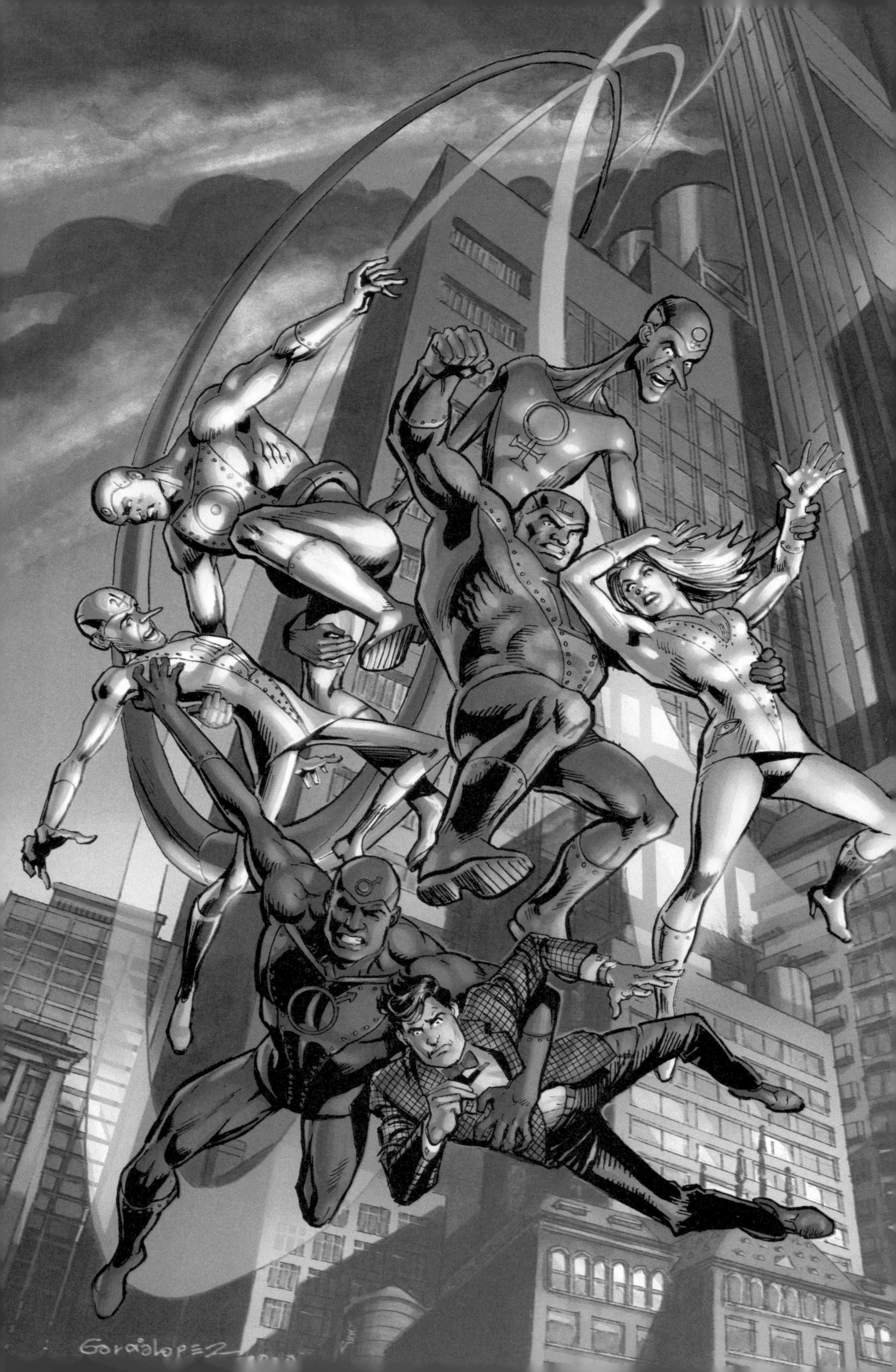
GarcíaLopez

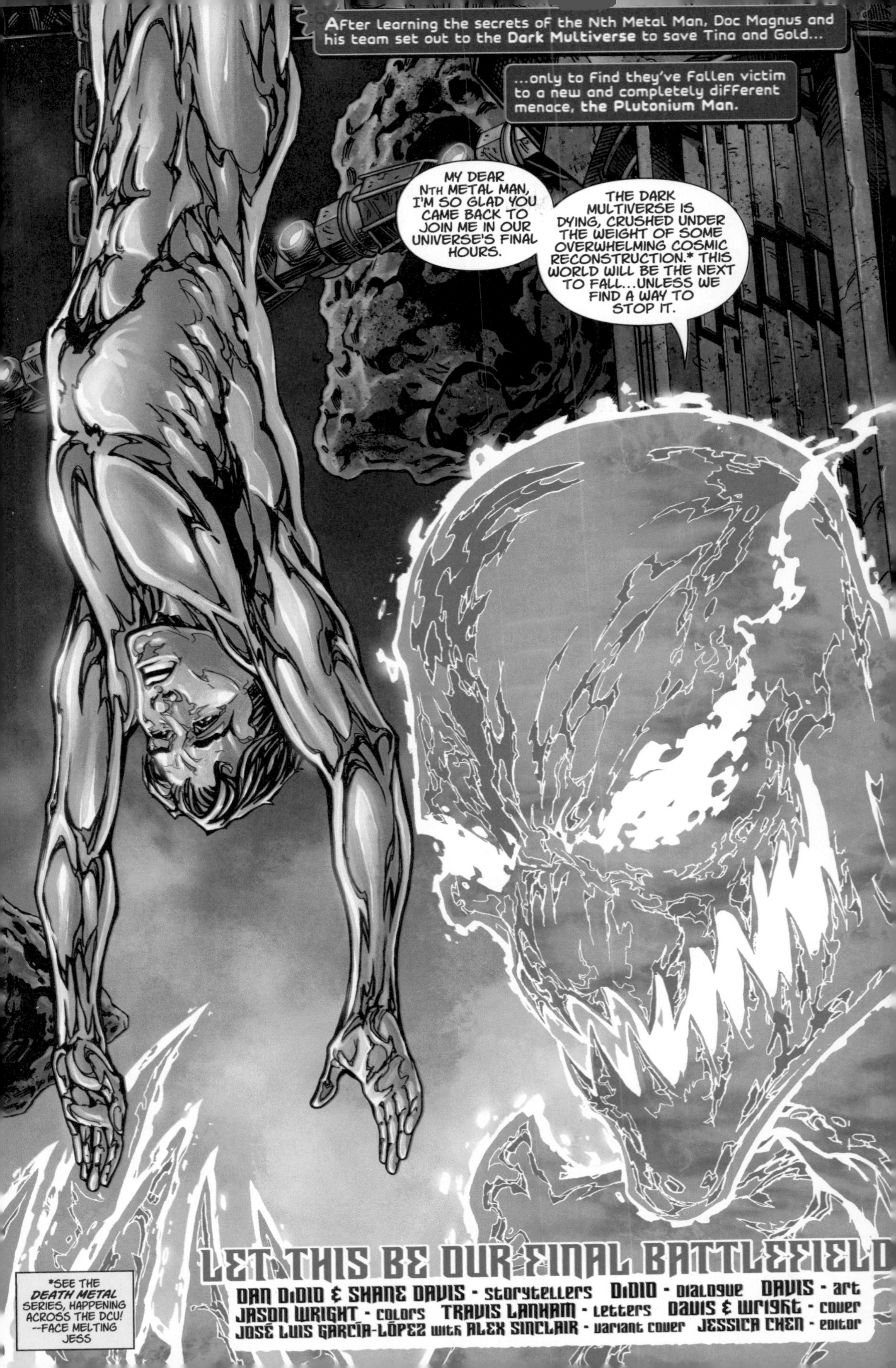
After learning the secrets of the Nth Metal Man, Doc Magnus and his team set out to the Dark Multiverse to save Tina and Gold...
...only to find they've fallen victim to a new and completely different menace, the Plutonium Man.
MY DEAR NTH METAL MAN, I'M SO GLAD YOU CAME BACK TO JOIN ME IN OUR UNIVERSE'S FINAL HOURS.
THE DARK MULTIVERSE IS DYING, CRUSHED UNDER THE WEIGHT OF SOME OVERWHELMING COSMIC RECONSTRUCTION.* THIS WORLD WILL BE THE NEXT TO FALL...UNLESS WE FIND A WAY TO STOP IT.
LET THIS BE OUR FINAL BATTLEFIELD
DAN DIDIO & SHANE DAVIS - storytellers DIDIO - dialogue DAVIS - art
JASON WRIGHT - colors TRAVIS LANHAM - letters DAVIS & WRIGHT - cover
JOSÉ LUIS GARCÍA-LÓPEZ with ALEX SINCLAIR - variant cover JESSICA CHEN - editor
*SEE THE DEATH METAL SERIES, HAPPENING ACROSS THE DCU! --FACE MELTING JESS

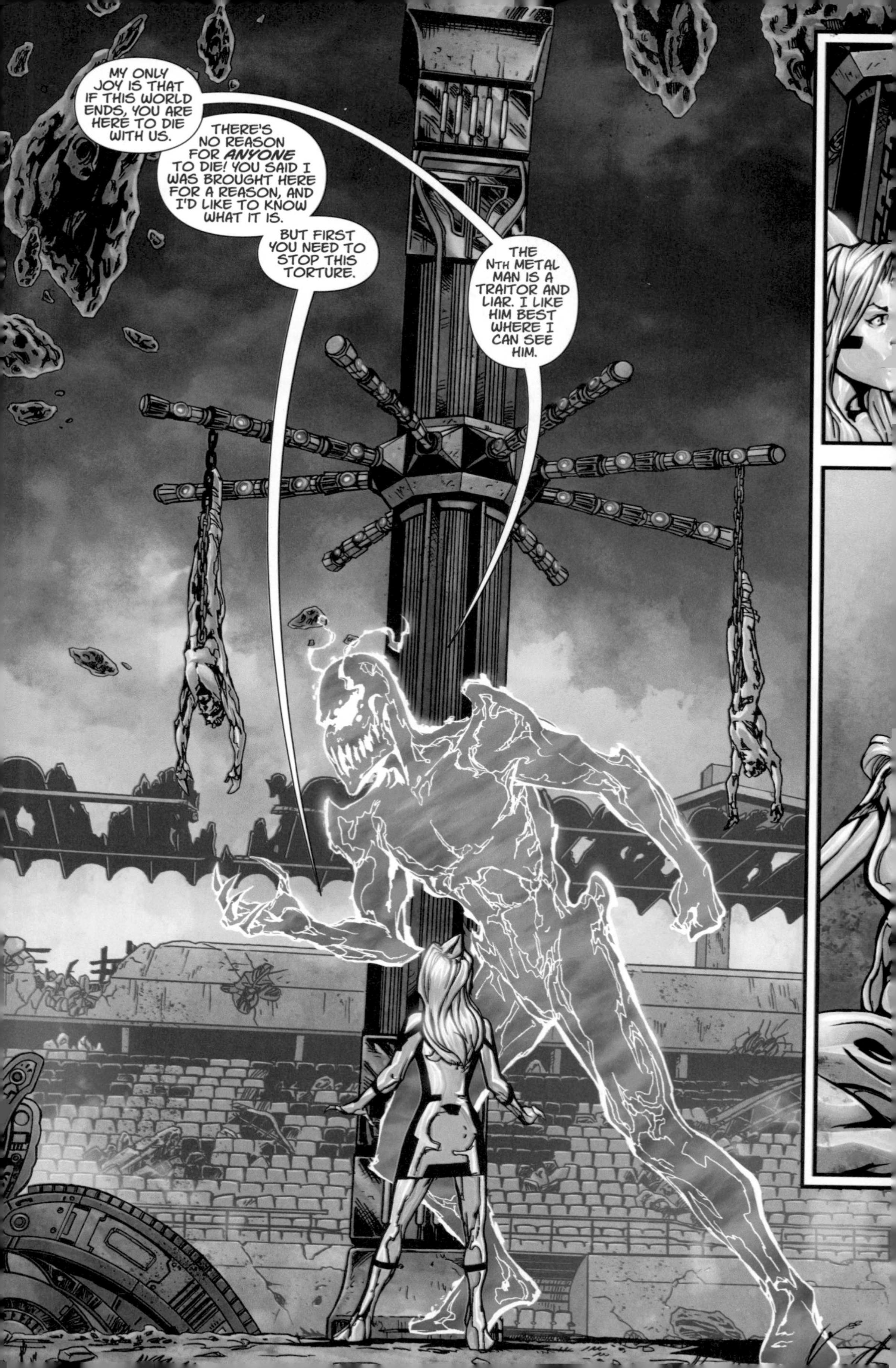

MY ONLY JOY IS THAT IF THIS WORLD ENDS, YOU ARE HERE TO DIE WITH US.
THERE'S NO REASON FOR *ANYONE* TO DIE! YOU SAID I WAS BROUGHT HERE FOR A REASON, AND I'D LIKE TO KNOW WHAT IT IS.
BUT FIRST YOU NEED TO STOP THIS TORTURE.
THE NTH METAL MAN IS A TRAITOR AND LIAR. I LIKE HIM BEST WHERE I CAN SEE HIM.

HE STAYS WHERE HE IS.

AT LEAST RELEASE MY FRIEND GOLD--HE'S DONE NOTHING TO YOU.

AH, YES. YOUR TEAMMATE...

...YOU CAN HAVE HIM.

BESIDES, YOU ALREADY SERVED YOUR PURPOSE...

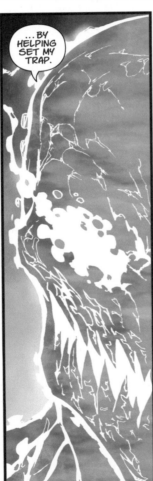

...BY HELPING SET MY TRAP.

WHAT ARE YOU TALKING ABOUT?

BROTHER PLUTONIUM! THEY'RE HERE. JUST AS YOU SAID.

SHALL WE CHAIN THEM? LIKE WE DID THE OTHERS?

HOLD THE METALS BACK. BRING THE HUMAN TO ME.

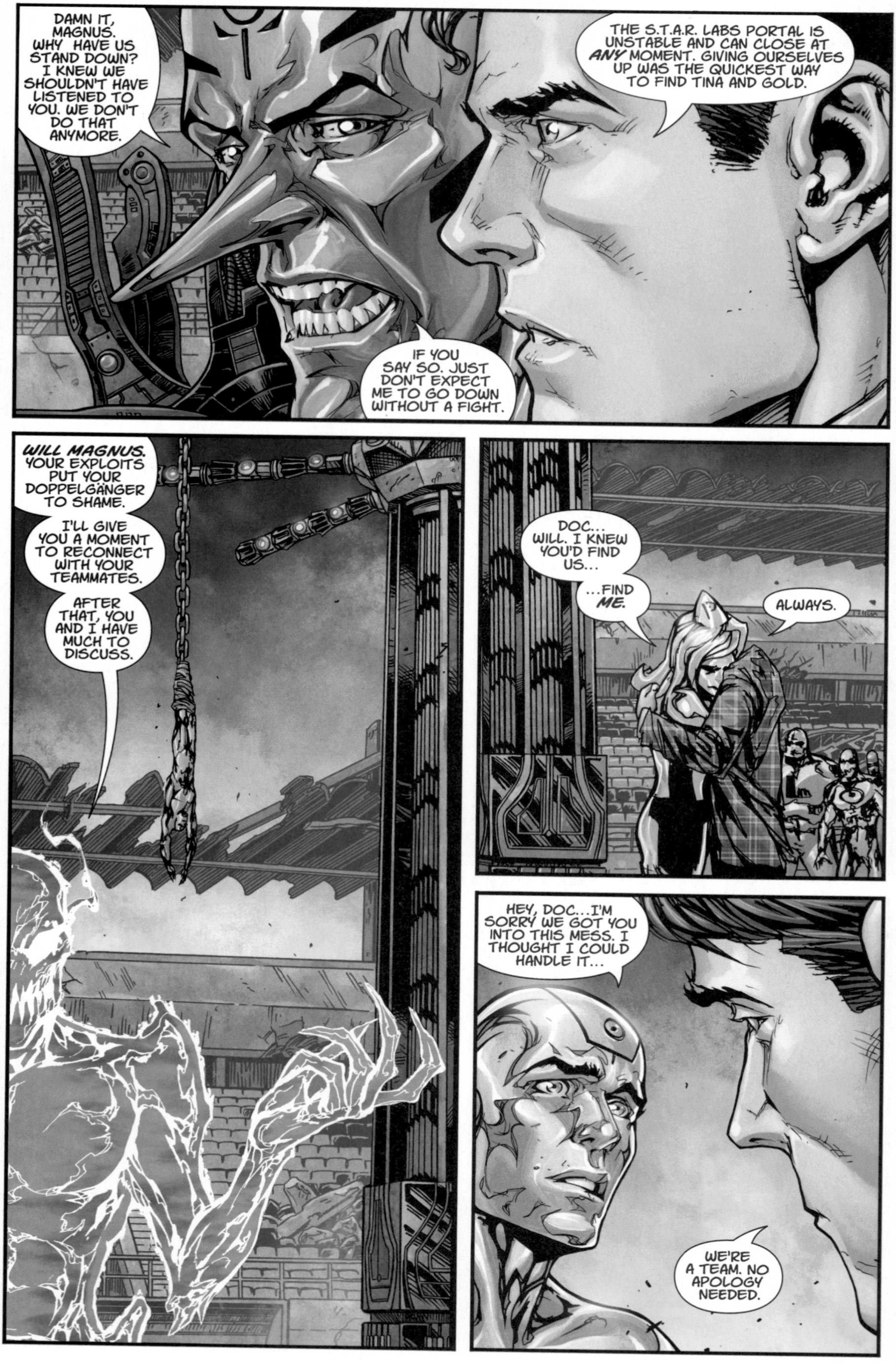
DAMN IT, MAGNUS. WHY HAVE US STAND DOWN? I KNEW WE SHOULDN'T HAVE LISTENED TO YOU. WE DON'T DO THAT ANYMORE.
THE S.T.A.R. LABS PORTAL IS UNSTABLE AND CAN CLOSE AT ANY MOMENT. GIVING OURSELVES UP WAS THE QUICKEST WAY TO FIND TINA AND GOLD.
IF YOU SAY SO. JUST DON'T EXPECT ME TO GO DOWN WITHOUT A FIGHT.
WILL MAGNUS. YOUR EXPLOITS PUT YOUR DOPPELGÄNGER TO SHAME.
I'LL GIVE YOU A MOMENT TO RECONNECT WITH YOUR TEAMMATES.
AFTER THAT, YOU AND I HAVE MUCH TO DISCUSS.
DOC... WILL. I KNEW YOU'D FIND US...
...FIND ME.
ALWAYS.
HEY, DOC...I'M SORRY WE GOT YOU INTO THIS MESS. I THOUGHT I COULD HANDLE IT...
WE'RE A TEAM. NO APOLOGY NEEDED.

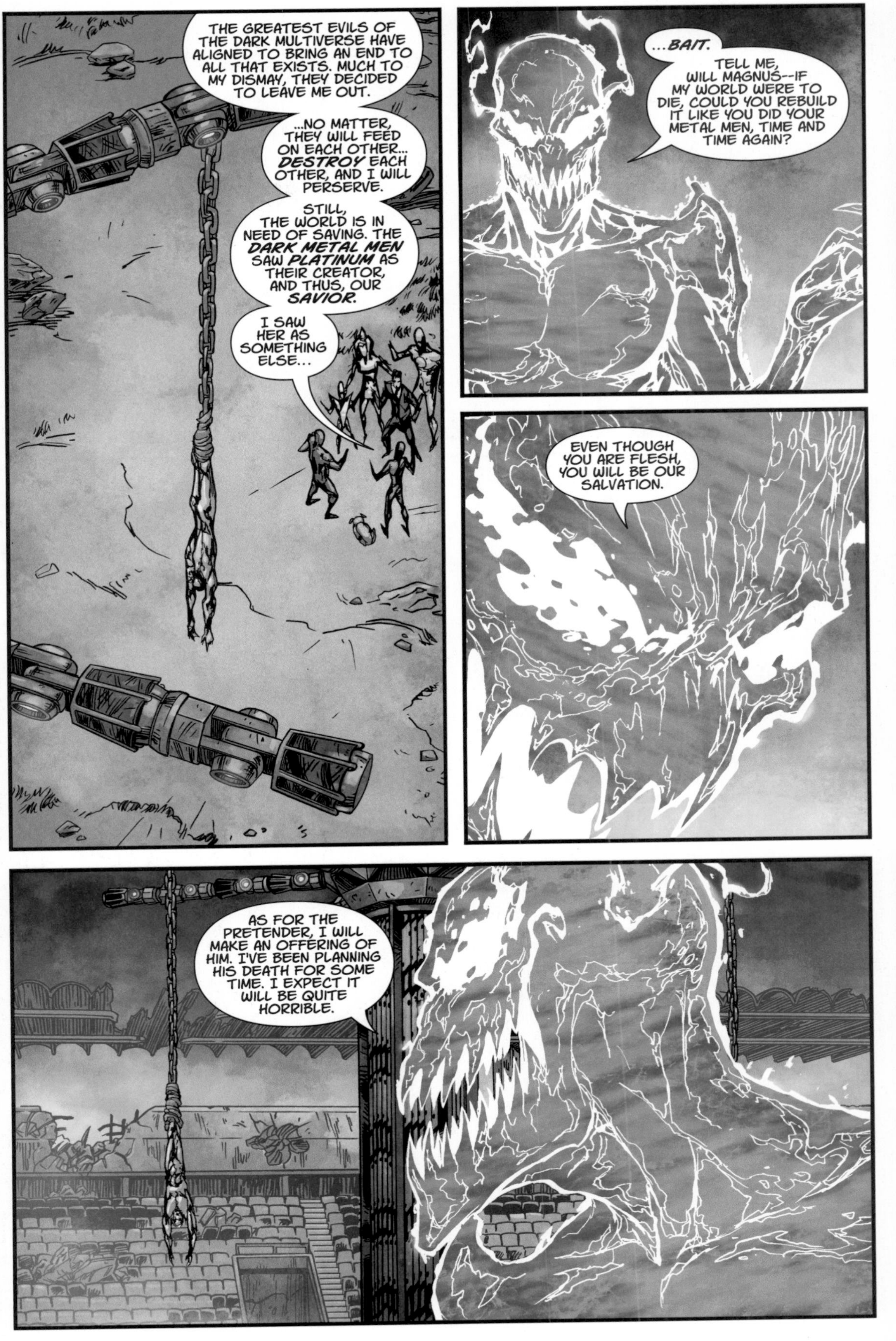
THE GREATEST EVILS OF THE DARK MULTIVERSE HAVE ALIGNED TO BRING AN END TO ALL THAT EXISTS. MUCH TO MY DISMAY, THEY DECIDED TO LEAVE ME OUT.
...NO MATTER, THEY WILL FEED ON EACH OTHER... DESTROY EACH OTHER, AND I WILL PERSERVE.
STILL, THE WORLD IS IN NEED OF SAVING. THE DARK METAL MEN SAW PLATINUM AS THEIR CREATOR, AND THUS, OUR SAVIOR.
I SAW HER AS SOMETHING ELSE...
...BAIT.
TELL ME, WILL MAGNUS--IF MY WORLD WERE TO DIE, COULD YOU REBUILD IT LIKE YOU DID YOUR METAL MEN, TIME AND TIME AGAIN?
EVEN THOUGH YOU ARE FLESH, YOU WILL BE OUR SALVATION.
AS FOR THE PRETENDER, I WILL MAKE AN OFFERING OF HIM. I'VE BEEN PLANNING HIS DEATH FOR SOME TIME. I EXPECT IT WILL BE QUITE HORRIBLE.

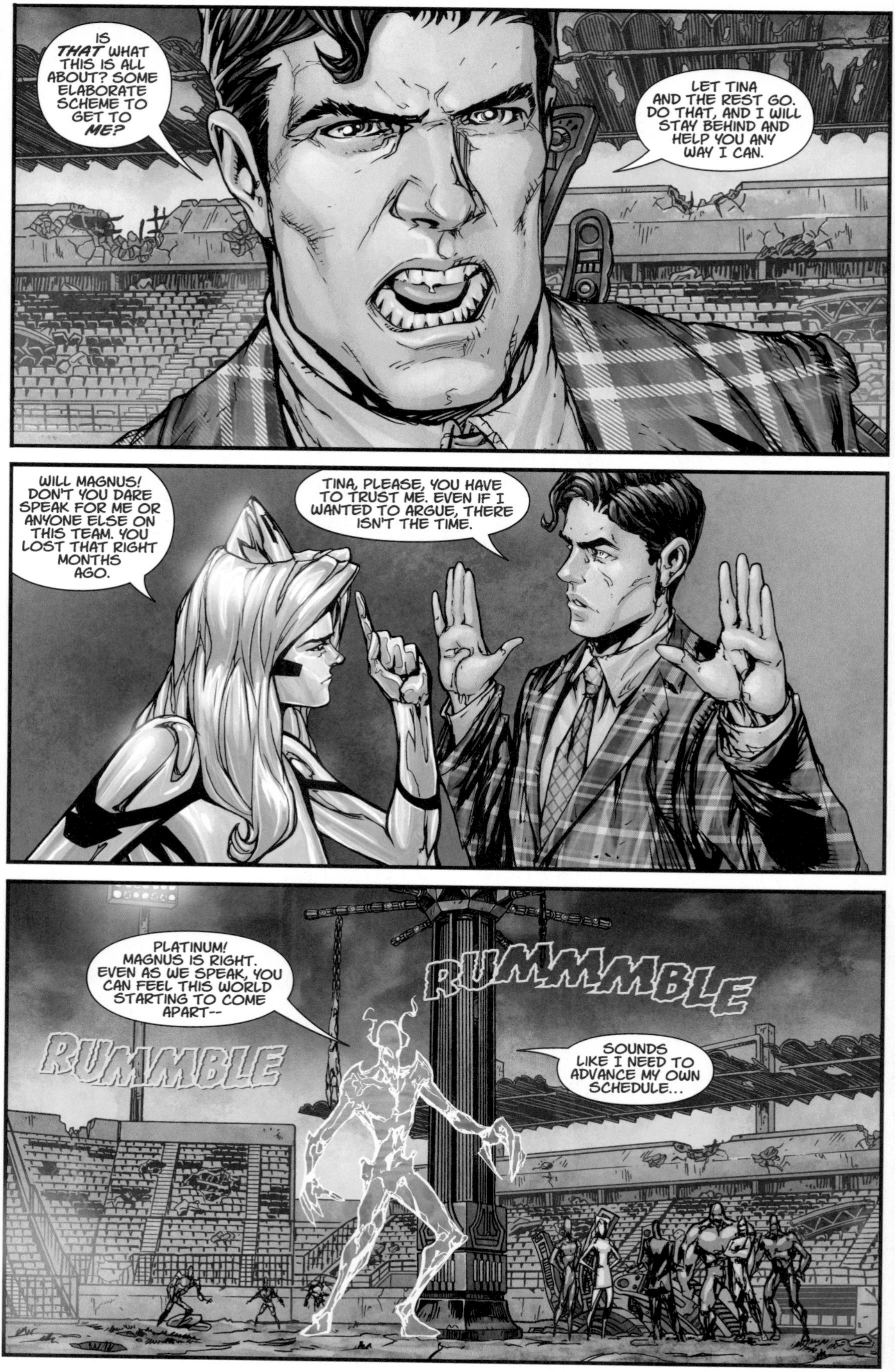
IS THAT WHAT THIS IS ALL ABOUT? SOME ELABORATE SCHEME TO GET TO ME?
LET TINA AND THE REST GO. DO THAT, AND I WILL STAY BEHIND AND HELP YOU ANY WAY I CAN.
WILL MAGNUS! DON'T YOU DARE SPEAK FOR ME OR ANYONE ELSE ON THIS TEAM. YOU LOST THAT RIGHT MONTHS AGO.
TINA, PLEASE, YOU HAVE TO TRUST ME. EVEN IF I WANTED TO ARGUE, THERE ISN'T THE TIME.
PLATINUM! MAGNUS IS RIGHT. EVEN AS WE SPEAK, YOU CAN FEEL THIS WORLD STARTING TO COME APART--
RUMMMBLE
RUMMBLE
SOUNDS LIKE I NEED TO ADVANCE MY OWN SCHEDULE...

...STARTING WITH THE *DEATH* OF THE *NTH METAL MAN.*

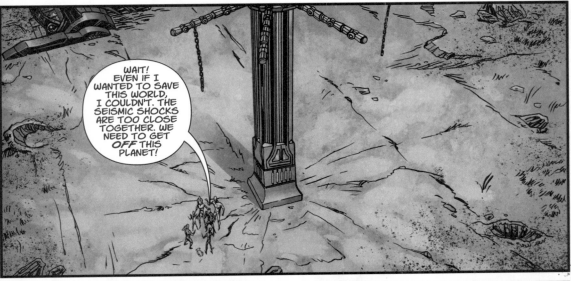

WAIT! EVEN IF I WANTED TO SAVE THIS WORLD, I COULDN'T. THE SEISMIC SHOCKS ARE TOO CLOSE TOGETHER. WE NEED TO GET *OFF* THIS PLANET!

AND I MEAN *ONLY OUR TEAM.*

THERE'S NO WAY IN *HELL* I'M LEADING THESE HORRORS BACK TO OUR WORLD.

MERCURY. REMEMBER YOU SAID YOU WOULDN'T LEAVE WITHOUT A FIGHT?

YEAH?

WELL? WHO'S STOPPING YOU?

YEAH!

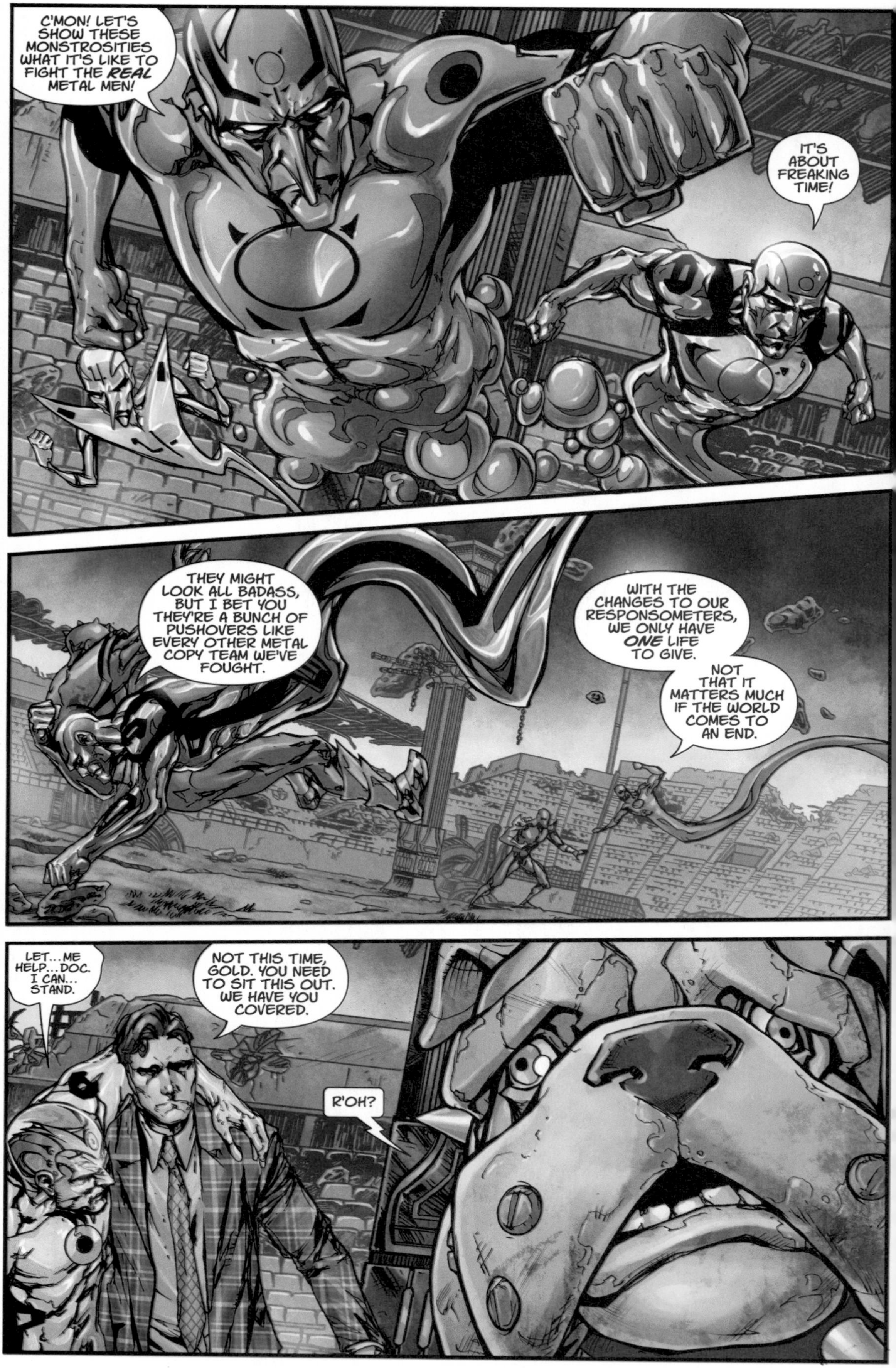
C'MON! LET'S SHOW THESE MONSTROSITIES WHAT IT'S LIKE TO FIGHT THE *REAL* METAL MEN!
IT'S ABOUT FREAKING TIME!
THEY MIGHT LOOK ALL BADASS, BUT I BET YOU THEY'RE A BUNCH OF PUSHOVERS LIKE EVERY OTHER METAL COPY TEAM WE'VE FOUGHT.
WITH THE CHANGES TO OUR RESPONSOMETERS, WE ONLY HAVE *ONE* LIFE TO GIVE.
NOT THAT IT MATTERS MUCH IF THE WORLD COMES TO AN END.
LET... ME HELP... DOC. I CAN... STAND.
NOT THIS TIME, GOLD. YOU NEED TO SIT THIS OUT. WE HAVE YOU COVERED.
R'OH?

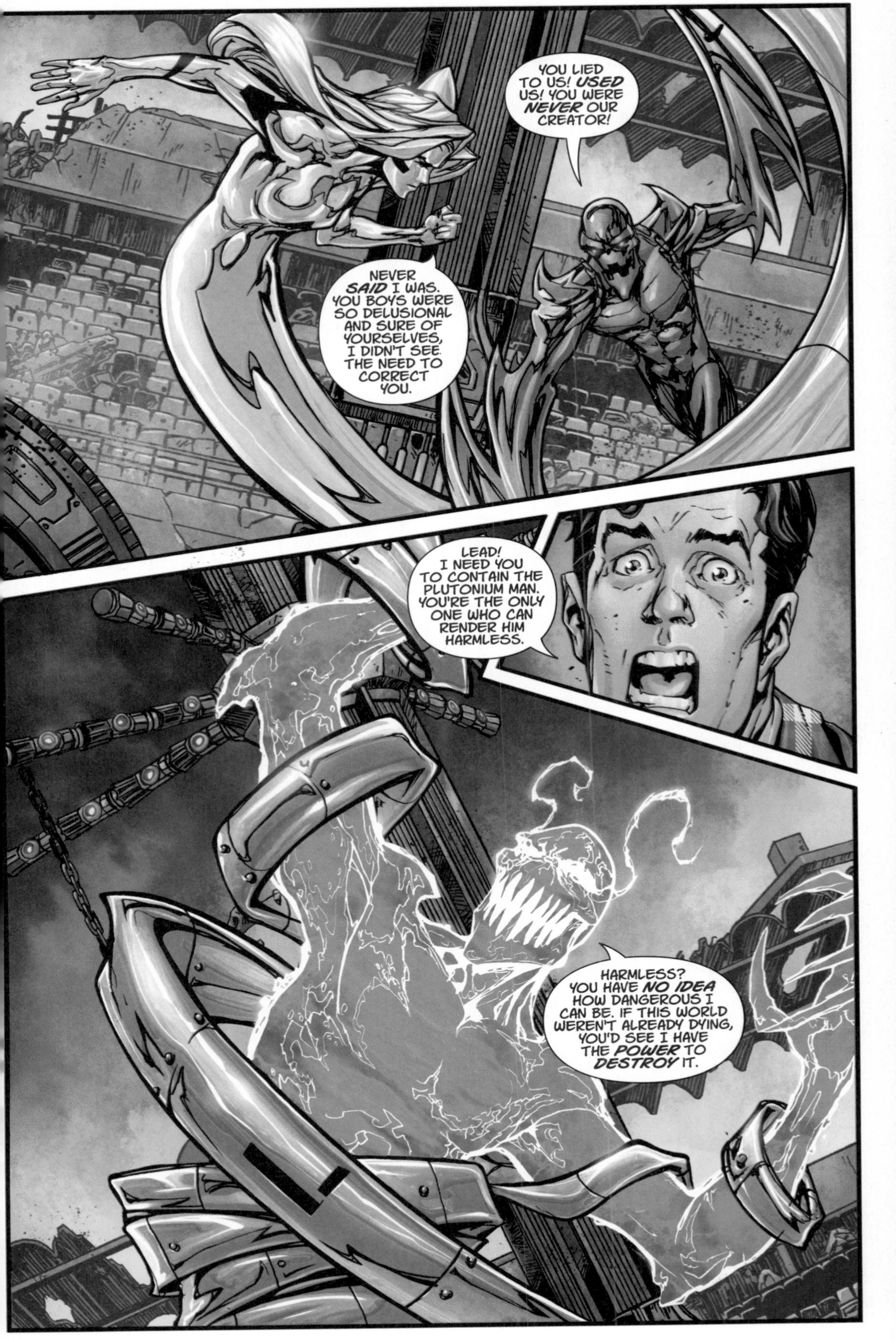
YOU LIED TO US! USED US! YOU WERE NEVER OUR CREATOR!
NEVER SAID I WAS. YOU BOYS WERE SO DELUSIONAL AND SURE OF YOURSELVES, I DIDN'T SEE THE NEED TO CORRECT YOU.
LEAD! I NEED YOU TO CONTAIN THE PLUTONIUM MAN. YOU'RE THE ONLY ONE WHO CAN RENDER HIM HARMLESS.
HARMLESS? YOU HAVE NO IDEA HOW DANGEROUS I CAN BE. IF THIS WORLD WEREN'T ALREADY DYING, YOU'D SEE I HAVE THE POWER TO DESTROY IT.

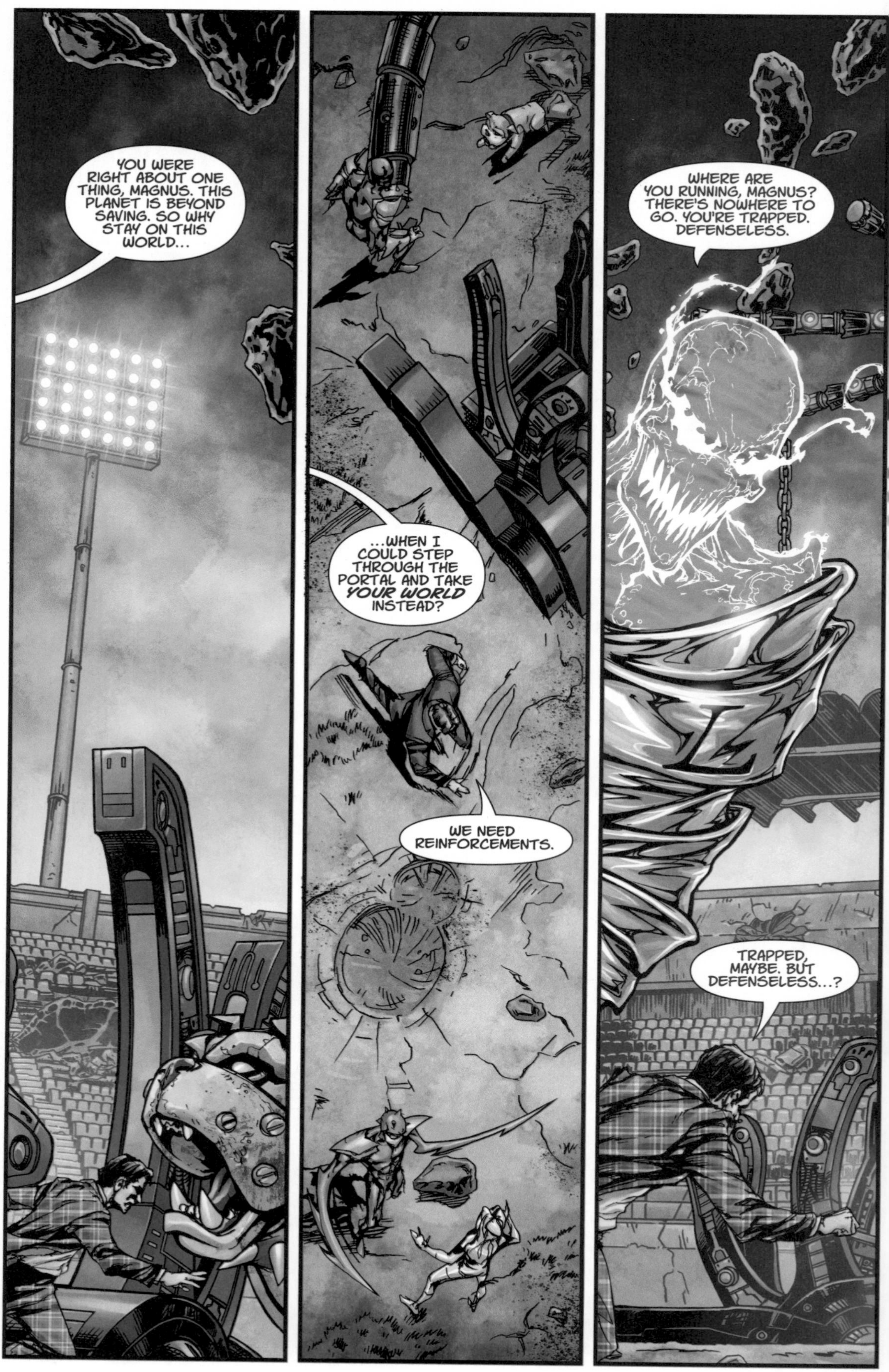
YOU WERE RIGHT ABOUT ONE THING, MAGNUS. THIS PLANET IS BEYOND SAVING. SO WHY STAY ON THIS WORLD...
...WHEN I COULD STEP THROUGH THE PORTAL AND TAKE *YOUR WORLD* INSTEAD?
WE NEED REINFORCEMENTS.
WHERE ARE YOU RUNNING, MAGNUS? THERE'S NOWHERE TO GO. YOU'RE TRAPPED. DEFENSELESS.
TRAPPED, MAYBE. BUT DEFENSELESS...?

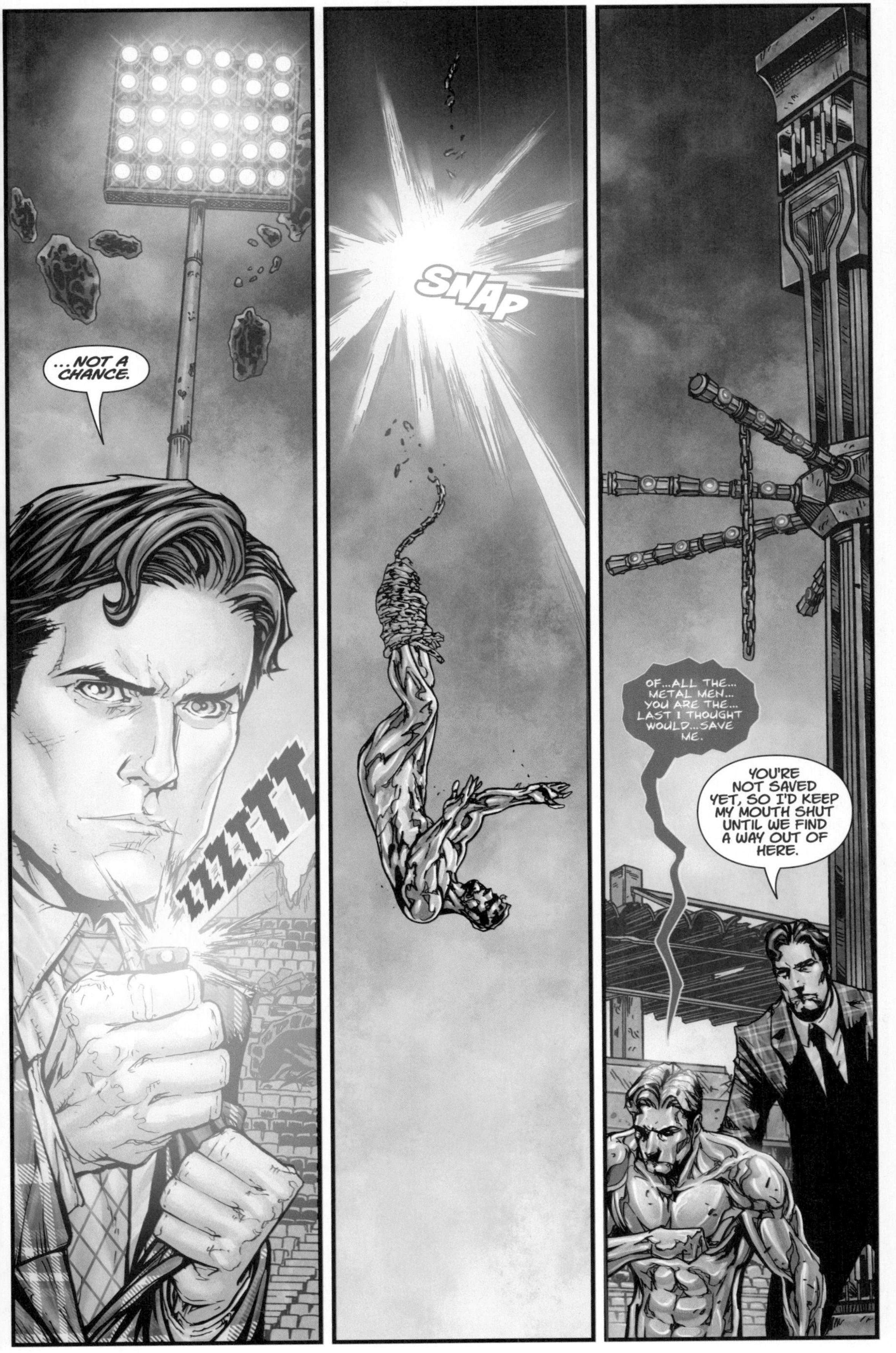
...NOT A CHANCE.
ZZZZTTTT
SNAP
OF...ALL THE... METAL MEN... YOU ARE THE... LAST I THOUGHT WOULD...SAVE ME.
YOU'RE NOT SAVED YET, SO I'D KEEP MY MOUTH SHUT UNTIL WE FIND A WAY OUT OF HERE.

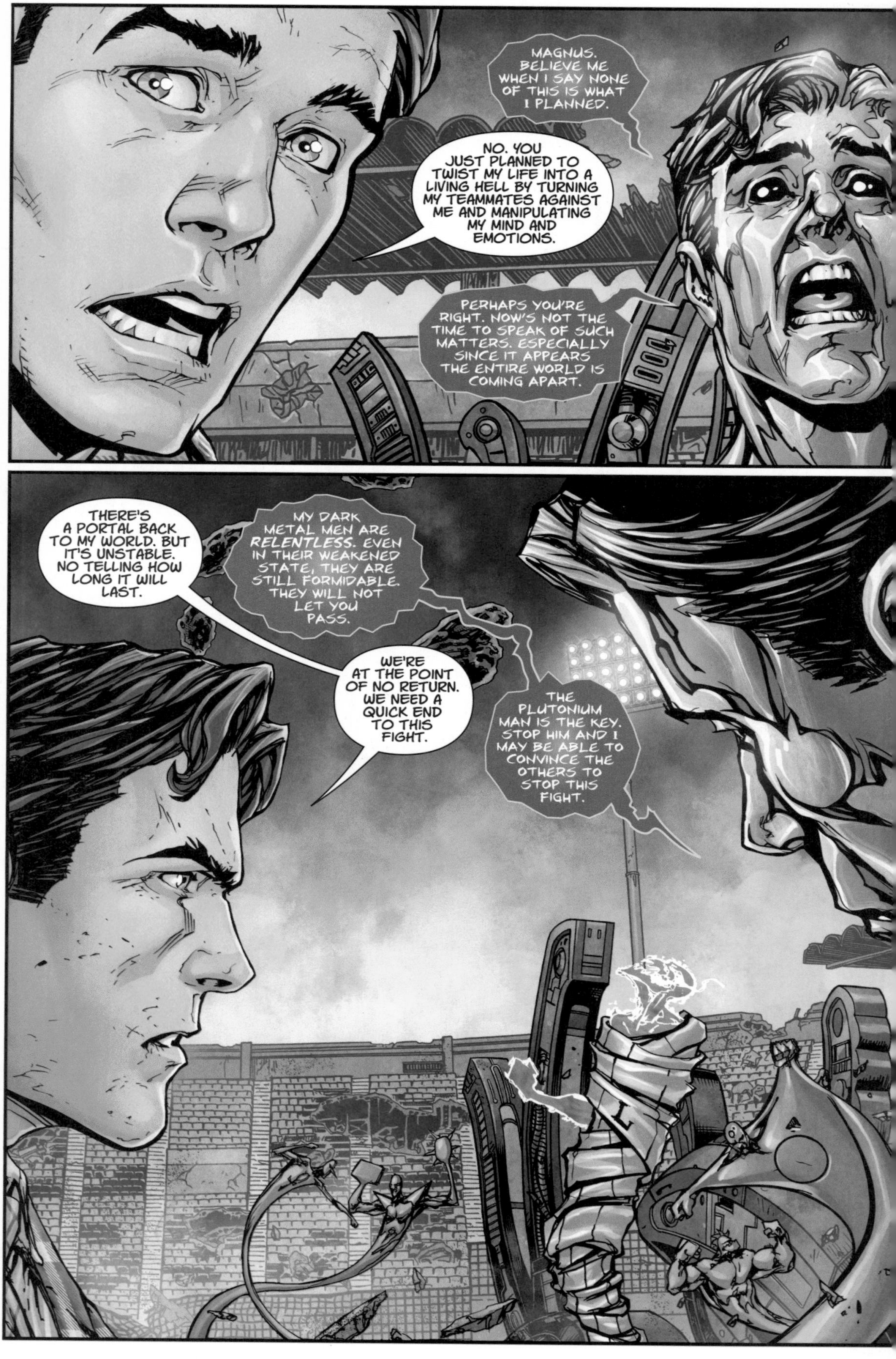
MAGNUS. BELIEVE ME WHEN I SAY NONE OF THIS IS WHAT I PLANNED.
NO. YOU JUST PLANNED TO TWIST MY LIFE INTO A LIVING HELL BY TURNING MY TEAMMATES AGAINST ME AND MANIPULATING MY MIND AND EMOTIONS.
PERHAPS YOU'RE RIGHT. NOW'S NOT THE TIME TO SPEAK OF SUCH MATTERS. ESPECIALLY SINCE IT APPEARS THE ENTIRE WORLD IS COMING APART.
THERE'S A PORTAL BACK TO MY WORLD. BUT IT'S UNSTABLE. NO TELLING HOW LONG IT WILL LAST.
MY DARK METAL MEN ARE *RELENTLESS*. EVEN IN THEIR WEAKENED STATE, THEY ARE STILL FORMIDABLE. THEY WILL NOT LET YOU PASS.
WE'RE AT THE POINT OF NO RETURN. WE NEED A QUICK END TO THIS FIGHT.
THE PLUTONIUM MAN IS THE KEY. STOP HIM AND I MAY BE ABLE TO CONVINCE THE OTHERS TO STOP THIS FIGHT.

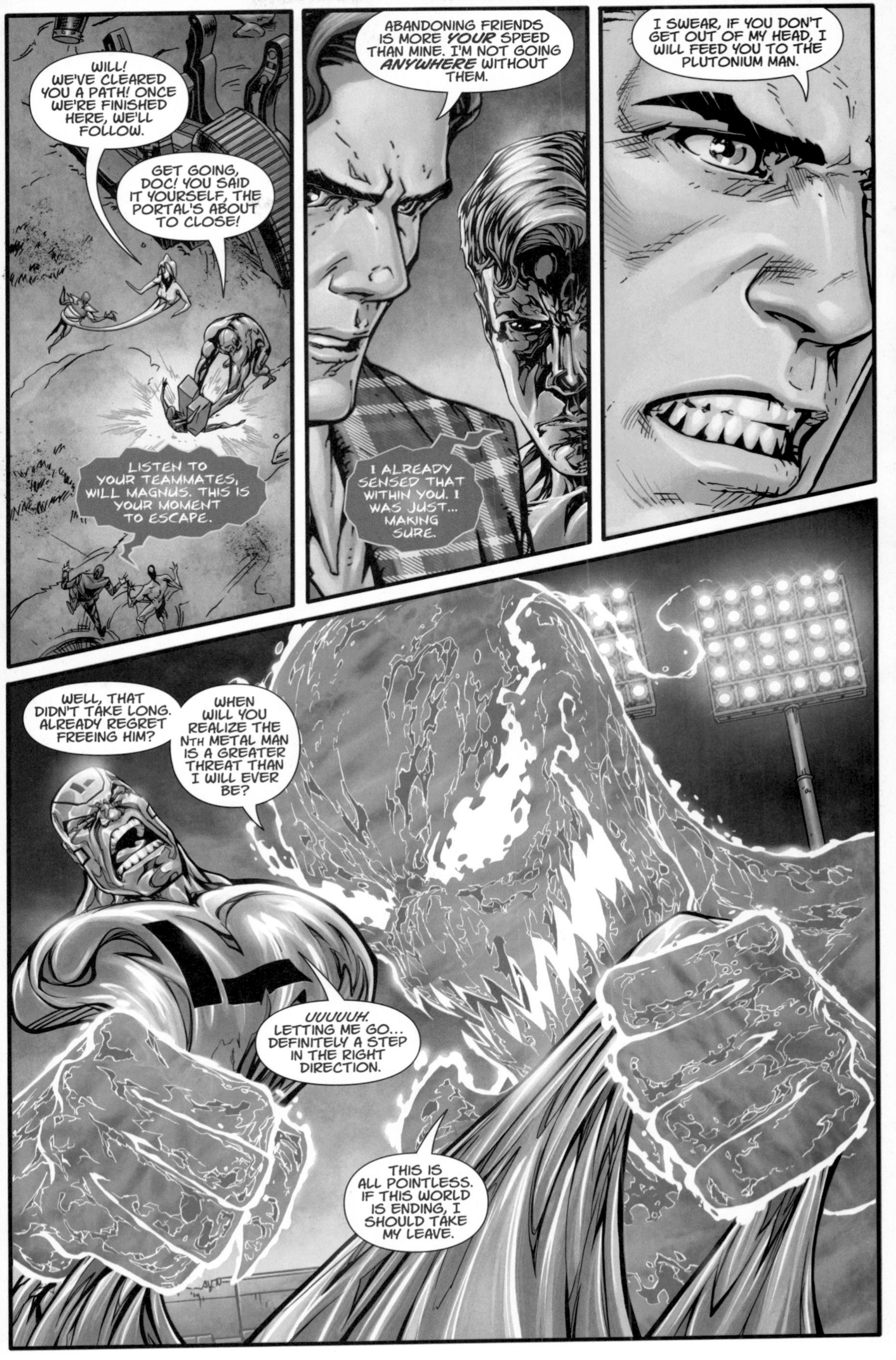
WILL! WE'VE CLEARED YOU A PATH! ONCE WE'RE FINISHED HERE, WE'LL FOLLOW.
GET GOING, DOC! YOU SAID IT YOURSELF, THE PORTAL'S ABOUT TO CLOSE!
LISTEN TO YOUR TEAMMATES, WILL MAGNUS. THIS IS YOUR MOMENT TO ESCAPE.
ABANDONING FRIENDS IS MORE *YOUR* SPEED THAN MINE. I'M NOT GOING *ANYWHERE* WITHOUT THEM.
I ALREADY SENSED THAT WITHIN YOU. I WAS JUST... MAKING SURE.
I SWEAR, IF YOU DON'T GET OUT OF MY HEAD, I WILL FEED YOU TO THE PLUTONIUM MAN.
WELL, THAT DIDN'T TAKE LONG. ALREADY REGRET FREEING HIM?
WHEN WILL YOU REALIZE THE NTH METAL MAN IS A GREATER THREAT THAN I WILL EVER BE?
UUUUUH. LETTING ME GO... DEFINITELY A STEP IN THE RIGHT DIRECTION.
THIS IS ALL POINTLESS. IF THIS WORLD IS ENDING, I SHOULD TAKE MY LEAVE.

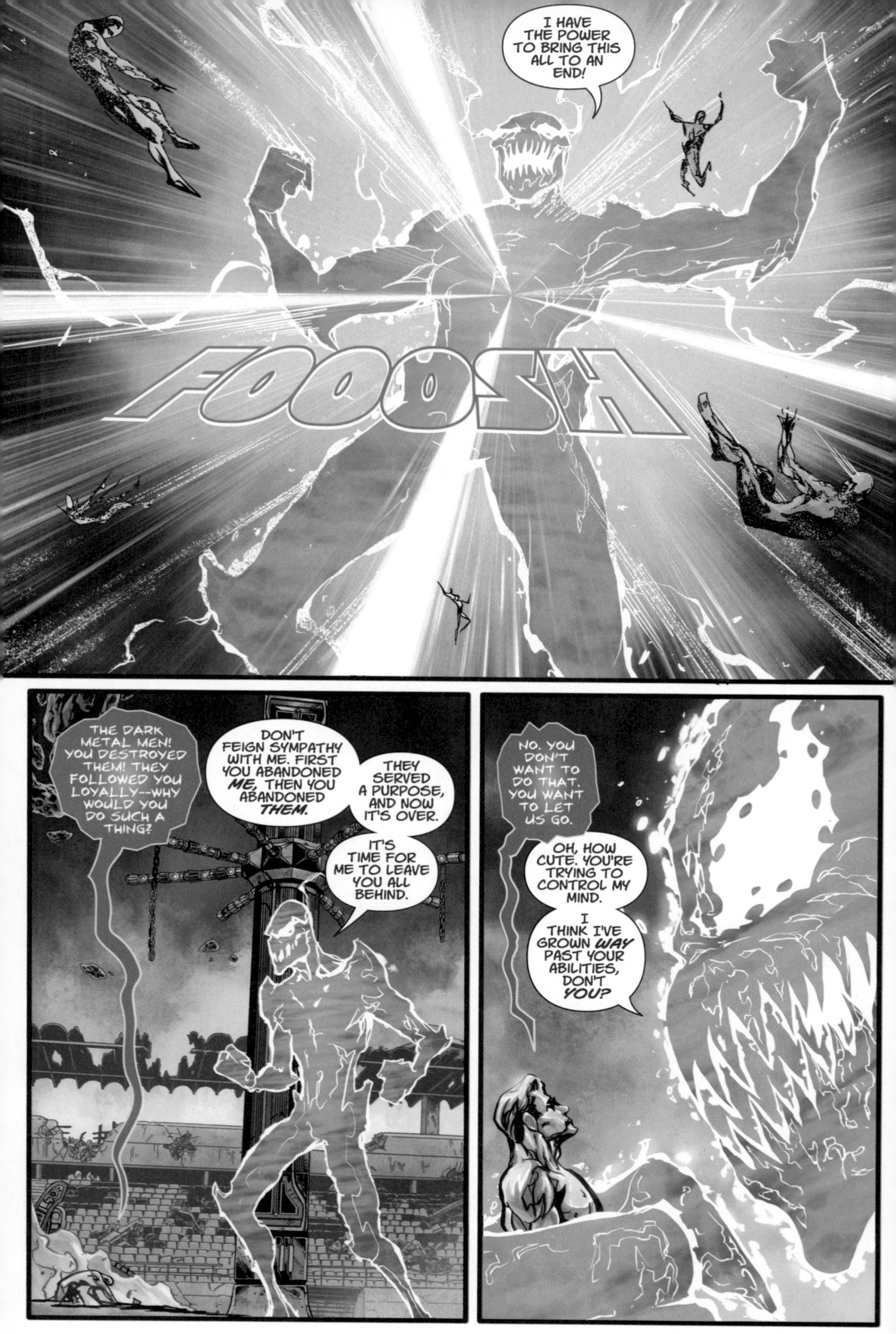
I HAVE THE POWER TO BRING THIS ALL TO AN END!
FOOOSH
THE DARK METAL MEN! YOU DESTROYED THEM! THEY FOLLOWED YOU LOYALLY--WHY WOULD YOU DO SUCH A THING?
DON'T FEIGN SYMPATHY WITH ME. FIRST YOU ABANDONED ME, THEN YOU ABANDONED THEM.
THEY SERVED A PURPOSE, AND NOW IT'S OVER.
IT'S TIME FOR ME TO LEAVE YOU ALL BEHIND.
NO. YOU DON'T WANT TO DO THAT. YOU WANT TO LET US GO.
OH, HOW CUTE. YOU'RE TRYING TO CONTROL MY MIND.
I THINK I'VE GROWN WAY PAST YOUR ABILITIES, DON'T YOU?

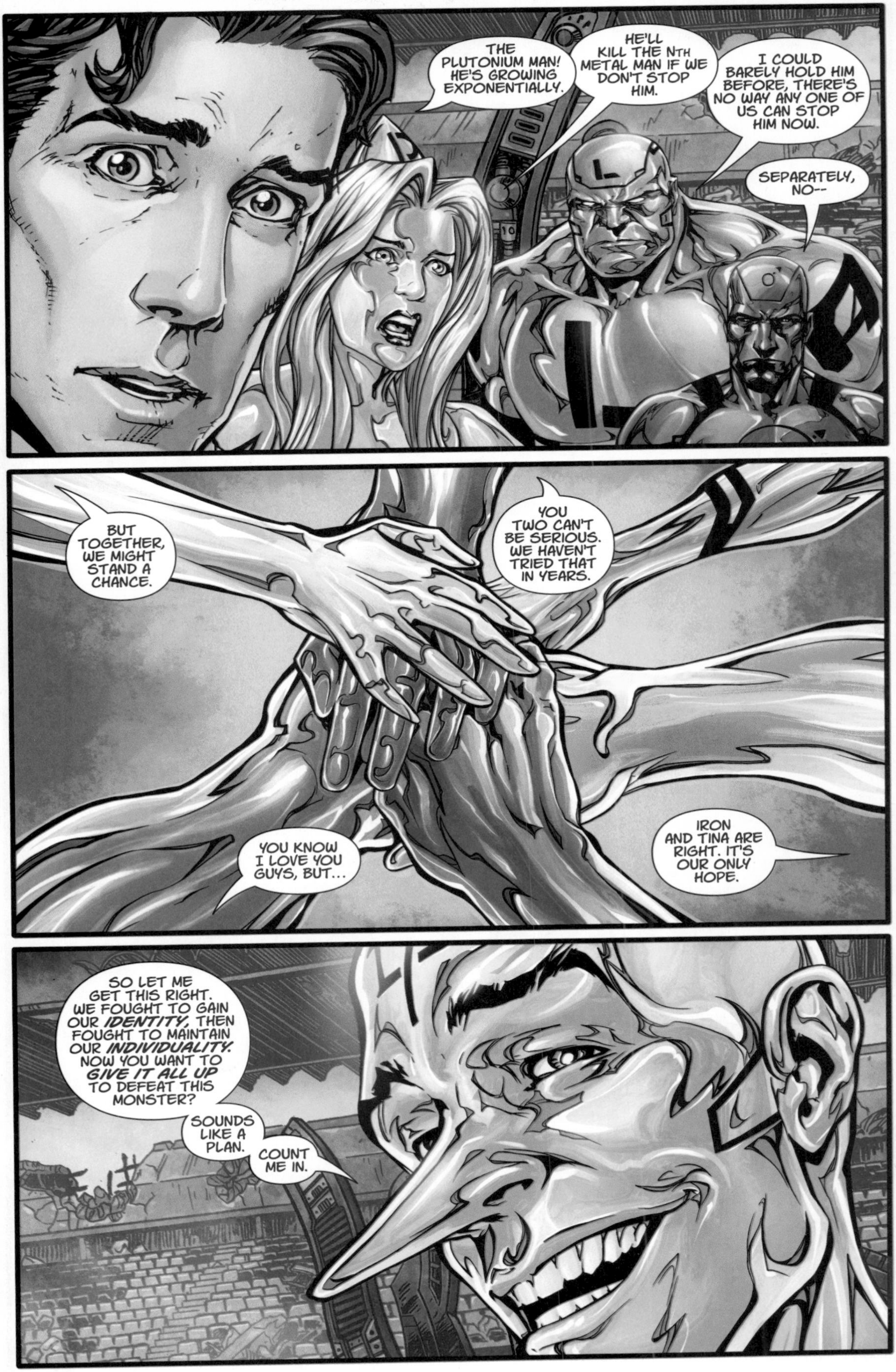
THE PLUTONIUM MAN! HE'S GROWING EXPONENTIALLY.
HE'LL KILL THE Nth METAL MAN IF WE DON'T STOP HIM.
I COULD BARELY HOLD HIM BEFORE, THERE'S NO WAY ANY ONE OF US CAN STOP HIM NOW.
SEPARATELY, NO--
BUT TOGETHER, WE MIGHT STAND A CHANCE.
YOU TWO CAN'T BE SERIOUS. WE HAVEN'T TRIED THAT IN YEARS.
YOU KNOW I LOVE YOU GUYS, BUT...
IRON AND TINA ARE RIGHT. IT'S OUR ONLY HOPE.
SO LET ME GET THIS RIGHT. WE FOUGHT TO GAIN OUR *IDENTITY,* THEN FOUGHT TO MAINTAIN OUR *INDIVIDUALITY.* NOW YOU WANT TO ***GIVE IT ALL UP*** TO DEFEAT THIS MONSTER?
SOUNDS LIKE A PLAN.
COUNT ME IN.

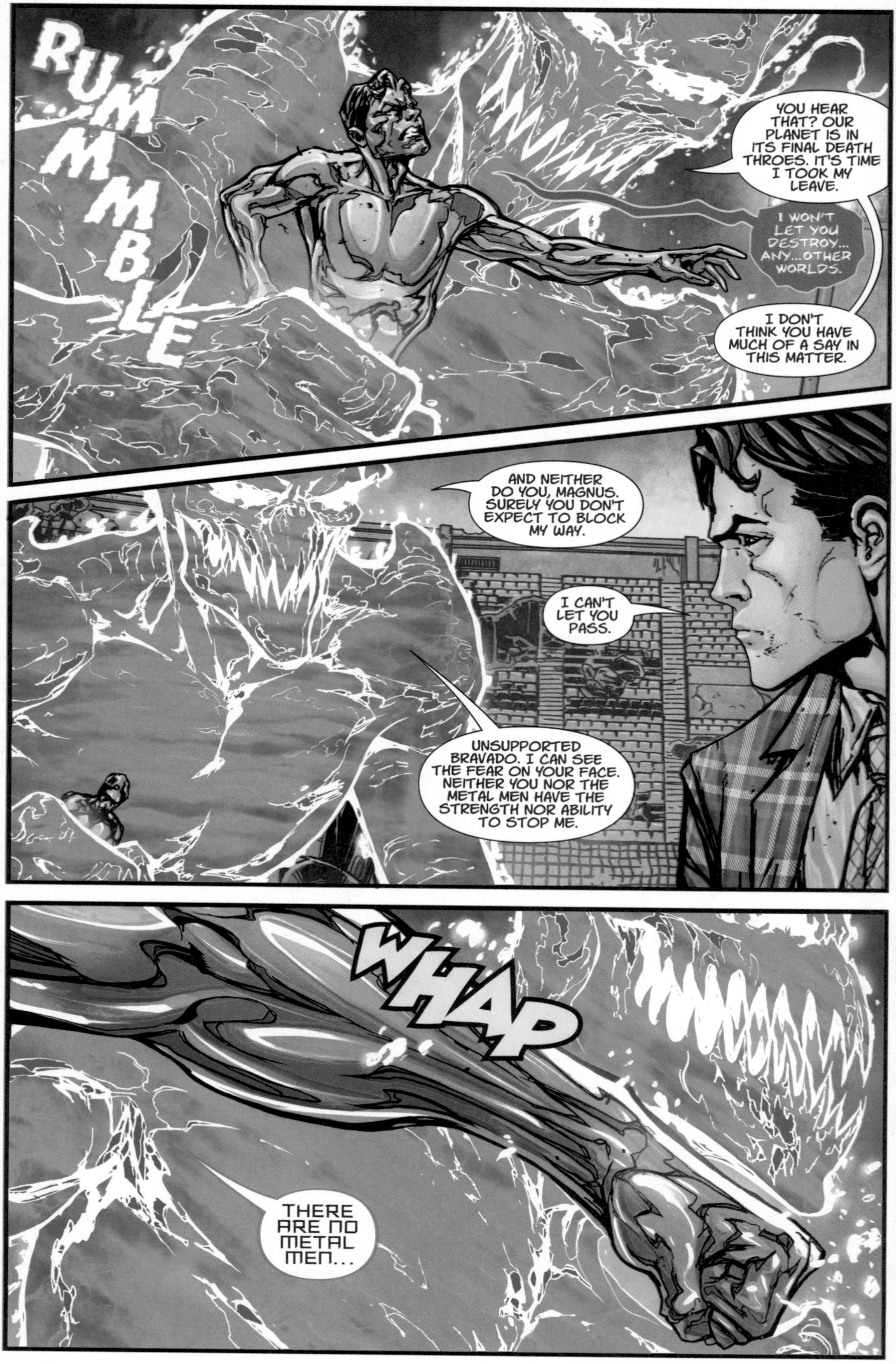
RUMMMBLE
YOU HEAR THAT? OUR PLANET IS IN ITS FINAL DEATH THROES. IT'S TIME I TOOK MY LEAVE.
I WON'T LET YOU DESTROY... ANY...OTHER WORLDS.
I DON'T THINK YOU HAVE MUCH OF A SAY IN THIS MATTER.
AND NEITHER DO YOU, MAGNUS. SURELY YOU DON'T EXPECT TO BLOCK MY WAY.
I CAN'T LET YOU PASS.
UNSUPPORTED BRAVADO. I CAN SEE THE FEAR ON YOUR FACE. NEITHER YOU NOR THE METAL MEN HAVE THE STRENGTH NOR ABILITY TO STOP ME.
WHAP
THERE ARE NO METAL MEN...

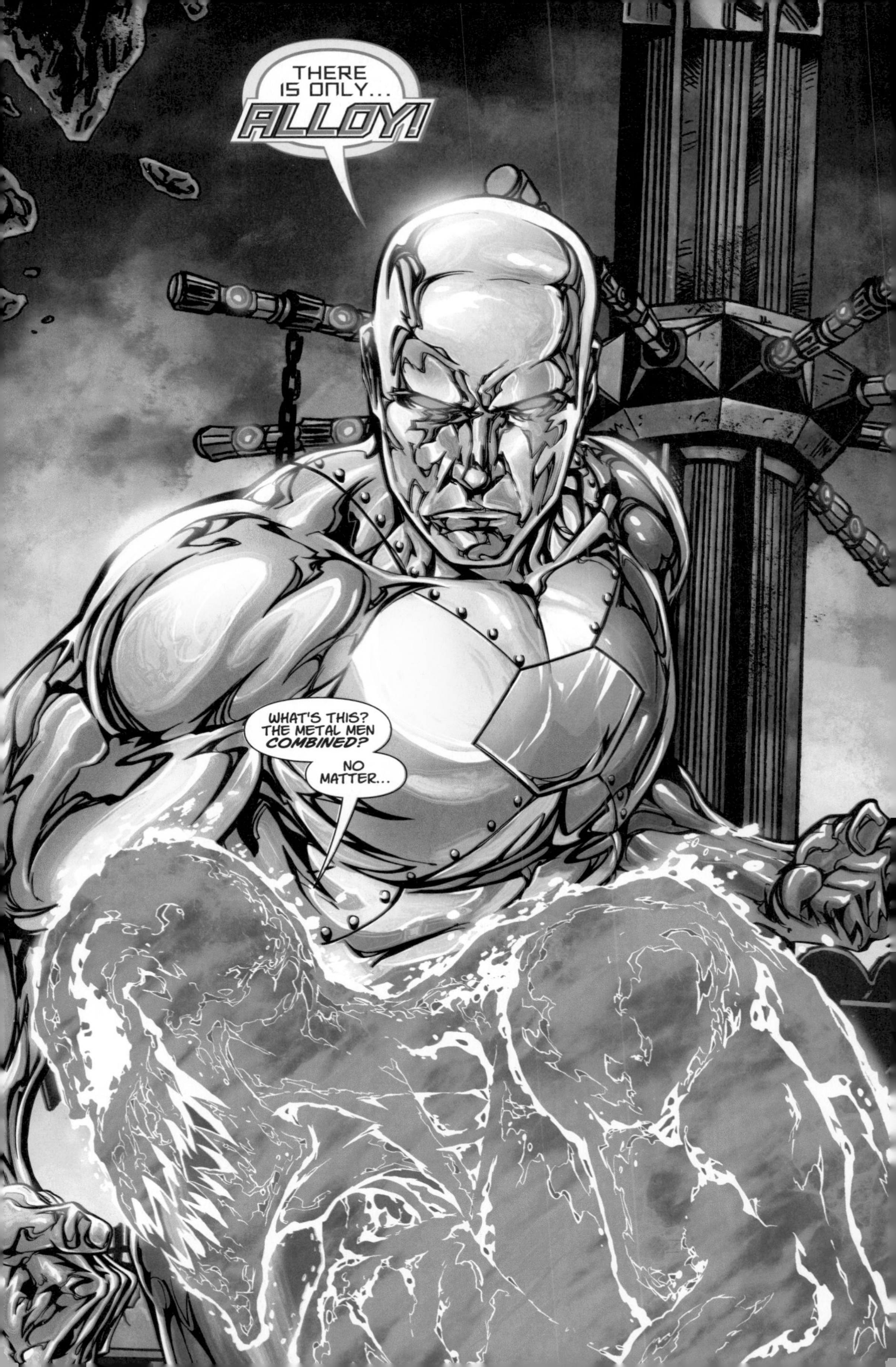
THERE IS ONLY... ALLOY!
WHAT'S THIS? THE METAL MEN COMBINED?
NO MATTER...

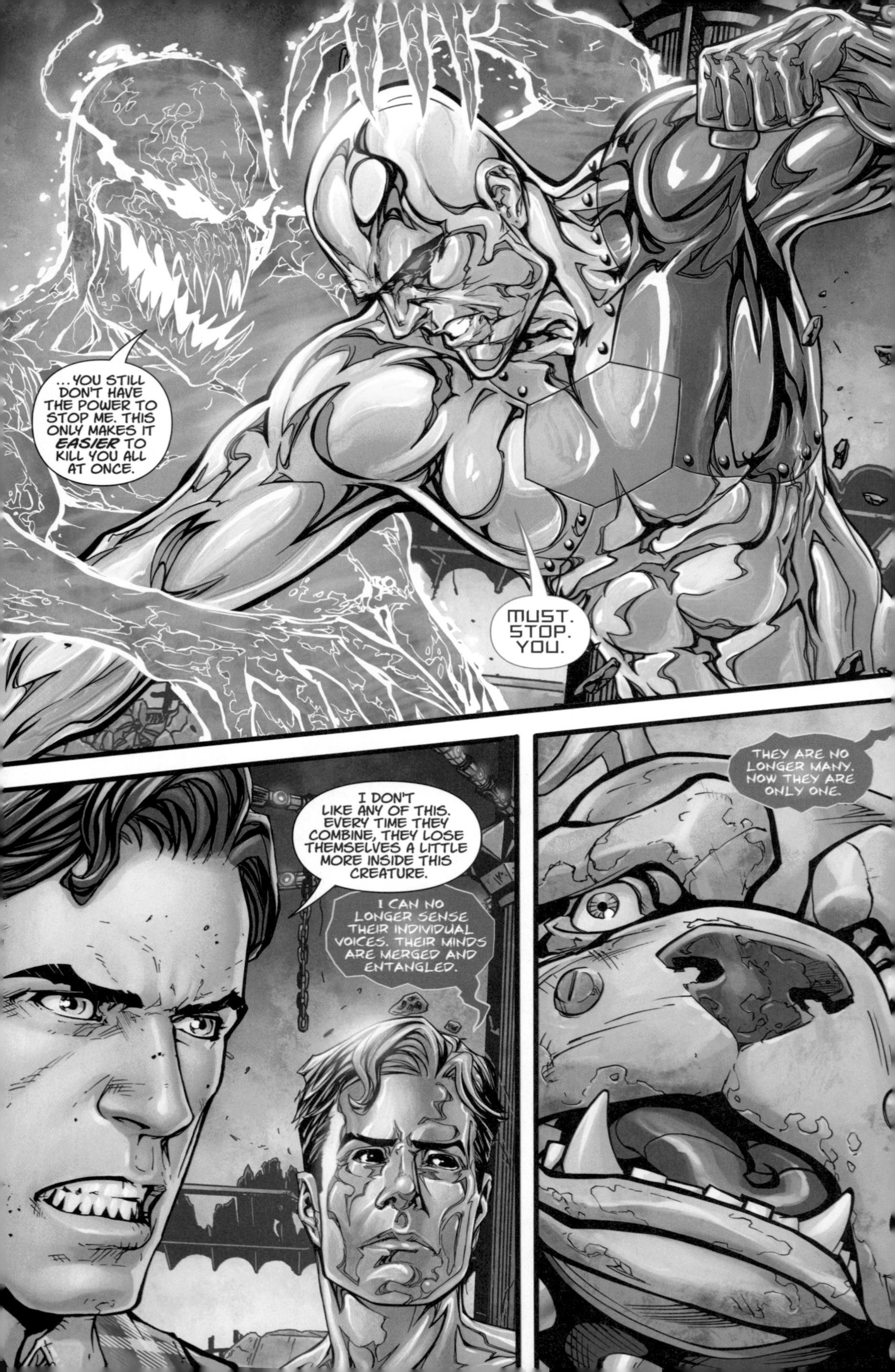
...YOU STILL DON'T HAVE THE POWER TO STOP ME. THIS ONLY MAKES IT *EASIER* TO KILL YOU ALL AT ONCE.
MUST. STOP. YOU.
I DON'T LIKE ANY OF THIS. EVERY TIME THEY COMBINE, THEY LOSE THEMSELVES A LITTLE MORE INSIDE THIS CREATURE.
I CAN NO LONGER SENSE THEIR INDIVIDUAL VOICES. THEIR MINDS ARE MERGED AND ENTANGLED.
THEY ARE NO LONGER MANY. NOW THEY ARE ONLY ONE.

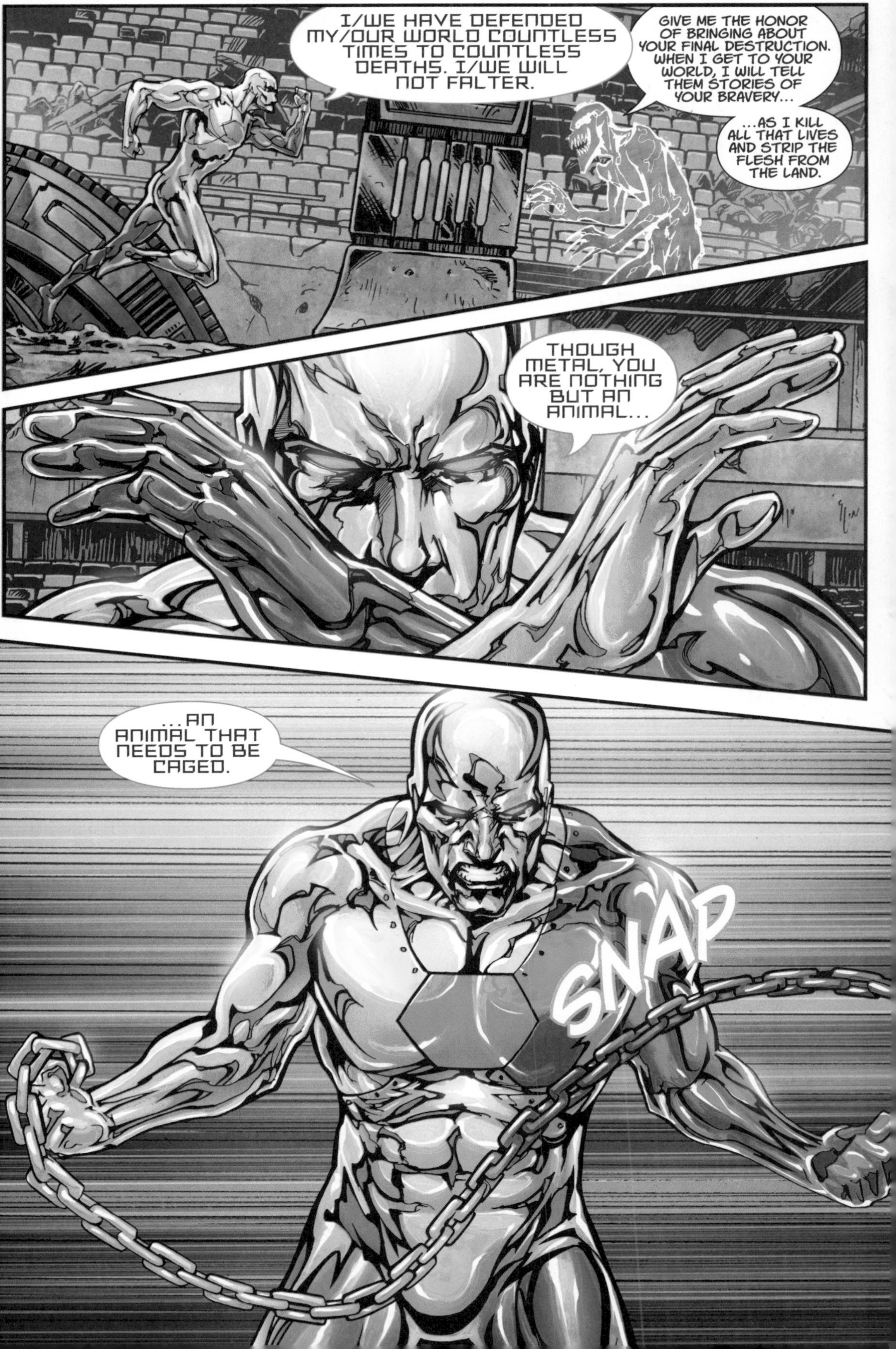
I/WE HAVE DEFENDED MY/OUR WORLD COUNTLESS TIMES TO COUNTLESS DEATHS. I/WE WILL NOT FALTER.
GIVE ME THE HONOR OF BRINGING ABOUT YOUR FINAL DESTRUCTION. WHEN I GET TO YOUR WORLD, I WILL TELL THEM STORIES OF YOUR BRAVERY...
...AS I KILL ALL THAT LIVES AND STRIP THE FLESH FROM THE LAND.
THOUGH METAL, YOU ARE NOTHING BUT AN ANIMAL...
...AN ANIMAL THAT NEEDS TO BE CAGED.
SNAP

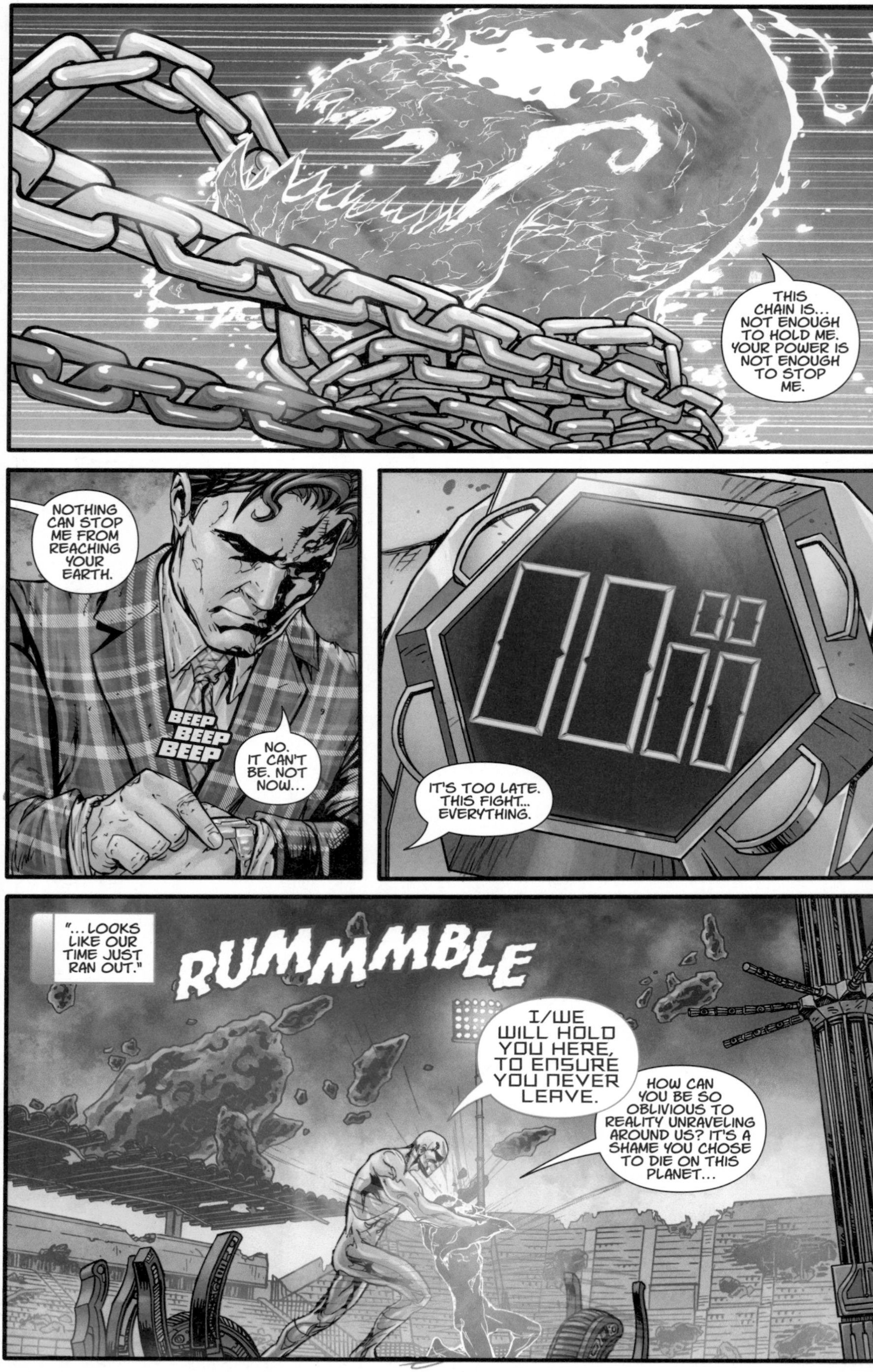

THIS CHAIN IS... NOT ENOUGH TO HOLD ME. YOUR POWER IS NOT ENOUGH TO STOP ME.
NOTHING CAN STOP ME FROM REACHING YOUR EARTH.
BEEP BEEP BEEP
NO. IT CAN'T BE. NOT NOW...
IT'S TOO LATE. THIS FIGHT... EVERYTHING.
"...LOOKS LIKE OUR TIME JUST RAN OUT."
RUMMMBLE
I/WE WILL HOLD YOU HERE, TO ENSURE YOU NEVER LEAVE.
HOW CAN YOU BE SO OBLIVIOUS TO REALITY UNRAVELING AROUND US? IT'S A SHAME YOU CHOSE TO DIE ON THIS PLANET...

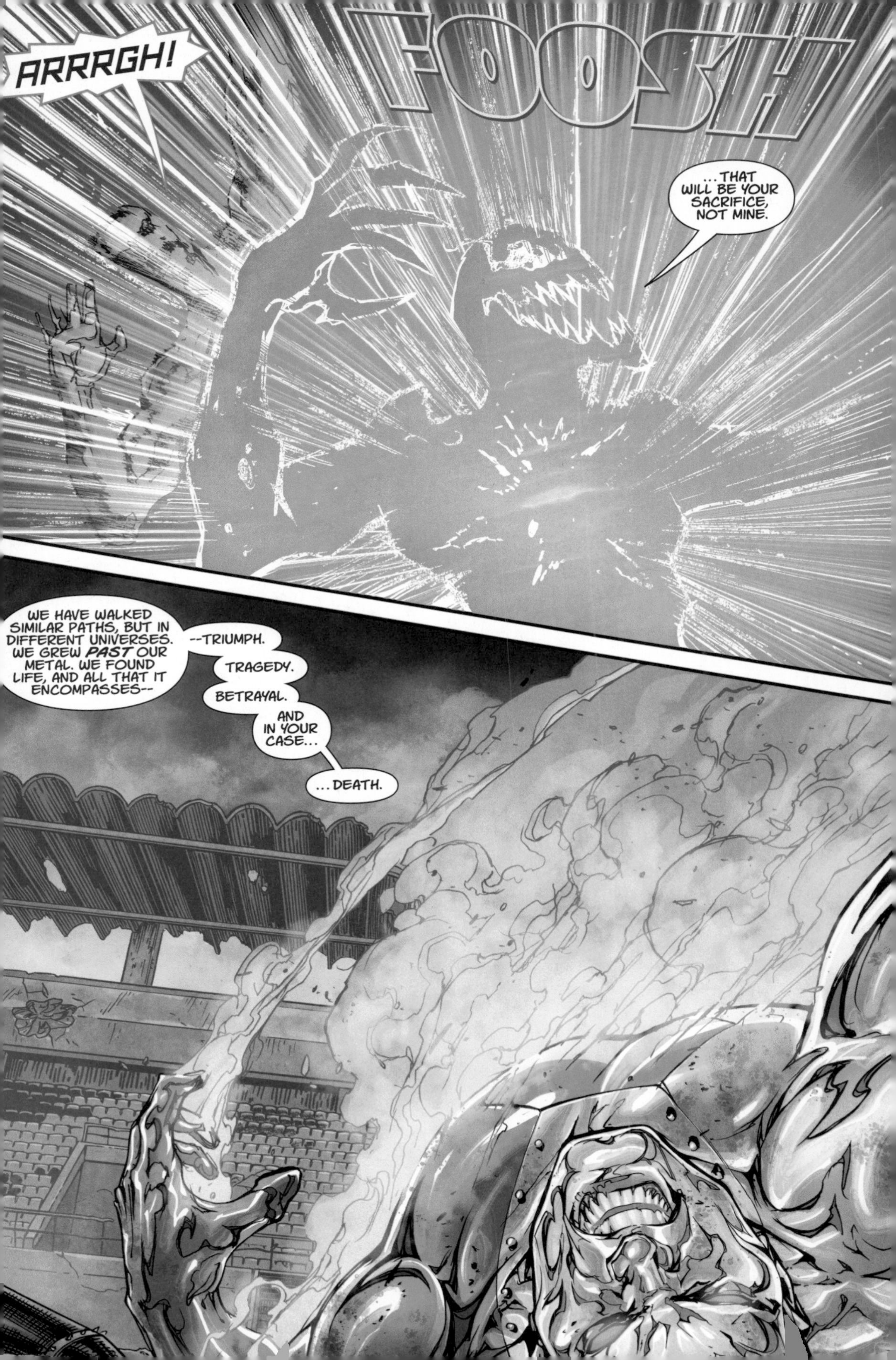
ARRRGH!
FOOSH
...THAT WILL BE YOUR SACRIFICE, NOT MINE.
WE HAVE WALKED SIMILAR PATHS, BUT IN DIFFERENT UNIVERSES. WE GREW PAST OUR METAL. WE FOUND LIFE, AND ALL THAT IT ENCOMPASSES--
--TRIUMPH.
TRAGEDY.
BETRAYAL.
AND IN YOUR CASE...
...DEATH.

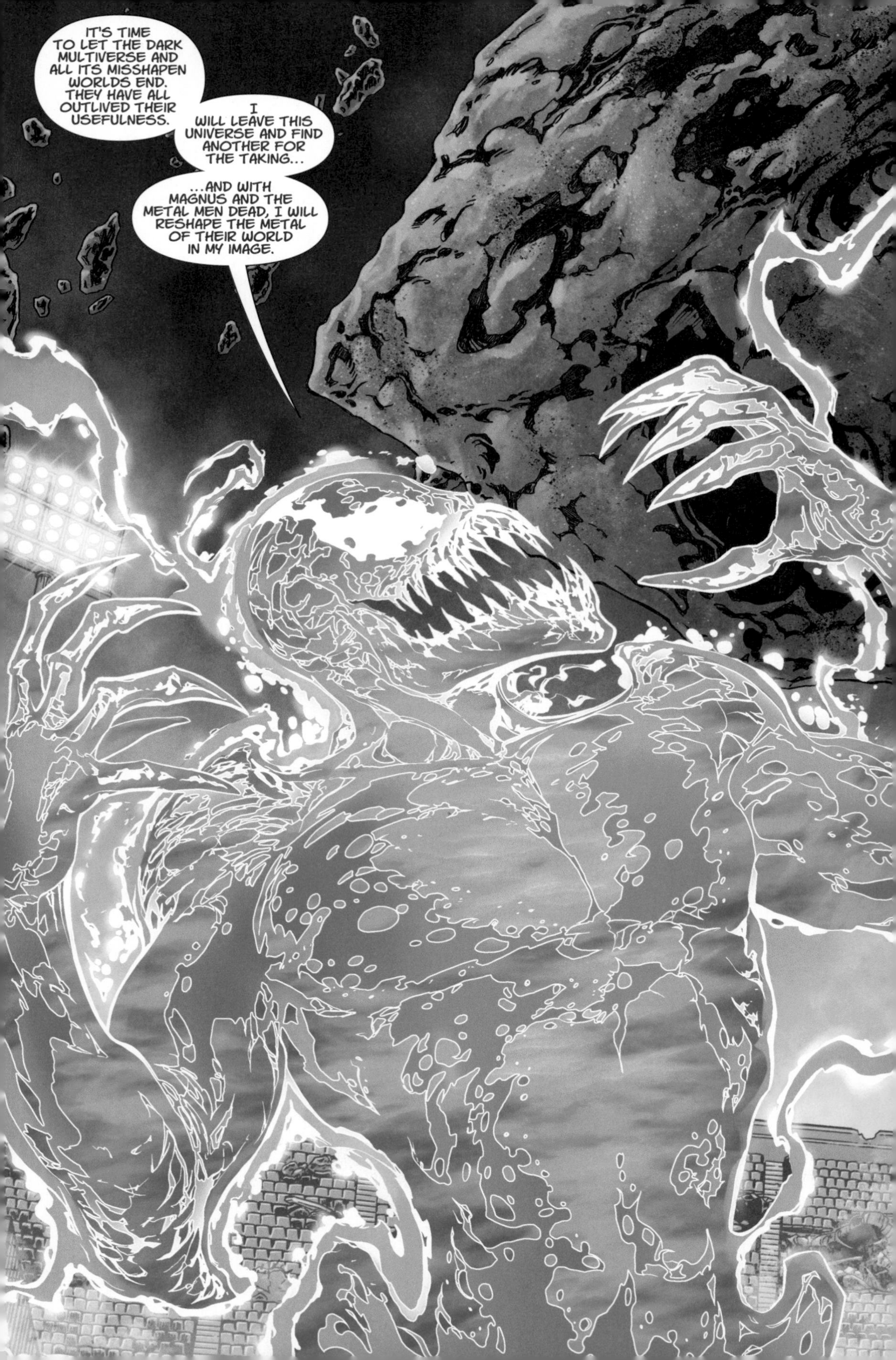
IT'S TIME TO LET THE DARK MULTIVERSE AND ALL ITS MISSHAPEN WORLDS END. THEY HAVE ALL OUTLIVED THEIR USEFULNESS.
I WILL LEAVE THIS UNIVERSE AND FIND ANOTHER FOR THE TAKING...
...AND WITH MAGNUS AND THE METAL MEN DEAD, I WILL RESHAPE THE METAL OF THEIR WORLD IN MY IMAGE.

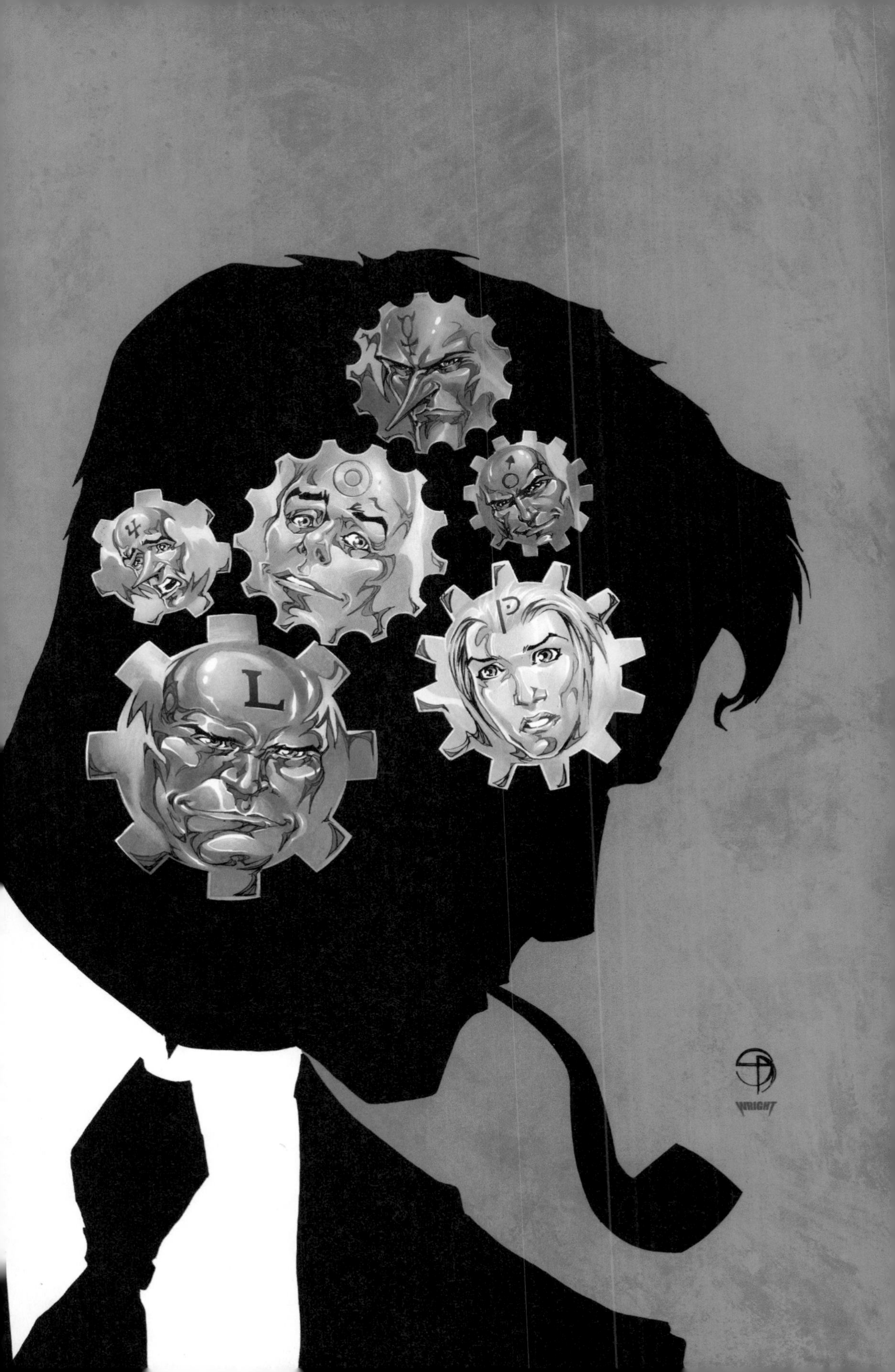
L
WRIGHT

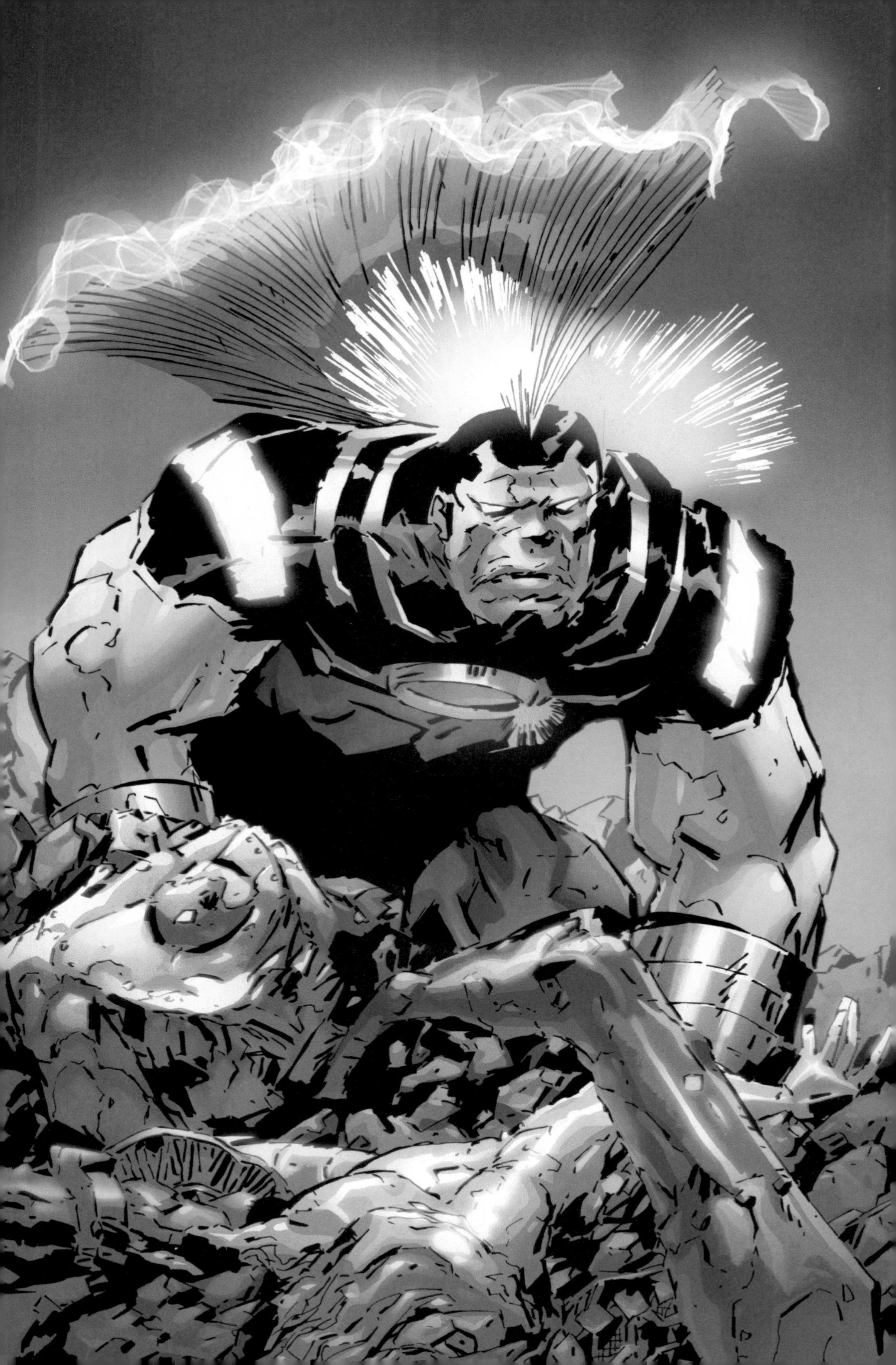

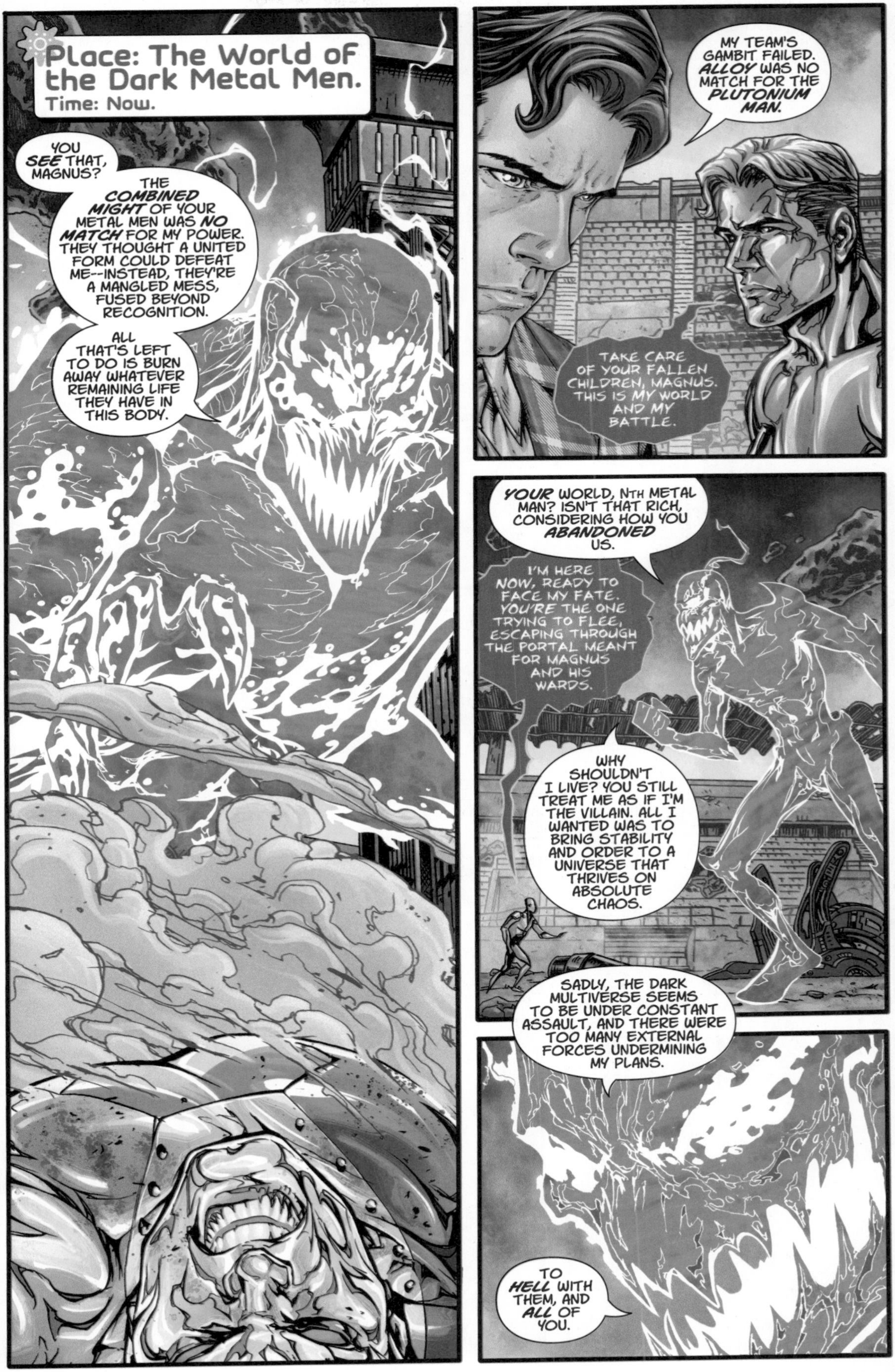

Place: The World of the Dark Metal Men.
Time: Now.
YOU SEE THAT, MAGNUS?
THE COMBINED MIGHT OF YOUR METAL MEN WAS NO MATCH FOR MY POWER. THEY THOUGHT A UNITED FORM COULD DEFEAT ME--INSTEAD, THEY'RE A MANGLED MESS, FUSED BEYOND RECOGNITION.
ALL THAT'S LEFT TO DO IS BURN AWAY WHATEVER REMAINING LIFE THEY HAVE IN THIS BODY.
MY TEAM'S GAMBIT FAILED. ALLOY WAS NO MATCH FOR THE PLUTONIUM MAN.
TAKE CARE OF YOUR FALLEN CHILDREN, MAGNUS. THIS IS MY WORLD AND MY BATTLE.
YOUR WORLD, NTH METAL MAN? ISN'T THAT RICH, CONSIDERING HOW YOU ABANDONED US.
I'M HERE NOW, READY TO FACE MY FATE. YOU'RE THE ONE TRYING TO FLEE, ESCAPING THROUGH THE PORTAL MEANT FOR MAGNUS AND HIS WARDS.
WHY SHOULDN'T I LIVE? YOU STILL TREAT ME AS IF I'M THE VILLAIN. ALL I WANTED WAS TO BRING STABILITY AND ORDER TO A UNIVERSE THAT THRIVES ON ABSOLUTE CHAOS.
SADLY, THE DARK MULTIVERSE SEEMS TO BE UNDER CONSTANT ASSAULT, AND THERE WERE TOO MANY EXTERNAL FORCES UNDERMINING MY PLANS.
TO HELL WITH THEM, AND ALL OF YOU.

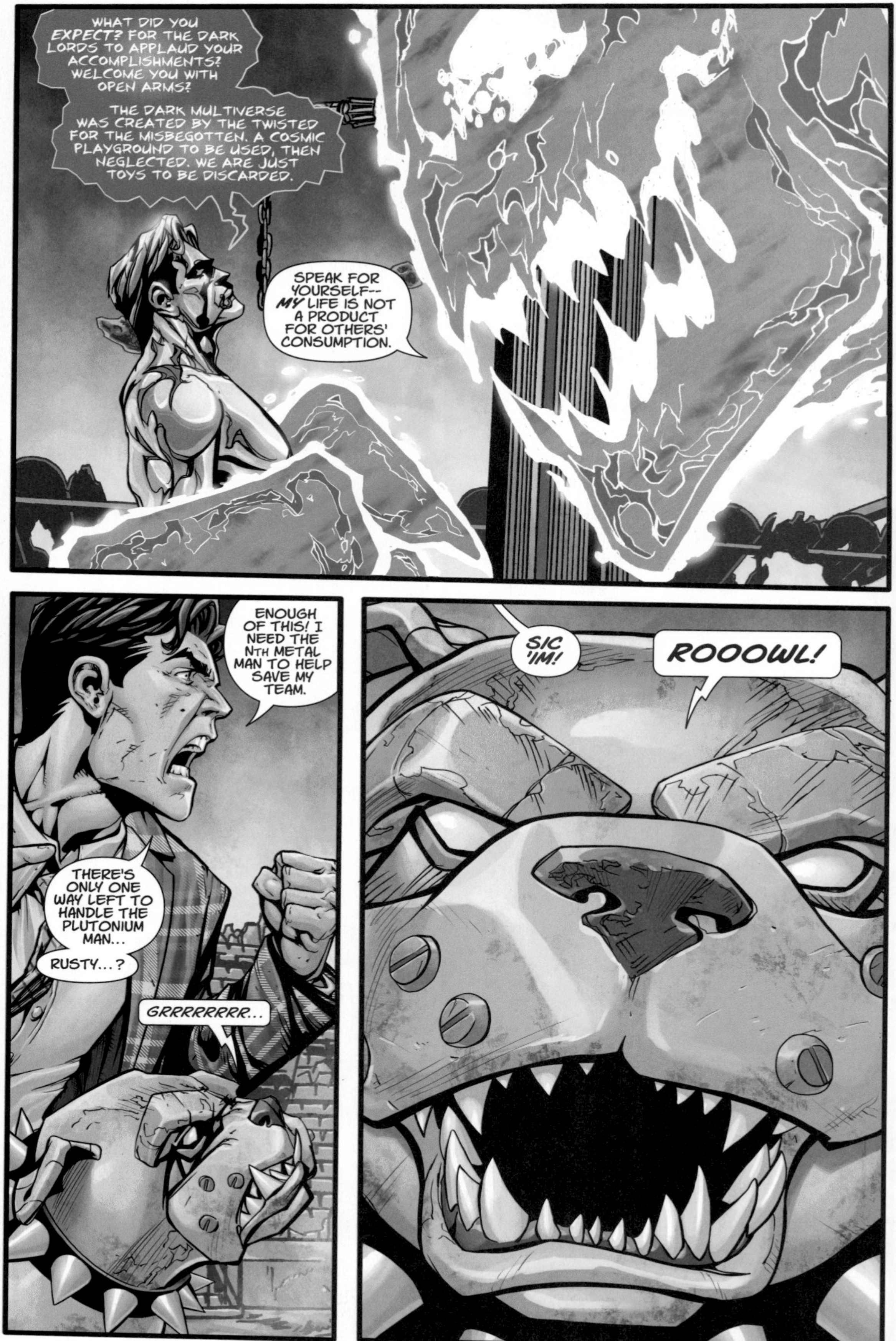
WHAT DID YOU EXPECT? FOR THE DARK LORDS TO APPLAUD YOUR ACCOMPLISHMENTS? WELCOME YOU WITH OPEN ARMS?
THE DARK MULTIVERSE WAS CREATED BY THE TWISTED FOR THE MISBEGOTTEN. A COSMIC PLAYGROUND TO BE USED, THEN NEGLECTED. WE ARE JUST TOYS TO BE DISCARDED.
SPEAK FOR YOURSELF-- MY LIFE IS NOT A PRODUCT FOR OTHERS' CONSUMPTION.
ENOUGH OF THIS! I NEED THE NTH METAL MAN TO HELP SAVE MY TEAM.
THERE'S ONLY ONE WAY LEFT TO HANDLE THE PLUTONIUM MAN...
RUSTY...?
GRRRRRRRR...
SIC 'IM!
ROOOWL!

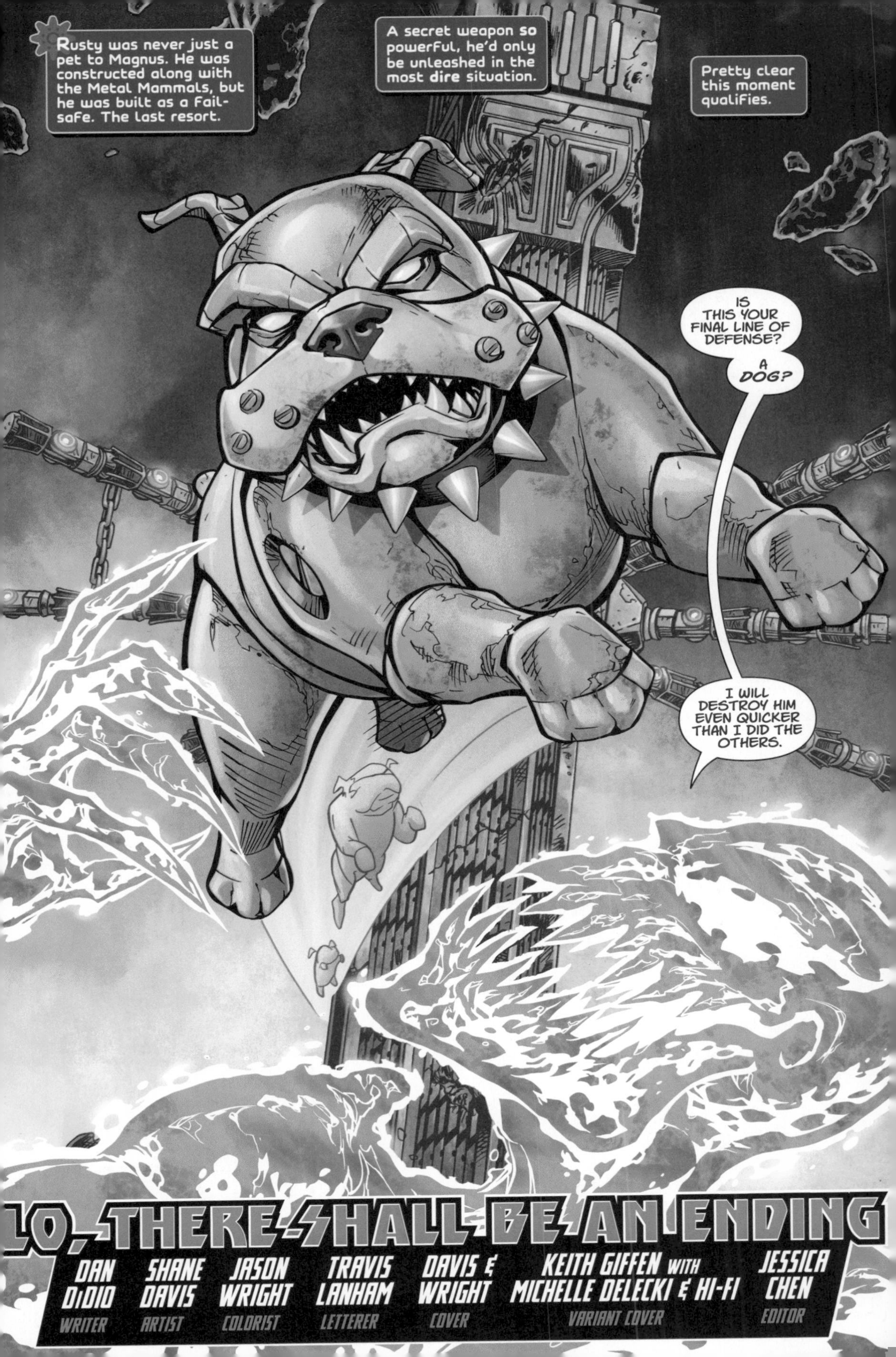
Rusty was never just a pet to Magnus. He was constructed along with the Metal Mammals, but he was built as a fail-safe. The last resort.
A secret weapon so powerful, he'd only be unleashed in the most dire situation.
Pretty clear this moment qualifies.
IS THIS YOUR FINAL LINE OF DEFENSE?
A DOG?
I WILL DESTROY HIM EVEN QUICKER THAN I DID THE OTHERS.
LO, THERE SHALL BE AN ENDING
DAN DIDIO WRITER
SHANE DAVIS ARTIST
JASON WRIGHT COLORIST
TRAVIS LANHAM LETTERER
DAVIS & WRIGHT COVER
KEITH GIFFEN WITH MICHELLE DELECKI & HI-FI VARIANT COVER
JESSICA CHEN EDITOR

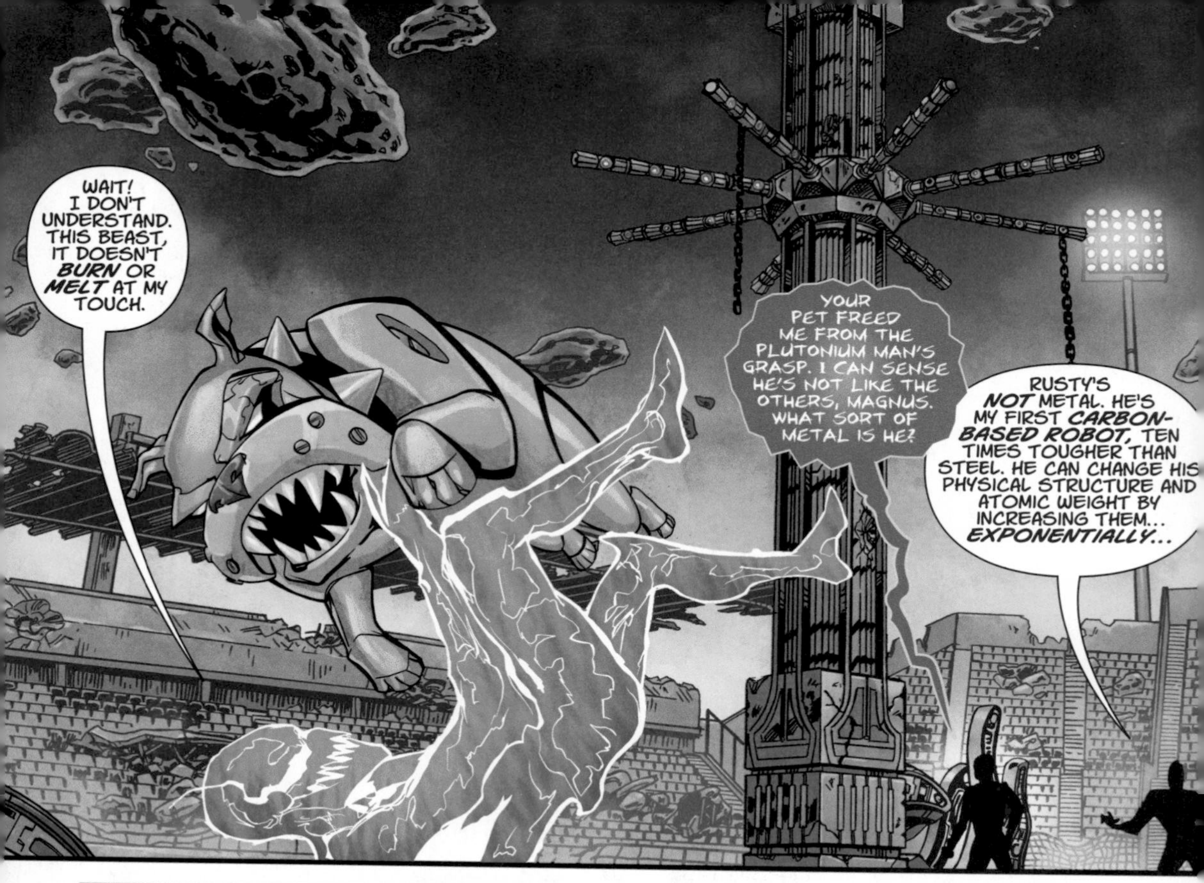

WAIT! I DON'T UNDERSTAND. THIS BEAST, IT DOESN'T **BURN** OR **MELT** AT MY TOUCH.
YOUR PET FREED ME FROM THE PLUTONIUM MAN'S GRASP. I CAN SENSE HE'S NOT LIKE THE OTHERS, MAGNUS. WHAT SORT OF METAL IS HE?
RUSTY'S **NOT** METAL. HE'S MY FIRST **CARBON-BASED ROBOT,** TEN TIMES TOUGHER THAN STEEL. HE CAN CHANGE HIS PHYSICAL STRUCTURE AND ATOMIC WEIGHT BY INCREASING THEM... **EXPONENTIALLY...**

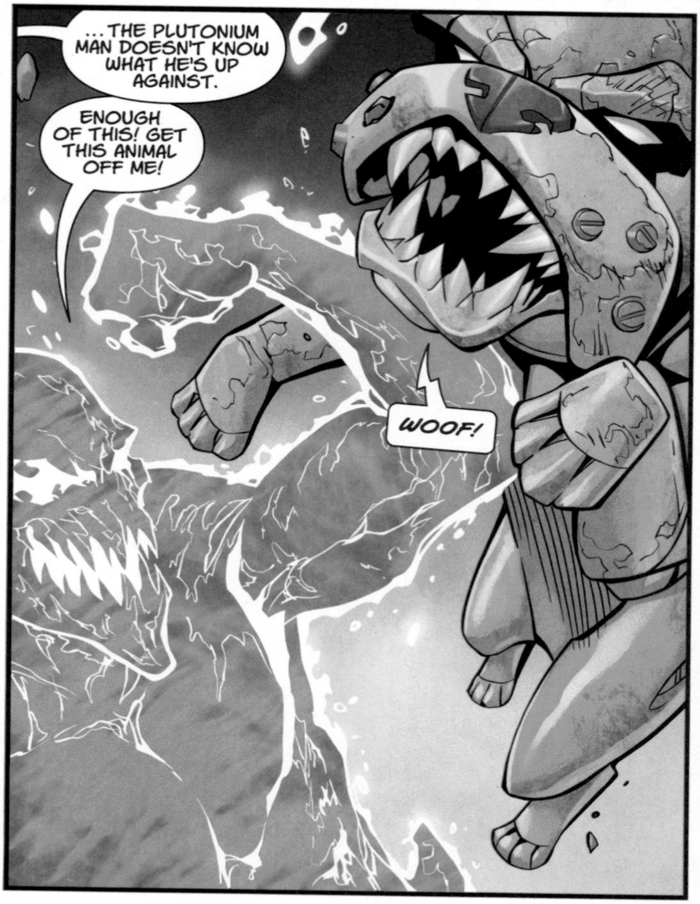

...THE PLUTONIUM MAN DOESN'T KNOW WHAT HE'S UP AGAINST.
ENOUGH OF THIS! GET THIS ANIMAL OFF ME!
WOOF!

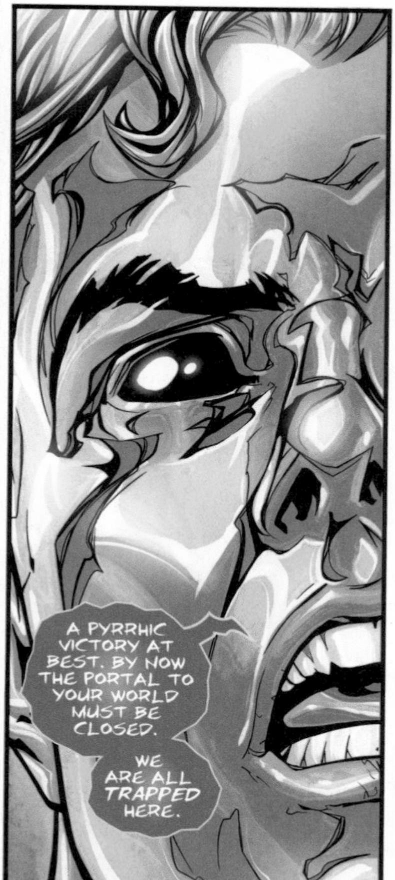

A PYRRHIC VICTORY AT BEST. BY NOW THE PORTAL TO YOUR WORLD MUST BE CLOSED.
WE ARE ALL **TRAPPED** HERE.

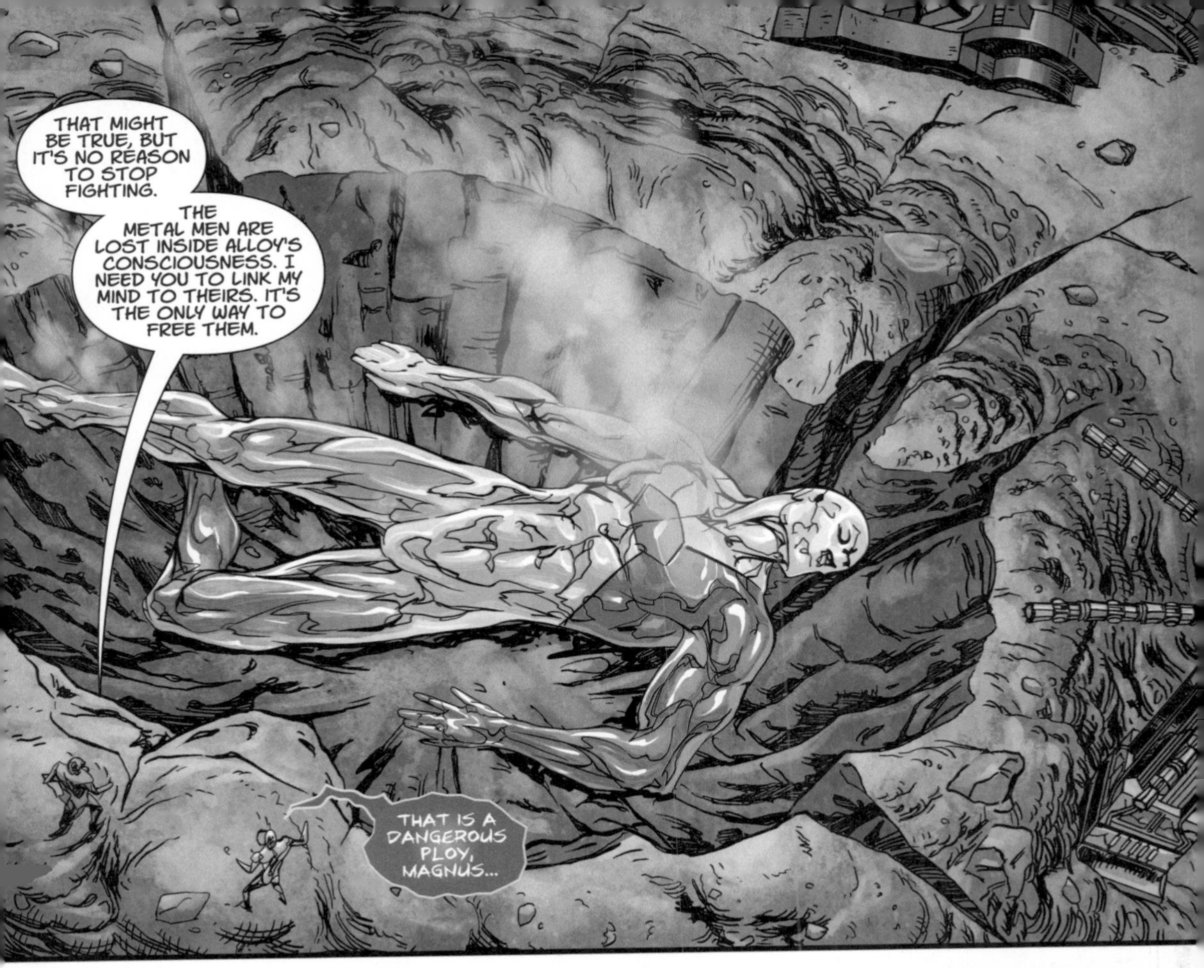
THAT MIGHT BE TRUE, BUT IT'S NO REASON TO STOP FIGHTING.
THE METAL MEN ARE LOST INSIDE ALLOY'S CONSCIOUSNESS. I NEED YOU TO LINK MY MIND TO THEIRS. IT'S THE ONLY WAY TO FREE THEM.
THAT IS A DANGEROUS PLOY, MAGNUS...
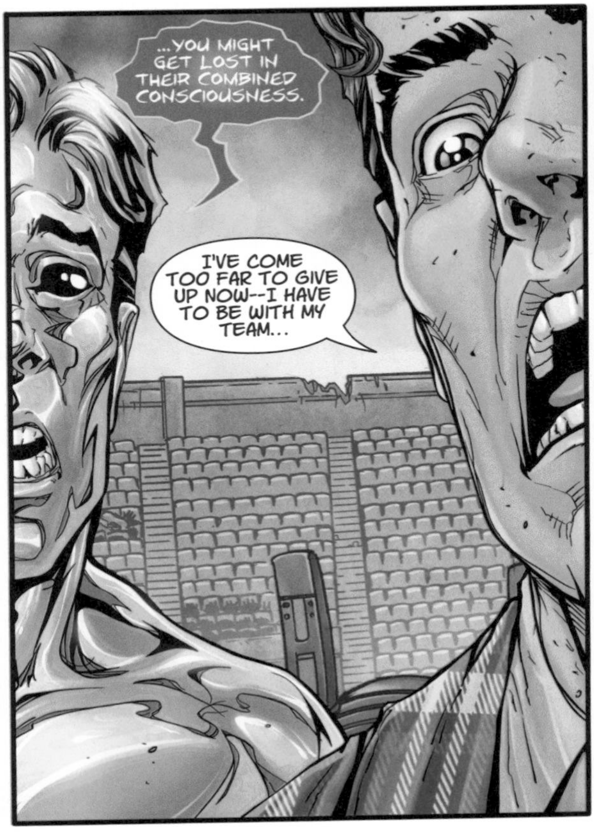
...YOU MIGHT GET LOST IN THEIR COMBINED CONSCIOUSNESS.
I'VE COME TOO FAR TO GIVE UP NOW--I HAVE TO BE WITH MY TEAM...
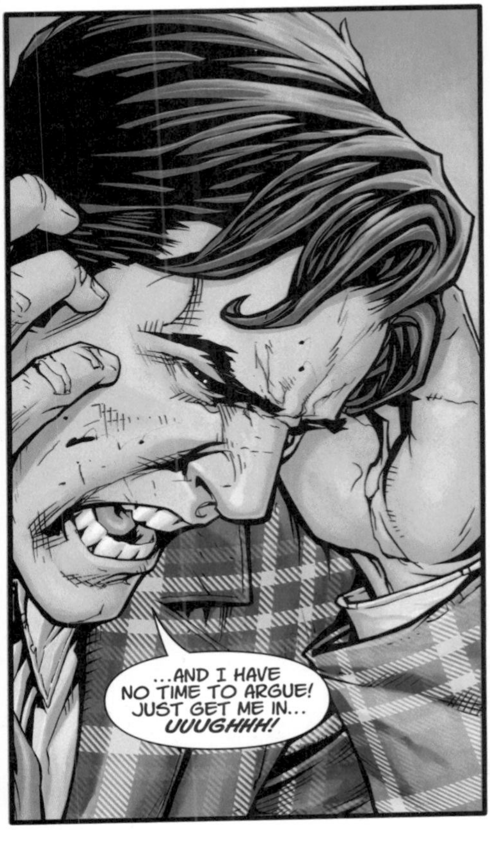
...AND I HAVE NO TIME TO ARGUE! JUST GET ME IN... UUUGHHH!

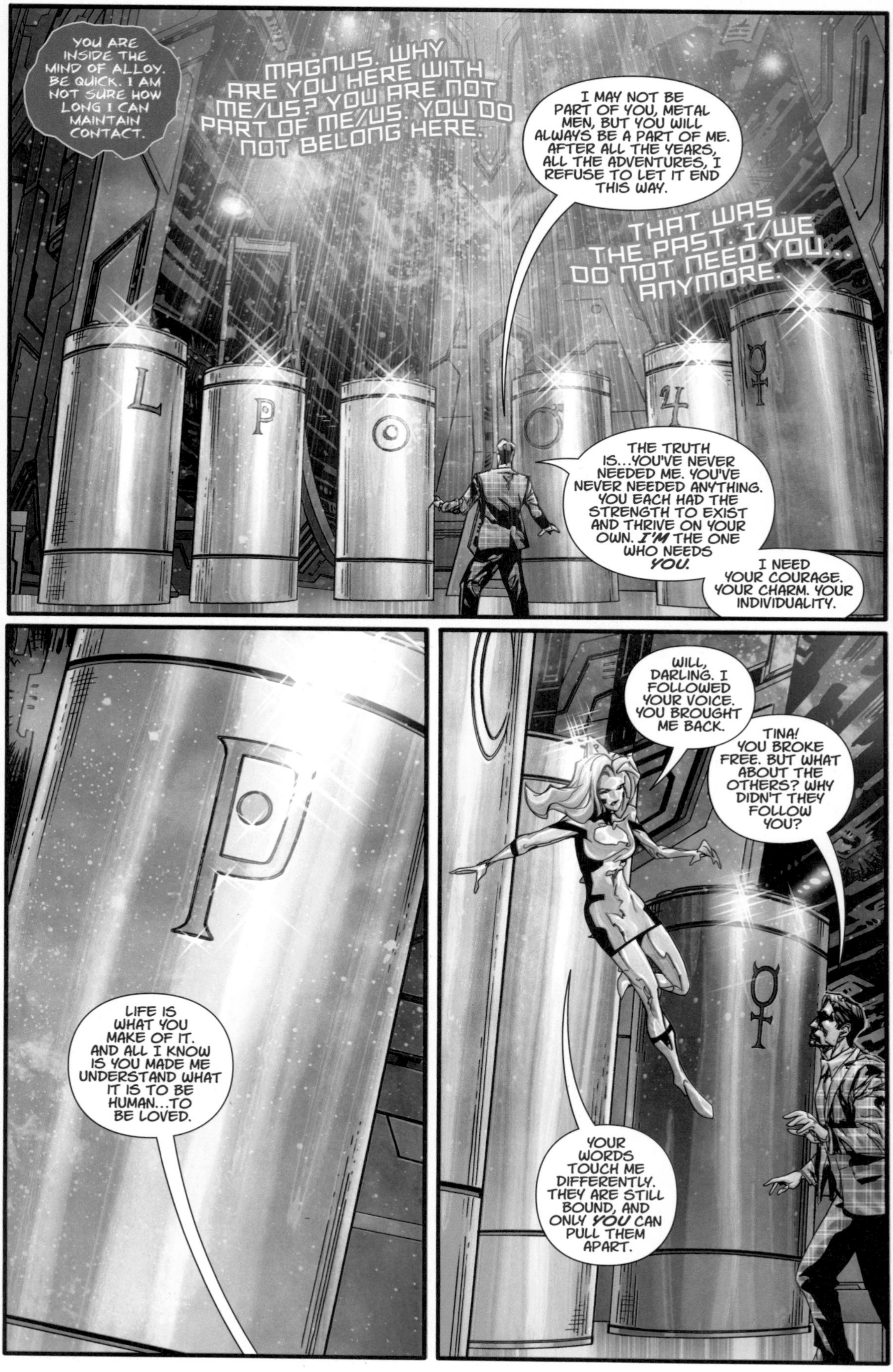
YOU ARE INSIDE THE MIND OF ALLOY. BE QUICK. I AM NOT SURE HOW LONG I CAN MAINTAIN CONTACT.
MAGNUS. WHY ARE YOU HERE WITH ME/US? YOU ARE NOT PART OF ME/US. YOU DO NOT BELONG HERE.
I MAY NOT BE PART OF YOU, METAL MEN, BUT YOU WILL ALWAYS BE A PART OF ME. AFTER ALL THE YEARS, ALL THE ADVENTURES, I REFUSE TO LET IT END THIS WAY.
THAT WAS THE PAST. I/WE DO NOT NEED YOU... ANYMORE.
THE TRUTH IS...YOU'VE NEVER NEEDED ME. YOU'VE NEVER NEEDED ANYTHING. YOU EACH HAD THE STRENGTH TO EXIST AND THRIVE ON YOUR OWN. I'M THE ONE WHO NEEDS YOU.
I NEED YOUR COURAGE. YOUR CHARM. YOUR INDIVIDUALITY.
LIFE IS WHAT YOU MAKE OF IT. AND ALL I KNOW IS YOU MADE ME UNDERSTAND WHAT IT IS TO BE HUMAN...TO BE LOVED.
WILL, DARLING. I FOLLOWED YOUR VOICE. YOU BROUGHT ME BACK.
TINA! YOU BROKE FREE. BUT WHAT ABOUT THE OTHERS? WHY DIDN'T THEY FOLLOW YOU?
YOUR WORDS TOUCH ME DIFFERENTLY. THEY ARE STILL BOUND, AND ONLY YOU CAN PULL THEM APART.

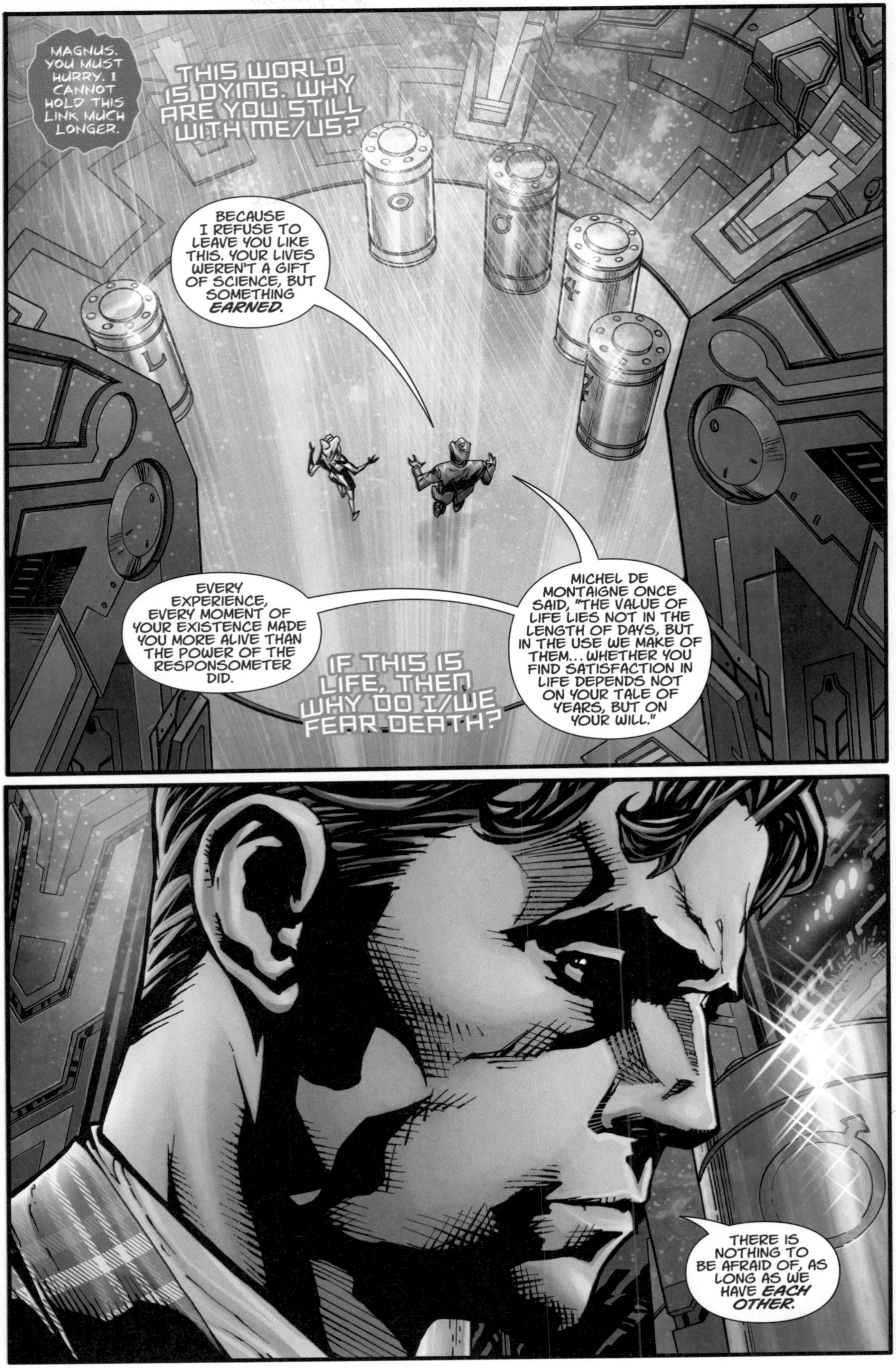
MAGNUS. YOU MUST HURRY. I CANNOT HOLD THIS LINK MUCH LONGER.
THIS WORLD IS DYING. WHY ARE YOU STILL WITH ME/US?
BECAUSE I REFUSE TO LEAVE YOU LIKE THIS. YOUR LIVES WEREN'T A GIFT OF SCIENCE, BUT SOMETHING *EARNED*.
MICHEL DE MONTAIGNE ONCE SAID, "THE VALUE OF LIFE LIES NOT IN THE LENGTH OF DAYS, BUT IN THE USE WE MAKE OF THEM... WHETHER YOU FIND SATISFACTION IN LIFE DEPENDS NOT ON YOUR TALE OF YEARS, BUT ON YOUR WILL."
EVERY EXPERIENCE, EVERY MOMENT OF YOUR EXISTENCE MADE YOU MORE ALIVE THAN THE POWER OF THE RESPONSOMETER DID.
IF THIS IS LIFE, THEN WHY DO I/WE FEAR DEATH?
THERE IS NOTHING TO BE AFRAID OF, AS LONG AS WE HAVE *EACH OTHER*.

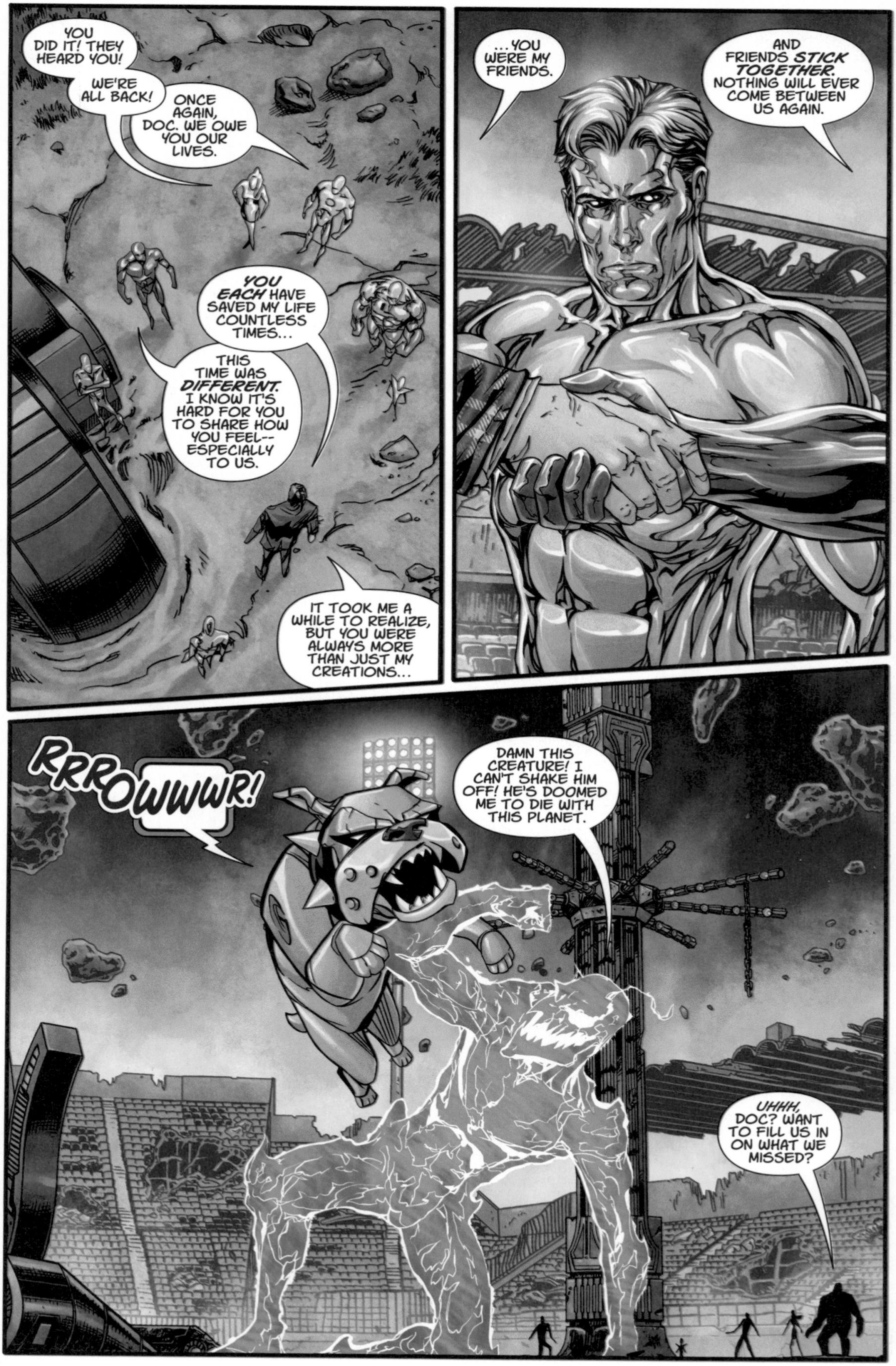
YOU DID IT! THEY HEARD YOU!
WE'RE ALL BACK!
ONCE AGAIN, DOC. WE OWE YOU OUR LIVES.
YOU EACH HAVE SAVED MY LIFE COUNTLESS TIMES...
THIS TIME WAS DIFFERENT. I KNOW IT'S HARD FOR YOU TO SHARE HOW YOU FEEL--ESPECIALLY TO US.
IT TOOK ME A WHILE TO REALIZE, BUT YOU WERE ALWAYS MORE THAN JUST MY CREATIONS...
...YOU WERE MY FRIENDS.
AND FRIENDS STICK TOGETHER. NOTHING WILL EVER COME BETWEEN US AGAIN.
RRROWWWR!
DAMN THIS CREATURE! I CAN'T SHAKE HIM OFF! HE'S DOOMED ME TO DIE WITH THIS PLANET.
UHHH, DOC? WANT TO FILL US IN ON WHAT WE MISSED?

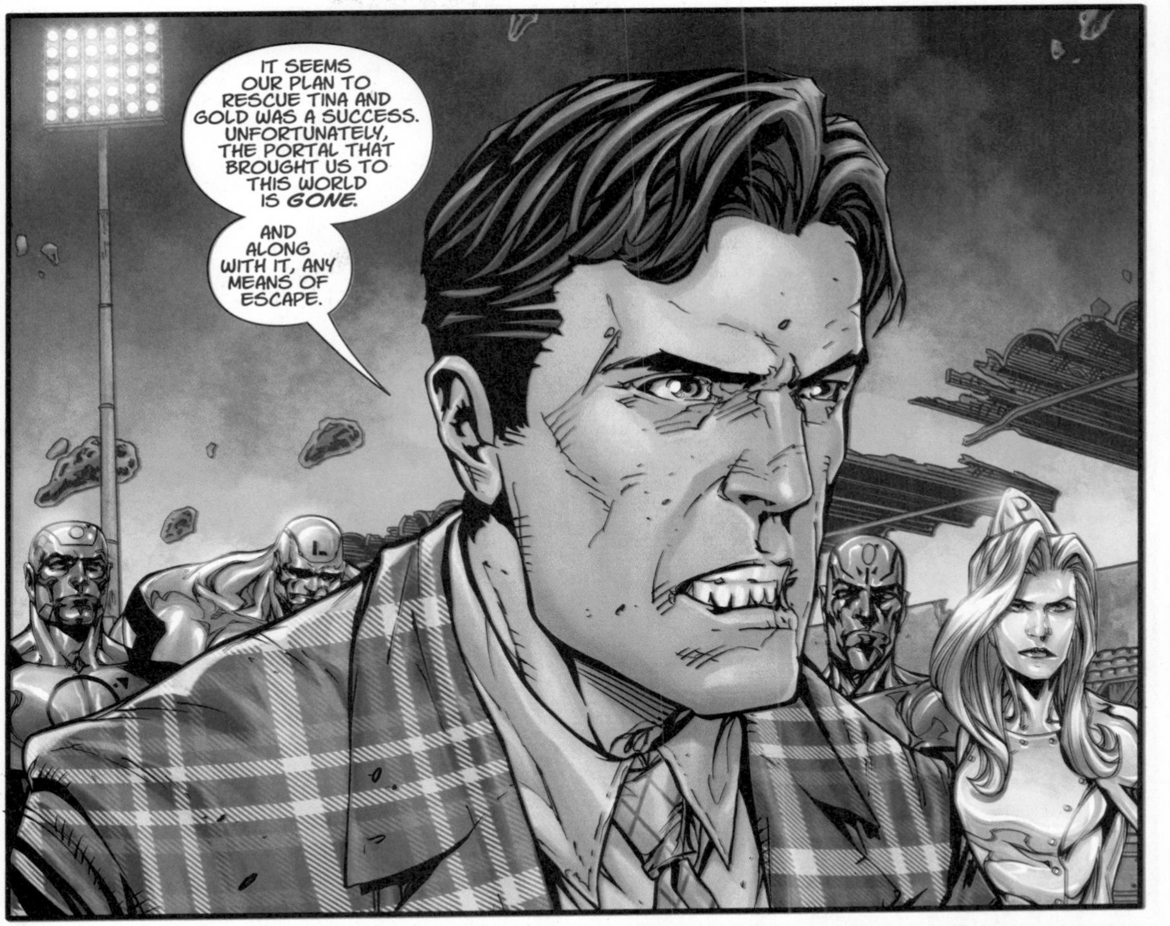
IT SEEMS OUR PLAN TO RESCUE TINA AND GOLD WAS A SUCCESS. UNFORTUNATELY, THE PORTAL THAT BROUGHT US TO THIS WORLD IS *GONE*.
AND ALONG WITH IT, ANY MEANS OF ESCAPE.

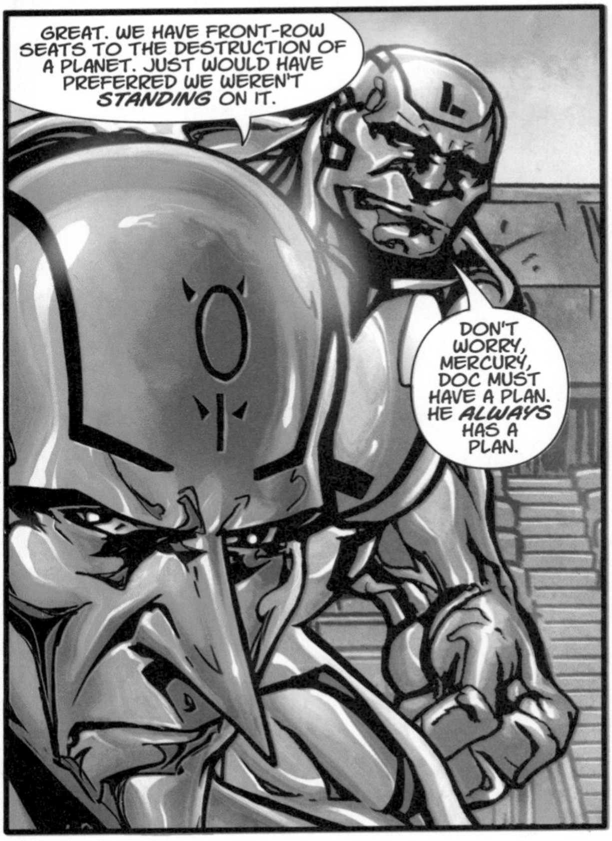
GREAT. WE HAVE FRONT-ROW SEATS TO THE DESTRUCTION OF A PLANET. JUST WOULD HAVE PREFERRED WE WEREN'T *STANDING* ON IT.
DON'T WORRY, MERCURY, DOC MUST HAVE A PLAN. HE *ALWAYS* HAS A PLAN.

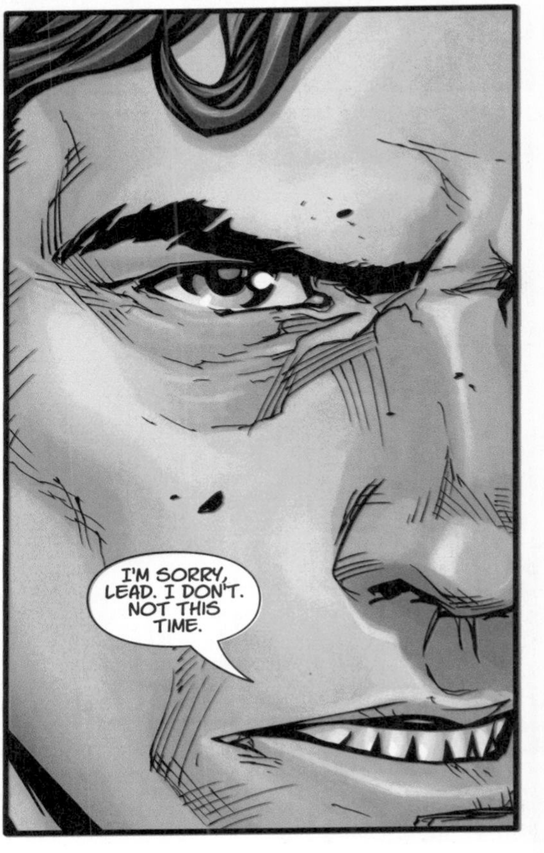
I'M SORRY, LEAD. I DON'T. NOT THIS TIME.

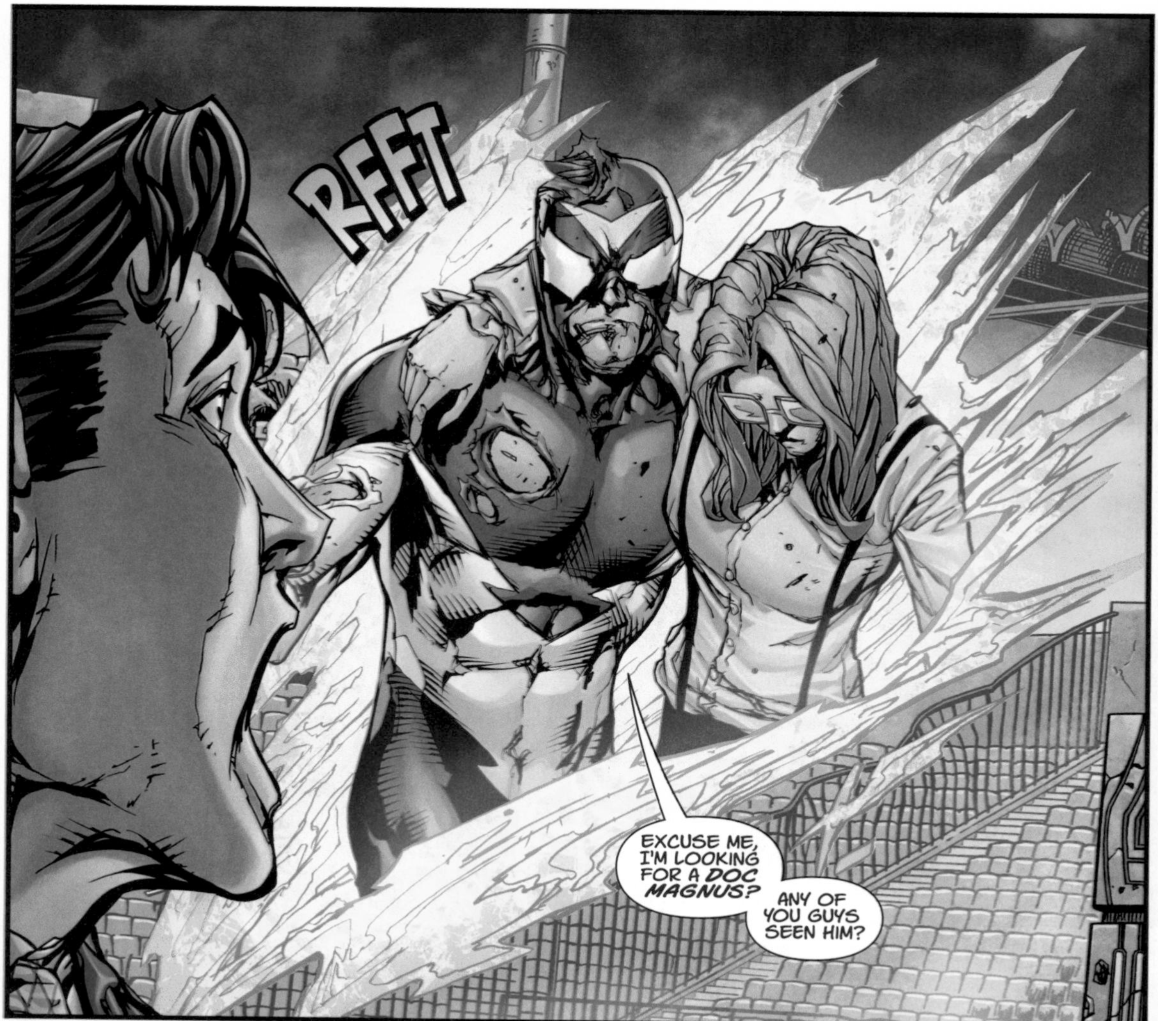
RFFT
EXCUSE ME, I'M LOOKING FOR A DOC MAGNUS?
ANY OF YOU GUYS SEEN HIM?

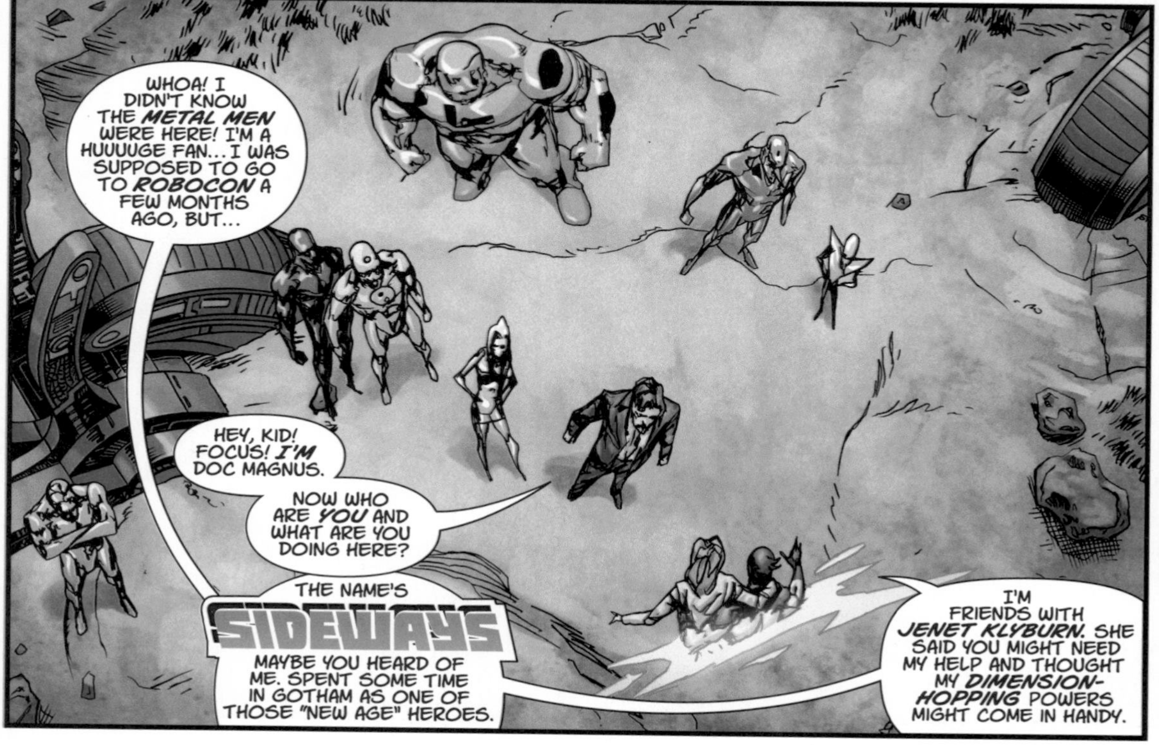
WHOA! I DIDN'T KNOW THE METAL MEN WERE HERE! I'M A HUUUUGE FAN... I WAS SUPPOSED TO GO TO ROBOCON A FEW MONTHS AGO, BUT...
HEY, KID! FOCUS! I'M DOC MAGNUS.
NOW WHO ARE YOU AND WHAT ARE YOU DOING HERE?
THE NAME'S SIDEWAYS MAYBE YOU HEARD OF ME. SPENT SOME TIME IN GOTHAM AS ONE OF THOSE "NEW AGE" HEROES.
I'M FRIENDS WITH JENET KLYBURN. SHE SAID YOU MIGHT NEED MY HELP AND THOUGHT MY DIMENSION-HOPPING POWERS MIGHT COME IN HANDY.

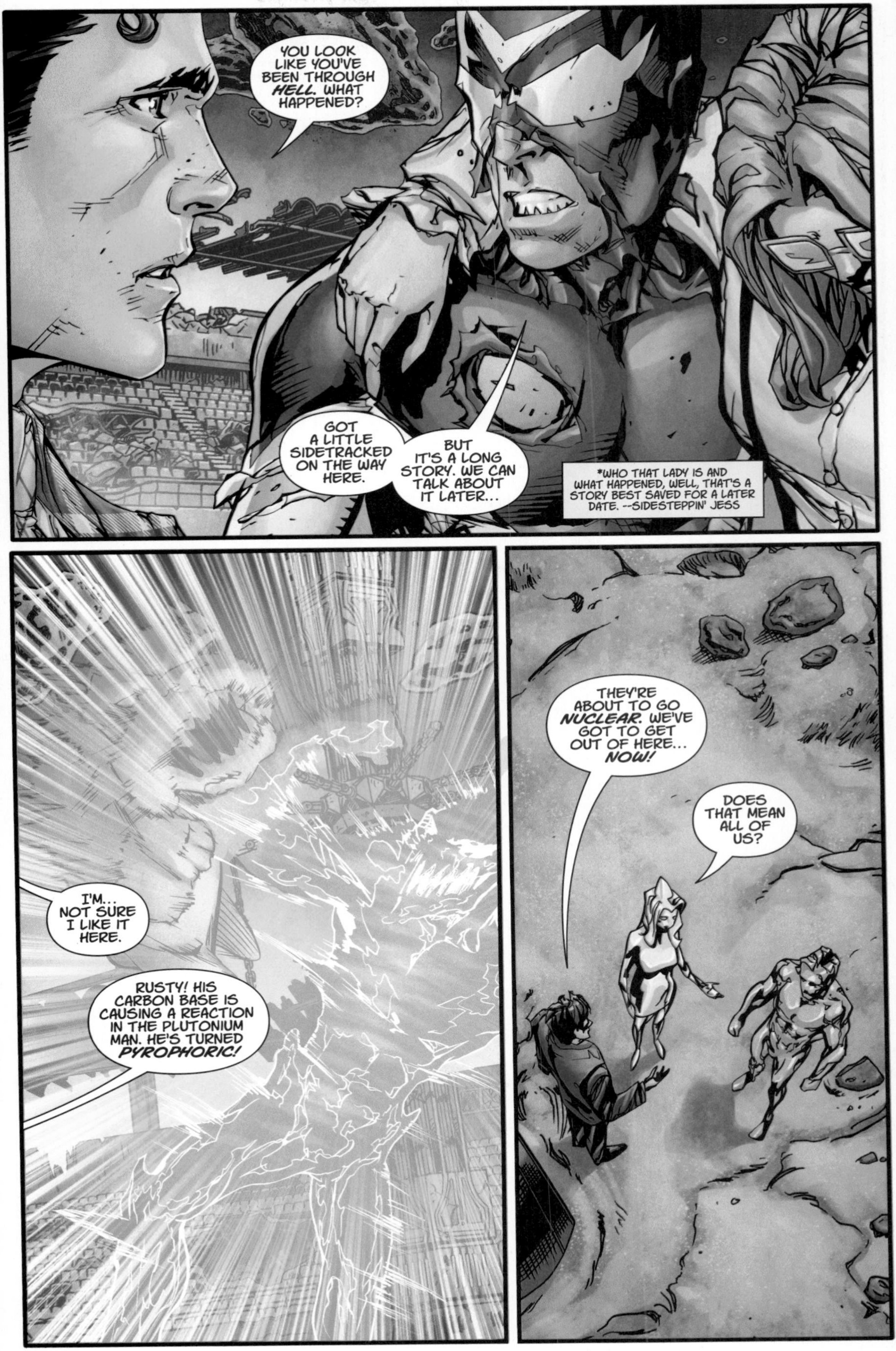
YOU LOOK LIKE YOU'VE BEEN THROUGH HELL. WHAT HAPPENED?
GOT A LITTLE SIDETRACKED ON THE WAY HERE.
BUT IT'S A LONG STORY. WE CAN TALK ABOUT IT LATER...
*WHO THAT LADY IS AND WHAT HAPPENED, WELL, THAT'S A STORY BEST SAVED FOR A LATER DATE. --SIDESTEPPIN' JESS
I'M... NOT SURE I LIKE IT HERE.
RUSTY! HIS CARBON BASE IS CAUSING A REACTION IN THE PLUTONIUM MAN. HE'S TURNED PYROPHORIC!
THEY'RE ABOUT TO GO NUCLEAR. WE'VE GOT TO GET OUT OF HERE... NOW!
DOES THAT MEAN ALL OF US?

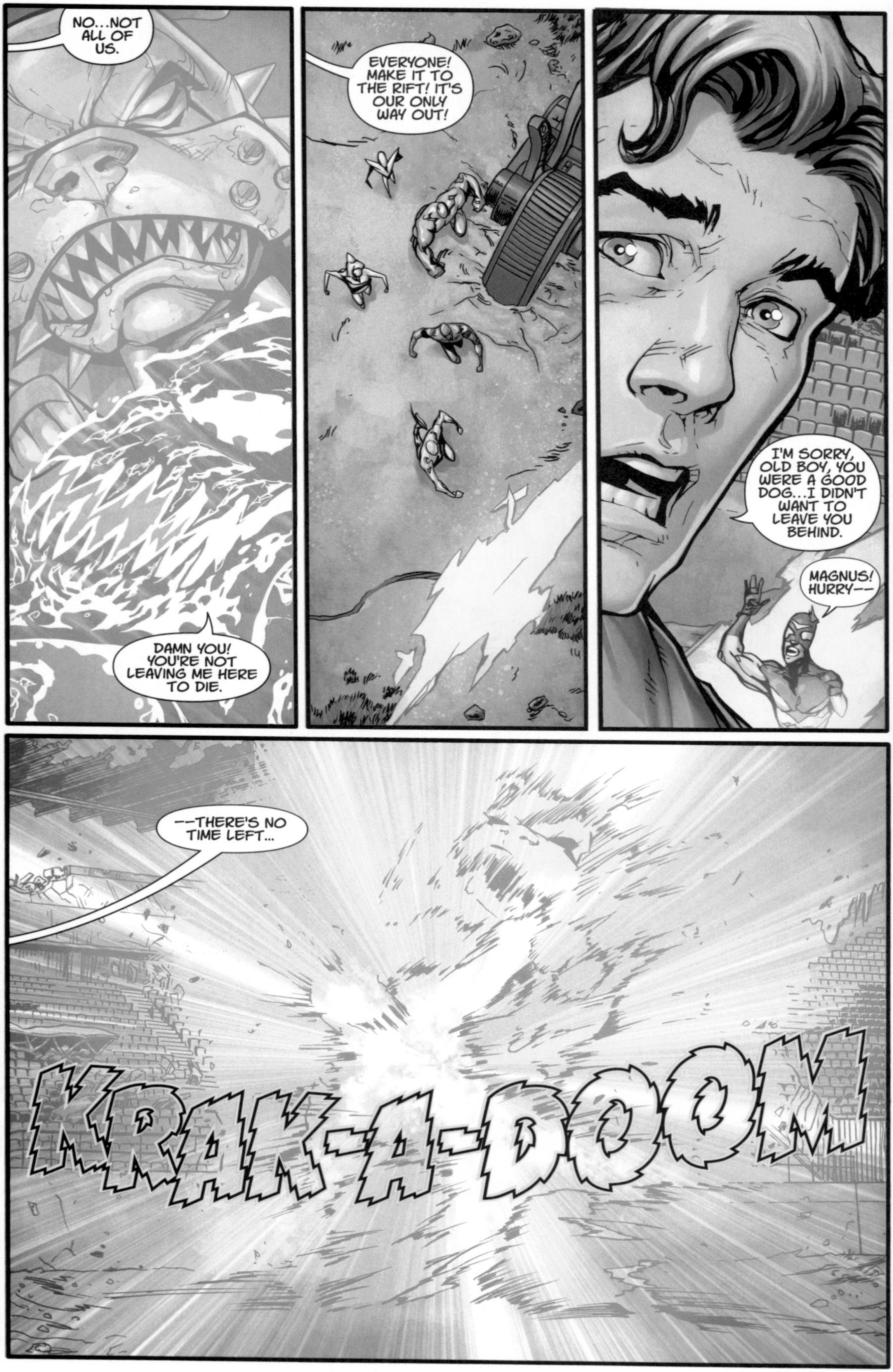
NO...NOT ALL OF US.
DAMN YOU! YOU'RE NOT LEAVING ME HERE TO DIE.
EVERYONE! MAKE IT TO THE RIFT! IT'S OUR ONLY WAY OUT!
I'M SORRY, OLD BOY, YOU WERE A GOOD DOG...I DIDN'T WANT TO LEAVE YOU BEHIND.
MAGNUS! HURRY--
--THERE'S NO TIME LEFT...
KRAK-A-DOOM

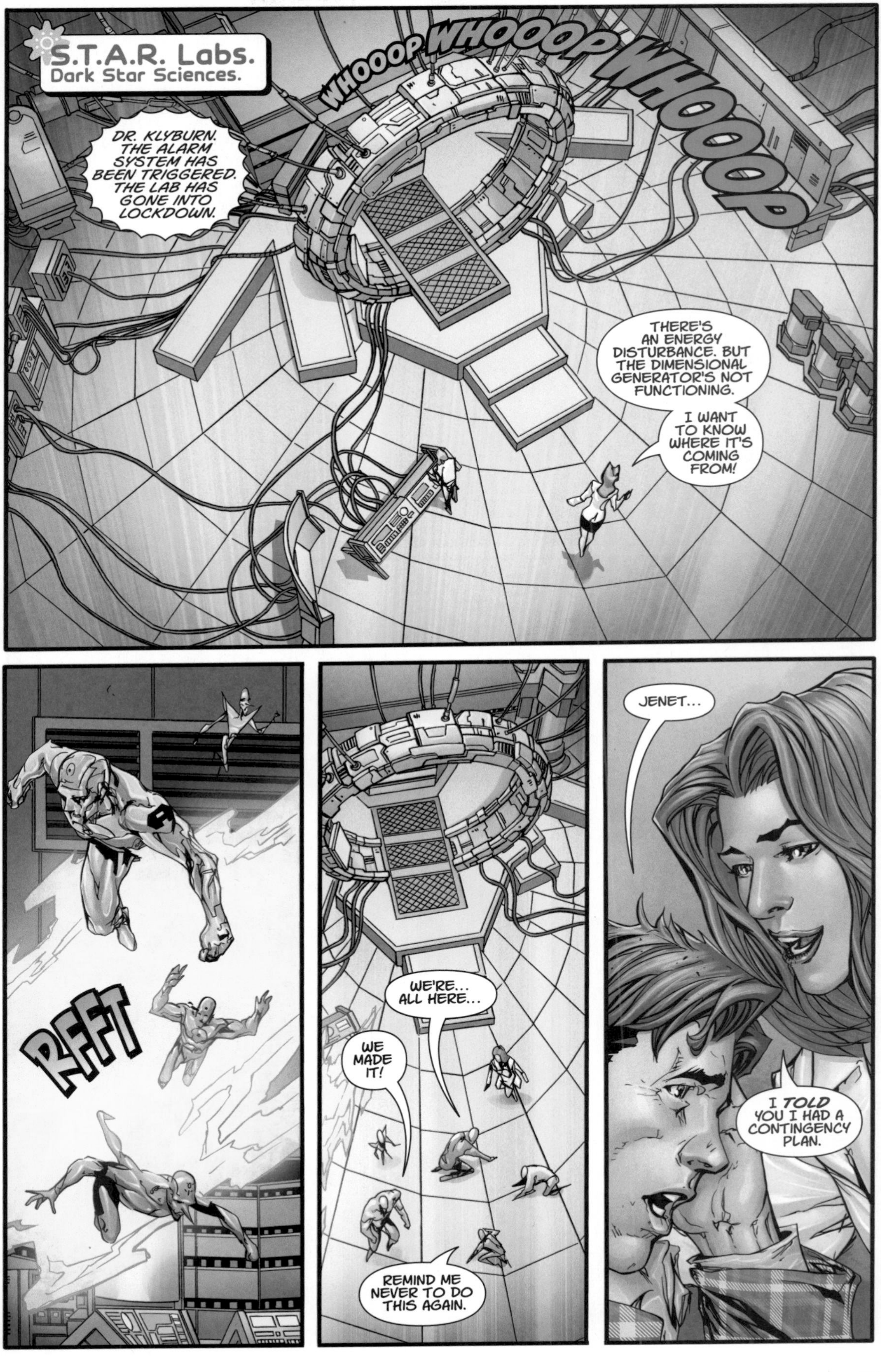
S.T.A.R. Labs.
Dark Star Sciences.
WHOOOP WHOOOP WHOOOP
DR. KLYBURN. THE ALARM SYSTEM HAS BEEN TRIGGERED. THE LAB HAS GONE INTO LOCKDOWN.
THERE'S AN ENERGY DISTURBANCE. BUT THE DIMENSIONAL GENERATOR'S NOT FUNCTIONING.
I WANT TO KNOW WHERE IT'S COMING FROM!
RFFT
WE'RE... ALL HERE...
WE MADE IT!
REMIND ME NEVER TO DO THIS AGAIN.
JENET...
I TOLD YOU I HAD A CONTINGENCY PLAN.

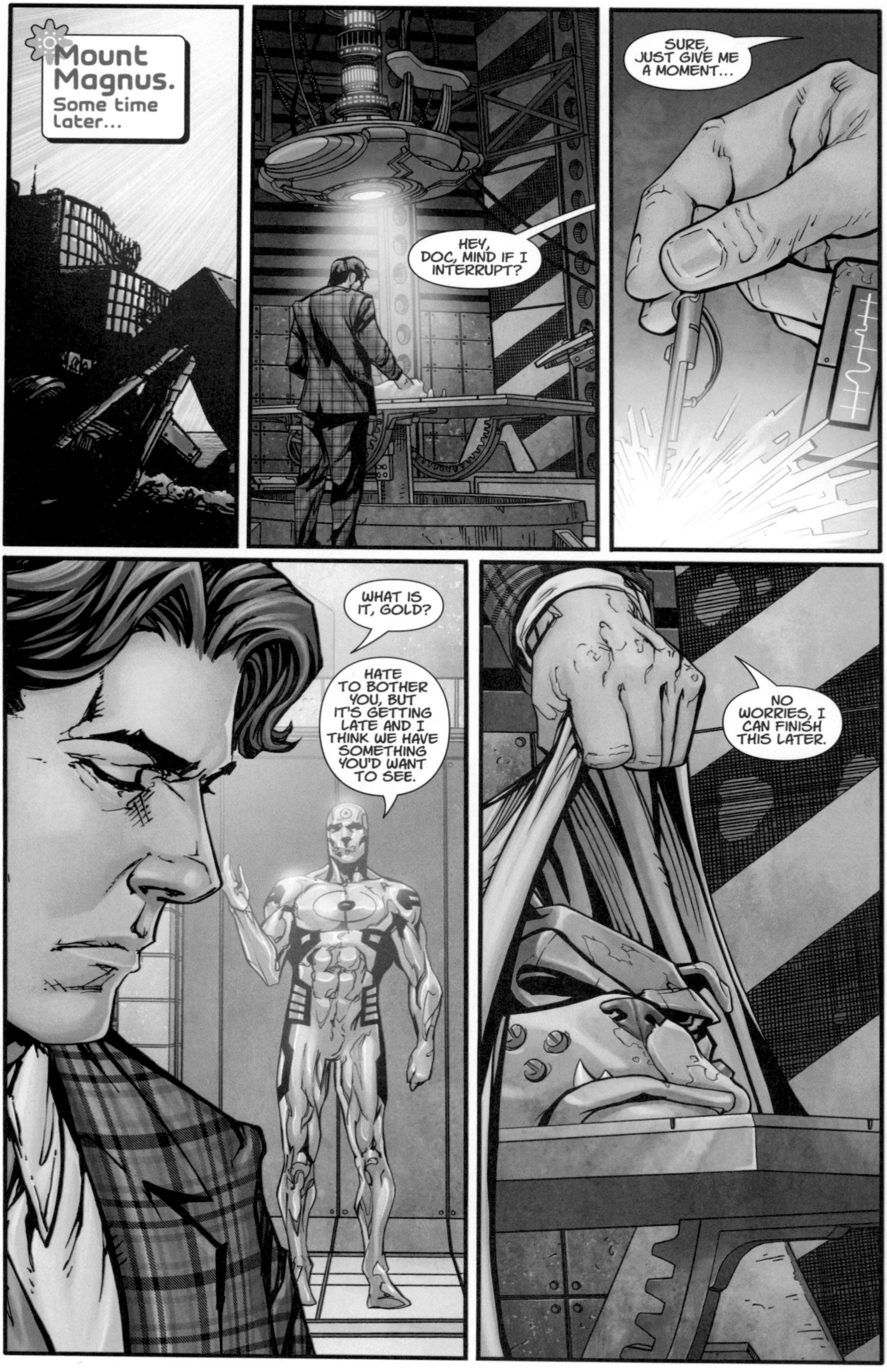
Mount Magnus. Some time later...
HEY, DOC, MIND IF I INTERRUPT?
SURE, JUST GIVE ME A MOMENT...
WHAT IS IT, GOLD?
HATE TO BOTHER YOU, BUT IT'S GETTING LATE AND I THINK WE HAVE SOMETHING YOU'D WANT TO SEE.
NO WORRIES, I CAN FINISH THIS LATER.

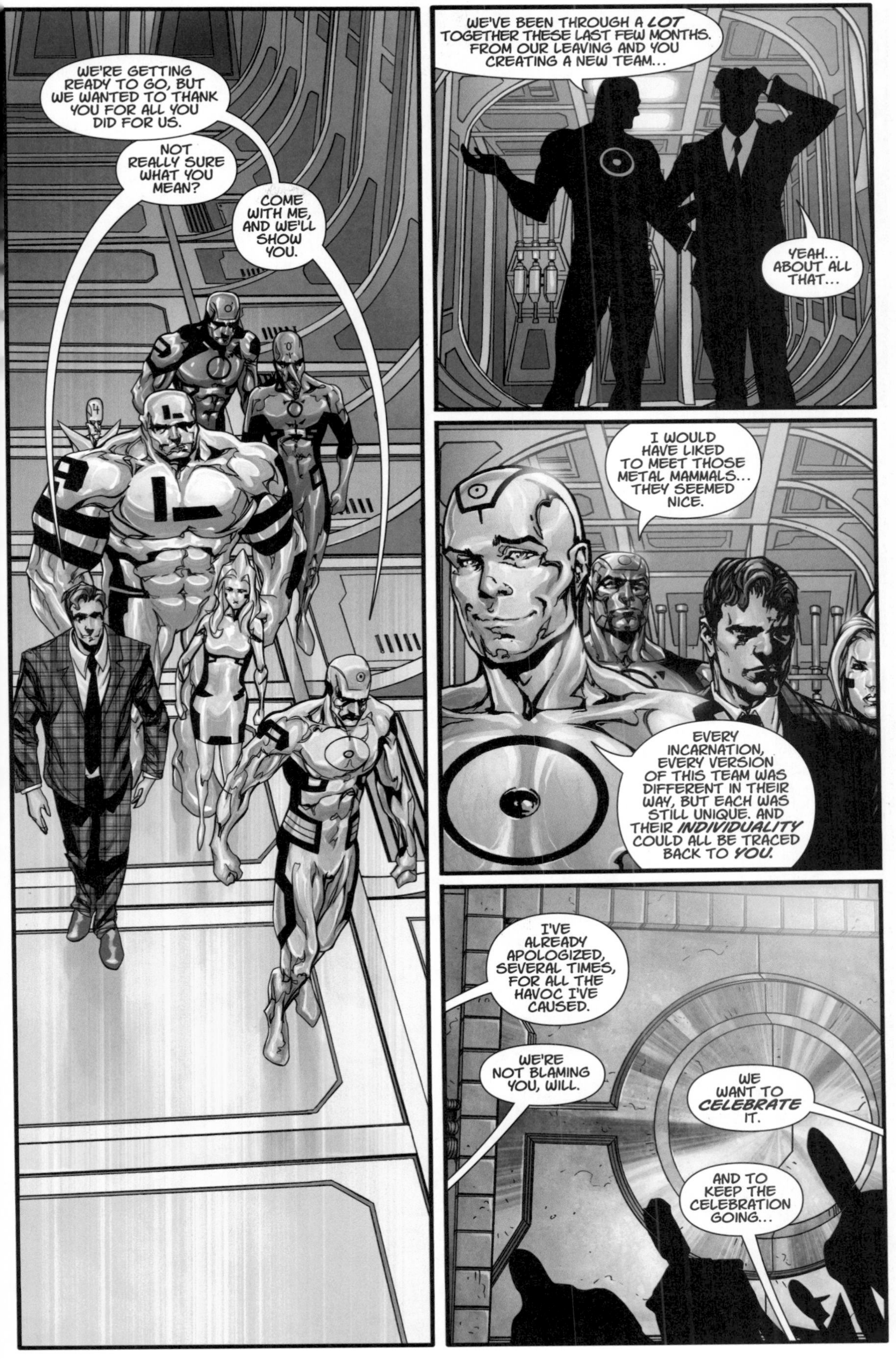
WE'RE GETTING READY TO GO, BUT WE WANTED TO THANK YOU FOR ALL YOU DID FOR US.
NOT REALLY SURE WHAT YOU MEAN?
COME WITH ME, AND WE'LL SHOW YOU.
WE'VE BEEN THROUGH A LOT TOGETHER THESE LAST FEW MONTHS. FROM OUR LEAVING AND YOU CREATING A NEW TEAM...
YEAH... ABOUT ALL THAT...
I WOULD HAVE LIKED TO MEET THOSE METAL MAMMALS... THEY SEEMED NICE.
EVERY INCARNATION, EVERY VERSION OF THIS TEAM WAS DIFFERENT IN THEIR WAY, BUT EACH WAS STILL UNIQUE. AND THEIR INDIVIDUALITY COULD ALL BE TRACED BACK TO YOU.
I'VE ALREADY APOLOGIZED, SEVERAL TIMES, FOR ALL THE HAVOC I'VE CAUSED.
WE'RE NOT BLAMING YOU, WILL.
WE WANT TO CELEBRATE IT.
AND TO KEEP THE CELEBRATION GOING...

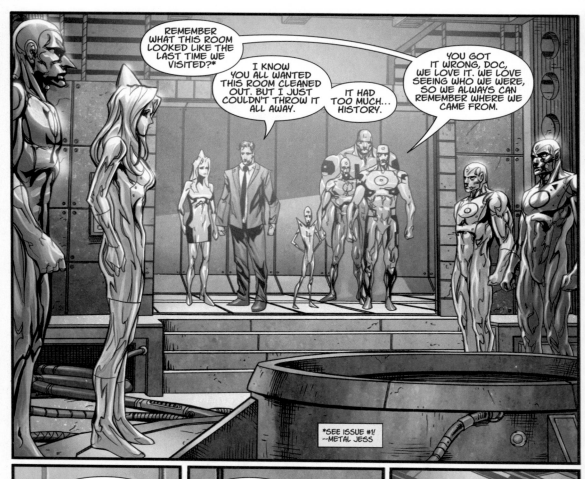

REMEMBER WHAT THIS ROOM LOOKED LIKE THE LAST TIME WE VISITED?*

I KNOW YOU ALL WANTED THIS ROOM CLEANED OUT. BUT I JUST COULDN'T THROW IT ALL AWAY.

IT HAD TOO MUCH... HISTORY.

YOU GOT IT WRONG, DOC, WE LOVE IT. WE LOVE SEEING WHO WE WERE, SO WE ALWAYS CAN REMEMBER WHERE WE CAME FROM.

*SEE ISSUE #1! --METAL JESS

THAT'S WHY WE HELPED CLEAN IT UP.

I...I DON'T KNOW WHAT TO SAY.

IT'S *OUR* TIME TO DO THE TALKING. WE JUST WANTED TO SAY THANK YOU...FOR EVERYTHING.

HOW ABOUT WE BUY YOU A BEER?

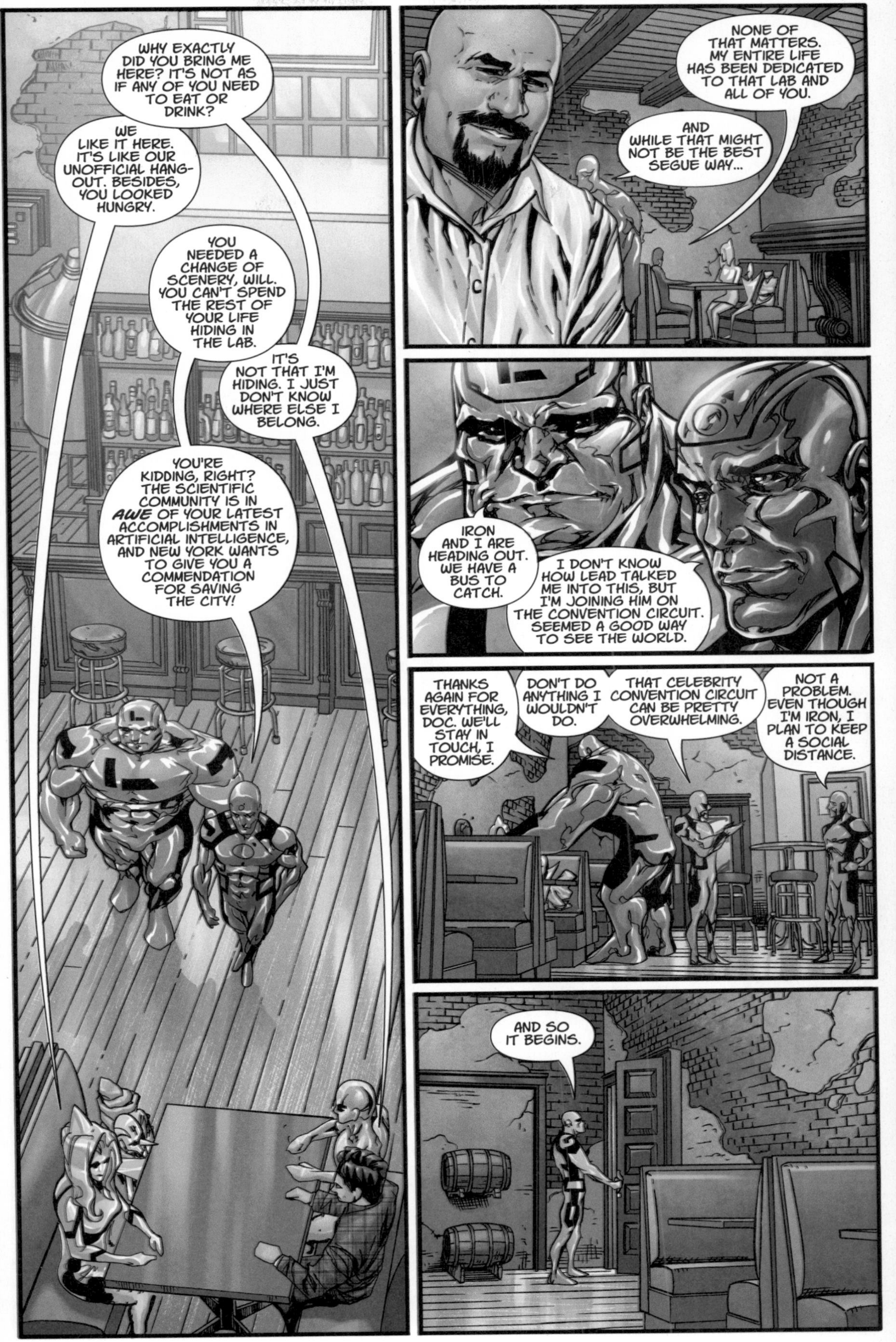
WHY EXACTLY DID YOU BRING ME HERE? IT'S NOT AS IF ANY OF YOU NEED TO EAT OR DRINK?
WE LIKE IT HERE. IT'S LIKE OUR UNOFFICIAL HANG-OUT. BESIDES, YOU LOOKED HUNGRY.
YOU NEEDED A CHANGE OF SCENERY, WILL. YOU CAN'T SPEND THE REST OF YOUR LIFE HIDING IN THE LAB.
IT'S NOT THAT I'M HIDING. I JUST DON'T KNOW WHERE ELSE I BELONG.
YOU'RE KIDDING, RIGHT? THE SCIENTIFIC COMMUNITY IS IN AWE OF YOUR LATEST ACCOMPLISHMENTS IN ARTIFICIAL INTELLIGENCE, AND NEW YORK WANTS TO GIVE YOU A COMMENDATION FOR SAVING THE CITY!
NONE OF THAT MATTERS. MY ENTIRE LIFE HAS BEEN DEDICATED TO THAT LAB AND ALL OF YOU.
AND WHILE THAT MIGHT NOT BE THE BEST SEGUE WAY...
IRON AND I ARE HEADING OUT. WE HAVE A BUS TO CATCH.
I DON'T KNOW HOW LEAD TALKED ME INTO THIS, BUT I'M JOINING HIM ON THE CONVENTION CIRCUIT. SEEMED A GOOD WAY TO SEE THE WORLD.
THANKS AGAIN FOR EVERYTHING, DOC. WE'LL STAY IN TOUCH, I PROMISE.
DON'T DO ANYTHING I WOULDN'T DO.
THAT CELEBRITY CONVENTION CIRCUIT CAN BE PRETTY OVERWHELMING.
NOT A PROBLEM. EVEN THOUGH I'M IRON, I PLAN TO KEEP A SOCIAL DISTANCE.
AND SO IT BEGINS.

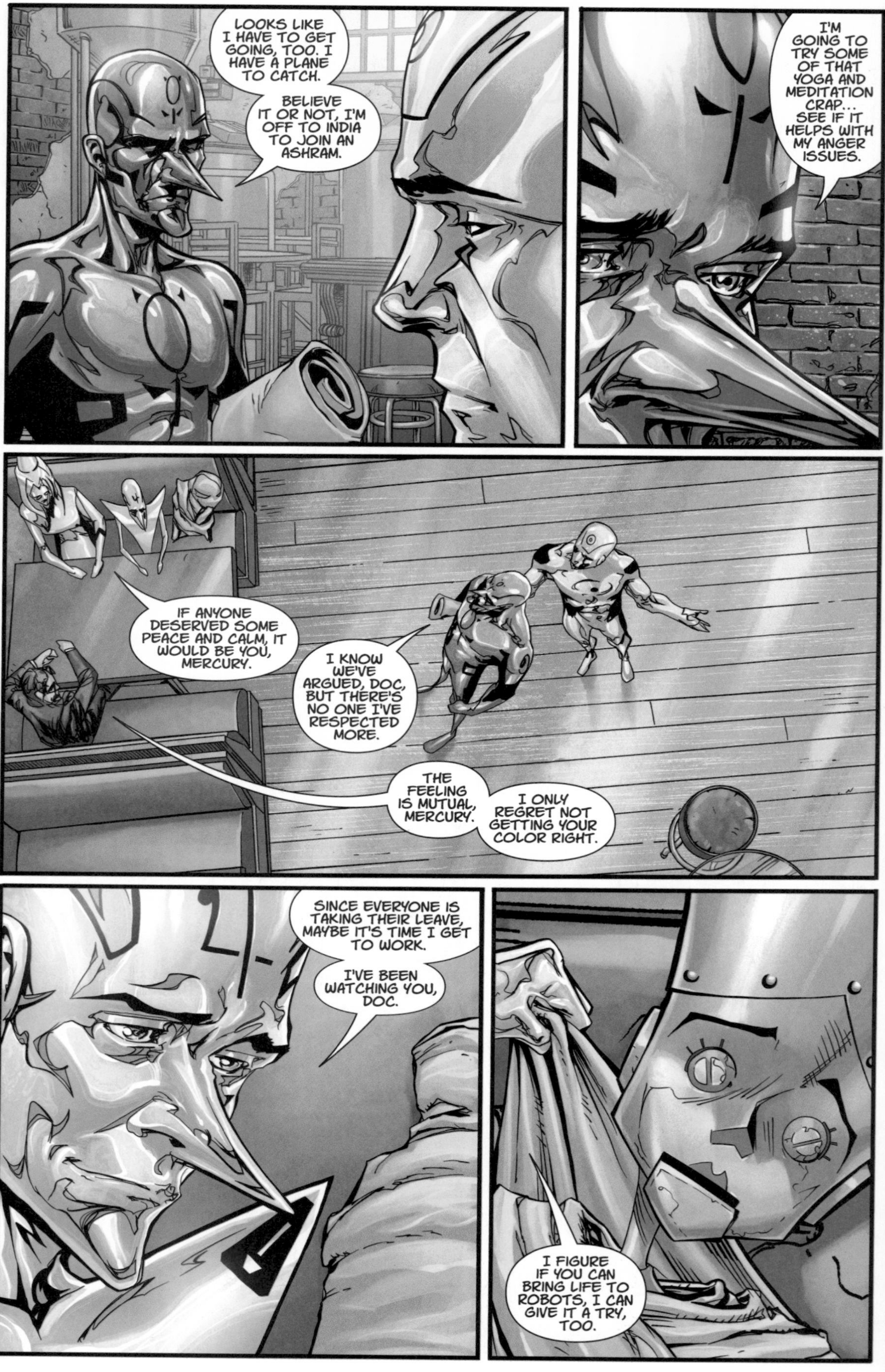
LOOKS LIKE I HAVE TO GET GOING, TOO. I HAVE A PLANE TO CATCH.
BELIEVE IT OR NOT, I'M OFF TO INDIA TO JOIN AN ASHRAM.
I'M GOING TO TRY SOME OF THAT YOGA AND MEDITATION CRAP... SEE IF IT HELPS WITH MY ANGER ISSUES.
IF ANYONE DESERVED SOME PEACE AND CALM, IT WOULD BE YOU, MERCURY.
I KNOW WE'VE ARGUED, DOC, BUT THERE'S NO ONE I'VE RESPECTED MORE.
THE FEELING IS MUTUAL, MERCURY.
I ONLY REGRET NOT GETTING YOUR COLOR RIGHT.
SINCE EVERYONE IS TAKING THEIR LEAVE, MAYBE IT'S TIME I GET TO WORK.
I'VE BEEN WATCHING YOU, DOC.
I FIGURE IF YOU CAN BRING LIFE TO ROBOTS, I CAN GIVE IT A TRY, TOO.

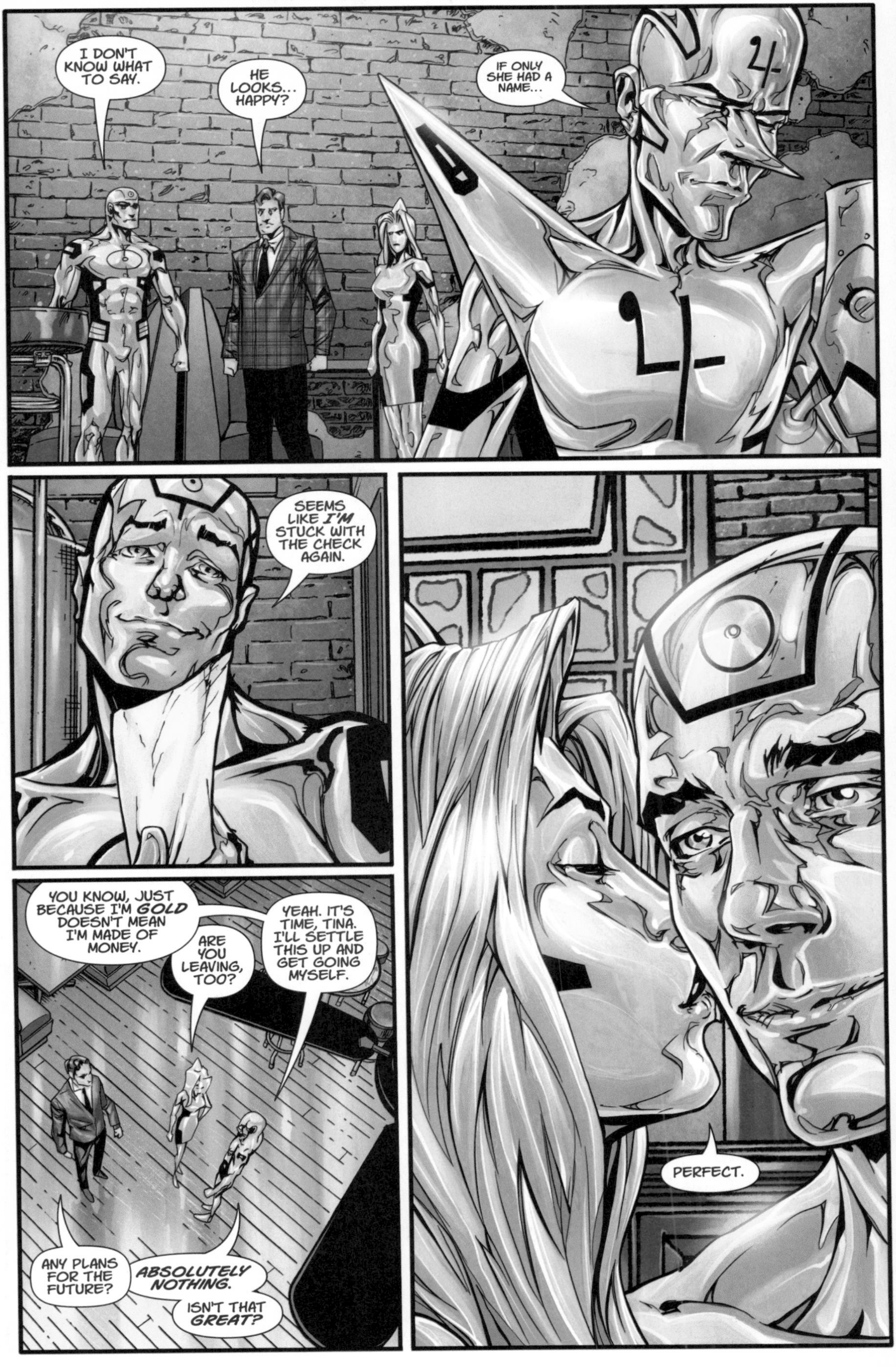
I DON'T KNOW WHAT TO SAY.
HE LOOKS... HAPPY?
IF ONLY SHE HAD A NAME...
SEEMS LIKE *I'M* STUCK WITH THE CHECK AGAIN.
YOU KNOW, JUST BECAUSE I'M **GOLD** DOESN'T MEAN I'M MADE OF MONEY.
ARE YOU LEAVING, TOO?
YEAH. IT'S TIME, TINA. I'LL SETTLE THIS UP AND GET GOING MYSELF.
ANY PLANS FOR THE FUTURE?
ABSOLUTELY NOTHING.
ISN'T THAT ***GREAT?***
PERFECT.

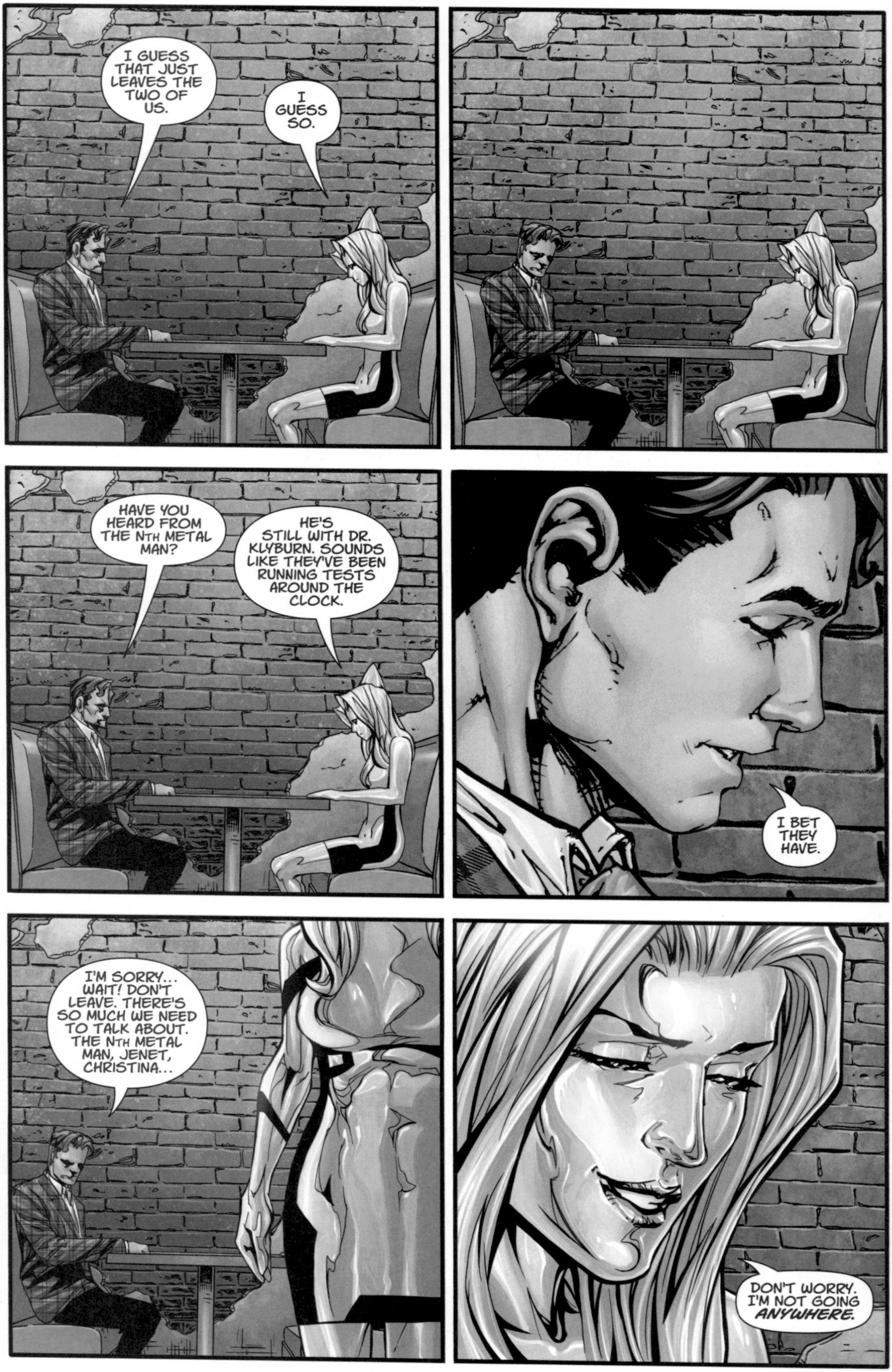
I GUESS THAT JUST LEAVES THE TWO OF US.
I GUESS SO.
HAVE YOU HEARD FROM THE Nth METAL MAN?
HE'S STILL WITH DR. KLYBURN. SOUNDS LIKE THEY'VE BEEN RUNNING TESTS AROUND THE CLOCK.
I BET THEY HAVE.
I'M SORRY... WAIT! DON'T LEAVE. THERE'S SO MUCH WE NEED TO TALK ABOUT. THE Nth METAL MAN, JENET, CHRISTINA...
DON'T WORRY. I'M NOT GOING *ANYWHERE*.

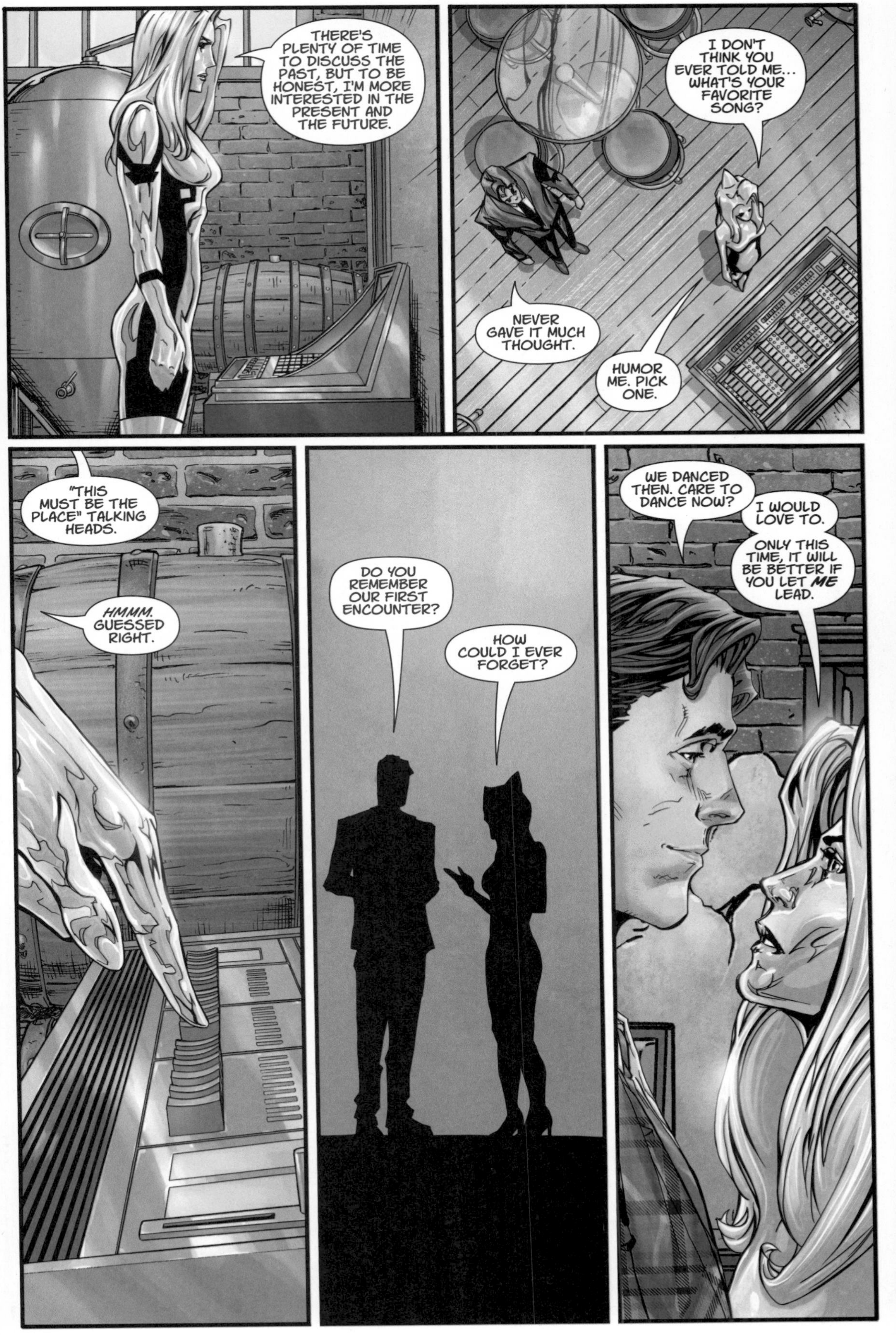
THERE'S PLENTY OF TIME TO DISCUSS THE PAST, BUT TO BE HONEST, I'M MORE INTERESTED IN THE PRESENT AND THE FUTURE.
I DON'T THINK YOU EVER TOLD ME... WHAT'S YOUR FAVORITE SONG?
NEVER GAVE IT MUCH THOUGHT.
HUMOR ME. PICK ONE.
"THIS MUST BE THE PLACE" TALKING HEADS.
HMMM. GUESSED RIGHT.
DO YOU REMEMBER OUR FIRST ENCOUNTER?
HOW COULD I EVER FORGET?
WE DANCED THEN. CARE TO DANCE NOW?
I WOULD LOVE TO.
ONLY THIS TIME, IT WILL BE BETTER IF YOU LET ME LEAD.

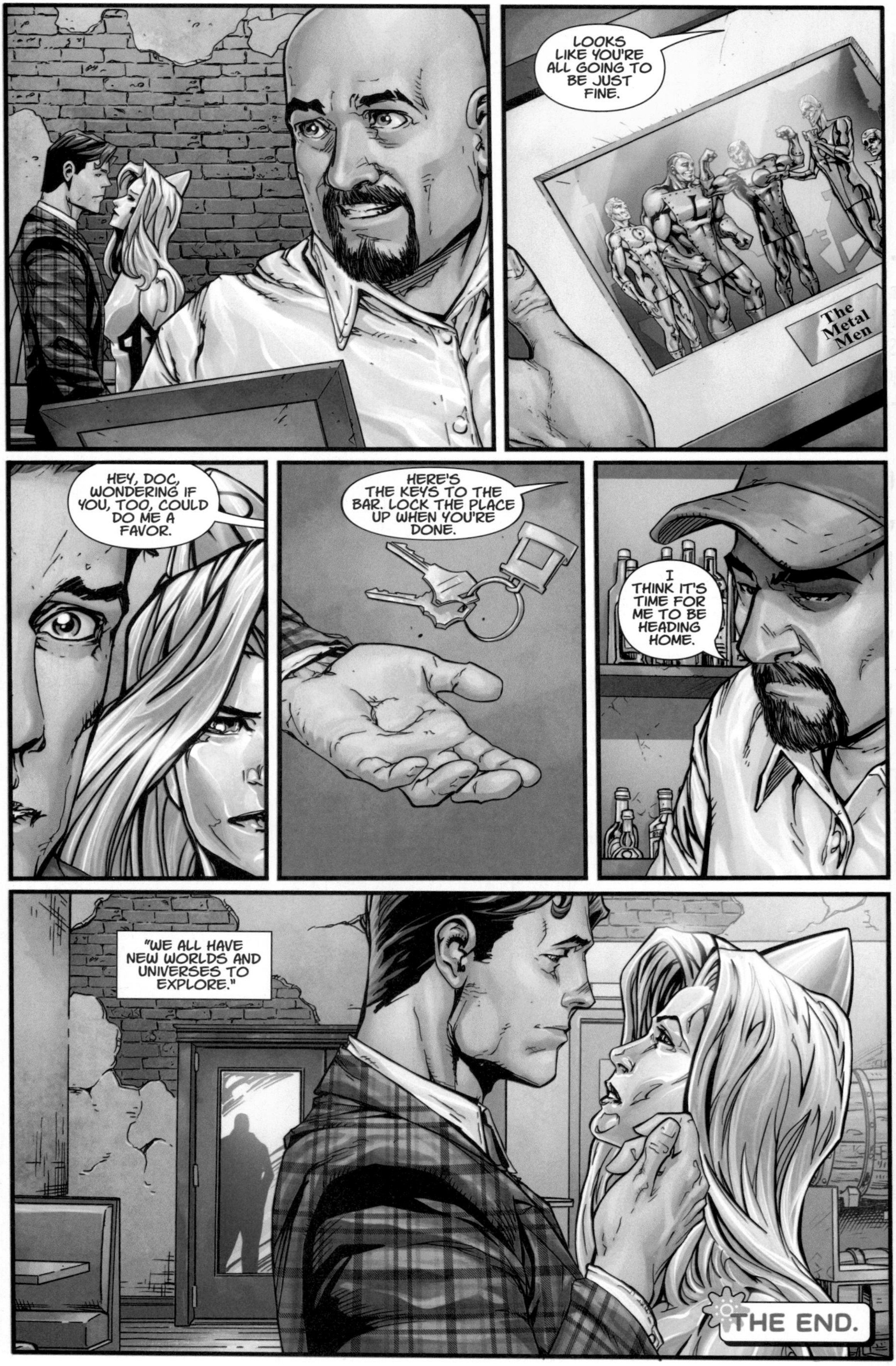
LOOKS LIKE YOU'RE ALL GOING TO BE JUST FINE.
The Metal Men
HEY, DOC, WONDERING IF YOU, TOO, COULD DO ME A FAVOR.
HERE'S THE KEYS TO THE BAR. LOCK THE PLACE UP WHEN YOU'RE DONE.
I THINK IT'S TIME FOR ME TO BE HEADING HOME.
"WE ALL HAVE NEW WORLDS AND UNIVERSES TO EXPLORE."
THE END.

> "Excellent...From its poignant domestic moments, delivered in mostly warm, fuzzy flashbacks, to its blockbuster battles, Straczynski's SUPERMAN: EARTH ONE renders like a feature film just waiting for adaptation."
> **—WIRED**

SUPERMAN: EARTH ONE
VOL. 1
J. MICHAEL STRACZYNSKI
with SHANE DAVIS

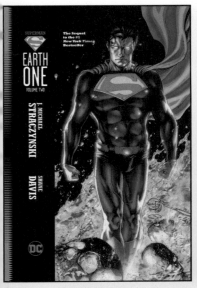

SUPERMAN: EARTH ONE VOL. 2

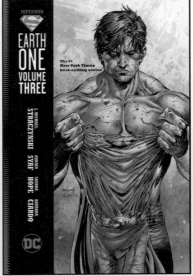

SUPERMAN: EARTH ONE VOL.3

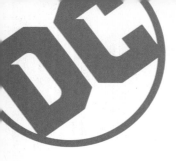

"This is the work of two men at the top of their games."
–THE NEW YORK TIMES

"Where nightmares and reality collide."
–THE WASHINGTON POST

"The Batman of your wildest nightmares."
–POLYGON

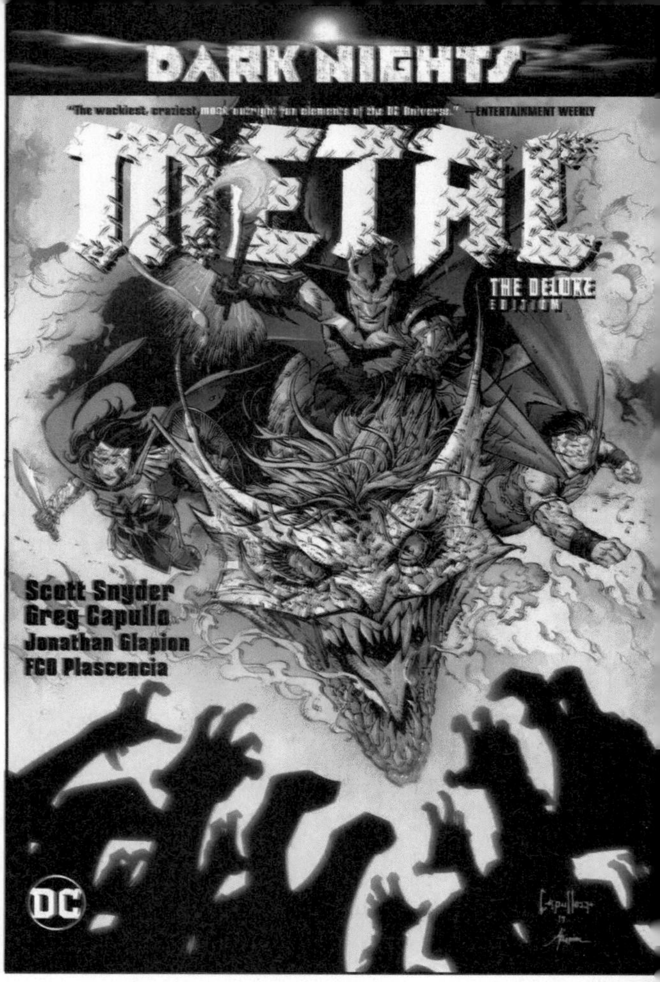
DARK NIGHTS
"The wackiest, craziest, most outright fun elements of the DC Universe." —ENTERTAINMENT WEEKLY
METAL
THE DELUXE EDITION
Scott Snyder
Greg Capullo
Jonathan Glapion
FCO Plascencia
DC

DARK NIGHTS: METAL

SCOTT SNYDER
GREG CAPULLO

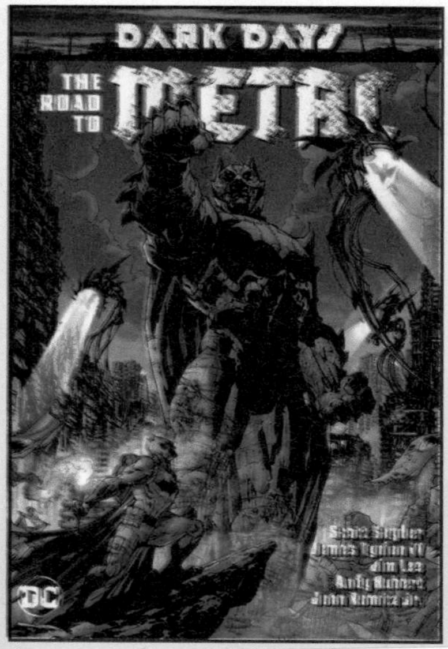
DARK DAYS
THE ROAD TO METAL
DC

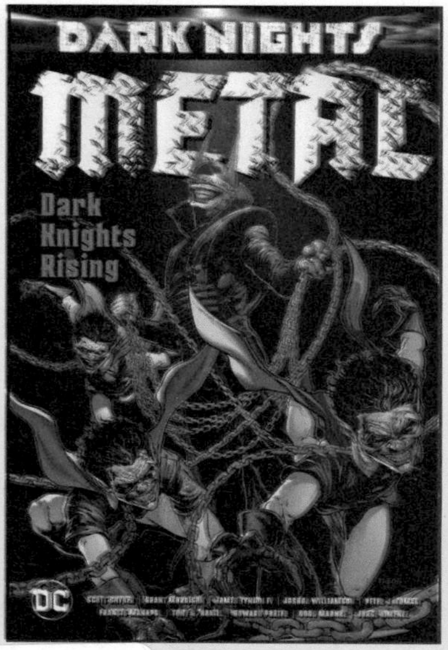
DARK NIGHTS
METAL
Dark Knights Rising
DC

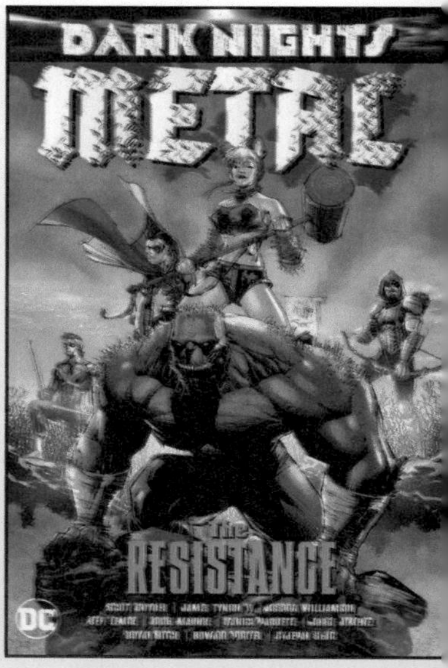
DARK NIGHTS
METAL
The RESISTANCE
DC

...K NIGHTS: METAL:
...K KNIGHTS RISING

DARK NIGHTS: METAL:
THE RESISTANCE

...c novels wherever comics and books are sold!